STUDIA ANSELMIANA
EDITA A PROFESSORIBUS ATHENÆI PONTIFICII
S. ANSELMI DE URBE

179

ANALECTA MONASTICA 20

Direttore: LÁSZLÓ SIMON O.S.B.

PONTIFICIO ATENEO S. ANSELMO – ROMA – 2019
Piazza dei Cavalieri di Malta, 5

MONASTICISM AND ECONOMY: REDISCOVERING AN APPROACH TO WORK AND POVERTY

Acts of the Fourth International Symposium
Rome, June 7-10, 2016
Study Days promoted and organised
by the Monastic Institute of the Faculty of Theology
of the Pontifical Athenaeum S.Anselmo

edited by
Isabelle Jonveaux
Thomas Quartier
Bernard Sawicki
Paolo Trianni

ROMA 2019

First impression 2019
ISBN 978-3-8306-7949-3

A catalogue record for this book is available from the German Library
http://dnb.ddb.de

EOS – Editions of Sankt Ottilien
www.eos-books.com | mail@eos-verlag.de
Printed in Germany

TABLE OF CONTENTS

WESTERN MONASTICISM

MONASTIC INSPIRATIONS

GOOD PRACTICES

FINAL LECTURE

ACRONYMS AND ABBREVIATIONS

AAS	*Acta Apostolicae Sedis*
ANA	Archief Nederlandse Augustijnen
BHG	*Bibliotheca Hagiographica Graeca*
BMFD	*Byzantine Monastic Foundation Documents. A Complete Translation of the Surviving Founders'* Typika *and Testaments*, I-V (Dumbarton Oaks Studies 35), éd. J. Thomas, A. Constantinides Hero, Washington 2000
BZ	*Byzantinische Zeitschrift*
Cf.	compare
Ed./edd.	editor/s
GCS	*Die griechischen christlichen Schriftsteller der ersten drei Jahrhunderte*
HTR	*Harvard Theological Review*
HUA	Het Utrechts Archief, Utrecht
Id.	*Idem*
JECS	*Journal of Early Christian Studies*
JGR	*Jus Graecoromanum*, 8 voll., édd. I. Zepos-P. Zepos, Athènes 1931
LCC	Library of Christian Classics (Philadelphia: Westminster Press)
LER	*Liber eremiticae regulae*, in *Consuetudo Camaldulensis. Rodulphi Constitutiones, Liber Eremiticae Regulae*, ed. P. Licciardello, Firenze 2004
MGH	*Monumenta Germaniae Historica*
NPNF	Nicene and Post-Nicene Fathers
ODB	*Oxford Dictionary of Byzantium*, edd. A. P. Kazhdan – *al.*, voll. 3 voll., Oxford University Press, New York – Oxford 1991.
OGHRA	*The Oxford guide to the historical reception of Augustine*, ed. K. Pollmann, Oxford University Press, Oxford 2013
OPD1	*Opera Omnia* di Pier Damiani
P. Cairo Masp	J. Maspero, *Papyrus grecs d'époque byzantine*, 3 voll., *Catalogue général des antiquités* égyptiennes *du Musée du Caire, nos. 67001-67359, Institut français d'archéologie orientale*, Le Caire 1911-1916

PG	*Patrologiae cursus completus. Series Graeca*, 161 voll., ed. J.-P. Migne, Paris-Montrouge 1857-1866
PL	*Patrologia Latina*
RB	*Rule of St. Benedict*
RGG	*Die Religion in Geschichte und Gegenwart*
ROC	*Revue de l'Orient Chrétien*
SC	*Sources Chrétiennes*, Cerf, Paris 1941
TWNT	G. KITTEL-G. FRIEDRICH, *Theologisches Wörterbuch zum Neuen Testament VII*, Stuttgart 1964
Vol./vols	volume/s

INTRODUCTION

A Benedictine monastery is primarily a place where God is the first one to be sought, the first to be served, loved and prayed to. The "spiritual arts" necessary to carry out this primary task are certainly practiced, but it is a place where other arts and crafts are practised as well.

Work in the monastery is not a simple pastime, though idleness is surely to be avoided; but it enters into the very definition of the monk, which is one who lives by the work of his own hands. Work is not a disturbance to prayer and contemplation. It also has an ascetic value; but in the end it is a reality that is necessary for the full realization of the human person, provided it is done in humility and obedience, without seeking only personal affirmation; because in this case it would become the primary purpose of monastic life which is notwithstanding and above all the search for God.

Monastic work is also motivated by charity towards the poor, pilgrims and members of the community itself; where the members must serve each other, and each must make himself useful to others. No one is exempted from work, because everyone should feel useful, but always with the discretion of balancing the burden of the work to the actual strength of each. Work is even allowed on public holidays, if in this way it is possible to avoid major disadvantages.

The "*ora, lege et labora*", this alternation of prayer, reading (for personal prayer and for study) and assiduous and productive work, in an atmosphere of peace, silence, order and harmony, where all differences and barriers are removed, and people are united harmoniously in the search and praise of God, in mutual service, and in fraternal welcome of the poor and pilgrims, has been a great turning point in history and has formed a model for the Church and the society that has spread throughout the world.

As can be seen in this volume "Monasticism and Economy: Rediscovering an Approach to Work and Poverty", the "*ora, lege et labora*" is not something relegated to the past; it can also now be a project for mankind and for organizations that actually and specifically focus on the human person. These three fundamental pillars (prayer, reading/study, work) in fact form a crossing between the transcendent dimension of life that looks beyond the ephemeral, transient and provisional, and the horizontal dimension of daily life. They also set limits to prevent a person's being overwhelmed by work and by destructive private ambition, while never escaping from reality and social commitment. They affirm the priority of the individual person over economic profit, while at the same time focusing on everyone's social responsibility and their consequent need to find a balance between activity and contemplation.

In line with this are Pope Francis's statements in his speech on Saturday 28 October 2017 to the participants at the "(Re-) thinking Europe" conference: «A Europe that rediscovers itself as a community will surely be a source of development for herself and for the whole world. Development must be understood in the terms laid down by Blessed Paul VI: "To be authentic, it must be well rounded; it must foster the development of each man and of the whole man. As an eminent specialist on this question has rightly said: 'We cannot allow economics to be separated from human realities, nor development from the civilization in which it takes place. What counts for us is man – each individual man, each human group, and humanity as a whole'"».

Work definitely contributes to this personal development, and this is clearly highlighted by the "*ora, lege et labora*", since, as mentioned above, work is seen as a reality necessary for the realization of human person, of his/her own "humanity". And this is true of any work, manual or intellectual; each job has its own dignity. However, such work can be lacking, and the increasing automation of work processes will surely reduce the number of people employed over time. The Pope continues in the same speech, "It would also be helpful to recover a sense of the need to provide concrete opportunities for employment, especially for the young. Today, many people tend to shy away from certain jobs because they seem physically demanding and unprofitable, forgetting how indispensable they are for human development… Governments also have the duty to create economic conditions that promote a healthy entrepreneurship and appropriate levels of employment. Politicians are especially responsible for restoring a virtuous circle that, starting from investments that favour the family and education, enable the harmonious and peaceful development of the entire civil community".

In this respect, it might also be useful to talk about "monastic poverty" which is a different concept from what we have now in the wake of the emergence of the so-called mendicant religious Orders. St. Benedict, in his Rule, does not deal explicitly with poverty, but with the manner of possessing goods. What is to be avoided is a style of possession that makes us slaves of the object possessed, as this closes on the object the horizon that must always be open to the infinity of God and which makes us and keeps us free. The remedies against a bad style of possession are to receive everything from the hands of the Abbot as a gift, and not to consider anything as our own but as held in common.

Access to goods held in common, then, gives to everyone, on the practical side of existence, the opportunity to train, to prepare, to keep oneself up to date, to learn a new business with the necessary economic security. Seen like this, such a form of common possession, is not far from those who today think in terms of a basic universal income to give everyone that financial security necessary to try new things and acquire new skills, as future society expects. This basic universal income is a form of security for citizens of a given society where all residents of a country receive a regular and unconditional sum of money, from the government or from a public institution, in addition to any income received elsewhere. This could be a way of addressing the generational challenge that awaits us, of creating new jobs and a renewed sense of purpose, and give the opportunity to engage in meaningful major projects.

Rome, 11th November 2017
Stefano Visintin, osb
Rector Magnificus

PREFACE

One can say that the International Monastic Symposia, organised by the Monastic Institute at Sant'Anselmo in Rome, begin to have their tradition. This book presents the papers prepared for the fourth of them. Such a symposium is always a time in which the scholars interested in monasticism may not only meet in the Benedictine University on the Aventine Hill to present their scientific researches, but also share their experiences, ideas and concerns. We are glad that, as usual, this Symposium also gathered quite a considerable international group of 55 speakers composed of different generations and coming from about 20 countries.

Obviously, the numbers are not of the greatest importance but they can say something about geography, distribution of fields of interests and methodological tendencies. It is difficult to say whether the theme itself or the specificity of our times caused, perhaps for the first time during these symposia, so huge a diversity of methodology and approach. It was definitively one of the greatest advantages of this event, besides the rich range of presented material.

The results of any symposium depend mostly on the selection of the theme as title and, simultaneously, as a main motive. Thinking of organising this Symposium, two years in advance, different proposals were taken into consideration. Finally, after some suggestions, both on the side of patristics and monasticism, the theme of economy was chosen – mostly in reference to Pope Francis' emphasis on problems of poverty. As a continuation of the previous two symposia, dedicated to monasticism in the context of society and culture, the focus on economy seemed to be a step forward: the concretisation and actualisation of the monastic message for the modern world. Even if monks do not take the vow of poverty, the vow of *conversatio morum* that they take instead means an integral approach towards God, neighbours and material goods which includes and implies a special respect for the resources we have and a sensibility for the right distribution of them.

Almost at the same time that the choice of the theme was being discussed, Pope Francis published his Encyclical *Laudato si*. Although this document deals with ecology, the awareness that "everything is (inter)connected", so much emphasised by the Pope[1], necessarily gives to ecology an economic

1 *Laudato si'*, 16, 42, 70, 91, 92, 111, 117, 138, 240.

dimension. Even if the Pope explicitly dedicates only one paragraph to the Benedictine tradition[2], his reflection inspires us to recall the huge and not always known contribution of monasticism to ecology, almost always having various economic implications. The symposium intended simply to do this, especially because monastic ecology has always been seen and practiced in an integrated, almost natural way, usually in a very concrete economic context. Perhaps that is why, although it has never been spectacular and visible, it, by no means, excludes its relevance for our days. On the contrary, the appeal of Pope Francis seems to urge the Benedictines to rediscover their tradition and to say that there has been already a long ecological tradition in the Church.

Thus, whilst programming and foreseeing the possible course of the symposium we had to focus, first of all, on the history of monasticism, because, from the very beginning, the monks had to deal with various economic challenges. To survive, they had to participate in an economic life with their surrounding society. Medieval monasteries were promoting a new material culture which included a wide range of achievements, from food products, administrative activities to innovative technical and architectural solutions. In this way, the monks, contributing so much to the spiritual heritage of Christianity, simultaneously – or rather "by the way" – were elaborating and implementing many various economic practices.

The Apophthegms offer a very refreshing and human vision of labour and management. Amazingly, for many centuries (up to the XII c.) the monastic communities were developing a material culture in parallel, and yet in an unusual harmony, with its spiritual achievements. The development of new forms of religious life and, at the same time, the great transformations of social structures stopped this integrated progress. Even if the successive centuries brought a marginalisation of monasticism, it did not cease to evolve and develop. It is enough to mention only some of its most radical forms, such as the Trappists or Camaldolese of Monte Corona.

More recent decades, in the context of a global and highly developed economy, seem to come back to the monastic ethos of economy. The Rule of S. Benedict has proved to be an excellent inspiration for people in business. Many monasteries actively and creatively participate, not only in local economic projects – as important tourist and cultural centres – but also as important employers. Monastic gastronomy and, usually organic, food products have become a base for a special culture for a modern, sobre and frugal style of

2 *Laudato si'*, 126.

being and welfare. The sharing economy and collaborative consumption seem to be an amazing application of monastic style in the practices of modern Western society. In this sense monasticism is really contributing to an understanding of economy as a locus of human interaction in society.

Looking at all these topics in the context of modern economic problems and in the light of Pope Francis' emphasis on a vast social and ecological framework of poverty, so clearly and strongly expressed in Laudate si', a multi-threaded reflection on the economy and its relationship with spirituality seems to be necessary. Monasticism seems to offer here something very important: a horizon of synthesis which could, paradoxically, reconcile various mutually exclusive and often radical options (poor Church for the poor/ distrust of wealth, radicalism/moderation, ethics /profit). The inter-relatedness of economic and spiritual lives in a specific monastic sense (for example the relationship between liturgy and work; cultural utterances and economic processes; spiritual awakening and productivity etc.) should also be taken into consideration. There are also monastic theological notions of economy, where interesting ideas have been developed in recent years, such as the heavenly economy as represented in the microcosm of a monastery; eschatological perspectives on economy (God's salvation) etc.

An elaboration and deepening of these perspectives became the main goal of the Symposium. It also implies that, with a full awareness of the importance of historic studies, a platform for multi-disciplinary research, reflection and exchange, as a place of permanent dialogue with modern sociology and economics turns out to be more than necessary. It could enrich not only the Church but also economy and the whole world.

Going along this line, to the traditional, geographical and generic sections of the symposium, such as Oriental, Western, Benedictine and Non- Monasticism (the categories inherited from the previous symposia), two new ones, reflecting practical and modern experience of monasticism, were added: Monastic Inspirations and Good Practices. The distribution of the papers admitted to the symposium says a lot about the profile of the reception and understanding of the theme. The two biggest sections were Western Monasticism (11 papers) and Monastic Inspirations (9 papers).Oriental Monasticism was represented by 7, General Practices by 5 papers, and Non-Christian monasticism only by 2 papers. Of course, these numbers mainly depended on the participants and, earlier, on the mechanisms of promotion of the symposium.

On the other hand, in some cases it was not easy to attribute a paper to a category, which shows the complexity of the phenomenon of monasticism especially in its reference to economy. However, to put an order in the Symposium, some criteria were necessary. Their choice – and eventual ambiguity related to this – signal methodological challenges in dealing with monasticism seen in a wider and socially relevant context. It was already visible during the previous symposium dedicated to the culture.

This time, the distance between a traditional, historically-textual approach toward monasticism and other, often more modern methodologies (archaeology, sociology and comparative studies) was very evident. Since it is natural in interdisciplinary researches of modern times one can say, that a new phase of study on monasticism has been inaugurated and with this Symposium validated, transforming eventually, original caution and reserve into a fruitful dialogue.

All this, as an unexpected but natural result of the Symposium, has very important and far reaching consequences not only for both monasticism and monastic spirituality but also, further, on theology:

1) Study of monasticism may become a laboratory of new methodologies enriching and supplementing the hitherto prevailing analysis of texts. A dialogue between patristics and archaeology, history and spirituality, economy and theology is more than necessary not only to understand the complex mechanisms generating essential social and cultural changes occurring within the course of history, but also to provide adequate tools for the description and interpretation of processes happening within modern societies.

2) A strong connection between theological discourse and spiritual and economic praxis is a new category of approaching spirituality and theology from the perspective of both personal and social experience. Interaction between individual and community, possible in this context, may become a new axis for ecclesiology.

3) The rather marginal position of monasticism in mainstream theological debate and politics of the Church gives a unique opportunity for a free appurtenance to form the vanguard of more practical than theoretical solutions. At the same time, the length of monastic tradition and its sensibility to external circumstances (due to the vote of stability) allow for bold and experimental connections between history and presence.

Does it seem, that there is here, a new perspective for monastic studies and monasticism itself? It looks like this could be the case. The fact that this theme is so vividly examined by young and lay scholars (they were the largest group participating in the Symposium) allows us to hope that, despite of an evident decline in monastic vocations in the world, the monastic tradition is still vivid and inspiring, more and more widely getting out of monasteries and exclusively monastic milieus. Slowly, it becomes a leaven of a new economic (and ecologic) culture, humbly but systematically whilst patiently offering a constructive alternative for the globalised world. This alternative, is not so much opposed to the world as open to it and ready to transform it – gently, discretely and successfully.

The Editors

BETWEEN MONASTICISM AND ECONOMY. FROM THE EXPERIENCE OF AN ABBOT

Notker WOLF

Monasteries are known as autonomous communities. Traditionally they are autarchic, self-sufficient. They intend to live from the income of the work of their own hands and don't like to depend upon the grace of other people or by hanging around begging. It is not a matter of pride but of self-responsibility. Monks should not be a burden on other people. Until modern times, it was possible to live on the income of the work of their own hands. But nowadays this is not so easy and monastics have become aware of the problems associated with livelihood and income. This problem is rather serious for a number of communities; in the end it will touch all of them. We have to be very realistic, facing and analysing the situation, by finding new ways, in our times, in order to retain our monastic ideals whilst finding the means of survival. Perhaps in some cases, the monastery alone can no longer be self-sufficient but will collaborate in local or regional corporations. Fortunately, a new awareness of this problems among monastics has emerged (cf. AIM Bulletin no. 110, 2016, pp.1-59).

The financial crash in 2008/9 has harmed a number of well- situated communities who lost up to half of their investments. Other monasteries, although juridically autonomous, have not yet reached their real economic autonomy. However, it is not healthy for a community to depend on donations from the founding monastery, nor for autonomous monasteries to depend upon continued donations from outside. S. Anselmo is a special case, because we have no greater resources of income than a number of other colleges. We are supported by the Confederation and this is sufficient only for the running costs, not for major repairs and construction work. Here, we have to find and rely upon people who see in the Benedictine Order an important contribution to the Church and to Society.

The usual way is to make products which sell well, to try to do most of the repair works by the monastics themselves in order to save expenses, and to live a frugal life. Nuns and sisters are far better at saving expenses. Men's monasteries need a higher budget.

1. LIVELIHOOD AND INCOME

The traditional basis of income has been agriculture. Monastics produced their own food and were able to sell a bit. Monks have been excellent farmers with their cattle, their fishponds, their fields and their forests. Nowadays, only a few monasteries continue with their agriculture, because for example in Europe, agriculture has become a field of hightech and you will need a big farm in order to get products which are still economically useful. But even here, monasteries have to be flexible. St. Ottilien in Bavaria, in spite of having 180 milk cows gains more from biogas and biomass energy than from the milk and milk products. It is a good development to see more and more monasteries changing to alternative energy like biogas or solar panels. The largest experimental solar farm in the upper Midwest/USA is located on the land of St. John's Abbey, Collegeville. The Abbey of Peramiho/Tanzania has a large solar plant. This creates a new sense of environmental responsibility. Besides saving and gaining money, especially in countries where nature is still exploited, it can become exemplary for the people of a whole region.

In situations where monasteries enjoy major woods, often times it is not the wood itself which will provide some income, but if it used for carpentry and buildings. Reforestation will be necessary in cases where wood is used for carpentry and timber. Monasteries have been exemplary in planting woods, esp. in the Middle Ages of Europe and nowadays in some places in Africa.

Processing products of agriculture will sometimes be more important than selling first products, like jam instead of fruits, or bread instead of wheat. We may also mention the production of wine and beer. Anyhow, in all this, communities will have to be very creative in order to survive. On the other hand, for communities a small scale agriculture enterprise is still possible and will provide food for the needs of the community, not forgetting the gardens. Even there, a recent development has turned over again to planting herbs, as in the Middle Ages or going back to African tradition for medical use. A number of monasteries have turned to organic farming.

Monastics have been and should become again, very creative as they have been in the past, be it through husbandry, fish, fields and crops, or reforestation. Starting with the Carolingian epoch, it was the monks who introduced the system of three-field-rotation replacing the two-field-rotation of the Roman period. Monastics have always had a sense for innovation and have become promotors of human culture and saving nature. It is true that in our modern times monks can no longer play that prominent role. Other people are better trained, we have universities for economy and for agriculture with many specialisations, and nowadays things are done on a larger scale, which needs more money than most of the monasteries could afford. Nevertheless, monasteries have to work for their survival and try to become exemplary in modern trends such as alternative energy, organic farming and herbal medicine.

Agriculture also had a double effect on community life. It does not only provide income, but it binds always a good number of monks to the place; it is a natural basis for the stabilitas loci. Animals need to be attended day by day. This challenges the stability of monks and creates also a natural rhythm for a community.

2. MANUAL LABOUR

"Monks must not become distressed if local conditions or their poverty should force them to do the harvesting themselves. When they live by the labour of their hands, as our fathers and the apostles did, then they are really monks" (RB 48,7-8). Labour of hands does not only mean agriculture but also different kinds of crafts. Crafts have been part of everyday life in monasteries. Monks made baskets and mats, copied books, and developed a great diversity of arts throughout history. They had their workshops, scriptoria, libraries. They were selling their products. St. Benedict only warned them about greed and fraud. Benedict calls those brothers not only "craftsmen", but "artisans". Monks have created beautiful art work, architecture, sculpture, books and music. But, also basic craftsmen have become important such as tailors, carpenters, plumbers, electricians and more recently IT-technicians.

These handicrafts especially have become important in constructing, maintaining and developing monasteries. This saves money and it is a pity that in our days only few monastics are still trained in crafts. Nowadays, in new foundations, monastics are used to move into completely new buildings. The young monks lack the psychological attachment to their monasteries and by consequence the spirit of maintenance. What you have created yourself, will be far more part of your concern. At the entrance to the church at St. Meinrad /USA you find a memorial stone: "We the monks with the help of many people have built this church." Of course, for major buildings monks will need the help of others, but the core of the work should be done by the monastics themselves. During a visit to the Abbey of Eichstätt in Germany, I saw a nun doing masonry and painting in their building. This happened outside all discussion of emancipation of women. The nuns simply take care of their own building.

The culture of maintenance is a particular heritage of the Benedictines, since St. Benedict warns the cellarer: "He will regard all utensils and goods of the monastery as sacred vessels of the altar, aware that nothing is to be neglected" (RB 31,10s.). I could imagine that this perspective might be an important contribution to some cultures and develop a sense of the importance of maintenance. Of course, this is the opposite of modern economic tendencies, e.g. our throwaway society On the other hand, people are calling for sustainability, a mere contradiction, but the stress on sustainability holds true and has been the quality of monastic culture. Monastics are also planting trees which they will never harvest in their own generation, but only later on. I was told in several places: "Why should we work for what we don't harvest?" Useless toil. But by this mentality, monks laid the ground for European development.

If monks should live by the work of their hands, they will have to be active, take initiatives, become creative. They cannot display a passive character and think that by this they are contemplative. We are no longer living in a feudal system of the Middle Ages when rich people founded a monastery in order to have monks to pray for the salvation of their souls, and monks would employ people to work for them in their fields. This is not according to the Rule of St. Benedict. This is the reason, why Robert of Molesme and his companions distanced themselves from Cluny, in order to revive the real spirit of Benedict. I found it rather strange when someone defended this feudal system and thought that this was real contemplative life: "They pay and we pray." I doubt whether this mentality is the spirit of St. Paul who wrote to the Thessalonians: "we were not idle when we were with you, and we did not eat anyone's bread without paying for it: but with toil and labour we worked night and day, so that we might not burden any of you" (2 Thess 3, 7-8).

Under this kind of mentality, there is hidden yet another one: There are people who think that a priest's collar around the neck, is more valuable than the yoke of the farmer or a hoe in one's hand. Clericalism has also entered into communities. But, as St. Paul insists : "There is no longer Jew or Greek, there is no longer slave or free, there is no longer male and female; for all of you are one in Christ Jesus" (Gal 3,28). In several cultures, such an attitude would mean baptising a culture. Cultures have grown on a different context than Christianity, and therefore can show elements which are not in conformity with the Christian ideals. Abbot John Kurichianil from Kappadu insists that his young monks have to work every day for some hours in the cow stable or in the fields in order to overcome the traditional cast system. Also, in Africa we can observe authoritarian structures where women have to take care of the fields. It would be highly desirable that monks give the example of hard work.

3. SCHOOLS

As I mentioned, monks in St. Benedict's monasteries had to be able to read and write. This was something quite new for many members. Monks were in need of books, in the church, at table and during Lent. But books could not be bought in bookstores. Schools had to be set up and scriptoria. Monks had to be educated and the whole development of Benedictine schools started. Many monasteries earned their income by teaching and welcoming students in boarding houses. Monastics have become outstanding specialists in science and publications like the monks of the Maurist Congregation in France in the 17th century by editing the Church fathers, although they insisted first of all in a renewal of Benedictine life, but combined it with literary and historical work. Serious Benedictine life is at the roots of cultural development, and not only by literary work but also by art.

Of course, this is a great challenge for formation. Monks need skills and qualifications in order to be up to date. Future teachers need a long preparation in universities or at professional schools. Are we still ready to face this sacrifice? In times of competition we need professionalism. There is the danger that we remain second class people in our societies. The general intellectual level in our monasteries is rather low. Monastics may say that we are made for spirituality, not for intellectual work. But what kind of spirituality is in our hearts if we are no longer capable of overcoming the troubles of serious studies? Yes, our societies are in need of spiritual input. But where are the qualified people? This holds true even more if we think of interreligious dialogue. Do we have specialists who know other spiritualities, who can be serious partners of spiritual people of other religions. Interestingly enough, the high moments of monastic life in history were always linked to a high level of education. Pope Benedict XVI underlines the need of philosophical training for priests. If we are not formed well, we are in danger of inclining towards superstition. Reason is the criterion joined with Faith.We have to prepare ourselves in order to be serious partners for our contemporary brethren. This has nothing to do with intellectualism; God has given us not only hands to pray but also some brains to think. Anti-intellectualism is an ideology and lowers the quality of our spiritual life.

Again, this needs sacrifices, and I doubt whether monastics are willing to do this. Outside of the monasteries, people are forced by sheer necessity of survival to accept such challenges. Many students are not too lazy to study foreign languages, even difficult ones such as Chinese of Arabic; they have to sit down to study physics, chemistry and many other conditions for their future. How can we make new monastic foundations in foreign cultures if we are not prepared to study these cultures and their languages?

4. GUESTHOUSES

Hospitality has become one of the main activities of a community. Nowadays, it means far more than just welcoming guests. Some monasteries try to live upon the income of their guest houses and give retreats and spiritual courses. A guest-house creates links with other people who may become also donors some day. As far as guesthouses run by monastics are concerned, they may create some income but hospitality as such was not meant by Benedict as a means of income; he admonishes the abbot to take care of the poor and the pilgrims (RB 53.15).

5. ADMINISTRATION

In the whole area of income and expenditure, investment and activity, the first prerequisite of economy is good administration. A procurator once told me: A solid administration is the best savings bank. The most simple principle is often neglected, i. e. to have an overview of the income and expenditure. Nowadays, the management of finances and taxes has become very complex and that even more, if a monastery has to take care of employees. Some monasteries have up to 1000 employees. Laws in different countries have become a thicket, for which you will need special training and ongoing formation. Therefore, a good number of monasteries in Europe have employed experts or at least consultants. The need of a secular cellarer creates another problem: He does not live with the community, he is not present all the time and has no natural authority regarding monks and other employees. This can make both sides feel uneasy and lead to power struggles.

Neither the abbot nor the administrator are the monastery, but the whole community has to be integrated into decision making. There is a natural gap of knowledge and expertise between the superior and cellarer on one side and the brethren on the other side. Ongoing information within the community will be necessary. Chapter 3 of the Rule of St. Benedict gives advice which unfortunately is often neglected. Monthly or yearly accounting is unavoidable. If a community is bankrupt all will have to suffer.

Often the principle of St. Benedict, that any kind of private property should be avoided seems to be very difficult. Confreres may get the impression that there is sufficient money for major projects and that the cellarer is stingy with regard to the smaller needs of the individual. A certain generosity will help. On the other hand, monastics have to develop a sense of common responsibility and avoid all kind of egoistic behaviour and private accounts.

This sense of being one family has to be developed especially in poorer countries. It is obvious that monks see the many advantages they have in their communities, in contrast with the situation of their families, and are tempted to misuse common goods in order to help their families. A Zimbabwean Jesuit told me: You Europeans cannot imagine how deep is our sense of responsibility in Africa toward our families. I can understand this way of reasoning. The family has worked for the well-being of the children, and one of their children "has made it." So, they expect some remuneration for their "investment" into the monk or nun. Nevertheless, they belong now to a new family. When a family gives away a daughter, it has to pay for her. In that sense, there should not be a problem. It is far more difficult for monks. It maybe, that a monastery will pay for another boy of that family or pay something for the parents. It is difficult for a European to give advice. The Africans themselves have to find the solution. In my personal case: My parents were poor, but whenever they came to my monastery, they brought some money to help the monasteries of poorer countries.

An administrator will be torn by such requests; on the other hand, he has to take care of the well- being of his community and try to save money. It will be up to the community to find rules according to the needs of their culture, but it can never be the question of just one individual. This also holds true for the poor who knock at the door of a monastery or are writing to some of the monastics. It is not down to the generosity of the individual to help; rather, it touches the whole community.

It is very important to have a well- trained cellarer within a community, and as we have seen, the question of finances should not only be the problem of an individual, but become more and more the question of the whole community. The community as such, has to develop some sense of entrepreneurship. Therefore, chapter 3 of the Rule of St. Benedict becomes more and more important. This does not mean that monks should become money-minded, but carry the common burden of survival and the future development of the community.

6. PARTICULAR QUESTIONS

There are still a few particular questions.

If a community needs more and more lay personnel, we have to train these persons in the sense and mentality of St. Benedict, as we are doing, for example, in the ICBE regarding our teachers. On the other hand, we have to develop an intensive collaboration and be humble, if e.g. the leader of a school or a printing press is a lay person and we are teachers or workers. I have heard sometimes: "I don't accept commands from a lay person. This is our business!" Collaboration can become a rather sensitive challenge for a community. There is much room for power struggle. We have to respect public laws when we employ lay people, and have to think twice, because if a lay person has an indefinite contract, he cannot easily be replaced by a monk.

Although monastics should live by the income of the work of their own hands, they often have to rely upon donors, especially for major projects. In some circumstances, this may even be justified. A community which serves the region by a school or a retreat house, the investment and running costs nowadays may surmount by far the financial capacities of a community. But, it is a service to the people. Private and public contributions or donations will be necessary. Some monasteries have a professional development office. The most important issue will be the continued contact with potential donors; they have to become friends of a monastery. They must see the spiritual, cultural and social contribution of a lively community to a region. Nevertheless, a community should at least provide its own livelihood.

New foundations will be in need of some considerable assistance for a longer period. Solid planning will avoid many frustrations. Important, first of all are accessibility, water, electricity, fertility of the land. One should not be shy to buy a sufficient plot. Later on, you can always give away or sell, but to buy new land can become very difficult. A master plan will be helpful. Right from the beginning, productivity should be one of the goals of the new foundation. It is obvious that a new foundation will be expensive. It will need constructions, and as soon as there are candidates, their formation will cost. In a rural area, young founders may plant good crops so that the investment will pay soon. Anyhow, right from the beginning the economic aspect is an important dimension. It is not healthy if a community drops into a "receiver" mentality. The founding group should develop their own responsibility by new initiatives. Sometimes, you cannot foresee the local possibilities. Which European would think of planting orchids in the Philippines or developing herbal medicine in Nigeria? It is the challenge of the founders themselves to find out the best ways.

CONCLUSION

The spiritual dimension must remain the first concern, but by our spiritual life, we cannot burden other people. We are human beings with souls and bodies.

"Ora et labora" therefore remains our motto, not forgetting the lectio. Jesus himself has given us the example of hard word as a carpenter. The superior needs a brave cellarer, in order to be free for his care of souls. In our times, we need not only responsibility of the individual in contributing to the livelihood of the community but we need to develop a spirit of common responsibility. Monastics should not become money-minded (cf. RB 57,7) but, on the other hand, do some serious work for the sake of their spiritual health (cf. RB 48, 1.22-24). Monastics have to be creative, not passive; hard-working, not lazy; saving nature not exploiting it; maintain their monasteries, not neglecting them; looking for income, whilst avoiding all kind of greed or stinginess. With regard to the poor, they have to be generous. And last but not least, autarchy should not become an ideology. We have to be humble and able to collaborate with lay personnel and with institutions of the region. If we follow these principles, I am sure that we shall create a place of peace inside the community and peace with our neighbours. The Pax Benedictina has always been a beacon of a region. We are not belonging to this world, but are living in this world (cf. John 17,13s.). This will remain the spiritual tension of monastic ideals and our life in this world. The problems will never be settled; we just have to go on, remaining open to change.

Abstract

Coming out from the Rule of Saint. Benedict and from history, the paper presents a general idea of work in Benedictine monasteries. At the same time, the present perspectives and challenges of such work are described. They are different in different regions and cultures. The particularly important fields of Benedictine activity today are hospitality and education. The need of efficient administration is indispensable. All this means the necessity of collaboration with lay people and constant attention towards social responsibility.

OPENING LECTURE

THE DEVELOPMENT OF THE CONCEPTOF POVERTY FROM ATHANASIUS TO CASSIAN

Mark Sheridan

Antony the Great died in the year 356 at an advanced age of over 100 years. The next year Athanasius, the great bishop and Pope of Alexandria wrote the first biography of a saint not a martyr. It is a highly complex work that owes much both to the Greek philosophical tradition and to the Hellenistic Jewish and Christian exegetical traditions. He rushed to complete it so that brethren visiting Egypt could take a copy with them before the end of the sailing season. The copy was probably the first Latin translation made simultaneously with the composition of the Greek.

In chapter 3 of his *Life of Antony*, Athanasius portrays Antony explaining that there are two reasons for the monk to work: to support himself and to have enough to give to the poor.: «He did manual labor, for he had heard that *he that is lazy, neither let him eat*. Some of his earnings he spent for bread and some he gave to the poor». This statement forms part of the basic program of monastic life to which chapter three is devoted. Athanasius wrote that Antony began to paid attention to himself (*prosoche*) and engaged in spiritual exercises (*askesis*)[1]. He sought to imitate the virtues of the older monks living in the vicinity and to strive against vice. The entire *Life of Antony* is in fact a didactic work aiming at the reform of monasticism as it then existed in Egypt, as Gregory Nazianzen recognized in his encomium of Athanasius[2]. The poverty envisioned in this pro-

---

Mark Sheridan, professor and rector emeritus of the Pontificio Ateneo S. Anselmo in Rome, patrologist and coptologist.

1 For the history of this pair of terms, see M. Sheridan, «The Spiritual and Intellectual World of Early Egyptian Monasticism», *Coptica* 1 (2002) 2-51, and Id., «Monastic Culture: a comparison of the concepts of askesis and asceticism» *(Monastic Symposium, Sant'Anselmo, 2011)* in Ph. Nouzille-M. Pfeifer, *Monasticism Between Culture and Cultures: Acts of the Third International Symposium. Rome, June 8-1, 2011* (Studia Anselmiana 159), Roma 2013.

2 Oration 21, 10. See Gregorius Nazianzenus, *Tutte Le Orazioni*, ed. Claudio Moreschini (Bompiani il pensiero occidentale), Milano 2000, 525.

gram was not the same as "non-ownership," something that could only be realized in a cenobitic community of the Pachomian type. It is also clear that Antony and Athanasius did not confuse religiously motivated poverty with real poverty, a poverty that is usually not only material but also cultural and social. People in such a situation can rarely raise themselves from it by their own efforts and so they need the help of those who like Antony have sought poverty for religious reasons – in the case of Christians, because they seek to imitate their Master, Jesus Christ.

Yet at the same time as he prescribed work for monks, Athanasius was well aware that external poverty was not the real goal. The goal was to be rid of the desire for unnecessary and superfluous possession, that is, the vice (*pathē*) of *philargyria*. In chapter 17 Athanasius has Antony say:

> We must further bear in mind that if we do not give up these things for virtue's sake, later we must leave them behind and often, too, as Ecclesiastes reminds us, even to persons to whom we do not wish to leave them. Then why not give them up for virtue's sake so that we may inherit a kingdom besides? Therefore, let none of us have even the desire to possess riches. For what does it avail us to possess what we cannot take with us? Why not rather possess those things which we can take along with us—prudence, justice, temperance, fortitude, understanding, charity, love of the poor, faith in Christ, meekness, hospitality? Once we possess these we shall find them going before us, preparing a welcome for us in the land of the meek[3].

«Let none of us have even the desire to possess riches», says Antony or his biographer. The goal is not just material poverty, but to eradicate the passion known as *philargiria*, literally, love of silver, or useless possessions, that is, luxury. It is a spiritual goal, that of passionlessness, or *apatheia*. To understand this concept, it is necessary to know that the Greek word *pathē*, always has a negative connotation. It is not the same as emotion. There are also good *pathē*, in Greek *eupatheia*. For Philo of Alexandria, God is *eupathes*, full of joy[4].

Pachomius had died already in 347. He was considerably younger than Antony and, unlike Antony, did not come from a Christian family. The story re-

---

3 Trans. from E.C.S. Gibson, *The Works of John Cassian. Translated, with Prolegomena, Prefaces, and Notes, by Rev. E.C.S. Gibson*, Oxford 1894.

4 See M. Sheridan, «The Controversy over *APATHEIA*: Cassian's sources and his use of them», in *From the Nile to the Rhone and Beyond: Studies in Early Monastic Literature and Scriptural Interpretation* (Studia Anselmiana 156), Roma 2012, 363.

corded in the lives of Pachomius and his successors is that, as a young recruit for the Roman army, he was being transported from Upper Egypt up the Nile and was imprisoned in a fortress overnight. The local Christians came and offered food to them. When young Pachomius saw them, he asked the men who were with him, «Why are these people so good to us when they do not know us» They answered, «They are Christians». Pachomius was so impressed that He withdrew to one side and spent the whole night praying before God saying, «My Lord Jesus the Christ, God of all the saints, may your goodness quickly come upon me, deliver me from this affliction and I will serve humankind all the days of my life».

After Constantine defeated Maxentius, the recruits were released. It is necessary to quote the Life at some length because it gives us the founding experience that characterizes Pachomian monasticism. It continues:

> Young Pachomius too went south until he arrived at a deserted village called Seneeet, scorched by the intensity of the heat. And he began to think about the place, in which there were not many but a few inhabitants. He went down to the river, into a small temple the ancients called Pmampiserapis. There he stood and prayed.' The Spirit of God seized him; 'Struggle and settle down here'. The thing pleased him and he settled down there, growing some vegetables and some palm-trees in order to feed himself or some poor man of the village or again some stranger who should happen to pass by in a boat or on the road[5].

At this point Pachomius was not yet a baptized Christian. Nevertheless many people came to consult him and the author says: «they would give up their homes to come and live in that village because of his way of encouraging them. It was really because of his attitude that many men made their dwelling in that place». The Life continues:

> After he had spent some days there, he was brought to the church and baptized' that he might be made worthy of the holy mysteries, that is to say of the body and blood of Christ. On the night he was baptized he had a dream. He saw the dew of heaven descend on his head, then condense in his right hand and turn into a honey- comb; and while he was considering it, it dropped onto the earth and spread out over the face of all the earth. As he was still disturbed, a voice came to him. from heaven, 'Understand this, Pachomius, for it will happen to you in

5 A. VEILLEUX, *Pachomian Koinonia 1*, vol. 1, Kalamazoo (Mich) 2010.

> a short time'. He made progress in that place by his charity for all. He was encouraging toward anyone who came to him, and his renown went out to many people, who came to live in that village because of him[6].

The story is long and we must make it short. When there was a serious outbreak of pestilence in that village, he would go out to serve them. After three years spent in that place, he realized that he was surrounded by many people to the point of being much inconvenienced, for they would never let him have a moment's peace.' Then he sought to become a monk and to give himself up to the anchoritic (*anachoresis* = withdrawn) life.

While he was still alive, he was surrounded by disciples, as Antony had been. The community grew, new houses were founded, the organization was extraordinary and the *koinonia* (the union of all the monasteries) grew wealthy. At the time of Pachomius' death it numbered about 1500 and continued to grow.

John Cassian was not yet born when Antony died in 356, but he arrived in Egypt about ten years after Athanasius, his biographer, died in 371. He had come with his friend Germanus first to Bethlehem in search of spiritual masters and had certainly passed through Jerusalem along with so many other famous pilgrims since the time of Constantine's mother Helena. At that time there were other famous monastic women living in or visiting Jerusalem. The rich lady from Spain, Egeria, had come about 384 to visit all the holy places and had seen the Sinai and many places in Syria as well. She described the Holy Week liturgy in Jerusalem[7]. And then Rufinus and Melania had already taken up residence on the Mount of Olives. After Gregory Nazianzen had been deposed as bishop of Constantinople in 381, the deacon Evagrius had come to the Mount of Olives and had been advised by Melania to go to Egypt to visit the famous monks with whom she was already acquainted through her previous travels in the deserts of Egypt. Cassian would hear about the marvels of Egyptian monasticism from Pinufius, who came to Bethlehem in order to flee from his own fame[8].

Eventually Cassian and Germanus asked permission of the seniors of the monastery in Bethlehem to go to Egypt to learn about the life of the monks there. They promised in the cave of the Nativity to return after three years. They returned after seven years and asked permission to return to Egypt again[9]. They

6 VEILLEUX, *Pachomian Koinonia 1,* vol. 1, 28-29.
7 EGERIA, *Pellegrinaggio in Terra Santa: Itinerarium Egeriae*, ed. N. Natalucci, Firenze 1991.
8 *Institutes*, 33-43.
9 *Conference* 17, 2-7.

remained in Egypt until the unfortunate Origenist – Anthropomorphist controversy of 399-400. Evagrius had died in 399. Then they left Egypt and went to Constantinople, where John Chrysostom was bishop. After his exile in 403, Cassian, who had been ordained deacon by John, went to Rome with letters appealing to the bishop of Rome on behalf of John Chrysostom. There John Cassian met the future Leo the Great, who was the archdeacon of the Roman Church. We know nothing about John until he resurfaced in southern Gaul about 415 and began to write his Institutes (*Institutiones*) and Conferences (*Collationes*).

At the end of the fourth book of the Institutes, he reports a homily by Pinufius for the clothing of a novice. Then he devotes the last eight books to the eight principle vices or passions. This brings us back to *philargyria*, the third of the vices after *gastrimargia* and *porneia*. Evagrius had also written of *philargyria* in his *Praktikos* and Cassian certainly knew this work and both of them knew the works of Origen who had given an allegorical interpretation of the seven nations that the Israelites had to conquer in order to enter thepromised land. Actually there were eight if Egypt is included. Egypt represents *gastrimargia* - the fleshpots of Egypt for which the Israelites longed in the desert.

Here we will treat only *philargyria,* the desire for riches, the struggle against greed. It is a perennial desire: the rich always seem to want more. As Thomas Piketty has described it so well for the last few centuries, there is a perennial accumulation of wealth in the hands of the few[10]. But Cassian was not aware of this and did not rail against the rich as John Chrysostom had done, one of the causes of his exile. Cassian was interested rather in the "inner man", a phrase he had found in St. Paul's letters. The development of the inner man is the real goal of the monastic life as Cassian saw it and repeatedly describes it. For example he writes regarding fasting:

> For it is no external adversary that we must fear: The foe is within us, and every day we wage an inner war. Once it has been conquered, everything that is outside will be weakened and all things will be subdued and subjected to the soldier of Christ. We shall not have an adversary outside of us to be afraid of if what is within us has been overcome and has yielded to the Spirit. And we should not believe that mere fasting from visible food can suffice for our perfection of heart and purity of body if a fasting of the soul has not also been joined to it[11].

10 T. Piketty, *Le Capital Au 21. Siecle*, Paris 2013.

11 *Institutes* 5, XXI. 1.

As he does with all of the eight principal vices or "thoughts" (*cogitationes = logismoi*), Cassian discusses their nature, how to recognize them, and how to cure them. Book 7 of the Institutes is devoted to the spirit of covetousness or greed. Cassian describes it:

> Our third conflict is against covetousness which we can describe as the love of money; a foreign warfare, and one outside of our nature, and in the case of a monk originating only from the state of a corrupt and sluggish mind, and often from the beginning of his renunciation being unsatisfactory, and his love towards God being lukewarm at its foundation. For the rest of the incitements to sin planted in human nature seem to have their commencement as it were congenital with us, and somehow being deeply rooted in our flesh, and almost coeval with our birth, anticipate our powers of discerning good and evil, and although in very early days they attack a man, yet they are overcome with a long struggle.

Greed is not natural like lust and anger; it is not rooted in the body. But it is particularly dangerous; as he observes: «this disease coming upon us at a later period, and approaching the soul from without, [...] if it is disregarded, is the more dangerous to everyone, for it becomes "a root of all evils"(1Tim 6,10) and gives rise to a multiplicity of incitements to sin». Monks should live from their own labor:

> Wherefore if we want to obey the gospel precept, and to show ourselves the followers of the Apostle and the whole primitive church, or of the fathers who in our own days succeeded to their virtues and perfection, we should not acquiesce in our own prescriptions, promising ourselves perfection from this wretched and lukewarm condition of ours: but following their footsteps, we should by no means aim at looking after our own interests, but should seek out the discipline and system of a monastery, that we may in very truth renounce this world; preserving nothing of those things which we have despised through the temptation of want of faith; and should look for our daily food, not from any store of money of our own, but from our own labors.

Not possessing anything or being materially poor is not enough. One must root out the desire from one's heart:

> For it is possible even for one who has no money to be by no means free from the malady of covetousness, and for the blessing of penury to do him no good,

because he has not been able to root out the sin of cupidity: delighting in the advantages of poverty, not in the merit of the virtue, and satisfied with the burden of necessity, not without coldness of heart. For just as the word of the gospel declares of those who are not defiled in body, that they are adulterers in heart;902 so it is possible that those who are in no way pressed down with the weight of money may be condemned with the covetous in disposition and intent. For it was the opportunity of possessing which was wanting in their case, and not the will for it: which latter is always crowned by God, rather than compulsion. And so we must use all diligence lest the fruits of our labors should be destroyed to no purpose. For it is a wretched thing to have endured the effects of poverty and want, but to have lost their fruits, through the fault of a shattered will.

How a monk can retain his poverty.

And we can only preserve this virtue unimpaired if we remain in a monastery, and as the Apostle says, having food and clothing, are therewith content. But we shall certainly not be suffered to do this, nor even to remain under the rule of a system, unless the virtue of patience, which can only spring from humility as its source, is first securely fixed and established in us. For the one teaches us not to trouble anyone else; the other, toendure with magnanimity wrongs offered to us.

Caring for the poor is a constant in the tradition from Antony to Pachomius and Shenute and to Cassian in the West and even to the Rule of Benedict. Monastic poverty is not indigence, but renouncing the desire for superfluous things.

Another constant is that monks must work! as Paul insists[12]. This remains true today, at least for the monks in Egypt. In 1993 I was present at a Wednesday evening audience of Pope Shenoute III in Cairo at which he answered questions from the congregation. One question was: «What should we think of monks who ask for money?» His answer was that real monks do not ask for money; they work.

In the fourth century in Cappadocia the wealthy land-owning aristocracy became Christians and produced the greatest Greek Christian literature of the patristic period: Basil the Great, Gregory of Nyssa, his younger brother, and his

12 1 Thes 4:10 Indeed, you do this for all the brothers throughout Macedonia. Nevertheless we urge you, brothers, to progress even more, 11and to aspire to live a tranquil life, to mind your own affairs, and to work with your [own] hands, as we instructed you,12 that you may conduct yourselves properly toward outsiders and not depend on anyone.

friend Gregory Nazianzen. They sought a withdrawn life on their family estates, but were pressed into service as bishops[13]. To this number should be added Melania the elder and Rufinus of Aquileia, who settled on the Mount of Olives. Wealth provided the education and the means for producing this literature in both Greek and Latin. To tell this story would require at least a whole book.

When we arrive in the early sixth century with the Rule of the Master and the Rule of Benedict, we see a notable shift in emphasis from the inner man to social control. The Master is suspicious of guests. The guest may be a burglar and so he is not even allowed to go to the lavatory in the middle of the night without a monk as escort to guide him through doorways and dark passages and to see that he does not steal the spoons. The monks have even locked the door and hidden the key to stop him from going our alone[14]. Although the Rule of Benedict is a notable improvement over that of the Master, there is, nevertheless an emphasis on social control. There are minute prescriptions to prevent any private ownership of anything, even a pen or tablet. The Abbot is told to search the beds frequently «lest private possessions be found there»[15]. One does not lose sight of the inner man completely, but the emphasis certainly on the external observance. The Prologue, ch. 4 (The Tools for Good Works) and ch. 7 (Humility) are exceptions and much of that material comes from Cassian.

As Owen Chadwick noted in 1980, there is a huge shift between the time of Cassian and the time of Benedict. For Cassian, the monastic cell is the place for praying, for working, for sleeping and eating. A hundred years later everything is to be done in common except for sleeping and reading. But even sleeping is done in a dormitory at least for the younger monks. Eating is not done in the refectory and praying in common in the oratory. Precise instructions are given for how the psalms are to be recited in the oratory[16]. This reflects not merely the difference between Egypt and southern Gaul or central Italy, but a change in culture and the breakdown of western society due to many factors. It is reflected

13 The catalogue alone of their works would cover many pages, but as examples, one may mention the Rules of Basil and his homilies, *The Life of Macrina* by Gregory of Nyssa, and the Sermons and poetry of Gregory Nazianzen.

14 O. Chadwick, *The Making of the Benedictine Ideal* (The Thomas Verner Moore Memorial Lecture for 1980), Washington (DC) 1981, 22: «the Master is very suspicious of guests... I can think of no more unpleasant house to stay a night». RM 78-79.

15 Rule of Saint Benedict, ch. 55. T. Fry, *Rb 1980: The Rule of St. Benedict in Latin and English with Notes and Thematic Index*, Collegeville (MN) 1981, 263.

16 Chadwick, *The Making of the Benedictine Ideal*, 12.

also in the figure of Cassiodorus, who had to write a book to teach his monks how to spell[17].

The emphasis on social control and personal non-ownership did not prevent the growth of institutional wealth, which culminates in the Cistercian invention of lay-brothers and the withdrawal from society. The early Cistercians were reacting to Cluny, which was heavily involved in the surrounding society and acquired landed wealth. R.W. Southern has described well how the Cistercians became wealthy despite their goals[18]. This had occurred also in the early cenobitic Pachomian communities. The fact is that any well-organized community dedicated to personal poverty will generate wealth.

Saint Francis and the early Franciscans revolted against institutional wealth. The original Rule of Saint Francis approved by the Pope in 1209 disallowed ownership of property, requiring members of the order to beg for food while preaching. The austerity was meant to emulate the life and ministry of Jesus Christ. However, the large numbers of men who flocked to Francis' new order made it impossible to live without buildings and careful administration of income, etc.

In a wide-ranging survey of attitudes toward wealth in the early church, Peter Brown in a recent book on riches and the church, *Making the camel pass through the eye of the needle*, says that the monasteries in antiquity were never self-sufficient[19]. This is certainly untrue. They were actually charitable institutions and provided employment opportunities to many as they do today in many countries including Egypt. In an otherwise excellent description of Cassian's program of renunciation, Brown omits one key element in Cassian's thought: the notion of the "inner man"[20].

Finally one must mention Jesus' own attitude as expressed when he was in Bethany in the house of Simon the leper:

> [6]"Now when Jesus was in Bethany in the house of Simon the leper, [7]a woman came up to him with an alabaster jar of costly perfumed oil, and poured it on

17 Cassiodorus, *De Orthographia: Tradizione Manoscritta, Fortuna, Edizione Critica*, ed. P. Stoppacci (Edizione nazionale dei testi mediolatini 25), Firenze 2010.

18 R.W. Southern, *Western Society and the Church in the Middle Ages*, Penguin, London 1990.

19 P. Brown, *Through the Eye of a Needle: Wealth, the Fall of Rome, and the Making of Christianity in the West, 350-550 Ad.*, 2014, 414-419.

20 See my forthcoming paper: «John Cassian's Understanding of the Nature of God» (https://www.academia.edu/17564000/John_Cassians_Understanding_of_the_Nature_of_God [access 11/11/2017]).

his head while he was reclining at table. [8]When the disciples saw this, they were indignant and said, "Why this waste? [9]It could have been sold for much, and the money given to the poor." [10]Since Jesus knew this, he said to them, "Why do you make trouble for the woman? She has done a good thing for me. [11d]The poor you will always have with you; but you will not always have me (Matt 26:6).

The three most virulent *pathē* are *porneia*, *philargiria*, (Paul also had something to say about this)[21] and the desire for power over others - this last one is also the most complex (it often involves vanity, pride, envy[22] and arrogance) and requires the help of modern psychology to understand it. These three lead to most of the conflicts in monastic communities, in the churches and in the civil society.

The late great scholar Owen Chadwick once wrote that the analyses of the problems of the human soul by Cassian are as subtle and refined as those of a modern psychologist[23]. This is true, but Cassian did not write the last word. No one ever does.

Finally it must be observed that in the monastic life and in the church there is no substitute for the love of learning and the desire for God, as another great scholar and professor of this Athenaeum, Jean Leclercq, once put it[24]. Love of learning and the desire for God characterizes much of the early monastic movement beginning at least with Origen of Alexandria and of Cesarea.

Abstract

This paper gives a general view on the understanding of work by the key figures of first centuries of Christian monasticism in, such as Anthony, Pachomius, Cas-

21 1 Tim 6:10: For the love of money is the root of all evils, and some people in their desire for it have strayed from the faith and have pierced themselves with many pains.

22 The bibliography on this subject begins with Plato and continues to this day. See https://plato.stanford.edu/entries/envy/#Bib [access: 11/11/2017] and J. Epstein, *Envy: The seven deadly sins*, Oxford University Press, New York 2003; F.J. Ninivaggi, *Envy Theory: Perspectives on the Psychology of Envy*, Rowman & Littlefield, Maryland 2010. P. Salovey, *The Psychology of Jealousy and Envy*, 1991; H. Schoeck, *Envy: A theory of social behavior*, Secker & Warburg, London 1969, R.H. Smith, *Envy: Theory and research*, Oxford University Press, New York 2008. K. Westhues, *The Envy of Excellence: Administrative Mobbing of High-Achieving Professors*, Edwin Mellen Press, Lewiston (N.Y.) 2004. C. Lindholm, *Generous Envy*, Digital Development Debates, issue 17 "Sharing" 2016.

23 Chadwick, *The Making of the Benedictine Ideal,* 5.

24 J. Leclercq, *The Love of Learning and the Desire for God: A Study of Monastic Culture*, New York 2014.

sian. For them any economic activity was not only necessary but also was to have a spiritual and moral dimension, referring, for example, to such ideas as *askesis* or *prosoche* are mentioned. Finally, the paper brings both a historical analysis and a theological critique of the RB in order to clear away some of the foggy thinking that surrounds the notions of poverty in Benedictine tradition.

ORIENTAL MONASTICISM

THE WORK OF THE ARTIST: THE ECONOMIC IMPLICATIONS OF ICON PRODUCTION IN MONASTERIES AND BYZANTINE ICONOCLASM

Barbara Crostini

When thinking about work in the monastery, activities such as the cultivation of land and the related production of wine, oil, beer, honey, and other consumables first spring to mind. These activities are perceived not only as a possible, but even as a desirable complement to contemplation and prayer, as famously stated in the Benedictine Rule. To an extent, the desirability of manual work, engaging the monk in practical tasks, is designed to balance the potentially totalizing abstraction of a life of prayer, and is therefore itself part of the spiritual discipline of monastic life; but from another angle, such activities are also necessary to the sustenance of the monastery, assuring its self-sufficiency. As such, they can be considered both appropriate and legitimate as a source of income for the community as a whole. The real nature of such a balancing act, and the tight grip placed on the healthy proportion between producing and consuming, rather than accumulating riches for their own sake, is addressed by other scholars in this volume.

Here, I would like to consider such economic issues from the perspective of another form of productive activity, namely that of artistic production. In particular, I will focus on the painting of sacred images and sacred books amongst other crafts that can be documented. I will argue that, insofar as such work is considered as an appropriate monastic activity from the spiritual viewpoint, it is also considered as an approved source of income. When, however, iconoclasm undermined the legitimacy of holy images in the Byzantine church, production of such goods was downgraded to an anti-Christian activity. As a consequence, the wealth generated by production of luxury handicrafts such as illuminated manuscripts and precious icons was undercut. In this way, iconoclasm had a del-

Barbara Crostini is Associate Professor at Uppsala University and works on Byzantine monasticism and manuscripts.

eterious economic impact on monastic institutions. This effect, moreover, need not have been merely a secondary consequence, but can be envisaged to be part of the iconoclasts' aims in reducing the growth of monasteries, their independence and therefore, also, their political weight.

Unlike the comprehensive article on craft production in early medieval Western monasteries by Francesca Dell'Acqua[1], who sets both the theoretical basis and the archaeological evidence for a broad range of artistic production, and to which I refer for a thorough and informed discussion of the spiritual basis for artistic activity in monasteries, my article will be more limited in scope. In the first section, I discuss the current trend in Byzantine art-historical scholarship to underplay the monastic contribution to these activities because of lack of evidence. One consequence of this attitude is that the economic impact of iconoclasm on monasteries in eighth- and ninth-century Byzantium is barely considered. In the second part, I examine the figure of Saint Lazarus the Painter through the available written and pictorial sources. I argue that this heroic figure was celebrated as emblematic of the targeting of monasteries and their artistic activity by the iconoclasts. These topics are certainly very limited, and would need to be further explored. They are only bare threads leading from monastic iconodule sentiments to artistic practice within monasteries, suggesting the possibility that anti-image policies were also meant to attack the economic foundations of monastic institutions.

1. THE WORK OF THE ARTIST

Unlike other examples of negative moral judgment over artistic activities, such as, for example, the theatre, it is the painted object rather than the painter who is the target of criticism during Iconoclasm. The Greek word for painter, in fact, *ζωγράφος*, highlights in its etymological composition the participation of the artist in the work of creation as writing life-like compositions. The open *Letter to Artists* that Pope John Paul II wrote in 1999[2] begins with a quotation from Genesis, and the connection between God's creative power and that of man is made clear at its outset:

1 F. Dell'Acqua, «Craft Production in Early Western Monasticism: Rules, Spaces, Products», in *Western Monasticism* ante litteram*: the Spaces of Monastic Observance in Late Antiquity and the Early Middle Ages*, ed. H. Dey, Turnhout 2011, 289-314, with a comprehensive bibliography of the work done in this field during the twentieth century.

2 Https://w2.vatican.va/content/john-paul-ii/en/letters/1999/documents/hf_jp-ii_let_23041999_artists.html [access: 11-11-2017].

> God therefore called man into existence, committing to him the craftsman's task. Through his "artistic creativity" man appears more than ever "in the image of God", and he accomplishes this task above all in shaping the wondrous "material" of his own humanity and then exercising creative dominion over the universe which surrounds him. With loving regard, the divine Artist passes on to the human artist a spark of his own surpassing wisdom, calling him to share in his creative power. Obviously, this is a sharing which leaves intact the infinite distance between the Creator and the creature [...].

The pope is keen to convey the sense that artistic creation is a special gift from God, but also that each human being is a creator when he takes the shape of his/her life into his/her hands. Thus, he says,

> Not all are called to be artists in the specific sense of the term. Yet, as Genesis has it, all men and women are entrusted with the task of crafting their own life: in a certain sense, they are to make of it a work of art, a masterpiece[3].

This self-awareness in the shaping of one's existence is particularly true of the monastic choice, where a specific lifestyle following well set-out rules is undertaken to achieve the goal of salvation. Consonance between a moral attitude and the capacity to produce approved paintings (icons) is developed as a condition for painting sacred art in later Orthodoxy[4].

Controversy rather stems from the images themselves. The two phases of Byzantine Iconoclasm (726-787; 814-842) questioned the validity of images, both of anthropomorphic images of God and of images of the saints. Representation of holy subjects was forbidden and condemned by the iconoclast emperors, and this position was made into ecclesiastical law at the Council of Heireia (754). Whether because of threat of persecution, political convenience or real conviction, a large part of the Byzantine church, including the patriarch, supported the iconoclast position. Active resistance to iconoclasm, however, was consistently found to come from two quarters: the monasteries and Rome. Amongst the causes for such a state of affairs, then, the question can be considered of whether the imperial anti-image policy was in fact a way of attacking monastic institutions

3 Https://w2.vatican.va/content/john-paul-ii/en/letters/1999/documents/hf_jp-ii_let_23041999_artists.html [access: 11-11-2017].

4 See the introduction by Mario Gallina to E. Fogliadini, *L'immagine negata. Il Concilio di Hieria e la formalizzazione ecclesiale dell'iconoclasmo*, Milano 2013, XII.

indirectly, undermining their power by making them, effectively, outlaws of the Empire. This idea can be supported by the monastic martyrs for this cause, and by invoking the figure of St Theodore of Stoudios (759-826), abbot of perhaps the most important monastery in Constantinople at the time, who suffered exile but nevertheless continued to preach and elaborate arguments in support of images. Besides this ideological undermining, it is likely that the attack on monastic power also entailed an economic aspect, since artistic work –including activities such as icon-painting, manuscript copying and decorating, etching, embroidering– were an economic asset for monasteries such as Theodore's.

Against this hypothesis stand two main factors. The first is the lack of evidence concerning the effects of iconoclasm in general; the second is the prevailing skepticism amongst modern scholars, that artists (of all the types mentioned above) cannot with any certainty be named as belonging to monastic institutions. The article by Alice-Mary Talbot is emblematic of this trend[5]. Despite displaying images of modern monks and nuns at work as painters in Orthodox monasteries, Talbot casts doubt on every piece of evidence surviving concerning Byzantine monastic art and artists. For example, she considers the portrait of the monk Theophanes in the Melbourne Gospels, inscribed with an epigram designating him as donor, scribe and illuminator of the manuscript he is presenting to the Virgin, as «only the donor, since it was a Byzantine convention for the patron to take credit for having "copied" or "painted" a manuscript»[6]. This skeptical trend in Byzantine historians is both common and disconcerting. Even if Theophanes were not himself the scribe and artist, the burden of proof lies on those who wish to show that this manuscript production is alien to the monastic milieu, rather than vice-versa[7]. By declaring himself scribe and artist, rather than simply the donor (or sponsor) of the book, Theophanes is representing himself as carrying out these tasks, of which he is clearly very proud[8],

5 A.-M. Talbot, «Byzantine Monasticism and the Liturgical Arts», in *Perceptions of Byzantium and Its Neighbors (843-1261)*, ed. O.Z. Pevny, New York 2000, 22-39.

6 Talbot, «Byzantine Monasticism», 24 and fig. 6.

7 On this ms, see H. Buchthal, «An Illuminated Byzantine Gospel Book of about 1100 AD», repr. in *Art of the Mediterranean World A.D. 100 to 1400*, Washington DC 2008, 140-149.

8 In the words of Antonio Iacobini, the choice of his self-presentation underscored «"la sua compiaciuta dichiarazione di paternità dell'opera": Libri per i monaci. Segni e immagini della committenza monastica nel mondo bizantino», *Rivista di studi bizantini e neoellenici* 43 (2006) 3-18, 16 figs. This article is a thorough survey of the monastic evidence for patronage, which broadly supports the view expressed in this paper.

before the Virgin. If the abbot is advocating for himself such practices, it is more likely that he would be usurping them from his brothers with their consent, rather than that he would be taking credit for the activity of an external and alien workforce.

While this extraordinary image confirms that monastics saw themselves as active producers of sacred, illuminated books, the observation by Buchthal that this manuscript had a limited progeny may also militate against its having been produced in a professional scriptorium. Rather, its unusual programme, including personifications of monastic virtues as part of the illuminated ornament, firmly anchors the book's audience to a monastic setting. According to Margaret Manion,

> The virtues are personal in emphasis: prudence, courage, thoughtfulness, alms-giving, well-doing, kindness of heart, exhortation, repentance, love, wisdom, contemplation and action. Juxtaposed with the calendar figures, they call for the living-out of the gospel ideal within the monastic environment[9].

One problem is that of distinguishing the milieu of production from the receiving end of the product. Whilst books of sacred and liturgical content would be most appropriate to the life of a community, some de-luxe productions appear to overstep the requirements for such needs in practice. The high cost of parchment manuscripts, increased by the use of gold and the painting of initials and miniatures, is also a factor to consider when imagining the prospective buyer. Often lay patrons are envisaged as more likely to be endowed with the means to acquire such books, although again patronage and final destination could be differentiated when a lay patron in turn donates such a book to an institution, either as direct sponsorship, or as a later gift. Artistic embellishment, either with or without a useful object –such as a book or a liturgical vessel–, covers a middle ground between the material and spiritual realms and is therefore a privileged place for exchanges between the monastic community and the world surrounding it.

In the eleventh century, elaborate figurative programmes were developed in biblical manuscripts connected with the monastery of Stoudios in Constantinople. Arguably, the theological depth in the relationship between the chosen images and the exegesis on the biblical text[10] presupposed a close collaboration

9 See M. Manion, http://www.ngv.vic.gov.au/essay/illuminating-words/ [access: 11-11-2017].

10 See for example C. Barber, *The Theodore Psalter*, Champaign (IL) 2000.

between monastics and professional scribes and artists, in the case that these manuscripts should be thought of as stemming from lay ateliers outside the monastery's doors. Even when the main scribes responsible for a family of related manuscripts are clearly monks, modern scholarship is unwilling to envisage the workings of an *"ergasterion"* or workshop within a monastic establishment. For example, the impressive study by Irmgard Hutter[11] that seeks out such family resemblances in tracing the belonging of a very large group of codices, all produced at Constantinople in the middle of the eleventh century, is reluctant to link such an extensive production either with Studios specifically, or with any monastic-driven enterprise in general:

> None of the manuscripts so far identified contains any undisputable indication as to the social status and the location of the anonymous ergasterion. [...] it is almost certain that it was not located in the monastery of Studiou [...]. In fact, I doubt that it was housed in any monastery at all, despite the fact that at least some of its scribes were monks, for the simple reason that there is no indication that monasteries ever operated a professional business of this proportion and on this calligraphic and artistic level[12].

While there is no reason to believe that such a vast production –on the scale of several hundred manuscripts produced within a couple of decades– came out of a single workshop at a single monastery, one ought to account at the same time both for the range of similarities highlighted by Hutter as well as for a consistent difference in details, including considerable codicological variation, for example in the ruling types. In other words, while the mass production of one type of text, such as the long collection of saints' Lives in ten volumes of the Metaphrastian menologion, well fits the picture of a semi-industrial serial production for profit purposes, the actual realization of each manuscript reflects individual choices since, as Hutter herself stresses, «not two of them are identical»[13]. Hutter admits that the workshop adapted each time to different requests: «Scribes and painters did not work at a production line but in reaction to the different demands of their clients as to the contents, format, price

11 I. Hutter, «Le copiste du Metaphraste: on a Center for Manuscript Production in Eleventh-Century Constantinople», in *I Manoscritti greci tra riflessione e dibattito: Atti del V Colloquio Internazionale di Paleografia greca*, ed. G. Prato, Firenze 2000, 535-586.

12 Hutter, «Le copiste du Metaphraste», 573-574.

13 Hutter, «Le copiste du Metaphraste», 571.

and prestige of the books»[14]. This explanation does not, of course, eliminate the possibility either that such patrons were in fact monastic institutions themselves, or that the artists came from or operated within a monastic milieu. In fact, it is not impossible to envisage a network of manuscript-producing monasteries at Constantinople, perhaps with a few more important and specialized centres, within which expertise, workmanship, labour and models could be exchanged. This *modus operandi* could explain variation, as well as the common characteristics between manuscripts, perhaps better than a one-workshop model, whether monastic or lay. While private libraries certainly existed, it is undoubted that in Constantinople, besides the imperial palace, ecclesiastical institutions such as the patriarchate and numerous monasteries were the primary depositaries as well as beneficiaries of the city's manuscript wealth[15].

Talbot treats Stoudios as an exception in the panorama of lay artistic endeavour in Byzantine icon and manuscript production, which she depicts as the norm. She nonetheless concedes that perhaps the isolation of Sinai and Athos gave rise to special local arrangements for the production of manuscripts, which could also be illuminated, and not just written, at monastic ateliers. On Sinai, special icons with a particular gilding technique may have been painted and thus such a special skill was developed in the monastery itself. But these exceptions are seen as confirming the rule that generally denies monasteries any pride of place in artistic production.

Invoking the lack of information concerning named monastic artists in Byzantium does not contribute much to supporting such a negative conclusion. Not only does the reasoning expose the weakness of any argument *e silentio*, but such absence of names is indeed expected during the entire medieval period in both East and West, when not only monastic, but also lay activity cannot be securely documented in this way. On the contrary, of the fairly long list of artists' names published by Anthony Cutler in the *Oxford Dictionary of Byzantium*, a good proportion are designated as "monk"[16]. Given the Byzantines' preference for short, elliptical colophons, even where present, such surprisingly rich data cannot be ignored.

14 HUTTER, «Le copiste du Metaphraste», 571.

15 On the necessary symbiosis between centres of copy and libraries, see G. DAGRON, «Centres de copie et bibliothèques», in *Byzantine Books and Bookmen*, Dumbarton Oaks, Center for Byzantine Studies, Washington DC 1975, 17-27, esp. 19, 22-23.

16 A. CUTLER, «Artist», in *Oxford Dictionary of Byzantium*, vol. 1, eds. A.P. Kazhdan-A.-M. Talbot-A. Cutler *et al.*, New York-Oxford 1991.

Cutler's remark that the Byzantine artist was not medium-specific leads us to expect versatility in the arts, so that the simultaneous production of, say, illuminated manuscripts and icons by the same artists was a definite possibility. Although neither materials, such as pigments used for icon and manuscript painting, nor other tools and equipment may have overlapped, costs of the more expensive production of books could have been defrayed by the easier revenues from the cheaper production of icons through the deployment of the same workforce. Thus, skilled craftsmen could be multi-tasking in the same place, or they might have had to exercise their artistry in different places at different times, since, of course, not all monasteries could and did run a scriptorium. The size of a community was one factor in determining the viability of a scriptorium enterprise that included the handling of expensive parchment and writing materials in great quantities. Francesco D'Aiuto has shown how therefore monk-artists travelled between communities even long-distance to establish profitable collaborations[17]. Moreover, their painting abilities could be used for manuscripts written in different languages, as in the case of a group of manuscripts whose "family resemblance" has been retraced across Greek and Georgian texts and communities[18]. Thus, both writing and painting were feasible and useful activities for the communities that wanted to specialize in them, and a high degree of collaboration was operative between centres of manuscript production and illumination by the eleventh century. Although we do not have comparable evidence for the earlier centuries, it is likely that to some extent this activity was also supporting monasteries earlier, and that iconoclasm saw in forbidding images an opportunity to effectively undercut this source of income for monasteries.

2. ST. LAZARUS THE PAINTER

While the championing of the iconodule cause by monastics such as Theodore Stoudite (759-826) is well-known, and his theological writings and diplomatic action are certainly part of the same discourse, the elevation of a monk/painter to the status of saint is significant in legitimizing and upholding this activity in monasteries to Byzantine eyes.

17 F. D'Aiuto, «Libro, scrittura e miniature fra Bisanzio e il Caucaso: qualche riflessione», in *Scrittura e libro nel mondo Greco-bizantin. Atti del Corso, Ravello, Villa Rufolo, 6-9 novembre 2007*, ed. C.C. Brach, Ravello 2012, 77-108.

18 D'Aiuto, «Libro, scrittura e miniature», 91-92. See at nn. 50-51 the citation of the Russian scholar, Alexander Saminsky, and of other researchers who have published work on this group of manuscripts.

St Lazarus the Painter was a champion of the iconodule cause in the second, ninth-century phase of iconoclasm. His figure, though not entirely minor, has generally been neglected in scholarship[19]. Although venerated as a saint, Lazarus was not assigned a BHG[20] number, since no full account of his Life is extant. Two short liturgical notices about him can be found in the Constantinopolitan Synaxarion and in the Menaion[21] on 17 November. However, despite the absence of a Life and unlike most saints, Lazarus enters the historical record in at least two places: in the Chronicle of Theophanes and in the official records of the popes[22]. There is no doubt, therefore, that his importance in the controversy, though perhaps in part mythologized, is real.

In the *Chronicle* by Theophanes, Lazarus is introduced as '*τὸν μοναχὸν Λάζαρον*' (ch. 13, l. 4)[23]. This status does not in itself set Lazarus apart: he is «renowned' (*περιβόητος*) for his artistic abilities and Emperor Theophilus is after him for this very reason, seeking to "eliminate from amongst all men all those who painted the divine images (*τὰς θείας ἐκτυποῦντας μορφὰς*)» (ch. 13, l. 1). Thus, Lazarus's life as a monk and a painter is pitched against the iconoclastic impetus of the ruler, who quickly resorts to torture in order to dissuade, and then physically to maim, the painter's skill. Lazarus emerges unscathed and undeterred from these attempts, and, as an example of resistance, sets up figural monuments around town. The word used twice to describe this activity by Theophanes is a rather unusual verb,

19 One notable exception is the discussion by C. Mango, «The Apse Mosaics of St. Sophia at Istanbul. Report on Work Carried out in 1964», *Dumbarton Oaks Papers* 19 (1965) 113-151, at 144-145, commenting on the traditional attribution of those mosaics to Lazarus. Mango considers the attribution unlikely not for reasons of chronology, but because of Lazarus' political allegiance to Photius' adversaries. Hence he was hardly the best candidate to have been chosen as the restorer of Photius' magnum opus. Mango considers that the attribution to him may have arisen "because he was the only famous painter ... [or] it may have been a deliberate invention calculated to deprive Photius of the credit of having restored the mosaics". See also L. Brubaker-J. HALDON, *Byzantium in the Iconoclast Era (ca 680850): the Source*, Aldershot 2001, 71-73.

20 *Bibliotheca Hagiographica graeca*, ed. F. Halkin (Subsidia hagiographica 8), 3 vols, Brussels, 1957.

21 Both these liturgical sources are pr. by Raasted (see n. 40 below) from the editions by Delehaye and Saliverou respectively. I present these texts in parallel columns as an appendix to this article in order to compare them and highlight their differences.

22 Concise biography and references to Lazaros the Painter in Dumbarton Oaks Online Database, *Introduction*, 61-62: http://www.doaks.org/research/byzantine/resources/hagiography-database/hagiointro.pdf [access: 27-01-2017].

23 *Chronographiae quae Theophanis Continuati nomine fertur Libri I-IV*, eds. M. Featherstone-J. Signes-Codoñer, Berlin 2015, ch. 13, 148 (Greek), 149 (English).

ἀναστηλόω, which, according to LSJ[24], means «to set up as a memorial», where the "stele" part contains in it the memorial function, as in a written slab or stone marking a site or a person's grave. The translators of the *Chronicle* into English have preferred to use "set out" and "set up" *tout court* in the respective instances. In the Dumbarton Oaks hagiography database this verb, with a question mark, is translated as "restored", when referred to Lazarus replacing the famous image of Christ at the Chalke Gate. The act of restoration seems to be a pertinent interpretation not only for the specific monument, whose earlier presence at this site is thus underlined[25], but also for the original semantics of this unusual verb as opposed to the more common *στηλόω* (also meaning "to set up as memorial"). Looking back to the first use, it is also possible to envisage that the "forms/images of the saints on panels" (*τὰς τῶν ἁγίων ἐν πίναξιν ... μορφάς*) were not erected *ex novo* either. The point of choosing this composite verb seems to be precisely that of stressing the return to tradition enacted through Lazarus's skill and his defiance of iconoclast power. One can also understand the act of restoration, not only as a re-placing, but also as a re-painting, i.e. improving the looks of discarded or ruined images for renewed use[26].

The account of Lazarus in Theophanes' *Chronicle* does not exactly overlap the synopsis of his Life in the two liturgical sources, which, despite small differences that we will analyze below, are essentially in agreement with each other. The *Chronicle* alone gives the detail that Lazarus's hands were burnt in the cruel tortures of the prison; the account exploits this detail in two ways: it describes Lazarus as «a spark (of inspiration) for posterity» (*τοῖς ὕστερον ἔναυσμα*)[27], thus reversing the effects of the torture through God's grace; and it emphasizes that his next painting, that of the icon of St John the Baptist for the homonymous monastery of Phoberos, where Lazarus had taken refuge after being released as good as dead, in turn became a source of healing. One cannot help but think of

24 H.G. Liddle-R. Scott, *Greek-English Lexicon*, Oxford [9]1996, s.v.

25 This point is debated by scholars. See M.-F. Auzépy, «La destruction de l'icône du Christ de la Chalcé par Léon III: Propagande ou Realité?», in Ead., *L'histoire des iconoclastes*, Paris 2007, 145-178, at 145, 177: «la destruction de l'icône du Christ à la Chalcé n'a pas eu lieu pour la bonne [177: excellente] raison que cette icône n'existait pas sous Léon III».

26 The bi- or tri-dimensional nature of these simulacra is perhaps debatable, as is the exact medium in which they were executed. For example, the Chalke icon of Christ may have been a mosaic; wooden panels may have been painted or sculpted; the word 'eikon' need not mean anything more than 'image' in a generic way.

27 The translation of this word as "a stimulus" misses the word-play on the fire theme introduced by the torture of burning.

those wonder-working icons whose definition of authenticity was that of not being painted by human hands[28]. This metaphor applies *a fortiori* to the temporarily handless Lazarus, whose creation appears as a miraculous event while his hands were maimed. That he also set up the Chalke icon «with his own hands» (*οὗτος χερσὶν*) is further picked up as a poignant detail in the *Chronicle*.

The *Chronicle* alone specifies the fact that Lazarus went into exile to the monastery of St John "called Fearful" (Phoberos). Mentions in Theophanes and in the chronicle by Cedrenus establish the existence of this foundation, probably located on the Asian shore of the Bosphoros, already in the ninth century, although details of the monastery's origin are otherwise not known for certain[29]. Its history of iconodule resistance may well have played a role in its re-establishment at the beginning of the twelfth century as a strongly independent foundation, capitalizing on the fame gained in the earlier period and thus countering, perhaps, a new wave of iconoclasm under the Komnenians[30]. Key to establishing continuity between the ninth-century vicissitudes and the later history of this foundation is the preservation of Lazarus' wonder-working icon of St John[31].

Neither of the liturgical accounts of Lazarus builds on or reproduces information found in this *Chronicle*. In them, only generic tortures and terrible punishments are mentioned without any naming of the emperor responsible. But whereas Theophilus is described periphrastically by Theophanes as «the tyrant who intended to eliminate from amongst men all those who painted the divine images or else [...] that they should spit upon them and cast them on the ground and trample on them as profane things and thus save themselves», this long periphrasis is wrapped up in only a few words in the Synaxarion: «*ἐπὶ τῆς βασιλείας τῶν εἰκονομάχων*». Later in the passage, the iconoclasts are described

28 On this theme, see G. Lingua, «Le acheropite e i fondamenti della teoria dell'immagine cristiana», in *Sacre immagini e oggetti "non fatti da mani d'uomo" nelle religioni*, ed. A. Monaci Castagno, Alessandria 2011, 113-128.

29 Robert Jordan's summary of R. Janin, *La géographie ecclésiastique de l'empire byzantine*, Première partie: *Le siège de Constantinople et le patriarcat œcuménique*, vol. 3: *Les églises et les monastères*, Paris 1953, 7-8, is rather misleading. He states that «Except for the information contained in the *typikon* itself, nothing else is known about this foundation»: DO Monastic Documents translations project, n. 30 (Phoberos), 872 (available online at doaks.org; access: 27-01-2017).

30 On iconoclastic tendencies in the eleventh century, see B. Pentcheva, *The Sensual Icon*, University Park 2010, 198-208.

31 As witnessed by Cedrenus: *Georgius Cedrenus Ioannis Scylitzae ope*, vol. 2, ed. E. Bekker, Bonn 1839, 112-113. The icon may have been kept in the church of Phoberou even through a period of decay of the monastic structures.

as «τῶν βδελυκτῶν καὶ ἀνοσίων εἰκονοκαυστῶν» by the Synaxarion and as «*ἀθέων εἰκονομάχων*» by the Menaion. Both passages equally throw into relief the heretical presuppositions of Lazarus' adversaries, calling them with the traditional names of the ancient heresiarchs, Eutyches, Nestorios and Dioskoros, as was common practice. Without mentioning the icon of Christ at the Chalke gate, the Synaxarion expresses the same Christological point with the succinct attribute «*θεανθρώπου*» used by Theophanes to describe it in the phrase «ὁμολογῶν τὸν Χριστὸν τέλειον θεὸν καὶ τέλειον ἄνθρωπον, ἀσυγχύτως, ἀτρέπτως, ἀναλλοιώτως». This elaboration, however, is omitted in the Menaion entry. The Synaxarion also specifies the grounds for the punishments inflicted on Lazarus which sounds as a reversal of the actions imposed by Theophilus: because he venerates and bows (προσκυνεῖν) before the venerable images (ἐκτυπώματα) of the saints and because he paints these skillfully (εὐφυῶς) on wooden boards with his own hands (οἰκειοχείρως)[32]. From the Synaxarion account, Lazarus emerges as an iconodule monk in all senses, orthodox in belief and practice, as well as a skillful painter. There is no sense that he took part in a wider programme of restoration, but rather simply that he was persecuted at a time when orthodoxy had been questioned by people with heretical beliefs.

Although short, both liturgical accounts add information to Theophanes' narrative. Both specify, in different words, that Lazarus became a monk from an early age, and the shorter account, that of the Menaion, further states that he learnt his skill as a painter in his first monastery. This is an interesting detail for our purposes. Although neither source names a specific monastery where Lazarus took the habit, there was no reason to add this information unless such practice was a reasonably expected occurrence. Since both sources end by naming the monastery of Evandros as Lazarus' place of burial, one could advance the hypothesis that he returned and was buried where he had begun his monastic life. The latter foundation, however, was relatively recent, making this hypothesis unlikely. According to Janin, Evandros was founded around 845 by the patrician Peter, an officer of Nikephoros's army against the Bulgarians[33]. This foundation date is compatible with the date of Lazarus' death, as discussed by Cyril Mango who posits a *post quem* of 865[34]. An independent witness to Lazarus' burial, the pilgrim Anthony of Novgorod, locates his tomb near the hospital of St Zoticus on the heights of

32 This word has only five parallels in TLG, among which Anna Komnena's *Alexiad*.

33 Janin, *La géographie*, vol. 3, 114.

34 C. Mango, «Documentary Evidence on the Apse Mosaics of St. Sophia», BZ 47 (1954) 397, as cited by Raasted (see below, n. 40), 129 and n. 15.

Galata[35]. According to the Synaxarion, Lazarus was placed to rest in the monastery τῶν Εὐάνδρου in the imperial city in the town of Pera (ἐν τῇ βασιλίδι τῶν πόλεων ... Πέραν τοῦ ἄστεος). While the Menaion printed by Saliverou does not give any specific location, the southern Italian manuscript, Vat. gr. 2046, 11th cent., with which I collated his text places Evandrou «near Constantinople» (πλησίον Κωνσταντινουπόλεως). This reading could be an addition for readers far from that geographical location; or it maybe should be restored to the text according to the similar specification of place in the Synaxarion. The two accounts differ in their telling of Lazarus' death, the shorter being the more precise in indicating a cause, however vague («a certain indisposition» or «malaise»)[36].

Thus, if we combine the account by Theophanes with the two short notices for Lazarus' feast day, no less than three monasteries come into play in the resulting picture: the monastery that Lazarus joined as a young man, where he learnt the art of painting; the monastery where he recovered from near-death (Phoberos) and produced a wonder-working icon of John the Baptist; and the monastery near Constantinople, in the Pera region (Euandrou), where, although he died (as we will see) on his second mission to Italy, he was taken back to and buried.

The historicity of Lazarus is confirmed beyond doubt by his involvement in a delegation to the pope at the time of iconoclasm. His name is mentioned in the very famous Letter of Pope Nicholas I to Emperor Michael III, dated 28 September 865[37]. It is somewhat peculiar that this historical fact should be commemorated by the liturgical sources, but ignored by Theophanes' *Chronicle*. While Theophanes is at pains to establish secure points of reference between

35 Janin, *La géographie*, vol. 3, 114; see also Mango, «Documentary Evidence on the Apse Mosaics», 142 and n. 40 and 144 on other testimonies by Anthony about Lazarus' activity in Constantinople.

36 Here too MS Vat. gr. 2046 has a variant reading. It uses the nominative rather than the genitive absolute, perhaps more consonant with the plain style of the note; and a more specific verb to describe the onset of the physical illness, as opposed to a generic auxiliary verb. On the origin of this manuscript from the area of Rossano or eastern Sicily, see Andrea Luzzi and Lidia Perria, 'Un sinassario-tipico italogreco *sui generis*: il *Vat. gr.* 2460', in *Calabria bizantina. Civiltà bizantina nei territori di Gerace e Stilo*, Soveria Mannelli 1998, 155-164.

37 MGH IV, Ep. 88, 477-478. See also M. McCormick, «La lettre diplomatique byzantine du premier millénaire», in *Byzance et le monde extérieur. Contacts, relations, échanges*, eds. M. Balard-É. Malamut-J.-M. Spieser, Paris 2005, 135-149, at 140 n. 17; M. McCormick, *Origins of the European Economy: Communications and Commerce AD 300-900*, Cambridge 2001, 935, n. 554.

Lazarus and the imperial city[38], both commemorations praise the international exploits of Lazarus in fighting for the cause of «the dogmas of the fathers and the apostles» in his diplomatic mission to Rome, where he was called by the pope to support the cause of Patriarch Ignatius. The Synaxarion even calls this journey an «apostolic service» (ἀποστολικὴν διακονίαν). One might well wonder if this mission made Lazarus in the end less popular in the East than might have been otherwise. It may thus not be a coincidence that his memory is mostly preserved in southern Italian liturgical books.

A curious piece of evidence might offer a connection between St Lazarus and a Western monastery, too, if Raasted's identification is correct. Raasted argues that a letter found in MS Sang. 902[39], dated to the ninth or early tenth century, could be about this Lazarus[40].

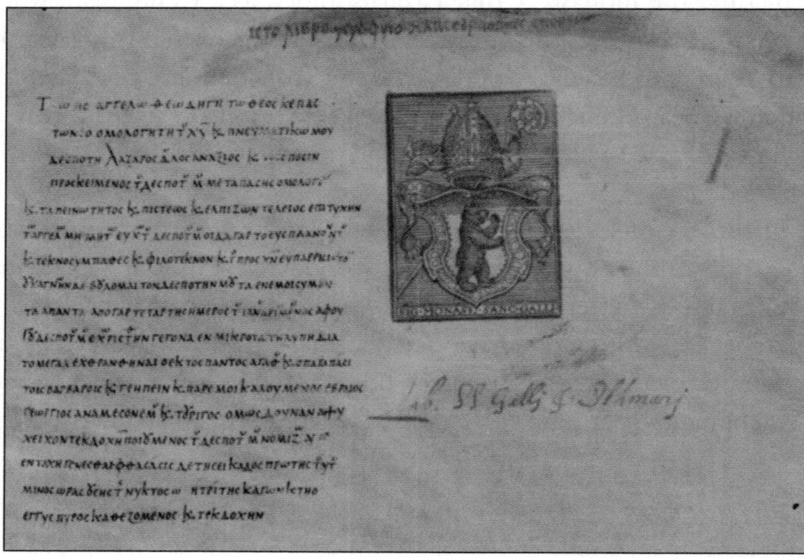

Fig. 1 Lazarus letter Sang. 902

38 To the evidence discussed above we must add the Theodora episode that concludes the passage in the *Chronicle*. It introduces a 'bon mot' on Lazarus' part with a proverbial ring to it modeled on narratives of saintly advice to emperors.

39 Neither the Letter on p. 7 nor Raasted's article are mentioned in the monastery's catalogue: A. von Euw, *Die St. Galler Buchkunst vom 8. bis zum Ende des 11. Jahrhunderts*, vol. 1: *Textband* (Monasterium Sancti Galli 3), St. Gallen 2008, 446-449, n. 119; http://www.e-codices.unifr.ch/en/description/csg/0902/ [access: 11-11-2017].

40 J. Raasted, «A Byzantine Letter in Sankt Gallen and Lazarus the Painter», *Cahiers de l'Institut du moyen-âge grec et latin* 37 (1981) 124-138.

Quite apart from the content of the Letter, which Raasted transcribes and translates, but whose contents are far from crystal clear, his argument depends on the early dating of the letter itself to the ninth century. Such date is fixed, according to Raasted, by the date of the manuscript. However, the manuscript is a composite of three authors and its structure does not appear unitary. Only the first part, containing a Greek-Latin text (pp. 8-68), is relevant here. The Letter is found on the recto of the first parchment leaf, at p. 7[41], while the verso, p. 8, has the beginning of the text of Dositheus' *Grammar* copied as a school text by the monks of St Gall.

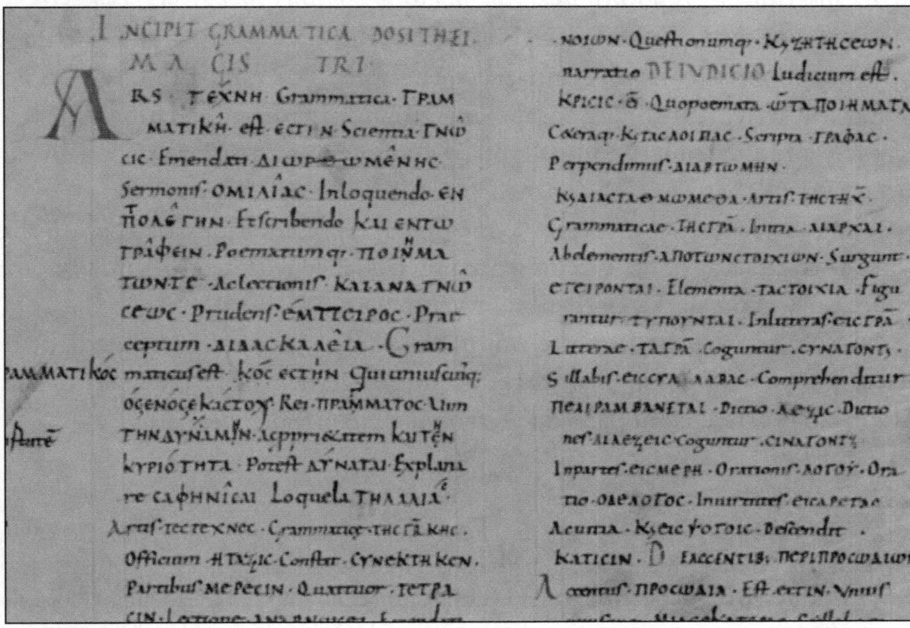

Fig. 2 Dositheus' *Grammar* in Sang. 902.

Although the ink colour of the Letter is a lighter brown than that of the main text, the style of writing in little uncials with singular morphologies is very similar and thus the letter cannot easily be dismissed as a later addition. If it was copied at the same time as the Dositheus text, perhaps by the same hand, it also probably came from the same model. Since Berschin notes that Dositheus'

41 As can be ascertained by consulting the facsimile at http://www.e-codices.unifr.ch/en/csg/0902 [access: 11-11-2017].

Grammar was originally written as a Latin grammar for Greeks[42], it is possible that the model in question was an Oriental manuscript written fairly close to the time of Lazarus' life. Another possibility is that the letter fragment was preserved at Saint Gall and then copied in this early manuscript. On this account, Raasted rightly judged the importance of this source and may well be correct in connecting it to Lazarus the painter. However, on the same page as the Letter, i.e. on p. 7, in the upper margin, there is also a note of possession written in a similar Greek uncial style but in a thicker pen and slightly different ink colour, subsequently rubbed unsuccessfully. It transliterates into Greek letters the following inscription: *Isto libro usus fuit magister Ioannes Sporer* (ΙΣΤΟ ΛΙΒΡΟ ΥΣΥΣ ΦΥΙΣ ΜΑΓΙΣΘΕΡ ΙΟΑΝΕΣ ΣΠΟΡΕΡ). According to Berschin, it was this schoolmaster from Vienna, active between 1453 and 1458, who copied the Lazarus letter[43]. If so, the compelling grounds for an early dating vanish irreparably and the seductive likelihood of a connection to St Lazarus disappears with them.

Besides these textual witnesses[44], one figural representation of St Lazarus has come down to us also. He is represented on a chalice with handles now kept in the Treasury of St Mark's Cathedral in Venice (fig. 3-4)[45].

St Lazarus is depicted on the rim of the chalice, whose cup is made of reused sardonyx sculpted in Classical Antiquity, together with a company of thirty-four saints arranged in pairs on rectangular enamel plaques.

42 W. Berschin, *Greek Letters and the Latin Middle Ages. From Jerome to Nicholas of Cusa*, transl. by Jerold C. Frakes, Washington DC 1988, 147 and n. 99.

43 My thanks to the librarian of Sankt Gallen, Cornel Dora, and to Karl Schmuki for helping find the relevant information about this page. Dr Schmuki provided this key reference to W. Berschin, «Griechische in der Klosterschule des Alten St. Gallen», *BZ* 84/85 (1991/92) 329-340, at 339.

44 Mango («The Apse Mosaics», 145 n. 56) cites two further witnesses to Lazarus's Roman mission: that of a letter from Stylianos to Pope Stephen V (Mansi, XVI, col. 428C) and that preserved by Cardinal Deusdedit in his compilation of extracts from the acts of the council of 861 (V. Wolf von Glanvell, *Die Kanonessamlung des Kardinals Deusdedit*, vol. 1, Paderborn, 1905, 608). I have not been able to follow up these references, though they are interesting in confirming the trail Lazarus left in historical sources of his period.

45 *The Treasury of San Marco Venice* (Milan: Olivetti/The Metropolitan Museum of Art, 1984), n. 10, 129-135 "Chalice of the emperor Romanos (with handles)". The detail of the handles is fundamental in distinguishing this object from the next one in this catalogue (n. 11, 136-140), which is also a "Chalice of the emperor Romanos (without handles)". Images of the latter are more commonly found on the web.

Fig. 3. "Chalice of the emperor Romanos (with handles)", after *The Treasury of San Marco Venice* (Milan: Olivetti/The Metropolitan Museum of Art, 1984), n. 10 (detail of St Lazarus).

Fig. 4. "Chalice of the emperor Romanos (with handles)", after *The Treasury of San Marco Venice* (Milan: Olivetti/The Metropolitan Museum of Art, 1984), n. 10.

It may be significant that Lazarus is here paired with Patriarch Nikephorus rather than with Ignatius, whose cause is usually thought to have been supported by the painter-monk[46]. Patriarch Ignatius does appear instead on a related object, together with a rare iconodule saint, Theophylact of Nicomedia[47].

An inscription dedicates this vessel to an emperor Romanos usually identified with Romanos II (r. 959-63). The chalice is part of a group of precious liturgical vessels that is associated with this emperor. Their style has been compared with the reliquary of Limburg an der Lahn executed under the patronage of Basil the Parakoikomenos. Coherently with Basil's concerns, these objects affirm the cult of saints and the legitimacy of their representation and veneration[48]. Poignantly, the saints join in partaking of the Eucharist, being depicted on precious chalices and patens, thus making visible the communion of saints. In this series of objects that depict defenders of icons on Eucharistic implements, the iconoclastic claims that divorce the sacrament from the veneration of images are thwarted and refuted.

CONCLUSION

In his treatise, *De idololatria*, Tertullian advocates the requalification of pagan artists into related fields, such as house decoration and building work, since he associates the making of statues with a form of worship[49] of the pagan gods–the artist cannot be morally detached from his product, even if it is carried out simply as a paid job. Reversing such fear, the iconodule makers of sacred books, icons and holy vessels adorned with images of Christ, Mary and the saints participate in the veneration by their making as well as through the results of their representations.

46 It is perhaps worth noting that the *Life of Ignatius* does not mention Lazarus despite dealing extensively with the case of Gregory of Syracuse. The earliest manuscript of this text is fourteenth century although scholars date its composition to the first decade of the tenth century. See the introduction by John Duffy in *The Life of Patriarch Ignatius = Vita Ignatii Patriarchae by Nicetas David*, ed. A. Smithies (Dumbarton Oaks texts 13/ Corpus fontium historiae Byzantinae 51), Washington DC 2013.

47 *The Treasury of San Marco*, 110.

48 L. Bevilacqua, *Arte e aristocrazia a Bisanzio nell'Età dei Macedoni*, Rome 2013, 193-227, surveys the role of Basil as sponsor of the arts and reviews all the objects attributed to him. See also Steve H. Wander, *The Joshua Roll*, Wiesbaden 2012, 96-103, with a recapitulative table of the works sponsored at 104-105.

49 Tertullianus, *De idololatria*, 8:1, eds. J.H. Waszink-J.C.M. Van Winden, Leiden 1987, 32-35.

Tertullian, who was wary even of Christian images, uses the analogy with Jews by saying that they only laid hands on Christ once, while "the makers of idols ill-treat his body daily"[50]. This comparison is turned on its head by the famous image of the Chludov Psalter, a ninth-century manuscript offering exegesis in the form of images drawn in the margins of the text, where Christ-slayers are likened to the iconoclasts who whitewash the icon of Christ. Such an analogy also works in cognitive terms, since neither the Jews (and Romans), nor the iconoclasts, were capable of recognizing God through the Christ they had before their eyes, whether in actuality or in a depiction. Although we have a limited amount of information concerning their actual making, the intense work of elaborating pictorial programmes that reflect a deeper meaning of the psalm verses, often according to sought-out patristic or liturgical references, points to monastic *concepteurs*, monastic scriptoria and indeed monastic audiences for their ultimate destination. Thus, although only few manuscripts are explicitly signed as monastic, extrapolating a richer monastic production from these complex procedures would not seem to be beyond the bounds of likelihood.

Icon and manuscript production can be seen as radically linked to monastic institutions as the defense of the iconodule position in its theological underpinnings. I suggest that this link rested on the accepted place of such activities as part of monastic work, and, further, that the income they generated was both legitimate and important for the life of monasteries. Thus, attacking the production of images also entailed attacking the economic wealth of monasteries, weakening their independence and curtailing a specific niche where the spiritual requirements met the material needs of the communities, especially in an urban setting such as Constantinople. Although the evidence adduced here is very partial, it is I hope enough for suggesting that this is a path of enquiry worth pursuing.

50 TERTULLIANUS, *De idololatria*, 7:2, 32-33.

Appendix: Liturgical texts on Lazarus the Painter

Synaxarion of Constantinople, ed. Delehaye	Menaion, ed. Saliverou; collated with MS Vat. gr. 2046, 11th cent., fol. 77r.
Τῇ αὐτῇ ἡμέρα· μνήμη τοῦ ὁσίου καὶ ὁμολογητοῦ Λαζάρου τοῦ ζώγράφου.	Τῇ αὐτη ἡμέρα· μνήμη τοῦ ὁσίου πατρὸς ἡμῶν Λαζάρου τοῦ ζώγράφου.
Οὗτος ὑπῆρχεν ἐπὶ τῆς βασιλείας τῶν εἰκονομάχων· ἔρωτι δὲ τῆς θείας τοῦ Χριστοῦ ἀγάπης τρωθείς· ῃρετίσατο ἐκ παιδόθεν ὑπελθεῖν τὸν μονήρη βίον, χαίρειν εἰπὼν πάσῃ ματαιότητι, ἀκτημοσύνην μετερχόμενος καὶ ἐλεημοσύνης ἐπιμελούμενος πρὸς τῇ σκληραγωγίᾳ καὶ ἐγκρατείᾳ καὶ ἀγρυπνίᾳ. Ἐν τούτοις τοῖς μεγίστοις πλεονεκτήμασι διαλάμπων,	Οὗτος νηπιόθεν τὸν μονήρη βίον ὑπέρχεται[51], καὶ τὴν ζωγραφικὴν ἐπιστήμην ἐκπαιδεύεται· καὶ πρὸς τῇ[52] σκληραγωγίᾳ καὶ ἐγκρατεῖᾳ καὶ τῆς ἐλεημοσύνης ἐπεμελεῖτο διὸ·
τοῦ τῆς ἱερωσύνης τετύχηκεν ἀξιώματος. Πλεῖστα δὲ κολαστήρια καθυπέμεινεν οὐ μόνον παρὰ τῶν τὰ Νεστορίου και Εὐτυχοῦς καὶ Διοσκόρου φρονούντων, ὁμολογῶν τὸν Χριστὸν τέλειον θεὸν καὶ τέλειον ἄνθρωπον, ἀσυγχύτως,	καὶ τὸ τῆς ἱεροσύνης ἀξίωμα δέχεται· ἐντεῦθεν κατὰ πασῶν τῶν αἱρέσεων ἀποδύεται· καὶ τοσαῦτας θλίψεις, οὐ μόνον παρὰ τῶν[53] τὰ Εὐτυχοῦς καὶ Νεστορίου καὶ Διοσκόρου φρονοῦντων[54].

51 ἦν· ἀπὸ ἐκ νεαρὰς ἡλικίας ἐν τῶ μονήρη βίον ἐγκαρτερῶν MS.

52 τὴν MS.

53 τὸν MS.

54 φρονοῦντος MS.

ἀτρέπτως, ἀναλλοιώτως, ἀλλὰ καὶ παρὰ τῶν βδελυκτῶν καὶ ἀνοσίων εἰκονοκαυστῶν πολλαῖς κατηκίσθη πληγαῖς καὶ βασάνοις, διά τε τὸ σέβεσθαι καὶ προσκυνεῖν τὰ τῶν ἁγίων σεβάσμια ἐκτυπώματα διά τε τὸ	ἀλλὰ καὶ παρὰ τῶν ἀθέων εἰκονομάχων[55] ὑπέμεινεν, ὅσα οὐδὲ ἔστι εἰπεῖν·
εὐφυῶς ζωγραφεῖν ταῦτα οἰκειοχείρως τοῖς πίναξιν καὶ οἷα βέλεσι τοὺς ἀλιτηρίους κατατοξεύειν.	
Οὗτος τὴν ἐπὶ τὴν πρεσβυτέραν Ῥώμην ὁδὸν στέλλεται ἀποστολικὴν ἐγκεχειρισμένος διακονίαν. Τῶν πατρικῶν φημι καὶ ἀποστολικῶν δογμάτων καὶ παραδόσεων ἕνεκεν· καὶ αὖθις ἐντεῦθεν μεγαλοπρεπῶς ὑποστρέφει· πάλιν δὲ εἰς τὴν αὐτὴν πορείαν πεμφθεὶς τῶν αὐτῶν ἕνεκεν ὑποθέσεων,	ἀλλὰ καὶ ἐπὶ τὸν πρεσβυτέραν Ῥώμην στέλλεται· τῶν πατρικῶν καὶ ἀποστολικῶν ὑπερμαχήσας δογμάτων καὶ μεγαλοπρεπῶς ὑποστρέψας· αὖθις τῶν αὐτῶν ἕνεκεν ὑποθέσεων ἐπὶ Ῥώμην ἀπαίρει·
περὶ τὰ μέσα που τῆς ὁδοῦ τὴν τιμίαν αὐτοῦ ψυχὴν τῷ Κυρίῳ παρέθετο. Τὸ μέντοι ἱερώτατον αὐτοῦ σῶμα τοῖς ποθοῦσιν ἀνακομισθὲν ἐν τῇ βασιλίδι τῶν πόλεων κατετέθη Πέραν τοῦ ἄστεος, ἐν τῇ μονῇ τῶν Εὐάνδρου.	καὶ περὶ τὰ μέσα που τῆς ὁδοῦ· ἀνωμαλίας τινος[56] αὐτῷ περὶ τὸ σῶμα γενομένης[57], τὸν βίον κατέλυσε· τὸ δὲ τίμιον αὐτοῦ σῶμα ἀνακομισθὲν ἐν τῇ μονῇ τοῦ Εὐανδροῦ[58] κατετέθη.

55 οἰκονομάχων MS.
56 ἀνωμαλία τις MS.
57 τὸ σώμα ἐνσκήψασα MS.
58 τῶν εὐανδρῶν πλησίον Κωνσταντινουπόλεως MS.

Abstract

The church's affirmation of artistic expression as part of the catechetical tools available for the preaching of the Gospel and its consequent rebuttal of iconoclasm have concrete consequences upon the flourishing of monastic communities.

This joint presentation (with Sister Manuela Scheiba) approached this issue from two complementary angles:

1) a historical perspective on icon production (including book illumination) in Byzantine monasteries; and

2) a modern reflection on the production and teaching of icon painting as appropriate income-generating work in a contemporary monastery, taking the example of St Gertrud monastery, Alexanderdorf, Germany.

The Byzantine tradition of icon painting plays a key role. The ninth-century iconoclastic struggle in Byzantium probably also aimed at attacking and weakening monastic life by removing a source of income from the monasteries in the form of icons and illuminated manuscripts. Looking at some examples of monastic representatives as icon defenders, such as St Theodore Stoudite and St Lazarus the painter, this paper argues for the double function of artistic production in monasteries as a spiritual and concrete asset.

DIVERGENT CONCEPTS OF WORK AND CREATION IN THE EARLY MONASTIC TRADITIONS

Ötvös Csaba

"with fear and trembling work out your own salvation"
Philippians 2: 12[1]

INTRODUCTION

St Paul in his Letter – that was written in prison, encourages the Church of Philippi to work on developing their way of life with Jesus Christ. In the quotation, the Apostle used the Greek verb κατεργάζομαι, *to work out* to emphasize the border of human side, the right methodology (with fear and trembling, φόβος and τρόμος) and the right target of human life that is salvation (σωτηρία). In the following verses Paul gives help to understand rightly his sentence, as he wrote: "For it is God who is working (ἐνεργῶν) in you (ἐν ὑμῖν) both to will and to do of his good pleasure" (2.13). In the next verse he describes believers as lights (2.15 φωστῆρες, as lights in the world) and in this way it is to allude to the creation story, precisely to the light of the first day of creation[2]. Paul declares that God himself is at work within us, provides the human being with both the desire and the ability to serve him, that is to work out his own salvation[3]. With the usage of verbs from the same root, the Apostle describes work as a common work, as a Pauline picture of synergy between God and man that is to be able to accomplish the common purpose which is involved in the symbol of light[4].

Ötvös Csaba, Hungarian researcher at the University of Debrecen. This paper was supported by the OTKA Project PD 112421.
Here I would like to express my gratitude for Professor Wipszycka for her generous help when she shared with me her articles and her comments on the paper also.

1 The quotations from the Bible here and later are from the KJV.

2 For this see, H.L. Strack-P. Billerbeck, *Kommentart zum Neuen Testament aus Talmud und Midrasch III*, München 1926, 621.

3 H.L. Willmington, *Willmington's Bible Handbook*, Tyndale House, Wheaton 1997, 712.

4 The Pauline usage and interpretation remains and appears later in the Christian tradition,

To see more clearly this cooperative relationship between God and man, we should turn to another Pauline verse and quote: *"We are fellow-workers (συνεργοί) with God"* (1 Cor. 3:9). Accepting Father Callistos' evaluation, we could say concerning Paul's teaching, that "If man is to achieve full fellowship with God, he cannot do so without God's help, yet he must also play his own part: man as well as God must make his contribution to the common work, although what God does is of immeasurably greater importance than what man does. The supreme example of synergy is the Mother of God"[5].

This sketched concept of synergy with this Scriptural quotation[6] stays at the centre of our present inquiry. More precisely, our question, based on the philological examination of the word οικονομία, does not have the aim to cover all occurences of the word[7], rather it comes from the side of theological investigation when it allows to point out the explanation of the divine economy in the early monastic traditions.

For this answer, the present examination turns firstly its attention to the examples concerning the theology of work[8] from the saying collections to illustrate the fathers' thinking concerning the work[9]. Next, based on the results of the close comments it considers the relation of work and economy in the early monastic traditions. Although these two objects that enchain and direct our steps are seemingly distant but the terminological and conceptual examination of the sayings aims to give as complete an account as possible of why and how

---

e.g.in the Const. App.2.54.4, Ath dial Trin 3.17 and Chrys hom 14.11 in Rom. For this see G.W.H. LAMPE, *A Patristic Greek Lexikon*, Oxford 1961, 1324a.

5 C. WARE, *The Orthodox Church*, Penguin Books, New York 1993, 263.

6 The term of συνεργοί occurs in the New Testament 13 times, always in plural, the verb of συνεργω in 5 times. In Mk. 16:20 the absolute genitives describe the Lord's working with the apostles by confirming their message with signs. For this see, G. KITTEL-G. FRIEDRICH, *Theologische Wörterbuch zum Neuen Testament VII*, Stuttgart 1964, esp. 871-875 (later TWNT).

7 LAMPE, *A Patristic Greek Lexicon*, 940B-943A, esp. 941B-942B.

8 The present paper focuses on the connection of work and creation and does not intend to present the whole picture of theology of work in the early monastic movements for two reasons. The first one is that the lecture of Professor Wipszicka deals with the questions of the beginning of the work and prayer in the monastic movements. The second reason is that while I was preparing this material I found a book but could not reach it, from B. HAYDON, *Divine Work: Theology of Work According to the Desert Fathers*, Irvine (CA) 2011.

9 On the socio-economic context of the early monasticism, see first of all Wipszicka, and J.R. BINNS, «The early Monasteries», *Mediavel History* 1/2 (1991) 12-22, J.E. GOEHRING, «The world Engaged: The Social and Econic World of Early Egyptian Monasticism», in *Gnosticism and the Early Christian World: In Honor of James M. Robinson*, eds. J.E. Gorhring-C.H. Hedrick-J.T. Sanders, Sonoma (Calif.) 1990, 133-144.

they had theological insights from them, how they could originate and develop a whole, coherent and comprehensive concept. In other words, the question is whether the founders and the first generations would reflect more closely and systematically on the theological concept on the divine economy during demonstrating the two pillars of Christian life. Keeping these challenges in mind, this approach does not propose to review the whole historical development of the concept under investigation; rather, it is a limited introduction.

1. THE FOUNDATIONS

"τὴν μελέτην, τὴν ψαλμωδίαν, καὶ τὸ ἐργόχειρον· ἅτινά ἐστι τὰ θεμέλια." "Meditation, psalmody, and manual labour, these are the foundations"[10]. This saying (from the Anonymous Collection) introduces the fathers' position and presents the prerequisites for the beginner or novice (ἀρχάριος) (or for fallen ones to whom the apophtegma is addressed) that is the simplest description of a rule that coordinates and sums up the daily routine of the monk[11]. We do not want to dissect this tripartite rule[12] nor involve ourselves in the question of practices of meditation and psalmody but only to concentrate on the last part of it and make an attempt to approach what they said about manual labour and why.

To start our inquiry with the terminology, it is worth noting that the Greek term ἐργόχειρον appears that can be translated either as manual labour or as handiwork. The connection of the sentence with our purpose comes with the usage of

10 The whole saying: "Meditation, psalmody, and manual labour, these are the foundations. For the novice needs to learn these things, for you need to start from (your) original status. AP N 168 transl by Wortley (ROC 13:54; trans. Ward, Wisdom, 8-9); cf. Verba Seniorum 5.18 (PL 73:877-878; LCC, 64). τὴν μελέτην, τὴν ψαλμωδίαν, καὶ τὸ ἐργόχειρον· ἅτινά ἐστι τὰ θεμέλια. Ὁ δὲ ἀρχάριος, ἐν ὅσῳ ταῦτα μανθάνει, ἔρχῃ σὺ εἰς τὴν πρώτην τάξιν.

11 The collection knows another tripartite rule but that presents the manual work as the fourth one. I quote John Kolobos 35 (350): "It was said of the same Abba John that when he returned from the harvest or when he had been with some of the old men, he gave himself to prayer, meditation and psalmody until his thoughts were re-established in their previous order" (transl. from B. Ward, *The Sayings of the Desert Fathers*, Kalamazoo [MI] 1975). Another four-parted example: Τέσσαρες εἰσὶν ἀρεταὶ προσκείμεναι τῷ ἀνθρώπῳ· ἡ νηστεία, ἡ προσευχή, τὸ ἐργόχειρον καὶ ἡ τοῦ σώματος σωφροσύνη (Quotation from Wortley o.c. 640.).

12 Another saying about the tripartite rule with similar point of view: N.500 He also said: "It is impossible to possess Jesus other than by labour, humility and ceaseless prayer". Εἶπεν πάλιν· Ἀδύνατον κτήσασθαι τὸν Ἰησοῦν, εἰ μὴ διὰ [f. 279ra] κόπου καὶ ταπεινώσεως καὶ προσευχῆς ἀπαύστου. Or in other case: μικρὸν ἐργόχειρον καὶ μικρὰν μελέτην, μικρὰν εὐχὴν (Wortley o.c. 556.).

the Greek term of foundation (θεμέλια) that could refer to Christ, to the Apostles and Prophets and to the Church,[13] but concerning the usage of the Old Testament, our term could hint back with its cosmological connotation to the foundation of the world. Although the sentence has many references, based on the terminology we hint only to the Psalm 81.5, where the Psalmist says: *They know not, nor understand; they walk on in darkness: all the foundations of the earth shall be shaken*, οὐκ ἔγνωσαν οὐδὲ συνῆκαν, ἐν σκότει διαπορεύονται· σαλευθήσονται πάντα τὰ θεμέλια τῆς γῆς" 81,5). Regarding the same usages of the terms and the similar associations, we raise that the sentence of the father could be an allusion to the Psalmist's saying or at least could be familiar with its use of words. Be as it may, our saying refers to the foundation of personal life and making the beginner and the fallen ones equal, gives instruction and guidance for reaching the foundation in the ascetic training. From this point of view, we should hint back to the former quoted Pauline sentence and raise our questions again on the role, the place and the target of work in the process of restoration and the economy.

In this example, we are facing not only practical advice, but also the beginning of the tradition that lives until now: the answers and the theological insights that are involved in them. Only two examples are to mention. The first quotation comes from John Cassian in his Institutes: "*eo enim feruore diuinarum scripturarum lectionibus orationimque et manuum operi diebus ac noctibus incubabant, ut ne escarum quidem adpetitus uel memoria*"[14] "For they gave themselves up to the reading of Holy Scripture and to prayers and to manual labour night and day with such fervour that they had no desire or thoughts of food" (II,5). According to the opinion of Goodrich: Manual labour was another of Cassian's additions to the story. He would later insist that all monks needed to work, both in order to support themselves and to foster prayer[15]. Concerning the manual work, the concept of Cassian is entirely within the Egyptian tradition. We could complement these statements with the note of the Greek tradition because in this corpus the same tripratite advice occurs: The task of a monk is the threefold activity that comprise manual work, study and prayer, in his words : Καθήμενοι δὲ ἐν τοῖς ἰδίοις κελλίοις, καὶ τῷ ἔργῳ καὶ τῇ μελέτῃ καὶ τῇ προσευχῇ μετὰ σπουδῆς προσέχοντες (Cassian the Sabaite, Const. 6)[16].

13 It occurs in the New Testament 16 times, for this se TWNT III 63-64.

14 *Iohannis Cassiani opera: De institutis coenobiorum*, ed. Michael Petschenig, Vindobonae 1886 (Corpus Scriptorum Ecclesiasticorum Latinorum, 13), 21.

15 R.J. Goodrich, «Contextualizing Cassian.Aristocrats, Asceticism, and Reformation», in *Fifth-Century Gaul*, Oxford 2007, 135.

16 The quotation is from P. Tzamalikos, *The Real Cassian Revisited: Monastic Life, Greek*

The other side of the foundations concerning the introductory role of the handiwork and its general and determinative relation to monastic life comes from the teachings on the spiritual ascent.

For our point of view it is enough to note the model of Evagrius – that was adapted later by Cassian. The structure of ascension is twofold, the praktikos is the cultivation of the virtues until reaching the apatheia and the gnostikos, the contemplation (of second nature, and of the logoi, of the first nature). This model was inherited by Cassian but there are other distinctions:

To point out more clearly the role of the manual work we turn to the example of John of Lycopolis – who was an adviser to Evagrius –, in the Historia monachorum:

> He is exceedingly good, for he is a man who puts the commandments into practice and does them. But he is occupied with earthly things. Better and greater than he is the contemplative, who has risen from active works to the spiritual sphere and has left it to others to be anxious about earthly things. Since he has not only denied himself but even become forgetful of himself, he is concerned with the things of heaven[17].

From the description of John is absent the speculative philosophical element that is in the Evagrian system. The structure is the same as in Evagrius and we could differentiate the stages of praktikos and theoretikos but there is no trace of the metaphysical speculation. For our point of view the introductory role of work is important on the one side, and on the other the spiritual ascension.

2. SAINT ANTONY

Concerning the beginning of the practice of work and prayer, we should quote an example as it is given and which bequeaths, in spite of the facts, that it is an enigmatic and arbitrary elaborated example from the hands of later editors with the wish to fulfil the Christian ideal.

Paideia, and Origenism in the Sixth Century, Leiden 2012, 189.

17 *Historia monachorum* 21.62-63, the translation from N. Russell, *The Lives of the Desert Fathers. Historia Monachorum in Aegypto*, Piscataway (NJ) 2009, 62, and for Greek text, A.J. Festugiére, *Historia monachorum in Aegypto: édition critique du texte grec et traduction annotée*, Bruxelles 1971, 34.

A few years later from that Sunday of the year of 270 or 271 in a small Egyptian village, when Christian monasticism began[18], Antony lived alone in the desert, probably in Wadi Arabi[19]. We quote with all certainty the most famous saying on the father of monks[20]:

> Ὁ ἅγιος ἀββᾶς Ἀντώνιος, καθεζόμενός ποτε ἐν τῇ ἐρήμῳ, ἐν ἀκηδίᾳ γέγονε καὶ πολλῇ σκοτώσει λογισμῶν·καὶ ἔλεγε πρὸς τὸν Θεόν· Κύριε, θέλω σωθῆναι, καὶ οὐκ ἐῶσί με οἱ λογισμοί· τί ποιήσω ἐν τῇ θλίψει μου; πῶς σωθῶ; Καὶ μικρὸν διαναστὰς ἐπὶ τὰ ἔξω, θεωρεῖ τινα ὁ Ἀντώνιος ὡς ἑαυτὸν, καθεζόμενον καὶ ἐργαζόμενον, εἶτα ἀνιστάμενον ἀπὸ τοῦ ἔργου καὶ προσευχόμενον, καὶ πάλιν καθεζόμενον καὶ τὴν σειρὰν πλέκοντα, εἶτα πάλιν εἰς προσευχὴν ἀνιστάμενον· ἦν δὲ ἄγγελος Κυρίου, ἀποσταλεὶς πρὸς διόρθωσιν καὶ ἀσφάλειαν Ἀντωνίου. Καὶ ἤκουσε τοῦ ἀγγέλου λέγοντος· Οὕτως ποίει, καὶ σώζῃ. Ὁ δὲ τοῦτο ἀκούσας, πολλὴν χαρὰν ἔσχε καὶ θάρσος, καὶ οὕτως ποιῶν ἐσώζετο.
> When the holy Abba Anthony lived in the desert he was beset by accidie, and attacked by many sinful thoughts. He said to God,' Lord, I want to be saved but these thoughts do not leave me alone; what shall I do in my affliction? How can I be saved?' A short while afterwards, when he got up to go out, Anthony saw a man like himself sitting at his work, getting up from his work to pray, then sitting down and plaiting a rope, then getting up again to pray. It was an angel of the Lord sent to correct and reassure him. He heard the angel saying to him, 'Do this and you will be saved.' At these words, Anthony was filled with joy and courage. He did this, and he was saved.

In this short story, that is a masterpiece among the apophthegmata, a struggle of Antony appears. In a literary sense, the story speaks of the father in desperation, under the attack of *accidie*[21] and other sinful thoughts. With the help of an angel, he found the way out and by following simple advice managed to

18 For this see, J. CHRYSSAVGIS, *In the Heart of the Desert. The Spirituality of the Desert Fathers and Mothers* (Treasures of Words Religions), Bloomington2003, 15.

19 As far as my knowledge Prof. Wipszycka made efforts to locate the places of Antony wandering. For this see, E. WIPSZYCKA, «A Look at the Origins of Monasticims in Egypt from a Geographic Point of View», *Przeglad Humanistyczny* 2 (2013) 109-126, 112.

20 The translation from WARD, *The Sayings of the Desert Fathers*, 2.

21 For the term and the concept of accidie, see E.G.J.-CH. NAULT, «Acedia. Enemy of Spiritual Joy», *Communio* 31 (2004) 236-258, A. CRISLIP, «The Sin of Sloth or the Illness of Demons? The Demons of Acedia in early Christian Monasticism», HTR 98/2 (2005) 143-69 and P. TOOHEY, «Acedia in Late Classical Antiquity», *Illinois Classical Studies* 15/2 (1990) 339-352.

recover his balance. Complementing this short comment, we can add to this, that the visitation gave the reason why Athanasius called Antony *theodidacta* in his encomiast biography (VA 66,2)[22].

Although, from the story we can learn all the important issues of the monastic life, but we should keep in mind that this is an invented and arbitrary created and emblematic paradigm as it was categorised in the modern literature. These issues describe a process that starts with the solitary life, from the temptations, through the heavenly help and the advice of the doublet of prayer and work and direct consequences: joy and courage and lastly the everlasting joy and courage, which is salvation. For now, it is enough to note that work appears as a key to salvation, in a form of a mediated knowledge or insight through an angel who helps and coordinates the monk regarding what is needed, and encourages him showing the right lifestyle to prepare the future salvation. These are the mosaic pieces of the emblematic life that became the archetype for the monks or the monastic way of life. This model that was mediated by the angel became the realized angelic life and this life is based on the double pillar of prayer and work.

Repeating Dysinger's words we could say: "Here Antony the Great is the archetype of the monk delivered from acedia through a simple practice: he is to regularly interrupt his manual labour by standing briefly for prayer. Although the apophthegm does not state that Antony is also to recite the psalms and other scriptures during the interval while sitting and working on his rope, this is probably presupposed; certainly, it had become the norm by the latter half of the fourth century in Evagrius' milieu. Palladius describes the chanting of psalms which could be heard coming from the cells of monks engaged in the manufacture of linen at Nitria"[23].

Concerning the role of work in the saying we could state shortly that it is in a balanced position with prayer.

The Vita shows another picture of Antony. Scholars have published volumes of works ranging the Vita from ancient biography through hagiography to myth. Quoting the opinion of a late contemporary, Gregory of Nazianzas, it exemplifies a monastic rule in narrative form[24]. In the modern literature, that we could refer to, for example, Meinardus' opinion who wrote: "The life, the attitudes, the words and works of this great hermit of the desert have influenced,

22 Και\ ἦν, κατά το\ γεγραμμένον, θεοδίδακτος γενόμενος ὁ μακάριος. The text from G.J.M. Bartelink, *Athanase d'Alexandrie, Vie d'Antoine* (SC 400) Paris 1994, o.c. 308.

23 *Psalmody and Prayer in the Writings of Evagrius Ponticus*, Oxford, 2005, 49.

24 W. Harmless, *Desert Christians*, Oxford 2004, 85.

and still influence, the lives of the desert fathers, be they anchorites or coenobitic monks."[25]. On the other hand, according to Goehring's words, it describes the life of "the first Egyptian monk" or the "father of monasticism[26] . There are good reasons to advocate the authenticity of Antony's life and adding to these Vivian's balanced opinion: "whether or not the details about Antony in the Life are 'biographically correct,' the Antony who lives and breathes in these pages is, on the whole, true to the way the early monks lived, thought, and believed"[27]. For our purpose, it is worth noting, regardless of the intense scholarly debate of the historicity and authorship of the *Vita Antoni*, that it witnessed the progressive emergence of the desert asceticism on the one hand and on the other the manual work appears in a similar way but in another dress that includes not only the rigorous training but other references also.

According to the description of St Athanasius (Vita 3,6)[28]:

> Εἰργάζετο γοῦν ταῖς χερσίν, ἀκούσας «Ὁ δὲ ἀργός μηδε- εσθιέτω.» Και- το- μὲν εἰς τὸν ἄρτόν, τὸ δὲ τοῖς δεομένοις ἀνήλισκεν. Προσηύχετο δὲ συνεχῶς, μαθών, ὅτι δεικατ̓ ἰδίαν προσεὺχεσται ἀδιαλείπτως.
> He worked, however, with his hands, having heard, 'he who is idle let him not eat' and part he spent on bread and part he gave to the needy. And he was constant in prayer, knowing that a man ought to pray in secret unceasingly[29].

The description shows the mentioned two motives in a broader sense. In this developed system, the balanced position remained, but new aspects occur with their reasoning: both present the aim to fulfil biblical, Pauline commands. The first one, to support himself and others in need, is based on 2 Thess 3:10 (*The*

25 O. MEINARDUS, *Monks and Monasteries of the Egyptian Desert*, Cairo 1999, 1.

26 J.E. GOEHRING, «The Origins of Monasticism», in *Ascetics, Society and the Desert: Studies in Early Egyptian Monasticism*, Trinity Press International, Harrisburg (PA) 1999, 18.

27 ATHANASIUS OF ALEXANDRIA, *The Life of Antony: The Coptic Life and the Greek Life*, ed. T. Vivian, Kalamazoo (MI) 2003, XXV.

28 The Greek text from BARTELINK, *Athanase d'Alexandrie, Vie d'Antoine*, 138.

29 Translation by H. Ellershaw from St ATHANASIUS, «Vita S. Antoni», in *Nicene and Post-Nicene Fathers, Second Series*, vol. 4: *Select works and letters. Athanasius*, eds. P. SCHAFF-H. WACE, Hendrickson, Peabody (Mass.) 1995. In the Coptic Life the text runs as follows: «He worked with his hands, for he had heard the scriptures say, "He who does not work, let him not eat". And he would spend what he earned from his handiwork rightly: he would spend part on bread and part on those in need. He prayed all the time, having learned that it is necessary to pray without ceasing». Translation from the Coptic by T. VIVIAN, «The Life of Anthony. by St. Athanasius of Alexandria», *Coptic Church Review* 15/1-2 (1994), 1047.

one who is unwilling to work shall not eat.), but the second one, the unceasing prayer in secret, bond into one rule the words of 1 Thess 5:17 (*pray unceasingly*) and Mt 6:6 (*But when you pray, go into your room, close the door and pray to your Father, who is unseen*). In this reading, the saint exemplified and personified the Pauline command whilst practising the two pillars of life.

A parallel reading of the two accounts indicate that the Antony in the collection had a different view from the Antony in the Vita, or at least different reason or theological intentions of the writers are manifested in the descriptions as we could distinguish the example of an angel (that was seen) and the commands of the Scriptures (that were heard). Complementing the picture of Vita we should also note that before our mentioned explanation there were a process, a stage by stage fulfilment of the removal from the inhabited land to the solitude where our Saint surely was trained in this way of life. From this point of view we could raise the question of how and how much was his own earlier experience, external help or earlier familiarity in creating the double order.

However, summing up shortly our step, we can say that in spite of the diverse particularities, the structure and the outcomes of the quotations are parallel and both bear witness of the daily routine that Antony adopted: manual work for himself and others and continuous prayer.

2.1. The work

Turning to the saying traditions, amongst the sayings we can find many examples where the practical pillar of the life of the desert monks and nuns appear as penetrating all segments of life.

To unveil the appreciated role and highly evaluated function of handiwork we can turn to another saying that expresses an extremity. According to John the Little (kolobos) (c. 339–409) who was one of the leading figures of Scetis in the late fourth and early fifth centuries, the monk is equal with the work he performs (saying 37): Ἐρώτησέ τις τῶν Πατέρων τὸν ἀββᾶν Ἰωάννην τὸν κολοβὸν, τί ἐστι μοναχός; Ὁ δὲ εἶπε· Κόπος Ὅτι ὁ μοναχὸς εἰς πᾶν ἔργον κοπιᾷ. Οὕτως ὁ μοναχός. "*One of the fathers asked abba John the Little, "What is a monk?" His answer: "He is work. The monk works at everything he does. That's what a monk is*"[30].

The Greek word that Harmless translated for work is the term of κόπος, that could mean work, hard work or exertion on the one hand but on the other, at

30 Translation from Harmless, *Desert Christians*, 199.

the same time its meaning extends to suffering, toil or beating[31]. Ward in his translation used the term toil.

Our term probably comes from the New Testament where it signs the apostolic work (2 Cor 6.5, 11.23 and 27.1, 1Thes 2.9, 2Thes 3.8). According to Miquel the kopos and the ponos are interchangeable[32]. This usage occurs in the Evagrian corpus and in the saying of the Fathers also.

From this lexical data, we can understand more exactly what is implied in the term of the manual work of the monachos. Based on this lexical result we could point out clearly its background that lies in the New Testament – as it was the case in Saint Antony – and, complementing this origin we have also an explanation of why and how could be the work an integral and necessary part of the divine economy. To make it absolutely understandable we should only refer to the statements of Keller who wrote the following: "Kopos the Greek word for "labour that expends physical energy", contributes God's continuing creation of the world and helps create a physical venue in which the monachos's spiritual labor can take place"[33].

The other essential aspect of the manual work can be illustrated with the teachings of Makarius. Accepting the opinions of the scholars we could say that he describes and identifies the ascesis or ascetical life with the weeping for tears (penthos) and hard work (ponos)[34]. These terms are most likely the embodiement of a biblical verse that shows the life as labor and sorrow (Ps 89.10). Macarius ascribes to divine grace the power to continue in the praxis or the performance of ascetical acts.

> "In the material world of things around us, the farmer works the earth. So also in the spiritual world there are two elements to be considered. It is necessary for man to work the soil of his heart by a free deliberation and hard work. For God looks to man's hard work and toil and labor. But if the heavenly clouds from above do not appear and the showers of grace, the farmer for all his labor avails nothing." (Hom 26,10).

---

31 For this see the verb κοπόω, e.g in LAMPE, *A Patristic Greek Lexikon*, 768.

32 P. MIQUEL, *Lexique du Désert. Etude de quelques mots-clés du vocabulaire monastique grec ancien* (Spirituealité Orientale 44), Bégrolles-en-Mauges 1986. 240.

33 D.G.R. KELLER, *Oasis of wisdom: the worlds of the desert fathers and mothers*, Collegeville (MN) 2005, 96.

34 For this see *Pseudo-Macarius. The fifty spiritual homilies; and, The great lette*, edited and translated with an introduction by G.A. Maloney, New York 1992, 186. footnote 20. For this point see also I. HAUSHERR, *Penthos la doctrine de la componction dans l'Orient chrétien* (Orientalia Christiana Analecta 132), Rome 1944 and J. DRISCOLL, «Penthos and Tears in Evagrius Ponticus», Studia Monastica 36 (1994) 147-163.

Even though the Christian must will to engage in ascetical practices, Macarius insists that the Christian cannot take pride in such exploits as though it depends solely on human effort. God's grace is always at work, even in bringing the individual Christian to will, and all the more, to persevere in the disciplines necessary to eradicate vices and to put on the virtues of Christ.

Macarius wrote in his Great Letter the following:

> "And we appear unworthy of the perfection to which the grace of the Spirit draws us. It is, therefore, to slacken off in undertaking hard work when we run away from the struggles of the race. Nor should we look back on what has been accomplished, but we should confine all that to oblivion, as the Apostle writes, "Let us strain ahead for what is to come" (Phil 3:13)".

The close context of the teaching is the temptation of pride but we could understand it in general sense. As Maloney wrote summing up shortly the teachings of Macarius: "Throughout this ascetical Great Letter, Macarius uses the term ponos for hard work, referring to any ascetical practices that involve great physical efforts in an attempt to bring the corporal powers under submission to the intellect and will, informed by grace. A more general word for asceticism that he also uses is ergon, which means "work." Macarius also uses the term kopos, which stresses the pain, suffering, and weariness that come from the physical ponos. St. Basil, whom Macarius follows greatly in writing on the ascetical life, explains how all spiritual goods come "through hard works (ponois) and sweat" (Hom. in principium Proverbiorum, 16; PG 31:421 A)[35].

A saying from Arsenius introduces the third basic aspect of the manual work when he examplifies the charity: "My thoughts trouble me, saying 'You can not fast or work; at least visit the sick, for this charity.'"[36]. But Arsenius recognized that the thought is a temptation from a demon and told the brother to "go and eat, drink and sleep, and do not work. He knew that "endurance of the cell puts a monk in order". In this example we are facing the topos of the cell as a place of temptation, of combat against thought. Endurance of the temptation to leave his cell proves a monk's capacity in the face of hardship and temptation itself.[37]

The saying has parallels in the collections but it is enough to point out the importance of charity.

---

35 Quoted by Maloney.

36 *Arsenius* 11.

37 G. Gould, *The Desert Fathers on Monastic Community*, Oxford 1993, 151.

Another aspect of this example can be illustrated by the saying of John Cassian. In his above mentioned Institutes he says the following:

> *His itaque exemplis per Aegyptum patres eruditi nullo modo otiosos esse monachos ac praecipue iuuenes sinunt, actum cordis et profectum patientiae et humilitatis sedulitate operis metientes, et non solum a nullo quicquam ad usum uictus sui accipere patiuntur, sed etiam de laboribus suis non tantum superuenientes ac peregrinos reficiunt fratres, uerum etiam per loca Libyae, quae sterilitate ac fame laborant, nec non etiam per ciuitates his, qui squalore carcerum contabescunt, inmanem conferentes dirigunt alimoniae uictusque substantiam, de fructu manuum suarum rationabile ac uerum sacrificium Domino tali oblatione se offerre credentes.* (X,22)
> And so taught by these examples the Fathers in Egypt never allow monks, and especially the younger ones, to be idle, estimating the purpose of their hearts and their growth in patience and humility by their diligence in work; and they not only do not allow them to receive anything from another to supply their own wants, but further, they not merely refresh pilgrims and brethren who come to visit them by means of their labours, but actually collect an enormous store of provisions and food, and distribute it in the parts of Libya which suffer from famine and barrenness, and also in the cities, to those who are pining away in the squalor of prison; as they believe that by such an offering of the fruit of their hands they offer a reasonable and true sacrifice to the Lord[38]

3. WORKS OF SOUL AND BODY

But, naturally the seemingly opposite side appears also where the manual work is underestimated. This opinion can be illustrated by the saying of abba Theodoros (11):

> Ὁ αὐτός ποτε παρέβαλε τῷ ἀββᾷ Ἰωάννῃ τῷ ἀπὸ γεννήσεως εὐνούχῳ· καὶ λαλούντων αὐτῶν, εἶπεν· Ὅταν ἤμην εἰς Σκῆτιν, τὰ ἔργα τῆς ψυχῆς ἦν τὸ ἔργον ἡμῶν, τὸ δὲ ἐργόχειρον ὡς πάρεργον εἴχομεν· νῦν δὲ γέγονε τὸ ἔργον τῆς ψυχῆς ὡς πάρεργον, καὶ τὸ πάρεργον ἔργον.
> The same abba came one day to see Abba John, a eunuch from birth, and during their conversation he said to him, 'When I was at Scetis, the works of the soul

38 Translation is from L. Dysinger: http://ldysinger.stjohnsem.edu/@texts/0415_cassian/00a_start.htm [access 12-12-2018].

> were our work, and we considered manual work to be subordinate; now the work of the soul has become subordinate and what was secondary is the chief work[39].

The change reflected in the saying, reacts on a move of Theodoros from Scetis to Pherme, after the first devastation of Scetis and this moving brings in itself the changed situation that could imply either the differences of the rules or economical changes or both, that made work necessary to a greater degree or created a new situation where there was more need for harder and more manual work. Be as it may, the change and the new emphasis on the manual work was condemned or rather disapproved in the saying.

Turning closer to the meaning of the saying it makes a clear and solid distinction between the types of work, using the words of ἔργον and πάρεργον to express that the place of manual work (ἐργόχειρον) is a secondary one after the work of the soul (τὸ ἔργον τῆς ψυχῆς). In other words, in the saying a subordination appears between the evaluation of the work of the soul and the manual work echoing an opposition between body and soul. In this case, the identification of the work of the soul remains uncertain but in another saying (the next one in the Apophtegma) our abba explains the works of the soul as work according to the commandment of God (Πάντα τὰ γινόμενα διὰ τὴν ἐντολὴν τοῦ Θεοῦ, ἔργον ψυχῆς ἐστι). This seemingly good solution is not a comforting one. The question remains open, and concerns the meaning of manual work because the father did not give other hints to unveil his teaching. Since, if we accept the solution with the help of the next saying, then our conclusion could be that the manual work (ἐργόχειρον) can not be according to the commandment of God or can not fulfil it. And this explanation is wrong.

The solution – as I can see it – is more simple and more personal. For this we should turn to the following lines of the next saying. The father said: "*Everything you do as a commandment of God is the work of the soul; but to work and to gather goods together for a personal motive ought to be held as subordinate*"[40]. To help to understand the brother, he exemplifies the first category and orders into it some duties of the monk (e.g visit the sick or help others, but prayer is absent from the list) and into the second one, the manual work.

In the light of these explanations we suppose that the distinction that was made by the father is in correspondence with the fulfilment of the commandment of God or personal interest. Based on the usages of the terms of εργον and πάρεργον

39 Translation from WARD, *The Sayings of the Desert Fathers*, 75.

40 Πάντα τὰ γινόμενα διὰ τὴν ἐντολὴν τοῦ Θεοῦ, ἔργον ψυχῆς ἐστι τὸ δε εἰς λόγον ἑαυτῶν ἐργάζεσθαι και συνάγειν, τοῦτο πάρεργον ἔχειν ὀφείλομεν.

we can state that the distinction is to make the subordination clear and not to create an opposition. The question is not concerning the value or the lack of value of any work but the emphasis is on the subordinate relation that is given between the soul and body, as between the work of the soul and work for personal interest[41].

3.1. Work and continual prayer

We saw in the example of Antonius the need and the biblical order of the union of continual prayer and manual labour because – as we know from the later followers – the work kept the monk awake and helped him carry out the injunction to pray without ceasing. Among the sayings there are some that belong clearly to this context.

Our first example comes from Cassian. In his Conferences – based on his experiences among the Egyptian and Palestinian monks –, describing the right methodology of prayer he makes a paralle between the manual labour and the prayer. According to the teaching of abba Isaac, who was the disciple of Cronius – who was a disciple of Athony the Great[42] – the right prayer is (9,2,1):

> *Omnis monachi finis cordisque perfectio ad iugem atque indisruptam orationis perseuerantiam tendit, et quantum humanae fragilitati conceditur, ad inmobilem tranquillitatem mentis ac perpetuam nititur puritatem, ob quam omnem tam laborem corporis quam contritionem spiritus indefesse quaerimus et iugiter exercemus. Et est inter alterutrum reciproca quaedam inseparabilisque coniunctio. Nam sicut ad orationis perfectionem omnium tendit structura uirtutum, ita nisi huius culmine haec omnia fuerint conligata atque conpacta, nullo modo firma poterunt uel stabilia perdurare.*
> The purpose of every monk and the perfection of his heart tends to continual and uninterrupted perseverance in prayer, and, as far as it is allowed to human frailty, strives to acquire an immovable tranquillity of mind and a perpetual purity, for the sake of which we seek unweariedly and constantly to practise all bodily labours as well as contrition of spirit. And there is between these two a sort of reciprocal and inseparable union. For just as the crown of the building of all virtues is the perfection of prayer, so unless everything has been united and compacted by this as its crown, it cannot possibly continue strong and stable[43].

---

41 Another example for this subordinate type comes from Evagrius (Praktikos 49) who makes a similar distinction between the relevances of prayer and work

42 Saint John Cassian, *On Prayer*, trans. by A.M. Casiday, Oxford 2006, 3.

43 The quotation and the translations are from Dysinger, with small modifications. http://

As it is well known and was presented formerly, the basis of daily monastic life which developed amongst the hermits was a round of meditation on the scriptures (*μελέτη*), psalmody (ψαλμῳδία) and manual labour (ἐργόχειρον). The value of the work was explained by abba Lucius when he was visited by a group of Euchites (or Messalians, the praying ones) who refused to work. He said:

> Παρέβαλόν ποτέ τινες τῷ ἀββᾷ Λουκίῳ εἰς τὸ Ἔνατον, οἱ λεγόμενοι Εὐκτῖται, μοναχοί· καὶ ἠρώτησεν αὐτοὺς ὁ γέρων· Τί τὸ ἐργόχειρον ὑμῶν; Οἱ δὲ εἶπον· Ἡμεῖς οὐ ψηλαφῶμεν ἐργόχειρον· ἀλλὰ, καθὼς λέγει ὁ Ἀπόστολος, ἀδιαλείπτως προσευχόμεθα. Καὶ λέγει ὁ γέρων· Οὐκ ἐσθίετε; Καὶ εἶπον· Ναί. Καὶ λέγει αὐτοῖς· Ὅτε οὖν ἐσθίετε, τίς εὔχεται ὑπὲρ ὑμῶν; Πάλιν οὖν εἶπεν αὐτοῖς· Οὐ κοιμᾶσθε; Καὶ εἶπον· Ναί. Καὶ λέγει ὁ γέρων· Ὅτε οὖν κοιμᾶσθε, τίς εὔχεται περὶ ὑμῶν; Καὶ οὐχ εὗρον πρὸς ταῦτα ἀποκρίνασθαι αὐτῷ. Καὶ εἶπεν αὐτοῖς· Συγχωρήσατέ μοι, ἰδοὺ οὐ ποιεῖτε καθὼς λέγετε. Ἐγὼ δὲ δεικνύω ὑμῖν, ὅτι ἐργαζόμενος τὸ ἐργόχειρόν μου ἀδιαλείπτως προσεύχομαι. Καθέζομαι σὺν Θεῷ βρέξας τὰ μικρά μου θαλλία· καὶ πλέκων αὐτὰ σειρὰν, λέγω· Ἐλέησόν με, ὁ Θεὸς, κατὰ τὸ μέγα ἔλεός σου, καὶ κατὰ τὸ πλῆθος τῶν οἰκτιρμῶν σου ἐξάλειψον τὸ ἀνόμημά μου. Καὶ λέγει αὐτοῖς· Οὐκ ἔστιν εὐχὴ τοῦτο; Καὶ εἶπον·Ναί.[44]
> Some of the monks who are called Euchites went to Enaton to see Abba Lucius. The old man asked them, 'What is your manual work?' They said, 'We do not touch manual work but as the Apostle says, we pray without ceasing.' The old man asked them if they did not eat and they replied they did. So he said to them, 'When you are eating, who prays for you then?' Again he asked them if they did not sleep and they replied they did. And he said to them, 'When you are asleep, who prays for you then?' They could not find any answer to give him. He said to them, 'Forgive me, but you do not act as you speak. I will show you how, while doing my manual work, I pray without interruption. I sit down with God, soaking my reeds and plaiting my ropes, and I say, "God, have mercy on me; according to your great goodness and according to the multitude of your mercies, save me from my sins." ' So he asked them if this were not prayer and they replied it was[45].

Abba Lucius adopts a view of prayer as virtuous life which includes manual work, because in this way the prayer could be unceasing. For our purpose it is important to note because comparing this saying with the aforementioned saying of Antony we could say that it seems to echo the former in a

ldysinger.stjohnsem.edu/@texts/0415_cassian/00a_start.htm [access 12-12-2018].

44 The Greek texts is from Diogenes.

45 The translation is from WARD, *The Sayings of the Desert Fathers*, 120-121.

slightly modified way. On the one hand, it plays an important role as witness of the tradition of the unceasing prayer[46], but on the other it could demonstrate well how the monks established their vivid affirmation of the double command of work and prayer[47]. Until now our abba gives the explanation of the parallel, when he is working, he is praying (quoting the Psalm 50,3). To demonstrate how he fulfils the precept of continual prayer and in the same time, to confute the wrong concept of the Euchites, the abba continues and says the following[48]:

> Καὶ εἶπεν αὐτοῖς· Ὅταν οὖν ἐμμείνω δι> ὅλης ἡμέρας ἐργαζόμενος καὶ εὐχόμενος, ποιῶ πλεῖον ἢ ἔλαττον δεκαὲξ νουμία· καὶ παρέχω ἐξ αὐτῶν εἰς τὴν θύραν δύο, καὶ τὰ λοιπὰ ἐσθίω· καὶ εὔχεται ὑπὲρ ἐμοῦ ὁ λαβὼν τὰ δύο νουμία ὅτε ἐσθίω ἢ ὅτε κοιμῶμαι· καὶ διὰ τῆς χάριτος τοῦ Θεοῦ πληροῦταί μοι τὸ ἀδιαλείπτως προσεύχεσθαι[49].
> Then he said to them: When I spend the whole day working and praying I make about sixteen numia, and I put two of them by the door, the rest is for my food. Who takes the two coins, prays for me while I am eating or sleeping, and so by the grace of God I attain continual prayer[50].

3.2. Work and prayer

Concerning the role of prayer we should mention the contemplation (θεωρία), especially because there are sayings where the contemplation and the manual work appear.

---

46 For the concept and the development of the unceasing prayer see e.g. K. Ware, *The Power of the Name. The Jesus Prayer in Orthodox Spirituality*, SLG Press, Convent of the Incarnation Fairacres Oxford 1974, 1986; I. Hausherr, *The Name of Jesus. The Development of the Jesus-prayer*, trans. by. C. Cumming, Kalamazoo 1978.

47 The same theological line affirmed by Basil the Great. He says: «In the midst of our work can we fulfil the duty of prayer, giving thanks to Him who has granted strength to our hands for performing our tasks and cleverness to our minds for acquiring knowledge, and for having provided the materials, both that which is in the instruments we use and that which forms the matter of the arts in which we may be engaged, praying that the work of our hands may be directed toward its goal, the good pleasure of God» (Reg. Brev. Tract. 37). The quotation is from A. Kordochkin, *John Climacus and the spiritual tradition of the IV-VII. Centuries*, Durham theses, Durham University, 2003 128. http://etheses.dur.ac.uk/3654/[access 12-12-2018].

48 Lucius 1.

49 The Greek text is from Diogenes.

50 Translation is from Ward, *The Sayings of the Desert Fathers*, 121, with small modification.

Our first example comes from abba Abraham:

Ἔλεγε περί τινος τῶν Σκητιωτῶν ὁ ἀββᾶς Ἀβραάμ, ὅτι γραφεὺς ἦν, καὶ οὐκ ἤσθιεν ἄρτον. Ἦλθεν οὖν ἀδελφὸς παρακαλῶν αὐτὸν γράψαὶ αὐτῷ βιβλίον. Ὁ οὖν γέρων ἔχων τὸν νοῦν αὐτοῦ εἰς τὴν θεωρίαν, ἔγραψε παρὰ στίχους, καὶ οὐκ ἔστιξεν. Ὁ δὲ ἀδελφὸς λαβὼν καὶ θέλων στίξαι, εὗρε παρὰ λόγους. Καὶ λέγει τῷ γέροντι· Παρὰ στίχους ἐστὶν, ἀββᾶ. Λέγει αὐτῷ ὁ γέρων· Ὕπαγε, πρῶτον ποίησον τὰ γεγραμμένα, καὶ τότε ἔρχῃ καὶ γράφω σοι καὶ τὴν λοιπάδα[51].
Abba Abraham told of a man of Scetis who was a scribe and did not eat bread. A brother came to beg him to copy a book. The old man whose spirit was engaged in contemplation, wrote, omitting some phrases and with no punctuation. The brother, taking the book and wishing to punctuate it, noticed that words were missing. So he said to the old man, 'Abba, there are some phrases missing.' The old man said to him, 'Go, and practise first that which is written, then come back and I will write the rest.'

At this point is important to note an unmentioned aspect of our question, namely that among the descriptions of the contemplation one can find examples of the usages of the word of economy although the word of manual work is absent.

Concerning our purpose we turn to the writings of Evagrius because if we rely on Frankenberg's retroversion we have some examples from him for our inquiry in his Gnostikos. These examples are not only connected to the contemplation but could use the Greek word of economy. In the 4th book he says: Τις απαγγελει περι της του θεου χαριτος και τις τους της οικονομιας αυτου λογους εξιχνιασει και οπως ο Χ. δια της των αγιων εντολων αυτου λατρειας την λογικην φυσιν εως της της αγιας τριαδος αυτου επιμιξιας παιδαγωγει. In Father Dysinger's translation (from the Guillaumont's Syriac S² version): Who will recount the grace of God? Who will scrutinize the *logoi* of providence and how the Christ leads the reasoning nature by [means of] varied worlds to the union of the Holy Unity?

A new level of meaning of our term occurs in the 5. book. I quote Dysinger's translation: One who sees the Creator according to the harmony of beings – it is not [God's] nature that he knows, rather he knows His wisdom by which He has made everything: and I do not mean the essential wisdom, but that which appears in beings, that which is called natural contemplation by those who are expert in these things. And if this is so, what is the madness of those who say

51 The Greek text is from Diogenes.

they know the nature of God! (V,51.). The Greek text is according to retroversion of Frankenberg: Ος εκ της των οντων οψεως εις τον θεον κατανοει ου την φυσιν αυτου οραι αλλα την της σοφιας αυτου οικονομιαν· ει δε τουτο ουτως εχει ποση εστιν η μανια των ειπειν οτι την θεου φυσιν γινωσκουσιν τολμωντων.

3.3. Work and prayer

From abba Cronius we inherited an example from the allegorical interpretation. Our abba joined Anthony the Great in Egypt and was his Greek interpreter. Later he become anchorite in Nitria and was ordained priest. The saying from him presents the allegorical interpretation of the bush in fire.

> Εἶπεν ὁ ἀββᾶς Κρόνιος, ὅτι Εἰ μὴ ἤγαγε Μωϋσῆς τὰ πρόβατα ὑπὸ τὸ ὄρος Σινᾶ, οὐκ ἂν ἔβλεπε τὸ πῦρ ἐν τῇ βάτῳ. Ἠρώτησεν ὁ ἀδελφὸς τὸν γέροντα· Εἰς τί λαμβάνεται ἡ βάτος; Καὶ λέγει αὐτῷ, ὅτι Ἡ βάτος λαμβάνεται εἰς τὴν σωματικὴν πρᾶξιν. Γέγραπται γάρ, ὅτι Ὁμοία ἐστὶν ἡ βασιλεία τῶν οὐρανῶν θησαυρῷ κεκρυμμένῳ ἐν ἀγρῷ. Λέγει ὁ ἀδελφὸς τῷ γέροντι· Οὐκοῦν ἐκτὸς καμάτου σωματικοῦ οὐ προκόπτει ἄνθρωπος εἴς τινα τιμήν; Λέγει αὐτῷ ὁ γέρων· Τέως γέγραπται· Ἀφορῶντες εἰς τὸν τῆς πίστεως ἀρχηγὸν καὶ τελειωτὴν Ἰησοῦν, ὃς ἀντὶ τῆς προκειμένης αὐτῷ χαρᾶς ὑπέμεινε σταυρόν. Καὶ πάλιν Δαβὶδ λέγει· Εἰ δώσω ὕπνον τοῖς ὀφθαλμοῖς μου, καὶ τοῖς βλεφάροις μου νυσταγμόν· καὶ τὰ ἑξῆς[52].
> Abba Cronius said, 'If Moses had not led his sheep to Mount Sinai, he would not have seen the fire in the bush.' The brother questioned the abba, 'What does the bush symbolize?' He said to him, 'The bush signifies bodily action. For it is written: "The kingdom of heaven is like unto treasure hid in a field.'". The brother said to the old man, 'So, man does not advance towards any reward without bodily affliction?' The old man said to him, 'Truly it is written: "Looking to Jesus, the Pioneer of and perfector of our faith who for the joy which was set before him, endured the cross." David also said: "I will not give sleep to mine eyes, nor slumber to my eyelids," until I find a place for the Lord'"[53].

According to our Father, the bush is the bodily action what we can understand as the manual work. At first sight the saying seems to be an explanation of the example of Moses and for this our Father uses the Lord's saying from the New and the Old Testament. With this methodology he creates a narrative that reaches the symbol of the place of the Lord. On the one hand we could

52 The Greek text is from Diogenes.

53 Translation from Ward, *The Sayings of the Desert Fathers*, with a small modofication.

accept the evaluation of Burton-Christie: "Abba Cronius ... interpreted Scripture allegorically in order to emphasize the importance of asceticism in the life of the monk."[54] but we should complementing this interpretation because we hesitate to accept that our Father's claim was that Moses' journey to the bush represented "bodily action" or asceticism."[55]. Adding to these, we could support his conclusion that "it has to do with what he sees as the aim of the monastic life: finding God" but with considering the early Christian exegetical tradition where the burning bush could symbolize either Christ himself in his abjection, with the bush crow in his head and in the same time, our Lady.

4. DIVINE WORK AND DIVINE ECONOMY

With the last example, we turn to Evagrius and the monks in Kellia. As it is known, he was a copyist or scribe already in Nitria[56]. This work was not a slavish copying but – as Casiday stated: "Obviously, Evagrius would have been able to produce copies of his own writings ... although it seems more likely that he would have been able to earn more money by copying out Scripture."[57]. Amongst the instructions for the copyist, for our purpose, the last chapter of the Gnostikos has relevance where he sums up and explains how he understands his work as copying sacred texts:

> Looking toward the archetype always, endeavour to scribe the images, Without omitting any of the things which complete the gaining of the one fallen. (translation from Young)[58].

---

54 D. Burton-Christi, *The word in the Desert*, Oxford 1994, 196.

55 Burton-Christi, *The word in the Desert*, 196.

56 As Palladius wrote: «he wrote gracefully in the oxyrynchus script» (Lausiac History 38); ἔγραψε τὸν ὀξύρυγχον χαρακτῆρα, *The Lausiac History of Palladius. II*, The Greek text edited with introd. and notes by E.C. Butler, Cambridge 1904, 120.

57 A. Casidy, *Reconstructing the Theology of Evagrius Ponticus*, New York 2013, 113.

58 The sentence has other translations: «Always endeavour to depict the images [εἰκόνας] by looking at the Archetype [ἀρχέτυπον], without omitting any of the factors that contribute to the reconstitution of the fallen [ἐκπεσοῦσαν] image» (I.L.E. Ramelli, *The Christian Doctrine of Apokatastasis*, Leiden 2013, page?) «Gazing fixedly upon the archetype, I strive to engrave the images without neglecting anything which might accomplish the gaining [back] of the fallen-away» (Dysinger) and «To the archetype looking always try to write the icons leaving out nothing of the things which contribute to the gaining of the one fallen». K. Corrigan, *Evagrius and Gregory: Mind, Soul and Body in the 4th Century*. (Ashgate studies in philosophy & theology in late antiquity), Ashgate Publishing Company, 2009, 162.

Πρὸς τὸ ἀρχέτυπον βλέπων ἀεὶ πειρῶ γράφειν τὰς εἰκόνας μηδὲν παρεὶς τῶν συντελούντων πρὸς τὸ κερδᾶναι τὴν ἐκπεσοῦσαν[59].

At first sight, in a literary sense, the chapter gives practical advice or instruction for his readers (for other scribes) about what he had to be aware of doing, whilst working as a scribe. Following Guillaumont's footnotes, on the level of the terms the sentence has a Platonizing reminiscence by using the term of archetype but the term of εἰκόνας hints to the biblical creation account, while the last part could allude to an Evagrian vision of the end. From this – so to say – theological point of view, the sentence embraces his protological and eschatological teaching.

According to my knowledge, in the scholarly literature the sentence has three different interpretations. Ramelli focused on the second part of the sentence and identified it as a trace of the eventual apokatastasis. In her reading (*without omitting any of the factors that contribute to the reconstitution of the fallen [ἐκπεσοῦσαν] image*) there is a clear reference to this – Origenian – tradition about the restoration of the fallen divine image in the human being. In her explanation: The eventual apokatastasis is seen by Evagrius, just as by Origen and especially by Gregory of Nyssa, as the restoration of the divine image in the human being, which had fallen and become blurred because of sin, and whose own seat is the intellect.[60]

In the interpretation of Corrigan "Despite its Platonic language", this is simple and direct. Evagrius worked as a copyist, copying sacred texts. As he worked, he also saw those who had come for spiritual guidance. As he worked or walked, he recited biblical texts. As he copied, he meditated on the text he was reading and writing... Chapter 50 sums up and is a vivid thought-picture of the reality of Evagrius' life on all those different levels: a divine reading that is a) simultaneously a form of human writing; b) a meditation that is simultaneously a form of being-with-others; c) a recollection that is an aid to memory in times of trouble; d) a stillness and silence that is also writing, inscribing, and spiritual direction; e) an archetype that includes surely those five wise teachers of the Church whose examples in the Gnostikos, Evagrius has just stressed, and who reflect Christ and scripture to others; and f) a prayer that is simultaneously inclusive of everyone."[61].

59 The Greek text from: Évagre le Pontique, *Le gnostique, ou À celui qui est devenu digne de la science*, éd. critique des fragments grecs, tr. établie au moyen des versions syriaques et arménienne, comm. par A. et C. Guillaumont (Sources Chrétiennes 356), Paris 1989, 192-193.

60 Ramelli, *The Christian Doctrine of Apokatastasis*, 501.

61 Corrigan, *Evagrius and Gregory*, 162.

Young re-examined the whole Gnostikos and established the sentence's place and meaning in relation to the whole. He argued for the solution of advice that is addressed to the Gnostikos with the aim to stimulate meditation. Young linked the sentence with the 11th one and stated: "the Gnostikos is commanded to look at Christ (Πρὸς τὸ ἀρχέτυπον) and to copy Christ (γράφειν τὰς εἰκόνας) onto his students."[62]. And later, he added: "Here, therefore, Evagrius links seeing the archetype with the demand for a Christlike condescension or synkatabasis, to rescue the fallen. In other words, looking at Christ shows the Gnostikos how to exercise the descent which was inherently perilous because it might become a habit"[63].

We should not follow further the different interpretations, because for our purpose all relevant details are together: 1.) In a literary sense, the sentence offers a practical advice for the scribe with pedagogic aim. 2.) if the scribe is the Gnostikos, the pedagogic aim is a mystagogic one, namely to lead the fallen one back to the original place. The terminology allows us to accept both solutions. 3.) At the same time, the terminology alludes to the platonic and biblical background, and if it is the case, we should take into account the theological solution and specifically that the sentence embraces the creation and the upcoming, but original situation. In other words, the references of the sentence extend to the level of the creation and the salvation. 4.) Based on these statements, we suppose that – at least in this Evagrian sentence – there is a detectable interpretation in which manual work was valued in analogy with the divine work. It means, in our case, that there is an analogy between the creative and salvific activities of God and copying sacred text. But in a broader sense, human work can imitate the divine work. In our proposed reading, this Evagrian sentence testifies also that human work partakes in the divine work and could imitate and serve, in this way, the divine economy.

One similar symbolic interpretation of the scribe appears in the Evagrian Great Letter where he describes the creative activity of God as the writing of letters (e.g.§ 6-7 and 17)[64]. This work exemplifies that our sketched teaching was not restricted to the ascetic writings.

62 R.D. Young, «Evagrius the Iconographer: Monastic Pedagogy in the Gnostikos», *JECS* 9 (2001) 53-71, 62.

63 Young, «Evagrius the Iconographer», 62.

64 At this point it is enough to hint at Casiday's clarification (Cassian, *On Prayer*, 153-154): in his Great Letter, Evagrius calls creation a "letter" from God – and he does so after explaining that a letter is a vehicle for making known to another party "those intentions and hidden secrets that are not for everyone and are not to be revealed to anyone except those who have a kindred mind".

CONCLUSION

This short paper, made an attempt to examine some different concepts of work and economy in the early monastic literature. Before the evaluation of our results, we should consider three basic statements of the scholarly literature. The first one is that the sayings as we received them had at least three significant stages of their development and after the centuries long process of collection, corrections, copying and editions from the oral traditions, the first edited written collections appeared towards the middle of the fifth century[65].

The second statement is a fact that should not be unmentioned and only its surface was touched in the paper concerning the monastic settlement where the sayings were born. The protagonists were not alone, but lived in a framework where this tradition was born together with them, from gatherings of monks in larger groups, then the foundations of the communities that were established in that time, and the whole environment rapidly changed profoundly and monastic complexes were being developed. Great efforts were made in the current scholarly literature to reach a new, more detailed picture of their daily life and economic activities, with focus on the monastic communities to unveil their huge range of economical, monetary activities that the lives and apophtegmas do not mention.[66]

The third general statement is that at first sight we could label the Desert Fathers as dualists because in the afore-mentioned sayings the physical world, the natural and the corporeal were rejected, and if not utterly, but held in low esteem on the one side[67]. On the other, there is the teaching of contemplation of the world, the created order that serves as basic idea and teaching in the spiritual life. We could mention also the tendency that is present e.g. in Athanasius, when he said that Antony was ashamed to be seen in the act of eating or sleeping. According to the scholars this motif appears in the Life of Plotinus where Porphyry says that "he was ashamed to be in a body" (VP 1,1) but as Brown stated,

---

65 For the more detailed description of this process see CHRYSSAVGIS, *In the Heart of the Desert. The Spirituality of the Desert Fathers and Mothers*, 9-10. In D.J. Chitty's terminology this period, in the early fifth century is the "diaspora" time, for this see his «The Books of the Old Man», *ECR* 6 (1974) 15-21 esp. 16-17 and ID., *The Desert a City*, Chretwood New York 1999, 67-68.

66 For the recent analysis, see e.g. E. WIPSZYCKA: «Resources and economic activities of the Egyptian monastic communities. (4th-8th Century)», *The Journal of Juristic Papyrology*, 41 (2011) 159-263.

67 Brown notes A.J. FESTUGIÈRE, *Antioche paienne et chrétienne*, Paris 1959, 309: Toute la spiritualité de ce temps est foncièrement dualiste.

in the intense struggle of retaining his body the monk also retained the will, and "seldom in the ancient world had the body been as more deeply implicated in the transformation of the soul; and never was it made to bear so heavy a burden. For the Desert Fathers, the body was not an irrelevant part of the human person, that could, as it were, be "put in brackets."".[68]. In the mortification of the flesh, or to say more exactly, the control of the body there were certainly extremists among the fathers and mothers in their asceticism but naturally the body was an integral part of the holiness[69]. For understanding the measure of the rigor and the violence to the body[70] it is enough to quote a saying from Antony (13): Once a hunter was haunting in the desert and saw Abba Anthony enjoying himself with the brethren and he was shocked. Wanting to show him that it was necessary sometimes to meet the needs of the brethren, the old man said to him, 'Put an arrow in your bow and shoot it.' So he did. The old man then said, 'Shoot another,' and he did so. Then the old man said, 'Shoot yet again,' and the hunter replied 'If I bend my bow so much I will break it.' Then the old man said to him, 'It is the same with the work of God. If we stretch the brethren beyond measure they will soon break. Sometimes it is necessary to come down to meet their needs.' When he heard these words the hunter was pierced by compunction and, greatly edified by the old man, he went away. As for the brethren, they went home strengthened.[71] Our abba gives the explanation about the measure how the monk could fulfill in a right way the work of God (τὸ ἔργον τοῦ Θεοῦ).

---

68 P. Brown, *The Body and Society: Men, Women and Sexual Renunciation in Early Christianity*, New York NY, 1988, 235.

69 For this term, see N. Russell, *The Doctrine of Deification in the Greek Patristic Tradition* Oxford University Press, Oxford 2004; *Theosis: Deification in Christian Theology*, eds. S. Finlan-V. Kharlamov, Cambridge 2006; *Partakers of the Divine Nature. The History and Development of Deification in the Christian Traditions*, eds. M.J. Christensen-J.A. Wittung, Michigan 2008; S. Thomas, *Deification in the Eastern Orthodox Tradition: A Biblical Perspective*, Piscataway (NJ) 2008.

70 For more details, see J. Pinsent, «Ascetic Moods in Greek and Latin Literature», in *Asceticism*, ed. W. Wimbush, Oxford 2002, 211-219, here 211. See also: H. Hunt, *Clothed in the Body. Asceticism, the Body and the Spiritual in the Late Antique Era*, Ashgate, Farnham 2012); N.G. Jennings, *Theology as Ascetic Act. Disciplining Christian Discourse*, New York 2010.

71 Ἠν δέ τις κατὰ τὴν ἔρημον θηρεύων ἄγρια ζῶα, καὶ εἶδε τὸν ἀββᾶν Ἀντώνιον χαριεντιζόμενον μετὰ τῶν ἀδελφῶν. Θέλων δὲ αὐτὸν πληροφορῆσαι ὁ γέρων, ὅτι χρὴ μίαν συγκαταβαίνειν τοῖς ἀδελφοῖς, λέγει αὐτῷ· Βάλε βέλος εἰς τὸ τόξον σου, καὶ τεῖνον· καὶ ἐποίησεν οὕτως. Λέγει αὐτῷ· Πάλιν τεῖνον· καὶ ἔτεινεν. Καὶ πάλιν φησί· Τεῖνον. Λέγει αὐτῷ ὁ θηρευτής· Ἐὰν ὑπὲρ τὸ μέτρον τείνω, κλᾶται τὸ τόξον. Λέγει αὐτῷ ὁ γέρων· Οὕτως καὶ εἰς τὸ ἔργον τοῦ Θεοῦ· ἐὰν πλεῖον τοῦ μέτρου τείνωμεν κατὰ τῶν ἀδελφῶν, ταχὺ προσρήσσουσι. Χρὴ οὖν μίαν μίαν συγκαταβαίνειν τοῖς ἀδελφοῖς. Ταῦτα ἀκούσας ὁ θηρευτὴς, κατενύγη, καὶ πολλὰ ὠφεληθεὶς παρὰ τοῦ γέροντος,

Coming closer to the topic, in general we could repeat the word of Rhee: Thus, whether one was an anchorite, semi-anchorite, or a cenobite, a monk did not necessarily live in destitution with "total" renunciation of private property, although other wandering monks in Syria who lived off of begging did choose a life of destitution with severe economic vulnerability. The monastic poverty in reality was more patterned after economic self-sufficiency than destitution"[72]. And later she continues: The ideal monk (whether a hermit or cenobite) should possess just enough to support oneself and to give alms (still out of surplus, however small that may be) to the economic poor, as almsgiving was a monastic obligation. In this context it is worth noting Evagrius's advice on the renunciation of possessions and on choosing poverty meant economic self-sufficiency for the monks through manual labor and the practice of inner detachment from desire and care of possessions—all as a demonstration of their dependence on God and their purity of heart[73]. Accepting Rhee's opinion This stance was much like the position of Clement of Alexandria earlier: "Give thought to working with your hands, and further that you may be able to offer donations, as the holy apostle Paul advised (1 Thess. 2:9; 2 Thess. 3:8).[74] But, It was not for nothing that "poverty" and "famine," "the poor" and "the starving" shared the same root in Coptic[75].

A monk worked for both practical and spiritual reasons. Quoting the opinion of Goodrich we could say that the most obvious practical reason was economic: the monk who had renounced all of his worldly possessions required some form of support. On the other side the value of manual labour was a means of cultivating humility and we should maintain with the fathers that the role of manual work was claimed obligatory next to the prayer because of the spiritual, unceasing process and struggle in which the monk has to restore the likeness by repentance and humility.

Turning to the sayings, two general and comprehensive results should be accentuated. The first one is that every example witnesses to the two aspects of work and prayer as two distinguishable but complementary aspects of the daily life that could cover the active and contemplative life. Furthermore, in the men-

ἀπῆλθε· καὶ οἱ ἀδελφοὶ στηριχθέντες ἀνεχώρησαν εἰς τὸν τόπον αὐτῶν.

72 H. Rhee, *Loving the Poor, saving the Rich.Wealth, Poverty and Early Christian Formation*, Baker Academic Grand Rapids (MI) 2012, 166.

73 See Evagrius of Pontus, T*he Greek Ascetic Corpus,* trans. R.E. Sinkewicz (Oxford Early Christian Studies), Oxford 2003.

74 Rhee, *Loving the Poor*, 167.

75 W.E. Crum, *A Coptic Dictionary*, Oxford 1939, 663-664. Quoted by Brown, *The Body and Society*, 218.

tioned examples, this twofold concept that lies in the background and developed as the result of the monastic movement whilst at the same time retaining its own frame, began to acquire distinctive features.

The second one could be that according to the sayings, the fathers' manual work was monotonous and simple, e.g. the making of rope, mats, baskets and sandals. Although Basil considered also weaving and shoe-making as ideal monastic occupations but building, carpentry, blacksmith and farming were recognized by him as necessary, though not ideal for a monk[76]. With every example, the ascetic value of manual labour was emphasized and articulated. This basic concept later – as far as the chronological order is estimable – expands into the theological and euchological concept, namely that work precludes thoughts that are prey for demons.

According to the sources, our first example that can not be underestimated, is the saying from Antony. The concept that stays in the center is common in the saying and the Vita but has different reasoning. As reported by both accounts, the Saint practiced the twofold life of prayer and work before he received the vision that is why we can not assert that the examined tradition hailed from his living experiences or from earlier traditions. As Chitty wrote in connection with this description: "He is assiduous in the work of his hands, to provide for himself and for those in need – no doubt that monotonous work, the making of rope, mats, baskets and sandals, from palm-blades and rushes, which became the staple industry of the monks because it fitted best the duty of unceasing prayer. It is a way of life that must have been known in the Church from the beginning."[77]. Based on the former observations, what can be stated with all certainty – if we accept that the saying testifies the earlier stage – is that the saying, in spite of being itself an arbitrary model and has only similarities with the account of the Vita, offers the prime concept that was adapted and adopted by the fathers who modified it through their experiences. Its influence and effectiveness can be demonstrated by the other examples.

The struggle for living a virtuous life appears in the example also where the indignation of abba Theodoros could reflect to the changed economical situation of the monastery. If we suppose that it was the case – may it be because of the changed role of manual work or just because of the glory of the past, our example could testify mundane, earthly economical connotations.

76 Saint Basil, *Long Rules* 38. For the Greek texts J.P. Migne (Patrologia Graeca 31), 1831, for the Latin text *The Rule of St Basil in Latin and English. A Revised Critical Edition*, trans. by A. M. Silvas, Collegeville (MN) 2013. For this question, see also E.F. Morison, *St Basil and his Rule. A Study in Early Monasticism*, Henry Rowde, Oxford University Press, 1912, esp. ch. IX. The monk at work, 79-85.

77 Chitty, *The Desert a City*, 2.

With the example from Evagrius, we investigate a concept of work that approached manual work as the imitation of the divine creative and redemptive work. In our reading, this concept exemplifies how manual work can partake or rather imitate the divine economy.

Keeping the different intentions in mind, we could state shortly, that work presents not only an important aspect of the writings and the daily life of the fathers, as it is shown by the assayed examples – and by the wealth of the unmentioned references to this question – but these allow us to state that the teachings concerning the work which we tried to evince, are rooted deeply in the fathers' experience and insights. At this point we hint back to our starting point, to the Pauline sentence in 1Cor. 3:9: *We are fellow-workers with God.*

In place of the conclusion of our inquiry, we turn to our last example to sum up why the desert father's teachings are essential when we try to approach the divine economy[78]: "An elder said: "The bee makes honey wherever it goes; likewise the monk too performs the work of God wherever he goes"[79].

Abstract

The Bible emphasises the importance of human creation. The created human – as God's image, steward and representative – is placed in having dominion over the material creation. Through sin, as a consequence of disobedience, we have lost our likeness to God. According to the sayings of the desert fathers, in the spiritual, unceasing process and struggle in which the monk has to restore the likeness by repentance and humility, the role of manual work was maintained and claimed obligatory.

In the earliest Christian traditions, among the differing attitudes to the meaning of work, the conceptualisation of work appeared as participation in God's creative activity.

This paper intends to investigate the questions of economy and work in the earliest traditions of monasticism. To make approachable the rich and manifold literature, the research is restrained to focus on work as a co-creative act of humanity. For the investigation, the closely related passages from the monastic literature would be examined, concentrating on the aspects of the monk's social and economic relationship to the world.

---

78 Anon. Sayings 255. the translation is from J. Wortley, *The anonymous sayings of the Desert Fathers*, Cambridge 2013.

79 The Greek text: 399. Εἶπεν [247vb] γέρων· Ἡ μέλισσα ὅπου ὑπάγει μέλι ποιεῖ. Οὕτως καὶ ὁ μοναχός, ὅπου ὑπάγει τὸ ἔργον τοῦ Θεοῦ ἐργάζεται.

"FROM HIS DESERT CAVE, A VOICE CRIES OUT IN THE WILDERNESS": SHENOUTE OF ATRIPE AND THE MANY FACES OF HOLINESS

Daniel LEMENI

INTRODUCTION

In this paper, we explore the multi-faceted picture of the holy man in late ancient community. In this context, we will refer to the relationship between monasticism and rural patronage in the vision of Shenoute (*c.* 348 – *c.* 466 A.D)[1] In

---

Daniel Lemeni, theologian and lecturer at the West University of Timişoara, specialist in Early Christian monasticism.

1 After Pachomius, St. Shenoute of Atripe (*ca.* 347 – 465 A.D) is the most important monastic figure of coenobitic monasticism in Egypt. He led one of the largest Christian monastic communities in late antique Egypt and was the greatest native writer of Coptic in history. More exactly, Shenoute of Atripe was the third leader of a notable monastic federation near Panopolis in Upper Egypt (present day Akhmim) that included two monasteries for male monks, the White Monastery (commonly known as Deir Anba Shenuda) and the Red Monastery (commonly known as Deir Anba Pšoi), and one for women in Atripe itself. There was very little academic attention given to Shenoute until ten to fifteen years ago when his literary corpus was reconstructed by Stephen Emmel. Therefore, the dossier of the monastic archimandrite Shenoute of Atripe (*c.* 350-465) provides rare firsthand documentation of a monk's often violent campaign against traditional religion in his context. See, S. EMMEL, *Shenoute's Literary Corpus*, 2 voll., Louvain 2004. Now, besides a few versions of Shenoute's biography, there are several academic studies extant, including translations of nine volumes of his *Canons*, eight volumes of *Discourses*, and a number of letters. There is also an international team of researchers at work, directed by S. Emmel, professor of Coptology at the Institute of Egyptology and Coptology at the University of Münster in Germany. This team is working on transcribing, editing, translating and studying these precious manuscripts in order not only to understand Shenoute and his monastic federation, but also to fill in the gaps of understanding concerning various other aspects of life in late antiquity with which Shenoute was involved. Books reflecting this interest include: *Selected Discourses of Shenoute the Great. Community, Theology, and Social Conflict in Late Antique Egypt*, edd. D. Brakke-A. Crislip, Cambridge 2015; B. LAYTON, *The Canons of Our Fathers: The Monastic Rules of Shenoute*, Oxford 2014; A. LÓPEZ, *Shenoute of Atripe and the Uses of Poverty: Rural Patronage, Religious Conflict, and Monasticism in Late Antique Egypt*, California 2013; R. KRAWIEC, *Shenoute and the Women of the White Monastery*, New York 2002,

the first section of our paper, we will focus on the essential features of the holy man as part of his charismatic authority, and then we will refer to the ascetic discourse that he put forward to promote and legitimize his active role in community. This role is essential for the understanding of the cultural significance of the holy man in the late antique world[2]. For the most part, this section is based on Peter Brown's brilliant analysis of the holy man.

In the second section, we point out the saint or holy man as a figure of importance in the social and economic context of late antiquity. Perhaps one of the most interesting aspects of Shenoute's monastic order was his involvement with the lay people of the Christian Mediterranean world. We explore here the public life of Shenoute of Atripe, and the discourse on poverty that he put forward to promote and legitimize his active role in society.

1. REVISITING THE HOLY MAN IN LATE ANTIQUITY: SHENOUTE OF ATRIPE, INSIDE AND OUTSIDE OF THE MONASTERY

The predominance of the holy man marked out Late Antiquity as a distinct phase of religious history. We know that in 1971, Peter Brown published his famous article, 'The Rise and Function of the Holy Man in Late Antiquity'[3], an essay that has

and Caroline T. Schroeder's *Monastic Body: Discipline and Salvation in Shenoute of Atripe*, Philadelphia 2007.

2 For this theme, see G. Anderson, *Sage, Saint and Sophist: Holy Men and Their Associates in the Early Roman Empire,* New York 1994.

3 P. Brown, «The Rise and Function of the Holy Man in Late Antiquity», *Journal of Roman Studies* 61 (1971) 80-101; reprinted in Id., *Society and the Holy in Late Antiquity*, Berkeley 1982, 103-152; now revised in P. Brown, *Authority and the Sacred: Aspects of the Christianisation of the Roman World*, Cambridge 1995: chapter 3 «Arbiters of the Holy: the Christian Holy Man in late antiquity», 57-78; P. Brown, «Town, Village and Holy Man: A Case of Syria», in Id., *Society and the Holy in Late Antiquity*, Univeristy of California Press, 1989, 153-165. In «The Rise and Function of the Holy Man in Late Antiquity» the holy man's public role as *patronus* becomes relevant, but subsequently Peter Brown offered some emendations to his position in «The Saint as Exemplar in Late Antiquity», *Representations* 1 (1983) 1.25, reprinted in *Saints and Virtues*, ed. J.S. Hawley, Berkeley 1987, 3-14. For assessments of the evolution of Brown's view of the holy man in Late Antiquity, see S. Elm, «Introduction», in «Charisma and Society: The 25th Anniversary of Peter Brown's Analysis of the Late Antique Holy Man. Conference Held at the University of California at Berkeley, March 13-16, 1997», *Journal of Early Christian Studies* 6 (1998) 343-351; and see Brown's own assessment, «The Rise and Function of the Holy Man in Late Antiquity, 1971-1997», *Journal of Early Christian*

transformed the way we think about saints in Late Antiquity. First of all, we say that in the Christian Mediterranean, a holy man crystallized the image of the charismatic sainthood, because he acted as a living mediator between earth and heaven[4].

In this section, we explore the central role of the holy man in late antiquity, and particularly Shenoute of Atripe, an extraordinary Egyptian monk from the middle of the fourth century and fifth century. The story of this spectacular holy man crystallized the image of the charismatic sainthood.

Therefore, we will focus in this section on the essential features of holy man as part of his charismatic authority. In this context, we stress that Shenoute not only served as abbot of the White Monastery, but he also worked as a prophet[5]. As Krawiec has remarked, Shenoute saw himself as a divinely appointed prophet, a "suffering servant", and a medium both of God's message and of God's judgment[6]. As prophet, his role in the community is to peel away the monks' false sense of security in their salvation and reveal what he believes to be the true spiritual state of the monastery. As Schroeder has remarked "he frames his censure of the monks' disobedience to the rule and of the leader's failure to exercise

---

Studies 6 (1998) 353–376. The *Journal of Early Christian Studies* 6 (Fall, 1998) is completely devoted to a re-assessment of Brown's holy man. The significance of Brown's original article is manifest from the fact that in March 1997 a conference was held in Berkeley, California, to celebrate the quarter-centenary of its publication, the proceedings of which were published in *Journal of Early Christian Studies* 6 (1998), and from the publication of a symposium inspired by Brown's article: J.Howard-Johnston-P.A. Hayward, *The Cult of Saints in Late Antiquity and the Middle Age*, Oxford 1999.

4 Generally, the works of D. Brakke and Peter Rousseau demonstrate the relationship between ascetics and world in Late Antiquity. On this subject, see Ph. Rousseau, «The World Engaged: The Social and Economic World», in *Ascetics, Society, and The Desert*, ed. J.E. Goehring, Harrisburg (PA) 1999, 49-51; D. Brakke, «Shenoute, Weber, and the Monastic Prophet: Ancient and Modern Articulations of Ascetic Authority», in *Foundations of Power and Conflicts of Authority in Late-Antique Monasticism: Proceedings of the International Seminar. Turin, December, 2-4, 2004*, edd. A Camplani-G. Filoramo, Leuven 2007, 47-73; Ph. Rousseau, «The Desert Fathers and Theire Broader Audience» in *Foundations of Power and Conflicts of Authority in Late-Antique Monasticism: Proceedings of the International Seminar Turin, December 2-4, 2004*, edd. A Camplani-G. Filoramo, Leuven 2007, 90-91; Id., «The Identity of the Ascetic Master in the Historia Religiosa of Theodoret of Cyrrhus: A New Paideia?» in *Mediterranean Archaeology* 11 (1998) 229-244.

5 David Frankfurter recognized the Egyptian Christian holy men as types of regional prophets, thus stressing the local and regional dimension of their cults. See D. Frankfurter, «Syncretism and the Holy Man in Late Antique Egypt», *Journal Early Christian Studies* 11 (2003) 339-385.

6 Krawiec, *Shenoute and the Women*, 55-72.

authority over the monks in the context of prophetic duty. He presents himself as the messenger of the truth who must uncover and extinguish the falsehood and hypocrisy concealed in the monastery"[7]. In other words, Shenoute preaches repentance on earth and intercedes for sinners at the divine court. Exposing sins, pronouncing judgment, interceding with Christ, as well as helping people with practical problems – these are the tasks of the prophet Shenoute, made possible by his clairvoyance[8], according to the *Life of Shenoute*[9].

Therefore, one of the interpretive keys to understand Shenoute, is his self-representation as a prophet for his community[10]. According to D. Brakke, "the revelations from God, constituted the essential element of Shenoute's authority as a prophet. It runs from his initial exposure of concealed sin in the monastery before he became its leader, through his interactions with his monks as their leader, including and especially the women, through his assertions of authority over persons outside the White Monastery (clergy, other monks, lay people). To know what God knows and to announce it to others – this was what it meant to be a prophet for Shenoute, and thus, there is a strong continuity between the authority that he sought to establish within the monastic community and that which he sought outside of it"[11].

7 C.T. SCHROEDER, *Monastic Bodies*, 49.

8 Heike Behlmer notes that clairvoyance, the «gift to search hearts», was an element in the holy man's prestige, and she sees the *Life* as multiplying the instances in which Shenoute displayed this miraculous ability (cf. H. BEHLMER, «Visitors to Shenoute's Monastery», in *Pilgrimage and Holy Space in Late Antique Egypt*, ed. D. Frankfurter, Leiden 1998, 357).

9 The portraits of Shenoute that work from Brown's holy man, all find themselves drawn to the *Life of Shenoute*, which provides the best material for a Shenoute who acts as a patron, dispenses divine blessings, and performs ritual acts that mimic as much as they reject traditional pagan religious behaviour. For more details, see BESA, *The life of Shenoute by Besa*, introd., trans., and notes by Daniel N. Bell, Kalamazoo 1983.

10 For example, in *Canon I*, Shenoute conforms to the literary and anthropological model of the biblical "peripheral prophet", a figure who stands outside of the community's primary religious and political authority system and speaks to the community from a marginal, but not wholly outside, position. For more details, see LAYTON, *The Canons of Our Fathers: Monastic Rules of Shenoute*. On the Shenoute as a prophet, see SCHROEDER, *Monastic Bodies* (ch. I, «Bodily Discipline and Monastic Authority: Shenoute's Earliest Letters to the Monastery», 24-53). On the figure of the biblical peripheral prophet, see R.R. WILSON, *Prophecy and Society in Ancient Israel*, Fortress Press, Philadelphia 1980. On the biblical tradition of prophecy in Christian Egypt, see also D. FRANKFURTER, *Elijah in Upper Egypt: The Apocalypse of Elijah and Early Egyptian Christianity*, Philadelphia 1993.

11 BRAKKE, «Shenoute, Weber, and the Monastic Prophet: Ancient and Modern Articulations of Ascetic Authority», 72.

By taking on the persona of a biblical prophet, Shenoute solidifies his reputation as a spiritual father. Therefore, he was spiritual guide, because he played a vital pastoral role in his community. As Bentley Layton has remarked, "Shenoute's most important business was undoubtedly seeing to the spiritual direction and spiritual formation of his monks and nuns – as distinct from their administrative care"[12].

From this perspective, Shenoute simultaneously places himself in the tradition of authoritative ascetics whose charisma or "ascetic authority"[13], and ascetic practice rendered them ascetic fathers worthy of disciples[14].

Essentially, the Christian saint of late antiquity ('the holy man' in Brown's terminology) belonged simultaneously to the earthly and the heavenly world. In Peter Brown's paradigmatic assessment, the late antique holy man is "an 'icon' who brought the holy into the world, a hinge person mediating between God and

---

12 LAYTON, *The Canons of Our Fathers: Monastic Rules of Shenoute*, 25.

13 The question of the relationship between asceticism and authority is rich in nuances throughout early Christian literature. Without referencing in detail the voluminous body of literature created by the discussion of the role of the 'holy man' in the late antique world, it is necessary to highlight at least a few of the more specific studies, which are immediately relevant as background to the present paper. Indispensable for situating the topic is Peter Brown's article «Arbiters of the Holy: The Christian Holy Man in Late Antiquity», in BROWN, *Authority and the Sacred: Aspects of the Christianisation of the Roman World*, 55-78. Concerning the nexus between asceticism and authority, see C. RAPP in *Holy Bishops in Late Antiquity: The Nature of Christian Leadership in an Age of Transition*, Berkeley 2005. For the question of ecclesial dimensions of ascetic authority, see S.J. COATES, «The Bishop as Pastor and Solitary: Bede and the Spiritual Authority of the Monk Bishop», *Journal of Ecclesiastical History* 47 (1996) 601-619; J. CHRYSSAVGIS, «Obedience: Hierarchy and Asceticism: The Concept of Spiritual Authority in the Church», *St Vladimir's Theological Quarterly* 34.1 (1990) 49-60; P. HENRY, «From Apostle to Abbot: The Legitimation of Spiritual Authority in the Early Church», *Studia Patristica* 17.2 (1982) 491-505; PH. ROUSSEAU, *Ascetics, Authority, and the Church in the Age of Jerome and Cassian*, Oxford 1978; and ID., «Spiritual Authority of the Monk Bishop: Eastern Elements in some Western Hagiography of the Fourth and Fifth Centuries», *Journal of Theological Studies* 22 (1971) 380-419. For a recent discussion of aspects of the question of the relationship between ascetic authority and ecclesiastical authority, see also D. CANER, *Wandering, Begging Monks: Spiritual Authority and the Promotion of Monasticism in Late Antiquity*, Berkeley 2002. On individual figures of spiritual authority see also J.W. DRIJVERS-J-W. WATT, *Portraits of Spiritual Authority: Religious Power in Early Christianity, Byzantium and the Christian Orient*, Leiden 1999.

14 One of the major themes in Shenoute's canons is the issue of monastic purity and holiness. This holiness was not just something considered at the level of the individual monk, but was seen collectively: in the sense that each monk's holiness affected the holiness of the entire community. On this theme, see B. LAYTON, *The Canons of Our Fathers: Monastic Rules of Shenoute*, Oxford 2015.

man"[15]. In other words, in the late Roman Mediterranean world, the divine comes to earth through the charismatic holy man[16]. Despite the discourse of ascetic isolation surrounding these figures, Peter Brown emphasises the degree to which the charismatic saint plays an integral social role as *patronus*[17] and mediator[18].

From this perspective, it is no exaggeration to say that Brown had transformed the way we think about saints in late antiquity. As Patricia Cox has argued, the "holiness" of these figures becomes a significant social factor in late antique life. "The *idea* of the holy man," Cox concludes, "became at least as important as the men themselves, for their existence (or, perhaps, their reputations) attested to the gods' concern for the welfare of humankind"[19].

In Late Antiquity, the saint encompasses a life of intense holiness, and an intensely public life. One common way in which holy persons become holy, comes from their ability to serve as a conduit between the world of the transcendent and the world of the mundane. In this sense the holy man appears as „a kind of hinge person, whose vertical axis linked him to the realm of celestial powers and whose horizontal axis separated him from social engagement and the daily round of the quotidian"[20]. In this context, we stress that one of the most interest-

---

15 Cf. J. Howe, «Revisiting the Holy Man: Review Article», *Catholic Historical Review* 86/4 (2000) 641.

16 The exegetical literature on the late-antique holy man is vast. For an introduction, P.C. Miller, *Biography in Late Antiquity: a Quest for the Holy Man*, Berkeley 1983; Rapp, *Holy Bishops in Late Antiquity: The Nature of Christian Leadership in an Age of Transition*; D. Satran, *Biblical Prophets in Byzantine Palestine: Reassessing the Lives of the Prophets*, Leiden 1994, 97-105. For some nuances in the multifaceted picture of the saint in late antique world, see especially the range of articles presented in Howard-Johnston-Hayward, *The Cult of Saints in Late Antiquity and the Middle Age*.

17 In Brown's account, the holy man remained sacred, but he was also a powerful patron in a world where mundane social, economic, and judicial responsibilities constituted the main sphere of his activity (cf. Brown, «The Rise and Function of the Holy Man in Late Antiquity», 1971, 80-101. The most visible manifestation of the holy man was obviously care for widows, orphans and the poor which contributed to the growing prominence and influence of his in cities (cf. P. Brown, *Poverty and Leadership in the Later Roman Empire*, Hanover [NH] 2002; R.D. Finn, *Almsgiving in the Later Roman Empire: Christian Promotion and Practice, 313-450*, Oxford 2006.

18 Peter Brown notes that the holy man's true power came from his role as a "mediator" in village life (cf. Brown, «The Rise and Function of the Holy Man in Late Antiquity», 89).

19 Miller, *Biography in Late Antiquity: A Quest for the Holy Man*, 19.

20 L.S. Cunningham, «Holy Men/Holy Women», in *The Blackwell Companion to the Study of Religion*, ed. R.A. Segal, 2006, 287.

ing aspects of Shenoute's monastic order, was his involvement with the lay people of that region. In contrast with the Pachomian *Koinonia*, Shenoute opened his monastery on Saturdays and Sundays to lay people and pilgrims and gave them religious instruction. He was quite generous in providing for the poor and in many cases acted as their patron, whilst at the same time he was robustly denouncing the wealthy, particularly the middle and upper classes of the local capital Panopolis, who he thought had a careless attitude to the physical and spiritual welfare of their local people[21].

The saint or holy man has long been recognised as a figure of importance in the social and religious history of late antiquity, with his role as patron in communities attracting particular attention. Like the prophets of the Bible, Shenoute denounced social and economic injustice, and in this case he was a powerful patron in a world where mundane social, economic, and judicial responsibilities constituted the main sphere of his activity.

In the next section, we will analyse Shenoute's welfare activities on behalf of the "poor" and we will track the emergence of a new economic discourse developed to justify the "miraculous" wealth acquired by large monasteries in the late antique Near East.

2. POVERTY IN LATE ANTIQUITY

In this section, we explore the public prominence of Shenoute of Atripe, and the discourse on poverty that he put forward to promote and legitimise his active role in society. From this perspective, as Ariel G. López has remarked "The contrast with the stars of the Egyptian monastic tradition – Antony, Pachomius, the monks of Nitria and Scetis – is clear. Notwithstanding their reputation and prestige, most of these monks were, in comparison with Shenoute, relatively harmless. Neither Antony nor Pachomius is known to have been involved in economic and religious struggles with the surrounding countryside"[22].

And indeed, one of the important features of Shenoute's life as ascetic was his huge involvement in the world outside his monastery. This significant social factor was neither common nor traditional among Egyptian monks, either before or after Shenoute's time. For to understand this new situation, the concept of the holy man as *patronus* (namely, public benefactor) becomes relevant, again. As we

21 López, *Shenoute of Atripe and the Uses of Poverty*, 57-62.

22 López, *Shenoute of Atripe and the Uses of Poverty*, 127.

know, public benefactors provided food in times of famine, helped Christians in distress, and pleaded with authorities for tax remission and other favours.

The concept of the holy man as *patronus* was introduced by Peter Brown to help explain the concrete role of holy men in the Syrian countryside. Brown pointed out that Syrian holy men – and the phenomenon can be seen in other regions as well – acted as advocates, and protectors with authorities on behalf of the rural population.

In similar terms, Shenoute of Atripe encompasses a life of intense holiness, and an intensely public life, because he was very active outside the walls of his monastery. Of Shenoute's career outside the monastery more is known. He now put to work the extraordinary charisma that he had acquired – effective both inside the ascetic world and outside in secular life[23].

As we know Shenoute's monastery has been described as one of the most important buildings in late antique Egypt. As Lopez has remarked the church that Shenoute constructed at the great White Monastery near Sohag was "the biggest monastic church built in the Mediterranean world during the late antique period"[24].

In this context, we stress that the monumental church building not only epitomized Shenoute's success as a monastic leader, it also broadcasted his importance and leadership to the wider world. As abbot of a great complex of monasteries, he was the equal of any lay patron[25]. Shenoute, who presented himself as the defender of "the poor", noted constantly the large number and diversity of the crowds who came to hear him preach in the church about four times each year.

Thus, the activity of Shenoute confirms the importance of the notion of patronage in Late Antiquity. Shenoute's role in practical matters was analogous to that of the *patronus* or public benefactor.

And indeed, Egyptian monasteries were also known to provide much more extensive aid to the poor in times of emergency. During times of famine, the poor

---

23 His public career will not be spelled out in detail. For details see especially the works of Stephen Emmel: Shenoute's Literary Corpus 1:6-14; «From the Other Side of the Nile»; «Shenoute the Monk»; «Shenoute's Place in the History of Monasticism»; «Christian Destruction of Temples». Emmel's foundational contributions are now supplemented by outstanding historical commentary on Shenoute's career in López, *Shenoute of Atripe and the Uses of Poverty*.

24 López, *Shenoute of Atripe and the Uses of Poverty*, 48.

25 Cf. P. Brown, *Treasure in Heaven: The Holy Poor in Early Christianity*, London 2016, 114.

would flock to the monasteries of the delta in search of alms, which they would of course receive. What is clear, in any case, is that Shenoute's monastery was far too big for the immediate needs of his monks. This was meant to be a public, not a monastic, community. On feast days, the monastic church would become a public stage[26]. For example, Shenoute indicates that every day special food was cooked for the poor, who gathered daily at the gates for their portions[27]. In Shenoute's monastery the capacity to care for the poor and homeless was considerable[28].

Thus, in the White Monastery, the care of the poor seems to be an aspect of the relationship between monasticism and local society. Ariel López, in *Shenoute of Atripe and the Uses of Poverty*, has published the only full-length study of the rural economy of Shenoute's work. López argues that Shenoute needed to justify his public role, which seemed to conflict with his monastic identity, and did so by portraying himself as the champion of the poor: "The public prominence achieved by self-made men like Shenoute was, in Egypt as elsewhere, problematic and fraught with tensions. This was particularly so in Shenoute's case, given his monastic status. Hence his constant need to explain himself and his actions. There were of course many self-made men in the later Roman Empire, and there were other monks in the fifth century who managed to gain power and influence over local society"[29]. As large monasteries became wealthy through donations (both imperial and private), they naturally took over charitable activities, especially in rural areas. And indeed, like guests or strangers, the poor were traditionally amongst the recipients of monastic charity.

Thus, one aspect of the White Monastery was to provide economic support for its members and the surrounding villages. The monks' labour contributed to

26 For more details López, *Shenoute of Atripe and the Use of Poverty*, 57-62.

27 See Besa, *Life of Shenoute*, 1983.

28 On the rules and organization of Shenoute's monastic community, see esp. B. Layton, «Rules, Patterns, and the Exercise of Power in Shenoute's Monastery: The Problem of World Replacement and Identity Maintenance», *Journal of Early Christian Studies* 15/1, 2007, 45-73; Id., «The Ancient Rules of Shenoute's Monastic Federation», in *Christianity and Monasticism in Upper Egypt*, vol 1: *Akhmim and Sohag*, eds. G. Gabra -H.N. Takla, Cairo 2008, 73-81; Id., «The Monastic Rules of Shenoute», in *Monastic Estates in Late Antique and Early Islamic Egypt: Ostraca, Papyri, and Essays in Memory of Sarah Clackson* (P. Clackson), eds. A. Boud'hors, *et al.* (American Studies in Papyrology 46), Ohio 2009, 170-77; Id., «Social Structure and Food Consumption in an Early Christian Monastery: The Evidence of Shenoute's *Canons* and the White Monastery Federation A.D. 385-465», *Museon* 115 (2002) 25-55.

29 López, *Shenoute of Atripe and the Uses of Poverty*, 128.

the monastery's ability to provide economic assistance both to themselves and those seeking hospitality and charity from them.

From this perspective, the monastery's administration was called the "administration of the poor", an ambiguous expression. This fame was well deserved. Shenoute's care of the poor and discourse of endless generosity had accomplished more than simply legitimising an unprecedented accumulation of wealth by monks. They had helped to establish his monastery as a public institution with a prominent role in local life. One characteristic of the White Monastery in Upper Egypt was the wide range of services that it provided, not just limited to medical care for the sick, but extending also to the poor, strangers, orphans, lepers, and elderly.

As Ariel G. Lopez has remarked "The language of poverty was above all a language of claims. Rather than a category with intrinsic meanings, the "poor" was a *relational* category often used with a polemical intent. Most of the time, it simply meant the "oppressed." Shenoute's attempt to define his ambivalent position in the "world" by referring to a vague and ill-defined notion made perfect political sense. Like "middle class" or "proletariat," the "poor" was a "social concept with variable geometry"[30].

Shenoute is depicted as a very compassionate man, with a particular concern for the poor and the destitute, whom he once relieved by a miraculous supply of bread:

> One day, our father the prophet abba Shenoute was engaged in their worship at night, and after he had completed the worship he rested for a little while and saw an apparition sent by the Lord. It was like this: he saw standing before him a man wholly filled with great glory. There was a great fragrance coming forth from his mouth and his face shone with light like the sun. The old man said to him: "Who are you, my Lord, surrounded as you are by this great glory?". The shining figure replied: "I am Paul, the apostle of Christ. Because you love charity and give alms to anyone that asks you and keep all the commandments in all ways because of the love (of God), behold! The Lord has sent me to you to comfort you because of what you do for the poor and the destitute". And he stayed talking with him like this until it was time to assemble in the church at night[31].

30 López, *Shenoute of Atripe and the Uses of Poverty*, 44.
31 Besa, *Life of Shenoute*, 80-81.

The public activity of Shenoute was called the "administration of the poor", although his public role went far beyond the care of the poor, strictly speaking. Shenoute's reputation consists in the fact that he saw himself as merely the instrument of God's will[32]. In this context, he was seen as an Old Testament prophet with a sacred mission[33].

Shenoute was a player within the power structures of late Roman Egypt. He exhibited no tension or conflict between ascetic withdrawal and active engagement in the world. To the contrary, his ascetic discipline, the size of his monastic federation, and his prophetic gifts legitimated his authority, destined to be exercised inside and outside his federation[34]. Strict ascetic discipline became the precondition for correct leadership of all Christians, ascetics and others, and such discipline had to increase in rigour the greater the monastic's involvement in the affairs of the world.

CONCLUSION

In conclusion, we say that Shenoute was a figure of importance in the social and economic history of late antiquity.

In this sense, we accept together with Ariel López that 'Shenoute was a monk of the "desert" heavily involved in the problems of the "world"'[35], so that "he may have been a cave-dwelling inhabitant of the desert, but the affairs of the world were still very much his concern"[36]. Briefly, Shenoute was an eminent monk and a strong *patron*, an example of the love of the poor. This is a duty that he has not chosen, but it has chosen him.

Moreover, this love of the poor defined the public role of Shenoute in the late antique world. Yet, it encouraged and legitimised a stronger and more active involvement outside the monastery.

32 For more details on this subject, see BRAKKE, «Shenoute, Weber, and the Monastic Prophet: Ancient and Modern Articulations of Ascetic Authority».

33 On the prophetic role of Shenoute, see KRAWIEC, *Shenoute and the Women*, C. SCHROEDER, «Prophecy and Porneia in Shenoute's Letters: The Rhetoric of Sexuality in a Late Antique Egyptian Monastery», *Journal of Near Eastern Studies* 65 (2006) 81-97, and BRAKKE, «Shenoute, Weber, and the Monastic Prophet: Ancient and Modern Articulations of Ascetic Authority».

34 On this subject, see J. TIMBIE, «The Education of Shenoute and Other Cenobitic Leaders: Inside and Outside of the Monastery», in *Education and Religion in Late Antique Christianity*, edd. P. Gemeinhardt,-L. Van Hoof-P. Van Nuffelen, Routledge 2016, 34-46.

35 LÓPEZ, *Shenoute of Atripe and the Uses of Poverty*, 23.

36 LÓPEZ, *Shenoute of Atripe and the Uses of Poverty*, 2.

From this perspective, Shenoute's texts are indeed an invaluable resource to study the antique economy of late Egypt. Moreover, perhaps, the insights offered by the Shenoute's work continue to constitute invaluable and most effective tools for the relationship between monasticism and economy in our times.

Abstract

In this paper, we explore the central role of the holy man in Late Antiquity, and especially the case of Shenoute of Atripe, an extraordinary Egyptian monk from the first half of the fifth century. Our major premise is that in the Christian communities of Late Antiquity, the saint (the holy man so well studied by Peter Brown) played a role comparable to that of the prophet: the axis of the community. In other words, the charismatic holy man transformed his territory into a sacred space and created a new site for the interrelation between society and the sacred. From this perspective, we offer a new interpretation of rural monasticism in early Egyptian monasticism. Our conclusion is that the monk becomes a significant economic factor in the late antique Mediterranean world.

THE WORK, PAIN AND OEUVRE IN THE FIRST PART OF THE MISSION OF PAPHNUTIUS / LIFE OF ONUPHRIUS

Marc MALEVEZ

The *Life of Onuphrius*, which we chose to rename the *Mission of Paphnutius* in accordance with the story as a whole, is well known as much in Latin as in most of the languages of the Christian East. Regarding the manuscripts of the Nile tradition, which we are the only ones to have studied to this day, the Pierpont Morgan M580, which is in New York and which we will call "S1" is a parchment in Sahidic Coptic. We are currently preparing its publication and French translation; however, it has already been translated into English by Tim Vivian[1]. This parchment is dated the year 606 of the Era of the Martyrs, i.e. years 889-890 of our calendar. The manuscript B.L. Oriental 7027, which we will call "S2" is also in Sahidic Coptic and is being preserved at the British Library. On paper dated 1004, it was first published and translated into English at the beginning of the 20th century by E.A.W. Budge. It was then recently translated again by Vivian, who, unfortunately, reproduces a number of his translation mistakes[2]. We have reviewed and edited Budge's version, with a new translation. Coptic manuscript on parchment n° 65[4] of the Vatican Library, dated 978-979 is in Bohairic. We

---

Mark Malevez, philologist and historian, specialist in Coptic language at the Free University of Brussels

1 L. DEPUYDT, *Catalogue of Coptic Manuscripts in the Pierpont Morgan Library*, vol. 1 (*Corpus van verluchte handschriften* 4-5), Louvain 1993, 322-324; T. VIVIAN, *The Life of Onnophrius: A New Translation*, in *Coptic Church Review*, 12/4, 99-111; re-published in T. VIVIAN, *Journeying into God. Seven Early Monastic Lives*, Minneapolis 1996, 166-187. We do not share the author's purely allegorical interpretation of the story.

2 The *Mission* covers the forty-two first pages of the manuscript B.L.Or. 7027; B. LAYTON, *Catalogue of Coptic Literary Manuscripts in the British Library Acquired since the Year 1906*, London 1987, 192-194; E.A.W. BUDGE, *Coptic Martyrdoms etc. in the Dialect of Upper Egypt*, London 1914, 205-223 and 455472; T. VIVIAN, *Histories of the Monks of Upper Egypt and The Life of Onnophrius by Paphnutius*, Kalamazoo 1993. Let us not forget the French translation of E.A.W. Budge's English version by S. CHAULEUR, *Saint Onuphre. Sa vie, d'après le Synaxaire copte, 16 Ba'ounah (10 juin) et le manuscrit Oriental n° 7027 du British Museum*, in *Les Cahiers Coptes*, 5 (1954) 3-15.

will call it "B". It was published and translated into French by Amélineau in 1884, except for the last verso[3]. This publication presents several mistakes and hence, was corrected and translated again. Various fragments in Sahidic Coptic were also preserved and will be called "R". We are preparing their publication in full, as well as their French translation.

As far as the work in Arabic is concerned, we were able to consult and translate three of the eight located manuscripts. The first one, and the most interesting one in many ways, is being preserved in Egypt, in the Monastery of the Syrians where it bears the reference «homilies n° 399». We were not allowed to read the manuscript itself or to see photographs of it. We had to work on an anonymous handwritten transcription which was inserted in a small booklet collecting the life stories of several Egyptian ascetics[4]. The author of this booklet, Father Ṣamū'īl as-Suryānī, declares having completed his transcription of the second part of the manuscript on 20 June 1959 (A1.193) and finished the first part five days later (A0.70). However, he does not provide any indication allowing us to date the manuscript he has copied. The only photographs we were able to obtain were of another copy of the second part made by Father Yehnes, a monk in the Monastery. His transcription was certified a «true copy» by Father Bigoul, the Monastery librarian. The photographs, which offer a text that is clearly closer to the manuscript's Arabic version, do not contain any colophon. It is therefore impossible to date the original or the copy. The manuscript of Paris 260[8] is an anonymous paper document, undated, even though Gérard Troupeau estimates it is from the 14th century[5]. We are preparing its publication and we have translated it. The same goes for manuscript n° 538, preserved at the Sainte-Catherine's Monastery in Sinai, which is also a paper document, and is dated 1211.

---

3 Vatican 65[4], fol. 99A-120B; É. AMÉLINEAU, «Voyage d'un moine égyptien dans le désert», in *Recueil de travaux relatifs à la philologie et à l'archéologie égyptiennes et assyriennes*, vol. 6, G. MASPERO (dir.), Vieweg, Paris 1885, 166-194. This manuscript was originally found in Cardinal Borgia's collection: G. ZOËGA, *Catalogus codicum copticorum manu scriptorum qui in Museo Borgiano Velitris adservantum. Avec une introduction historique et des notes bibliographiques par Joseph-Marie Sauget*, Hildesheim-New York 1973, 14-19 (1st edition: Bologne 1785). It is worth noting that Amélineau also reproduces Zoëga's mistakes. See also catalogue by A. HEBBELYNCK-A. VAN LANTSCHOOT, *Codices coptici Vaticani, Barberiniani, Borgiani, Rossiani*, vol. 1: *Codices coptici Vaticani*, Vatican 1937, 472-473.

4 من سير الآباء السواح عن مخطوطات الميامر بدير السريان, s.l., s.d.

5 G. TROUPEAU, *Catalogue des manuscrits arabes. Première partie: manuscrits chrétiens*, t. 2, *Manuscrits dispersés entre les n° 780 et 6933*, Paris 1972, 223-224.

Finally, for the Ethiopian tradition, there are five known manuscripts. One of them, dated the last quarter of the 16th century, is preserved at the British Library (manuscript B.L. Oriental n° 763², folios 125A-131A). It was the only published manuscript to this day[6]. This version really needed the revision we provided. The Ethiopian Manuscript Microfilm Library in Addis Abäba (EMML) and the Hill Museum and Manuscript Library of the Saint John University in Collegeville, US (HMML) have a copy of a parchment manuscript of the *Mission*, which is being preserved at the Institute of Ethiopian Studies, in the Ethiopian capital city. It is the only manuscript that has kept a colophon, but no date unfortunately. This manuscript probably dates back to the first half of 16th century at the latest. Three other manuscripts, preserved in Paris, belong to Abbadie's collection, in which they are numbered as follows : n° 85³, fol. 2A-20B, 91³, fol. 87A-102B, and 94¹, fol. 159A-164B. These manuscripts do not have a colophon and the Ethiopian writing does not really help the dating process. Nr 85³ clearly is from 18th or 19th century. The other two are from the end of 14th century or the first half of 15th century. Nr 94¹ presents the most ancient Ethiopian text, and therefore it is the manuscript ('E1') on which we base the review we are preparing.

The *Mission of Paphnutius*, traditionnally called the *Life of Onuphrius*, is the story of a journey; it tells us about a monk from Scetis called Paphnutius and his travelling to the Libyan desert. After having first stopped in a cave where he discovered the natural mummy of a hermit, he encountered another wanderer named Timothy. The second part is about Paphnutius meeting Onuphrius and, while travelling back to Scetis, his encounter with two groups of other brothers who lived in the desert.

The *Mission of Paphnutius / Life of Onuphrius* seems to be completely devoid of any mention of manual work, except for this first part of the story.

When he meets Paphnutius, Timothy starts by explaining his cenobitic life in his first monastery. He was, of course, performing some manual work there, S2 being the only manuscript from the Nile tradition we had access to which does not mention this fact.

S1.36 – ϫⲉⲁⲛⲟⲕ ⲟⲩⲙⲟⲛⲁⲭⲟⲥ · ⲉⲓⲟⲩⲏϩ ϩ̇ⲛⲟⲩⲥⲟⲟⲩϩⲥ̇ ⲙ̇ⲙⲟⲛⲁⲭⲟⲥ · ϩ̇ⲛⲛ̇ⲧⲟϣ ⲛ̇ⲑⲏⲃⲁⲉⲓⲥ · ⲉⲓⲣϩⲱⲃ ⲉⲧⲙ̇ⲛⲧ̇ϩⲁⲣⲥⲓⲕⲁⲣⲓ̈ⲟⲥ

6 F.M. Esteves Pereira, *Vida de Santo Abunafre (S. Onuphrio). Versão ethiopica*, Lisbonne 1905; W. Wright, *Catalogue of the Ethiopic Manuscripts in the British Museum Acquired since the Year 1847*, London 1877, 173-175; a note on the front page of the folio 124 specifies that the manuscript is the work of a certain Mathieu and that it was written in the 24th year of Sarsa Dengel's reign, e.i. in 15861587.

«I was a monk living in a monastic community in the nome of Thebaid, working in basketry.»

B.26 – ϪⲈⲀⲚⲞⲔ ⲞⲨⲘⲞⲨⲚⲀⲬⲞⲤ ⲈⲚⲀⲒϢⲞⲠ ⲠⲈ ϦⲈⲚⲞⲨⲀⲂⲎⲦ ⲠⲈ ϦⲈ(Ⲛ)ⲪⲘⲀⲢⲎⲤ ⲈⲒⲈⲢϨⲰⲂ ⲈⲐⲘⲈⲦⲐⲀⲢⲤⲒⲔⲀⲢⲒⲞⲤ

«I was a monk staying in a community in the South, working in basketry.»

E1.35 - ወይቤለኒ ፡ አንሰ ፡ በስምሰ ፡ መነኮስ ፡ ወነበርኩ ፡ ውስተ ፡ ምኔት ፡ ምስለ ፡ ጉባኤ ፡ መነኮሳት ፡ ወእትገበር ፡ በእደዊየ ፡፡

«And he said to me: certainly, by name I am a monk and I have lived in a monastery with a community of monks and I worked with my hands.»

A0.24 - نم ةعامج هيف ريد يف مسإلاب ابهار تنك» : يل لاقف
.نولمعي امك يديب لمعأ ،نابهرلا

«And he said to me: by name I was a monk in a monastery where a community of monks lived; I was working with my hands like they were working.»

ديعصلا دلبب ريد يف ابهار مسإلاب يرمع ميدق يف تنك انأ ينباجأف
- A2.31.ناتكلا لمعأو انطوتسم

«And he answered: me, I was, in my former life, monk by name, living permanently in a monastery in the area of Upper Egypt, and I worked linen.»

تارايدلا ضعب يف تنك يتينابهر)ءادتبا يف انأ يخأاي الئاق ينباجأف
-A3.31 ناتكلا لمع ةعنص يدي يف ناكو انكاس سطانبلا

«And he answered, saying: Oh my brother, me, at the beginning of my monastic life, I lived among Cells (?) and a manual work was in my hands, the work of linen».

According to S1 and B, we are talking about basketry, whereas A2 and A3 mention the work of linen, considered more «luxurious» and, therefore, sometimes seen as representing a superior risk of Pride.

The monk then decides to leave the monastery and live alone. He thinks he will then «profit» more from his manual work.

S1.37 - ⲀⲨⲘⲈⲈⲨⲈ ⲚⲦⲈⲒⲘⲒⲚⲈ ⲈⲒ ⲈⲠⲀϨⲎⲦ · ϪⲈⲦⲰⲞⲨ̈Ⲛ ⲀⲘⲞⲨ ⲈⲂⲞⲖ Ϩ̇ⲘⲠⲈⲒϪⲀⲒ̈Ⲉ Ⲛ̇Ⲅ̇ϬⲰ ⲘⲀⲨⲀⲀⲔ Ϩ̇ⲘⲠⲈⲔⲘⲀⲚϢⲰⲠⲈ · ⲀⲨⲰ Ⲕ̇ⲚⲀⲈⲤⲨⲬⲀⲌⲈ · Ⲛ̇ⲔⲀⲚⲀⲬⲰⲢⲈⲒ̈ Ⲛ̇Ⲅ̇ϢⲰⲠⲈ Ⲙ̇ⲘⲀⲒϢ̇ⲘⲘⲞ · ⲀⲨⲰ Ⲕ̇ⲚⲀϬⲒⲚⲈ ⲚⲞⲨϨⲞⲨⲞ ⲂⲈⲔⲎ Ϩ̇ⲘⲠ̇ϨⲰⲂ Ⲛ̇ⲚⲈⲔϬⲒϪ

«A thought of that sort came to my mind: get up, go out in the desert and stay alone in your home and you will live in *ἡσυχία* and anachoresis and you will be welcoming and you will find more profit in the work with your hands.»

S2.38 - ⲀⲨⲘⲈⲈⲨⲈ ⲈⲒ ⲈⲠⲀϨⲎⲦ ⲚⲦⲈⲒϨⲈ ϪⲈⲦⲰⲞⲨⲚ ⲀⲘⲞⲨ ⲈⲂⲞⲖ ⲚⲄϬⲰ ϨⲘⲠⲈⲔⲘⲀ ⲘⲀⲨⲀⲀⲔ ⲀⲨⲰ ⲔⲚⲀⲈⲤⲨⲬⲀⲌⲈ ⲘⲘⲞⲔ ⲚⲄⲀⲚⲀⲬⲰⲢⲈⲒ ⲚⲄϢⲠⲚⲈⲤⲚⲎⲨ ⲈⲢⲞⲔ ⲚⲄⲢⲘⲀⲒϢⲘⲘⲞ ⲈⲘⲀⲦⲈ ⲀⲨⲰ ⲔⲚⲀϬⲒⲚⲈ ⲚⲞⲨϨⲞⲨⲞ ⲃⲉⲉⲕⲉ ϩⲙⲡϩⲱⲃ ⲛⲛⲉⲕϭⲓϫ. ⲁⲩⲙⲉⲉⲩⲉ ⲉⲓ ⲉⲡⲁϩⲏⲧ ⲛⲧⲉⲓϩⲉ ϫⲉⲧⲱⲟⲩⲛ ⲁⲙⲟⲩ ⲉⲃⲟⲗ ⲛⲅϭⲱ ϩⲙⲡⲉⲕⲙⲁ ⲙⲁⲩⲁⲁⲕ ⲁⲩⲱ ⲕⲛⲁⲉⲥⲩⲭⲁⲍⲉ ⲙⲙⲟⲕ ⲛⲅⲁⲛⲁⲭⲱⲣⲉⲓ ⲛⲅϣⲡⲛⲉⲥⲛⲏⲩ ⲉⲣⲟⲕ ⲛⲅⲣⲙⲁⲓϣⲙⲙⲟ ⲉⲙⲁⲧⲉ ⲁⲩⲱ ⲕⲛⲁϭⲓⲛⲉ ⲛⲟⲩϩⲟⲩⲟ ⲃⲉⲉⲕⲉ ϩⲙⲡϩⲱⲃ ⲛⲛⲉⲕϭⲓϫ.

«A thought thus came to my mind: get up, go out and stay alone in your place and you will live in ἡσυχία and anachoresis and you will invite the brothers to your home and you will be very welcoming and you will find more profit in the work with your hands».

B.27 - ⲁⲟⲩⲙⲉⲩⲓ ⲓ̄ ⲉⲡⲁϩⲏⲧ ϫⲉⲧⲱⲛ[ⲕ] ⲁⲙⲟⲩ ⲉⲃⲟⲗ ϧⲉⲛⲡⲁⲓⲁⲃⲏⲧ ⲛⲧⲉⲕϩⲉⲙⲥⲓ ⲙⲙⲁⲩⲁⲧⲕ ϧⲉⲛⲡⲉⲕⲙⲁⲛϣⲱⲡⲓ ⲟⲩⲟϩ ⲛⲧⲉⲕⲱⲣϥ ⲛⲧⲉⲕⲉⲣⲁⲛⲁⲭⲱⲣⲓⲧⲏⲥ ⲛⲧⲉⲕϣⲉⲡⲛⲓⲥⲛⲏⲟⲩ ⲉⲣⲟⲕ ⲛⲧⲉⲕⲉⲣⲙⲁⲓϣⲉⲙⲙⲟ ⲛⲧⲉⲕϭⲓⲃⲉⲭⲉ ⲛϩⲟⲩⲟ ϧⲉⲛⲡⲉⲕϩⲱⲃ ⲛϫⲓϫ.

«A thought came to my mind : get up, leave this community and stay alone in your home and live in ἡσυχία and anachoresis, and invite the brothers to your home and be welcoming et you will receive more profit from in your manual work.»

A2.32 and 33 - لبقأو ادرتفم نكسأو ريدلا كلذ نم جرخأ نأ تيأترإف
ارفاوتم ارجأ هللا نم لانأ نأ يصرح ناكو ءابرغلاو نابهرلا

«And I decided to get out of that monastery and live as a recluse and invite the monks and the strangers. And it was my desire to obtain from God an abundant reward.»

A3.32 -
فيضأ اميكل ةدحولا يف نوكأو نكاس هيف تنك يذلا ريدلا نم جرخأ نأ تيأرف
يذلا يريد نم رثكأ حيسملا دنع باوثو رجأ يل نوكي ىتح) ء(ابرغلا لبقأو
هيف تنك

«And I thought of getting out of the monastery in which I lived and to be in solitude to be welcoming and invite the strangers so that there would be for me salary and reward from the Christ, more than in the monastery in which I was.»

Of course, we have to see here the expression of a spiritual profit rather than a financial one. A3, however, mentions both. For A2, God's «reward» certainly is, in the first place, a spiritual one. It is worth noting that the Ge'ez versions and A0 only mention his will to live as a recluse.

Timothy then starts his «solitary» life as a «sarakôte». During that period of his life, many people come to him to offer him some manual work.

S1.40 and 41 - ⲁϩⲁϩ ⲛⲣⲱⲙⲉ ⲉⲡⲓ̈ⲧⲁⲥⲥⲉ ⲛⲁⲓ ⲛ̇ϩ̇ⲛϩⲱⲃ ⲛ̇ϭⲓϫ · ⲁⲩⲱ ⲁⲓϭⲓⲛⲉ ⲛⲟⲩϩⲏⲩ ⲙ̇ⲛⲟⲩⲁⲛⲁⲭⲱⲣⲏⲥⲓ̈ⲥ ⁘ⲁⲩⲱ ⲛⲉⲧⲉϣⲁⲓ̈ϫⲡⲟⲟⲩ ⲙⲙⲏⲛⲉ · ⲛⲉⲓϯ ⲛ̇ⲛϣ̇ⲙⲙⲟ ⲙ̇ⲙⲛ̇ⲧⲛⲁ

«A crowd of men ordered manual work from me and I found profit and anachoresis. And what I had obtained, every day, I gave it to strangers in charity.»

S2.41 - ⲁⲩⲁⲡⲥ ⲛⲣⲱⲙⲉ ⲉⲡⲉⲓⲧⲁⲥⲥⲉ ⲛⲁⲓ ⲛϩⲱⲃ ⲛϭⲓϫ ϣⲁⲓⲧⲁⲁⲩ ⲙⲙⲛⲧⲛⲁ ⲛⲛϣⲙⲙⲟ

«A great number of men ordered manual work from me and I gave it in charity to strangers.»

B.28 to 30 - (...) ⲁⲓⲕⲱⲧ ⲛⲏⲓ ⲙⲡⲓⲙⲁⲛϣⲱⲡⲓ ⲁⲓϩⲉⲙⲥⲓ ⲛϧⲏⲧϥ ϩⲁⲛⲙⲏϣ ⲛⲣⲱⲙⲓ ⲁⲩⲓ̅ ϣⲁⲣⲟⲓ ⲉⲑⲃⲉⲡⲓⲕⲟⲩϫⲓ ⲛϩⲱⲃ ⲛϫⲓϫ ⲟⲩⲟϩ ⲁⲓϭⲓ ⲛⲏⲓ ⲛⲟⲩⲛⲓϣϯ ⲛϩⲏⲟⲩ ⲛⲉ[ⲙⲟⲩ]ⲁⲛⲁⲭⲱⲣⲓⲥⲓⲥ ⲛⲏ ⲉϣⲁⲓϫⲫⲱⲟⲩ ϣⲁⲓⲧⲏⲓⲧⲟⲩ ⲛⲛⲓϩⲏⲕⲓ ⲉⲑⲙⲉⲧⲛⲁⲏⲧ ⲛⲉⲙⲛⲏ ⲉⲧⲉⲙⲙⲟⲛ ⲛⲧⲱⲟⲩ

«(...) I built this home for myself and I lived there and crowds of men came to me for small manual work. And I found for myself great profit and anachoresis. Those things that I acquire, I give them in charity to the poor and to those who do not have any.»

E1.37 - ወወፃእኩ፡እንከ፡እምደብር፡ወሐነጽኩ፡ሊተ፡በዐተ፡ወነበርኩ፡ባቲ፡ወተገበርኩ፡በእደዊየ፡ወኮንኩ፡አስተዋፅአ፡ዘእነሥኦ፡ለሕሙማን፡ወለምቱራን፡ወለነግዳን፡ወረባሕኩ፡በውእቱ፡ሠናየ፡ረብሐ።

«And I went out of the monastery and bought myself a cell and lived there and worked with my hands and I gave what I acquired to the suffering and amputated and strangers and I made a good profit from it.»

A0.27 and 28 - وبنيت لي قلاية، وأقمت فيها، وعملت بيدي،
وصرفت ما أعمله على الضعفاء والغرباء والمنقطعين وإيقنن أنني ربحت
بذلك ربحا عظيما

«And I built myself a cell and I stayed there and worked with my hands; and I distributed what I made to the weak, the strangers and the amputated. And be convinced that I made a great profit from it.»

A2.35 and 36 -
وكان قوم كثيرون يقصدونني منجل صناعتي فحصل لي كسبا ليس
يسيرا فكنت أعطيه للمساكين والمحتاجين والمتغربين.

«And a numerous crowd was seeking me out because of my work which resulted in a significant profit for me. And I gave it to the poor and to the destitute and to the expatriate.»

A3.33 - فبنيت لي قلاية صغيرة وسكنتها وحدي
أعمل بيدي وأعيش
وكانوا آناس يأتون إلي ويشترون عملي وكنت أتقوا منه وأعيش منه
المحتاجين والذين يضيفون بي

«And I built myself a small cell and lived there alone, working with my hands, and I lived and some people came to me and they bought my work which made me stronger and I used it to help the destitute and those who were guests at my place.»

Let us note, that here in the case described by J.E. Goehring as less frequent in the literature, i.e. that of a monk receiving orders in his cell, in this case, in great quantity[7]. If it is rarely written, it is because it does not correspond to the ideal of anachoresis and it is indeed how we should see it here : the author wants to emphasise the fact that Thimothy's πολιτεία is not ideal and will facilitate his fall into Lust. However, he still does find «profit and anachoresis» in that life, at first. He gives the benefits of his work to strangers and poor people. A3 is very interesting, because it mentions that he gets «stronger»; in other words, work probably feeds him, unless we need to consider here a spiritual strength. Nevertheless, the first option seems preferable as the sentence continues with the fact that he helps the destitute and his guests, bringing here another side of charity, hospitality. The «Profit» mentioned in various versions is, of course, of a spiritual kind, except for A2 where the phrasing is unclear : either what he gives away is his profit, which is therefore purely economical, or it is his work, and in this sense, it is most likely about spiritual profit. Considering what precedes in the previous paragraph, the second approach would be more appropriate. Please note sentence A2.34 which clearly indicates that it was the anchorite's «trade», just as for any other Egyptian worker.

A2.34 - ةفيطل ةيالق تينب يريرس يف اذه ترمضأ املف
يتعنص الماع يدحو اهتنكسو

«And when I conceived this deep within myself, I built a pleasant cell and I lived there alone, practicing my trade.»

The manuscripts then mention the devil's jealousy vis-à-vis the wanderer's divine reward. The Ge'ez (E1.38) and Arabic (A0.29, A3.34) versions only say that the reward will be obtained in exchange for what the wanderer has done, without any more details, A2.37 being even more vague. S2 however specifies that it is in exchange for his «manual work», whereas S1 mentions «labour», the «effort» from his hands. While B.31 seems to reconnect the divine grace to the wanderer's charity, made possible through his work. B.32 however links the Enemy's jealousy to the monk's «labour», his «manual work» for God.

S1.42 - ⲡϫⲁϫⲉ ⲇⲉ ⲡⲣⲉϥⲙⲉⲥⲧⲉ ⲡⲉⲧⲛⲁⲛⲟⲩϥ ⲛⲓⲙ · ⲁϥⲕⲱϩ ⲉⲣⲟï ⲙ̇ⲡⲉⲟⲩⲟⲉⲓϣ ⲉⲧ̇ⲙⲙⲁⲩ ⲉϫⲙⲡⲃⲉⲕⲏ ⲉϯⲛⲁϫïⲧϥ̇ ⲉⲃⲟⲗ ϩïⲧⲙ̇ⲡⲛⲟⲩⲧⲉ

7 J.E. Goehring, «The World Engaged : The Social and Economic World of Early Egyptian Monasticism», in Id., *Ascetics, Society, and the Desert. Studies in Early Egyptian Monasticism*, Harrisburg 1999, 46, n. 32.

· ⲉⲧⲃⲉⲡⲉϯⲉⲓⲣⲉ ⲙ̇ⲙⲟϥ ⲛ̇ⲛϣ̇ⲙⲙⲟ ⲙ̇ⲛ̇ⲛ̇ⲕⲟⲟⲩⲉ ⲉⲧⲣ̇ϭⲣⲱϩ · ⲉϥⲛⲁⲩ ⲉⲡϩⲓⲥⲉ ⲛⲛⲁϭⲓϫ. ⲉⲓⲥⲡⲟⲩⲇⲁⲍⲉ ⲉⲓϯ ⲙ̇ⲙⲟϥ ⲙ̇ⲡ̄ⲛⲟⲩⲧⲉ

«And the Enemy – the one who hates everything that is good – was jealous of me at that moment of the reward I will receive from God because of what I do for the strangers and others in need, seeing the labour of my hands, applying myself and giving it to God».

S2.42 - ⲡⲇⲓⲁⲃⲟⲩⲗⲟⲥ ⲇⲉ ⲁϥⲕⲱϩ ⲙⲡⲉⲟⲩⲟⲉⲓϣ ⲉⲧⲙⲙⲁⲩ ⲉⲡⲃⲉⲉⲕⲉ ϯϫⲡⲟ ⲙⲙⲟϥ ⲙⲡⲙⲧⲟ ⲉⲃⲟⲗ ⲙⲡϫ̄ⲥ̄ ϩⲁⲡⲉⲧⲉⲓⲣⲉ ⲙⲙⲟϥ ⲛⲛϣⲙⲙⲟ ⲙⲛⲛⲕⲟⲟⲩⲉ ⲉⲧⲣϭⲣⲱⲱϩ ⲉϥⲛⲁⲩ ⲉⲑⲉ ⲉϯⲥⲡⲟⲩⲇⲁⲍⲉ ⲉⲡⲁϩⲱⲃ ⲛϭⲓϫ.

«And the devil was jealous at that moment of the reward that I received before the Lord because of what is done for the strangers and the others in need, seeing the way I apply myself to my manual work.»

B.31 and 32 - ⲁⲡⲓϫⲁϫⲓ ⲡ[ⲓⲇ]ⲓⲁⲃⲟⲗⲟⲥ ⲭⲟϩ ⲉⲣⲟⲓ ⲙⲡⲓⲉϩⲟⲟⲩ ⲉⲧⲉⲙⲙⲁⲩ ⲉⲑⲃⲉⲡⲓⲃⲉⲭⲉ ⲉϯⲛⲁϭ[ⲓⲧϥ] ⲛⲧⲟⲧϥ ⲙⲫ̄ϯ̄ ϧⲁⲫⲏ ⲉϯⲓ̄ⲣⲓ ⲙⲙⲟϥ ⲛⲛⲓϩⲏⲕⲓ ⲛⲉⲙⲛⲏ ⲉⲧⲟⲓ ⲛϧⲁⲉ ⲉϥⲛⲁⲩ ⲉϯⲥⲡⲟⲩⲇⲏ ⲛⲧⲉ ⲡⲁϧⲓⲥⲓ ⲉⲧϧⲉⲛⲛⲉⲛϫⲓϫ. ⲙⲫ̄ϯ̄ (...)

«The Enemy – the devil – was jealous of me at that moment because of the reward that I will receive from God because of what I do for the poor and those in need. Seeing the diligence of my labour, in my manual work for God, (...)»

The ruse used by the demon proves that the economical relations could be made with women, even if they were nuns.

S1.43 - ⲁϥⲕⲱϩ ⲇⲉ ⲉⲣⲟⲓ ⲉⲧⲃⲉⲡⲉϯⲉⲓⲣⲉ ⲙ̇ⲙⲟϥ · ⲁϥⲃⲱⲕ ϣⲁⲟⲩⲥϩⲓⲙⲉ ⲙ̇ⲙⲟⲛⲁⲭⲏ ⲉⲥⲛⲏⲩ ϣⲁⲣⲟⲓ · ⲉⲥⲉⲡⲓ̈ⲧⲁⲥⲥⲉ ⲛⲁⲓ ⲛ̇ϩ̇ⲛⲕⲟⲩⲓ ⲛ̇ϩⲱⲃ ⲛ̇ϭⲓϫ.

«And he was jealous of me because of what I do and he went to a woman monk coming to me to order some manual work».

S2.43 - ⲁϥⲕⲱϩ ⲉⲣⲟⲓ ⲉⲙⲁⲧⲉ ϩⲁⲡⲉⲧⲉⲓⲣⲉ ⲙⲙⲟϥ ⲁϥⲃⲱⲕ ⲉϩⲟⲩⲛ ⲉⲩⲥϩⲓⲙⲉ ⲙⲙⲟⲛⲁⲭⲏ ⲉⲥⲛⲏⲩ ϣⲁⲣⲟⲓ ⲉⲁⲥⲧⲁⲥⲥⲉ ⲛⲁⲓ ⲛϩⲉⲛϩⲱⲃ ⲛϭⲓϫ.

«And he was very jealous of me because of what is done and he went inside to a woman monk coming to me to order manual work.»

B.32 – (...) ⲁϥⲭⲟϩ ⲉⲣⲟⲓ ⲉⲑⲃⲉⲡⲉϯⲓ̄ⲣⲓ ⲙⲙⲟϥ ⲁϥϩⲱⲗ ⲉϧⲟⲩⲛ ⲉⲟⲩⲥϩⲓⲙⲓ ⲙⲙⲟⲩⲛⲁⲭⲏ ⲉⲥⲛⲏⲟⲩ ϣⲁⲣⲟⲓ ⲉⲑⲃⲉϩⲁⲛϩⲱⲃ ⲛϫⲓϫ.

«(...) he was jealous of me because of what I do and he went inside to a woman monk coming to me for manual work.»

E1.39 and 40 - ወቦአ፡ ውስተ፡ ብእሲት፡ መነኮሳይት፡ ወኮነት፡ ትመጽእ፡ ኀቤየ፡ ትሳየጥ ፡ እምኔየ፡ ዘእትገበሮ፡ በእደዊየ፡ ወእሁብ፡ ሊተ፡ ዐስባ፡ ወኮነት፡ ዘትኄውጸኒ፡ ኀቤየ።

«And he went inside to a woman monk and she came to me to sell for me what I produced with my hands. And I gave her her salary and she visited me in my home.»

A0.29 - ةبهار ةأرما يف لخدف ،هتلعف ام ىلع ريخ ناك ودع ينَدسحف
يديب هلمعأ ام ينم يرتشت يتيالق ىلإ ءيجت تناك

«And the Enemy of what is good was jealous of me because of what I was doing, and he went inside to a woman monk who was coming towards my cell to buy what I made with my hands».

A2.39 and 40 - ةبهار تناك ام ةأرمإ لقع يف لجدف

«And he went inside the spirit of a certain woman. She was a nun (...)»

A3.36 - يرتشتو يلإ يتأت تناك ةبهار ةأرماب يلع لاتحأف
ةريثك تاعفد يلمع نم

«And he used a ruse against me by means of a woman monk who came to me and bought some of my work many times.»

A0 and A3 (A2 is incomplete here) clearly demonstrate that these are commercial exchanges since they are talking of buying something. The Ge'ez texts provide a very interesting version: the woman here seems to be a go-between who, in exchange for a «salary», helps the monk sell his goods on the village market without leaving his cell. Even if it is probably the Ethiopian translator's interpretation (although he may have read a version in Arabic containing these terms), it must have corresponded to the reality enabling the wanderer, either through the use of a delegate who was paid to sell the goods himself, or by bulk selling to a go-between, to preserve his anachoresis while limiting to the minimum the number of visits to his cell in the context of his manual work.

When Paphnutius asks Timothy about the beginning of his stay in the desert, he asks him about the «pain» he encountered there.

S1.64 - ϫⲉⲁⲣⲁ ϩⲛ̀ⲧⲉϩⲟⲩⲉⲓⲧⲉ ⲛ̀ⲧⲁⲕⲉⲓ ⲉⲡⲉⲓⲙⲁ · ⲁⲕϩⲓⲥⲉ ⲧⲱⲛⲟⲩ ϫⲉⲙ̀ⲡⲉ

«At the beginning when you came to this place, did you have a lot of pain or not?»

S2.64 - ⲁⲓϫⲛⲟⲩϥ ϫⲉⲁⲣⲁ ⲧⲁⲣⲭⲏ ⲛⲧⲁⲕⲉⲓ ⲉⲡⲉⲓⲙⲁ ⲁⲕϩⲓⲥⲉ ⲧⲱⲛⲟⲩ

«I asked him: at the beginning when you came to this place, did you have great pain?»

B.43 - ⲁⲓϣⲉⲛϥ ⲇⲉ ⲟⲛ ϫⲉϩⲁⲣⲁ ϧⲉⲛϯⲁⲣⲭⲏ ⲉⲧⲁⲕⲓ̄ ⲉⲡϣⲁϥⲉ ⲁⲕϧⲓⲥⲓ ϩⲓⲧⲉⲛⲡⲓⲱϫⲉⲃ (...)

«And I also asked him: at the beginning when you came to the desert, did you feel pain because of the cold ? (...)»

E1.51 - ወእቤሎ፡ጻመውከኑ፡እስከ፡በጻሕከ፡ኀበ፡ዝየ።

«And I told him: did you have pain until you arrived here ?»

A0.42 - تئج امل تبعت له« هل تلقف
«؟ انهه ىلإ

«And I told him : did you have pain when you came here ?»

امل كـئادتـبا يف هاتـبأ اي الئاق هتلأس سيدقلا كلذ نم مالكلا اذه تعمس املف
- A3.47 ال مأ ريثك بعت كقحل انهاه ىلإ تيتأ

«And when I heard that speech from that saint, I asked him, saying: Oh father, at the beginning, when you came here, did a great pain affect you or not ?»

We are not dealing here with a question regarding the wanderer's manual work, but rather a question regarding his suffering due to the harshness of the place, as clearly demonstrated in B which mentions the cold. The Coptic term ϩⲓⲥⲉ, «pain», is moreover used on its own, without any genitival relation to the term ϭⲓϫ, «hand». Similarly, the Arabic version does not use the term عمل, «work», but rather تعب, «fatigue, pain». The chapter is missing in A2. It is worth noting that the «pain» seems to be related to the beginning of his stay in the desert.

The wanderer's response demonstrates that it is about physical pain.

S1.65 - ⲛ̇ⲧⲟϥ ⲇⲉ ⲡⲉϫⲁϥ ⲛⲁⲓ̈ ϫⲉⲁⲓϩⲓ̈ⲥⲉ ⲧⲱⲛⲟⲩ ⲛ̇ⲧⲉⲣⲓⲉⲓ ⲉⲡⲉⲓⲙⲁ · ϩⲱⲥⲧⲉ ⲉⲧⲣⲁⲛⲟϫⲧ̇ ⲉϫ̇ⲙ̄ⲡⲕⲁϩ ⲉⲧⲃⲉⲡ̄ⲧⲓ̈ⲧⲕⲁⲥ ⲙ̇ⲡⲁϩⲏⲧ

«And he said to me: I felt such great pain when I came to this place that I threw myself on the ground because of my insides' affliction.»

S2.65 - ⲡⲉϫⲁϥ ⲛⲁⲓ ϫⲉⲁϩⲉ ⲁⲓϩⲓⲥⲉ ⲧⲱⲛⲟⲩ ⲱ ⲡⲁϣⲏⲣⲉ ϩⲱⲥⲧⲉ ⲛⲛⲁϣⲛⲟϫⲧ ⲉⲡⲕⲁϩ ⲉⲧⲃⲉⲡⲙⲕⲁϩ ⲛϩⲏⲧ ⲉⲓⲱϣ ⲉϩⲣⲁⲓ ⲉⲡϫ̅ⲥ̅ ⲉⲧⲃⲉⲛⲁⲛⲟⲃⲉ ⲉⲧⲟϣ

«He said to me: yes, I felt such great pain, oh my son, that I threw myself on the ground because of the affliction to my insides, screaming towards the Lord because of my numerous sins.»

B.43 – (...) ⲛⲑⲟϥ ⲇⲉ ⲡⲉϫⲁϥ ⲛⲏⲓ ϫⲉⲁⲓϧⲓⲥⲓ ⲧⲟⲛⲁ ϧⲉⲛϯⲁⲣⲭⲏ ϩⲱⲥⲇⲉ ⲛⲧⲁⲥⲁⲧⲧ ⲉϫⲉⲛⲡⲓⲕⲁϩⲓ ⲛⲧⲉⲛϯⲙⲉⲧⲁⲧϫⲟⲙ

«(...) And he said to me: I felt such great pain at the beginning that I threw myself on the ground out of weakness.»

E1.52 - ወይቤለኒ ፡ እወ ፡ አማን ፡ ጻመውኩ ፡ ጥቀ ፡ እስከ ፡ ኮንኩ ፡ እገድፍ፡ዲበ፡ምድር፡እምንዳቤ፡ሕማማት፡ዘውስተ፡ከርሥየ፡ወእቤጽሐ ፡ለመዊት ፡ እስከ፡ ኮንኩ፡ እጼሊ፡ ወአነ፡ ግዱፍየ፡ ዲበ፡ ምድር ፡፡

«And he said to me: Yes, in truth, I felt such great pain that I threw myself on the floor because of the affliction of the suffering in my insides, and being at the door of death, so much that I prayed while I was on the ground.»

A0.43 - فقال لي : «نعم حقا، كنت قد تعبت في أول مجيئي، حتى
أنني كنت ألقى نفسي على الأرض لشدة ما أجده من الألم والحرقة في فؤادي

«And he said to me: Yes, in truth, I felt such pain at the beginning of my stay, that I threw myself on the ground because of the intensity of the suffering I endured and the affliction to my insides».

A3.48 -
نم ىتح ميظع ابعت يخأ اي تبعت يـئادتبا يف ءيش لوأ الئاق باجأف
يبلق نم عجوتم ضرألا ىلع طقسأ تنك يعاجوأ ةرثك

«And he answered, saying: Firstly, at my beginning, I felt such intense pain, oh my brother, that, due to the extent of my suffering, I fell on the ground, suffering in my insides.»

In some versions, what succeeds immediately after confirms it, too.

S1.66 - ϩⲱⲥⲧⲉ ⲉⲧ̇ⲙⲧⲣⲁⲉϣϭⲙ̇ϭⲟⲙ ⲉⲉⲓⲣⲉ ⲛ̇ⲛⲁⲥⲩⲛⲁⲝⲓⲥ ⲉⲓⲁϩⲉ ⲣⲁⲧ · ⲁⲗⲗⲁ ⲁⲛⲉⲓⲛⲏϫ ⲉϫ̇ⲙⲡ̄ⲕⲁϩ ⲉⲧⲃⲉⲡ̄ⲧⲓⲧⲕⲁⲥ ⲙ̇ⲡⲁϩⲏⲧ · ⲉⲓⲱϣ ⲉϩⲣⲁï ⲉⲡⲛⲟⲩⲧⲉ ⲉⲧⲃⲉⲛⲁⲛⲟⲃⲉ ⲉⲧⲟϣ · ⲁⲓϩⲓⲥⲉ ⲧⲱⲛⲟⲩ ϩ̇ⲛⲟⲩⲛⲟϭ ⲙ̇ⲙⲟⲕϩ̇ⲥ

«To the point that I didn't find the strength to do my synaxes standing up anymore, but I was lying on the ground because of the affliction of my insides, screaming towards God because of my numerous sins; I felt great pain and great suffering».

S2.66 - ⲁⲓϩⲓⲥⲉ ⲇⲉ ⲟⲛ ϩⲛⲟⲩⲛⲟϭ ⲙⲙⲟⲕϩⲥ ⲉⲧⲃⲉⲡⲉⲧⲕⲁⲥ ⲉⲧϩⲓϫⲱⲓ

«And I continued to feel pain in great suffering because of my affliction.»

A3.49 -
تنكو ضرألا ىلع احورطم تنك لب امئاق يلصأو يسأر عفرأ ردقأ سيلو
ريثك بعت ىلع تربصو ياياطخ ةهج نم بلق حرفب دئادشلا هذه ىلع ربصأ

«And I could not lift my head again and pray standing up, but I was lying on the ground and endured these adversities with a joyful heart, on the account of my sins and I endured a great pain».

The term «pain», meaning «suffering», appears again in S1 and B during the visit of the surgeon angel who will then heal the wanderer's ill liver.

S1.67 - ⲁⲥϣⲱⲡⲉ ⲇⲉ ⲛⲟⲩϩⲟⲟⲩ ⲉⲓϩ̇ⲙⲟⲟⲥ ⲉⲣⲉⲡ̄ⲧⲓ̈ⲧ̇ⲕⲁⲥ ϯϩⲓ̈ⲥⲉ ⲛⲁï ⲉⲡⲉϩⲟⲩⲟ · ⲁⲓϭⲱϣⲧ ⲁⲓⲛⲁⲩ ⲉⲩⲣⲱⲙⲉ ⲉϥϩⲁⲉⲟⲟⲩ ⲙ̇ⲙⲁⲧⲉ · ⲁϥⲉⲓ ⲁϥⲁϩⲉ ⲣⲁⲧϥ̇ ⲙ̇ⲡⲁⲙ̇ⲧⲟ ⲉⲃⲟⲗ

«And it happened one day, sitting down, the affliction giving me pain to excess, that I looked and saw a man in great glory; he came and stood in my presence.»

B.45 - ⲁⲓⲱϣ ⲉϩⲣⲏⲓ ϩⲁⲫ̄ϯ̄ ⲉⲑⲃⲉⲛⲁⲛⲟⲃⲉ ⲉⲧⲟϣ ⲛⲉⲙⲛⲁϣⲱⲛⲓ ⲉⲁⲓϧⲓⲥⲓ ϧⲉⲛⲟⲩⲛⲓϣϯ ⲛϧⲓⲥⲓ ⲁⲓϫⲟⲩϣⲧ ⲁⲓⲛⲁⲩ ⲉⲟⲩⲣⲱⲙⲓ ⲉϥϧⲉⲛⲟⲩⲛⲓϣϯ ⲛⲱⲟⲩ ⲉϥⲟϩⲓ ⲉⲣⲁⲧϥ ⲛⲁϩⲣⲁⲓ (...)

«I screamed towards God because of my numerous sins and my illnesses, suffering in great pain, and I looked and saw a man in great glory, standing in front of me (...)»

Once healed by the angel, he did not feel anymore physical «pain» in the desert. A3 does not use this term, but rather the term «suffering».

S1.74 - ⲁⲩⲱ ⲛ̇ϫⲓⲛⲡⲉϩⲟⲟⲩ ⲉⲧ̇ⲙⲙⲁⲩ ⲁⲓ̈ⲗⲟ ⲉⲓϣⲱⲛⲉ ⲉⲡⲁϩⲩⲡⲁⲣ · ϯϣⲟⲟⲡ ⲇⲉ ϩ̇ⲙⲡⲉⲓϫⲁⲓ̈ⲉ ⲭⲱⲣⲓⲥ ϩⲓ̈ⲥⲉ · ϫⲓⲛⲡⲉϩⲟⲟⲩ ⲉⲧ̇ⲙⲙⲁⲩ

«And since that day, I have stopped suffering from my liver; and I have lived without pain in this desert since that day.»

S2.76 - ϫⲓⲛⲡⲉϩⲟⲟⲩ ⲉⲧⲙⲙⲁⲩ ⲁⲛⲉⲧⲡⲁⲥⲁ ⲛϩⲟⲩⲛ ⲧⲏⲣⲟⲩ ⲟⲩϫⲁⲓ ⲁⲩⲱ ⲁⲓⲗⲟ ⲉⲓϣⲱⲛⲉ ⲉⲡⲁϩⲏⲡⲁⲣ ϯϣⲟⲟⲡ ϩⲙⲡⲉⲓⲙⲁ ⲛϫⲁⲓⲉ ⲭⲱⲣⲓⲥ ϩⲓⲥⲉ

«Since that day, all my insides were in good health and I ceased suffering from my liver and I live in this desert place without pain.»

B.52 and 53 - ⲟⲩⲟϩ ⲓⲥϫⲉⲛⲡⲓⲉϩⲟⲟⲩ ⲉⲧⲉⲙⲙⲁⲩ ⲁⲛⲏⲉⲧⲥⲁϧⲟⲩⲛ ⲙⲙⲟⲓ ⲧⲏⲣⲟⲩ ⲟⲩϫⲁⲓ ⲟⲩⲟϩ ⲁⲓⲕⲏⲛ ⲉⲓϣⲱⲛⲓ ⲉⲡⲁϩⲩⲡⲁⲣ ϯϣⲟⲡ ⲇⲉ ϧⲉⲛⲡⲁⲓϣⲁϥⲉ ⲭⲱⲣⲓⲥ ϧⲓⲥⲓ ⲓⲥϫⲉⲛⲡⲓⲉϩⲟⲟⲩ ⲉⲧⲉⲙⲙⲁⲩ (...)

«And since that day, all my insides were in good health and I ceased suffering from my liver. And I have lived in this desert without pain since that day (...)»

E1.64 and 65 - ወእምውእቱ ፡ ጊዜ ፡ ሐይወ ፡ ዘኮንኩ ፡ እረክቦ ፡ ዘውስተ ፡ ከርሥየ ፡ ወጥዕየ ፡ ከብድየ ። ወነበርኩ ፡ ውስተ ፡ ገዳም ፡ ዘእንበለ ፡ ጻማ ፡ እምውእቱ ፡ ዕለት ።

«And since then, what I received that was in my insides was healthy and my liver was in good health. And I have lived in this desert without pain since that day.»

A0.55 - بعت الب ةيربلا هذه يف تيقبو تيفوعف
نآلا ىلإو مويلا كلذ نم

«And I was healed and lived in this desert without pain since that day and until now».

A3.60 - ريغب تباث ينإو يعاجوأ نم تيفوع اذه يتقو ىلإ مويلا كلذ نمو
هنسحت ةرثكل هركشأو هلل حبسأ عجو

«And, since that day until this instant, I was healed from my sufferings and, I, relieved of all my suffering, I glorified God and gave him thanks for the abundance of his kindness».

After his stay with Timothy, Paphnutius wishes to imitate his «œuvre», as described by the Ge'ez, in A2 and A3. However, as demonstrated in B, it is more about imitating his way of life, his πολιτεία, his anachoresis and his practice, his search for the two ξενιτείαι, which Paphnutius will not achieve, incapable of keeping to his cell and therefore of maintaining anachoresis and overcoming Acedia. A0 only mentions the will to imitate the elder, without more precision.

B.60 - ⲉⲑⲃⲉⲛⲏ ⲉⲧⲁⲓⲥⲟⲑⲙⲟⲩ ⲉⲃⲟⲗ ϧⲉ(ⲛ)ⲣⲱϥ ⲛⲁⲃⲃⲁ ⲧⲓⲙⲟⲑⲉⲟⲥ ⲫⲏ ⲉⲑⲟⲩⲁⲃ ⲛⲧⲉ ⲫ︦ϯ︦ ⲁⲓⲉⲣⲟⲩⲙⲏϣ ⲛⲉϩⲟⲟⲩ ⲉⲓϫⲟϩ ⲉϯϫⲓⲛⲉⲣϩⲱⲃ ⲛⲧⲉ ⲫⲏ ⲉⲧⲉⲙⲙⲁⲩ ⲉⲧⲁⲓⲛⲁⲩ ⲉⲣⲟⲥ ⲉⲓⲟⲩⲱϣ ϩⲱ ⲉⲉⲣⲡⲉϥⲣⲏϯ ⲡⲉ

«Because of these things I had heard in the mouth of abba Timothy – the one who is a saint of God –, I spent many days trying hard to imitate the way of life of that one I had seen, willing myself to resemble him.»

E1.78 - ፈተውኩ ፡ ከመ ፡ እትመሰል ፡ ቦቱ ፡ በምግባራቲሁ ፡ ወኢክህልኩ ፡ ነቢረ ፡ ውስተ ፡ በዓት ።

«I wished to imitate him in his œuvre, but couldn't live in the cave.»

A0.65 - واشتهيت أن أتشبه به، فلم أطق
ولا استطعت

«And I wished to imitate him, but did not have the strength and was not capable of it.»

A2.48 - ولبثت مفتكرا في هذه الأمور أياما ليست قليلة مشتاقا أن
أتبع أفعال ذلك الصديق المرضية لله

«And I continued to think about those things for many days, ardently wishing to follow this companion's œuvre that satisfies God».

A3.71 - فثبتت علي هذه الفكر أياما كثيرة أتفكر به جدا وأشتاق أن
أعمل أعمال ذلك الرجل الصديق المرضي لله

«And this thought maintained itself in me for many days, reflecting intensely within myself and wishing ardently to accomplish this man's œuvre, the companion who satisfies God».

In conclusion, the manual works only appear in the first part of the story, with Timothy starting to practice them in his cenobite monastery before being ordered by some during his stay in his first cell in the nearby desert, works for which the spiritual profit provoked the devil's hatred, when he came to tempt him under the appearance of a nun. Let us note that even though it is said that – according to the various versions – he practiced basketry or the work of linen in the monastery, there are however no mentions of what type of manual work he performs when he lives by himself. Let us assume that it is most probably the same type of work.

The term «pain» does not refer here to manual work in its meaning of «effort», but essentially to physical suffering related to the harsh living conditions in the desert, especially at the beginning of the anchorite's stay, before acquired tolerance is reached. It can also refer to physical suffering or fatigue, or to the hardness of travelling in the desert.

The term «œuvre» does not refer to manual work either. The «œuvre» essentially expresses the πολιτεία, the monastic approach in its most generic sense, i.e. the pursuit of the two ξενιτείαι.

There is a clear link between the «pain» and the «œuvre», the former being indissociable from the latter, since it is related to the wanderer's living conditions in the desert. An apothegm incidentally shows us this relation when Macarius the Great proclaims not to say: «maybe those who accept the pain (= bother) and those who don't are one and the same thing», after having declared: «fight (...), do not look at the crowd that eats, drinks and sleeps without having any remorse»[8].

Abstract

We are studying the *Mission of Paphnutius/Life of Onuphrius* in its Nile tradition. We are therefore using the three complete and well-preserved Coptic manuscripts: the sahidic manuscript from the Pierpont Morgan Library, the sahidic manuscript from the British Library, and the bohairic manuscript from the Vatican. We are also using three Arabian and five Ethiopian manuscripts.

The texts do not present any mention of manual work, except in its first part. Timothy starts by explaining his coenobitic life in the monastery, where he was indeed performing some manual work. According to the Coptic version, it was basketwork, whereas the Arabian version mentions the work of linen, considered more «luxurious» and therefore, sometimes interpreted as a more likely source of Pride. Timothy then starts his «solitary» life as a «sarakôte». During that period of his life, many people come to him to offer him some manual work. When Paphnutius asks Timothy about the beginning of his stay in the desert, he asks him about the «pain» he encountered there. The question is not related at all to the wanderer's manual work, it is actually about the pain he suffered due to the harshness of his environment. The term «pain», meaning «suffering», appears again with the arrival of the surgical angel who will cure the wanderer's diseased liver. At the end of his stay with Timothy, Paphnutius wishes to imitate his «work», however he means imitating his πολιτεία, his anachoresis and his practice, which Paphnutius will not achieve.

8 Am 167,12 (L. Regnault, *Les sentences des Pères du désert. Troisième recueil et tables*, Sablé sur Sarthe 1976, 174-175).

ECONOMY OF NUBIAN MONASTICISM. A PRELIMINARY ASSESSMENT

Artur Obłuski

1. NUBIA

In its most simple definition, Nubia is the part of the Nile Valley between Aswan and Khartoum. A large part of it is now submerged by the waters of two artificial lakes, formed as a result of the construction of the Aswan High Dam on the first Nile cataract and Hamdab Dam on the fourth Nile cataract. Nubia is a heuristic tool used to designate the territory along the Nile where abundant archaeological cultures flourished almost since the beginning of mankind. In the period under consideration, after the final demise of the Meroitic Empire around the middle of the fourth century AD, in a time of uncertainty and dissolution of state institutions, three new states emerged in Nubia. In geographical order, from the border with Egypt southward, they were: Nobadia, Makuria and Alodia. However, these political designations were created by Byzantine historians, who were then followed by the Arabs and by modern scholars, and are not equivalent to indigenous names, which were Migi for Nobadia, Dotawo for Makuria and Alwa for Alodia. At the end of the sixth or the beginning of the seventh century at the latest, Nobadia and Makuria merged into one political entity.

Medieval Nubian kingdoms are a forgotten part of the Christian *koine*, mostly disregarded in the studies of Christianity, despite being one of the political entities which accepted new monotheistic religion at a very early date. All three of the kingdoms converted to Christianity during the course of the sixth century: first Migi, ca. 540, then Dotawo and Alwa both around 570. The northernmost and southernmost kingdoms could have been evangelized before the official conversion of the royal courts. Although this is not attested in the sources, we may expect that some role in those processes was played by monastic communities.

Artur Obłuski, Director of the Research Center in Cairo, Polish Center of Mediterranean Archaeology, University of Warsaw; Coptic Visiting Professor in Egyptology, American University in Cairo.

2. SOURCES

There are textual and archaeological sources at our disposal to study Nubian monasticism. The archaeological sources come from the fully excavated monasteries: Ghazali[1] and Qasr el-Wizz[2], two partially excavated ones: Monastery on

Fig.1 Ghazali monastery kite photo, M.Bogacki

1 The four-volume final publication of the Ghazali monastery is in preparation. For now, the results are available in: P.L. SHINNIE.-N.H. CHITTICK, *Ghazali, a Monastery in the Northern Sudan* (Occasional papers of Sudan Antiquities Service 5), Khartoum 1961; A. OBLUSKI-G. OCHALA, «La redécouverte d'un monastère nubien : premiers résultats des fouilles polonaises à el-Ghazali», in *Actes de la Seizième Journée d'études coptes, Genève 19-21 juin 2013*, edd. N. Bosson-A. Boud'hors (Études coptes 14), Paris 2016, 63-79; A. OBŁUSKI, «Ghazali Site Presentation Project 2012-2014 preliminary results», *Der Antike Sudan. Mitteilungen der Sudanarchäologischen Gesellschaft zu Berlin e.V. 25* (2014) 197-204; A. OBŁUSKI *et al.*, «Al-Ghazali Monastery 2012. The First Preliminary Report», *Polish Archaeology in the Mediterranean 24* (2015) 425-435 .

2 For Qasr el-Wizz, see: G.T. SCANLON, «Corrigenda. Excavations at Kasr el-Wizz. A Preliminary Report. II», *The Journal of Egyptian Archaeology* 60 (1974) 78; ID., «Excavations at Kasr el-Wizz. A Preliminary Report. I», *The Journal of Egyptian Archaeology* 56 (1970) 29-57; ID., «Excavations at Kasr el-Wizz. A Preliminary Report. II. Part II. The Monastery», *The Journal of Egyptian Archaeology* 58 (1972) 7-42.

Kom D[3] and Monastery on Kom H, both at Old Dongola, and two hermitages: one in the vicinity of Faras[4], the other in the modern village of Zuma[5].

Textual sources – crucial for understanding of the monasticism in other regions – are unfortunately scarce in Nubia. Suffice it to say that at the fully excavated monastery of Ghazali, I have found pieces of almost two hundred tombstones, over one thousand inscribed sherds (unfortunately mostly holy names,

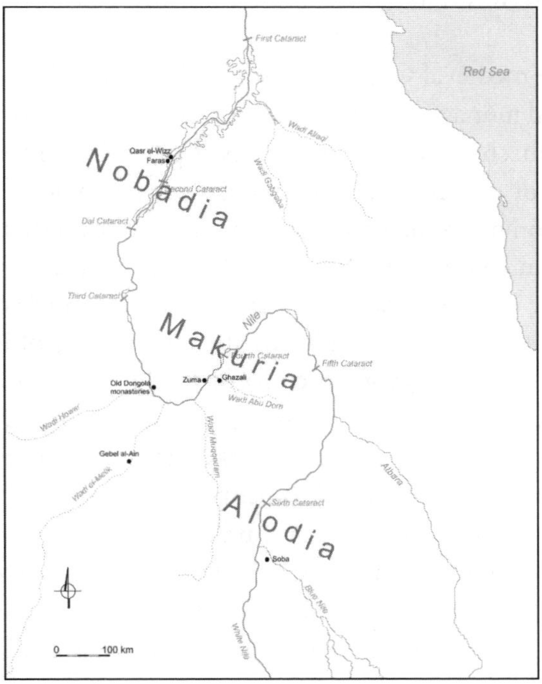

Fig. 2 Map of Christian Nubian kingdoms

3 For the bibliography regarding results of excavations of both monasteries at Old Dongola and further annual publications in the Polish Archaeology in Mediterranean, see: *Dongola-Studien. 35 Jahre polnisher Forschungen im Zentrum des makuritischen Reiches*, edd. S. Jakobielski-P. Scholz, Warszawa 2001.

4 F.Ll. Griffith, «Oxford Excavations in Nubia», *University of Liverpool Annals of Archaeology and Anthropology* 14 (1927) 57-116; U. Monneret de Villard, *La Nubia medioevale* (Mission archéologique de Nubie 1), vol. 1, Le Caire 1935, 251.

5 A. Łajtar, «Inscriptions from the Anachorite grotto at Ez-Zuma», in *Survey and Excavations between Old Dongola and Ez-Zuma. Southern Dongola Reach of the Nile from Prehistory to 1820 AD Based on the Fieldwork Conducted in 1997–2003 by the Polish Archaeological Joint Expedition to the Middle Nile*, edd. B. Żurawski *et al.* (Nubian Voices 2), Warsaw 2003, 512-517.

names and titles of the owners of vessels) and only two ostraca, while Egyptian hermitages delivered hundreds of documents. The excavations at Qasr el-Wizz were more successful in that respect: over two hundred textual finds were recorded; unfortunately, only several of them are documentary and can benefit the study of the subject under consideration[6].

3. AN OVERVIEW OF NUBIAN MONASTICISM

According to the medieval Coptic historian Abū al-Makārim, there were plentiful churches and monasteries in Nubia. For the southernmost Alwa, he quotes four hundred churches[7]. While the numbers given by him were exaggerated, still the number of churches must have been considerable if it drew his attention. The evolution of Nubian monasticism differed from that of the other parts of the Christian community due to the lack of processes and/or events that shaped Byzantine and Egyptian monasticisms, like iconoclastic crises and the resurgence of monasteries in Byzantium after the victory of iconodules or the introduction of Islam in Egypt. In contrast to the neighboring Egypt, where monasticism emerged as a predominantly peasant movement, it does seem that the Nubian monasticism was imported by the elites in a well-defined coenobitic form in the second half of the sixth century. A dozen monasteries are known from the written sources and a similar number of archaeological sites may hide the remains of Christian monasteries. It is almost impossible to verify the latter information, without archaeological research at the sites, but several of them are likely candidates for monasteries[8]. One such site is al-Ugal, where Derek Welsby identified a dormitory-like structure[9]. Some sites will never be verified, since they are flooded by the Nubian Lake.

The earliest monasteries were established in northern Nubia, in the territory of Nobadia. One of them was the Qasr el-Wizz monastery, located on the outskirts of the Nobadian capital city of Pachoras (Faras), founded probably

6 See A. Tsakos, «Textual Finds», in *Excavations at Qasr El-Wizz, George T. Scanlon, Director*, ed. A. Obłuski, Chicago, forthcoming.

7 Abū al-Makārim, *The Churches and Monasteries of Egypt and Some Neighbouring Countries*, trans. B. T.A. Evetts-A.J. Butler, Oxford 1895.

8 For the list of sites see: J.R. Anderson, «Monastic Lifestyles of the Nubian Desert», *Sudan and Nubia* 3 (1999) 72-8 or P. Jeute, «Monasteries in Nubia– An open issue», *Nubica* 3 (1994) 59-97.

9 D.A. Welsby *et al.*, *Life on the Desert Edge. Seven Thousand Years of Settlement in the Northern Dongola Reach, Sudan*, vol. 1 (BAR international series 980), Oxford 2001, 21-25.

in the late sixth century. Two known monasteries from the Makurian capital, Dongola, one on Kom D and the other on Kom H were likewise located on the fringes of the city. The first can be tentatively dated to the seventh century[10], while the latter had to be built before 28 April 668, which is the date of the death of Joannes, bishop of Syene, who was subsequently buried in the monastic church[11]. Radiocarbon dating suggests the time span of 680–720 for the construction of the Ghazali monastery. The latest clearly monastic activity from Ghazali is dated between 1225 and 1275[12]. This, however, does not mark the end of Nubian monasticism in general, as it is attested by the so-called scrolls of bishop Timotheos, which mention him as a hegoumenos of a monastery located in Qasr Ibrim before becoming a bishop in 1372[13].

There are three types of monastic life attested in Nubia: anchoritic, laura and coenobitic. There are three firmly confirmed hermitages in Nubia: the so-called Anchorite Grottos in Faras[14], Toshka East[15] and Zuma[16] and tentatively suggested in el Allaqi[17].

Several small walled enclosures in the region of Batn el-Hajar – like Akasha (21-N- ll), Kulb (21-R-3), Kulubnarti (21-S- 10) Ukma (21-N-7, -9) – could have been laura-like communities, as suggested by Julie Anderson[18]. They could have housed up to seven monks and were tentatively identified as lauras due to the lack of common spaces like one dormitory or refectory. I add to this group a

10 Dating of the monastery on Kom D suggested in: S. Jakobielski, «Old Dongola 1989-1990», *Polish Archaeology in the Mediterranean* 2 (1991) 65-73, 68.

11 S. Jakobielski-J. van der Vliet, «From Aswan to Dongola. The Epitaph of Bishop Joseph (Died AD 668)», in *Nubian Voices. Studies in Christian Nubian Culture*, edd. A. Łajtar-J. van der Vliet (The Journal of Juristic Papyrology Supplements 15), Warsaw 2011, 15-37.

12 A. Obłuski-M. Korzeniowska, «First Look at the History of the Dormitory of the Ghazali Monastery », in *Across the Mediterranean – Along the Nile. Studies in Egyptology, Nubilology and Late Antiquity Dedicated to László Török on the Occasion of His 75th Birthday*, vol. 2, edd. T. A. Bács-B. Ádám-V. Tivadar, 2017, 601-612.

13 M.J. Plumley, *The scrolls of Bishop Timotheos. Two Documents from Medieval Nubia (Texts from Excavations)*, London 1975.

14 Griffith, «Oxford excavations in Nubia».

15 Monneret de Villard, *La Nubia medioevale*, I, 121-122; W.K. Simpson, *Heka-Nefer and the Dynastic Material from Toshka and Arminna*, New Haven-Philadelphia 1963, 19-20.

16 Monneret de Villard, *La Nubia medioevale*, I, 251; Łajtar, «Inscriptions from the anachorite grotto at Ez-Zuma».

17 C.M. Firth, *The Archæological Survey of Nubia. Report for 1910-1911*, Cairo 1927, 111.

18 Anderson, «Monastic Lifestyles of the Nubian Desert», 82.

building (Einsedlung E) from Bietak and Schwarz's excavations at Naga es-Sheima[19], because of its structural affinity to other lauras, even though it was also considered a quadruple hermitage[20].

The Nubian monasteries we know so far do not seem to have accommodated large number of monks. On the basis of dormitories and refectories we can estimate that an average Nubian monastic community consisted of twenty monks, whilst the largest dormitory excavated so far could have housed thirty-six monks[21]. However, we need to bear in mind that a monastery was permanently and temporarily occupied also by lay people, who had not yet become monks or who were supporting the monks voluntarily or as slaves[22].

The topic of economy and monasticism can be approached from various perspectives and reflected upon on different levels. As stated by Platte, Late Antique monasticism was part of the productive economy of the Roman Empire[23]. Monasteries were responsible for the upkeep of their own members as well as for charitable actions which supported the local Christian communities, and thus needed to produce even more than it took to be self-sufficient. They required a combination of productive activities and investments and smart administration to meet their social obligations. Hence, apart from the economy of a single monastery and the way it functioned in the economic system in a specific region in the particular point or period in time, one can also ponder the place of monasticism in the economy of the contemporary world whether medieval or modern. The data regarding the Nubian economy is very limited in general. Thus, in this paper, I tackle the topic of the economics of Nubian monasteries on the level of a single community and, adapting a comparative perspective, I try to present how it might have provided for its subsistence and development rather than discuss the place of monasticism in the state economy. The economy of monasticism in the East is a topic studied in numerous publications: by

---

19 M. Bietak-M. Schwarz, *Nag' el-Scheima, eine befestigte christliche Siedlung und andere christliche Denkmaler in Sayala - Nubien*, (Denkschriften. Österreichische Akademie der Wissenschaften. Philosophisch-Historische Klasse 191), Wien 1987, 187-199.

20 Jeute, «Monasteries in Nubia», 60.

21 Obłuski-Korzeniowska, «First look».

22 P. Hatlie, *The Monks and Monasteries of Constantinople, ca. 350-850*, Cambridge-New York 2007, 148, note 50, draws our attention to John of Ephesus, who in *Lives*, 328-9, mentions John of Hephaestopolis, abbot of Ta Anthemiou, as recipient of an allowance and a slave.

23 E.L. Platte, *Monks and Matrons s. The Economy of Charity in the Late Antique Mediterranean*, Doctoral Dissertation, University of Michigan 2013 [access: 25-02-2017], http://hdl.handle.net/2027.42/99823.

Patlagean for the entire East[24], by Hatlie[25] and Morris[26] for the capital city of Constantinople; by Tchalenko[27], Vööbus[28], Peña[29] and Villeneuve[30] for Syria, by Hirschfeld[31], Binns[32] for Palestine and Wipszycka's numerous publications as concerns the economic activities of Egyptian monks[33].

There was only a limited number of monastic economic activities as represented in textual and archaeological sources that was not shared or doubled by other entities and can thus be seen as the hallmark of monastic economy. Manual labor, craftsmanship, food production, land possession, alms, grants, gifts or trade were not monopolized by the monks. In each of these activities a single monk or a monastic community could participate either on the receiving or on the delivering end of the transaction. There are some activities where we do expect monks to be solely on the receiving end (land or extensive and generous donations or gifts) or exclusively on the delivering end (spiritual services: guidance, offering prayers; healing/magical services). Sometimes, it is hard to differentiate between these two categories – for example, gifts were often an expression of gratitude for monks' endeavors and it is hard to separate them from the delivery of the service. Only the spiritual services seem to be a category performed exclusively by monks and, less often, by other

24 E. Patlagean, *Pauvreté économique et pauvreté sociale à Byzance, 4e-7e siècles* (Civilisations et sociétés 48), Paris 1977.

25 Hatlie, *The Monks.*

26 R. Morris, *Monks and Laymen in Byzantium, 843-1118*, Cambridge-New York 1995.

27 G. Tchalenko, *Villages antiques de la Syrie du Nord. Le massif du Bélus à l'époque romaine* (Bibliothèque archéologique et historique 50), Paris 1953.

28 A. Vööbus, *History of Asceticism in the Syrian Orient. A Contribution to the History of Culture in the Near East* (Corpus Scriptorum Christianorum Orientalium 184), Louvain 1958.

29 I. Peña-P. Castellana-R. Fernández, *Les cénobites syriens* (Studium Biblicum Franciscanum 28), Jerusalem 1983.

30 F. Villeneuve, «L'économie rurale et la vie des campagnes dans les Hauran antique (Ier siècle avant J.-C. – Vie siècle après J. C.)», in *Hauran I: recherches archéologiques sur la Syrie du Sud à l'époque hellénistique et romaine*, ed. J.M. Dentzer (Bibliothèque archéologique et historique), P. Geuthner, Paris 1985, 63-136.

31 Y. Hirschfeld, *The Judean Desert Monasteries in the Byzantine Period*, New Haven 1992.

32 J. Binns, *Ascetics and Ambassadors of Christ. The Monasteries of Palestine, 314-631* (Oxford Early Christian Studies), Oxford 1994.

33 E. Wipszycka, *Les ressources et les activités économiques des églises en Égypte du IVe au VIIIe siècle* (Papyrologica Bruxellensia 10), Bruxelles 1972; Ead., *Moines et communautés monastiques en Égypte (IVe-VIIIe siècles)* (The Journal of Juristic Papyrology Supplements 11), Varsovie 2009; Ead., «Resources and Economic Activities of the Egyptian Monastic Communities (4th–8th Century)», *The Journal of Juristic Papyrology* 41 (2011) 159-263.

church officials. Monks could participate in exchanges as individuals; however, the economic power of monasteries was based on the overall volume of wealth accumulated, as well as on deliveries and/or procurements of a community of monks and lay people associated with a monastery – and it is this aspect that made them important partakers in every local, if not regional, economy and exchange network.

4. ECONOMIC ACTIVITIES OF NUBIAN MONASTERIES

The following part of the article is devoted to a review of several categories of economic activities of Nubian monasteries, analysed in a comparative perspective, using as a benchmark Byzantine monasticism, and Egyptian monasticism, Palestinian and Syrian in particular. I have distinguished the following economy-related activities of monastic communities, which allowed them to provide for their subsistence and to produce surpluses vital for their perseverance and outreach work within the society:

1. Land possession and cultivation
2. Alms, grants and gifts
3. Manual labor, craftsmanship and services
4. Food production and processing
5. Expert services (demanding special education and talent)

4.1. Land possession and cultivation

The majority of the Nubian monasteries were located in the Nile valley and thus it would be unreasonable to presume that they were not land holders, since we know that private property and real estate market existed in Nubia, or – being precise – at least in its northern part. The textual evidence is unfortunately – but in the case of Nubia, not surprisingly – scarce. At the monastery of Qasr el-Wizz, George Scanlon[34] found in one of the cells (Room II-E) a unique document written in Coptic on a single folded leaf of parchment. It lists land property of the monastery of Apa Dioskoros (probably the monastery of Qasr el-Wizz) and the estimated annual output expected from them in wine and pro-

34 Textual finds documented by Marek Marciniak have never been published except an inscription on the wall of baptismal tank, see: J. Barns, «A Text of the "Benedicite" in Greek and Old Nubian from Kasr el-Wizz», *The Journal of Egyptian Archaeology* 60 (1974) 206-211. I currently head the project whose aim is to prepare complete publication of excavations at the site. The textual finds will be published in the volume: Tsakos, «Textual Finds».

bably bread. There are several intriguing issues regarding this document. First of all, it is the sole document from this monastic milieu regarding its property. Secondly, the monastic property is spread over the distance of ca. 100 km along the Nile, upriver from the city of Primis (Qasr Ibrim). Thirdly, most likely it is the list of rented property not the land plots cultivated by the monastic community itself, suggesting limited direct involvement of monks in agriculture in Nubia. Location of some monasteries: like tentative monastery at Gebel al-Ain[35] in Wadi al-Malik in the Western Desert considerably limits the possibility of land cultivation by Nubian monasteries and this in turn leads to the assumption that at least some communities had to rely on provisions of staple food. Whether monks secured those on their own or were provided with sustenance in the form of alms or gifts cannot be ascertained now. The lack of involvement of monks in cultivation works is in agreement with the *Apophthegmata Patrum*, where Abba Poemen[36], one of the most respected fathers, discourages monks from taking part in such activities, since they should withdraw from the world and, as harvest and agricultural works were communal works, monks could be tempted. Yet this ideal depiction of a monastic life in Egypt did not have a lot in common with reality. Monks possessed plots of land since a very early period[37], while the Pachomian *koine* cultivated not only the land it owned but also the one it leased. The monasteries were important land owners and cultivators in Late Antique Egypt, as attested, for example, in the dossier from Bawit[38].

4.2. Alms, grants and gifts

This category is not transparent and does not have clearly defined, rigid limits. Grants and gifts were almost always given with an expectation of reciprocity. What is then the difference between grants and payments for services? The

35 J. Eger, «Ein mittelalterliches Kloster am Gebel al-Ain?», *Der Antike Sudan. Mitteilungen der Sudanarchäologischen Gesellschaft zu Berlin e.V.* 22 (2011) 115-120.

36 Apophthegm Poemen 22 (596), after: Wipszycka, «Resources and economic activities», 200-202.

37 M. Choat, «Property Ownership and Tax Payment in Fourth-Century Monasticism», in *Monastic Estates in Late Antique and Early Islamic Egypt. Ostraca, Papyri and Studies in Memory of Sarah Clackson*, edd. A. Boud'hors *et al.* (American Studies in Papyrology 46), Cincinnati 2009, 129-158.

38 S.A. Richter, «The Cultivation of Monastic Estates in Late Antique and Early Islamic Egypt. Some Evidence from Coptic Land Leases and Related Documents», in *Monastic Estates in Late Antique and Early Islamic Egypt: Ostraca, Papyri and Essays in Memory of Sarah Clackson*, edd. A. Boud'hors *et al.* (American Studies in Papyrology 46), Cincinnati 2009, 205-215.

latter are provisions linked directly to the delivery of a particular, most often spiritual service and examples of them follows in the services section. Grants had a more general character and were aimed at providing for subsistence. The relevant question here is whether the receiving individual or group relied on this charity to survive or whether he/it ensured his/its needs in other ways as well. Generous contributions by the wealthy for the benefit of the community were characteristic to the Graeco-Roman world. With its increasing number of followers, the Church became an important recipient of charitable donations. For instance, in the sixth century, the great Metanoia monastery of Canopus, a suburb of Alexandria, received an annual grant of 5.759 artabae of grain from the imperial taxes of the village of Aphrodito[39]. Palladius mentions in *Historia Lausiaca* an *oikonomos* that received as a gift from Melania a chest containing 300 silver coins[40]. When we approach this phenomenon from the perspective of social science, it is clear that in each and every society there is a more or less sophisticated mechanism of food and wealth redistribution. It definitely existed in medieval Nubia, too, but we do not know how it worked or to what extent it was linked to religion. There is no direct confirmation for gifts/grants for the monasteries in Nubia yet the charitable activities of the Christian community are well known. There are several attestations of:

- churches being recipients of goods[41],
- churches being owned and most probably founded by individuals, like a deacon, priests (also a daughter of a priest), bishops, high court officials and a king[42],
- foundation and restoration of churches done by the bishops[43].

39 M.J. Hollerich, «The Alexandrian Bishops and the Grain Trade. Ecclesiastical Commerce in Late Roman Egypt», *Journal of the Economic and Social History of the Orient* 2 (1982) 187-207: 205-206.

40 Palladius, «Historia Lausiaca», in Palladius, *Palladiusz. Opowiadania dla Lausosa (Historia Lausiaca)*, ed. M. Starowieyski, tr. S. Kalinkowski, Kraków-Tyniec 1996, 96.

41 A. Łajtar-G. Ochała, «Two Wall Inscriptions from the Faras Cathedral with Lists of People and Goods», in *Nubian Voices*, vol. 2: *New Texts and Studies on Christian Nubian Culture*, edd. A. Łajtar-G. Ochała-J. van der Vliet (The Journal of Juristic Papyrology Supplements 27), Warsaw 2016, 73-102.

42 A. Łajtar-J. van der Vliet, «Rich Ladies of Meinarti and Their Churches with an Appended List of Sources from Christian Nubia Containing the Expression: "Having the Church of So-and-So"», *Journal of Juristic Papyrology* 28 (1998) 35-53.

43 Like in the case of the cathedral of Pachoras, see: J. van der Vliet, *Catalogue*, 3-15; and edition princeps: S. Jakobielski, «Two Coptic Foundation Stones from Faras», in *Mélanges offerts à Kazimierz Michałowski*, ed. M.L. Bernhard, Warszawa 1966, 103-109.

It would be surprising if the monasteries were not to be the recipients of such pious donations as well. Some clues regarding the benevolent donations for monastic communities are also discernible in the archaeological evidence. The Qasr el-Wizz and al-Ghazali monasteries were built as the result of the same type of foundation: one single act, founding a ready-to-operate monastery, not a small set of buildings then gradually evolving into a full-blown monastery. The first can be dated to the late sixth century; Ghazali, built about a hundred years later, is comparable to the monastery of St. Catherine in the Sinai Peninsula, which was an imperial (Justinian) foundation. In search for the willing founders, the scale of the investments leads us to the upper echelons of the medieval Nubian society, and especially directly to the ruler, since the new religion was not embedded deeply enough to mobilize such resources from lower levels of Nubian society. There is one type of donation we can exclude in Nubia, namely donations in money, since Nubia lacked a monetary economy. So, the monks could not have received grants like, for instance, their counterparts from the monastery of Saint John the Baptist, with an annual income of six solidi each offered by Emperor Anastasius[44].

Monks played an important role in the delivery of several types of social services, including provisions for the handicapped and the society in general. A good example is offered by the life of Georgios (†1113), the archimandrite of a monastery and archbishop of Dongola, described in his epitaph as "loving the poor, conscious about the local community, the mildest father of the orphans"[45]. This epithet can be of a panegyric and rhetorical character, but to some extent must reflect the charitable activity of the deceased.

4.3. Manual labor, craftsmanship and services

The economic activities of monks appear very early in monastic literature, for instance in *Apophtegmata Patrum* and Basil of Caesarea's instructions on ascetic life, in which he encouraged monks to work for their living[46]. Howe-

44 Theodosius, *De situ Terræ Sanctæ*, 20, after: N. Heiska, *The Economy and Livelihoods of the Early Christian Monasteries in Palestine*, Master of Arts thesis, University of Helsinki, 2003 [access: 25-02-2017] http://ethesis.helsinki.fi/julkaisut/hum/kultt/pg/heiska/theecono.pdf., 66.

45 A. Łajtar, «Georgios, Archbishop of Dongola (†1113) and His Epitaph», in *Euergesias Charin. Studies Presented to Benedetto Bravo and Ewa Wipszycka by Their Disciples*, edd. T. Derda-J. Urbanik-M. Węcowski, Warsaw 2002, 159-192.

46 See for instance: St Basil, Bishop of Caesarea, *Ascetical Works*, Fathers of the

ver, Constantinopolitan monks were engaged in manual labor only in the Mar Mare monastery. The founder led them by example by doing hand crafts and later agricultural work. We do not know whether the same emphasis was put on manual work in other monasteries in Constantinople[47]. Manual labor was, however, one of the fundamental features of the Egyptian monasticism, both coenobitic and anchoritic, along with the most important ones: prayer, self-denial and fasting. This was not only for economic reasons; manual labor was also a "practical component of monastic prayer, as certain tasks enabled the monastic to retain a meditative state through their repetitive nature"[48]. The endeavors of the Theban monks, attested in texts and in the archaeological record, included the following[49]:

- basketry: ropes, baskets,
- textile weaving: linen shrouds and keiriai (strips of linen), linen garments,
- making leather goods : certainly codex bindings,
- copying manuscripts.

John Moschos recounts that anchorites of Sketis had a habit of seeking employment in the estates during the harvest time.[50] There are references to Palestinian monks who temporarily left their monasteries and worked for secular employers[51]. A monk of the monastery of Abba Severian was sent to work in a farm in the district of Eleutheropolis[52]. There is also a story of a monk, Theodore, who worked on the construction of a reservoir to earn money to pay for a Bible[53].

In Nubian monasteries, the evidence for manual labor and crafts is delivered only by archaeology. There are no texts describing the everyday activities of Nubian monks as in the narratives regarding, for instance, Egyptian monasticism – there are no Nubian *Apophtegmata Patrum*. The archaeological finds have not

Church 9, ed. M. Wagner, Washington 1962, 306-311, Long rules, 37. Whether prayer and psalmody ought to afford a pretext for neglecting our work, what hours are suitable for prayer, and, above all, whether labor is necessary.

47 Hatlie, *The Monks*, 148.

48 A. T. Crislip, *From Monastery to Hospital. Christian Monasticism & the Transformation of Health Care in Late Antiquity*, Ann Arbor 2005, 3.

49 Wipszycka, «Resources and Economic Activities», 229.

50 J. Moschus, *The Spiritual Meadow = Pratum spirituale*, tr. J. Wortley (Cistercian Studies Series 139), Kalamazoo 1992, 183.

51 Heiska, *The Economy*, 66.

52 Moschus, *The Spiritual Meadow*, 39.

53 Moschus, *The Spiritual Meadow*, 134.

been discovered in big numbers but are present at the monasteries of Qasr el-Wizz, Ghazali and on Kom H at Old Dongola and include: spindle whorls, punchers, and scraps of leather, probably leftovers from production of monastic aprons and sandals, which suggests that monks might have been involved in spinning and leatherwork.

Apart from relatively simple forms of labor, like spinning or leatherwork, monks were involved in delivery of services which demanded a good education, e.g. serving as notaries, or experience, like iron smelting or clay object production. The contiguity of the monastery and one of the iron smelting centres in the area of Ghazali and the fact they are concurrent with each other offer strong grounds for a claim about the monks' association with this industry. Even the superstructures of some of the monks' tombs were made of slag and leftovers from iron production. At Banganarti, a mysterious site 8 km south of Dongola, the capital of Makuria, there is an inscription which may mention a blacksmith monk (Adam Łajtar, *personal communication*). Blacksmiths appeared in Egypt on the list of monks working in the Pachomian monastery at Panopolis (seven out of three hundred were blacksmiths)[54], and in Shenoute's congregation[55]. There is also a mention of a blacksmith monk in Bawit[56]. Ewa Wipszycka is cautious to state that there really were monk-blacksmiths, but I am inclined to accept that three testimonies make the case[57].

Production of clay objects was reported by Bogdan Żurawski in Room 8 in the NE corner of the monastic complex on Kom H at Dongola. According to the excavators, the room could have been used in a minor ceramic industry which produced peculiar objects, such as inscribed terracotta, sepulchral crosses and ceramic sepulchral stelae[58]. In Room 2 of the same complex a pottery stamp was found. The stamp was definitely used to impress the bottoms of pottery bowls, which are attested all over Nubia[59].

54 Palladius, «Historia Lausiaca», 156 (32,9).

55 Reproofs and monastic rules, VIII, 1: Besa, *Letters and Sermons*, , ed. K. H. Kuhn, Leuven 1956, 33.

56 E. Drioton-J. Maspero, *Fouilles de Baouît*, ed. É. Drioton (Mémoires publiés par les membres de l'Institut français d'archéologie du Caire 59), Le Caire 1931-43, no. 428.

57 Wipszycka, «Resources and economic activities», 186.

58 B.T. Żurawski, «The Service Area in North-Eastern Corner of the Monastery on Kom H in Old Dongola. A Preliminary Report», *Nubica* 3 (1994) 319-360, 337.

59 Żurawski, «The Service Area in North-Eastern Corner of the Monastery on Kom H in Old Dongola. A Preliminary Report», 340, fig. 15.

Two intriguing objects were recovered from the excavations of the Ghazali monastery. Both of them, are fragmentarily preserved terracotta figurines of monks made of fired clay[60]. Their meaning is quite problematic. It is hard to believe that monks made such figurines for themselves; it seems most probable that they were devotional items taken from the holy site by the visiting pilgrims. Yet, for this thesis to be positively confirmed, such figurines would have to be found on at least one archaeological site other than the Ghazali monastery, where they were supposedly produced or at least commissioned by the monastery and then sold/given away.

These devotional items bring us to an important spiritual but also economic phenomenon in which the Nubian monastic communities took part: the pilgrimage. While at Ghazali except for the figurines there is no other irrefutable material evidence for pilgrimage, such evidence is present at the monastery of Qasr el-Wizz. At the turn of the 11th century an architectural alteration took place[61]. The sacred part of the monastery was enlarged by addition of a second church east of the original one. It was a small construction with a hierateion limited to a small room, built over the entrance to the crypt where most likely the relics of a local saint were laid. The altar that room is furnished with, was moved to the corner, as the monks expected that more than one body would be buried in the crypt, which consisted of a vertical shaft and two burial chambers. An ambo abutted the outer faces of the southern wall of the room and openings were made in the eastern wall of the main church to facilitate the movement of the pilgrims. The number of visitors must have grown considerably, since a new food production annex was supplemented in the north-west corner of the monastery as well.

Pilgrim-oriented alterations to the sites of pilgrimage were also made in other parts of the Christian *koine*. In Syria, for instance, in the fourth to sixth centuries, monasteries were designed specifically for pilgrims, with huge colonnaded spaces to accommodate their numbers, like at Qal'at Sim'an. The layout of these sites suggests that their builders were much more concerned with catering for pilgrims than with providing space for the permanent religious communities[62]. A later example of this is likewise provided by pilgrim churches built by the Crusaders in the Holy Land. Split level churches, in which pilgrims had access

---

60 Shinnie-Chittick, *Ghazali, a Monastery*, 26, pl. 9.

61 A. Obłuski, «Nobadian and Makurian Church Architecture. Qasr el-Wizz, a Case Study», in *Aegyptus et Nubia Christiana. The Włodzimierz Godlewski Jubilee Volume on the Occasion of his 70th Birthday*, edd. A. Łajtar-A. Obłuski-I. Zych, Warsaw 2016, 481-51.

62 W. Braunfels, *Monasteries of Western Europe. The architecture of the orders*, Princeton 1973, 15-18.

Fig. 3 Plan Qasr el-Wizz, drawing S. Maślak, after W. Kołątaj.

to the lower floor and members of the orders upstairs, were one of the solutions adopted to allow access to pilgrims without interrupting monastic services[63].

4.4. Expert services

Nubian monks were also involved in rendering services which demanded a high level of education, such as those of a *notarios*. In Byzantium, a *notarios* was originally an official responsible for preparation of the minutes of important meetings, then his duty was to register transactions and certify documents. Then, by the 14th or 15th century notarioi assumed the role of public notaries[64]. Anthony Cutler estimated that in the 10th and 11th centuries about 50 percent of them were monks[65]. Monks were also employed in the state administration, like John Vincomalos, who was at the same time a government servant and a monk in the monastery of Bassianou[66]. The same phenomenon seems to have occurred in Nubia and is attested in:

63 D. Pringle, «The Planning of Some Pilgrimage Churches in Crusader Palestine», *World Archaeology* 3 (1987) 341-362.

64 A. Kazhdan-A. Cutler, «Notary», in *Oxford Dictionary of Byzantium*, edd. A.P. Kazhdan *et al.*, vol. 3, New York-Oxford 1991, 1495.

65 A. Cutler, «The Social Status of Byzantine Scribes, 800–1500. A Statistical Analysis Based on Vogel-Gardthausen», *Byzantinische Zeitschrift* 74 (1981) 328-334.

66 Hatlie, *The Monks*, 104, note 47.

- Epitaphs of Marianou[67] and Georgiou[68], bishops of Phrim (Primis, Qasr Ibrim). Both of them are called *abba*, which is tantamount to calling someone a monk[69]. Marianou during his career was the *archinotarios* (chief of notaries) of the eparch; Georgiou was a *notarios* of the eparch.
- Inscription about *abba* Joseph from Anba Hadra monastery in Aswan, who served not only as a notarios but also as a *nauarches*[70] and advisor to the kings[71].
- Epitaph with the *cursus honorum* of Stephanos, archimandrite of the monastery of Maria in Timaeie[72].

A document found in one of the cells at the monastery of Qasr el-Wizz suggests that monasteries could have served as chancelleries of state officials or that the monks were hired by the elites for their knowledge of languages and skill of writing. The document is a letter sent from one high-ranked Makurian official to another: from the eparchos of Nobadia and Seven Lands to another eparchos[73].

4.5. Spiritual and magical services

There is no direct and decisive proof for involvement of Nubian monks in magical and spiritual services, which were abundant for Egyptian monasticism, as evidenced for instance by two collections of magic spells: one found in the monastery of Epiphanius[74]; the other in a monk's cell at Naqlun[75].

---

67 A. Łajtar-J. van der Vliet, *Qasr Ibrim. The Greek and Coptic Inscriptions* (The Journal of Juristic Papyrology Supplements 13), Warsaw 2010, 77-85, no. 21.

68 Łajtar-van der Vliet, *Qasr Ibrim*, 68-77., no. 20.

69 T. Derda-E. Wipszycka, «L'emploi des titres abba, apa et papas dans l'Égypte byzantine», *Journal of Juristic Papyrology* 24 (1994) 23-56.

70 The *nauarches* is a title of the commander of a river fleet of a Nubian town

71 Adam Łajtar, personal communication, who shared with me draft of his reedition of this inscription. Editio princeps of this inscription: F.Ll. Griffith, *The Nubian Texts of the Christian Period* (Abhandlungen der Königlich preussichen akademie der wissenschaften. Phil.-Hist. Classe 8), Berlin 1913, 57-58.

72 A. Łajtar-A. Twardecki, *Catalogue des inscriptions grecques du Musée national de Varsovie* (The Journal of Juristic Papyrology Supplements 2), Varsovie 2003, 304-309, no. 110.

73 The eparch is a title of the head of local territorial Makurian administration. For publication of the text see: A. Obłuski, *Excavations at Qasr el-Wizz, George T. Scanlon, Director*, Chicago, forthcoming exc. no. 65-11-103.

74 H.E. Winlock, *The monastery of Epiphanius at Thebes*, vol. 2 (Publications of the Metropolitan Museum of Art Egyptian Expedition 3), New York 1926, 21, 207.

75 W. Godlewski, «Naqlun: Excavations 1997», *Polish Archaeology in the Mediterra-*

Apart from this ambiguous activity, monks also delivered what we may call spiritual services – like prayers for someone or something or posthumous commemoration – for which the monks received gifts in money or in kind. For example, one of the papyri states that in exchange for a donation the physician from Antinoe will be buried at the monks' cemetery and his name will be entered in the list of the deceased for whom the monks offer their prayers[76]. Another piece of evidence is a reference to a man from Aila who gave a monk named Joseph three silver coins so that Joseph would pray for his ship, which he had sent to Ethiopia[77]. A Theban monk named Frange more than once openly demands gifts in the form of foodstuffs in exchange for prayers for various intentions. For instance he asks one of his supplicants:

> "Je demande à Votre Charité que, quand mon frère Thomas viendra à vous avec la tablette de mon humilité, pour l'amour de Dieu et le salut de votre âme et de votre bétail, vous lui donniez du bon vin pour qu'il me l'apporte"[78].

Two small fragments of parchment from Qasr el-Wizz[79] and a potsherd from Ghazali, both bearing the names of the Forty Martyrs of Sebaste, suggest both of them served magical purposes. The specific function of the names of the martyrs is confirmed by the fact that the piece of parchment on which they were written is cut at the corners, suggesting it was put in an enclosed, limited space, probably an amulet. There are also several other amulets found in Christian Nubia, yet they cannot be unquestionably linked to the monks. Further evidence is the apotropaic cross or eight-pointed star marked on one of the monastic tombs at Qasr el-Wizz, as well as numerous cryptograms and monograms on various artefacts from the monastic milieu. A quite spectacular testimony comes from the crypt found in the Annex to the monastery on Kom H at Old Dongola, where apart from the canonical texts (the gospels), used to secure the passage of the soul from our world to eternity, there

---

nean 9 (1998) 77-86: 79.

76 J. Maspero, *Papyrus grecs d'époque byzantine*, vol. 2 (Catalogue général des antiquités égyptiennes du Musée du Caire), Institut français d'archéologie orientale, Le Caire 1913, no. 67151, after Wipszycka, «Resources and Economic Activities», 167, note 11.

77 L. Regnault, *Les Sentences des Pères du désert, nouveau recueil, apophtegmes inédits ou peu connus*, Solesmes 1970, 191.

78 A. Boud'hors-C. Heurtel, *Les ostraca coptes de la TT 29. Autour du moine Frangé*, vol. 1: *Textes* (Études d'archéologie thébaine 3), Bruxelles 2010, 98, O. 290840.

79 Tsakos, «Textual Finds», exc. np. 65-11-104.

are less orthodox elements, like the Sator Square[80]. Even some material evidence may imply delivery of spiritual and magical services, we cannot firmly state if the monks produced amulets and talismans.

4.6. Food production

One of the most important issues from the communal perspective is the production and distribution of food. There were no common dietary rules for ascetics in the Christian *koine* during Late Antiquity and the Middle Ages. The communities may have created their own regulations following the food practices of the region in which they lived. For example, according to the historical sources, the Pachomian monks in Egypt ate a fish soup made of crushed small fish[81], whilst the Palestinian monks considered fish nourishment reserved rather for the sick[82]. From Egypt there are confirmed monastic purchases of: cereals – like wheat, barley, lentils and bread – oil, wine, honey, salt, (sheep milk) cheeses, fish preserves, cardamom and garlic[83].

We do not know whether there existed any rules of this kind in Nubian monasticism. The first analyses will be carried out on the basis of the results of excavations at the Ghazali monastery and its cemetery. The excavations unveiled some evidence which is of paramount importance for the reconstruction of everyday life of the monks in Nubia. The bio-archaeological material shows no traces of trauma induced by extensive physical labor. There is no evidence of malnutrition or lack of rudimentary human diet components. The life expectancy (35-50 years) is also higher than at the lay cemeteries studied in Nubia (20-35 years)[84].

The excavations at Ghazali unearthed finds that are unique in terms of monastic studies in the Nile Valley. Recovered in the food production compound were the only example of an oil press, and the second example of mill and grain

80 Łajtar-van der Vliet, «Wall Inscriptions».

81 M. Dembinska, «Diet. A Comparison of Food Consumption between Some Eastern and Western Monasteries in the 4th-12th Centuries», *Byzantion* 55 (1985) 431-462: 441.

82 Hirschfeld, *The Judean Desert Monasteries*, 88.

83 Wipszycka, «Resources and Economic Activities», 242.

84 J.A. Ciesielska-A. Obłuski-R.J. Stark, «The Cemeteries of Ghazali, season 2015/2016», *Archaeological Bayuda Conference Proceedings of the First International Conference on the Archaeology of the Bayuda Desert*, edd. A. Lohwasser-T. Karberg-J. Auenmuller, 257-271.

storage facilities known in the Nile Valley's monastic contexts (aside quern stones from the monastery of Anba Hadra in Aswan[85]). Apart from finds at Ghazali, there is only one document testifying to the existence of a monastic *elaiourgeion* – it belonged to the Oasiton monastery, which had a *diakonia* with an oil press in Aphrodito[86]. Monasteries must have had grain mills, as in Antiquity the object of sale was grain, not flour[87]. Both grain and oil were of utmost importance for the monastic communities with restricted diets. According to specialists, one artaba of grain (30–33 kg) provided the existential minimum for one person for a month. The need for oil was certainly considerable, since it was the only source of lipids in the monastic diet. Since the cultivation of olives is not attested in Nubia, one may assume that oil was made of some other plants like sesame and/or castor.

CONCLUSIONS

The results of comparative analysis suggest a picture of Nubian monks not very dissimilar to what we could observe in the Byzantine Empire. Even though the monastic communities did not play such an important role in the state economy, we can still assume that they were amongst the most durable Nubian institutions: the Ghazali monastery persisted for over five hundred years.

The Nubian monastic economies were rather small and they probably did not impact regional markets, but could shape the local ones to a considerable extent. The Nubian monks' economic activities did not differ considerably from their counterparts in other Christian regions. They were involved in manual labor and food production, as well as the delivery of various services demanding good education, literacy and involvement in elite social networks (royal and eparch courts). They ran chancelleries of high-ranked officials and *abba* Joseph even became chief of the city's fleet and was the king's advisor.

Inside the monasteries engagement in economic activities varied, depending probably on the skills and competences of an individual monk. In well managed organisations, there was no place for waste of resources and the heads of monasteries definitely took advantage of the potential at their disposal. It also depended on the volume of the other works in which the monastery as a whole

85 U. Monneret de Villard, *Il monastero di S. [i.e. Santo] Simeone presso Aswân*, Milano 1927.

86 Wipszycka, «Resources and Economic Activities», 196.

87 L.A. Moritz, *Grain-mills and Flour in Classical Antiquity*, Oxford 1958.

was involved, e.g., scribal work, which might have brought more profits than simple labor. In the case of monasteries, one always must ask the question if the archeological evidence speaks in favor of the involvement of the monks themselves or the lay people who were present at the monasteries, be they novices, lay people hired by the monks or even slaves. The end of monasticism in Nubia correlates with the considerable weakening of central and regional authorities and impoverishment of Nubian society due to instability and frequent Mameluk invasions at the end of the 13th century. This seems to be a clear indicator of strong reliance of monastic milieu on state support.

Abstract

Monasticism found its way to Nubia at the end of the sixth and the beginning of the seventh century and it appeared there in a well-organized coenobitic form. The anchoretic way of life probably had never been very popular. S According to the medieval Coptic historian Abū al-Makārim, there were plentiful churches and monasteries in Nubia. For the southernmost Alwa, he quotes four hundred churches. While the numbers given by him were exaggerated, still the number of churches must have been considerable if it drew his attention. The evolution of Nubian monasticism differed from that of the other parts of the Christian community due to the lack of processes and/or events that shaped Byzantine and Egyptian monasticisms, like iconoclastic crises and the resurgence of monasteries in Byzantium after the victory of iconodules or the introduction of Islam in Egypt. This paper is the first attempt to tackle the important topic of the economy of Nubian monasteries. It surveys the economic activities of monks in Christian East in a comparative perspective. The textual and archeological evidence from Nubia suggest close relationship of monks and state elites and limited involvement of monks in physical labor.

The publication came into existence thanks to the grant 2014/13/D/HS3/03829 “Nubian Monasticism. Religious institutions in the fringes of the Byzantine world.” founded by National Science Centre, Poland.

LE « PRIX » DE L'HABIT MONASTIQUE À BYZANCE. RECHERCHES SUR LES DONS DES POSTULANTS À L'ENTRÉE AU MONASTÈRE

Daniel OLTEAN

L'habit monastique n'a pas de prix. Comme le baptême, la foi ou la grâce divine. Tout au long de l'histoire byzantine, l'entrée au monastère et la profession monastique ont été décrites en termes enthousiastes : on parle souvent du « saint » habit, du « grand » habit, de l'habit « parfait », qui a le pouvoir d'effacer les péchés de celui qui le revêt et de l'introduire dans une nouvelle réalité spirituelle.

Néanmoins, on constate que cet habit est souvent donné dans un contexte économique très concret : après avoir renoncé à ses biens et les avoir distribués aux pauvres, le postulant offre une part de sa fortune et la dépose dans les mains de l'higoumène. S'agit-il d'une recommandation ? D'une obligation ? D'une coutume ? Ou bien cette procédure est-elle une exception qui transgresse la règle, comme quelques textes byzantins le suggèrent ? Pour clarifier la question, notre texte propose un examen des éléments économiques de l'engagement monastique, afin de donner quelques réponses concernant la motivation du don, le moment où il est apporté, son montant. En essayant de distinguer entre réalité, mimétisme littéraire et rhétorique, on analysera les différents types de sources (textes juridiques, *typika* monastiques, vies des saints, actes de la pratique, textes patristiques) qui gardent des données à ce sujet.

1. LE RENONCEMENT AUX BIENS DANS LE MONACHISME BYZANTIN

Dans un apophtegme bien connu, Antoine donne un conseil inattendu à un novice qui avait gardé une partie de ses biens pour son propre usage : « Si tu veux devenir moine, va dans tel village, achète de la viande, mets-la sur ton corps nu, puis reviens ici ». Et lorsque le frère revient chez le vieillard avec tout son corps lacéré par les chiens et les oiseaux, le grand ascète lui dit : « Ceux qui renoncent

---

Doctorant à l'École des hautes études en sciences sociales, Paris et à l'Université de Thessalonique (cotutelle).

au monde et veulent garder des richesses sont déchirés ainsi par les démons qui les combattent »[1].

Ce texte exprime bien la pensée des premiers moines égyptiens concernant la possession de biens. Leurs principes de vie sont en évidente opposition avec les coutumes rencontrées dans le monachisme de type familial des premiers siècles chrétiens. Pour les moines qui vivaient en dehors des villes, le renoncement aux biens est ainsi devenu une condition obligatoire pour l'entrée au monastère. « Si on ne renonce pas à toutes les choses du monde, on ne peut pas devenir moine », dit Macaire dans un autre apophtegme[2], tandis que dans le même milieu, un frère qui avait gardé cent pièces de monnaie est renvoyé dans le monde, trois fois consécutives, avec les mots : « Va, renonce au monde, puis viens demeurer dans ta cellule »[3]. Dans les communautés cénobitiques de Pacôme[4], Basile de Césarée[5] ou Schenoute d'Atripé[6], la renonciation à tous les biens personnels est déjà une règle imposée aux candidats. Dans l'hagiographie, les exemples sont également nombreux. Selon Théodoret de Cyr, Publius, un homme riche issu du milieu sénatorial, vend tous ses biens hérités de ses parents avant de partir au monastère, c'est-à-dire « sa maison, ses terres, ses troupeaux, sa garde-robe, sa vaisselle d'argent et de bronze et tout ce qu'il pouvait avoir encore »[7]. Cette ligne de conduite est reprise tout au long de l'histoire du

1 *Apophthegmata Patrum*, Antoine 20, *PG* 65, 81C-D, trad. L. Regnault, *Les Sentences des Pères du désert. Collection alphabétique*, Solesmes 1981, 18.

2 *Ibid.*, Macaire 2, *PG* 65, 260D, trad. Regnault, 174.

3 *The Anonymous Sayings of the Desert Fathers*, 17, éd. et trad. J. Wortley, Cambridge 2013, 16-17.

4 *Règle de Pacôme, Praecepta* 49, in *Pachomiana latina*, éd. A. Boon (Bibliothèque de la Revue d'Histoire ecclésiastique 7), Louvain 1932, 25, trad. P. Deseille, *L'esprit du monachisme pachômien* (Spiritualité orientale 2), Bégrolles-en-Mauges 1968, 23.

5 Basile de Césarée, *Grandes regles*, 8-9, *PG* 31, 933D-944B, in Basile de Césarée, *Les règles monastiques*, trad. L. Lèbe, Éditions de Maredsous, 1969, 68-74 ; Id., *Petites règles*, 85, *PG* 31, 1144A, trad. Lèbe, 221 : « Celui qui prétend donc avoir quelque chose en propre s'exclut lui-même de l'Église de Dieu et de la charité du Seigneur, lui qui, dans ses paroles et dans ses actes, apprend à donner sa vie pour ses amis, et non pas seulement les biens extérieurs ».

6 Schenoute, *Canons*, 243, éd. et trad. B. Layton, *The Canons of our Fathers: Monastic Rules of Shenoute* (Oxford Early Christian Studies), Oxford 2014, 190-191; *Ibid.*, 464, 292-293 ; Besa, *Lettres et sermons*, 31, 1, 2-3, éd. et trad. K.H. Kuhn, *Letters and Sermons of Besa* (Corpus Scriptorum Christianorum Orientalium 157-158, Scriptores Coptici 21-22), Louvain 1956, 104-105, trad. 101 ; *Ibid.*, 32, 8, 1-2, 111, trad. 107-108.

7 Théodoret de Cyr, *Histoire des moines de Syrie*, 5, 1, éd. et trad. P. Canivet-A. Leroy-Molinghen, 2 voll. (Sources chrétiennes 234, 257), Paris 1977-1979, 328-331.

monachisme. Le droit canonique et civil et les *typika* l'incorporent parmi les réglementations pour les moines[8].

1.1. Distribution des biens avant l'entrée

Pour ceux qui possédaient des biens, la réalisation pratique de ce principe ascétique impliquait certains détails concrets. Selon la législation de Justinien, avant qu'il parte au monastère, le futur moine devait assurer à ses éventuels enfants un quart de ses biens et à sa femme la dot initiale et les avantages prévus dans le contrat nuptial en cas de décès du mari. Après l'entrée au monastère, le moine ne disposait plus de sa fortune, mais la partie qui revenait aux enfants pouvait être réclamée par ceux-ci même après la mort de leur père[9]. Ces dispositions sont réaffirmées par Léon VI et la jurisprudence ultérieure[10].

Mais les moines riches gardaient parfois une part de leurs biens[11]. Deux textes du Code Théodosien évoquent bien cette réalité. Une constitution de Valentinien et Valens datant de 370 ou 373 impose à ceux qui s'étaient retirés dans le

8 *Synode prime-second de Constantinople, Canons*, 6, in *Discipline générale antique*, vol. 1/2 : *Les canons des synodes particuliers (IIe-IXe s.)*, éd. et trad. P.P. Joannou (Fonti IX), Rome-Grottaferrata 1962-1964, 457 : « Les moines ne doivent rien posséder en propre, et tous leurs biens doivent être adjugés au monastère » ; *Testament de Matthieu Ier de Constantinople*, éds. I.M. Konidares-K.A. Manaphes, « Ἐπιτελεύτιος βούλησις καὶ διδασκαλία τοῦ οἰκουμενικοῦ πατριάρχου Ματθαίου Α΄ », *Ἐπετηρὶς Ἑταιρείας Βυζαντινῶν Σπουδῶν* 45 (1981-1982), 462-515, ici 489, trad. A.-M. Talbot, « *Testament* of Patriarch Mathew I for the Monastery of Charsianeites Dedicated to the Mother of God *Nea Peribleptos* », in *Byzantine Monastic Foundation Documents. A Complete Translation of the Surviving Founders'* Typika *and Testaments*, I-V (Dumbarton Oaks Studies 35), éds. J. Thomas-A. Constantinides Hero, Washington 2000 (= *BMFD*), IV, n° 60, 1625-1666, ici [B12]-[B13], 1646. Pour l'Occident voir *Règle du Maître*, 87, 12-24, éd. et trad. A. de Vogüé, 2 voll. (Sources chrétiennes 105-106), Paris 1964, II, 356-359 ; *Règle de Benoît*, 58, éds. et trad. A. de Vogüé-J. Neufville, 2 voll. (Sources chrétiennes 181, 183), Paris 1972, II, 630-633.

9 Justinien, *Novelles*, 5, 5 ; 76 ; 123, 38 = *Basiliques*, 4, 1, 9.

10 Léon VI, *Novelles*, 5, éd. et trad. P. Noailles-A. Dain, *Les Novelles de Léon VI le Sage*, Paris 1944, 24-29 ; *Prochiron*, 24, 2, in *Jus Graecoromanum*, vol. 2, éds. I. Zepos-P. Zepos, Athènes 1931 (= *JGR*), 172 ; Constantin Harménopoulos, *Hexabible*, 5, 4, 2, éd. C.G.Pitsakis:ΚΩΝΣΤΑΝΤΙΝΟΥΑΡΜΕΝΟΠΟΥΛΟΥ,*ΠρόχειροννόμωνἢἙχαβίβλος*,Athènes1971, 287.

11 Sur les biens des premiers moines égyptiens voir E. Wipszycka, *Moines et communautés monastiques en Égypte (IVe-VIIIe siècles)* (The Journal of Juristic Papyrology, Supplement XI), Varsovie 2009, 493-494.

désert à renoncer à leurs biens, s'ils veulent rester dans ce genre de vie[12]. Selon une autre loi, datée de 434, les biens des moines et des moniales morts sans laisser de testament et sans parenté y ayant droit, entrent en possession de l'Église[13].

À l'époque byzantine, les exemples sont également nombreux. Dans la *Vie* d'Iôannikios, un moine très pieux nommé Thomas est prévenu par le grand ascète de sa mort imminente. Devant l'annonce, Thomas distribue tous ses biens aux pauvres, signe qu'il ne l'avait pas fait jusqu'à ce moment[14]. Plus tard, l'un des conseils de Syméon le Nouveau Théologien adressés aux novices mentionne : « Mieux vaut être pauvre, étranger et en avoir la réputation que de distribuer des richesses et de donner aux pauvres, lorsqu'on n'est que novice »[15]. La distribution des biens à l'entrée au monastère n'est donc pas une règle si stricte et les moines gardaient une certaine liberté concernant cet aspect. Ainsi, parmi les moines de cette catégorie, la *Vie* de Lazare de Galèsion nous donne l'exemple d'un certain Cosmas Politès, qui garde une part de son argent pour la distribuer aux pauvres[16].

Parfois, les candidats riches préservent une part de leur fortune pour servir aux futures fondations monastiques. Les cas de Théophane le Confesseur et Théodore Stoudite sont bien connus. De la même manière, après la mort de son père, Michel Maléïnos libère les esclaves et donne aux pauvres les biens mobiliers de la fortune qui lui est revenue en héritage. Concernant les propriétés foncières, il les vend à son frère, peut-être pour les garder à l'intérieur de sa famille. Une moitié de l'argent obtenu parvient dans les mains de son maître spirituel, pour agrandir le monastère et pour la distribuer aux moines et aux pauvres. La deuxième moitié est gardée. Michel achètera avec elle une propriété sur le mont Kyminas, où il bâtira son propre monastère[17].

---

12 *Code Théodosien*, 12, 1, 63.

13 *Code Théodosien*, 5, 3, 1.

14 *Vie d'Iôannikios par Pierre* (*BHG* 936), 65, éd. I. van den Gheyn, *Acta Sanctorum Nov.*, II, 384-435, ici 427, trad. D. Sullivan, « Life of St. Ioannikios », in *Byzantine Defenders of Images. Eight Saints' Lives in English Translation*, éd. A.-M. Talbot (Byzantine Saints' Lives in Translation 2), Washington 1998, 243-351, ici 333.

15 Syméon le Nouveau Théologien, *Chapitres théologiques, gnostiques et pratiques*, I, 25, éd. et trad. J. Darrouzès (Sources chrétiennes 51bis), Paris 1996, 54-55.

16 *Vie de Lazare de Galèsion* (*BHG* 979), 193, *Acta Sanctorum Nov.*, vol. 3, éd. H. Delehaye, 508-588, ici 566, *The Life of Lazaros of Mt. Galesion: An Eleventh-Century Pillar Saint*, trad. R.P.H. Greenfield, (Byzantine Saints' Lives in Translation 3), Washington 2000, 283-284.

17 *Vie de Michel Maléinos* (*BHG* 1295), 11, éd. L. Petit, « Vie et office de saint Michel Maléinos, suivis d'un traité ascétique de Basile Maléinos », *Revue de l'Orient chrétien* 7

Pour résoudre cette contradiction entre l'idéal de la pauvreté monastique et l'utilité de l'argent apporté par les débutants, Pallade nous donne un très bon exemple. Les frères Paësios et Isaïe choisissent deux modalités différentes de renonciation à leurs parts de biens : l'un donne tout aux églises, monastères et prisons, sans rien garder pour lui ; en restant en solitude, il gagnait son pain par le travail de ses mains ; en revanche, l'autre préserve son argent, l'utilisant pour bâtir un monastère cénobitique, où il commence à aider les pauvres, les étrangers, les vieillards et les infirmes. Concernant ce cas, Pallade exprime une opinion équilibrée : les frères ont assuré leur place au paradis, car chacun a accompli, dans sa propre façon, la volonté de Dieu et les exigences de l'Évangile[18].

1.2. Les biens obtenus après l'entrée au monastère

Si un moine était l'héritier de certains biens de sa famille, l'état monastique lui imposait le refus de l'héritage. Théodore de Sykéôn agit de cette façon à la mort de sa mère[19]. Les textes canoniques s'expriment dans cette ligne : après leur entrée au monastère, les moines ne pouvaient plus s'occuper de leurs biens ou en disposer. S'ils ne respectaient pas la règle, ils seraient punis et les biens confisqués par le monastère. Le synode prime-second ajoute en ce sens que les propriétés étaient vendues devant témoins et l'argent était distribué aux pauvres[20].

Par ailleurs, Léon VI intervient avec une réglementation intéressante à ce sujet. Selon l'une des *Novelles*, le moine dispose de toute la liberté d'administrer ses biens et le monastère n'a pas le pouvoir d'intervenir ; seulement dans le cas où le moine n'ait rien apporté à son entrée, un tiers de la nouvelle fortune reste dans le patrimoine de la communauté, tandis que les autres deux tiers peuvent être utilisés à son propre gré[21]. S'agit-il d'un désir de sanctionner les abus ou de

(1902) 543-603, ici 557-558, trad. S. Métivier in *Économie et société à Byzance (VIIIe-XIIe siècle). Textes et documents* (Byzantina Sorbonensia 24), éd. Ead., Paris 2007, 47-48.

18 Pallade, *Histoire lausiaque*, 14, in Palladio, *La Storia Lausiaca*, éd. G.J.M. Bartelink, trad. M. Barchiesi (Vite dei santi 2), Vicence 1985, 58-63.

19 *Vie de Théodore de Sykéôn* (*BHG* 1748), 33, éd. et trad. A.-J. Festugière, 2 voll. (Subsidia Hagiographica 48), Bruxelles 1970, vol. 1, 30, trad. vol. 2, 32.

20 *Synode prime-second de Constantinople, Canons*, 6, éd. et trad. Joannou, 458 : « Si quelqu'un est convaincu de posséder une propriété, qui ne fut pas adjugée au monastère, et se rend ainsi esclave de la passion de posséder, la propriété sera reprise par l'higoumène ou par l'évêque et vendue devant témoins et l'argent sera distribué aux pauvres et indigents ».

21 Léon VI, *Novelles*, 5, éd. Noailles-Dain, 28-33 : « S'il est prouvé que quelqu'un, au moment où il a choisi la vie monastique, a consacré une partie de ses biens à l'Église, il pourra,

limiter le pouvoir des monastères ? Quelle que ce soit la réponse, la disposition sera reprise dans la législation byzantine ultérieure[22].

La pratique est en accord avec ce dernier texte. Le moine Syméon, fils de Marie la Jeune, décide avec son frère de consacrer la fortune laissée par leurs parents à la construction d'un nouveau tombeau pour les reliques de sa mère et d'un couvent dans le village natal[23]. En 1012, avec l'accord de son higoumène, le moine Théodoret de Lavra donne un petit monastère à Skyros au couvent de la Théotokos de Bouleutèria conduit par son neveu Athanase. Théodoret avait reçu ce monastère de la part de la nonne Glykéria suite aux pressions et « misères » de l'évêque du lieu[24].

2. DONS À L'ENTRÉE

En règle générale, les dons (*ἀποταγαί*) ne sont pas exigés à l'entrée au monastère, mais ils sont acceptés. Le candidat offre ce don et le monastère a le pouvoir de l'utiliser selon son intérêt. Cette attitude est la plus répandue. Néanmoins, elle est complétée par deux autres coutumes. Selon la première, le monastère refuse d'une manière catégorique le don ou les biens apportés sont vendus et l'argent est distribué aux pauvres. À l'inverse, l'attitude opposée est aussi possible : un don est demandé à l'entrée ou au moment de la tonsure monastique. La première coutume est rencontrée dans les monastères de tradition plus ascétique, la seconde, dans les couvents plus proches de l'esprit du monde[25].

---

en ce qui concerne les biens acquis postérieurement, décider librement et souverainement de la façon dont il entend disposer de l'ensemble. »

22 *Epanagoge aucta*, 30, 4, in *JGR*, VI, 148 ; *Synopsis minor*, N, 39, in *JGR*, VI, 475 ; CONSTANTIN HARMÉNOPOULOS, *Hexabible*, 5, 4, 3, éd. Pitsakis, 287-288.

23 *Vie de Marie la Jeune* (*BHG* 1164), 27, *Acta Sanctorum Nov.*, IV, 692-705, ici 702, trad. A. Laiou, « Life of St. Mary the Younger », in *Holy Women of Byzantium. Ten Saints' Lives in English Translation*, éd. A.-M. Talbot (Byzantine Saints' Lives in Translation 1), Washington 1996 (= TALBOT, *Holy Women*), 239-289, ici 280-281.

24 *Actes de Lavra*, éds. P. Lemerle *et al.*, 4. voll. (Archives de l'Athos 5, 8, 10, 11), Paris 1970-1982, vol. 1, 16, 141-144.

25 Sur les dons offerts à l'entrée au monastère voir E. HERMAN, « Regelung der Armut in den byzantinichen Klöstern », *Orientalia Christiana Periodica* 7 (1941) 406-460, ici 438-450 ; J.P. THOMAS, *Private Religious Foundations in the Byzantine Empire* (Dumbarton Oaks Studies 24), Washington 1987, 145 ; 183 ; 207-208 ; I. KONIDARIS, Το δίκαιον της μοναστηριακής περιουσίας από του *9ου* μέχρι και του *12ου* αιώνο, Athènes 1979, 87-95 ; K. SMYRILIS, *La fortune des grands monastères byzantins (fin du Xe-milieu du XIVe siècle)* (Travaux et Mémoires, Monographies 21), Paris 2006, 136-138. Pour l'Occident voir J.H. LYNCH, *Simoniacal Entry into Religious Life from 1000 to 1260: A Social, Economic,*

2.1. Refus du don

Selon Basile de Césarée, les présents que pourraient offrir les parents d'un jeune postulant ne doivent pas être acceptés[26]. Selon Jean Cassien, les Tabennésiotes refusaient de recevoir de la part des postulants l'argent qui « servirait pour les besoins du monastère »[27]. La tradition est gardée dans les communautés ascétiques de l'Orient, comme celle syro-orientale de Babaï au mont Izla, au début du VIIe siècle. Selon sa règle, le nouveau moine n'avait aucune obligation envers la communauté, et même s'il apportait quelque chose, l'offrande était refusée[28].

Cette ancienne tradition est rarement rencontrée à Byzance. Une référence singulière se trouve dans le *Testament* du patriarche Matthieu Ier de Constantinople, qui impose dans son couvent le refus des dons. L'argument invoqué concerne à la fois l'intérêt faible du donateur pour les exigences de la vie monastique et la distinction sociale générée par cette procédure au sein de la communauté[29].

2.2. Acceptation du don

Plus souvent, le don est accepté, sans être imposé. Il est compris comme un signe visible du sacrifice que le candidat apporte pour sa nouvelle communauté. Un certain droit de l'Église sur la fortune ou une partie de la fortune de celui qui voulait devenir moine est ainsi sous-entendu. Selon Basile de Césarée, « celui qui renonce à toute propriété dans un tel but, ne peut cependant pas agir avec mépris vis-à-vis de ses biens. Il doit au contraire en prendre scrupuleusement soin, parce qu'ils sont désormais consacrés au Seigneur »[30]. La consécration monastique implique donc la consécration des biens à la communauté où le candidat voulait s'intégrer.

Ainsi, au IVe siècle, le don d'Épiphane de Chypre pour l'entrée de sa sœur au monastère de Bérénice est de mille *nomismata*. Pour lui-même, Épiphane garde

and Legal Study, Columbus (Ohio) 1976.

26 Basile de Césarée, *Petites règles*, 304, *PG* 31, 1300A-B, trad. Lèbe, 340-341.

27 Jean Cassien, *Institutions cénobitiques*, 4, 4, éd. et trad. J.-C. Guy (Sources chrétiennes 109), Paris 1965, 126-127.

28 *Règle de Babaï*, 19, éd. et trad. A. Vööbus, *Syriac and Arabic Documents regarding legislation relative to Syrian Asceticism* (Papers of the Estonian Theological Society in Exile 11), Stockholm 1960, 176-184, ici 182 : « It is not necessary that he takes the trouble after this to make a gift to the brothers ; and even if he has this ready, this shall not be accepted from him ».

29 *Testament de Matthieu Ier de Constantinople*, éd. Konidaris-Manaphes, 490-491, trad. Talbot, [B15], 1647.

30 Basile de Césarée, *Grandes règles*, 9, *PG* 31, 941B, trad. Lèbe, 73.

quarante pièces, avec le but précis d'acheter des livres spirituels, tandis que le reste est donné aux pauvres[31]. Probablement dans la même période, un solitaire égyptien s'adresse à un certain prêtre en le sollicitant à donner l'habit monastique à son disciple Dios, porteur du message. Le texte, conservé sur un ostracon du monastère d'apa Phoibammon, mentionne qu'une dette antérieure du prêtre sera effacée à cette occasion[32]. Euphrosyne d'Alexandrie offre cinq cents *nomismata* à son entrée au monastère[33], tandis que la jeune fille d'un sénateur, qui reçoit l'habit monastique dans le désert de Juda, laisse au vieil ascète qui l'avait tonsurée trois cents *nomismata* pour son habit et pour deux livres, probablement l'Ancien et le Nouveau Testament[34]. Au VIIIe siècle, Michel le Syncelle conduit sa mère et ses deux sœurs dans un monastère à Jérusalem auquel il consacre beaucoup de leurs propriétés. Puis il distribue ses biens aux pauvres en gardant pour lui une petite somme d'argent, donnée à l'higoumène de Saint-Sabas, pour la distribuer selon les nécessités du monastère[35].

À Byzance, le deuxième concile de Nicée réaffirme l'ancienne tradition selon laquelle toutes les admissions des candidats devaient être faites sans cadeaux préalables à l'higoumène ou à tout autre membre de la direction du monastère. La coutume entre aussi dans la législation civile[36]. Les biens que le novice apportait à l'entrée ou que les parents donnaient en dot à leur enfant restaient la propriété du monastère selon la promesse du candidat, « que celui-ci reste ou quitte le monastère, à condition que l'higoumène n'ait rien à se reprocher pour le départ »[37].

L'hagiographie nous présente plusieurs cas. Après la mort de son époux, Théodora de Thessalonique partage ses biens en trois parties : la première est donnée aux pauvres pour le repos de l'âme de son mari défunt, une deuxième partie de cent monnaies d'or est apportée à son entrée au monastère, le reste et trois servantes sont offerts seulement après sa tonsure[38]. Les gens aisés arrivés à Iviron au temps de

31 *Vie d'Épiphane de Chypre* (*BHG* 596), 8, *PG* 41, 33A.

32 *O.CrumST*, n° 310, 83-84 = *O.Vind.Copt.*, n° 287, trad. W.C. Till, « Zu Crums Varia Coptica », *Le Muséon* 53 (1940) 111-122, ici 119.

33 *Vie d'Euphrosyne* (*BHG* 625), 10, éd. A. Boucherie, « Vita Sanctae Euphrosynae », *Analecta Bollandiana* 2 (1883) 195-205, ici 200.

34 B. Flusin, J. Paramelle, « De Syncletica in deserto Iordanis (*BHG* 1318w) », 11, *Analecta Bollandiana* 100 (1982) 313-314.

35 *Vie de Michel le Syncelle* (*BHG* 1296), 3, éd. et trad. M. Cunningham, *The Life of Michael the Synkellos* (Belfast Byzantine Texts and Translations 1), Belfast 1991, 48-51.

36 *Peira*, 15, 15, in *JGR*, IV, 54.

37 *Concile de Nicée II, Canons*, 19, in *Discipline générale antique*, vol. 1/1 : *Les canons des conciles œcuméniques*, éd. et trad. P.P. Joannou, 278-279.

38 *Vie de Théodora de Thessalonique* (*BHG* 1737), 20, éd. et trad. S. Paschalidis, *Ὁ Βίος τῆς ὁσιομυροβλύτιδος Θεοδώρας τῆς ἐν Θεσσαλονίκῃ. Διήγηση περὶ τῆς μεταθέσεως τοῦ Τιμίου*

l'higoumène Euthyme, au début du XIe siècle, font aussi des dons importants. Parmi eux, un diacre « fils de gens illustres, qui avait donné au monastère une somme d'argent non négligeable »[39] et Athanase P'eritureli et son fils, propriétaires d'un monastère à Karyès, pour lequel Iviron obtient 340 pièces d'or. Quant à Syméon le Nouveau Théologien, sa famille amène deux livres d'or (= 144 *nomismata*) pour l'entrée de leur fils à Stoudios, dans la deuxième moitié du Xe siècle[40]. Selon la *Vie* de Léontios de Jérusalem, un certain Anastase, devenu moine à Patmos, amène avec lui des livres sacrés, des icônes, et une grande somme d'argent, « en se consacrant lui-même et tout ce qu'il avait à Dieu »[41].

Les *typika* monastiques attestent également cette pratique. Selon Athanase de Lavra, les dons sont acceptés[42]. Le *typikon* de la *Théotokos* Évergétis précise qu'il est interdit de demander des dons, « car il ne faut pas trafiquer la grâce de Dieu », mais ils étaient acceptés lorsque les candidats les apportaient de leur propre gré[43]. Le texte sera souvent repris dans les *typika* ultérieurs[44]. La *diataxis* de Michel At-

---

Λειψάνου τῆς Ὁσίας Θεοδώρας, Thessalonique 1991, 104-106, trad. anglaise A.-M. Talbot, « Life of St. Theodora of Thessalonike », in EAD., *Holy Women*, 159-237, ici 181.

39 *Vie de Jean et Euthyme d'Iviron*, 51, trad. B. Martin-Hisard, « La Vie de Jean et Euthyme et le statut du monastère des Ibères sur l'Athos », *Revue des études byzantines* 49 (1991) 67-142, ici 117 ; *Ibid.*, 54, 118 ; 57, 119.

40 *Vie de Syméon le Nouveau Théologien* (*BHG* 1692), 11, éd. I. Hausherr, trad. G. Horn, *Un grand mystique byzantin. Vie de Syméon le Nouveau Théologien (949-1022)* (Orientalia Christiana 12, n° 45), Rome 1928, 18-19.

41 *Vie de Léontios de Jérusalem* (*BHG* 985), 49, éd. et trad. D. Tsougarakis, *The Life of Leontios, Patriarch of Jerusalem* (Medieval Mediterranean 2), Leiden 1993, 88-89.

42 *Typikon de Lavra*, éd. P. Meyer, *Die Haupturkunden für Geschichte der Athosklöster*, Leipzig 1894, 102-122, ici 119, « *Typikon* of Athanasios the Athonite for the Lavra Monastery », *BMFD*, trad. G. Dennis, I, n° 13, 245-270, ici [49], 263.

43 *Typikon de la Théotokos* Évergétis, 37, éd. et trad. P. Gautier, « Le typikon de la Théotokos Évergétis », *Revue des études byzantines* 40 (1982) 5-101, ici 78-81 : « Ceux qu'on a jugé bon d'admettre, on ne les contraindra pas à verser une dot ou une offrande, car il ne faut pas trafiquer de la grâce de Dieu ou la vendre pour de l'argent ... Mais si quelqu'un qui va être tondu décide de son plein gré d'offrir quelque chose, on l'acceptera ».

44 *Typikon de la Théotokos Kécharitôménè*, 7, éd. et trad. P. Gautier, « Le typikon de la Théotokos Kécharitôménè », *Revue des études byzantines* 43 (1985) 5-165, ici 42-43 ; *Typikon de la Théotokos Kosmosôteira*, 55, éd. L. Petit, « Le Monastère de la Kosmosoteira près d'Aenos (1152) », *Izvestiia Russkago Archeologicheskago Instituta v Konstantinople (Bulletin de l'institut archéologique russe à Constantinople)* 13 (1908) 17-75, ici 47, trad. N. Patterson Ševčenko, « *Typikon* of the *Sevastokrator* Isaac Komnenos for the Monastery of the Mother of God *Kosmosoteira* near Bera », *BMFD*, II, n° 29, 782-858, ici 823-824 ; *Typikon de Phobéros*, 53[A], éd. A. Papadopoulos-Kerameus, *Noctes Petropolitanae*, Saint-Pétersbourg 1913, réimp. Leipzig 1976, 1-88, ici 64-65, trad. R. Jordan, « *Rule* of John for the Monas-

taliate ajoute que ces dons sont bienvenus lorsqu'il s'agit de « gens capables de rendre service à l'Église, ou de notaires, ou de secrétaires ». Les donations étaient ainsi utilisées en conformité avec l'intérêt immédiat du monastère : constructions, restaurations ou achats de terrains[45]. Sans imposer des règles, Lazare de Galèsion accepte l'entrée libre au monastère, mais il ne refuse pas les dons et n'impose pas un renoncement total aux biens pour ceux qui ne le désirent pas[46]. Selon le *typikon* de Machairas, le candidat apportait lui-même le don à l'autel le jour de sa tonsure ou il amenait seulement le document de donation[47].

Les exemples de dons faits à l'entrée au monastère sont nombreux dans les actes des grands monastères. Au VIIIe siècle, en Égypte, un certain Moïse donne à son entrée au monastère de Paul la somme de 20 sous pour être distribuée aux pauvres après sa mort[48]. En 1012, grâce à son héritage consacré au monastère d'Iviron, un moine géorgien obtient le droit de mener une vie anachorétique[49]. Au XIIIe siècle, au monastère de Lembos, les moines Maxime Planitès, Théodore Gordatos et Lucas Tzouroulos donnent des biens importants à l'occasion de leur tonsure[50]. C'est aussi la procédure utilisée par Zoé Siropoulina à l'entrée

tery of St. John the Forerunner of *Phoberos* », *BMFD*, III, n° 30, 872-953, ici 929-930 ; *Typikon de Saint-Mamas*, 5, éd. S. Efstratiadis, « Τυπικὸν τῆς ἐν Κωνσταντινουπόλει Μονῆς τοῦ Ἁγίου μεγαλομάρτυρος Μάμαντος », Ἑλληνικά 1 (1928) 245-314, ici 267, trad. A. Bandy, « *Typikon* of Athanasios Philanthropenos for the Monastery of St. Mamas in Constantinople », *BMFD*, III, n° 32, 973-1041, ici 1000 ; *Ibid.*, 22, 279, trad. 1010 ; *Typikon d'Élegmoi*, 5, éd. A. Dmitrievski, *Описанiе литургическихъ рукописей хранящихся въ библiотекахъ православнаго Востока, I, III :* Τυπικά (*Description des manuscrits liturgiques de l'Orient orthodoxe, I, III : Typika*), Kiev 1895, Saint-Pétersbourg 1917, réimp. Hildesheim 1965, I, 715-769, ici 726, trad. A. Brandy, « *Typikon* of Nikephoros *Mystikos* for the Monastery of the Mother of God *ton Heliou Bomon* or *Elegmon* », *BMFD*, III, n° 33, 1042-1091, ici 1057 ; *Ibid.*, 22, 739, trad. 1067 ; *Typikon de Machairas*, 57-58, *Κυπριακά Τυπικά*, éd. I. Tsiknopoulos, Nicosia 1969, 1-68, ici 29-30, « *Rule* of Neilos, Bishop of Tamasia, for the Monastery of the Mother of God of *Machairas* in Cyprus », trad. A. Bandy, *BMFD*, III, n° 34, 1107-1175, ici 1140-1141.

45 *Diataxis de Michel Attaliate*, [28], éd. et trad. P. Gautier, « La Diataxis de Michel Attaliate », *Revue des études byzantines* 39 (1981) 5-143, ici 58-59 ; *Ibid.*, [30], 62-63.

46 *Vie de Lazare de Galèsion*, 192, éd. Delehaye, 566, trad. Greenfield, 282-283.

47 *Typikon de Machairas*, 58, éd. Tsiknopoulos, 29-30, trad. Bandy, 1140.

48 A. Schiller, *Ten Coptic Legal Texts*, New York 1932, 21. Cf. E. Wipszycka, « Le fonctionnement interne des monastères et des laures en Égypte du point de vue économique », *Journal of Juristic Papyrology* 31 (2001) 169-186, ici 176.

49 *Actes d'Iviron*, éds. J. Lefort-N. Oikonomidès-D. Papachryssanthou *et al.*, 4 voll. (Archives de l'Athos 14, 16, 18, 19), Paris 1985-1995, vol. 1, 17, 193-200.

50 *Actes de Lembos*, 20, éds. F. Miklosich-J. Müller, *Acta et diplomata graeca medii aevi sacra et profana*, Vienne 1860-1890, vol. 1, 1-289, ici 67 ; *Ibid.*, 58, 125-126 ; 69, 137.

au monastère de Néa Pétra, près de Volos[51]. Au XIVe siècle, Démétrios, fils de Nicolas Pechlambos, devient moine à Vatopédi avant sa mort, offrant au monastère deux terrains et une vigne en friche[52], tandis que Michel Kalamitzènos et son fils Denys font don au même monastère et pour le même but de quatre maisons à étage à Thessalonique[53]. Au moment de leur entrée, en 1328 et 1329, Georges Kalampakès et Théodore Sarakenos font d'importantes donations au monastère Saint-Jean-Prodrome de Serres[54].

En acceptant les dons, les monastères essaient souvent de garder le sens spirituel de ces offrandes. L'attention est orientée principalement sur la conduite monastique de celui qui les amène, car les dons ne doivent pas lui procurer d'avantages à l'intérieur de la communauté. Les supérieurs des monastères pacômiens de la fin du IVe siècle désiraient ainsi « que l'assurance de cette offrande ne le gonfle et qu'il ne daigne plus vivre à égalité avec des frères plus pauvres »[55]. Selon Athanase de Lavra, si les dons conduisent au souhait de certains avantages, ils seront offerts aux pauvres[56]. Le *typikon* de la *Théotokos* Évergétis critique la pensée répandue parmi les moines selon laquelle « celui qui a fait un versement vaut mieux que celui qui n'en a pas fait »[57]. Il faut toujours garder l'égalité entre les membres de la communauté, car « la dot détruit l'obéissance et engendre quantité de discordes ». Pour cette raison, Michel Attaliate semble préférer les candidats de condition modeste, mais d'une conduite monastique correcte[58]. Le *typikon* du Christ Pantocrator contient le même principe : il ne faut pas que les dons créent une distinction entre les différentes catégories sociales des frères :

> On ne demandera d'*apotagè* à personne, pour ne pas donner par ce moyen licence de recevoir au monastère n'importe qui, car la conduite de chacun, son degré d'instruction, son habileté dans les affaires et sa richesse en vertu seront

51 *Actes de la Théotokos Makrinitissa et Néa* Pétra, 27, éds. Miklosich-Müller, *Acta et diplomata*, vol. 4, 330-430, ici 395.

52 *Actes de Vatopédi*, 43/XXI, éds. J. Bompaire-J. Lefort-V. Kravari *et al.*, 2 voll. (Archives de l'Athos 21, 22), Paris 2001-2006, vol. 1, 254.

53 *Actes de Vatopédi*, 85, éds. Bompaire-Lefort-Kravari, vol. 2, 176-179.

54 *Actes de Saint-Jean-Prodrome de Serres*, in *Le Codex B du monastère Saint-Jean-Prodrome (Serres)*, éds. L. Bénou-P. Odorico, (Textes, Documents, Études sur le monde byzantin, néohellénique et balkanique 2), Paris 1998, vol. 1, 83, 158-159 ; *Ibid.*, 89, 164-165.

55 Jean Cassien, *Institutions cénobitiques*, 4, 4, éd. Guy, 126-127.

56 *Typikon de Lavra*, éd. Meyer, 119, trad. Dennis, [49], 263.

57 *Typikon de la Théotokos* Évergétis, 37, éd. Gautier, 80-81.

58 *Diataxis de Michel Attaliate*, [28], éd. Gautier, 58-59.

mieux estimés que de l'or ou des présents quelconques, et tous les frères feront l'objet d'une égale considération[59].

Des considérations de ce type sont également rencontrées dans d'autres *typika* : l'obéissance est plus importante que le don[60] ; il ne faut pas que le candidat soit reçu à cause du don qu'il offre ou d'une influence extérieure[61] ; celui qui avait apporté un don important doit se comporter comme il n'aurait apporté aucune contribution, respectant l'égalité et la règle commune[62]. En outre, la règle d'Attaliate impose une qualité « morale » des dons : ceux apportés par les querelleurs, chicaneurs, prétentieux, déloyaux ou cruels n'étaient pas acceptés[63].

Mais ce type de discours suggère que cette égalité parfaite des chances n'est pas toujours respectée et qu'il veut simplement combattre une pratique opposée bien répandue. Les dons offraient des privilèges aux aristocrates arrivés au monastère, car ils bénéficiaient d'un logement spécial ou de serviteurs[64]. Une stratification sociale à l'intérieur du monastère est toujours observée. Théodore Prodrome nous donne l'image d'une telle distinction : celui qui arrive au monastère avec dix livres d'or est traité d'une manière préférentielle par rapport à celui qui ne possède rien[65]. Au XIVe siècle, le *Testament* de Chariton de Kutlumus accepte que les Valaques qui voulaient devenir moines dans son monastère gardent une auto-

59 *Typikon du Christ Pantocrator*, [17], éd. et trad. P. Gautier, « Le typikon du Christ Sauveur Pantocrator », *Revue des études byzantines* 32 (1974) 26-130, ici 60-61.

60 *Typikon d'Areia*, M[10], éd. G. Chora, *Ἡ Ἁγία Μονὴ Ἀρείας*, Athènes 1975, 245-252, ici 242, trad. A.-M. Talbot, « *Memorandum* and *Typikon* of Leo, Bishop of Naulia, for the Monastery of the Mother of God in *Areia* », *BMFD*, III, n° 31, 954-972, ici 962 ; *Ibid.*, T[6], 247, trad. 966.

61 *Typikon d'Athanase Ier de Constantinople*, 7, trad. T. Miller, « *Rule* of Patriarch Athanasios I », *BMFD*, IV, n° 55, 1495-1504, ici 1502.

62 *Typikon de Lips*, 14, éd. H. Delehaye, *Deux typica de l'époque des Paléologues*, Bruxelles 1921, 106-136, ici 114, trad. A.-M. Talbot, « *Typikon* of Theodora Palaiologina for the Convent of Lips in Constantinople », *BMFD*, III, n° 39, 1254-1286, ici 1269 ; *Typikon de Manuel II Paléologue*, 1, 14-15, éd. D. Papachryssanthou, *Actes du Prôtaton* (Archives de l'Athos 7), Paris 1975, n° 13, 254-261, ici 257, trad. G. Dennis, « *Typikon* of Manuel II Palaiologos for the Monasteries of Mount Athos », *BMFD*, IV, n° 59, 1613-1624, ici 1618 ; *Ibid.*, 12, 68-70, 260, trad. 1621.

63 *Diataxis de Michel Attaliate*, [28], éd. Gautier, 58-59.

64 *Typikon de la Théotokos Kosmosôteira*, 55, éd. Petit, 47, trad. Patterson Ševčenko, 824 ; *Typikon de Saint-Mamas*, 26, éd. Efstratiadis, 282, trad. Bandy, 1012-1013.

65 Théodore Prodrome, *Contre les higoumènes*, 94-191, éd. et trad. H. Eideneier, *Ptochoprodromos*, Köln 1991, 139-175, ici 144, trad. française R. Bouchet, *Satires et parodies du Moyen Âge grec*, Paris 2012, 25-38, ici 27.

nomie par rapport à la communauté s'ils apportent des dons importants, suffisants pour leur entretien. Dans ce cas, le monastère leur assurait une pension fixe, et les moines avaient le droit d'organiser leur vie selon leurs préférences[66].

Un dernier aspect est lié à la possibilité de réclamer les dons apportés par ceux qui pensaient abandonner la vie monastique. Les textes normatifs veulent bien sûr éviter cette situation et mettent en garde les supérieurs. Jean Cassien avait déjà pensé que l'abandon du monastère est encore une raison pour refuser le don à l'entrée[67]. Les principes invoqués par les *typika* byzantins sont simples : « ce qui a été consacré à Dieu une fois pour toutes ne peut être repris »[68] et « c'est un sacrilège d'essayer de prendre comme sien le don que le moine a apporté à son entrée »[69].

2.3. Imposition du don

Il y avait également le cas où le don était obligatoire. Nous avons déjà remarqué le lien étroit entre la consécration monastique et la consécration des dons au monastère. Parfois, cette correspondance est exprimée plus clairement. Dans l'un de ses canons monastiques, Schenoute demande aux candidats qu'ils renoncent à tous leurs biens en faveur de la communauté[70]. La même pensée est rencontrée dans les *Novelles* de Justinien et de Léon VI, qui imposent que toute la fortune des candidats sans enfants arrive au monastère[71]. Sans avoir de nombreuses situa-

---

66 *Testament de Chariton de Kutlumus*, in *Actes de Kutlumus*, éd. P. Lemerle (Archives de l'Athos ²2), Paris 1988, n° 29, 113-121, ici 120, 119-122, trad. G. Dennis, « *Testaments* of Chariton for the Monastery of Christ Savior of Koutloumousi on Mount Athos », *BMFD*, IV, n° 51, 1408-1432, ici [B16], 1423.

67 Jean Cassien, *Institutions cénobitiques*, 4, 4, éd. Guy, 126-127 : « Mais c'est aussi pour éviter que, si cette vanité l'empêche de descendre jusqu'à l'humilité du Christ et qu'il ne puisse persévérer sous la règle du monastère, il ne cherche, en le quittant une fois devenu tiède, à récupérer avec un esprit sacrilège et à exiger, non sans faire tort du monastère, ce que au début de son renoncement il y avait apporté, enflammé de ferveur spirituelle. »

68 *Typikon de la Théotokos* Évergétis, 37, éd. Gautier, 80-81.

69 *Typikon de Manuel II Paléologue*, 1, 15-20, éd. Papachryssanthou, 257-258, trad. Dennis, 1618.

70 Schenoute, *Canons*, 243, éd. Layton, 190-191 : « And any who comes to us to become a monastic whether male or female, shall first renounce all the things that they possess unto the Diakonia. » Cf. B. Layton, « Rules, Patterns, and the Exercise of Power in Shenute's Monastery: The Problem of World Replacement and Identity Maintenance», *Journal of Early Christian Studies* 15/1 (2007) 45-73, ici 60 et n. 85.

71 Justinien, *Novelles*, 123, 38 = *Basiliques*, 4, 1, 9 : « Si un individu de l'un ou de l'autre sexe choisit la vie monastique, et entre dans un monastère sans avoir d'enfants, nous

tions concrètes, nous remarquons que, selon la règle d'Attaliate, le jour de la profession monastique les candidats étaient invités de verser dix *nomismata* pour « l'encens, la table des frères et le reste »[72]. Dans d'autres cas, ils devaient payer au moins le cierge[73]. En outre, même si Attaliate n'impose pas les dons à l'entrée au monastère, il y avait une exception notable. En affirmant que le couvent est réservé aux eunuques, le fondateur précise aussi que les hommes barbus qui appartenaient à sa famille, âgés de plus de cinquante ans, de mœurs irréprochables et qui apportaient un bien foncier étaient aussi reçus dans la communauté. Dans ce cas, le don devient en réalité une condition pour l'entrée[74]. Lorsqu'un monastère était donné en *charisticariat*, les dots étaient souvent gardées par les *charisticaires*[75], parfois grâce au droit donné d'une manière contractuelle par les propriétaires[76]. Plus clairement, à l'arrivée au monastère de Sabas, Lazare de Galèsion est obligé de payer douze *nomismata*, règle en vigueur pour les novices et pour les moines étrangers. Après sa fuite dans le désert, lorsqu'il revient au monastère, l'higoumène l'accepte grâce à l'insistance de l'archidiacre du monastère d'Euthyme, et après avoir payé encore douze *nomismata* « comme à la première entrée »[77]. La même règle était valable en 1220 dans un monastère d'Épire, qui demandait 24 *nomismata* à l'entrée dans la communauté[78].

On peut imaginer que cette liberté d'agir a conduit parfois à des abus. Au temps du deuxième concile de Nicée, les excès des higoumènes étaient nombreux, car un canon exprime l'inquiétude des participants concernant ce sujet :

> La passion honteuse de l'amour de l'argent s'est tellement répandue parmi les chefs des églises et des monastères, que certains hommes et femmes parmi ceux qu'on es-

ordonnons que ses biens appartiennent à ce monastère. » ; Léon VI, *Novelles*, 5, éd. Noailles-Dain, 26-27 : « Une fois tonsuré, on ne doit plus leur permettre de faire un testament, mais toute leur fortune doit aller à l'Église dans laquelle ils ont reçu la tonsure ».

72 *Diataxis de Michel Attaliate*, [28], éd. Gautier, 58-59.

73 Théodore Prodrome, *Contre les higoumènes*, 97, éd. Eideneier, 144, trad. Bouchet, 27.

74 *Diataxis de Michel Attaliate*, [30], éd. Gautier, 64-65.

75 J. Darrouzès, « Dossier sur le charisticariat », in *Polychronion : Festschrift Franz Dölger zum 75. Geburstag*, éd. P. Wirth, Heidelberg 1966, 150-165, n° 6, 160.21-25, trad. 164 et n. 13.

76 *JGR*, I, 347 (*Coll.* IV, *Nov.* 37).

77 *Vie de Lazare de Galèsion*, 16-17, éd. Delehaye, 514, trad. Greenfield, 96-98.

78 A. Papadopoulos-Kérameus, « Συμβολὴ εἰς τὴν ἱστορίαν τῆς ἀρχιεπισκοπῆς Ἀχρίδος », in *Sbornik statej posvjaščennych počitatieljam akademiku i zaslužennomu professoru V. I. Lamanskomu*, Saint-Pétersbourg 1907, I, 227-250, ici 244, cf. Smyrilis, *La fortune des grands monastères byzantins*, 137 et n. 310.

time pieux, oubliant le précepte de Dieu, se laissent induire en erreur et font payer à prix d'argent la réception des candidats à la vie cléricale ou à la vie monastique.[79]

La *Vie* de Cyrille le Philéote mentionne également que le supérieur qui recevait de l'argent des postulants pour être admis dans le monastère devait être déposé[80]. Dans la même période, l'empereur Alexis Comnène essaie de réglementer le problème, interdisant ce don[81]. Mais la coutume reste en vigueur et les efforts législatifs n'arrivent pas à l'annihiler. Au XIVe siècle, le patriarche Athanase Ier de Constantinople demande encore à ses métropolites d'excommunier celui qui avait reçu de l'argent pour la tonsure d'un moine[82].

CONCLUSION

On constate donc une large variété de pratiques, allant du refus du don jusqu'à son imposition. Néanmoins, la coutume la plus répandue est de ne pas imposer le don, laissant à la latitude de chacun l'initiative et le montant de l'offrande. La pratique nous semble tout à fait normale, compte tenu de la diversité sociale des candidats à la vie monastique : on ne peut imposer la même règle à la fois pour les aristocrates et pour les pauvres. En fonction à la fois de sa ligne de conduite spirituelle et de ses richesses, chaque monastère prescrit une procédure pour la réception des postulants et pour les dons qu'ils doivent offrir.

Sans imposer de règles claires, le monachisme byzantin a toujours laissé une certaine indépendance aux communautés locales au sujet de l'organisation interne et de la vie pratique. La diversité des procédures appliquées aux postulants n'est ainsi que l'un des aspects concrets de cette liberté.

Abstract

This study focuses on the 'economic' elements of the monastic commitment in the Byzantine monastic milieu. It provides an analysis of admission procedures encountered in different types of sources: legal texts, monastic typika, and lives of saints. According to those texts, the donations were forbidden, as well as ac-

79 *Concile de Nicée II, Canons*, 19, éd. Joannou, 277-278.

80 *Vie de Cyrille le Philéote* (*BHG* 468), 39, 10, éd. et trad. E. Sargologos, *La vie de saint Cyrille le Philéote, moine byzantin († 1100)* (Subsidia Hagiographica 39), Bruxelles 1964, 173.

81 *JGR*, I, 346-348 (*Coll.* IV, *Nov.* 37).

82 *Les Regestes des actes du Patriarcat de Constantinople, I : Les actes des Patriarches, IV : Les Regestes de 1208 à 1309*, éd. V. Laurent, Paris 1971, n° 1747/23, 527.

cepted, and even required. Trying to distinguish between reality, literary mimesis, and rhetoric, the study provides some answers on the motivation of the donation, on the time when it was brought, on the amount. Regional monastic contexts and social position of the applicant are also taken into question.

MONKS AND MONEY IN THE EARLY MODERN MUSCOWY: VOW OF POVERTY AND MONASTIC TESTAMENTS

Anastasia Preobrazhenskaya

Preserved from the seventeenth century, a corpus of documents that relates to Muscovite monasticism is vast and embraces a range of manifold texts such as acts, literary works, formal and official records, correspondence and testaments[1]. The latter bring to the foreground various issues of interest, both for a historian and a philologist. Above all, the very fact of an ascetic monk legally bequeathing money and possessions and documenting it in a will demonstrates a certain gap between formal monastic rules, which on a regular basis included the vow of poverty and non-possession, and real monastic practices. On the one hand, as we see from archived sources, it was not uncommon for a monk to compose and get approved a testament, thus bringing his worldly life into order before death; on the other hand, these monastic testaments were obviously to come into a conflict with a holy order of testator and with existing monastic rules, either oral or written. My principal goal in this article is to enhance our understanding of practical and conceptual aspects of monastic life of the seventeenth-century Muscovy through discussing real practices of observation, neglection, and re-interpretation of the vow of poverty and non-possession by individual monks, as represented in their testaments – acts of last will. The study focuses on a peculiar document – a testament of a monk Simeon of Polotsk (1629-1680), a court poet and preacher of the Tzars Aleksei Mikhailovich (1629-1676) and Fedor Alekseevich (1661-1682). Simeon's testament illustrates one of the ways in which monks used to reconcile worldly riches with keeping the vow and gives a glimpse of the everyday life of a monk, highlighting the ways in which money was earned and spent in monasteries.

Anastasia Preobrazhenskaya, PhD candidate in Russian and Comparative Literature at National Research University Higher School of Economics.

1 For a digitalized corpus of seventeenth-century texts see for example "Vostochnaya Literatura" [Eastern Literature]. Available at: http://www.vostlit.info/Texts/Dokumenty/Russ/xvii.htm [access: 12-09-2016].

1. XVIITH-CENTURY MONKS AND MONASTERIES: INCOME, POSSESSIONS, AND WEALTH

In the Orthodox monastic tradition, a vow of poverty and non-possession is one of three vows taken by novices when tonsured, and one of the essential maxims of monastic life. The perception of the vow amongst monastics and Church leaders changed dramatically over centuries and local traditions. Monastic rules of pre-Petrine Russia demonstrate various attitudes towards the vow – from a complete and absolute non-possession imposed on an individual monk to tolerating large monasteries becoming influential economic actors. Whilst no universal monastic rule existed and codes of conduct were often oral, defined by custom and tradition, real monastic practices of dealing with earnings, income, money, and possessions could and did tremendously differ from theoretical conceptions and ideas. The everyday life of individual monks and monasteries as institutions included various economic activities, some of which could sometimes go far beyond vital necessity and earning a living.

In general, pre-Petrine Russian monasteries had two principal sources of income, that varied greatly depending on the epoch: they were monastery estates and state provision. Chantries, contributions of newly accepted novices and monks; private donations coming from the royal family, nobility and peasants also formed significant, though unstable and highly unpredictable earnings. Famous and widely known convents received more donations while small and less famed monasteries often experienced a lack of money and had to survive by trade, craft, and occasional donations.

By the second half of the seventeenth century, large convents were growing in power as active economic actors – they owned and managed large estates, entered into lawsuits, maintained and augmented their monetary and material wealth. Though a monetary profit was not the goal of a monastery activity, certain convents would often not only trade but lend out money to peasants and lower nobility, usually with interest. Receipts and payment books of Russian monasteries of the sixteenth and seventeenth centuries preserve numerous debt documents from which we learn that monasteries, that acted as corporations, and even individual monks [primarily Fathers Superior, treasurers, cellarers, but sometimes also common monks and monk-priests] lent money to people living around and thus earned money and accumulated wealth.

The Moscow Novodevichii nunnery could serve as a vivid example of such a convent of the discussed period. Run by energetic Mothers Superior from Belarus, the nunnery, where dwelt more than 150 nuns, enjoyed vast estates over which it entered various lawsuits with other landlords. As sources show, one of the lawsuits, over a fishing holding, was finally lost by the nunnery, but the procedure lasted for four years and during that period the fishing holding was in the use of the nunnery[2].

2. MONASTIC TESTAMENTS OF THE XVIITH CENTURY TRADITIONS AND INNOVATIONS

Interpretations of the vow of poverty and non-possession and attitudes towards it are hard to study due to the character of sources we have at hand. Information provided by respectively well-preserved official documents on the topic, such as ecclesiastical compilations of laws, decrees of Patriarchs and so on, give a one-sided view of the problem since they record an ideology and prescriptive; in other words – how it should be, that was not necessarily equal to the actual situation. Financial documents of convents and monasteries contain factual data, with no explanation or interpretation, and could serve as supportive evidence only. Compared to the first group of sources, these documents stand on the opposite side of the scale, for they reflect how the things were, leaving aside ideological matters. Private documents such as memoirs, diaries, and correspondence that could help in bridging the gap between the two, are almost inaccessible for the Russian seventeenth century for two principal reasons: non-occurence of these genres in the Russian literary culture of the time and low preservation of sporadic private writings such as letters, for example. The only sources that could serve our goal in understanding private lives and the economic behaviour of monks and clergy are their testaments[3] or written last wills.

These fragmentary studied and highly informative documents reflect real, private monastic practices of dealing with money and possessions in the context of the vow of poverty and non-possession. Monastic testaments and testaments of clerical authorities, together with testaments of peasants and lower nobility, form one of the most numerous groups of preserved wills from the seventeenth century. Part of these documents originates from South-Western regions

2 M.V. Chistiakova, *Monakhini s «Beloi Rosi» v Novodevich'em monastyre* [Nuns from «White Russian» in Novodevichii nunnery], Moscow 2000, 59.

3 In literature testaments are often called «the most private documents». Look Iu.M. Eskin, «Zaveshchanie kniazia Dmitriia Pozharskogo» [The Testament of kniaz' Dmitrii Pozharskii], *Otechestvennaia istoriia* 1 (2000) 144. U. Augustyniak, «Wizerunek Krzysztofa II Radziwiłła jako magnata-ewangelika w świete jego testamentów», *Przegląd historyczny* 81(1990) 461-477.

of Muscovy, i. e. from the territories of present-time Ukraine and Belarus. It should be noted here, that monastic life in the mentioned territories considerably differed from that in the Muscovy state. Whilst experiencing a long and rather strong influence of the Catholic church, Orthodox clergy in these territories developed an individual tradition, that in some aspects reflected those of the Polish Catholic clergy.

Clerical status of a testator in many respects predefined linguistic layout and juridical aspect of a testament. Wills of common monks and clerical hierarchs differed greatly, with the former being private acts and the latter – public documents. Vow of poverty and holy order together with a significant position within the church hierarchy imposed more limitations on contents of testaments of metropolitans and Fathers Superior than on testaments of regular monks. Obligatory usage of certain document structures and linguistic formulae was prescribed mainly by a custom, not by a testator's status.

Thus, testaments of Church and monastic leaders were characterised as «publicistic in nature and socially important in contents and goal, since they were addressed to public»[4]. These testaments were not private acts, but rather socially important documents. Their title, «a spiritual charter», [*dukhovnaia gramota*] closely reflected their contents – almost purely spiritual in character. Testaments of the Church and monastery authorities could embrace, besides spiritual instructions blessings, and forgiveness, commandments to fellow clergy and congregation[5], or even to a secular government; rules for a convent or a monastery; last requests of the testators. Feodosii, the Father Superior of Maniavskii v chest' Vozdvizheniia Kresta Gospodnia Skete monastery, divided his testament into twenty chapters containing instructions about love, humility, placability, obedience, patience, various crafst and making bread[6]. Money matters were usually marginally mentioned, sometimes with the reference to inventories, which co-existed with testaments and were meant for economic and household arrangements. The Russian Patriarch Ioakim in his vast testament wrote about his cell belongings, naming among them only «money and clothes»[7].

4 Panich T.V, «Drevnerusskie dukhovnye zaveshchaniia XV–XVII vv. v agiograficheskom povestvovanii» [Old-Russian Testaments of the XVth-XVIIth Centuries in Autobiographic Narrative], *Gumanitarnye nauki Sibiri* 3 (2013) 34.

5 Panich, «Drevnerusskie dukhovnye zaveshchaniia XV–XVII vv. v agiograficheskom povestvovanii», 34.

6 See *Akty, otnosiashchiesia k istorii Iuzhnozapadnoi Rusi* [Acts related to History of South-West Russia], ed. P.A. Petrushevich, Lviv 1868, 56-98.

7 I.E. Zabelin, *Zhitie i zaveshchanie sviateishego patriarkha moskovskogo Ioakima* [Life

Testaments of Muscovite monks from the seventeenth century primarily dealt with personal items [clothes, dishes, sometimes books] and debts: money they owed to somebody and money owed to them; funds collected in such a way were supposed to be spent on funeral ceremony. For example, an elderly monk Iosif Koptev from Prilutskii monastery wrote in his testament in 1608: «And I, an elderly monk Iosif, do not owe anything to anybody, I do not have any debt, onerous or nor»[8].

In the seventeenth century, under the influence of Baroque and West European, particularly Polish, cultural traditions, testaments of clergy and laity began to change, acquiring features unusual for the traditional Old-Russian style. Now testaments were perceived is an indispensable attribute of the conception of *ars bene moriendi* – good, or proper, death of a faithful Christian. It was believed that a person who remembered about death during all his life and who thus did not sin, was well-prepared for the eternal life. Written wills allowed a person to finalise and put into order all their worldly deeds and to prepare for an after-life. Testaments as literary and official texts embodied two conflicting spheres of human life – material and spiritual. While *dispositio* (distributions made by the testator) formed an economic core of the testament, preamble and conclusion framed money matters with the testator's confession and repentance. Confessional introduction combined with a careful, business-like listing of funds, belongings, beneficiaries, and distributions constitute the conceptual nature of the testament as a genre, providing a rich source for studying. It is interesting to note, that Muscovite monks and monastic leaders who usually served as mediators in transfer of a new, Baroque art style from West Europe and Poland to Russia, almost escaped its influence themselves, and only those who were close to an ecclesiastical and secular elite, assimilated new style late in the seventeenth century.

3. SIMEON OF POLOTSK: A MONK AT THE TZAR'S COURT

The second half of the seventeenth century witnessed several waves of population migration to Muscovy from regions of present-time Belarus and Ukraine, caused by often military campaigns and religious instability. At that time, Polish

and Testament of the Holy Patriarch Ioakim], Saint-Petersburg 1879, 113.

8 Arkheograficheskaia komissiia, *Akty iuridicheskie, ili sobranie form starinnogo deloproizvodstva* [Juridical Acts, or a Collection of Forms of Ancient Records], Saint-Petersburg 1838, 459.

traditions were coming into vogue at the court of the Russian Tzar, and educated and crafted migrants from the Polish-Lithuanian Commonwealth (Rzeczpospolita) were particularly welcomed by the Muscovy elite.

At that time, many convents and individual monks moved to Moscow «at the Tzar's name» (the phrase literary meant «with the Tzar's permission»). The large Epiphany convent of Kuteino, that played an important role in the cultural life of the South-West region, was relocated to Muscovy together with its printing facilities. With the blessing of the Russian Patriarch Nikon[9] part of brethren, the Father Superior and the printing facility of the convent moved to Valdaiskii Iverskii Monastery. The monastery's printing facility was later moved to the Moscow Printing House (Pechatnyi Dvor).

Individual monks, with the permission of their Fathers Superior and the Patriarch, or often even invited by the Tzar or his courtiers, moved to Moscow in search of a better life. However, after the campaign, when Malorossja was annexed to Russia, relocations for monks was simplified, and many of them moved to Muscovy monasteries even without special permissions[10]. In 1656, during his Riga war campaign, the Russian Tzar Aleksei Mikhailovich visited many monasteries and convents in Belarus, including the Kuteino Epiphany monastery and the Polotsk Epiphany monastery. Two wood carvers were invited into the service of the Muscovite Tzar from the Kuteino monastery. In Polotsk, the Tzar Aleksei Mikhailovich met a young and well-educated monk, Simeon Petrovskii-Sitnianovich who taught in the primary school at the Polotsk Epiphany monastery. Together with the Father Superior, other brethren, and school students, Simeon gave to the Tzar a welcome oratory address, composed in a Polish Baroque style. Aleksei Mikhailovich enjoyed the performance, and several years later Simeon relocated to Moscow, where he became the first Russian court poet and preacher.

A monk Simeon Petrovskii-Sitnianovich, Samuil by his secular name, was known to his contemporaries and researchers as Simeon of Polotsk, the first in Russia court poet. Simeon was one of the most unique figures at the Muscovy Tzar court of the last quarter of the seventeenth century. Born in Polotsk, Belarus in 1629, he got his education in Kyiv and then in a college somewhere abroad

9 S.E. Somov, *Orthodox Convents and Monasteries of Belarus*, Minsk 2003, 91-92. Available at: http://orda.of.by/.lib/pmb/3 [access: 25-08-2016].

10 K.V. Kharlampovich, *Malorossiiskoe vliianie na velikorusskuiu tserkovnuiu zhizn'* [Malorussian influence on Muscovite Church Life], 1, Kazan 1914, 251.

[presumably Vilno college in the Grand Duchy of Lithuania][11] and, back to Polotsk in 1656, he took his vows and was accepted as an instructor at a school of the Epiphany Monastery.

Simeon's social status at the feudal and still in many respects medieval court of the Muscovy Tzar was far from being common. Throughout his life Simeon remained in the status of a hieromonk, or a monk-priest, one of the lowest positions in the monastery hierarchy. Nevertheless, when in Moscow he was appointed a teacher of the royal children, he got a permission to found his own typography, where he printed books without patriarchal licence, and was admitted to the selected company of boyars and Church authorities.

His financial situation and behaviour, examined in the context of his holy order and therefore – of his vow of poverty and non-possession, deserve a special attention, since they demonstrate how monastic rules could be accommodated to real practices and life style. Unlike other monks, Simeon did not rely for his living on the Zaikonospasskii monastery [a monastery he was assigned to when in Moscow]. We know from Simeon's petition letters to the Tzar[12] that he received a modest monetary allowance. In addition to that, Simeon was entitled to a material pension that included everything necessary for living such as food, forage, paper and so on. It is also possible to suggest that Simeon may have received some monetary aid from his home Polotsk Epiphany monastery. In the *intitulatio* of his testament Simeon states: «I, a sinful servant of God, Simeon Petrovskii-Sitnianovich *a monk-priest of the Polotsk monastery of the Saint God's Epiphany*»[13] [*cursive is mine*]. In the seventeenth century, monks could travel to other convents and another places with the permission of a Father Superior and stay there for a defined period of time; however, Simeon's relocation was not a mere visit, or a trip, or a pilgrimage – he moved to Moscow in order to stay there for the rest of his life. In that case, the juridical aspect of such relocation is rather unclear – did he continue to be formally affiliated with the Polotsk monastery where he took his vows? What then was his status at the Moscow Zaikonospasskii monastery? Was he allowed to take up any post in that monastery [some of

11 A.N. Robinson, *Simeon Polotskii i ego knigoizdatel'skaia deiatel'nost'* [Simeon of Polotsk and his Book-printing Work], Moscow 1982, 9.

12 Pis'ma Simeona Polotskogo [Letter of Simeon of Polotsk], *Vestnik Evropy* 162 part 17 (1828) 43.

13 State Historical museum, Moscow. Department of manuscripts. Collection of the count A. S. Uvarov, № 247-4° (GIM OR Uvar. sobr. №247-4°).Testament of Simeon of Polotsk. f. 10 r. Hereinafter the folios from the manuscript are indicated in brackets in the text. Translation is mine.

Simeon's biographers state that he was the head of the monastery[14] or even a Father Superior][15] In any case, the position of Simeon, as well as his financial situation, in the Moscow society of the second half of the seventeenth century was unique; and preserved sources about Simeon's life in Moscow contain precious information on the vow of poverty and real monastic practices.

4. «LET NOT MY VICIOUS POSSESSIONS PERISH VICIOUSLY»

Unfortunately, only few documents concerning the material side of Simeon's life survived until our day. They are limited to his epistolary legacy [more than 200 various letters and epistles[16]] with petition letters to the Tzar containing requests for money and food allowance being the most informative[17]; two records from the court chronicle[18] about gifts Simeon got from the Tzar; and finally, the testament of Simeon – a unique document, that provides a glimpse at his economic practices in the context of the monastic vow of poverty.

There are two known copies of the document, all dating back to roughly the same time period, from 1679 to the very end of the seventeenth century[19]. Both are scribal copies without seals and signatures, no original document is known. The first copy has been known to researchers from the second half of

14 In the pre-Petrine Russia we have several terms that stand for a Father Superior; hegumen, archimandrite and a monastery builder. The latter was used to indicate a head person of a monastery who contributed much to the monastery construction or whose monastery was under the command of another convent. Here in the article we use the term «head of the monastery» for the matter of simplicity. The difference between a hegumen and archimandrite was recorded only in the eighteenth century, when monasteries were divided into three classes, and Fathers Superior of the lowest class convents were called hegumens. Again, for the matter of simplicity, the term Father Superior is used in the article.

15 A. Kovalev, *Istoricheskoe opisanie Zaikonospasskogo monastyria v Moskve* [Historic Description of the Zaikonospasskii monastery in Moscow], Moscow 1887. P.M. Stroev, *Spiski ierarkhov i nastoiatelei monastyrei Rossiiskoi tserkvi* [Lists of hierarchs and Fathers Superior of the Russian Church], Saint-Petersburg 1877, 158.

16 State Historical museum, Moscow. Department of manuscripts. Synodal collection, №130-2° (GIM OR Sin. sobr. №130-2°).

17 1828. Pis'ma Simeona Polotskogo [Letter of Simeon of Polotsk], 43.

18 *Dopolneniia k Tomu III-mu dvortsovykh razriadov* [Supplement to the 3rd Volume of the Court Records], ed. II otdelenie sobstvennoi Ee Imperatorskogo Velichestva Kantseliarii, Saint-Petersburg 1854, 474.

19 State Historical museum, Moscow. Department of manuscripts. Collection of count A. S. Uvarov, №247-4° (GIM OR Uvar. sobr. №247-4°).

the nineteenth century[20]. I found the second copy[21], from manuscript №167-4°, collection of the count A. S. Uvarov, State Historical museum, Moscow, that was written presumably later than the copy in the manuscript №247-4°, and was copied from another draft version of the testament to serve as a sample [numerals were written there as figures, various titles and names were abbreviated].

From the literary point of view, the layout and genre of Simeon's testament stands out from Muscovy monastic and clergy testaments of the time. Presumably, the structural and linguistic layout of the testament, chosen by Simeon, originates in the South-West Russian [Ukrainian and Belarussian] and Polish traditions. Unlike the wills of Muscovite Church and monastery authorities, which were discussed above, testaments of metropolitans and Fathers Superior from the South-West Russian territories combined both spiritual and money matters in a single text. For example, the last will of the Father Superior Iliia Torskii had both distributions and didactic instructions for his brethren[22]. This tradition of composing a testament was brought to Muscovy by relocating monks and was partly adopted by a Muscovite clergy elite and some regular monks. Simeon's testament has a theological and a slightly biographical introduction, a preamble, and a clearly structured executive part that deals with money bequeathed to funeral matters [funeral ceremony, charity, chantries], etiquette contributions to convents and monasteries, monetary donations to family and friends, and personal belongings bequeathed to various parties. The testament concludes with a damnation to those who would dare not to obey the testator's last will.

20 I. A. Tatarskii, *Simeon Polotskii: (Ego zhizn' i deiatel'nost')* [Simeon of Polotsk: (His Life and Work)], Moscow 1886, 319-322.

21 For detail see my articles A.A. Preobrazhenskaia, «Prezhde smerti naipache vnezapnyia i naprasnyia»: dukhonaia gramota Simeona Polotskogo [«Before Death Sudden and Vain»: a Testament of Simeon of Polotsk], *Drevniaia Rus'. Voprosy medievistiki* 2 (2015) 115-132. Available at: http://www.drevnyaya.ru/vyp/2015_2/part_10.pdf [access: 28-08-2016]. A.A. Preobrazhenskaia, *K interpretatsii odnoi dukhovnoi gramoty XVII veka: chastnaia zhizn' Simeona Polotskogo* [To the Interpretation of One Testament: Private Life of Simeon of Polotsk], ed. Srednevekovaia lichnost' v pis'mennykh i arkheologicheskikh istochnikakh: Moskovskaia Rus', Rossiiskaia Imperiia i ikh sosedi: materialy nauch. konf. Institut rossiiskoi istorii RAN, Beliaev L. A. [Medieval Personality in Written and Archaeological Sources: Muscovite Rus', Russian Empire and their Neighbors: Proceedings of an Academic Conference of the Institute for Russian History of Russian Academy of Science], Moscow 2016, 178-183.

22 O. Bodianskii, *Letopisets o pervom zachatii i sozdanii sviatyia obiteli monastyria Gustynskogo v leto bytiia mira 7108, ot voploshcheniia zhe boga slova tysiashcha shestisotnoe* [Chronicle about the First Origins of Gustynskii Monastery in year AM 7108, in year AD 1600], Moscow 1848, 46.

The preamble of Simeon's testament is not extensive and includes a laconic discussion of the testator's possessions and funds, supported by elaborately selected quotations from the Bible[23] and a work by Saint Augustine[24]. The preamble defines an emotional and conceptual mood of the whole text, explicitly demonstrating and at the same time accommodating for an acute conflict of a holy order of the testator and his vow of non-possession and poverty and amount of bequeathed money and belongings. The first biographer of Simeon, Ierofei Tatarskii mentioned this preamble, which he called an introduction, in his study, claiming its unique character: «This introduction is crafted in fervent rhetoric and is so vast and peculiar, that one can treat it as a special general part for the whole testament»[25].

It should be noted that Simeon's preamble stands out from both the Russian and Polish testamentary traditions, though clearly following the latter. Whilst a motif of *memento mori* is included in the narration, the mystery of death or the Day of Atonement are not discussed. However, a Baroque literary tradition is still present in the text and manifests itself in the image of the testator and the entire narration. The testator is presented as a person who neglected his vows during his earthly life and did not remember about death and the Day of Atonement, but who suddenly realized that his life was coming to an end and who then repented his sins: «I did not remember about the last: death, the God's judgment, the hell and the heaven; and lived as if I would never have to pay the debt of death» (f. 9 r.). Realization comes to the testator in a peculiar way: he hears a prophet that speaks to him eye-opening words: «[I] have remembered the prophet calling» (f. 9 r.), states Simeon. He directly states that he has neglected his vows: «I have disdained my holy order, and have cherished my fortune, though when taking my vows I promised to keep poverty and non-possession» (f. 9 v.).

The preamble also contains the reason why the testament was written – an *arenga*. In order to state his motives, Simeon uses a very specific formula, not found in other contemporary wills, that takes into consideration and balances both his holy order and the purely economic goal of the document. An eco-

23 The preamble of Simeon's testament contains the following exact quotations and periphrases from the Bible: Gen 18,27; Lk 1,25; Mt 21, 28-32 or Lk 23, 40-43 or Mt 2, 25; Gen 3, 14; Ps 102, 15. The Psalms here are referred to in Greek numbering.

24 The phrase in the testament, attributed by Simeon to Saint Augustine, was impossible to identify, since Simeon presumably rendered it in his own translation. The phrase could be roughly translated as "there is no time, when one could fill utero with worldly sweets and have at the same time the eternal kingdom in heaven" (f. 9 v.).

25 Tatarskii. *Simeon Polotskii*, 320.

nomic reason for writing the testament is put by the author in such a way that makes it sound a spiritual one. Simeon states that he fears to multiply his sins by leaving his wealth, though vicious, unattended: «before death sudden and vain, fearing to multiply my sins, [I] decided to write this testament, in my own hand. Let not my vicious fortune perish viciously» (f. 10 r.-10 v.).

The extensive executive part of the testament takes nine folios that makes more than half of the whole text. Structural layout and linguistic characteristics of distributions closely resemble those of Polish monks and clergy of the seventeenth century. The very existence of this part in a testament of a regular Muscovite monk highlights Simeon's uncommon position in the Russian feudal society. Being a professional writer and a court servant, Simeon neglected to a certain degree his holy order and acted as a secular person. The information that we learn from the distributions provided sheds light on Simeon's everyday life and demonstrates his attitude towards money and numerous belongings.

It is remarkable how Simeon lists all his distributions and beneficiaries. In his testament, money and possessions turn from a marginal subject to a conceptual core of the text. A scrutiny of the inventory of chantries to monasteries, money and property distributions to relatives are stated directly; no abstract or generalised points are made (compare for example an article on monastery chantries in the testament of the Patriarch Ioakim: «To priests in cathedrals and to appropriate monasteries and convents give from the treasury for the forty days' prayers by the aforetime custom»[26].

The total amount of money Simeon bequeathed to various beneficiaries is rather large for a regular Russian monk-priest of the time. During sixteen years of service at the Tzar's court, he managed to save 700 hundred roubles in silver, 600 golden ducats and some other silver coins, presumably talers; that in total amounts to approximately 1500 silver roubles. Ducates and talers were not in circulation in Russia, but presumably they could be changed into roubles[27]. Most of the money was distributed to monastery chantries, funeral expenditures, to his executors, and only a small amount – to his relatives and friends. How did Simeon manage to accumulate this money?

Let us turn to Simeon's work at the court of the Tzar, in order to learn about his income in roubles. It is known that Simeon did not have any formal court

26 I.E. Zabelin, *Zhitie i zaveshchanie sviateishego patriarkha moskovskogo Ioakima* [Life and Testament of the Holy Patriarch Ioakim], Saint-Petersburg 1879, 114.

27 M.F. Kotliar, *Narysy istorii' obigu j lichby monet na Ukrai'ni XIV-XVII st* [Essays on history of circulation and count of coins in Ukraine in XIVth-XVIIth centuries], Kyiv 1981, 239.

position or rank, since monks and clergy were not allowed to take up secular posts. However, he got paid as any other courtier: first of all, he received a monetary allowance of 15 kopeks per day thus making 54 roubles per year[28] from the Tzar; secondly, he was now and then presented with money gifts from the Tzar and boyars for his service or on special occasions [celebrations of name-days, baptism]; and finally, it is reasonable to suggest, though no direct indications survive, that he got paid for his literary work [i. e. for composing documents, poems, sermons, etc.].

Simeon's funds in ducats cannot be explained as simply. Two curious and unclear articles found in Simeon's testament allow to suppose that he lent money with interest and kept money deposited by third parties, safe at his lodgings, probably for some payment also. In the preamble, Simeon confessed that he was eager to save and earn money, but he eluded any details. In one of the distributions, Simeon instructed his executors to give away all letters of deposits he had free of charge (f. 14 v.). In the seventeenth century when money was lent, letters of deposits were composed, that guaranteed creditors paying their debts. The scheme was rather simple: a person would get money upon the security of some property: a letter of deposit would document the deal. In addition to that, Simeon had the money of a Philipp Tarasow: «[I] hold money of Philipp Tarasov in safe custody, over twenty ducats, some silver coins, there is my letter with the money, return to him intact» (f. 14 v.).

Another issue that should be addressed in relation to Simeon's finance refers to the attitude of the Muscovy Church authorities to these ways of earning and the situation with a regular monk bequeathing large amounts of money in general. Simeon himself called his fortune «vicious». It is obvious that the court service and literary work could be easily tolerated by the Church, since even metropolitans often turned to Simeon's service[29]. We know that Simeon composed three more testaments in the same style as his own – they were meant for three metropolitans: Pitirim, Pavel, and Ilarion[30]. Lending money with interest, on the contrary, was common for the seventeenth century monasteries but was not regarded as a proper practice. Various monastery documents often contained articles about lending money: «the archimandrite, and the cellarer,

28 State Historical museum, Moscow. Department of manuscripts. Synodal collection, № 130 (GIM OR Sin. sobr. № 130). ff. 181 r.-181 v.

29 TATARSKII. *Simeon Polotskii*, 102, 110.

30 Look for example at N.V. PONYRKO, «Zhitie protopopa Avvakuma kak dukhovnoe zaveshchanie» [Life of the protopope Avvakum as his testament], *Trudy otdela drevnerusskoi literatury*, 39 (1985) 382.

and the treasurer, and the avener, and all the brethren lent [us] with monastery public money»[31].

Money was not the only asset of Simeon: his «viciously acquired» fortune included personal items, some of which were not common for regular monks and thus serve as evidence of Simeon's unique position at the court. He possessed a large library, some household items and church ware, and even a horse with a coach. Horses and coaches usually belonged to a monastery as a community; a monk could not possess them as private belongings. However, for the South-West Russian testaments we know several cases where Fathers Superior would administer monastery property as their own. The aforementioned Iliia Torskii had «a horse with a coach» and bequeathed it in his testament on his own discretion[32.]

Simeon owned so many things, obviously precious, that even a cellar for keeping them was needed. In one of his petition letters to the Tzar, Simeon asked to provide him with a cellar in the city wall to keep his belongings safe from fires[33.] We could assume that the cellar was needed primarily for Simeon's library. He enjoyed a vast collection of books in Old Church Slavonic, Latin, Polish, German, English[34.] He brought some books with him from Polotsk, the rest were acquired whilst in Moscow. Amongst other possessions of Simeon were several fur coats; many copper and tin dishes, two precious thin Persian carpets, in vogue at that time, and church ware which also originated from Belarus.

In most cases, by providing precise calculations in various currencies and consistent enumeration of distributions, Simeon proved to be not only a learned monk and poet, but also, a good man of business, capable of managing his funds and property.

***

Interpretation and implementation of the vow of poverty and non-possession in real monastic practices in pre-Petrine Russian changed over time. Whilst the fifteenth and sixteenth centuries witnessed the rise of ascetic trends, with absolute rejection of private belongings and money of a monk, secularisation and the

31 *Akty feodal'nogo zemledvladeniia i khoziaistva. Akty moskovskogo Simonova monastyria (1506-1613 gg)* [Acts of Feudal Landowing and Economy. Acts of Moscow Simonov monastery (1506 – 1613)], ed L.I. Ivina, Leningrad 1983, 166.

32 Bodianskii. *Letopisets o pervom zachatii i sozdanii sviatyia obiteli monastyria Gustynskogo v leto bytiia mira 7108*, 45.

33 State Historical museum, Moscow. Synodal collection, № 130 (GIM OR Sin. sobr. № 130). F. 181 r.

34 A. Hippisley-E.V. Luk'ianova, *Simeon Polockij's Library: A Catalogue*, Böhlau 2005.

strong influence of monastic traditions of the South-West Russia and Catholic Poland led to certain neglection of the vow of poverty and non-possession. Monastic testaments preserved from that period demonstrate various traditions of perceiving the vow of poverty by regular monks and monastic leaders. Whilst Muscovite monks included debts in their testaments and Fathers Superior and Church hierarchs barely mentioned any worldly business at all, their fellows from the South-Western regions of Russia composed proper testaments with lists of money and property distributions. Active migration of monks from these territories to Moscow led to a transfer of a new tradition that was adopted by the society's elite. The first in Russia court poet and preacher, a monk Simeon from Polotsk was one of the most active mediators of the tradition in Moscow. Simeon's testament clearly shows an expansion and circulation of a new for Muscovite monasticism of the seventeenth century tradition of interpretation and attitude towards the vow of poverty and non-possession – i. e. the tradition of including money matters in the very texts of a «spiritual charters». His testament embraces both spiritual matters and discussion of a «viciously acquired» fortune – money and property. Whilst purely spiritual issues are moved to the background, the core part of the document deals with distribution and beneficiaries. This mode of writing testaments was later in the century copied by Church hierarchs. However, after the rules and reforms of Peter the Great juridical practices for monastics changed dramatically: written codes of conduct and codes of laws were issued, and testamentary tradition was significantly altered.

Abstract

With the vow of non-possession being an essential concept in Russian monasticism, real monastic practices of the 17th-century Muscowy, as we can perceive relying on preserved documents, demonstrated certain negligence of the vow. Large monasteries acted as corporations that produced goods and traded them to cover living expenses. Although, in theory a monetary profit was not the goal, certain monasteries would often not only trade, but lend out money, sometimes even with interest.

By the second half of the seventeenth century in Muscowy, there existed not only monastic communities, but also independent monks only formally affiliated with some Moscow monastery. As a rule, they were natives of the South-Western regions of Russia (modern territories of Belarus and Ukraine). In general, they were educated in Poland or in the Grand Duchy of Lithuania, took their vows in home monasteries and then moved to Moscow in search of a better life or due to war or social instability in homeland. They would enjoy greater mobility and freedom in their activities than a common monk would – they were employed at the Tzar's court, interacted with boyars and church leaders.

One of the most well-known monks of the type was the first Muscowy court poet and preacher Simeon Polotsky (1629-1680). His manifold background and experiences, as well as his preserved archives, inspired me to look into his financial situation: ways in which he earned and accumulated money, expenditures he may have faced during his life in a Moscow monastery and his service at Tzar's court, currency of his savings. I will address in detail Simeon's last will – a unique document, providing an extensive data on the financial sphere of Simeon's life. The study is meant to be comparative, thus giving a general perspective on Simeon's place in the economic structure of the Muscowy Tzar court and Moscow monastic and clerical communities.

WESTERN MONASTICISM

THE SUBSISTENCE OF MARTIN OF TOURS' MARMOUTIER

Matheus Coutinho FIGUINHA

In the *Life of Saint Martin*, Sulpicius Severus tells that after his hero was ordained as bishop to the see of Tours in 371, he made use of a cell attached to the city church. Sometime later, however, because of the disturbance caused by the frequency of people seeking his audience, Martin retreated to the monastery he founded two miles outside the city, later called Marmoutier. In Sulpicius' words:

> This spot was so secret and retired that he enjoyed in it the solitude of a hermit. For, on one side, it was surrounded by a precipitous rock of a lofty mountain, while the river Loire had shut in the rest of the plain by a bay extending back for a little distance; and the place could be approached only by one, and that, a very narrow passage. Here, then, he possessed a cell constructed of wood. Many also of the brethren had, in the same manner, fashioned retreats for themselves, but most of them had formed these out of the rock of the overhanging mountain, hollowed into caves. There were altogether eighty disciples, who were being disciplined after the example of the saintly master. No one there had anything which was called his own; all things were possessed in common. It was not allowed either to buy or to sell anything, as is the custom among most monks. No art was practiced there, except that of transcribers, and even this was assigned to the brethren of younger years, while the elders spent their time in prayer. Rarely did any one of them go beyond the cell, unless when they assembled at the place of prayer. They all took their food together, after the hour of fasting was past. No one used wine, except when illness compelled them to do so. Most of them were clothed in garments of camels' hair. Any dress approaching to softness was there deemed criminal, and this must be thought the more remarkable, because many among them were such as are deemed of noble rank. These, though far differently brought up, had forced themselves down to this degree of humility and patient endurance, and we have seen numbers of these afterwards made bishops.

Matheus Coutinho Figuinha, historian, specialist in Antiquity, post-doctoral fellow at the University of São Paulo (Brazil).

For what city or church would there be that would not desire to have its priests from among those in the monastery of Martin?[1].

Because of the absence of manual labour in Marmoutier, scholars have relied on a passage of Sulpicius' *Dialogues* to discuss the subsistence of the monastery:

He [Lycontius] also offered a hundred pounds of silver, which the blessed man neither rejected nor accepted; but before the amount of money touched the threshold of the monastery, he had, without hesitation, destined it for the redemption of captives. And when it was suggested to him by the brethren, that some portion of it should be reserved for the expenses of the monastery, since it was difficult for all of them to obtain necessary food, while many of them were sorely in need of clothing, he replied, «Let the church both feed and clothe us, as long as we do not appear to have provided, in any way, for our own wants»[2].

This passage has been variously interpreted. Scholars do not agree if the subsidy of the church of Tours was either regular or sporadic, or if Marmoutier

1 Sulpicius Severus, *Vita sancti Martini* 10.4-9, in *Vie de saint Martin*, vol. 1, ed. J. Fontaine, SC 133-135, Paris 1967-1969, 274: «*Qui locus tam secretus et remotus erat, ut eremi solitudinem non desideraret. Ex uno enim latere praecisa montis excelsi rupe ambiebatur, reliquam planitiem Liger fluuius reducto paululum sinu clauserat; una tantum eademque arta admodum uia adiri poterat. Ipse ex lignis contextam cellulam habebat, multique ex fratribus in eundem modum; plerique saxo superiecti montis cauato receptacula sibi fecerant. Discipuli fere octoginta erant, qui ad exemplum beati magistri instituebantur. Nemo ibi quicquam proprium habebat, omnia in medium conferebantur. Non emere aut uendere, ut plerisque monachis moris est, quicquam licebat; ars ibi, exceptis scriptoribus, nulla habebatur, cui tamen operi minor aetas deputabatur: maiores orationi uacabant. Rarus cuiquam extra cellulam suam egressus, nisi cum ad locum orationis conueniebant. Cibum una omnes post horam ieiunii accipiebant. Vinum nemo nouerat, nisi quem infirmitas coegisset. Plerique camelorum saetis uestiebantur: mollior ibi habitus pro crimine erat. Quod eo magis sit mirum necesse est, quod multi inter eos nobiles habebantur, qui longe aliter educati ad hanc se humilitatem et patientiam coegerant; pluresque ex eis postea episcopos uidimus. Quae enim esset ciuitas aut ecclesia, quae non sibi de Martini monasterio cuperet sacerdotem?*» Tr. A. Roberts, NPNF, *Sulpitius Severus on the Life of St. Martin*, 2nd series, 11, New York 1894, 9.

2 Sulpicius Severus, *Dialogi* 3.14.5-6, in *Gallus. Dialogues sur les «vertus» de saint Martin*, edd. J. Fontaine-N. Dupré, SC 510, Paris 2006, 346: *Centum etiam argenti libras obtulit, quas uir beatus nec respuit nec recepit; sed priusquam pondus illud monasterii limen adtingeret, redimendis id captiuis continuo deputauit. Et cum ei suggereretur a fratribus ut aliquid ex eo in sumptum monasterii reseruaret — omnibus in angusto esse uictum, multis deesse uestitum: «Nos, inquit, ecclesia et pascat et uestiat, dum nihil nostris usibus quaesisse uideamur»*. Tr. Roberts, *The Dialogues of Sulpitius Severus*, NPNF, 2nd series, 11, 52.

depended either entirely or only in part on the patrimony of its wealthy members, the many nobles mentioned by Sulpicius in the *Life*[3]. Indeed, since the publication of Jacques Fontaine's commentary on the *Life* in the late 1960's, the supposed presence of many nobles in the monastery has had a huge weight in the discussions on the economic situation of the monastery, in particular, and on Martinian monasticism, in general.

My purpose in this paper is to reconsider the subsistence of the community of Marmoutier at the time of Martin (*c.* 372-397). For purposes here, I define the subsistence of the monastery as the supporting of the monks' expenses, no matter what they could have been (food, clothes, domestic tools, books, etc.). I argue that Marmoutier did not count on the properties of its wealthy members. For its needs, it depended regularly on the resources of the church of Tours, on the donations of the faithful, and on the salaries of the monks ordained clerics.

We should not forget that the information we have on Martin's practice and promotion of monasticism are limited and almost always dependent on Sulpicius' works. Sulpicius was not only a sincere and enthusiastic admirer of Martin, but also an advocate who wrote in defense of his hero and his ideas. Because of that, the information he provides on Martin and his monasticism was accurately selected and elaborated. Even Sulpicius' informants, Martin himself and his monks, had already internalised the lived or witnessed events through their own religious conceptions. Despite Sulpicius' stylisations and exaggerations, Jacques Fontaine and Clare Stancliffe have brilliantly argued for the reliability of a *noyau historique* in all stories, even in the thaumaturgical ones[4]. In my opinion, however, Sulpicius' presentation of the monks of Marmoutier and their lifestyle in the tenth chapter of the *Life* has been taken too literally. It is necessary to cross-reference that presentation, whenever possible, to other passages of the *Life* and the *Dialogues* and to Sulpicius' public and purposes in both works.

3 Cf. J.-M. BESSE, *Les moines de l'ancienne France (période gallo-romaine et mérovingienne)*, Archives de la France monastique 2, Paris 1906, 13; E.-C. BABUT, *Saint Martin de Tours*, Paris 1912, 241; R. LORENZ, «Die Anfänge des abendländischen Mönchtums im 4. Jahrhundert», *Zeitschrift für Kirchengeschichte* 77 (1966) 1-61, 14; *Vie*, ed. Fontaine, vol. 2, 676-677.685 and vol. 3, 991; C. STANCLIFFE, *St. Martin and His Hagiographer. History and Miracle in Sulpicius Severus*, Oxford 1983, 25-26; H. OUDART, «Marmoutier au IVe siècle, un exemple de vie érémitique?», *Revue Mabillon* 65 (1993) 109-132, 128; A. DE VOGÜÉ, *Histoire littéraire du mouvement monastique dans l'antiquité. IV. Sulpice Sévère et Paulin de Nole (393-409), Jérôme, homéliste et traducteur des «Pachomiana»*, Paris 1997, 146-147.153; FONTAINE-DUPRÉ, *Gallus*, 347; R.J. GOODRICH, *Contextualizing Cassian. Aristocrats, Asceticism, and Reformation in Fifth-Century Gaul*, Oxford 2007, 192-193.

4 *Vie*, ed. Fontaine, 3 voll.; STANCLIFFE, *St. Martin*.

Let us start by examining how many of Martin's disciples were nobles[5]. Other than the tenth chapter of the *Life*, there are no indications, even in Sulpicius' own writings, that many nobles inhabited Marmoutier. We have anecdotes of only two aristocrats, who were not members of the highest senatorial class, but in all likelihood local aristocrats. The first one is Clarus, identified by Sulpicius as an *adulescens nobilissimus*, «a most noble youth». The term *nobilissimus* has here an undeniable social meaning, for Sulpicius stated that Clarus «had abandoned all» to follow Martin and presented him as the witness of a miracle of his master. But the term also has a moral meaning, indicated by the sentence: «He [...] in a short time became distinguished for the most exalted faith, and for all sorts of excellence»[6]. Clarus' own name conveys these two meanings. Consequently, scholars do not cast doubt on his nobility[7]. Fontaine has gone so far as to say that «his history is that of another Paulinus of Nola»[8]. But there is a significant difference between abandoning «all» and abandoning «great possessions» (*summis opibus abiectis*), as Sulpicius himself said about Paulinus[9]. The term «all» is vague, for it does not necessarily indicate that Clarus was wealthy, but only that he had goods, which could be quite modest. «Great possessions», on the other hand, gives unambiguously the idea of a rich patrimony. I contend, therefore, that Clarus was a member of a local aristocratic family that claimed a distant noble ancestry[10].

5 I treat this question with more detail in M.C. Figuinha, «O monasticismo de Martinho de Tours e as aristocracias na Gália do século IV», *Revista Brasileira de História* 36 (2016) 13-33.

6 Sulpicius Severus, *Vita sancti Martini* 23.1, in *Vie*, vol. 1, ed. Fontaine, 302: «*Clarus quidam adulescens nobilissimus [...] cum, relictis omnibus, se ad Martinum contulisset, breui tempore ad summum fidei uirtutumque omnium culmen enituit*». Tr. Roberts, *Sulpitius*, 15.

7 Babut, *Saint Martin*, 241; K.F. Stroheker, *Der senatorische Adel im spätantiken Gallien*, Tübingen 1948, 161; *Vie*, vol. 3, ed. Fontaine, 989-992; M. Heinzelmann, «Gallische Prosopographie, 260-527», *Francia* 10 (1982) 531-718, 584; F. Ghizzoni, *Sulpicio Severo*, Università degli Studi di Parma, Istituto di Lingua e Letteratura Latina 8, Roma 1983, 73; Stancliffe, *St. Martin*, 31; *Prosopographie chrétienne du bas-empire. IV. Prosopographie de la Gaule chrétienne (314-614)*, vol. 1, edd. L. Pietri-M. Heijmans, Paris 2013, 479.

8 *Vie*, ed. Fontaine, vol. 3, 991.

9 Sulpicius Severus, *Vita sancti Martini* 25.4.

10 As Ausonius did. Cf. S.J.B. Barnish, «Transformation and Survival in the Western Senatorial Aristocracy, *c.* AD 400-700», *Papers of the British School at Rome* 56 (1988) 120-155, 122, for the references. Cf. also M.R. Salzman, «Competing Claims to "Nobilitas" in the Western Empire of the Fourth and Fifth Centuries», *Journal of Early Chris-

The second aristocratic inhabitant of Marmoutier was Gallus. He declared to have abandoned school to follow Martin,[11] but he did not indicate if he was a teacher or only a student. Because of the great quality of his speeches in the *Dialogues*, some scholars have espoused the first option[12]. Gallus, indeed, is called *scholasticus*, a term that could be used deprecatingly, meaning «pedantic», but that could also designate the teachers of rhetoric and those graduated at the schools of rhetoric[13]. We cannot assume, however, that the *Dialogues* reproduce Gallus' precise words. Sulpicius certainly corrected and selected the speeches of all those who participated in the sessions in defense of Martin — assuming, of course, that they are not simply a literary invention.

We know that Gallus was from the civil diocese of Gauls, for, playing with his name, he presented himself as being less educated than the Aquitanians[14]. He might have been, more precisely, from Trier, having converted during one of Martin's visits to the imperial court. If he were a teacher, he could hardly be as rich as a great senator. An edict promulgated in 376 by Valens, Gratian and Valentinian stipulated that, in Trier, teachers of rhetoric should receive thirty *annonae*. In the other cities of the diocese, they should receive twenty four *annonae*[15]. Both were good salaries, but did not allow a person to go beyond *mediocritas*. To the eyes of a wealthy senator, therefore, teachers of rhetoric were only the «unprepossessing members of the local elite»[16]. If, differently, Gallus was a student, he might have searched an education as an opportunity for social ascension. For he was nephew of Evanthius, a man presented in the *Dialogues* as «a highly Christian man, although occupied in the affairs of this world» (*uir, licet saeculi negotiis occupatus, admodum Christianus*). Gallus attests that Martin once cured Evanthius of «a very serious illness» (*grauissima aegritudine*) and a boy of his family of a snakebite[17]. The reference to a house and domestic slaves shows that Evanthius was a respectable man. But considering the contacts of

---

tian Studies 9 (2001) 359-385, for the use of the term *nobilitas* by Christian authors.

11 Sulpicius Severus, *Dialogi* 2.1.1.

12 Fontaine-Dupré, *Gallus*, 42-44; R. Alciati, *Monaci, vescovi e scuola nella Gallia tardoantica*, Roma 2009, 51-53.

13 Alciati, *Monaci*, 20.

14 Sulpicius Severus, *Dialogi* 1.27.2; *Prosopographie*, vol. 1, edd. Pietri-Heijmans, 847.

15 *Codex Theodosianus* 13.3.11.

16 R.A. Kaster, *Guardians of Language. The Grammarian and Society in Late Antiquity*, The Transformation of the Classical Heritage 11, Berkeley-Los Angeles 1988, 123. For the status and salaries of grammarians, cf. Kaster, *Guardians*, 99-134; H. Sivan, *Ausonius of Bordeaux. Genesis of a Gallic Aristocracy*, London-New York 1993, 74-93.

17 Sulpicius Severus, *Dialogi* 2.2.3. Tr. Roberts, *The Dialogues*, 38.

Martin,[18] we can go further and assume that Evanthius was a local aristocrat who pursed a career at the imperial court[19]. In short, either as a teacher or a student, Gallus might have come from a local aristocratic family.

Sulpicius is more silent about the social origins of Martin's disciples than we would like him to be. But his silence is in itself an indication. Sulpicius visited Marmoutier many times, so that he met all the monks who lived there[20]. It was from those monks that he learned of most of Martin's miracles[21]. At the same time, Sulpicius did his best to stress Martin's contacts with aristocrats, for they were the best witnesses he could present to the authenticity of Martin's miracles[22]. When Sulpicius presents the monks of Marmoutier as witnesses to Martin's miracles, he mentions only their clerical position (when they had one); Clarus is the only exception. Therefore, Sulpicius is silent about the social origins of most of Martin's disciples simply because he had nothing to say about it.

Sulpicius composed the *Life* not only for admirers of Martin[23]. When he says that many nobles inhabited Marmoutier, surrounded by books and often promoted to the episcopal office, that they had renounced a life of comfort for a life of modesty and mortification, he intended, firstly, to defend Martin's monasticism. He had in mind pagans who regarded monasticism as madness and Christians who suspected any excesses. He also needed to answer those who accused Martin of being a non-declared Priscillianist. Sulpicius is telling his audience that the discipline of Marmoutier was rational and had nothing to do with heresy, for it was molded by the most perfect moral principles. To those skeptics about Martin's miracles, Sulpicius intended to show that, through that restricted and irreprehensible discipline, Martin was a true friend of God and, therefore, had certainly performed miracles. Sulpicius also intended to promote Martin's monasticism to aristocratic readers, for he is implying that they did not

18 On these, cf. J. Matthews, *Western Aristocracies and Imperial Court, AD 364-425*, Oxford 1975, 154-160.

19 FONTAINE-DUPRÉ, *Gallus*, 223, unjustifiably assume that Evanthius and Eventius, whose epitaph was discovered in Rome (*L'année épigrafique*, 1953, 200), were the same person. HEINZELMANN, «Galliche Prosopographie», 605, had already differentiated the two men. On the epitaph, cf. H.-I. MARROU, «L'épitaphe vaticane du consulaire de Vienne Eventius», *Revue des études anciennes* 54 (1952) 326-331.

20 *Vie*, ed. Fontaine, vol. 1, 29, and vol. 3, 1050; STANCLIFFE, *St. Martin*, 71.318.

21 On Sulpicius' informants, cf. *Vie*, ed. Fontaine, vol. 1, 183-205; STANCLIFFE, *St. Martin*, 160-173.

22 GOODRICH, *Contextualizing Cassian*, 29.

23 On Sulpicius' public, cf. *Vie*, ed. Fontaine, 3 voll.; STANCLIFFE, *St. Martin*; GHIZZONI, *Sulpicio*, 121; GOODRICH, *Contextualizing Cassian*, 21-26.

have to abandon their social standing and their literary culture if they embraced monastic life. And, finally, Sulpicius intended to criticise the supposedly mundane Gallo-Roman episcopate. While Martin and his disciples dedicated themselves to a perfect ascetic life, Gallo-Roman bishops were in the search of material benefits. In Sulpicius' criticism, the presence of many nobles in Marmoutier intended precisely to raise the degree of material renouncement of Martin's disciples: they would have been great aristocrats who had abandoned many things, not poor men who had nothing to abandon.

In this way, Sulpicius' assertion that many nobles lived in Marmoutier fits all too well into his portrait of Martin. Two passages from Sulpicius' own writings, however, contradict his assertion. In the *Life*, from a sermon to Sulpicius on the necessity to abandon «the allurements of this world and secular burdens», Martin gave «as an admirable example in present circumstances the conduct of that distinguished man Paulinus», saying that, «by parting with his great possessions and following Christ, as he did, he showed himself almost the only one who in these times had fully obeyed the precepts of the Gospel»[24]. Fontaine suggests that Martin, referring to Paulinus' example as rare, might have intended to spare «the other members of the Gallo-Roman aristocracy» who lived in Marmoutier[25]. Nevertheless, Martin's words are much more meaningful if we accept that aristocrats of Paulinus' pedigree did not live in the monastery. Martin was truly impressed because he had not had news before of the conversion of a rich senator to monasticism.

The passage of the *Dialogues* on the donation of Lycontius also contradicts Sulpicius' own assertion. The monks asked Martin to save part of the money that Lycontius had given him to buy food, insufficient for all, and clothes, needed by many. Hervé Oudart is right to say that the phrase *omnia in medium conferebantur* (literally: «all things were brought to the middle») of the *Life* is a possible reference to the goods donated by the postulants to the monastery[26]. But if Marmoutier descended into such a dramatic situation, it is because the donations were insufficient to guarantee the subsistence of the monastery. And, if the do-

24 Sulpicius Severus, *Vita sancti Martini* 25.4, in *Vie*, ed. Fontaine, vol. 1, 310: *Sermo autem illius non alius apud nos fuit quam mundi inlecebras et saeculi onera relinquenda, ut Dominum Iesum liberi expeditique sequeremur; praestantissimumque nobis praesentium temporum inlustris uiri Paulini, cuius supra fecimus mentionem, exemplum ingerebat, qui, summis opibus abiectis Christum secutus, solus paene his temporibus euangelica praecepta conplesset [...].* Tr. Roberts, *Sulpitius*, 16.

25 *Vie*, ed. Fontaine, vol. 3, 1059.

26 Oudart, «Marmoutier», 127.

nations were insufficient, the postulants could not share Paulinus' pedigree. In this way, we cannot consider that many nobles inhabited Marmoutier, much less that the monastery depended on the resources of its wealthy members.

Oudart argues that the penury of Marmoutier is the proof that the church of Tours did not provide for the monks' needs. Martin's use of the subjunctives *pascat* and *uestiat* would have denoted only the potential, not the institutionalised, character of the church's contribution. Martin would have meant, therefore, that the church would have contributed only if the monks showed that they had not asked for anything[27]. Oudart's hypothesis is suggestive, but far from conclusive. Martin's subjunctives could in reality manifest a command, a possibility that is much more suited to the tone of reproach of the sentence. Consequently, the subsistence of Marmoutier could already depend on the church of Tours on a regular basis and Martin can only have endorsed that situation to the monks who felt the need to get part of Lycontius' donation.

In any case, we should not rely too much on Martin's words, for the *Dialogues* may not transcribe them precisely. They were probably retouched by Sulpicius or even by the monks who kept the memory of the story. It is more fruitful to consider Martin's monastic experiences before the foundation of Marmoutier, for they give important hints on how he conceived the monastic life.

It is possible that Martin initiated his monastic career among the clerics of Hilary, in the summer of 356[28]. Even before Hilary was exiled to the East, in that same year, Martin departed to Sabaria, his homeland, in order to convert his parents. In Illyria, where Constantius established his court in October 357, «he was publicly scourged, and at last was compelled to leave the city» (*et publice uirgis caesus est et ad extremum de ciuitate exire conpulsus*), because of his energetic fight against Arianism[29]. Martin then «established a monastery for himself at Milan» (*sibi monasterium statuit*). Sulpicius attests that he was

27 Oudart, «Marmoutier», 128.

28 Cf. Besse, *Les moines*, 7; C. Courtois, «L'évolution du monachisme en Gaule de St Martin à St Colomban», in *Il monachesimo nell'alto medioevo e la formazione della civiltà occidentale (8-14 aprile 1956)*, Settimane di studio del Centro Italiano di Studi sull'Alto Medioevo 4, Spoleto 1957, 47-72, 47; Lorenz, «Die Anfänge», 13; *Vie*, ed. Fontaine, vol. 2, 547.560; Id., «L'ascétisme chrétien dans la littérature gallo-romaine d'Hilaire à Cassien», in *La Gallia romana. Atti del colloquio promosso dall'Accademia Nazionale dei Lincei in collaborazione con l'École française de Rome (Roma, 10-11 maggio 1971)*, Roma 1973, 87-115, 95-98; Id., «L'aristocratie occidentale devant le monachisme aux IVème et Vème siècles», *Rivista di storia e letteratura religiosa* 15 (1979) 28-53, 39.

29 Sulpicius Severus, *Vita sancti Martini* 5.3 and 6.3-4. Tr. Roberts, *Sulpitius*, 7. Cf. Fontaine's comments in *Vie*, ed. Fontaine, vol. 2, 579-590.

«bitterly persecuted» (*grauissime insectatus est*) by bishop Auxentius, «the originator and leader of the Arians» (*auctor et princeps Arianorum*), certainly because of his engagement in the homoousean resistance. Sulpicius describes Martin's retreat to the Gallinaria island as a personal decision «to yield to circumstances» (*cedendum itaque tempori ratus*), but he was most probably sentenced to deportation to a desert island[30]. There he had the company of a priest, probably the leader of the homoousean community since the exile of bishop Dionysus, in 355[31]. In 361, after having met Hilary in Poitiers, Martin «established for himself a monastery not far from the town» (*haud longe sibi ab oppido monasterium conlocauit*), almost certainly where nowadays is the Saint-Martin of Ligugé abbey[32]. The geological, toponymic and archaeological evidence suggests that, at that time, there was at the place a sanctuary dedicated to the main Gallic divinity, Lug. Martin may have established a monastery at the place, after having destroyed the sanctuary, in order to Christianise the territory. In this sense, he may have acted as a legate of Hilary[33]. And, finally, after he was ordained bishop of Tours, Martin inhabited a cell adjacent to the church for a certain period[34].

Almost all these instances suggest that for Martin, monasticism was deeply intertwined with the active fight against Arianism and paganism[35]. We do not see

30 Sulpicius, *Vita sancti Martini* 6.4, also says that Auxentius assailed Martin «with many injuries» and «violently expelled him from the city» (*Auxentius ... multisque adfectum iniuriis de ciuitate exturbauit [Martinum]*). Tr. Roberts, *Sulpitius*, 7.

31 Sulpicius Severus, *Vita sancti Martini* 6.4-5. Cf. *Vie*, ed. Fontaine, vol. 2, 590-600.

32 Sulpicius Severus, *Vita sancti Martini* 7.1.

33 For a description of the remains found in the archaeological surveys conducted between 1952 and 1954, cf. J. Coquet, «Découvertes archéologiques à l'abbaye de Ligugé (octobre 1952-avril 1953). Un "martyrium" martinien?», *Revue Mabillon* 44 (1954) 45-94; Id., «L'inscription tumulaire de Ligugé (fin du VIIe siècle)», *Revue Mabillon* 44 (1954) 97-104; Id., «Les édifices religieux du haut moyen âge à l'abbaye de Ligugé», *Revue Mabillon* 45 (1955) 75-147; Id., «Les fresques romanes de Ligugé et leur rôle dans la chronologie locale», *Revue Mabillon* 48 (1958) 245-248; Id., «Les carrelages vernissés du VIIe siècle à l'abbaye de Ligugé et les témoins étrangers au site», *Revue Mabillon* 50 (1960) 109-140; Id., «Fouilles de Ligugé. I. L'inscription d'Ariomeres. II. Pierres à décor mérovingien», *Revue Mabillon* 51 (1961) 54-75; Id., *L'intérêt des fouilles de Ligugé*, Ligugé 1968[2]. The remains of the Gallo-Roman monuments have incited many debates on their meaning. I here follow the proposition of L.-J. Bord, *Histoire de l'abbaye Saint-Martin de Ligugé, 361-2001*, Paris 2005, 11-43.

34 Sulpicius Severus, *Vita sancti Martini* 10.3.

35 Martin continued his fight against paganism after his election to the see of Tours. Cf. Sulpicius Severus, *Vita sancti Martini* 11-15, and Fontaine's comments on each chapter.

him struggling to be economically independent from the church or the Christian community, as John Cassian recommended some decades later[36]. Sulpicius, it is true, was not concerned with Martin's sustenance. But he would certainly have told us if economic independence were one of his hero's monastic precepts. In all likelihood, therefore, Martin depended on the church for his needs.

As for Marmoutier, the archaeological surveys conducted under the abbey church by Charles Lelong between 1974 and 1983 and by Élisabeth Lorans since 2005 brought to light the remains of two Gallo-Roman buildings. Lelong proposed that they belonged to a villa destroyed in the third century and that Martin reused some of its structures to found Marmoutier[37]. Lorans has alternatively suggested that the villa had been continuously occupied since the first-second century and that it had thus passed to the patrimony of the church of Tours before the foundation of the monastery[38].

The possible foundation of Marmoutier in a suburban villa would reinforce the idea that the monastery was mostly self-sufficient and that Martin's disciples dedicated themselves to *otium* while servants provided for their needs[39]. Lorans, however, has recently abandoned the hypothesis of a suburban villa. First, there were very few villas on the banks of the Loire and they were generally not connected with a long-distance road (Sulpicius' *arta admodum uia*)[40]. And second, geological and geophysical surveys revealed that, up to the seventh-ninth centuries, the *planities* between the river and the cliff was very narrow, so that

36 Cf. Goodrich, *Contextualizing Cassian*, esp. 198-200. However, many Egyptian monks could not sustain themselves only on the basis of manual labor. Cf. E. Wipszycka, «Les aspects économiques de la vie de la communauté des Kellia», in *Le site monastique copte des Kellia: sources historiques et explorations archéologiques. Actes du Colloque de Genève, 13 au 15 août 1984*, ed. P. Bridel, Genève 1986, 117-144, reprinted in E. Wipszycka, *Études sur le christianisme dans l'Égypte de l'antiquité tardive*, Studia Ephemeridis Augustinianum 52, Roma 1996, 337-362; Id., «When Did Work and Love Begin to Be Part of the Life of the Egyptian Monks?», in this volume.

37 C. Lelong, *L'abbaye de Marmoutier*, Chambray 1989, 15.134-140.

38 «Le site de l'abbaye de Marmoutier (Tours, Indre-et-Loire)», ed. É. Lorans, reports 2009, 18-20, and 2010, 15-16, both available on http://citeres.univ-tours.fr/spip.php?article1305; Id., «Aux origines du monastère de Marmoutier: le témoignage de l'archéologie», in *Les abbayes martiniennes en Europe*, *Annales de Bretagne et des Pays de l'Ouest (Anjou, Maine, Poitou-Charente, Touraine)* ed. B. Judic, 119 (2012) 177-203, 196-201; L. Pietri-É. Lorans, «Tours», in *Topographie chrétienne des cités de la Gaule des origines au milieu du VIIIe siècle*. XVI. *Quarante ans d'enquête (1972-2012)*, vol. 1, edd. F. Prévot-M. Gaillard-N. Gauthier, Paris 2014, 286-288.

39 This idea is most blatantly defended by Goodrich, *Contextualizing Cassian*, 192-193.

40 On that road, cf. Lorans, «Aux origines», 183-184.

it could not accommodate a large construction[41]. The remains unveiled at the site since 2013 are indeed incompatible with the existence of a continuously occupied suburban villa. They suggest an intense artisanal activity between the second and the fourth centuries and successive building destructions[42]. The material remains, however, are too scarce for us to propose any reliable hypotheses regarding the occupation of the site before the 370's and the circumstances of the foundation of Marmoutier. In any case, there are no indications at all that allow us to suppose that the monastery counted on the resources of a suburban villa for its subsistence. It is much more likely that Martin maintained a material condition similar to what he had experienced before the foundation of Marmoutier: he and his disciples depended on the subsidies of the church.

Aside from the church's support, offerings of the faithful, especially of Martin's aristocratic admirers, also contributed to the subsistence of the monks. In the anecdote of Lycontius' donation, Martin shows a little reserve, expressed by the paradox «neither rejected nor accepted», and decided to use all the money for the redemption of captives. Sulpicius also tells in other passages that Martin refused the *munera* offered by Valentinian and that he did not accept *xenium* or *munus* from any source[43]. With that, Sulpicius intended to contrast a bishop deeply concerned about the maintenance of his poverty with the supposed corrupted clerics of Gaul, who expected to receive presents when they had no properties of their own[44]. Lycontius' donation, however, shows that Martin could receive offerings from his admirers[45] and the sentence «before the amount of money touched the threshold of the monastery» suggests that such offerings were naturally destined to Marmoutier. It was either an extraordinary situation or the will to get rid of so much money that made Martin alter the destination of the gift. «A hundred pounds of silver» was certainly an exceptional donation for a monk[46] and that is why, in the end, Sulpicius told the anecdote: it proved

41 I thank Professor Lorans for kindly presenting me the reasons that led her to abandon the villa hypothesis in a letter dated from August 5th, 2016.

42 «Le site de l'abbaye de Marmoutier (Tours, Indre-et-Loire)», edd. É. Lorans-T. Creissen, reports 2013, vol. 1, 27-29, 2014, vol. 1, 21-29, and 2015, vol. 1, 13-21, all available on http://citeres.univ-tours.fr/spip.php?article1305.

43 Sulpicius Severus, *Dialogi* 2.5.10 and 2.12.6.

44 Sulpicius Severus, *Chronica* 1.22.

45 Sulpicius Severus, *Dialogi* 2.12.6: Martin also accepted the *xenium* of a nun who hid from the view of all men.

46 Such an amount could also be invented. Fontaine-Dupré, *Gallus*, 346, observe that *centum libras* are also the amount of the mixture of myrrh and aloes that Nicodemus brought to embalm Jesus' body (Jn 19:39).

that Martin had been duly acknowledged by the aristocrats who benefited by his miracles. More frequently, the monks of Marmoutier might have counted on modest donations, similar to those that sustained the churches of the time[47].

The absence of manual labour and the importance of continuous prayer in Marmoutier is a reminiscence of Messalianism, as some scholars have already observed[48]. Some Messalian ideas might indeed have come to Martin's knowledge through Hilary, who was sent into exile to Phrygia in 356[49]. In his *Homily on the Psalms*, composed shortly after his return to Poitiers in 360, Hilary states that the Christian community should provide for the daily nourishment of renunciants[50]. It strongly suggests that he took knowledge of Messalian ideas during his exile and later put them into practice in Gaul. But Martin might have had contact with Messalian ideas even before 360. In the fourth century, many dealers and monks from Syria criss-crossed Gaul and Spain[51]. The presence in Marmoutier of the Syrian Anatolius[52] is a strong argument for contacts of Martin with ideas from the Eastern provinces. It is quite possible, therefore, that Martin was influenced by Messalianism and such a possibility reinforces the notion that Marmoutier was maintained by subsidies of the church and donations of the faithful.

Another source of income was the salary that the monks ordained clerics at the church of Tours received. Adalbert de Vogüé is right to suppose that they donated it to the monastery, in order to keep the ideal of community of goods mentioned by Sulpicius in the *Life*[53]. Sulpicius reports that Brice, Martin's disciple and his successor at the see of Tours, was accused of buying horses and slaves (including young and beautiful girls)[54]. Brice could only do that — should the

47 P. Brown, *Poverty and Leadership in the Later Roman Empire*, Hannover-London 2002, 54-55.

48 J. Gribomont, «L'influence du monachisme oriental sur Sulpice Sévère», in *Saint Martin et son temps. Mémorial du XVIe centenaire des débuts du monachisme en Gaule, 361-1961* (Studia Anselmiana 46), Rome 1961, 137; Stancliffe, *St. Martin*, 260-261; Fontaine-Dupré, *Gallus*, 70. On Messalianism, cf. C. Stewart, *«Working the Earth of the Heart». The Messalian Controversy in History, Texts, and Language to AD 431*, Oxford 1991.

49 Sulpicius Severus, *Chronica* 2.42.1.

50 Hilary, *Tractatus super Psalmos* 52.13.

51 Cf. P. Lambrechts, «Le commerce des "syriens" en Gaule du haut empire à l'époque mérovingienne», *L'antiquité classique* 6 (1937) 35-61; H. Chadwick, *Priscillian of Avila. The Occult and the Charismatic in the Early Church*, Oxford 1976, 167.

52 Sulpicius Severus, *Vita sancti Martini* 23.2. Cf. *Vie*, ed. Fontaine, vol. 3, 994-995.

53 De Vogüé, *Histoire*, 147.

54 Sulpicius Severus, *Dialogi* 3.15.2.

accusations be true — with the salary he received as a priest, for he was of poor origins. Sulpicius blames him, therefore, not only for adopting an extravagant and sexually compromising lifestyle, but also for refusing to share his salary with the other monks: he disobeyed important precepts of his master.

Modern interpretations on Martinian monasticism are much too dependent on Sulpicius' assertion that many nobles inhabited Marmoutier. However, there are no clear indications that corroborate it; there is only evidence for two local aristocrats who were known to have lived in the monastery. Sulpicius' portrait of Marmoutier was carefully designed for those who despised monasticism, those who accused Martin of heresy, those who did not believe in his miracle stories, learned aristocrats, and the supposedly mundane clergy of Gaul. In this way, we cannot rely on Sulpicius' assertion to discuss the subsistence of the monastery. The idea that Marmoutier depended on the donations of its wealthy members or that the monks dedicated themselves to *otium* while servants cultivated the land must be discarded. The passage of the *Dialogues* on the donation of Lycontius allows us to suppose quite confidently that most of the resources of the monastery regularly came from the church of Tours. But the faithful also made contributions. Great offerings, as that of Lycontius, might have been unusual. Most of the time, the monks might have counted on modest donations, in a similar condition to that of the churches of the time. It is quite possible that Martin's disciples, who were ordained clerics, donated the salary they received to the monastery. Marmoutier, therefore, depended on different sources of income for its subsistence. But that situation was not sufficient to avoid hard times and the monks might well have faced the possibility of having to abandon the monastery because of the lack of resources.

Abstract

In his *Vita sancti Martini*, Sulpicius Severus attested that Martin inhabited a cell connected with the city church after his ordination to the see of Tours in 371. Some time later, however, because of the disturbance caused by the frequency of people seeking his audience, Martin retired to the monastery that he founded two miles outside the city, later known as Marmoutier. The disciples he gathered there could not buy or sell anything and did not practice manual labour: only the youngest were devoted to the copying of manuscripts, whilst all the others stayed in their cells praying. Scholars have considered that the subsistence of the monks of Marmoutier, in such circumstances, depended either on the church of Tours or on the patrimony of the «many nobles» who, in Sulpicius' words, lived in the monastery. The purpose of this paper is to reconsider the subsistence of Martin's disciples. It argues that they were not nobles – there is evidence of only two local aristocrats – and, therefore, that Marmoutier could not count on their patrimony. Instead, the monks depended on the resources of the church of Tours, on the donations of the faithful, and on the salaries of those ordained clerics.

This research was financed by FAPESP, a Brazilian government agency. I am most grateful to Patrícia D. Meneses, Guido Clemente and Edward M. Schoolman, whose corrections and comments helped me to improve this paper. Any errors are my own.

«WHAT YOU DID FOR ONE OF THESE LEAST ONES, YOU DID FOR ME». CARING FOR THE POOR AND THE SICK IN EARLY MEDIEVAL SAINT GALL

Cornel DORA

The Abbey of Saint Gall lasted from 612/719 to 1805 and was for more than a thousand years the most important monastery in what is today Switzerland. It was designated a UNESCO world heritage site in 1983, on the grounds of its unique documentary heritage and the well preserved baroque complex of architecture with the beautiful Abbey Church and the breath-taking Abbey Library as highlights[1].

Saint Gall is located in the Lake Constance region. In the Middle Ages, there were two more religious institutions of major importance in the area: the monastery of Reichenau, and the bishop's see of Constance. The abbeys of Reichenau and Saint Gall followed the *Regula Benedicti.* They are known as the pair *eremus* and *insula,* characterising the Abbey of Saint Gall as the ascetic hermit, and the Abbey of Reichenau as the mild insula[2].

The Abbey Library of Saint Gall, going back to the early 7th century, holds one of the most important collections of manuscripts in the world. Especially where the early medieval period is concerned, Saint Gall is unique and on a par with the biggest libraries in the western world in Rome, Paris, London, Vienna or Munich. The difference is, that here, the precious material still is where it was produced or collected in the first place. In no other location, is there such a density of transmission for the time span between the 8th and the 11th century referring to a single spot. In all, there are 400 manuscripts relating to this period in the library, and 850 charters in the Abbey Archives. The latter holds the largest collection of charters before 1000, north of the Alps[3].

Cornel Dora, historian, Director of the Abbey Library of Saint Gall, Switzerland.

1 J. GRÜNENFELDER, *Der Stiftsbezirk St. Gallen – Kulturhistorischer Führer*, Lindenberg im Allgäu 2012, 6.

2 W. BERSCHIN, *Eremus und Insula. St.Gallen und die Reichenau im Mittelalter. Modell einer lateinischen Literaturlandschaft*, Wiesbaden ²2005.

3 E. TREMP-J. HUBER-K. SCHMUKI, *Stiftsbibliothek St. Gallen. Ein Rundgang durch*

Tough the character of the Saint Gall transmission has a religious, cultural and juridical focus, there is also a wealth of information about the economic and social questions we are discussing at this conference. This paper tries to provide an outline of what we know about the economy of the monastery, and especially of what the monks did for the poor and the sick in Saint Gall.

Let us start with some basic moral considerations. Why did monastic communities pay special attention to caring for the poor and the sick? The answer lies, as we will see, in the Bible and some basic monastic texts, notably the *Regula Benedicti*. After this, we will take a brief look at the economic base that was necessary to be able to support people who needed help. The question here is: Where did the financial and material resources come from and how were they put in place?

After these more theoretical considerations we will turn to practical aspects and focus on three examples at Saint Gall which are related to our theme. They are dating from the 8th, 9th and 10th centuries respectively: Firstly, Saint Otmar, the founder of the monastery, who acted as a father to the poor and the sick in the 8th century; secondly, the infrastructure for the reception of guests and for medical treatment in the 9th century, as shown on the famous plan of Saint Gall; and, thirdly, the healing practice of the best known physician of the period, Notker medicus, during the 10th century.

At the end, we will summarise the main points and draw a few conclusions.

1. THE RELIGIOUS AND MONASTIC BASE

According to Christian ethics, caring for the sick and the poor became the duty of every individual in the first centuries of Christianity. This meant that the suffering and the poor were no longer at the mercy of families and patrons only, as they had been in antiquity. These new ethics were based on the idea that we meet Christ in every human being, particularly in those who are sick or poor, but also in strangers, and that before God there is no difference between rich and poor, man and woman, or healthy and sick, because every human being has a soul, a divine light within[4].

Geschichte, Räumlichkeiten und Sammlungen, St. Gallen ^{2}2007; Grünenfelder, *Der Stiftsbezirk St. Gallen – Kulturhistorischer Führer*, 80-132.

4 C. Dora, «Christliche Krankensorge», in *Abracadabra. Medizin im Mittelalter*, St. Gallen 2016, 60-71.

The root of this is in the Bible. When it comes to caring for the poor and the sick, Christ is the example to follow. There are numerous examples in the Gospels of how He helps the poor and heals the sick – both mentally and physically. From the scenes of faith healing in the Bible, the church fathers developed the idea of *Christus Medicus*: Christ is the doctor of mankind. Whenever someone performs healing, it is in fact Christ who does so[5].

Another basic Christian ideal taken from the Gospels is the altruistic love of fellow human beings, the Christian «Love of one's neighbour». The most impressive example of this belief is the story of the Good Samaritan, recounted by Luke in Chapter 10. Also important in this context is Matthew 25, 40: «What you did for one of these least brethren, you did for Me». This applies to the poor as well as the sick. As we will see, this phrase appears in the *Regula Benedicti* and also in the *Life of Saint Otmar* to legitimize helping activities in the monastic world.

The ideas derived from the Bible were put into practice by the leaders and teachers of the church, and especially by monastic communities, from the 6th century onwards. The most influential normative text in this respect is certainly the *Regula Benedicti,* where caring for the poor, the stranger and the sick is mentioned as an important task of the abbot and of all the members of the community.

As an example, we may look at chapter 36 concerning the sick.

> Before all things and above all things, care must be taken of the sick, so that they will be served as if they were Christ in person; for He Himself said, «I was sick, and you visited Me», (Mt 25, 36) and, «What you did for one of these least ones, you did for Me». (Mt 25, 40) (*Regula Benedicti,* 36)[6]

As the passage shows, every Benedictine monastery needed to have facilities for the sick: a separate room and somebody responsible for them. It is interesting by the way, that Benedict does not cite Matthew 25, 40 completely, but leaves out the word «brethren»: «What you did for one of these least ones, you did for Me»[7].

---

5 R.W. Moser, *Jesus Christus, der Arzt. Krankheit und Heilung in der Bibel*, Freiburg CH 2012.

6 Regula Benedicti 36, transl. St. Benedict's Rule for Monasteries, http://www.gutenberg.org/files/50040/50040-h/50040-h.html [access: 15.10.2016].

7 See A. Böckmann, *Geeint in Christus. Exegetischer Kommentar zur Regel Benedikts*, vol. 2, Sankt Ottilien, 2013, 367-374.

For the reception of guests, Benedict formulates the requirements in similar terms in chapter 53:

> «Let all guests who arrive be received like Christ, for He is going to say, ‹I came as a guest, and you received Me› (Mt 25, 35). And to all let due honour be shown, especially to the domestics of the faith and to pilgrims»[8].

And a little later, the rule stresses the fact that the poor need special attention:

> In the reception of the poor and of pilgrims the greatest care and solicitude should be shown, because it is especially in them that Christ is received; for as far as the rich are concerned, the very fear which they inspire wins respect for them». (*Regula Benedicti,* 53)[9]

2. THE ECONOMIC BASE

Up to now we have seen that the normative texts, the Bible and the *Regula Benedicti* made caring for the poor, for guests and the sick, one of the most important tasks in a monastery. However, in order to carry out this task, the monasteries needed an economic base. We know more about the material resources at Saint Gall than at any other early medieval monastery, thanks to the rich transmission in the Abbey Archives and Library. The sources include:

1. The Charters in the Abbey Archives, the largest collection north of the Alps, going back before the year 1000, edited in the *Chartularium Sangallense,* currently being published in a second edition.
2. The literary sources in the Abbey Library, especially the lives of the local saints (Gallus and Otmar) and the chronicles *Casus Sancti Galli.*
3. The annals that have survived, both in the Abbey Library and Archives.

The economy of the monastery that counted between 80 and 120 monks in the 9th and 10th century, was analysed by Hermann Bikel in 1914[10]. Even though

---

8 Regula Benedicti 53, transl. St. Benedict's Rule for Monasteries, http://www.gutenberg.org/files/50040/50040-h/50040-h.html [access: 15-10-2016].

9 Regula Benedicti 53, transl. St. Benedict's Rule for Monasteries, http://www.gutenberg.org/files/50040/50040-h/50040-h.html [access: 15-10-2016].

10 H. Bikel, *Die Wirtschaftsverhältnisse des Klosters St. Gallen von der Gründung bis zum Ende des XIII. Jahrhunderts,* Freiburg im Breisgau 1914.

it was published a century ago, Bikel's study is still very valuable. He lists the most important material resources of the monastery.

According to Bikel, the property and income of the monastery of Saint Gall came almost exclusively from the following sources:

- gifts to the altar, for the celebration of Mass, etc.
- gifts of land, charges and taxes
- forest clearance[11].

In Saint Gall, the property of the monastery largely consisted of gifts that provided regular income. The community was rich. The amount of land the abbey owned already in the 9th century, is quite unique, and laid the ground for the development of the state of Saint Gall as a political body then and during the centuries to come. According to Bikel it owned around 160,000 acres of land around the year 900, property that was able to provide a living for 4000 families[12].

Because Saint Gall was not situated on one of the important travelling and trading routes, it was not so often visited by emperors and kings. So, it did not need financial liquidity as much as for example the Abbey of Reichenau or other abbeys the same size that were closer to the political itineraries of the time. These monasteries had to house their powerful guests for free[13].

Given this, it is clear that the wealthy community of Saint Gall was not only able to support 80 to 120 monks plus the monastery staff, but moreover there were sufficient resources left to support poor and sick people as well as pilgrims and guests.

A few charters show that sometimes special donations were made to fund the facilities for the poor, the sick and the guests: There are five charters documenting such gifts to the *domus peregrinorum*, the *hospitium*, the *hospitium peregrinis et pauperibus*, *ad hospitalem* and *in ministerio hospitarii*[14].

Even though we enjoy access to rich sources at Saint Gall, it is still impossible to provide exact figures for the income of the monastery in the early medieval period – at least up to now there is no study that supplies information in this respect. And it is even more difficult to ascertain the expenditure. Therefore, we have no exact answer to the question as to how much was spent on the poor and

11 Bikel adds swaps, purchases and sales but notes that these were of no great importance in Saint Gall. BIKEL, *Die Wirtschaftsverhältnisse des Klosters St. Gallen*, 18-75.

12 BIKEL, *Die Wirtschaftsverhältnisse des Klosters St. Gallen*, 74-75.

13 Thanks to Anthony John Lappin, with whom I was able to discuss this matter at the conference.

14 BIKEL, *Die Wirtschaftsverhältnisse des Klosters St. Gallen*, 201-202.

the sick. Instead, we can at least try to say something about the welfare facilities provided at the monastery and the organisational structures.

3. ORGANISATION

On the one hand, the monastery had a *hospitium* for pilgrims and the poor. The *hospitium* was a kind of guest infrastructure providing food, shelter and a place to stay for a while. According to Rupert Schaab, who carried out a study on the monastery of Saint Gall in the 9th century, the *hospitium* probably supported twelve *provendarii* on a regular basis. Furthermore, there was also a hospice for twelve pilgrims on the Viktorsberg, a place about fifty kilometres east of Saint Gall for a few decades in the 9th century[15].

As far as organisation is concerned, we have, on the one hand, the sphere of pilgrims and the poor. The *hospitarius* was responsible for looking after them and giving them a suitable reception. The *hospitarius* is sometimes also called *procurator pauperum*. He must have had some staff to receive the guests, to provide food and drink for them and to give them further assistance if necessary. It seems that he was supported by the *portarius* (porter), another office in the monastery, if necessary[16].

On the other hand, we have the sphere of the sick. The *infirmarium* was under the guidance of a *magister infirmorum*, a «master of the sick», who also had some staff and – more importantly – a certain amount of medical expertise (doctors) at hand. The monastery had an *infirmarium*, a hospital, which was run according to the *Regula Benedicti*. The *infirmarium* provided care for sick monks and monastery staff, as well as for people from outside the monastery who required medical care, and probably also for people staying at the hospice[17].

From what we see, we may be tempted to draw the conclusion that there were two offices in the monastery of Saint Gall dealing with the two spheres of charity: The *hospitarius* for the poor and the *infirmarius* or *magister infirmorum* for the sick. It seems, however, that at Saint Gall, these two tasks were both carried out by the same person. It is likely that the *hospitarius* and the *magister infirmorum* were the same person[18]. The infrastructures for the poor, the sick and guests seem to have been managed together – at least to a certain extent.

---

15 R. Schaab, *Mönch in St. Gallen. Zur inneren Geschichte eines frühmittelalterlichen Klosters*, Ostfildern 2003, 206-208.

16 Schaab, *Mönch in St. Gallen*, 205-207.

17 C. Dora, «Das Spital», in *Abracadabra. Medizin im Mittelalter*, St. Gallen 2016, 72-87.

18 Schaab, *Mönch in St. Gallen*, 207.

Now let us look at three special contributions from early medieval Saint Gall on the theme of this conference. We will start with Saint Otmar.

4. OTMAR, PATER PAUPERUM

In 612, the Irish monk Gallus had settled in the wilderness in what later became Saint Gall. After he died, his grave became a place of worship, and in 719 Otmar, a nobleman who had been educated in the region of Chur, transformed the monastic community existing there since 612 into an abbey, that grew rapidly and became important. Otmar was an excellent leader, but he also was a champion of the poor and the sick. After his death, he was referred to as *pater pauperum,* the «Father of the Poor»[19].

An interesting side of Otmar's charitable activities was that he focused on leprosy. The *Life of Saint Otmar,* written by Walahfrid Strabo around 835, offers precious details:

> He had such compassion for the poor that he made every effort to care for them personally, rather than delegating this duty to others. Indeed, when it came to almsgiving, there was no-one more compassionate than Otmar. He established a small hospital for lepers, who at that time were shunned by society and had to live in isolation. The hospital was not far from the monastery, but away from the habitations where other poor people were received.
> He was so eager to provide every kind of care personally that he often left the monastery, even at night, in order to minister to them with selfless devotion. He washed their hair and feet, cleansed their festering wounds and gave them a means of subsistence. He always bore in mind what the Righteous Judge said to those who had showed mercy: «What you did for one of these least brethren, you did for Me».[20]

Let us take a closer look at what Otmar did:[21]

- He visited and nursed the lepers personally.
- He also visited them at night.
- He washed them.

19 *Sankt Otmar. Die Quellen zu seinem Leben lateinisch und deutsch*, ed. J. Duft, Zürich 1959; Johannes Duft, Sankt Otmar in Kult und Kunst, St. Gallen 1966, 54-57.

20 W. Strabo, «Vita Sancti Otmari Abbatis», in *Sankt Otmar. Die Quellen zu seinem Leben lateinisch und deutsch,* ed. J. Duft, Zürich 1959; Johannes Duft, Sankt Otmar in Kult und Kunst, St. Gallen, 26-27, translation by Jenifer Horlent.

21 Dora, «Das Spital», 74-76.

- He cleansed their wounds and dressed them.
- He took care of their livelihood: that means he gave them food, clothes and a house to live in.

If we look at the nursing profession today, the basic requirements were already developed in Otmar's action. He was indeed a pioneer in caring for the poor and especially in the care of lepers for the Lake of Constance region. His hospital is one of the earliest documented *leprosoria* in Western Europe. Otmar is an early example of how Christian ideas encouraged charitable action and infrastructure in concrete life.

5. CARITATIVE FACILITIES ON THE PLAN OF SAINT GALL

The famous Plan of Saint Gall proves, that the facilities that we have seen in the first half of this paper were in fact existing in one way or the other in a big monastery at the time.

Before turning to the details, we must be sure that this plan is a concept that was never executed in Saint Gall. Excavations have only for the church provided some evidence that the drawing may have had some influence on the building process[22].

The plan may have copied a few things from the monastery of Reichenau, where it was compiled, and it gives us an idea of how a large monastery could have been imagined at the time. But it was never fully realised as a building[23].

When we look closer, we see seven different facilities for pilgrims, the poor and the sick:[24]

1. *Templum*: the church with the grave of Saint Gall, the focus of attraction for the numerous pilgrims, including poor and sick people;
2. *Domus peregrinorum et pauperum*: the guest house with a storeroom, bakery and brewery;
3. *Pausatio procuratoris pauperum*: a room of rest for the *hospitarius*;
4. *Domus hospitum ad prandendum*: a house for more noble guests;
5. *Culina hospitum*: kitchen, bakery and brewery for noble guests;
6. *Ad sedendum cum hospitibus*: a place in the refectory for the guests to sit;
7. *Infirmarium*: the hospital. This we need to look at more closely.

22 C. Dora, «Skriptorium und Bibliothek auf dem St. Galler Klosterplan», in *Im Paradies des Alphabets. Die Entwicklung der lateinischen Schrift*, St. Gallen 2016, 66-75.

23 Dora, «Das Spital», 80.

24 Dora, «Das Spital», 80-85.

The hospital section on the plan of Saint Gall is quite large and comprises six units:

1. The chapel for the sick: It is, of course, important in the practice of healing. Following the concept of *Christus Medicus,* prayers, benedictions and other rituals were an integral part of medicine.
2. The *infirmarium* itself: It is built as a small cloister with three wings and a crossway in the middle. This is where sick or handicapped monks would have been accommodated. We must not forget that there may have been a considerable number of crippled or blind brethren who could no longer live with the regular community. The plan indicates a *camera,* a *refectorium,* a room for the *Magister infirmorum*, a room for the *valde infirmorum* (the very sick), a *dormitorium* and a community room with heating. We also find toilets.
3. Kitchen and baths: They are located to the west of the hospital. According to the *Regula Benedicti,* the sick are allowed to eat meat and to bathe more often than the healthy monks. Of course, both eating meat and the taking of usually very long baths of several days length aim at supporting the healing process.
4. The house for bloodletting: North of the baths, there is a large building for the most popular healing therapy of the time, that is to say: bloodletting. Throughout the Middle Ages, bloodletting was frequently performed. According to the four-humour theory, it allowed the withdrawal of superfluous blood and the renewal of the bodily fluids. The patient's age, gender and lifestyle would be taken into account, as would the climate, time of year, astrological constellation and direction of the wind.
5. *Domus medicorum:* This building is very interesting. It is reserved for the most sophisticated treatments and for surgery. We can see a *mansio medici ipsius,* and a *locus valde infirmorum,* where surgery could be conducted. By the northern wall an *armarium pigmentorum* provides the medication needed.
6. *Herbularius:* The herbs for the pharmaceutical treatments are at least to some extent produced in the famous herb garden, the *herbularius* next to the *domus medicorum.* Every bed is inscribed with the herb that is supposed to be planted there.

The plan of Saint Gall is an important witness to the history of medicine because this schematic drawing shows us the kind of hospital infrastructure that would have been available at a large monastery at the time. It makes clear, that a wide range of therapies existed and medicine played an important role in monastery life.

The plan moreover, shows that the anti-clerical narrative of medicine history, according to which the early medieval «monks' medicine» was inefficient and inferior to the arabic world, is not true[25].

6. NOTKER THE PHYSICIAN

Notker the Physician lived from c. 905 until 975. He is certainly the early medieval healer in the West with whom we are most familiar, owing to Ekkehart IV who devoted a whole chapter to him in the abbey chronicle *Casus Sancti Galli* compiled in 1050, 75 years after Notker's death[26].

Notker acted as a physician not only at Saint Gall, but also at the royal and imperial court of Otto the Great. The date of his death (12 November 975) is recorded in the oldest capitulary of the Abbey of Saint Gall.

Ekkehart praises Notker as a physician who is noted for his reliable diagnoses, his knowledge of medicines and antidotes, and his ability to cure even serious diseases. Ekkehart's style is superb[27]:

> In medicine, Notker wrought marvellous and amazing cures; for he was singularly learned in medical aphorisms and antidotes. For example, in the matter of the urine sample of Duke Henry (of Bavaria). The duke craftily set out to deceive Notker by giving him a urine sample that was not his own, but that of a maid. After inspecting the sample, Notker told the duke: «God is now about to work a portentous and unheard-of miracle, that a man should give birth to a child. For it shall come to pass that, about the thirtieth day from this present time, the duke shall be brought to bed of a son and lay the child to his breast».[28]

So much about Otmar, the Plan of Saint Gall and Notker the Physician.

25 For example the articles in Wikipedia, Klostermedizin: https://de.wikipedia.org/wiki/Klostermedizin [access: 15.10.2105] or Medizin des Mittelalters: https://de.wikipedia.org/wiki/Medizin_des_Mittelalters [access: 15.10.2105].

26 F. Schnoor, «Notker der Arzt», in *Abracadabra. Medizin im Mittelalter*, St. Gallen 2016, 88-97.

27 Schnoor, «Notker der Arzt», 93.

28 Ekkehart IV., *Casus Sancti Galli*, 123, edition and translation into German: Ekkehard IV., *St. Galler Klostergeschichten*, ed. H.F. Haefele, Darmstadt 2013, 238-241; translation by J. Horlent.

Summary

Let us conclude with a summary of the main points:

Because of the unique quality and quantity of its sources, Saint Gall is the best documented example of a monastic community – even for a human community in general – for the time between 700 and 1000 in Europe.

1. The evidence shows, that monasteries were not only religious and cultural centres, but also points of attraction for the poor and the sick. In the monasteries, the poor found help, the pilgrims were received as friends and the sick were able to get medical treatment.
2. To provide these services, the monasteries needed, first of all, a religious base. The Bible, the *Regula Benedicti* and other normative texts not only legitimated but strongly encouraged charitable activities.
3. Additionally, the charitable infrastructures in the monasteries needed an economic base. Big monasteries such as Saint Gall held a large amount of property, from which they were able to draw the necessary resources to care for the poor and the sick. They also received gifts specifically for the benefice of the hospices.
4. Saint Gall has unique evidence of practical charity from the 8th to the 10th centuries, including caring for lepers, the poor and the sick.
5. On the *Plan of Saint Gall*, we find some important information about the establishment and maintenance of hospices and hospitals, including a large complex of hospital buildings.
6. There is a very fine testimonial of practical charity in the example of Otmar, who is indeed a model for caring for the poor and the sick in the early medieval period.
7. The narratives of Ekkehart IV about Notker the Physician give us the best example of a monk acting as a sophisticated doctor in the 10th century.

If we ask why the monasteries took care of the less privileged and the sick we must remember the basic and genuine Christian belief, according to which every human being has a soul, every human being is therefore a little bit like God, and every person has the right to be respected. In a Christian society compassion and the commandment to love one's neighbour as oneself are the duty of every person towards every other human being.

This idea is expressed in short in Matthew 25, 40, a passage we came across several times. In the version of Benedict, who leaves out «brethren»:

«What you did for one of these least ones, you did for Me».

Abstract

The Abbey of Saint Gall in Switzerland was a place of prayer and culture from 612 to 1805. The Abbey Library and the Abbey Archives together hold the richest transmission of documents from the 8th to 11th centuries, referring to a single place, including charters, chronicles, lives of saints and the famous Plan of Saint Gall. The paper shows what we can draw from these documents for the topic of charity and healing. Caring for the poor and the sick in Saint Gall as elsewhere was rooted in normative Christian texts, certainly the Bible – for example the story of the good Samaritan – and also the Benedictine Rule – especially chapter 36. To pursue the goal of charity the monastery needed a material basis. The financial resources of the Abbey of Saint Gall are documented by the charters who in a few cases also testify to the existance of charitable institutions, especially of a hospice in the monastery. Probably the hospice and the infirmery were directed by the same person. The life of Otmar by Walahfrid Strabo gives interesting information about the practical social activities of abbot Otmar, who was called "father of the poor", in the first half of the 8th century. Otmar took care of the lepers in the region, for whom he built one of the earliest known leprosories and hospitals in Western Europe. The Plan of Saint Gall of c. 820 is proof for the fact, that Western monastic medicine was better than its reputation in some of the histories of medicine. The buildings on the plan testify to a considerable repertory of medical treatments, including bathing, blodletting, the use of pharmaceutical drugs and surgery. The plan also mentions a *medicus,* that is a qualified person in charge of the medical sector. Finally, Saint Gall was also home to the best known physician between 800 and 1100, Notker medicus (c. 905-975). We get to know him as a sophisticated doctor with a humourous mind. There is no doubt that Christian ideas proved stimulating for caritative action and the development of medicine in the early medieval period.

WORK *FOR* OR *AGAINST* MONASTIC LIFE? OBSERVATIONS ABOUT THE PERILS AND OPPORTUNITIES OF *LABORA* TODAY

Bernhard A. ECKERSTORFER

Monasticism is often employed as a model of a decent life-work-balance. However, in Western monasticism it is all too easy for a monk to lose the sound rhythms of his vocation due to overwork. The individual or even whole communities run the danger of burn out. On the other hand, monks do not have to be too preoccupied about their own income, relying on the common wealth of the monastery. But, this can lead to attitudes which they could not afford in secular life. Conversely, others use the demands and pressures of their work to justify a lack of commitment and spirituality.

The author's field of expertise is not the study of work in monastic sources, nor does he know a whole lot about the sociology of work. Specialising in fundamental theology before entering Kremsmünster Abbey, his main interest has, since 2000, been monastic formation under current circumstances and what the role of monasticism might be in contemporary culture. Looked at it in this perspective, the theme of the symposium and its acts in this volume show one of the central issues for the renewal of monastic life. Among the chief topics chosen for Benedictine conventions of any kind is the one under investigation in this book. Thus, this article aims to entertain some thoughts about work and monasticism in today's context, limited to the perspective of an Austrian monk at the beginning of the 21st century. It may be read as a small contribution to a phenomenology of monasticism in the midst of a vastly changing world.

1. THE MONASTERY AS A PASTORAL CENTRE

There is a new awareness of the monastery as the place of pastoral significance in its own right. Formerly, Benedictine monks in Austria defined their existence in the wake of the enlightenment to a very high and at times unbalanced degree by

---

Bernhard A. Eckerstorfer, Austrian monk of Benedictine Abbey Kremsmünster and priest, theologian, speaker, author and formator

means of their work – even to the extent that they ceased communal prayer. For 1,200 years, Kremsmünster Abbey existed pretty much without interruption but at a price: Church and state were for the most part interwoven, politics not only supported the abbey but also intervened in its affairs. For Emperor Joseph II (†1790) religious life had to be useful, otherwise it should not have a place in the modern world.

For the sake of clarity, it might be helpful to speak of a post-modern emphasis that perceives monasticism differently: For contemporary men and women, religious life does not have to justify itself primarily by means of pointing out its utility. Rather, our culture seems to welcome and appreciate anew alternative forms of existence. Where the modern, uniform foundations are being questioned, they are viewed as sometimes an expression of a pluralist world. Monasticism might seem absurd and fascinating at one and the same time: it certainly has its place amongst other ways of life, with no superiority or claim to truth attached to them. Monastic existence adds to the colourful life of our world, at least as it is envisioned.

The form of religious life makes sense in itself and exerts a certain role merely by its being. Timothy Radcliffe, when general superior of the Dominican Order, said in his address to the Benedictine Abbots from around the world in their Jubilee Congress of 2000 in Rome:

> The most obvious fact about monks is that you do not do anything in particular. You farm but you are not farmers. You teach, but you are not school teachers. You may even run hospitals, or mission stations, but you are not primarily doctors or missionaries. You are monks, who follow the rule of Benedict. You do not do anything in particular. Monks are usually very busy people but the business is not the point and purpose of your lives. Cardinal Hume once wrote that, "we do not see ourselves as having any particular mission or function in the Church. We do not set out to change the course of history. We are just there almost by accident from a human point of view. And, happily, we go on 'just being there'". It is this absence of explicit purpose that discloses God as the secret, hidden purpose of your lives. God is disclosed as the invisible centre of our lives when we do not try to give any other justification for who we are. The point of the Christian life is just to be with God[1].

1 T. Radcliffe, *The throne of God. A Talk for the Congress of Abbots*, Sant'Anselmo September 2000. See: http://www.dominicains.ca/english/Documents/masters_order/Radcliffe/abbots.htm, [access: 15-10-18].

Here we detect room for the *vacare Deo*, a liberty to a "re-collection" of the pillars of monastic life. Seen against the background of decades, even centuries of intense work in parishes and schools, there has been a remarkable shift in the Constitutions of the Austrian Benedictine Congregation within the last 20 years: Both the constitutions of 1986 and 2006 have a chapter heading "Die Aufgaben des Klosters", a section which deals specifically with the principal occupation of a Benedictine monastery in Austria. In constitution No. 227 it says that our vocation has at its core an apostolic character. The main service to the world is pastoral work (No. 228), and the underlying suggestion is that this means that monks fulfil pastoral duties outside the walls of the monastery. According to this rather functional view, community life serves as a source of strength for the monk's successful work in parish, school or research. No. 229 says bluntly that community life can be an aid to the individual monk to be refreshed for his work, that is, for his individual endeavours outside the cloistered realm.

The constitutions issued 20 years later have a quite different definition under the same headline. Here, we read that the Benedictine monks see their monastery as a spiritual centre (No. 239). No. 240 urges each monastery of the Austrian congregation to evaluate old and new tasks to be appropriate to the needs of the church in our time. No. 241, which follows, is also newly written; it suggests priorities according to which the monastery's workforce should be organised: The prime focus should be on the monastery as a spiritual centre. Hence, the first and foremost task of a Benedictine community is to offer a lively and liveable place for the individual monk. His vocation should flourish in his community in a certain setting. Secondly, the monks should be there for people who visit their monastery (liturgy, pastoral counselling, retreats). Thirdly, the employees should be offered the same sources that are vital for the monks themselves – a wonderful line saying that the people who work in and for the monastery should drink from the same well as do the monks. Only as a final point do the constitutions also mention tasks outside of the monastery, such as work in a parish, insofar, as these jobs can be carried out without compromising the primary purpose of the monastery.

Consequently, the monastery is a pastoral centre, where monastic life itself is the main occupation – the principal work! – of the monks[2]. This new emphasis

2 For a broader reflection see Bernhard A. Eckerstorfer OSB, «Das Kloster als pastoraler Ort. Die Bedeutung des benediktinischen Lebenszeugnisses», *Geist und Leben* 82 (2009) 321-335. Translated by Terrence Kardong, O.S.B. as «The Monastery as a Pastoral Site: The Meaning of Benedictine Living Witness», *American Benedictine Review* 65 (2014) 94-109.

is reflected in the younger generation's desire to be first of all monks. A survey conducted by the Centre for Applied Research on the Apostolate at Georgetown University in Washington, D.C. gives hard data to this assumption: The study, sponsored by the National Religious Vocation Conference based in Chicago, can show convincingly that young people who have entered religious life since 1993 expect from their new form of life an explicit dedication to God in a genuine Christian community where prayer plays the key role. Work, on the other hand, is considered a minor question that follows naturally from this primary aim[3].

The new emphasis on the monastery as a pastoral place can be actually read as a return to the sources. One of the pioneers of the liturgical movement, the Austrian Jesuit Joseph Andreas Jungmann, put this view in a programmatic statement that can well be applied to monasticism: "The lively celebration of the liturgy has for centuries been the most important form of pastoral ministry"[4].

2. IS WORK UNDERMINING MONASTIC LIFE?

The famous Melk Abbey near Vienna has more parishes than monks and a school with nearly 1,000 pupils, not even to count the numerous tourists. Overwork for the monks is at hand, not just in Austria. In Western monasticism, it is all too easy for a monk to lose the sound rhythms of his vocation due to overwork. The individual or even whole communities run the danger of burn out. The noted Benedictine scholar Terrence Kardong, for one, asserts in his article *Work is Prayer: Not!* that overwork is one of the most pressing issues of monastic life in the Western world[5].

In the course of the translation of this article into German[6], Terrence Kardong made an interesting observation to me:

---

3 The study «Recent Vocation to Religious Life», stemming back to the year 2009, can be easily found under www.nrvc.net. For the German-speaking world I summarized and interpreted this eminent survey in «Die junge Generation in den Orden. Reflexionen über eine Studie aus den USA», *Erbe und Auftrag* 90 (2014) 32-52 and more recently in „Junge Ordensleute? Erneuerung unserer Gemeinschaften", *Ordenskorrespondenz* 57 (2016) 21-28.

4 «Die lebendig gefeierte Liturgie ist durch Jahrhunderte die wichtigste Form der Seelsorge gewesen» See Jungmann, «Seelsorge als Schlüssel der Liturgiegeschichte» in *Erneuerung der Liturgie aus dem Geist der Seelsorge unter dem Pontifikat Papst Pius XII. Akten des Ersten Internationalen Pastoralliturgischen Kongresses zu Assisi*, ed. J. Wagner, Trier 1957, 48-65, citation 63.

5 Http://www.osb.org/gen/topics/work/kard1.html and http://www.osb.org/gen/topics/work/kard2.html.

6 T. Kardong, «Arbeit ist Gebet – nein! Eine Verteidigung der Muße», *Erbe und Auf-*

> What I worry about is not so much individual, personal cases of overwork, but whole monastic SYSTEMS that simply assume overwork. For example, we have schools in which the monks teach full-time five days a week, and then they go to a parish on Saturday afternoon and return home Sunday afternoon. In my opinion, that is overwork! But they have done it for a hundred years and see no problem with it. Have you ever heard of an abbot disciplining a monk for overworking?

"What are you *doing* in your monastery?" This question in an everyday context is very telling – it is all about work. At least many assume it is. In German the point can be made more clearly. The question can also be put this way: "Was *sind Sie* in Kremsmünster", literally translated: "What/Who are you in Kremsmünster?", meaning: "What is your work there?" This is a hint that our being has been absorbed by our work. Both on the individual and on the community level, we identify ourselves mainly with what we do rather than how we are. Also as monks.

Yet, a daunting question is whether it is really the work itself that undermines monastic life. What if this is primarily a spiritual question? Therefore, we have to ask: Do not monks use the demands and pressures of their work to justify a lack of commitment and spirituality? Or, to put it differently: Does work not excuse everything and thus become an easy way to escape the demanding question of how to live a decent monastic life?

3. REGAINING A BALANCED FORM OF LIFE

Monasticism is often employed as a model of a decent life-work-balance. Work is, then, seen as integrated into the form of life. The life-style of a monk conveys: Work is prayer and even more so: prayer is work. From a phenomenological point of view, the beauty of such a unity is easy to detect. *Labora* includes *ora*.

That work is a necessary part of the monastic day is amply testified to from desert monasticism onward. One telling example will do:

> A brother went to see Abba Silvanus on the mountain of Sinai. When he saw the brothers working hard he said to the old man, "Do not labour for the food which perishes. (John 6.27) Mary has chosen the good portion." (Luke 10,42) The old man said to his disciple, "Zacharias, give the brother a book and put him in a cell

trag 85 (2009) 407-417.

> without anything else." So, when the ninth hour came, the visitor watched the door expecting someone would be sent to call him to the meal. When no-one called him he got up, went to find the old man and said to him, "Have the brothers not eaten today?" The old man replied that they had. Then he said, "Why did you not call me?" The old man said to him, "Because you are a spiritual man and do not need that kind of food. We, being carnal, want to eat, and that is why we work. But you have chosen the good portion and read the whole day long and you do not want to eat carnal food." When he heard these words, the brother made a prostration saying, "Forgive me, abba." The old man said to him, "Mary needs Martha. It is really thanks to Martha that Mary is praised"[7].

Monks rely on the common wealth of the monastery. They do not have to be too preoccupied about their own income. This can lead to attitudes which they could not afford in secular life. What, then, does poverty mean for monastic life? Monks have to be self-critical whether their life-style is in accordance with their vows, and they should attentively watch people outside the monastery and see how they try to raise their children, find a decent income, cope with financial problems.

On the other hand, work should not become the main focus of monastic life. Monks have to be counter-cultural, their whole being a sign of God's abundant blessing that puts everything on earth in relative terms. The rediscovery of *lectio divina* in recent decades can be contemplated in the context of work and its overwhelming priority that does not halt in front of the gates of the monastery. The cry for *lege* in the midst of *ora* and *labora* might be a sign that work has become too prominent in the monastic schedule of every day life.

The word leisure and what is generally associated with this term could serve as a concept for putting *lectio divina* as one of the cores of monastic life. According to the German Catholic philosopher Josef Pieper (1904-1997) leisure is a means to state clearly that work is not everything, it is "Nicht-Aktivität", not activity[8]. "It is a form of silence. Leisure is precisely the kind of silence that is a precondition for listening." Pieper then talks about the "Geöffnetsein der Seele", the opening up of the soul that we never achieve by means of any spiritual work ("geistliche Arbeit").

7 *The Sayings of the Desert Fathers. The Alphabetical Collection* (Silvanus 5), trans. B. Ward, Kalamazoo 1975, 223.

8 J. Pieper, «Der freie Raum inmitten der Arbeitswelt», in *Lesebuch*, München 1981, 155-163 (The following citation was translated by B.E.).

Leisure is not merely a pause, an intermission. Pausing means to recreate oneself from work to take up work afterwards. Leisure, however, is something very meaningful, "etwas in sich selbst Sinnvolles". Pieper concludes that out of such an understanding of leisure, cult and liturgy emerge.

At this point, we can turn to another great German thinker who had Italian roots: Romano Guardini made an important distinction in his seminal work *Vom Geist der Liturgie*[9]: He distinguishes between "Zweck" and "Sinn", purpose and sense/meaning. Things (*Dinge*) have their meaning in what they are ("das zu sein, was sie sind"). They are purposeless, but meaningful ("zwecklos, aber doch sinnvoll"), "a reflection of the eternal God".

On this point, it might be enlightening to turn once again to Terrence Kardong[10]. His remedy seems to be principally to work less. However, reduction of the time dedicated to work might turn out as a mere outward change that does not necessarily affect the inward life. Perhaps it is not so much the amount of work but rather the right attitude. This can be gauged when we look at RB 57,1-3 where St. Benedict writes:

> If there are artisans in the monastery, they are to practice their craft with all humility, but only with the abbot's permission. If one of them becomes puffed up by his skillfulness in his craft, and feels that he is conferring something on the monastery, he is to be removed from practicing his craft and not allowed to resume it unless, after manifesting his humility, he is so ordered by the abbot[11].

An all too individualistic notion of work considers tasks undertaken for the monastery as one's little realm where nobody should interfere, not even know what I am exactly doing, let alone suggest what would better suit the purpose of the common good. Here poverty comes in as a call not to rely only on oneself but to see everything as a gift. The monk should be ultimately accountable to God. How can this be achieved?

First of all, work has to recapture in monastic life its communal value. Far from building up and jealously maintaining one's own kingdom, it is "our" project, not "mine". Secondly, recognition should not only – or even not mainly – be granted by one's work; on a name day or jubilee of vows, what seems to be in the centre of speeches or intercessions are the (external) achievements accom-

9 R. Guardini, *Vom Geist der Liturgie*, Freiburg 1983, 90-93.

10 See above notes 5 and 6.

11 *RB 1980. The Rule of St. Benedict in English*, Collegeville 1982.

plished over the years. Consequently, a monk can justify almost everything with work, even the frequent absence at communal prayer. Thirdly, the work load often does not seem to be justly distributed.

The goal is not necessarily the reduction of the time someone devotes to work. I doubt whether monks in our age and hemisphere really work more than contemporary men and women. The solution to the right balance is, rather, a new monastic culture with its own unique style. Of course, questions have to be raised about how to deal with technology, especially in the cells of monks, or whether it is bearable to wear many hats and increasingly put more work on fewer shoulders. However, the question of overwork that seems to entail that monks stay up late at night etc. needs to be treated primarily as a spiritual problem: If there is no vision, then activism is an easy and respected way to avoid the deeper questions, indeed to suppress the need of conversion. Work is certainly a core issue for the future of Western monasticism, but it has to be seen as a part of monastic life that needs a new foundation for the times and challenges to come.

Abstract

Monasticism is often employed as a model of a decent life-work-balance. However, in Western monasticism it is all too easy for a monk to lose the sound rhythms of his vocation due to overwork. The individual or even whole communities run the danger of burn out. Monks do not have to be too preoccupied about their own income, relying on the common wealth of the monastery. But this can lead to attitudes which they could not afford in secular life. Conversely, others use the demands and pressures of their work to justify a lack of commitment and spirituality. What, then, does poverty mean for monastic life? – A contribution to a phenomenology of contemporary monasticism.

PENURIA NOMINUM AND LANGUAGE *RECTITUDO*. LINGUISTIC ECONOMY IN SAINT ANSELM OF CANTERBURY

Riccardo FEDRIGA – Roberto LIMONTA

The role that language holds in Anselm's thought can hardly be underestimated, for what concerns both his philosophical and logical arguments (as in *De grammatico, De veritate* and *Cur Deus Homo*) and his more strictly theological reflections (in the *Monologion* and *Proslogio*n above all). Indeed, it may be argued that the crux of Anselm's thought precisely resides in the intimate tie between language analysis and Trinitarian theology, so that it is not possible to elucidate one without elucidating the other, and vice-versa. In the light of Anselm's conception of language, therefore, we shall advance an analysis of the term *paupertas* and all its semantic ramifications, showing how the term and the concept it conveys stand at the core of a theoretical construction that organically and seamlessly connects logical-linguistical terms (e.g. *cogitatio vocum* and *cogitatio rerum, significatio per se* and *per aliud*), theological and philosophical principles (such as *Verbum, intima locutio* and *veritas*), and monastic values that belong to the ethical, social and political context, such as silence and *rectitudo*.

1. PAUPERTAS AND TACITURNITAS: THE LANGUAGE OF THINGS

If we consider the occurrences of the terms belonging to the semantic area of *paupertas* in Anselm's work (*paupertas, pauper, paupero*), we see that they constantly oscillate between two extremes. On the one hand, we have *paupertas* in its more commonly understood sense: that expressed in the formula "pauper est anima mea", which indicates a condition of poverty; its opposite is represented by the *dives*, the rich person who owns much. On the other hand, there is the *paupertas* that characterises the monks and, in a different way, the *pauperes spi-*

Riccardo Fedriga, professor at the Alma Mater Studiorum – University of Bologna, scholar of epistemology and philosophy of language in medieval thought; Roberto Limonta, honorary fellow (cultore) at the Alma Mater Studiorum – University of Bologna, scholar of medieval philosophy of language.

ritu, to whom the Kingdom of Heaven belongs. In this sense, the term is equivalent to "necessary", as the right measure between lack and excess. Thus, in *De Veritate* XI, for example, the right definition is labelled «that which does not contain nothing more and nothing less than what is needed»[1]. *Paupertas*, therefore, is linked to a condition of *simplicitas* and *rectitudo*.

In line with Anselm's overall conception, *simplicitas* is both a logical and a theological principle: it is not only a moral virtue, by analogy with God's simple nature; it also constitutes the *modus operandi* of human intellect when it does not scatter itself around to follow the *multiplicitas phantasmatum* (*Epistula de Incarnatione Verbi*), the *verba vana* (*Regula* IV)[2] or *verba otiosa* (*Regula* VI)[3]. *Paupertas*, therefore, amounts to simplicity in the act of reference: it is a logical rule that operates on both a mental and a social level – like the Benedictine rule, though in a different sense; it shows the proper norms of behaviour to the monk who wants to make a righteous use of his interior and exterior language, both in the dialogue with God and with men.

In order to be true, the *significatio* that connects its linguistic sign to its reference must satisfy two requirements: (1) it must connect on the logical level what is connected on the level of reality, and (2), it must do so correctly (*recte*). The mode in which the linguistic reference happens provides the condition for the cognitive act to grasp its object. In geometry, a straight line is the shortest distance needed to connect two points: similarly, the shorter the distance between a term and its object, the straighter, righter and thus more truthful the cognitive act. When such a distance is equal to zero, the *verbum* coincides with the *res* and is thus eminently true because eminently simple.

Within the realm of language, the *verbum cordis* – as Anselm defines it, following Augustine in the *De Trinitate*[4] – holds a special place: the formula describes an

1 «*Nempe nec plus nec minus continet ista definitio veritatis quam expediat*» *De veritate*, XI, 121, ll. 21-22. All the latin quotes of Anselmian works are from Sancti Anselmi Cantuariensis Archiepiscopi, *Opera omnia* ad fidem codicum recensuit 6 voll., F.S. Schmitt, Edinburgi 1946-1961.

2 «*Os suum a malo vel pravo eloquio custodire, multum loqui non amare, verba vana aut risui apta non loqui, risum multum aut excussum non amare*» *Regula*, IV, 51-54, in *La regola di san Benedetto e le Regole dei Padri*, ed. S. Pricoco, Milano 1995, 146.

3 «*Nam loqui et docere magistrum condecet, tacere et audire discipulum convenit. [...] Scurrilitates vero vel verba otiosa et risum moventia aeterna clausura in omnibus locis damnamus et ad talia eloquia discipulum aperire os non permittimus*» *Regula*, VI, 6-8, in *La regola di san Benedetto e le Regole dei Padri*, ed. Pricoco, 152.

4 Cf. *Trin*. X, 17-18: «*Nam etsi verba non sonent, in corde suo dicit utique qui cogitat [...] quaedam ergo cogitationes locutiones sunt cordis*». This *verbum*, *qua* interior, is «*similli-*

inner kind of word, a different way to talk about things that has to do with "what" and "how" one speaks rather than to whom. The *verbum cordis* avoids "linguistic scattering", as it were, by establishing a straight and right relationship between terms, meaning and reference. Let us consider Book 10 of the *Monologion*, for example. Here, Anselm distinguishes three different manners of speaking, which correspond to three forms of human words: first, when we speak by employing perceptible signs (for instance, when we use the term "man" to indicate the person in front of us); secondly, when we imperceptibly think to ourselves those same signs (i.e. when we repeat the term "man" in our mind); thirdly, when we «inwardly and mentally speak of the objects themselves» (*Monologion* X)[5]. While all the three modes make use of words, the third one is the only one that employs universal words (*verba naturalia*), which are the same for all peoples.

The *verba naturalia* are the matrix of every historical language with which men have tried to (conventionally) express natural terms. Such a *locutio* says things in their being, for

> «no other word seems so similar to the object for which it is a word, and [no other word] so expresses that object, as does that likeness which is expressed in the acute gaze of the mind as it conceives the object itself. Therefore, the natural word is rightly to be called the principal and most proper word for an object (*rei verbum*)»[6]

The *verbum cordis* does not talk *about* things, but *says* them, by producing terms that indicate things rather than representing them by reproducing them as mental images. *Simplicitas* in reference is the rule of such a language: its terms are perfect *similitudines* of things, as they adhere to them without any distortion or mediation. The *verbum cordis* is a sign insofar as it refers to something else and makes it know-

---

mum rei notae» (*Trin.* XV, 12, 22). Cf. also *Trin.*, XV, 12, 21. About *verbum,* see also *De magistro* (particularly *mag.* 1.2); cf. A. Bisogno, *Il* De magistro *di Agostino. Introduzione, testo, traduzione e commento,* Roma 2014, 62-92 and, from a different point of view, C. Kirwan, *Augustine's philosophy of language* in *The Cambridge Companion to Augustine*, edd. E. Stump-N. Kretzmann, Cambridge 2006, 186-204.

5 *«pro rerum ipsarum diversitate intus in nostra mente dicendo» Monologion*, X, 25, ll. 3-4.

6 *«Exceptis namque rebus illis, quibus ipsis utimur pro nominibus suis ad easdem significandas, ut sunt quaedam voces velut, a vocalis, exceptis inquam his nullum aliud verbum sic videtur rei simile cuius est verbum, aut sic eam exprimit, quomodo illa similitudo quae in acie mentis rem ipsam cogitantis exprimitur. Illud igitur iure dicendum est maxime proprium et principale rei verbum» Monologion*, ll. 17-22.

able, according to the definition provided by Augustine in *De Doctrina Christiana*: «a sign is a thing which, over and above the impression it makes on the senses, causes something else to come into the mind as a consequence of itself»[7].

Within this semiotic model, linguistic signs perform a function that is purely reproductive, not productive, of knowledge. They establish a relationship between the *verba cordis* of the interlocutors, so that their value is purely indicative, as a track is indicative of an animal or smoke is indicative of fire.The mental language of the *verbum cordis* thus holds a privileged position, linking as it does the utterances of all historical languages – of which it is matrix – to the level of *res*. Such a privileged position is due to the fact that the *verbum cordis* is eminently analogous to the perfect example of the divine *Verbum* of the *Genesis*, which is an "interior language", a silent word (*intima locutio*): «it is equally certain, as reason teaches, that whatever the Supreme Substance made, it made through no other than through itself and that whatever it made, it made through its own inmost Expression (whether by uttering different things with different words or else by uttering all things at once with a single word)» (*Monologion*)[8]; lastly, it is simple (*unum verbum*)[9]. Consequently, if unity and simplicity are the features of divine order, if it is through unity and simplicity that the world testifies to the nature of its Creator, then also the human word that aims to approximate God and its order must be unitary and simple[10].

From *Regula* VI (*De Taciturnitate*) on, the logical-linguistic inquiry meets the Benedictine tradition of silence. *Taciturnitas* describes, in the first instance,

7 *«Signum est enim res, praeter speciem quam ingerit sensibus, aliud aliquid ex se faciens in cogitationem venire»*, *Doctr. chr.*, II.1.1.

8 *«Sed cum pariter ratione docente certum sit, quia quidquid summa substantia fecit, non fecit per aliud quam per semetipsam, et quidquid fecit, per suam intimam locutionem fecit, sive singula singulis verbis, sive potius uno verbo simul omnia dicendo»* *Monologion*, XII, 26, ll. 26-29.

9 *«Non igitur constat pluribus verbis, sed est unum verbum per quod facta sunt omnia»*, *Monologion*, XXX, 48, ll.11-12.

10 About Word and languages in Anselm's works, cf I. Rosier Catach, *The Augustinian Threefold Word and Angelic Mental Speech* in *The Word in Medieval Logic, Theology and Psychology. Acts of the XIIIth International Colloquium of the Société Internationale pour l'Étude de la Philosophie Médiévale. Kyoto, 27 September-1 October 2005*, edd. T. Shimizu-C. Burnett, Turnhout 2009, 20-21; L. Valente, *The Notion of the Mental Word in Twelfth-Century Theology* in *The Word in Medieval Logic, Theology and Psychology. Acts of the XIIIth International Colloquium of the Société Internationale pour l'Étude de la Philosophie Médiévale. Kyoto, 27 September-1 October 2005*, edd. T. Shimizu-C. Burnett, Turnhout 2009, 369-371; E. Sweeney, *Anselm of Canterbury and the Desire for the Word*, Washington DC 2012.

the condition of possibility for a true language: this is identified with a mental space in which the vain words of human language are silenced and utterances can therefore become true, as intellect can tune in with that wavelength, so to speak, that allows it to grasp the *res* and indicate them. Silence is intellect's mode of acting when it thinks *in veritate*, when it grasps the thing that stands at the other end of the straight line and thus constitutes it as the object of its cognition[11].

Secondly, silence is the very nature of the divine *Verbum* itself, insofar as it is language of things: existence and meaning in this case coincide; things have a meaning due to a reference act that is inherent to their nature and not due to a conventional signification (*appellatio*, in Anselm's words): «by the very fact that they are, [things] declare that they ought to be» (*De Veritate* IX)[12]. This coincidence of levels reveals *paupertas*, along with *rectitudo* and *simplicitas*, as the essential rule for the logical use of language and the foundation for an ethics of speaking.

2. BETWEEN VOX AND VERBUM

Anselm's philosophy of language is organised around a number of distinctions, which all go back to the seminal one between *vox* and *Verbum*: the former indicating the human word, the latter the divine one. The utterances of human language are, in Anselm's view, propositional *complexa* whose terms and syntactical structures are functional to the *usus loquendi*, that is, to the daily practice of language. Anselm assigns such a mode of speaking to the category of *vox*, thus signalling both its insubstantiality, as the *flatus voci* that is somehow consumed by use in the communicative act, and its semantic vagueness, that is, the inability of language to establish a term that univocally ties its reference to the level of *res*.

In common usage, language moves on the edge between use and abuse of words: words are often an example of *multum loqui* (*Regula Sancti Benedicti* IV),

11 About the role of *taciturnitas* in Anselm's philosophy of language, see M.L. COLISH, «St. Anselm's Philosophy of Language Reconsidered», *Anselm Studies. An Occasional Journal* 1 (1983) 113-123, S. VANNI ROVIGHI, *Introduzione ad Anselmo*, Chapter IV, «Logica e filosofia del linguaggio», Roma-Bari 1987, 63-79, P. KING, *Anselm's Philosophy of Language* in *The Cambridge Companion to Anselm*, edd. B. Davies-B. Leftow, Cambridge 2004, 84-110, and R. LIMONTA, «Linguaggio e spazio del silenzio in Anselmo d'Aosta» *Dianoia* 18 (2013) 163-190. See also, for a broader sense of *taciturnitas* in medieval monastic tradition, S.G. BRUCE, *Silence and Sign Language in Medieval Monasticism. The Cluniac Tradition c. 900-1200*, Cambridge 2007, particularly 1-27, and A.G. WATHAN, *Silence: The Meaning of Silence in the Rule of Saint Benedict*, Washington DC 1973.

12 «*eo ipso quia est, dicit se debere esse*», *De Veritate*, IX, 189, l. 25.

and are as redundant as «a resounding gong or a clanging cymbal» (1*Cor* 13,1). Although terms are plentiful, they are incapable of securely connecting to things: under the pressure of the practical functions of language, terms become signs whose references are uncertain; thus, linguistic proliferation becomes in fact the mark of a *penuria nominum* and a semantic poverty that are integral to *voces*.

In the case of *usus loquendi*, the appellative function of a term, that is, its reference, is established within a framework of linguistic rules that is determined by the social context. Words belong to the entirely conventional level represented by the historical languages that arose after Babel, and wear out with use, so to speak.

In Anselm's account, linguistic signification has two modes: *per se* and *per aliud*. The distinction is developed in its most complete form in the dialogue *De Grammatico*. Here, Anselm takes into consideration the case of appellative terms, i.e. those concrete terms that derive from an abstract one, like *grammaticus* derives from *grammatica* and *pauper* from *paupertas*, and inquires into their nature, asking whether they designate a substance (a man who is poor), a quality (poverty), or both. In Anselm's view, in utterances like "homo est pauper", the term *pauper* is the object of a double signification: one that is linked to the substance (*per aliud*) and one that is linked to the quality (*per se*)[13].

However, one signification does not entail the other:

> «It is not the case that the name "expert-in-grammar" signifies as a single thing man and expertise-in-grammar; rather, of and by itself (*per se*) it signifies expertise-in-grammar, and on the basis of something else *(per aliud)* it signifies man. Moreover, although the name "expert-in-grammar" is appellative of (a) man, nevertheless it is not proper to say that it signifies man; and although "expert-in-grammar" signifies expertise-in-grammar, nevertheless it is not appellative of expertise-in-grammar» (*De Grammatico,* XII).

Direct (or: *per se*) signification, therefore, indicates the quality of being poor (*paupertas*) in the poor man; it is thus the most proper kind of signification, insofar as it is a semantic property that is inherent to terms and precedes their use.

13 «*Grammaticus vero non significat hominem et grammaticam ut unum, sed grammaticam per se et hominem per aliud significat. Et hoc nomen quamvis sit appellativum hominis, non tamen proprie dicitur eius significativum ; et licet sit significativum grammaticae, non tamen est eius appeliativum. Appellativum autem nomen cuiuslibet rei nunc dico, quo res ipsa usu loquendi appellatur. Nullo enim usu loquendi dicitur: grammatica est grammaticus, aut: grammaticus est grammatica; sed: homo est grammaticus, et grammaticus homo*», *De grammatico*, XII, 157, 1-8.

Since *per se* signification is the logical frame that underlies grammatical form, it is the object of Anselm's inquiry as he strives to provide a secure foundation, and thus truth, to human language, making it as close as possible to the divine *Verbum*. Indirect (or: *per aliud*) signification, on the other hand, is tied to the *usus loquendi* and indicates (*appellat*) the term's reference, i.e. the man who is an expert in grammar. The term *pauper*, therefore, signifies (*significat*) poverty and is appellative (*appellat*) of the man who is poor.

The divine *Verbum* represents the other form of language, whose simplicity and *summa paupertas* reside in *rectitudo*. This concept is key to Anselm's thought, as it marks the transition from human language to God's *Verbum*. Let us trace this shift. In *De Grammatico*, we observed how the relationship between linguistic signs and their references is defined by the capacity, or lack thereof, to connect to the things' substance (to *paupertas*, therefore, or to the *homo pauper*).

The criterion that determines this capacity is *rectitudo*. Discussing the long tradition of such a complex notion is beyond the scope of this paper; however, some remarks on the role of *rectitudo* in connecting these two dimensions of language are in order[14].

Rectitudo is a multifaceted notion: it is an ethical and theological value, an ontological principle, a logical-linguistic property and a truth-value. The latter two are the most relevant to our argument. *Rectitudo* is the mode of the cognitive act when it connects to the level of *res* thus granting true knowledge: in this case, the linguistic term is not a mental object that reproduces the real one, but an intentional act by way of which intellect correctly (*recte*) aims at its reference.

Linguistic rectitude is thus much more than the mere correctness of reference within the framework of a certain language or a rule of correspondence between the *res* and its concept (in accordance with the model of *adaequatio rei et intellectus*). As rectitude activates the natural capacity of language to direct itself towards things, it is the only factor that allows what Anselm calls *cogitatio rerum*, in contrast with the *cogitatio vocum* that is vainly performed on linguistic functions and not on real objects. The *penuria nominum* thus turns into semantic *paupertas*, which results from the rectitude of the cognitive act and is at the same time guarantee of its truth. In order to approach the divine *Verbum* model, human language must proceed by subtraction rather than by addition. Once

14 Cf. R. Pouchet, *La Rectitudo chez Saint Anselme. Un itinéraire Augustinien de l'Ame à Dieu*, Paris 1964 and B. Goebel, *Rectitudo, Wahrheit und Freiheit bei Anselm von Canterbury: Eine philosophische Untersuchung seines Denkansatzes*, Münster 2001.

they are deprived of their multiple meanings, human words are made "poorer", and, thus, truer.

3. LINGUISTIC ECONOMY: THE MONASTIC COMMUNITY AS A CONVERSATIONAL COMMUNITY

The nature of Anselm's reflection on language should not lead us to conclude that his aim is to elaborate an exclusively logical model. For the normative force that *taciturnitas* and *rectitudo* exercise on interior language is also projected outwards, to structure the daily linguistic practice of the monastic community. First, we saw how the theological significance of *taciturnitas* supports its function as the norm that regulates the correctness of linguistic reference; now, we get to see that once such rule attains its ultimate form, that is, silence, it becomes the proper linguistic model for the monastic community. Here, language ceases to be a mere communicative practice to become the spiritual exercise *par excellence.*

Indeed, meaning is not only a concept in Anselm's view, but also an event, a social object. It is determined in the context of a reading practice (or a writing practice, we might add), along the lines reconstructed by Stanley Fish: «The communication takes place within a situation, and [...] finding oneself in a situation means to already possess (or be possessed by) a framework of assumptions and practices that were established as appropriate to certain goals and objectives [...] Such a framework, on the other hand, is not abstract and independent, but social»[15].

For the monastery – and in a broader sense, the whole network of Benedictine communities that include the Bec Abbey[16] –, must be understood as a "conversational community", in which literary sources are far more mobile than what the Benedictine vow of stability would lead us to suppose. With the phrase "conversational community" we mean a context characterised by the recurrence of certain themes, terms and concepts, which, although allowing for a certain degree of variety in individual positions and modes and manners of discussion, are consistent enough with one another to define a common theoretical field[17]. The latter must not be understood as a doctrinal framework aimed at rigidly

15 S. FISH, *Is There a Text in This Class? The Authority of Interpretative Communities*, Cambridge Massachussets 1980, 157-158.

16 Cf. R.W. SOUTHERN, *Saint Anselm: a portrait in a landscape*, Cambridge University Press, Cambridge 1990, particularly Chap. II and Chap. XIII.

17 We refer here to the use and meaning of the term "conversational community" adopted by Hester Gelber in H.G. GELBER, *It Could Have Been Otherwise: Contingency and Necessity in Dominican Theology at Oxford, 1300-1350*, Leiden-Boston 2004.

defining the field of orthodoxy and rule out any deviation from it as a heresy. Rather, through the sharing of texts and cultural practices, this model allows that *conversatio* that Gilson identified as the very condition and rule of monastic life[18]. It is this rich network of relationships that emerges from Anselm's letters[19].

Anselm envisages in linguistic *rectitudo* and *paupertas* the rule of the monastic community that is gathered around his authority and his word. Not only must the *verbum cordis* be rooted in the interior language with which man dialogues with God; it must also constitute the fundamental norm that regulates the linguistic exchange between monks and monastic communities, functioning as the exterior trace and mark of a deeper, inner rule of life.

Epistolary exchanges are especially revealing of such forms of communication. Anselm's letters, in particular, are packed with references to the need of overcoming verbosity and linguistic proliferation, as they are useless in relation to the truth of the word that is characterised by *rectitudo* and *paupertas.* Letter 41, addressed to the fellow monk Gondulf, reads as follows:

> «Both my inner Gondulf and your inner Anselm are witnesses of the fact that neither you or I need to explicitly declare our mutual affection in our letters. [...] Why should I describe on paper my affection for you, when its true image is safely guarded within the casket of your heart? [...] Thus your desire, which I know very well, suggests me to write you something, to overcome the distance that physically separates us; but as we are no strangers to one another and, furthermore, we are fully present to one another in spirit, I will limit myself to wish you that God may grant you what he knows to be pleasing to Him and useful to you» (*Letters*, 41)[20].

18 Cf. E. Gilson, *Héloïse et Abélard*, Paris 1938.

19 About the cultural relationships between Bec's Abbey and other Benedictine monasteries, see also G.H. Becker, «Catalogi Bibliotecharum Antiqui», Bonnae 1885, J. Hamesse, «Les florilèges à l'*époque de saint Anselme*», *Rivista di storia della filosofia* 3 (1993) 477-495 and R. Fedriga-R. Limonta, «La debolezza di volontà in Anselmo e le sue fonti», *Rivista di storia della filosofia* 3 (2016) 357-386, particularly 372-383.

20 *«Et meus Gondulfus et tuus Anselmus est testis quia ego et tu nequaquam indigemus, ut mutuos nostros affectus per epistolas nobis invicem indicemus. [...] Cur autem tibi dilectionem meam describam in carta, cum eius veram imaginem assidue serves in cordis tui arca? [...] Invitat igitur me nota mihi tua voluntas, ut propter corporalem nostram absentiam aliquid tibi scribam; sed quia nobis noti sumus per animarum praesentiam, nescio quid tibi dicam, nisi deus tibi faciat quod ipse scit sibi placere et tibi expedire»*, *Epistola 41*, 52-53, ll. 4-15.

When the communication takes place in the terms of the *verbum cordis*, its guiding rule is linguistic economy: it employs a word that says *all* that needs to be said because it says *only* what needs to be said; a word that *says* only what *is*, and nothing more. Letter 4 is again addressed to Gondulf, who lives in England and would like to receive as many letters from Bec as possible:

> «Why are you so distressed, and why do you complain so much about not seeing my letters, and why do you lovingly ask to receive more of them, when my conscience is always with you? Certainly, if you stay silent, I understand that I am in your heart; so when I keep quiet, "You know that I love you" [Gv 21, 16]» (*Letters*, 4)[21].

Anselm writes to Gondulf again in Letter 28: «It is not necessary for my mouth to speak much to him whom I know to be another heart of mine, thanks to the love that binds us to one another»[22]. Silence speaks, and only says what is essential.

The transition from the simplicity of language to the *verbum cordis*, and finally to silence as the sublimation of words, is explicit. The rule of linguistic *paupertas* thus reaches through to the core of Anselm's theology. In Letter 77, Anselm defends his *Monologion*, which got a rather cold reception from his master Lanfranc, by claiming that his work has at least the virtue of presenting a "shorter argument" (*breviori ratiocinatione*)[23].

Even in official letters, which require specific formulas of address to respect the institutional etiquette, Anselm lingers on an apology of linguistic simplicity – a paradoxically verbose one, it must be said –, complaining about the archbishop Lanfranc's use of phrases such as «lord and father» or «yours *qua* yours» (Letter 57). Such circumlocutions appear to Anselm as deprived of an objectual reference, and thus unable to reach through to his *verbum cordis*, which, he suggests, contains far truer words.

In writing to his beloved monks of the Bec Abbey from Canterbury, where he is now archbishop, Anselm restates the idea that two modes of language ex-

21 «*Praeterea cur – sicut audio – tanto maerore quereris quod numquam litteras meas videas, et tanto amore quaeris ut eas saepe accipias, cum meam conscientiam tecum semper habeas? Te quippe silente ego novi quia diligis me; et me tacente "tu scis quia amo te"*», *Epistola 4*, 104, ll. 16-19. See also *Epistola 16*.

22 «*Non est opus ut multa de incolumitate pristinae amicitiae loquatur os meum illi, quem in mutua dilectione scio esse alterum cor meum*», *Epistola 28*, 135, ll. 3-4.

23 Cf. *Epistola 77*, 199, ll. 25-26.

ist: «Each written or uttered word, which you individually or collectively send to me, your most beloved and cherished friend, with the liveliest affection of your heart, and which no tongue or pen might ever express, is clearly impressed within my heart (*in corde meo*)» (Letter 148)[24].

The same concept returns in a letter to Matilde, countess of Tuscany: «Lips and pen are unable to express what my heart feels»[25] (Letter 325). The word that Anselm reads and turns over in his mind, again and again, in the solitude of his inner dialogue with God, is the *verbum cordis*. In comparison with it, the language of the *usus loquendi* reveals all its inadequacy: «When confronted with such an intimate spiritual union, souls reach such a high degree of mutual knowledge that no tongue or pen could ever manage to express» (Letter 178)[26].

When speaking to Aimon and Rainal, two relatives of his that have come from afar to visit him in Bec, Anselm cannot but encourage them to embrace the monastic life. But as the two are still outside of the *monachica conversatio*, Anselm's words sound hollow, insufficient (*nulla verba sufficiunt*) and ineffective, laden as they are with Anselm's excitement and impatience at the thought of the happiness his relatives would have access to. Anselm thus turns to the power of interior language, which is true and effective: «Talk to their heart, dear Jesus – without you no word (*vox*) can affect their ears; tell them to leave everything behind to follow you» (Letter 120)[27].

The value of linguistic simplicity recurs in a number of letters, with minuscule variations: in Anselm's view, terms are signs that are functional to rousing the *verba cordis* in the interlocutors' souls; thus, when the distance separating them is equal to zero, words become useless, as they lie directly on the thing itself, so to speak. When this happens, language reaches a level of synctatic parsimony that amounts to semantic fullness. The conversational community in which Anselm acts, thinks and writes is founded on a word of this kind and a corresponding reading and discussion practice. The *paupertas* that grounds and supports such linguistic economy is thus set against the world's spiritual poverty,

24 *«Quaecumque scripta vel dicta communiter vel singuli de affectu cordis vestri mittitis dilectissimo et desideratissimo vestro, et quae nec lingua potest exprimere nec calamus: omnia expresse et aperte scripta sunt in corde meo»*, *Epistola 148*, 3, ll. 4-6.

25 *«os et stilus ad proferendum quod cor sentit non sufficit»*, *Epistola 325*, 256, ll. 17-18.

26 *«Ubi enim tanta cordis est et animarum unitas, plus ipsae sibi invicem sunt notae conscientiae, quam lingua aut stilus possit exprimere»*, *Epistola 178*, 61, ll. 11-12.

27 *«Dic tu, o bone Iesu, cordibus eorum, sine quo nulla vox valet auribus eorum, dic illis ut relinquant omnia et sequantur te»*, *Epistola 120*, 259, 45-46.

in the framework of an economy of Salvation to which all other forms of political, social and economic order must, in Anselm's view, submit.

Abstract

The topics of language and dialectic argumentation have a pivotal role in Anselm's thought. They constitute the theoretical context in which we proceeded with a semantic analysis of the term *paupertas;* it should be understood under a thought where logical-linguistic terms (*appellatio, cogitatio vocum* e *rerum, significatio*) are related to ethical and social principles as monastic silence and *rectitudo,* in particular. Indeed, Anselmian idea of poverty moves on the ridge between the *paupertas* as *penuria nominum,* typical of the human language merely capable of producing *voces* for the *usus loquendi*, and the Divine Word (*Verbum*), a "poor" word, where "poor" means unique, simple, pure and real. The *Verbum* will be, at the same time, a linguistic and ethical model for the human language to avoid the *multiloquium* and to properly connect words and things. Reduced to a line that directly moves from the word to his corresponding thing, the linguistic signification thins all his redundant references and becomes right, that is simple. This kind of language aims at the monastic silence of chapter six of the *Regula Sancti Benedicti* as his higher and very true form. So, the *paupertas* has to be intended, in the Anselmian philosophy of language, as a value against the mundane poverty of spirit, in the broader context of the Salvation of the soul's economy.

SINT VOBIS OMNIA COMMUNIA. CONCEPTIONS OF RELIGIOUS POVERTY AMONG THE DUTCH AUGUSTINIAN FRIARS, 1886-2006

Brian Heffernan

Augustinian friars, when they make their vows, promise obedience, chastity, and «to live without property and in perfect communal life»[1]. This formula, terse as it is, hints at two different conceptions of religious poverty. The first, *vivere sine proprio*, echoes the advice that Jesus gives the rich young man in the gospel: «if you wish to be perfect, go and sell your possessions ... then come, follow me»[2]. The second, *et in perfecta vita communi*, on the other hand, echoes the description in the Acts of the Apostles of the life of the early Christian community: «and all who shared the faith owned everything in common»[3]. This second interpretation is the one most characteristic of Augustine of Hippo's (354-430) conception of the religious life, to the extent that it features more prominently in his Rule (397/400)[4]. In religious communities, he says, no one must call anything their own, but everything should be possessed in common: *sint vobis omnia communia*[5].

Whether or not the first interpretation is stricter than the second is a question that has occupied members of the Order of Hermits of Saint Augustine

---

Various sections of this article have appeared previously in Dutch as part of my book *Een kleine orde met allure. De augustijnen in Nederland, 1886-2006,* Hilversum 2015).

Brian Heffernan is a historian and is currently working on a book on the Discalced Carmelite Sisters in the Netherlands.

1 See text in *Sacrae caeremoniae ex variis auctoribus et caeremonialibus collectae juxta ritum Sanctae Romanae Ecclesiae usui Fratrum Eremitarum S. Augustini aliorumque Romano ritu utentium accomodatae quas pluribus emendatis et additis edi mandavit Rmus Pater Magister Fr. Pacificus Neno Augustiniani Ordinis Commissarius Generalis* (3d edition; Rome: Della Pace, 1881), 521.

2 Matthew 19,21, cf. Mark 10,21 and Luke 18,22.

3 Acts 2,44-5.

4 On this document, see M.D. Ponesse, «Regula», in *The Oxford guide to the historical reception of Augustine* [=OGHRA], ed. K. Pollmann vol. 1, Oxford 2013, 462-7, at 463.

5 See text in *Regula et constitutions Ordinis Fratrum S. Augustini iussu Rev.mi P. Fr. Michaelangeli Orcasitas Prioris Generalis eiusdem Ordinis editae*, Rome 1990, 5-6.

from time to time. Either way, the evangelical counsel of poverty is an important touchstone of the radicalism of the religious life, because it is a self-conscious rejection of what human beings ordinarily strive for. It is a «counter-witness» against the spirit of the age, a critique of society. The attitude of *contemptus mundi* went out of fashion in the Catholic Church after the Second Vatican Council (1962-1965) declared that the «joys and hopes, the grief and anguish of the people of our time ... are [those] of the followers of Christ as well»[6]. In fact, however, most Catholics up to the 1960s had been taught to believe that their joys and hopes were not much like those of the world at all.

What this article proposes to do is to use changing Dutch Augustinian conceptions of religious poverty as a measuring rod to gauge their self-understanding as religious. It will do this for three distinct periods: from the 1880s to 1920, the age of mass mobilisation, from 1920 to 1950, an «ideological» age, and from 1950 to the present, a consumerist age. Precisely because the radicalism of the religious life was meant to be a testimony against the world, more specifically the modern world, it is hoped that this endeavour will also shed light on a wider question: that of the place of religion in modernity. Modernity, understood as industrialised, urbanised society dominated by bourgeois and popular culture and politics, has often been regarded as an inevitable solvent of religion. The hypothesis underlying the current article, however, is that this view is quite mistaken. By showing how one radical marker of the anti-modern otherness of religion was subject to constant reinterpretation under the influence of societal change, it intends to make the case that the religious life fulfilled a modern function in modern society[7].

1. AUGUSTINIANS AND RELIGIOUS POVERTY

First, however, it must be explained why the Augustinian Friars are a good case study. As an average-sized clerical order that went from very small membership figures in the 1880s to four hundred by 1960, before falling to a few dozen currently, it is typical of many similar institutes in the Netherlands. As parish ministers and, especially, as teachers in their six secondary schools, the Augustinians

6 SECOND VATICAN COUNCIL, *Pastoral Constitution on the Church in the Modern World (*Gaudium et spes*)*, 7 December 1965.

7 Cf. U. ALTERMATT, *Katholizismus und Moderne. Zur Sozial- und Mentalitätsgeschichte der Schweizer Katholiken im 19. und 20. Jahrhundert*, Zürich 1989 and S. Hellemans, *Strijd om de moderniteit. Sociale bewegingen en verzuiling in Europa sinds 1800*, Leuven 1990.

were a small, but not insignificant elite group in Dutch Catholic society. Despite their name, the Augustinians have no known historical link to Augustine. Instead their origins lie in the high middle ages, in the *vita apostolica* movement. Various newly founded orders of hermits were joined together by the pope in 1256. They were given the Rule of Augustine, and from this – and from the need to claim a prestigious founder figure – the new order soon developed a strong cult of Augustine[8].

The Augustinians had a number of houses in the Low Countries, but those in the Northern provinces had all disappeared by the 1580s as the Calvinist government suppressed monasteries. In the eyes of the Catholic Church, the Dutch Republic became a mission territory. A handful of Augustinian missionaries established themselves in the Republic from the 1620s onwards. They engaged in pastoral ministry in so-called *staties*: mission stations tolerated by the authorities. Catholics achieved legal emancipation in 1795, when all disabilities for non-Catholics were abolished, but legal restrictions on the religious life remained in place. These were retained by the government of the new Kingdom of the Netherlands in 1813, and it was only when a liberal constitution was adopted in 1848 that full religious freedom was achieved. For the Catholic community, this meant the end of its missionary status, as Pope Pius IX (1846-1878) established dioceses and appointed bishops in 1853. The Augustinians by mid-century numbered nine, all of them parish ministers[9].

2. AUGUSTINIAN CONCEPTIONS OF RELIGIOUS POVERTY IN AN AGE OF CATHOLIC MASS MOBILISATION, 1886-1920

These friars were formally missionaries, but this must not mislead us into thinking of them as gaunt and impoverished men doing heroic work among an unpromising heathen population. During the nineteenth century, priests enjoyed high status in the Netherlands, even amongst enlightened non-Catholics, who viewed them as instruments for the moral elevation of the people. They generally came from well-to-do families and felt they were entitled to maintain a state of life that befitted their position[10]. This was no different for religious priests,

8 E.L. Saak, *High way to heaven. The Augustinian platform between reform and Reformation, 1292-1524*, Leiden-Boston-Cologne 2002.

9 Heffernan, *Kleine orde*, 45.

10 M. Monteiro, «Mannen Gods: historische perspectieven op clericale identiteit en clericale cultuur», in *Mannen Gods. Clericale identiteit in verandering*, edd. G. Ackermans-M. Monteiro, Hilversum 2007, 9-32, at 17-18.

and it can be shown of several Augustinians of the late nineteenth century that they came from relatively wealthy backgrounds[11]. But this began to change from the 1860s onwards. As the Catholic middle classes expanded, the social backgrounds of priests became more diverse[12]. Between 1856 and 1956 the number of Catholics in the Netherlands tripled, but the number of priests increased more than six-fold: Catholics were able to support more priests per capita[13]. Becoming a priest was an important form of social mobility for Catholic young men of the lower strata of society[14].

All this brought significant changes to the Augustinian mission. By the 1880s it was attracting recruits at a good rate, and by 1895 it had enough members to form a separate province. The elite of the province continued to be drawn from wealthy families, and the networks of these friars were important for the province. Thus, the fundraising capabilities of Ambrosius Hoorneman (1818-1889), parish priest in Amsterdam from 1860 to 1889, were legendary and financed much of the province's expansion[15]. But increasingly, friars were recruited from the *petite bourgeoisie*, whilst novices with an agricultural background no longer came exclusively from wealthy farming families[16].

It is in the context of this social shift in the priesthood that an important transformation took place in Augustinian conceptions of religious poverty and in their self-understanding more generally. New sees had been established in 1853 and the bishops appointed to them lost no time in becoming masters in

---

11 See for instance W. Verhoeven, «Pater Bernardus Johannes van Eert (1839-1905). Provinciaal en grondlegger van de Nederlandse augustijnen provincie», *Van Vehchele tot Veghel. Periodiek van de Heemkundekring Vehchele*, 25, 85 (2006) 6-18, at 8; Alph. J. Claesen, *Ter vrome herinnering aan den hoogeerwaarden pater Gregorius F.J.P. van Etten, Ord. Er. S. Aug., magister in de H. Godgeleerdheid, oud-procurator-generaal, oud-provinciaal, eersten definitor der Nederlandsche ordesprovincie*, z.j. Eindhoven 1909; P. Jansen, «Bijdrage tot het Archief van de kerk "De Star" te Amsterdam voorafgegaan door eenige Opmerkingen nopens de Hollandsche Paters Augustijnen» (1924) 25 (Het Utrechts Archief, Utrecht [HUA], 1392-2: Archief Nederlandse Augustijnen [ANA], 4374).

12 Jos M.M. Leenders, *«Zijn dit nu de handelwijzen van een herder...!» Hollands katholicisme 1840-1920*, Nijmegen 2008, 117-120.

13 Th.A.J. Jansen, *De pater op de pastorie. Het aandeel van de regulieren in de parochiële zielzorg van Nederland 1853-1966*, Nijmegen 1976, 118-120.

14 J.J. Dellepoort, *De priesterroepingen in Nederland. Proeve van een statistisch-sociografische analyse*, The Hague 1955, 232.

15 «Geschiedenis der St. Monica-Priorij der Augustijner Eremieten te Utrecht (1866-1954 (1977)», 10-11 (HUA, 1392-2: ANA, 3968).

16 See examples in Heffernan, *Kleine orde*, 75.

their new house. They did this by putting an end to the independence of priests, and particularly to that of religious priests. This circumstance, combined with a wider medieval-oriented spirit of monastic revival, led to a policy of what might be called «monasticisation» amongst the old orders. It involved building new priories in addition to presbyteries, wearing the habit instead of clerical attire, recruiting lay brothers to do the work of female housekeepers, et cetera.

A very important measure was the drive to restore the common life – or specifically: community of property[17]. The friars in their mission stations had not practiced it, and it had disappeared in many other houses of the order[18]. It became an important aspect of a worldwide revival of the order from the 1880s onwards. General Tomás Rodríguez (1898-1920) wrote to all Augustinians in December 1897 that «where the common life flourishes, «... there work is more ardent and more fruitful», and he described the custom of owning private possessions as a «woodworm that slowly consumes the foundation of even the most solid virtue»[19]. The transition to the *vita communis perfecta* understandably came as somewhat of a shock. In the years before the founding of the first priory in the Netherlands in 1886, Dutch friars had been accustomed to receiving an annual stipend – the *peculium* – usually from the parish where they worked[20]. In addition, they were allowed to keep any personal donations from parishioners. In the newly founded priories, community of property was part of life from the start, but during a visitation in 1891, General Sebastiano Martinelli (1889-1898) also prescribed it for the presbyteries[21].

Somewhat predictably, it proved difficult to ensure observance of this measure, especially in the priories that served as presbyteries, and it is no surprise that it had frequently to be repeated[22]. But young friars often embraced it with ardour. In a speech given to his class fellows in 1905, the seminarian Ugolinus Goll (1883-1957) described «community of property, obedience, poverty and chastity» as

17 For this section, see also B. HEFFERNAN, «"Spiritus ordinis nostri paulatim reviviscere incepit". Dutch Augustinian revival in the Netherlands, 1886-1920», in *La ripresa dell'ordine. Gli agostiniani tra 1850-1920*, ed. L.M. de San Martín, Rome 2012, 349-373.

18 Cf. P. van Geest, «Asceticism», in POLLMANN, *OGRHA*, vol. 2, 572-577, at 574.

19 Circular letter Rodríguez, 8 December 1897 (HUA, 1392-1: ANA, 424).

20 JANSEN, «Bijdrage», 16-17 (HUA, 1392-2: ANA, 4374).

21 Acts of visitation Martinelli, 21 August 1891 (HUA, 1392-1: ANA, 438).

22 «Liber Visitationum a Rev. Priore Provinciali peractarum. 1915, Oct. – 1935, Juli», 1-14 (HUA, 1392-1: ANA, 502); Van Eert to local priors, 4 November 1901 (HUA, 1392-1: ANA, 101); Acts provincial intermediate chapter, 1909 (HUA, 1392-1: ANA, 28) and Acts provincial chapter, 1911 (HUA, 1392-1: ANA, 5); Act of visitation, Beke, undated (HUA, 1392-1: ANA, 502).

weapons that Augustine had taken up to combat the heresy and the «destructive persecution urge» of his day[23]. Goll saw the *vita communis perfecta* as a weapon religious could use in their struggle for the cause of Catholicism in the Netherlands.

Monasticisation represented a search for a new identity vis-à-vis the secular clergy. But it had an equivalent among the secular clergy: diocesan seminaries were little different from religious seminaries and young diocesan priests were taught very similar values[24]. In fact, the priesthood in general became more regimented, less independent, and poorer. And a more disciplined, more frugal clergy meant a cheaper, and therefore a more numerous clergy. Having more priests per capita was an important strategy in the mass mobilisation process that was taking place and to which Goll's words were testimony. Moreover, if the Catholic masses were to be the church's new support base, then it was necessary for its ministers to be men from all classes. It is no coincidence that the church was, at this time, engaging in a concerted campaign to create a Catholic subculture or «pillar» that catered not only to the religious needs of its members, but also to their political, educational, cultural and social needs[25]. This was its answer to the modernisation of Dutch society. Monasticisation was part of a wider phenomenon.

3. AUGUSTINIAN CONCEPTIONS OF RELIGIOUS POVERTY IN AN IDEOLOGICAL AGE, 1920-1950

According to the standard historical view of Dutch twentieth-century history, «pillarisation» had by 1920 produced a society in which the loyalties of a large part of the population were claimed by four «pillars» – Catholicism, Protestantism, socialism and liberalism. Although right-wing ideologies managed to attract some support during the 1930s, the social, cultural and political landscape did not fundamentally change. Historians have recently emphasised that to speak of society as «pillarised» in this way is to take a post-war reformist caricature of the past at face value[26]. In fact, the unity within their own communities that the various elites strove for was often more desired than real. Thus

23 U. Goll, «De H. Vader Augustinus», Cassiciacum speech, 25 November 1905 (HUA, 1392-1: ANA, 3588).

24 Leenders, *Handelwijzen*, 29-217.

25 H. Righart, *De katholieke zuil in Europa. Het ontstaan van verzuiling onder katholieken in Oostenrijk, Zwitserland, België en Nederland*, Amsterdam-Meppel 1986, 237-244.

26 P. van Dam, *Staat van verzuiling. Over een Nederlandse mythe*, Amsterdam 2011.

there were competing groups within the Catholic community and divisions also ran through the Augustinian province.

Apart from numerical expansion, the most important change to occur in the province during this period was the rise of a new generation of intellectuals. The province needed university-trained friars for its own seminary, and young friars had been sent to university for degrees in the sacred disciplines since the late nineteenth century[27]. It also needed them to teach at secondary school, as this was fast becoming one of its main apostolates. Catholic schools were eligible for state funding if they met certain conditions, one being that teachers must hold university degrees. By the 1920s and 1930s, these two developments had produced a pool of young intellectuals.

These friars did not look kindly on the ideals and achievements of their elders: monasticisation had been about building up external structures and mobilising large groups of people, not about achieving spiritual depth. The young felt that the devotional life of the older generation was sentimental and unmanly – mawkish statues, feminine piety, all the superficial plasterwork of parish religiosity. When the order's commemoration of the fifteenth centenary of Augustine's death in 1930 offered a glimpse of something totally different – of true *spirituality* – the intellectuals jumped at the opportunity. The interwar years saw the rediscovery of Augustinian spirituality. Its focus was on the community ideal of Augustine's Rule: *anima una et cor unum in Deum*: one soul and one heart toward God. Through articles, seminars, books, and letters, the notion was disseminated that the communal life was the special mark of the Augustinian Order, just as poverty was the special mark of the Franciscans[28]. To communicate to humanity the community ideal, not just for the religious life, but also for the church generally and even for society – this was the vocation of the Order[29].

For friars who cherished the ascetical aspect of their monastic training, the community ideal was not radical enough. It emphasised fraternal charity, but their desire was for something more demanding, something more virile – conscious as they were of right-wing critics of Catholicism who jeered that a celibate was only half a man. These friars looked to the eremitical heritage of the order for an answer. They did not reject the community ideal, but attempted to «asceticise» it: living in community required spiritual self-abnegation. And this

27 Heffernan, *Kleine orde*, 212.

28 Valentinus Hutjens, *De monniken van Sint Augustinus*, De Toorts 1948, 39.

29 Cf. Prospectus «juvenaat», undated [late 1930s] (HUA, 1392-1: ANA, 755).

was much more difficult, one protagonist contended, than the merely material self-abnegation practiced by the Franciscans in their pursuit of poverty[30].

What consequences did this discovery have for their perceptions of religious poverty? Poverty for these young friars was never an end in its own right, but the «hard» aspect of communal life – the self-renunciation required in subordinating one's own interests to those of the community – included indifference to material things. Alphons Claesen (1867-1937), an early protagonist, explained in 1929 that he owned only a few books, despite being a professor, because he did not wish to withdraw resources from the community: as an Augustinian, he said, «I believe I must place greater importance on the communal than on the individual and personal»[31]. Provincial Servus Makaay (1893-1959) pointed out in a circular letter in 1932 that the Augustinian community ideal meant that friars should stop thinking in terms of «rich» and «poor» houses in the province. They all belonged to the same community, and should all be prepared to serve in poor or in rich houses[32].

This community ideal was consciously constructed as a Catholic answer, even an antidote, to the right-wing ideologies of the time. When the German invasion of the Netherlands was imminent, in February 1940, Makaay warned the province that the years ahead might bring the «partial or total destruction of everything that we built up over the course of the years». But, he added, whatever the future might hold, «our *inner* disposition, our charity, our ideals no created power can take from us»[33]. This was characteristic of his generation of young intellectuals: their faith and their religious life were about spirituality, and this implied indifference to the material things their fathers had built.

4. AUGUSTINIAN CONCEPTIONS OF RELIGIOUS POVERTY IN A CONSUMERIST AGE, 1950-2006

There is little doubt that the emergence of an affluent, consumerist society has had a profound impact on the practice of religion in post-war Western Europe. It fostered the rise of individualism, as people could now afford to go their own way without reference to authorities to which they had previously been

30 HUTJENS, *Monniken*, 39-40.

31 Claesen to Jurgens, 23 January 1929 (HUA, 1392-1: ANA, 2295).

32 Circular letter Makaay, 9 October 1932 (HUA, 1392-1: ANA, 106).

33 B. HEFFERNAN, «Dutch Augustinians and the Second World War», *Analecta Augustiniana* 78 (2015) 161-191, at 171.

beholden, such as churches or «pillarised» institutions[34]. Hugh McLeod has summarised developments by commenting that «collective identities and communal institutions of all kinds ... were weakened»[35]. In addition, the state took over social tasks that religious had previously been doing out of charity.

None of this boded well for the evangelical counsel of poverty, and in fact it was the age in which the Dutch Augustinian province declined almost to extinction. But before it declined, it peaked. It peaked numerically, at nearly 400 in 1960. But the 1950s and 1960s were also a heyday in another respect. The expansion of the province's activities throughout the country was greater than it had ever been and Augustinian intellectuals contributed to public debates to a degree that had never been seen before[36]. New ideas about the church and modern society, the *aggiornamento* of the Second Vatican Council, and hopes of reform of the religious life seemed to promise a bright future for a reinvigorated church and order. It is tempting to view this late vigour as an anomaly, the last flourishing of a cultural phenomenon doomed to disappear. In fact, the high ideals of this last generation were creative, if ultimately unsuccessful responses to societal change.

The emphasis that the intellectual friars of the interwar years had placed on authenticity and personal commitment had unexpected and far-reaching consequences. Before the war, this emphasis was strongly ascetic: it was meant to be a demanding alternative to the shallow mediocrity of traditional Catholic spirituality[37]. The intellectuals of the 1930s had set the bar high: the religious life was about personal appropriation of uncompromising ideals. Their pupils, the post-war generation, believed that many of their fellow friars did not in fact meet this standard. Instead, this generation considered, they unthinkingly conformed to what was demanded of them, and were weighed down under the burden of vexatious rituals whose meaning they did not understand. Suddenly, the radical, «unadjusted» aspects of the religious life no longer seemed part of the solution, but part of the problem. Demanding ascetical practices, poverty, obedience – did these not encourage shallow formalism rather than deep spirituality? This thought made the young intellectuals of the 1950s anxious: how could the order

34 See H. McLeod, *The religious crisis of the 1960s*, Oxford 2007, 104; M. Gauvreau, *The Catholic origins of Quebec's Quiet Revolution, 1931-1970*, McGill-Queen», Montreal and Kingston 2005; C.G. Brown, *The death of Christian Britain. Understanding secularization, 1800-2000*, Abingdon 2001.

35 McLeod, *The religious crisis of the 1960s*, 123.

36 E. Simons-L. Winkeler, *Het verraad der clercken. Intellectuelen en hun rol in de ontwikkelingen van het Nederlandse katholicisme na 1945*, Baarn 1987, 159-160, 448-449.

37 Heffernan, *Kleine orde*, 199.

survive on conformism in an existentialist and consumerist age? If the religious life were to survive, it would have to be modernised and adapted. Everything that was an obstacle to true, personal commitment would have to go[38].

In 1963 the order symbolically divested itself of its eremitical heritage by dropping the word *Eremitarum* from its official name *Ordo Eremitarum Sancti Augustini*. Instead the order turned to Augustine's community ideal, the «charism of the founder»[39]. In the Dutch province, a study meeting on Augustinian poverty in late 1960 confirmed that ascetical perceptions of poverty were no longer in favour. The theme was that Augustinian poverty was not «characterised by hard self-denial and deprivation for the sake of penance», but was simply the «cutting away of what was superfluous and excessive»[40]. Soon the very process itself of studying the Rule or of trying to interpret what Augustine's ideal of the religious life meant was vitiated, as more radical reformers argued that a truly authentic religious life could be achieved only by discarding any normative standards at all[41]. The high-water mark came in 1969, when the provincial council proposed a radical transformation of the province into a federation of loosely associated persons, on the basis not of vows or hierarchy, but of personal commitment and experimentation[42].

The proposal was rejected at the 1970 provincial chapter, but its spirit lived on. Idealistic young friars created «experimental communities», which admitted non-Augustinians and practiced a radically egalitarian common life. These groups did not survive very long, and the most enduring legacy of the liberation was the emergence of the solitary Augustinian. Many friars moved out on their own – a third of the province in 1978[43]. The chapter of 1974 redefined the practice of communal property to reflect this new situation. Those who continued to live in community pooled their possessions, although the role of the prior was de-emphasised in favour of more democratic mutual agreements. Solitary friars were to control their own finances, but agreed to transfer any excess funds to the province[44].

38 Heffernan, *Kleine orde*, 206-207, 309-311.

39 Circular letter L. Rubio, 26 April 1963, *Acta Ordinis Sancti Augustini. Commentarium officiale* 8/1 (1963) 7.

40 Visitation speech Lucas Hoogveld, December 1959/January 1960, *Analecta Augustiniana Provinciae Hollandicae* 87 (1960) I-VIII, at IV.

41 See examples in Heffernan, *Kleine orde*, 313.

42 Heffernan, *Kleine orde*, 325-331.

43 L. van Gelder, «Komt de "E" weer in de "OSA"? De alleen wonende en/of levende religieus» *Nederlandse Analecta OSA* (August/September 1978) 1.

44 Finantieel statuut [1974] (HUA, 1392-1: ANA, 310).

Friars had been no less appreciative than laypeople of the good things that affluence had brought[45]. Middle-class normality became an ideal for many friars in the 1960s: compared to the modern layman – well-educated, well-off, sexually liberated, the master of his own destiny – reform-minded Augustinians felt inadequate. Many left the religious life, others stayed and cheered the dismantling of anything that set them apart from «normal» people. But by the 1980s a small group of friars forged what may be called a minor reaction against what they saw as their confrères' «passive conformism to middle-class prosperity» and «lack of evangelical radicalism»[46]. They advocated a return to tradition. By the 1990s, the province had rediscovered Augustine, not this time as the *magne pater* of the order, but as a spiritual master who might be «marketed» to an appreciative lay audience of spiritual seekers[47]. This late rediscovery of Augustine led to new initiatives, even if it was powerless to stave off the end of the province[48].

CONCLUSION

The changes in Augustinian conceptions of poverty identified in this paper reflect the evolving place of religion in Dutch society. The most recent episode has seen the rebranding of Augustine and his community ideal as a «spirituality» that can be practiced and enjoyed even apart from any permanent commitment to a particular belief system or organised religion. As such it has had some success. Several scholars have pointed to the popularity of religious «bricolage», and there is certainly a market for Augustinian spirituality, as there is for other schools of spirituality[49]. But what will remain of this once the last Dutch Augustinian has moved to a nursing home?

---

45 See example in HEFFERNAN, *Kleine orde*, 272.

46 M. SCHRAMA, «Zaken in orde brengen» *Nederlandse Analecta OSA* (April/June 1980), 3-4, at 3.

47 B. HEFFERNAN, «Van Groote Vader tot inspiratiebron. De Nederlandse augustijnen en Augustinus sinds de negentiende eeuw», in *Verlangen naar geestelijke schoonheid. Opstellen aangeboden aan Martijn Schrama, O.S.A.*, edd. J. van Neer-B. Heffernan, Bergambacht 2014, 157-168.

48 HEFFERNAN, *Kleine orde*, 391.

49 W. DAMBERG-P. PASTURE, «Restoration and erosion of pillarised Catholicism in Western Europe», in *The transformation of the Christian churches in Western Europe 1945-2000/La transformation des églises chrétiennes en Europe occidentale*, edd. L. Kenis-J. Billiet-P. Pasture, Leuven 2010, 55-76, at 73.

The story told here is one of constant – and often successful – adaptation of Augustinian religious life, capitalising on opportunities offered by modernity. The question is whether the last adaptation has not been too successful for its own good, whether the post-conciliar retreat from the radical, unadjusted aspects of the religious life has not been detrimental to it. Perhaps the Dutch Augustinians have recently been too eager to promote Augustinian spirituality, whilst neglecting to promote themselves. Sometimes reading the signs of the times can be important precisely because it allows one to go in the *opposite* direction.

Abstract

As do other monastic rules, the Rule of Saint Augustine stipulates that those who live in community must not call anything their own, but should possess everything in common. The practical application of this precept is an important touchstone of the radicalism of the religious life, and gauging conceptions of religious poverty is therefore a significant heuristic device for the historian of religious institutes. As Dutch Catholicism experienced a revival in the nineteenth century, it discovered the mobilising force of those aspects of Catholic tradition that were least acceptable to non-Catholic society, one of them being a more radical ideal of the religious life. For the «old orders» of mendicant friars, many of whom had been exclusively involved in parish ministry for centuries, revival came in the form of a campaign of «monasticisation». The introduction of the *vita communis perfecta* was an important aspect of this campaign.

This historical paper examines this process by taking the Dutch Augustinian Friars as a case. It starts with their founding of a first post-Reformation Augustinian priory in the Netherlands in 1886, and analyses their changing perceptions of religious poverty in the 120 years that followed. «Monasticisation» gave way in the interwar years to the search for a sophisticated spirituality in which the concepts of community and communal property played an important role. After the Second World War, and particularly in the 1960s, Dutch Augustinians looked critically at all aspects of their religious heritage. Many discarded traditional interpretations of the precept of religious poverty as being restrictive of free individual commitment and personal fulfilment. This changed again as interest in the spirituality of Augustine experienced a revival in the province from the 1980s onwards. In describing conceptions of religious poverty among the Dutch Augustinians, this paper shows how changing interpretations of this particular evangelical counsel can point to underlying shifts in the place of religion in modern Western society.

ALLOGGIARE, SFAMARE, PROVVEDERE DUE VOLTI FEMMINILI DELL'ECONOMIA CISTERCIENSE

Michaela PFEIFER

Per fondare un monastero, chi comincia a fare i conti, i fondatori o i patroni? Quando si tratta di comunità femminili, può essere un terzo gruppo, gli stessi membri futuri. È accaduto otto cent'anni fa, in Baviera, quando un gruppo di beghine, insieme con la Maestra, ha chiesto di essere ammesso nell'Ordine Cistercense la cui irradiazione spirituale e ascetica ha avuto la meglio sull'indipendenza della sua vita comunitaria al servizio dei poveri. Così nacque il monastero di Oberschönenfeld incorporato, trent'anni dopo, nell'Ordine[1]. Similmente, nel 1980, il monastero delle cistercensi di Valserena (PI) si è deciso di mandare delle monache in Angola per far nascere e sostenere una comunità di vita contemplativa; solo quest'anno, dopo quattro tentativi, ci si prepara all'insediamento nel monastero sulla collina del Soke nella diocesi di Huambo[2]. Queste iniziative da parte delle abitanti dei futuri monasteri non sono rare, ma non sempre sono coronate di successo. Mancava l'impianto economico adeguato?

Nella relazione seguente, si tratta meno della storia variegata delle due fondazioni tanto diverse che non dell'amministrazione economica che, pure in tempi e luoghi diversissimi, segue sempre un certo ordine: all'inizio stanno le iniziative per l'alloggio e l'alimentazione. Garantiti questi, si potrà pensare al futuro. Un tale procedimento non contraddice la concezione d'economia? Quali indicazioni si trovano nella Regola di S. Benedetto (= RB) e nelle costituzioni cistercensi?

All'ultima domanda sarà dedicato il primo breve passo. Seguirà l'esposizione del rovesciamento dell'economia del monastero bavarese, dopo il resoconto del-

---

Michaela Pfeifer, cistercian nun, theologian, ex-professor and ex-coordinator of the Monastic Institute at Sant'Anselmo Athenaeum in Rome

1 Cf. W. SCHIEDERMAIR, «Das Zisterzienserinnenkloster Oberschönenfeld von 1211 bis 2011. Ein geschichtlicher Abriss», in *Kloster Oberschönenfeld*, ed. ID., Lindenberg im Allgäu ^{2}2011, 28-35.

2 Riguardo al monastero Nostra Signora Regina della Pace cf. il resoconto «Angola: La communauté de la Reine de la Paix - Nasoma Y' Ombemwa», *Bulletin de l'A.I.M.* 102 (2012) 119-120, e l'altro sotto la voce «Valserena», *Liens cisterciens* 29 (2015) 41-47, soprattutto 44-45.

la faticosa costruzione di un impianto economico presso le monache in Angola. Alla fine si cercherà di paragonare questi due sviluppi con il traguardo di ogni gestione economica nel monastero, vale a dire la premura di dare consistenza a una vita comune che si dedica alla lode di Dio in povertà.

1. LE FONTI MONASTICHE, LETTERALMENTE, NON PARLANO DI "ECONOMIA"

Trattandosi di un gruppo di persone, bisogna concepire l'economia, in primo luogo, come "l'insieme delle risorse che possono essere utili alla produzione: la terra ecc.; è anche l'attività diretta all'utilizzazione di queste risorse: la coltivazione e la raccolta, la produzione, la distribuzione, la vendita e il consumo"[3]. All'attività, però, si aggiungono, sempre nell'arco dell'economia, la gestione e l'etica[4]. Per quanto riguarda la produzione e il consumo, li ritroviamo nella RB: il lavoro (RB 48; 57) procura quanto è necessario per la vita dei monaci (vitto, abbigliamento, alloggio e assistenza – cf. RB 39; 40; 55) e rende possibile il dispendio per i poveri (RB 53; 55; 66). Esiste pure un minimo di distribuzione e di vendita (RB 67; 57). La gestione di queste attività spetta all'abate (RB 2; 64), aiutato dal cellerario (RB 31), dal consiglio (RB 3), dai decani (RB 21) e dal priore (RB 65). Questa comprende anche il controllo, la resa dei conti, delle ammonizioni ed eventualmente pure delle punizioni (*passim*). Per quanto riguarda l'economia etica, nel capitolo degli artigiani (RB 57) si chiede di vendere i prodotti "un po' più a buon mercato dei secolari" (v. 8). Nel monastero, difatti, "la salvezza delle anime" (RB 2,33-36) è più importante delle sostanze, e promesso uno stile di vita ascetico, spetta a ciascuno e a tutta la comunità, amare e conservare la povertà . Questa, S. Benedetto la chiama "frugalità"; perciò insiste che ognuno prenda cura dei beni del monastero (*passim*). Non di meno l'economia monastica deve produrre un certo profitto per sostentare i membri che non possono ancora o non più lavorare: i novizi, gli anziani, deboli e ammalati. Inoltre l'orario nel monastero raramente permette un lavoro che superi sei ore. Ci vuole molta destrezza per trovare un lavoro remunerativo idoneo. Spesso s'impiegano salariati ovvero si accettano, in monastero, dei fratelli e sorelle converse; nei monasteri femminili, fino al 1960, si richiedeva a chi entrava, una dote.

3 Cf. la voce «Economia» nel sito www.treccani.it, nella rubrica *Domande e risposte*, [accesso: 18-5-2016].

4 Cf. la voce «Economia» nel *Dizionario Italiano Sabatini Coletti*, Firenze 1997, 818-819, spec. n. 6 ("economia politica").

L'ordine cistercense, primo "ordine" religioso, come padroneggia questo stato di fatto complesso? È l'anno 1098; i primi monaci s'installano a Cîteaux per vivere una vita monastica in un luogo appartato, "poveri con il povero Cristo", lavorando con le proprie mani. Perciò decidono di osservare esattamente la Regola di S. Benedetto. Questo vale anche per la loro vita economica, come lo dice il Piccolo Esordio:

> Siccome non trovavano, né nella Regola né nella Vita di s. Benedetto, che il loro maestro abbia posseduto chiese, altari, contributi, sepolture, decime di persone straniere, fornaci, mulini, villaggi o servi della gleba..., anche loro vi rinunciarono...In tal modo, poveri con il povero Cristo, disprezzarono le ricchezze di questo mondo. Come nuovi soldati di Cristo cominciarono a riflettere secondo quale progetto, con quale mestiere o con quale attività avrebbero potuto sostenere se stessi che vivevano così, nonché gli ospiti che sarebbero arrivati, prescrivendo la Regola di accettarli come Cristo, siano poveri o ricchi[5].

Il risultato di queste riflessioni è la decisione di accettare dei fratelli conversi nel monastero. Questi avrebbero continuato il lavoro, quando loro stessi si recavano all'ufficio, e sarebbero vissuti anche fuori della clausura nelle grange per coltivare i campi più remoti. Il nuovo Ordine Cistercense è riuscito a fare a meno di benefattori ricchi e a realizzare l'ideale dell'autonomia benedettina? Gli ultimi studi storici provano che non ci sono riusciti, nemmeno nei primi cinquant'anni[6]. Allora come si viveva nei monasteri femminili dell'Ordine dove le regole di clausura restringevano ancora le possibilità di lavoro?

2. GESTIRE UN'ECONOMIA ALLA LODE DI DIO PER OTTOCENTO ANNI: L'ABBAZIA BAVARESE DI OBERSCHÖNENFELD

Fin a oggi, gli esperti della storiografia cistercense non sono d'accordo sul modo in cui l'Ordine, nel XIII secolo, si è comportato di fronte all'incorporazione dei mo-

---

5 *Il Piccolo Esordio* (*Exordium parvum*), ed. Goffredo Viti, cap. XV, nel sito http://www.cistercensi.info/testi/fonti.php, [accesso: 18-5-2016].

6 Cf. C.H. Berman, «Les Cisterciens et le tournant économique du XIIe siècle», in *Bernard de Clairvaux. Histoire, mentalités, spiritualité*, Paris 1992, 155-177. Riguardo all'economia dei cistercensi e alla discussione dei loro attributi d'innovatori, pionieri o primi capitalisti cf. E. Jamroziak, *The Cistercian Order in Medieval Europe 1090-1500*, London-New-York 2013, Chapter 6.«Economy: not just Sheep and Grain», 183-307.

nasteri femminili. Lo fece soltanto perché obbligati dalle autorità ecclesiastiche? Ovvero visto la mole delle richieste, ci voleva unicamente del tempo per stabilire le condizioni d'ammissione?[7] Stefano Harding e Bernardo di Chiaravalle, nella prima metà del XII secolo, avevano appoggiato la fondazione dei monasteri Jully e Tart; fra gli statuti dei capitoli generali, però, solo nel 1237 e 1257 si trovano i primi statuti per monasteri femminili[8]. Ecco i punti decisivi: I monasteri maschili e femminili sono equiparati e formano l'unico ordine cistercense; anche dal punto di vista economico, hanno la stessa struttura. Dall'altra parte vi si scorge la posizione della donna nella società medievale[9]. Accanto alle leggi severe della clausura, ogni monastero femminile è sottoposto a un abate, al "padre immediato". Questi vi fa la visita canonica annuale ed elegge un cappellano per la cura d'anima delle monache. Secondo la loro situazione economica, stabilisce il numero massimo delle monache[10], accetta la loro professione come quella dei fratelli e sorelle converse ed esercita un influsso notevole sulla gestione dei possedimenti e delle finanze a carico dell'abbadessa; inoltre controlla le attività dei conversi incaricati con i numerosi contatti con l'esterno.

7 Cf. «Die älteste Gesetzgebung des Generalkapitels für die Zisterziensernonnen», in *Neuerung und Erneuerung. Wichtige Quellentexte aus der Geschichte des Zisterzienserordens vom 12. bis 17. Jahrhundert*, edd. H. Brem-A. M. Altermatt (Quellen und Studien zur Zisterzienserliteratur VI), Langwaden 2003, 71-101, qui 77-78; JAMROZIAK, *The Cistercian Order* (nota 6), 124-155, qui 124-132.

8 *Neuerung und Erneuerung* (nota 7) riproduce nelle pp. 82-101 una sinossi latino-tedesca degli statuti di 1237 e di 1257.

9 Cf. W. RÖSENER, «Haushalt und Gebet–Frauenklöster des Mittelalters als Wirtschaftsorganismen», in *Krone und Schleier. Kunst aus mittelalterlichen Frauenklöstern. Ruhrlandmuseum: Die frühen Klöster und Stifte. Kunst- und Ausstellungshalle der Bundesrepublik Deutschland: Die Zeit der Orden 1200-1500*, edd. Jutta Frings-Jan Gerchow, München 2005, 79-87, qui 82-84.

10 In questo contesto bisogna anche parlare della dote, importante per la manutenzione del monastero scelto dalla novizia e in uso fino agli anni sessanta del Novecento. Obbligatoria dal Cinquecento, fu regolata dal diritto canonico nell'Ottocento, cf. F. CUBELLI-G. ROCCA, «Dote», in *Dizionario degli Istituti di Perfezione* (=DIP) 3 (1976) 968-972. Grazie alla situazione economica dei monasteri europei odierni, nella maggioranza dei casi non è più necessaria, anche perché molte novizie hanno già una formazione professionale. Secondo il Codice Orientale, però, la dote rimane una possibilità a seconda del diritto particolare degli istituti (*Codex Canonum Ecclesiarum Orientalium* [=CCEO] c. 79 PA). Cf. Br. PRIMETSHOFER, *Ordensrecht auf der Grundlage des Codex Iuris Canonici* (=CIC) *1983 und des CCEO unter Berücksichtigung des staatlichen Rechts der Bundesrepublik Deutschland, Österreichs und der Schweiz*, Freiburg im Breisgau [4]2003, 197-198.

In tutto ciò appare una caratteristica tipicamente medievale, la tripartizione della società in chi fa la guerra, chi prega e chi lavora ovvero in *bellatores – oratores - aratores*[11]. L'aristocrazia ha bisogno d'intercessori presso Dio la cui preghiera allevia la pena per tutti i peccati perpetrati in terra e dopo la morte, ottiene la salvezza delle loro anime in cielo[12]. La preghiera delle monache ha una forza speciale, perché è la preghiera di vergini. Perciò i nobili fondano o istituiscono dei monasteri femminili dove si prega per loro quotidianamente e dove la loro tomba, più tardi, sarà posta ai gradini dell'altare. Dall'altro canto, questi monasteri devono sostituirli nella cura per i poveri, costruendo ospedali e scuole. Molti mandano loro le figlie per l'educazione. Questo legame dura tutta la vita; proteggono il monastero con il loro aiuto giuridico e militare. L'abbadessa, da parte sua, tutela come amministratrice della proprietà fondiaria del monastero i suoi diritti non solo civili, ma anche ecclesiali, quando si tratta di chiese, pievi e cappellani, appoggiandosi sull'aiuto dei benefattori.

L'abbazia bavarese di Oberschönenfeld, nei pressi di Augusta, era un tale organismo economico medievale. Fondato nel 1211 dal duca di Dillingen, fu incorporato nel 1248 nell'Ordine cistercense e sottoposto all'abate di Kaisheim. Grazie alle donazioni dei ministeriali di Kemnat e di altri nobili, già nel 1262 si poté far consacrare la chiesa. Da questa data fino alla sua soppressione nel 1803, ha vissuto le peripezie di un patrimonio fondiario che si estendeva fino al Danubio[13]. Di continuo bisognava, tramite lettere e libelli di protezione, confermare i possedimenti e resistere ai conflitti armati.

Nella guerra delle città del XIV secolo, la chiesa e il monastero furono distrutti; per sopravvivere, le monache dovevano fare elemosina. L'anno 1525 fu l'inizio di quattro periodi di esilio nel quale le monache si salvarono prima dalle guerre dei contadini, poi da quelle della Riforma. Alla fine ritornarono in tre. Mentre cercavano di ricostruire le rovine, presero una decisione a lungo termi-

11 Cf. G. Constable, «The Orders of Society», in Id., *Three Studies in Medieval Religious and Social Thought*, Cambridge 1998, 249-323.

12 Cf. H. Röckelein, «Gründer, Stifter und Heilige – Patrone der Frauenkonvente», in *Krone und Schleier. Kunst aus mittelalterlichen Frauenklöstern. Ruhrlandmuseum: Die frühen Klöster und Stifte. Kunst- und Ausstellungshalle der Bundesrepublik Deutschland: Die Zeit der Orden 1200-1500*, edd. Jutta Frings-Jan Gerchow, München 2005, 66-77.

13 Cf. P. Fried-G. Fürmetz, «Obrigkeit und Ökonomie: Grundzüge der herrschafts-, sozial- und wirtschaftsgeschichtlichen Entwicklung des Klosters Oberschönenfeld bis zur Säkularisation», in *"Kloster Oberschönenfeld"*, ed. Schiedermair, 36-45; G. Fürmetz, «Kloster Oberschönenfeld: Übersicht über die Grund- und Gerichtsherrschaft am Ende des Alten Reiches (um 1800)», *Ibid.* 46-49.

ne: mancando le vocazioni nobili, d'ora in poi si accettavano anche delle novizie borghesi. Le abbadesse del tempo, quindi, abolirono le residenze in cui alcune monache nobili abitavano con proprio personale di casa, e introdussero le suore converse. Si elesse la prima abbadessa borghese, Barbara II Elchinger (+1601), la "restauratrice del monastero"; fece rinnovare gli edifici, secondo le leggi del Concilio di Trento osservò strettamente la clausura e iniziò delle confraternite di preghiera con altri monasteri. Anche le sue succeditrici cercavano di ristabilire gli ideali dell'Ordine: si comprò un organo con i risparmi privati delle monache, si organizzarono delle lezioni di canto e s'introdussero gli esercizi spirituali annuali.

La guerra dei trent'anni (1618-1648) fu ancora più devastatrice. Prima le monache dovevano pagare dei contributi alla guerra, poi sopportare un esilio di tre anni nel Tirolo. Tornate a casa, bisognava ricostruire le rovine e implorare l'imperatore di confermare l'abbazia e i suoi possedimenti. Nel 1654 l'Abate Generale dell'Ordine Claude Vaussin visitò l'abbazia e disse: "È tornato uno spirito eccellente." Difatti, fu l'opera dell'abbadessa più famosa nella storia del luogo, Elisabeth Herold (+1646): abbellì l'ufficio divino "alla gloria di Dio", iniziò la galleria delle abbadesse e redisse, per confortare le consorelle, la cronaca dell'abbazia fin dalle sue origini[14]. Fu, però, solo la succeditrice a consolidare l'economia con la costruzione degli edifici adibiti all'economia. Pochi decenni dopo, i soldati della guerra di successione spagnola (1701-1714) scacciarono le monache e fecero bottino del monastero. Tutte, però, ritornarono e si misero alla ricostruzione.

Alla fine del XVIII secolo, nonostante le numerose costruzioni barocche, i debiti dell'abbazia erano pochi, e l'ultima abbadessa prima della soppressione lodò "la bella unanimità in comunità". Nel 1803 arrivò il colpo della secolarizzazione: si perse non solo tutto il patrimonio ma si vietarono sia l'elezione di un'abbadessa sia l'ammissione di novizie. Solo nel 1836, ridotto il numero delle monache a sei, si ricevette il permesso di riprendere la vita regolare. Pezzo per pezzo, si ricomprò quanto era necessario per la vita; nel 1918 l'abbazia fu riconfermata e nel 1922 si elesse di nuovo un'abbadessa. Il regime nazionalsocialista minacciava ripetutamente di sopprimere il monastero. Infatti, gli anni 1944-1946 furono più pesanti: bisognava alimentare i fuggitivi e poveri con il pane della propria fornace. Dal 1948 rifiorì la comunità che poté fondare tre

14 *Kloster Oberschönenfeld - Die Chronik der Elisabeth Herold* mit dem Titel *Geschichte des Klosters Oberschönenfeld von dem Jahr nach Christi Geburt 1211 bis aufs Jahr 1633, nebst einer Ergänzung bis zum Jahr 1657*, ed. W. Schiedermair, Lindenberg im Allgäu 2011.

monasteri nel Brasile[15]; dal 1973 al 1991, grazie a una nuova gestione economica e all'aiuto della sovrintendenza ai beni culturali, gli edifici storici, la chiesa e il convento furono sottoposti a un restauro generale.

L'anno di svolta era 1971, sei anni dopo la chiusura del Concilio Vaticano II. Si decise, per motivi di mancanza di redditi, di dare in affitto due terzi dei 150 ettari di superficie agricola insieme con il permesso di caccia, con l'esercizio della pesca nello specchio d'acqua e nel torrente, e con gli edifici dell'economia e il ristorante; rimasero nel possesso 50 ettari di foresta e il giardino del convento. Per gli stessi motivi si chiuse, nel 1985, il pollaio e nel 1989, l'asilo per gli anziani, troppo piccolo perché si adeguasse alle nuove leggi sanitarie. Dopo il Concilio fu anche cambiata la clausura papale in quella costituzionale; perciò le monache incominciarono a prender cura se stesse degli ospiti in foresteria; nel 1977, le novizie proposero di vendere, accanto al loro famoso pane cotto in forno a legna, anche degli articoli attinenti alla vita monastica[16]. Così si aprì un negozio di letteratura e arte religiosa. Oggi i pilastri dell'economia di Oberschönenfeld sono l'affitto, la fornace, il negozio, i contributi della sovrintendenza e dell'associazione degli amici del monastero nonché la foresteria. Lì si offrono anche dei corsi per i quali alcune sorelle si sono specializzate. Nella situazione attuale, l'abbadessa, l'economa e la contabile possono essere fiduciose: "Se non accadono delle catastrofi, il futuro delle nostre ventuno monache sembra essere assicurato." Non si potrebbe cuocere ancora più pane e allargare la foresteria? La comunità dice di no; bisogna preservare il carattere di una piccola impresa gestibile. Si cerca, invece, la produzione biologica dei generi alimentari, il commercio equo-solidale e la cura dei poveri alla porta del monastero[17].

---

15 Si tratta dei monasteri di Itararé (1965), Monte Castelo (1973), Campo Grande (1976). Cf.. B. Esser, «Die Abtei Oberschönenfeld und ihre Tochtergründungen in Brasilien», in *Kloster Oberschönenfeld - Die Chronik der Elisabeth Herold* mit dem Titel *Geschichte des Klosters Oberschönenfeld von dem Jahr nach Christi Geburt 1211 bis aufs Jahr 1633, nebst einer Ergänzung bis zum Jahr 1657*, ed. W. Schiedermair, Lindenberg im Allgäu 2011, 194-195.

16 Cf. «Arbeitsbereiche im Kloster Oberschönenfeld heute – Gästebetreuung, Buch- und Kunsthandlung, Bäckerei und Paramentenwerkstatt», in *Kloster Oberschönenfeld - Die Chronik der Elisabeth Herold* mit dem Titel *Geschichte des Klosters Oberschönenfeld von dem Jahr nach Christi Geburt 1211 bis aufs Jahr 1633, nebst einer Ergänzung bis zum Jahr 1657*, Lindenberg im Allgäu 2011, 182-185; W. Schiedemeyer, «Die Zusammensetzung des Konvents von Oberschönenfeld», in *Ibid.* 51-59, spec. 59.

17 Ecco alcune osservazioni orali in merito fatte da parte dell'abbadessa emerita di Oberschönenfeld M. Ancilla Betting: Accanto al pane di segale cotto nel forno a legna, si coltivano anche il legume e la frutta nel modo biologico. Nel lavoro, le monache sono

Poco tempo fa il cosiddetto "Weiherhof", il maso nel quale vivevano le beghine prima di traslocare, ben otto cento anni fa, nel "bel campo superiore" ("Oberschönen-feld"), è stato restituito al monastero. La comunità decise di metterlo a disposizione dei profughi, secondo il principio dell'economia benedettino-cistercense di provvedere sia al proprio mantenimento, sia all'aiuto dei poveri.

È diversa la situazione delle consorelle a Soke nell'Angola. Qui il passato doloroso del paese è sempre presente.

3. TRENT'ANNI DI VITA MONASTICA IN PUNTA DI PIEDI. IL PRIORATO CISTERCENSE DI NASOMA Y' OMBEMBWA

Fin dalla fondazione a Huambo, nel 1980, il priorato cistercense di Nasoma Y' Ombwemba[18] sta aspettando il trasloco definitivo in un monastero. Non è mai mancato il lavoro. Durante gli anni di guerra civile bisognava sfamare non solo se stesse, ma anche, con l'aiuto di benefattori italiani, i bambini e gli anziani delle vicinanze e costruire delle capanne per i rifugiati[19]. Più tardi, le monache cominciarono, nonostante le strade minate, a uscire dalla città in punta di piedi e a piantare il mais a Cuando. Trasferitesi, poi, nella *fazenda* più spaziosa di Cambiote, vi piantarono banane, fragole, un frutteto e un orto. Furono, però, i militari a raccogliere. Le monache fuggirono e trovarono rifugio presso i Padri missionari di Kakuti dove ricevettero un campo per l'orto. Nell'anno della pace 1992, s'installarono su una *fazenda* di 4000 ettari a Bailundo, a 80 km da Huambo, per dissodare, seminare e progettare un monastero. Misurando un geometra italiano il terreno, i guerriglieri della vicinanza accusarono le monache di tradimento e minacciarono di rapirle. Queste caricarono sul loro camioncino i tetti delle loro due case, delle coperte di lana, due mobili e 20 giovani alberi da frutta e si rimisero in strada.

---

assecondate da tre impiegati maschili e cinque femminili. L'approvvigionamento energetico, purtroppo, non è ancora sostenibile. Siccome l'area del monastero fa parte del parco naturale "I boschi occidentali" del distretto rurale di Augusta, è vietata l'installazione di torri eoliche, panelli solari e fotovoltaici che muterebbero l'aspetto del paesaggio.

18 Accanto alle fonti citate nella nota 2, la relazione presente si appoggia sul periodico quadrimestrale dell'Associazione Nostra Signora della Pace ONLUS Guardistallo (Pi) «Il Seme. Lettera agli amici» e sulle notizie dell'Internet sotto i due indirizzi http://www.valserena.it/angola.html e http://www.trappisteangola.org/. Sul sito dell'Ordine Cistercense dell'Osservanza Stretta (www.ocso.org) si trovano le indicazioni necessarie e 21 fotografie dello stato attuale sotto la voce Huambo che corrisponde al n. 55 del catalogo.

19 Riguardo ad Angola, cf. la voce «Angola» in *Die Religion in Geschichte und Gegenwart* (=RGG)^{4} 1 (1998) 494-495, e in *Meyers großes Taschenlexikon* 1 (^{8}2001) 198-199.

Si trovò nel mezzo di un'antica *fazenda* di 2000 ettari, la collina di Soke. Era stata la proprietà di un signore portoghese; durante la guerra aveva servito a entrambi i partiti come quartiere militare, adesso, però, era inabitabile a causa delle mine. Le autorità la cedettero alla comunità che pagò i militari perché la sminassero. In punta di piedi si ricominciò a dissodare e piantare. Si costruì una casa di fango per farvi abitare un primo gruppo di monache. Scoppiò di nuovo la guerra civile, e tutto era perso. Tornata la pace, il cappellano brasiliano P. José incoraggiò la comunità a costruire il monastero. Dopo la sua morte improvvisa, fu il suo successore, un monaco architetto, a presentare un nuovo progetto. Iniziati i lavori nel 2011, tre anni dopo la prima parte era finita, e il laboratorio artigianale, finora installato a Huambo, poteva trasferirsi. Difatti, già dal 1994 era iniziata la produzione, simile al mezzo di sostentamento nella casa madre, di prodotti farmaceutici e cosmetici a base naturale per la quale alcune monache si erano preparate tramite corsi specializzati in Italia. Ora potevano lavorare sul posto insieme con le altre consorelle. Finalmente nel 2014 è cominciata la costruzione del monastero stesso[20]. Le venti monache sperano di poter toccare, dopo 27 anni di continui traslochi, il porto sicuro, tanto necessario per le consorelle anziane e per quelle in formazione.

A questo punto saranno esclusi i poveri? La Regola di S. Benedetto, nei cap. 53 e 66, ammonisce di accogliere poveri e stranieri, mettendo alla porta del monastero un fratello saggio e abile a rispondere ai loro bisogni. Difatti, accanto al monastero, Soke è diventato, sempre grazie ai benefattori italiani, un centro sociale per aiutare la gente povera in campagna. Quella, purtroppo, anche dopo l'accordo di pace, non approfitta dello sviluppo nel paese – uno dei più ricchi dell'Africa –, perché la corruzione impoverisce sempre i poveri. A Soke, i contadini seguono l'esempio delle monache: nell'azienda agricola del monastero guadagnano la loro vita, coltivando banane, caffè e mais. Nei villaggi vicini sono stati creati scuole e appartamenti per gli insegnanti, una distribuzione di medicinali, sussidi per nuove case, un centro parrocchiale e una formazione scolastica per ragazze adolescenti e giovani a Huambo. Dal 2012, le monache consegnarono le scuole, i due posti medici e il collegio di quaranta ragazzine a due congregazioni di vita attiva[21]. Trasferita la responsabilità, si potevano ritirare nel silenzio della loro clausura.

20 L'organizzazione dell'*Alliance InterMonastères* ha aiutato la costruzione con un contributo notevole.

21 Difatti, sono stati consegnati i centri sociali di cui le trappiste erano responsabili, alle "Suore di Tchilonga" di origine messicana, "Instituto de Coadjutoras do Apostolado So-

Filtrando da questo resoconto commovente i dati sobri dell'economia monastica, ne spiccano tre attributi: essa è allo stesso tempo sociale, economica ed ecologica. Il tratto sociale è, dall'una parte, la distribuzione di viveri e di medicine ai poveri, dall'altra l'esempio delle monache che incoraggia i contadini angosciati a prendere la zappa in mano. Il lato economico e provvedente si scorge nei due pilastri del guadagno, l'azienda agricola e quella artigianale. Inoltre, l'attività nel laboratorio si adatta specialmente alla spiritualità cistercense, poiché tutte le monache, nel silenzio, mettono i loro talenti diversi a disposizione dell'opera comune. Per finire, il fatto che i prodotti del laboratorio sono a base naturale, è un segno del fine ecologico e duraturo di quest'economia. Questo si rispecchia anche nel fatto che la produzione si è spostata dalla città in campagna, alle radici del popolo angolano. Per quanto concerne il fine primario di un'economia monastica, bisogna costatare: Nasoma Y' Owembwa non può ancora sostenere se stesso. Visto la situazione politica e sociale attuale del paese[22], per lungo tempo dipenderà ancora dalla casa madre europea Valserena.

CONCLUSIONE

Prima di paragonare l'economia dei due monasteri femminili, bisogna costatare per entrambi le case: nessuna potrà amministrare i beni in un modo tanto eccellente da arricchirsi. Nei secoli passati è esistito il pericolo che la diligenza delle monache, tutte quante persone celibi e senza posteri, superi il rigore del voto della povertà[23]; oggigiorno è inconcepibile, non solo a causa delle condizioni di vita precarie come nell'Angola, ma anche sotto le condizioni dello stato europeo assistenziale. I suoi obblighi civili prevedono non solo delle tasse ma anche dei contributi sociali di tale altezza che ogni casa religiosa ha bisogno di un certo sovrappiù per sostenere i suoi membri che non lavorano ancora o non più. Inoltre, nel caso dell'abbazia bavarese, bisogna contribuire al mantenimento degli edifici storici con una certa quota.

"Alloggiare, sfamare, provvedere" è il titolo di questo contributo. Il fine principale di una proficua gestione economica, in un monastero, è il consolidamento delle sostanze in vista del futuro, come lo dice la parola *oikonomia* stessa: il governo della casa. Tante volte, nel corso della storia delle due comunità, questo "provvede-

cial" (I.C.A.S.), e dal 2014, alle Suore di S. Giuseppe di Cluny (S.J.C.) che si presenta nella rivista *Il Seme* n. 41 (maggio 2016). A Huambo fu creato anche un legame con l'"Opera Don Calabria" per bambini orfani e andicappati. Le tre congregazioni ricevono un sopporto finanziario da parte di Valserena.

22 Cf. K. Maier, *Angola: Promises and Lies*, London 2013.

23 Cf. «Economia», in *DIP* 3 (1976) 1011-1047, qui 1011.

re" fu trascurato quando bisognava salvarsi la vita. Non di meno, le monache angolane e bavaresi erano sempre spinte, appena giunto un posto sicuro, a salvaguardare l'alloggio e l'alimentazione in vista della loro promessa di stabilità. La brama di sopravvivere e l'intesa in comunità si coniugavano con i principi della vita monastica sì da cercare e realizzare con coraggio, talvolta con audacia, nuovi modi di un'economia duratura. Ne risulta un'economia aperta ai bisogni sociali, provvidente ed equo-solidale che corrisponde alla concezione di sostenibilità nella *Responsabilità sociale d'impresa (Corporate Social Responsibility* [CSR][24].

Secondo l'appartenenza delle comunità, quella dell'Angola alla Stretta Osservanza Cistercense, quella bavarese alla Comune Osservanza, le soluzioni economiche adoperate si dirigono, sul piano spirituale, in sensi opposti, l'una per ritornare alla vita contemplativa, l'altra per aprirsi di più al mondo. Oberschönenfeld è stato costretto, dalla secolarizzazione, a passare dalla "garanzia del possedimento fondiario"[25] al sostentamento personale produttivo. Le cistercensi angolane, capitate nel mezzo della guerra civile, dovevano, nei primi trent'anni, occuparsi dei poveri; finalmente arrivate a Soke e grazie a una buona amministrazione dell'aiuto e dei fondi da parte di benefattori, stanno oggi per insediarsi nel proprio monastero nel quale, in silenzio, possono dedicarsi alla contemplazione. Amministrare economicamente un monastero non dipende solo dai tempi ma anche riflette, spesso a sua insaputa, le sue caratteristiche sociali, artistiche e spirituali. Riflette pure il modo in cui il proprio Ordine, anch'egli legato al proprio tempo, interpreta e vive la tensione fra l'"Opera di Dio" al quale "niente deve'essere anteposto" (RB 43,4), e i poveri "che non mancano mai nel monastero" (RB 53,16).

Abstract

Nell'ordine cistercense, si può parlare di economia in senso stretto? I suoi testi legislativi primitivi non la conoscono né la Regola di S. Benedetto. Benché la storiografia parli del "miracolo economico cistercense", la presente conferenza

24 Secondo Wikipedia [accesso: 10/10/2016], la *Responsabilità sociale d'impresa* è definita, nel 2011, dall'Unione Europea, come «La responsabilità delle imprese per il loro impatto sulla società». Fra i manuali citati sono A. Beretta Zanoni, «Le relazioni con gli stakeholder e gli obiettivi istituzionali d'impresa. Un approccio strategico - nuovi strumenti per la CSR», in *La teoria degli stakeholder*, edd. E.R. Freeman-G. Rusconi-M. Dorigatti, Milano 2007 e F. Perrini-A. Tencati, *Corporate Social Responsibility. Un approccio strategico alla gestione d'impresa* (La cultura d'impresa), Milano 2008.

25 A. Duval, «Economia monastica femminile», in «Economia», in *DIP* 3 (1976) 1042.

si limita ai tre scopi di base di ogni economia monastica, "alloggiare, sfamare, provvedere", per ricercarli presso due monasteri femminili dell'ordine.

L'abbazia bavarese di Oberschönenfeld, nei suoi ottocento anni, sopravvisse a distruzioni e soppressioni. Dal proprietario terreno di allora si è trasmutata in un centro artigianale, culturale, artistico e spirituale nei dintorni di Augusta, guidata dalle monache formate ed esperte nelle diverse discipline.

Il priorato trappista di Nasoma Y'Ombembwa fu fondato nel 1980 in Angola, prima della ricomparsa della guerra civile. Fuggite quattro volte dai militari e dai campi minati, le monache ora si avviano alla costruzione di un monastero a Soke; lì è già costruito un laboratorio farmaceutico dalle cui rendite vive la comunità. L'appoggio costante dell'abbazia fondatrice di Valserena (PI) e dell'associazione di benefattori sostengono e forniscono i mezzi per aiutare la gente povera del paese.

Dando un primo sguardo retrospettivo alle due storie, il verbo "alloggiare" che occupa il primo posto nel titolo, nell'Angola, cede il passo allo "sfamare", al bisogno vitale. Nei termini della Regola, la "stabilità" necessita un minimo di sussistenza. È evidente, poi, l'impatto formativo dell'economia "ad extra", soprattutto a Soke dove le monache, lavorando nei campi, mostrano come sopravvivere. A Oberschönenfeld, oggi, si tratta piuttosto di un'irradiazione spirituale del posto che diventa un antidoto contro l'angoscia diffusa medio-europea.

L'impatto formativo dell'economia "ad intra" è l'urgenza di formazione professionale coniugata con l'accettazione di ogni strato sociale in comunità. Così è più facile evitare i pericoli della clausura stretta femminile, l'ideologizzazione e la deresponsabilizzazione. Un *desideratum* rimane l'autonomia femminile economica presso le autorità dell'Ordine.

CAMPUS AMABILIS. AMBIENTE, LAVORO E CONTEMPLAZIONE NELLA TRADIZIONE EREMITICA CAMALDOLESE

Lorenzo Saraceno

1. LA PROSPETTIVA NELL'APPROCCIO

L'eremo di Camaldoli (da *campus amabilis*?[1]) nella sua storia ormai millenaria si è configurato coniugando il suo insediamento con un ambiente naturale, la circostante foresta casentinese, la quale sembra avere avuto un ruolo importante per definire la percezione della sua identità propria, come forse per poche altre realtà monastiche, dove maggior rilievo ha assunto la edificazione di strutture murarie importanti entro cui collocare i *claustra monasterii*. Sta di fatto che, pur con il mutare delle sensibilità degli eremiti che ci hanno vissuto e con l'evolversi nel tempo dei gusti estetici, l'eremo è rimasto sostanzialmente semplice dal punto di vista degli edifici, e nello stesso tempo gli eremiti sono stati molto attenti a creare e conservare l'ambiente della foresta circostante come lo spazio della loro separatezza e il confine della loro *conversatio* monastica. Per questo si suol dire che la gestione della foresta è apparsa sempre come un aspetto connaturato alla vita dell'eremo, e la peculiarità del cosiddetto "Codice forestale", integrato alle costituzioni camaldolesi ad opera di Paolo Giustiniani nel 1521[2], da questo

---

Lorenzo Saraceno, monaco camaldolese, insegnante, autore, editore, collaboratore della cattedra di Lingua e letteratura latina medievale dell'Università di Verona.

1 Come noto, il toponimo Camaldoli sembra riferirsi alla definizione di *campus amabilis* in riferimento al sito dell'Eremo che fu oggetto della donazione da parte del vescovo Tedaldo nel 1024. Solo un secolo dopo (nel quadro di un conflitto di patronato insorto tra il vescovo di Arezzo e la feudalità laica), nasce la leggenda di un *campus Maldoli*, che fa di un certo conte Maldolo, non altrimenti documentato, il donatore del terreno; cf. G. Vedovato, *Camaldoli e la sua congregazione dalle origini al 1184. Storia e documentazione*, (Italia Benedettina XIII) Cesena 1994, 15-23.

2 Per la questione della genesi e della applicazione del Codice forestale camaldolese si veda G. M. Cacciamani, *L'antica foresta di Camaldoli: storia e codice forestale*, Camaldoli, Edizioni Camaldoli, 1965; V. Merlo, *La foresta come chiostro. Influsso delle idee cristiane sull'ambiente vegetale*, Cinisello Balsamo, 1997, 109-129; *Il codice forestale camaldolese: legislazione e gestione del bosco nella documentazione d'archivio romualdina*, ed. Francesco

punto di vista potrebbe essere inteso come il punto di arrivo di una coscienza ormai radicata. Secondo alcuni in tutto questo si potrebbe infine scorgere nel lungo periodo il definirsi di una sorta di *genius loci*, e di riflesso di una sensibilità in qualche modo ecologica *ante litteram*. Ci si può chiedere allora se il fissarsi a futura memoria di una tradizione di cura, di adattamento e armonizzazione degli insediamenti materiali e del sistema di vita nell'ambiente ha comportato ricadute nella concezione del lavoro e della economia di una comunità monastica semianacoretica quale quella di Camaldoli. Proprio intorno ad alcune dimensioni di questo *genius loci*, tra idealizzazione e realtà, si vogliono porre le osservazioni che seguono.

In anni recenti ho già studiato alcune delle immagini della vita eremitica in qualche modo tipiche della più antica tradizione camaldolese e avellanita, con l'intento di individuare alcuni tratti ideali nella coscienza dei suoi protagonisti. A partire dalle mie competenze, di ordine linguistico e letterario, ho fissato la mia attenzione su tipologie testuali di carattere latamente poetico (per esempio le *laudes crucis* o *heremi* di Pier Damiani), che si pongono in modo esplicito a un livello alto di espressione. In questo contesto si era posto già un mio studio del 2007 riguardo ad alcuni aspetti del mito della cella come luogo privilegiato della contemplazione in Pier Damiani[3]. In quella sede utilizzavo, non senza una certa vena provocatoria, la parola mito: nella rappresentazione retoricamente elevata e talvolta stilisticamente lussureggiante che si fa dell'eremo e della cella si concentra un mondo di aspirazioni, di tensioni e di valori di riferimento che, nella loro dimensione concettuale ed esistenziale, mediante l'analisi critica e la ricostruzione storica, possiamo certo sottoporre a un sano processo di demitologizzazione[4]; ma è anche vero che la rappresentazione mitizzante in quanto

---

Cardarelli, Roma, Ente italiano della montagna – Bologna 2009; *Codice forestale camaldolese. Le radici della sostenibilità* [Roma], I.N.E.A, 2010; *Foresta e monaci di Camaldoli : un rapporto millenario tra gestione e conservazione. Codice forestale camaldolese*, edd. C. Urbinati-R. Romano, [Roma], INEA [2012].

3 Cf. L. Saraceno, «Il mito della cella come luogo privilegiato della contemplazione. Una lettura della *Laus heremi* nella lettera 28 (*Dominus vobiscum*) di Pier Damiani», in *La grammatica di Cristo di Pier Damiani. Un maestro per il nostro tempo*, ed. G.I. Gargano e L. Saraceno, S. Pietro in Cariano 2009, 184-219.

4 Come si potrebbe fare anche per alcune forme parossistiche di ascesi: poteva il Loricato andare da Fonte Avellana a Osimo conciato nella maniera descritta da Pier Damiani nella lettera 112? O poteva Pier Damiani digiunare con il il rigore da lui prescritto quando affrontava i suoi viaggi a cavallo, quand'anche affermi che la legazione in Francia avvenne nel rispetto delle norme del digiuno (cf. *Iter Gallicum, vel De Gallica Petri Damiani profectione et eius ultramontano itinere*, edd. G Schwartz-A. Hofmeister, in *Monumenta Germaniae*

tale resta pur sempre un polo attrattivo in grado di definire identità, di orientare scelte, di animare percorsi spirituali, di darne le parole e la grammatica di riferimento. Noi monaci, che lottiamo contro le nostre chiacchiere più o meno futili (quando non vane) che sembrano sfigurare questa rappresentazione; noi, che ben conosciamo le tante banalità del nostro vivere quotidiano; noi monaci insomma, un po' smagati, sorridiamo forse nel vedere quale forza di suggestione e di seduzione esercita ancora la nostra vita nelle attese che essa suscita, eppure dobbiamo riconoscere che, al di là o giusto proprio nel seno stesso della nostra mediocrità più o meno evitabile, qualcosa di quel mito vive e si trasmette anche nel nostro concreto interpretare la vita monastico-eremitica: ciò evidentemente è detto non per abbassare, ma per alzare il tiro della tensione rappresentata da questa trasfigurazione ideale.

2. LA CELLA COME MITO EDENICO E IL CONCRETO DEL SUO PORSI IN UNA REALTÀ NATURALE

Ogni mito che si rispetti, nel suo proporre un immaginario, trasfigura, ma di necessità suppone, più o meno direttamente, una realtà concreta. Per questo la mia considerazione delle rappresentazioni dell'eremo parte da una osservazione secondo me imprescindibile, che ho già avuto occasione di segnalare e che qui richiamo per cenni. La cella eremitica fin dalle origini è sempre stata posta in relazione con due riferimenti ambientali in qualche modo connaturali. In primo luogo, per antonomasia, con il deserto. In secondo luogo, per una sorta di ossimoro, con il giardino edenico: l'eremo è come un fiore che rende fecondo, trasforma in giardino il deserto. Il modo poi in cui questi riferimenti si articolano e si modulano cambia nel tempo e nello spazio[5]. Certo, il deserto dai padri antichi era inteso primariamente come luogo emblematico soprattutto per esprimere la separazione dal mondo e la rudezza nel combattimento spirituale. Tuttavia è stato osservato che nell'occidente tardo-antico e medievale proprio l'immaginario che si connette al valore religioso del deserto conosce una trasfor-

---

Historica, SS, XXX, 2, Hannoverae 1934, 1039-40)? Anche Pier Damiani era tra gli *infirmi* che si adattava a bere un po' di vino, se dice nella *Vita Odilonis* (PL 144, 933D-934B) che costui trasformò in vino ottimo quello che era acido, come spesso avviene a Roma: segno per lo meno che lo stesso Damiani ne aveva una conoscenza non per sentito dire, pur facendosi scrupolo di vivere nei soggiorni romani osservando uno stile ascetico di vita.

5 Per una trattazione complessiva tra tardo antico e alto Medioevo si può far riferimento a F. MARAZZI, *La città dei monaci. Storia degli spazi che avvicinano a Dio*, Milano 2015.

mazione profonda[6], che non è senza conseguenze sulla stessa idea di eremo e di cella eremitica che ne deriva: il luogo in cui piuttosto ci si nasconde, ci si ritira, e che per questo si continua a chiamare deserto, diventa dapprima l'isola (per esempio Lérins), poi la foresta, la quale per parte sua è certo luogo di separazione dal mondo, ma per così dire in un eccesso di natura, di fecondità smisurata e disordinata[7]. Per questo il monaco eremita altomedievale in occidente si trova a compiere il suo combattimento spirituale nella naturalità radicale e indistinta della selva, per fare di essa non, come topicamente si è portati a pensare, il luogo per antonomasia dell'erranza, il labirinto in cui perdersi, ma quello dell'armonia della creazione ricomposta. L'ambiente da lui abitato diventa così una sorta di selva edenica, al cui centro ricreare un giardino che evochi quello primordiale in cui il progenitore dà nome alle cose, e dunque non ne è schiavo. Per questo la letteratura cortese e cavalleresca, nei secoli successivi, tante volte farà incrociare i suoi personaggi erranti – si chiamino Perceval, Angelica o Erminia per dire qualche nome fatidico – con qualche figura di eremita, il quale, più o meno ispirato da motivi religiosi, vive in una radura irrigata da una sorgente al centro di una foresta. Lì questi cavalieri scoprono uomini che hanno saputo prendere le loro misure, che hanno preso le loro distanze e hanno assunto una nuova prospettiva di sguardo rispetto al mondo comune, con tutte le sue contraddizioni, siano esse di carattere spirituale o profano. La semplicità di quel luogo e di quell'incontro riconducono quei personaggi errabondi, per più versi inquieti se non disperati, a una nuova percezione di sé e della realtà, e a relativizzare le proprie pene. Certo in quel luogo ameno in cui quei personaggi incontrano un vecchio saggio solitario c'è molto del Virgilio delle Bucoliche e delle Georgiche, ma rivisitato dai racconti dei santi asceti medievali, i quali nel distacco dal mondo e nel combattimento spirituale hanno creato in sé e intorno a sé una armonia e una sapienza fatta di semplicità, sobrietà e autosufficienza materiale. Una autarchia che a sua

---

6 Cf. J. Le Goff, *Il meraviglioso e il quotidiano nell'Occidente medievale*, Bari 1983, 27-35.

7 Cf. Ch. Higounet, «Les forêts de l'Europe occidentale du Ve au XIe siècle», in *Agricoltura e mondo rurale in Occidente nell'alto Medioevo*, XIII Settimana del CISAM, Spoleto 1966, 384, M. Pastoreau, *La forêt médiévale: un univers symbolique*, in *Le chateau, la chasse et la forêt*, Luçon 1990, 83-85. R. Grégoire, «La foresta come esperienza religiosa», in *L'ambiente vegetale nell'Alto Medio Evo*, XXXVII Settimana del CISAM, Spoleto 1989, 678-682. S. Boesch Gajano, «Alla ricerca dell'identità eremitica», in *Ermites de France et d'Italie (XI-XIV siècle)*, ed. A. Vauchez (Collection de l'EFR 313), Rome 2003, 486-487 fa per parte sua opportune osservazioni sulla dimensione di asprezza che all'immaginario della foresta si connette, ma non mi sembra che questo contraddica la dimensione idealizzante che esso comporta (come già del resto avviene nella Bibbia e nella letteratura delle *Vitae patrum* per il deserto).

volta è specchio di un'armonia interiore, espressione di quel dominio di sé che non è, si badi, il risultato soprattutto di uno sforzo dell'io, pur necessario, quanto piuttosto frutto dello spirito, accoglienza di un dono di grazia che aiuta a regolare le proprie inquietudini e riscattare i propri limiti.

Ora, per entrare più direttamente nel tema, non è inutile rammentare che in particolare l'eremo di Camaldoli è costituito da un insieme cintato di celle, ciascuna con il suo giardino: come un accampamento posto in una radura trasformata in giardino, nel mezzo di una foresta, la più che millenaria foresta a cavaliere dell'Appennino tosco-romagnolo; al suo interno, ora coperta da una cappellina, sgorga una sorgente. Pur nella sua singolarità nel suo essere *campus amabilis*, irripetibile in altre condizioni ambientali, questo eremo ha costituito di fatto l'archetipo di tutti gli insediamenti monastico-eremitici che sono germogliati su quel ceppo. La cella e l'eremo nel suo complesso, il vivere in luogo solitario, nel conseguente processo di idealizzazione hanno così trovato un loro modo proprio di riferirsi al giardino edenico, quasi ponte verso il cielo, anticipazione del paradiso. Insomma, se questo tipo di correlazione di certo non è nuova nella tradizione monastica di oriente e di occidente[8], in quel particolare contesto ambientale sembra essere diventato particolarmente pregnante. Basti pensare alle splendide miniature e stampe che ci rappresentano il sogno di Maldolo ovvero di Romualdo su cui è costruito il mito fondativo di Camaldoli[9]. Diverso il discorso che andrebbe fatto per Fonte Avellana, l'altro luogo-matrice della tradizione eremitica camaldolese, o forse meglio della tradizione eremitica dell'occidente cristiano, grazie al ruolo ivi esercitato alle origini da Pier Damiani, senza dubbio il più importante teorico latino della vita eremitica a cavallo tra alto e basso medioevo: il suo insediamento, pure così fascinoso oggi per noi, non sembra abbia esercitato allora e in seguito una simile suggestione. A giudicare da una ricerca di riscontri testuali da me intrapresa almeno per

8 Il tema di per sé è legato al *topos* classico della spiritualità monastica costituito dalla scala di Giacobbe (cf. Gen 28). In oriente il referente maggiore è evidentemente la *Scala Paradisi* di Giovanni Climaco, peraltro sconosciuta alla tradizione latina fino al XIV secolo, quando si diffonde grazie alla traduzione di Angelo Clareno; in occidente si suole individuare il riferimento principale in Gerolamo, (*Epistulae*, 125,7 [CSEL 56,I, 125]): *Quamdiu in patria es, habeto cellulam pro Paradiso*. La presenza nella tradizione romualdina di questo tema è attestata nella cosiddetta piccola regola di Romualdo secondo Bruno di Querfurt (Brunonis Querfurtensis *Vita quinque fratrum*, XXXII, ed. J. Karwasinska, MPH II,IV,3, Warszawa 1973, 83): *Sede in cella tua quasi in Paradiso*.

9 Ora un'analisi di molti di questi aspetti e della configurazione architettonica che ne è derivata è reperibile in *Architettura eremitica. Sistemi progettuali e paesaggi culturali. Atti del Terzo Convegno Internazionale di Studi. Camaldoli 21-23 settembre 2012*, edd. S. Bertocci-S. Parinello, Firenze 2012

sondaggi pilota, sembra almeno doversi osservare il fatto che Fonte Avellana nella sua specificità di luogo all'interno di uno spazio e di un paesaggio definito non è mai tratteggiato nelle lettere del suo priore.

3. L'IMMAGINARIO DEL GIARDINO: I FIORI DELLE VIRTÙ NEL *DOMINUS VOBISCUM* E IL *GENIUS LOCI* DI CAMALDOLI

In questo contesto problematico si vuol porre lo specifico assunto della prima parte di questo studio: verificare il modo in cui viene idealizzato l'eremo nella scrittura di Pier Damiani e nei testi fondativi della esperienza romualdino-camaldolese, vedendo, anche per raffronto, il modo in cui la tradizione ha coniugato le proprie origini con la realtà naturale circostante, e come eventualmente ha modulato la propria rappresentazione simbolica appunto nella figura del giardino.

Con due osservazione preliminari che si impongono.

La prima: sono ben consapevole che almeno in questa prima parte ragionerò su testi tra loro molto diversi dal punto di vista del genere letterario, per cui in particolare nei documenti legislativi sarà difficile trovare più di qualche spunto indiretto sul contesto ambientale in cui gli eremi si collocano.

La seconda: nelle prime *Costituzioni* di Camaldoli scritte verso la fine del secolo XI da Rodolfo I[10], l'opera di Pier Damiani è già posta per la nascente congregazione eremitica come una delle fonti ispirative principali, sia direttamente, mediante l'evocazione iniziale della sua *Vita Romualdi* a testimonianza dell'azione del santo come fondatore di eremi, sia indirettamente, in virtù della citazione (pur senza indicazione del suo autore) della «Regola eremitica» damianea[11]. Ciò rende Pier Damiani il referente istituzionale che fa autorità quando si tratta di enunciare gli usi e costumi praticati dagli abitanti dell'eremo.

A partire dalla prospettiva di osservazione che abbiamo assunto, si deve prendere in considerazione un importante elemento di tipo strutturale, che sembra assumere un carattere si direbbe topico, e che passa direttamente dalla lettere 18 e 50 di Pier Damiani (le «Regole eremitiche» appunto) alle costituzioni di Rodolfo I: della vita eremitica in realtà non si scrivono regole, ma si propone appunto un vissuto da preservare, un modello da non corrompere affinché non si

10 Edita in *Consuetudo Camaldulensis. Rodulphi Constitutiones, Liber Eremiticae Regulae*, ed. P. Licciardello, Firenze 2004. D'ora in poi RC.

11 Cfr. RC V,33; trattasi delle lettere 18 e 50, che si possono leggere rispettivamente in Pier Damiani, *Lettere (1-21)*, edd. G.I. Gargano-N. D'Acunto, Roma 2000, e *Lettere (41-67)*, Roma 2002) (OPD [Opera Omnia di Pier Damiani] 1/1, 3).

abbia in futuro a ridurne l'asprezza e la radicalità[12]. Insomma, più che di regola si dovrebbe parlare di una lode degli eremi di cui si afferma l'esemplarità: appunto si contribuisce a configurarne una immagine mitica nel senso sopra precisato. Già questo dato mi sembra importante, al di là dei contenuti specifici dei documenti che stiamo considerando. In questo quadro il giardino edenico assume in più di un caso un ruolo portante.

Ciò è vero in particolare per la lettera 28 (il *Dominus vobiscum*)[13], la quale non ha, è vero, un fine normativo, ma ben esprime i toni e le forme della mitizzazione. Notiamo per lo meno che qui la figura del giardino segna ai due suoi estremi la *Laus heremi*, la parte conclusiva di tutta la lettera di cui costituisce il vertice anche retorico.

Così infatti si apre la *Laus*, con una vera e propria cesura di tono e di stile rispetto al discorso precedente:

> L'eremo infatti è un *paradiso di delizie*, dove spira la fragranza odorosa delle virtù come profumati petali, come splendidi fiori aromatici. Qui le rose della carità fiammeggiano di color rosso fuoco, qui i gigli della castità biancheggiano candidi come la neve; assieme a loro non temono l'assalto dei venti le viole dell'umiltà, fintanto che se ne stanno così vicine al suolo. Qui stilla la mirra della mortificazione perfetta ed esala incessante l'incenso di una assidua preghiera[14].

E alla fine così si chiude:

> E che più dirò di te, o vita eremitica, vita santa, vita angelica, vita benedetta, *giardino di anime*, scrigno di gemme celesti, consesso di un senato spirituale? Il tuo profumo supera la fragranza di tutti gli aromi; il tuo sapore, più dei favi stillanti, più di ogni qualità di miele addolcisce il gusto di un cuore illuminato[15].

La *solitudo pluralis* dell'eremita[16] argomentata in precedenza nella lettera è qui rappresentata per immagini che evocano una vita di uomini collocati in una

12 Nel caso delle RC questa fotografia, a sua volta fondata principalmente proprio sull'autorità Pier Damiani come sopra ricordato, è per di più sancita solennemente da un documento collegiale, forse utilizzando il *topos* monastico delle *collationes* (RC V,33).

13 Cf. P. Damiani, *Lettere (22-40)*, edd. G.I. Gargano-N. D'Acunto, Roma 2001 (OPD1/2), 112-153.

14 Damiani, *Lettere (22-40)*, 143.

15 Damiani, *Lettere (22-40)*, 153.

16 In altro contesto ho posto in luce il fatto che l'espressione non andrebbe mai disgiunta

armonia naturale che certamente richiama il giardino dell'Eden. Così gli eremiti ritrovano attorno a sé, nella luce del sabato di Dio, il creato ricondotto all'ordine e alla sua funzionalità di essere d'aiuto per l'uomo stesso. La vita eremitica appunto costituisce un giardino di anime. Siamo ai vertici dell'idealizzazione, di per sé comunque rigorosamente nella linea tradizionale della letteratura monastica, cui si faceva cenno: sono le virtù che rendono giardino l'eremo, luogo che nella sua concretezza resta tuttavia senza un volto definito[17]. Il giardino edenico è certo, come si è accennato, funzionale alla rappresentazione della cella eremitica come un microcosmo[18], ma anche è tutto già metafora, e forse proprio per questo per così dire astratto nella sua rappresentazione. Di più ancora nelle due lettere 18 e 50, che la tradizione ci ha trasmesso come «Regole di vita eremitica»[19]: lì il luogo in cui quegli eremiti vivono si direbbe assolutamente irrilevante.

Che ne è di questo tema nelle più antiche costituzioni camaldolesi?

Sembrerebbe poco appariscente, se non del tutto assente, nella prima legislazione scritta di Camaldoli, le *Rodulphi Constitutiones*[20] del secolo XI. Forse potrebbe essere meno netta l'impressione nella lettura del *Liber eremiticae regulae* del secolo successivo[21], dove il *genius loci*, evocato nel racconto della leggenda

---

dalla sua speculare *moltitudo singularis* (cf il mio «Solitudine e comunione: la dimensione pneumatica e il ruolo ecclesiale del carisma eremitico. Romualdo e Pier Damiani tra carisma e istituzione», *Sacris Erudiri* 43 (2004) 261-279.

17 Lo stesso per la cella, salvo le panche cui l'eremita sembrerebbe rivolgersi dicendo *Dominus vobiscum*, cf. Lett. 28,2, Damiani, *Lettere (22-40)*, 112.

18 Cf. Lett. 28, 21: «Come poi l'uomo in greco si definisce microcosmo, cioè mondo in piccolo [*Sicut autem homo Greco aeloquio dicitur microcosmus, hoc est minor mundus*], in quanto per la sua costituzione fisica consta dei medesimi quattro elementi di cui si compone tutto l'universo, così anche ciascuno dei fedeli appare, per così dire, una Chiesa in piccolo [*ita etiam unusquisque fidelium quasi quaedam minor esse videtur aecclesia*] », Ibid., 128.

19 Tradizione viva già all'altezza degli anni '80 del secolo XI, come ci testimoniano, come si è detto, le Costituzioni del Beato Rodolfo.

20 Cf. nota 10.

21 Edito anch'esso in *Consuetudo Camaldulensis*; d'ora in poi LER. Una osservazione *a latere* mi sembra tuttavia doverosa: il *Dominus vobiscum* sembra ignoto a entrambi i Rodolfi legislatori di Camaldoli. In sé nulla di stupefacente in questo, se si pensa alle complesse variabili della trasmissione manoscritta delle opere medievali. Ma resta almeno significativo un fatto: Pier Damiani è noto, e come si diceva fa da *auctoritas*, a Camaldoli in quanto agiografo del fondatore Romualdo e in quanto legislatore delle pratiche devozionali del digiuno e della disciplina che caratterizzano l'eremitismo del secolo XI; invece questa opera coeva alle «Regole», così ricca di implicazioni teologico-spirituali per l'identità eremitica, non sembra aver varcato l'Appennino, o essere comunque nota a Camaldoli per altre vie. Forse perché ormai la *Laus heremi* si era avviata ad avere una fortuna indipendente dal

fondativa del *Campus Maldoli*[22] sembrerebbe aver segnato la prospettiva spirituale e l'autocoscienza degli eremiti che l'hanno eletto a loro luogo di vita; ma la ricerca lessicale che ho condotto, sia pur parziale, non mi è parsa particolarmente ricca di frutti. Si intuisce un ambiente concreto di vita solo per il fatto che c'è qualcuno al servizio dei monaci che vi lavora, pur osservando un regime ascetico semi monastico, tanto che se ne vede in filigrana il germinare dell'istituzione dei monaci conversi, come peraltro si intravvede anche per Fonte Avellana[23].

Una prima conseguenza da mettere in rilievo è che una considerazione del lavoro da parte degli eremiti sembra essere piuttosto evanescente, sia nella tradizione camaldolese sia in quella avellanita. Nel LER, l'unico tra i testi più o meno formalmente legislativi che parla esplicitamente di impegni possibili di lavoro, i riferimenti sono limitati sostanzialmente al cap. XXXIII, in cui si precisa che i lavori manuali si possono fare solo quando non si fa astinenza, in quaresima due giorni la settimana dopo sesta, fuori quaresima anche il sabato tra nona e vespri (dunque d'estate non più di tre ore): il lavoro come tale sembra insomma molestare la tranquillità eremitica; al cap. XXIV in cui sono elencati i lavori possibili: legna, orto, fieno. Salvo l'orto, attività estiva ma continua, gli altri sono lavori periodici, per certi versi eccezionali. Del resto già in LER XXXII, quando si dice che non si deve stare in cella senza far niente, e che questo è importante per la stabilità dell'anima e contro le tentazioni, poi le attività previste sono la pre-

resto della lettera, fino a diventare, sotto il nome di Basilio Magno, uno dei *livre de chevet* della tradizione certosina, per cui cf. B. Gain, «L'opuscule *De laude Vitae solitariae* de Pierre Damien attribué à s. Basile de Cesarée», *Benedictina* 41 (2004) 437-462? Fa comunque riflettere il fatto che anche Giovanni da Lodi non utilizzi mai la lettera 28 per i suoi *Collectanea*, sebbene gli dovrebbe essere nota visto che è presente nel *Vaticanus latinus 3797*. Il *Dominus Vobiscum* non sembra insomma essere stato una tessera importante del ritratto di Pier Damiani lasciato alla memoria storica da parte dei suoi discepoli più vicini. E di fatto Rodolfo II-III, così raffinato ed erudito nello spettro delle sue conoscenze teologico-spirituali, deve attingere altrove per costruire il suo proprio mito dell'eremo.

22 LER X, 1.2, 30: *Nam, cum pervenisset ad partes Aretini territorii, locum idoneum huic proposito cupiens invenire, occurrit ei quidam vir nomine Maldulus, dicens se campum habere amenum in Alpibus positum, ubi cum aliquando dormiret, instar Iacob patriarche scalam vidit excelsam, celum quasi suo vertice tangentem, per quam splendentium atque albescentium videbatur ascendere multitudo. Quo audito vir Dei, tamquam divino illustratus oraculo, mox campum petiit, locum vidit, cellas ibidem construxit.*

23 Cf. lett. 18,4, vedi Damiani, *Lettere (1-21)*, 329, 331. A proposito del tema dei conversi in Pier Damiani e a Camaldoli si può vedere F. Salvestrini, «"*Recipiantur in choro [...] qualiter benigne et caritative tractantur*". Per una storia delle relazioni fra Camaldolesi e Vallombrosani (XI-XV secolo)», in *Camaldoli e l'Ordine Camaldolese dalle origini alla fine del XV secolo*, edd. C. Caby-P. Licciardello, Cesena 2014, 53-96.

ghiera, la lettura, la pratica delle metanie e delle flagellazioni: il lavoro sembra sostanzialmente estraneo alla giornata ideale dell'eremita. Almeno nel caso del LER, va comunque rilevato che si tiene conto che la selva circostante è luogo da cui attingere legname per i bisogni primari, e che dunque almeno questa attività contempla un momento di lavoro serio[24].

Estendendo il campo di osservazione, certo sarebbe improprio cercare nel testo una descrizione paesaggistica, e lo stesso diffuso ricorrere a metafore di carattere naturale e particolarmente vegetale[25] non sembra particolarmente originale, ma topico da parte di un autore di buone e ricche letture. Ma per lo meno è interessante scoprire che uno dei momenti chiave dell'idealizzazione dell'eremo, quello in cui il settenario delle virtù è modulato su un settenario di alberi[26], è introdotto dalla più esplicita formulazione dell'archetipo edenico, sviluppata non a caso a partire da una citazione del Cantico dei Cantici (Ct 2,7):

> «Vi scongiuro per le gazzelle e i cervi dei campi, non svegliate la mia diletta, finché essa non lo voglia»! Quanto più questo scongiuro è assurdo alla lettera, tanto più è glorioso nel suo significato spirituale; è un frutto dalla buccia ruvida, ma dalla polpa dolcissima. Le gazzelle per natura sono eccellenti per agilità nella corsa, hanno vista acuta, scelgono cibo ricercato; anche i cervi non sono meno

24 Nessuno osi uscire da solo a raccogliere legna o per altri lavori manuali, ma vadano insieme tre o più, LER XXXIV,1, 53.

25 Ne segnalo i riferimenti più indicativi: LER III,1, 27 (Noi raccogliamo le erbe salutari dall'orto della dottrina spirituale); LER III,9, 29 (Se tuttavia ci succedesse talvolta di raccogliere simili erbacce, di seguire tali esempi); XXXVI tutto il capitolo, 55-57 (in partic.: 2. *quieto et perseveranti suavitatis refrigerium, silentium beatitudinis tamquam portionem exhibet Paradisi*; 4. *In eis quippe tamquam inter spinas et tribulos, paliuros, rannos sciebant se posse prefocari*); XXXVIII,7 (i religiosi e i contemplativi a volte vi aspirano in modo lodevole, per trovare dove far risplendere la loro virtù e santità, produrre frutti profumati di onestà e rendere buona testimonianza a quelli di fuori); XXXIX,1-6 (L'umiltà, radice e custode di ogni virtù; infatti, come dalla radice della superbia pullulano i vizi, così dal seme dell'umiltà nascono i virgulti delle virtù [con ciò che segue]); XL,1 (l'obbedienza, prima e principale compagna dell'umiltà, come frutto maturo o virgulto nato da un'ottima radice); XLV,1-9 (Come scongiurano coloro che vivono nella pace: cf. la descrizione del *locus amoenus);* il capitolo è utile premessa a XLVI, dove i sette alberi nel loro simbolismo costituiscono il vertice del *locus amoenus*; XLVVII,5, 75 («Oh, se qualcuno mi desse le ali, come una colomba, per poter volare e rifugiarmi nella santa solitudine, e meritassi di cogliere un ramoscello da quegli alberi, anzi virtù!»); XLIX,3, 77 (Dio non ha creato l'uomo perché governasse gli uomini, ma perché governasse gli uccelli del cielo, gli animali della terra e i pesci del mare, cioè i superbi, gli avidi e i curiosi, sui quali dominano l'avidità della carne cioè i superbi, gli avidi e i curiosi).

26 LER cap. XLVI sotto citato.

veloci, e hanno doti straordinarie: uccidono i serpenti, portano pesi a vicenda, bevendo acqua neutralizzano veleni mortali. In questi due generi di animali sono rappresentati due ordini degli spiriti beati, angelici ed umani. Essi infatti sono tanto rapidi da saltare senza difficoltà o indugio tra gli opposti, tanto perspicaci da vedere Dio, tanto ricercati da nutrirsi di cibo celeste, gustando e vedendo quanto dolce è Dio. Scacciano i serpenti infernali, soccorrono il bisogno altrui, con l'acqua salvifica della sapienza allontanano il veleno dei vizi. Che c'è di strano, se l'anima santa e quieta dell'uomo contemplativo non vuole privarsi della vista di coloro, che è abituata a frequentare? È giusto che ci scongiuri con l'autorità di coloro dei quali ama la compagnia, imita la natura, contempla la grazia, gusta la soavità, desiderando riposare nella loro meditazione piuttosto che abitare nelle tende dei peccatori.[27]

Pochi insomma sono i risultati dello spoglio sui testi fondativi della *forma vitae* di Camaldoli, che pur meriterebbero ulteriori verifiche; meno ancora quelli che si ricavano da un raffronto tra le costituzioni di Camaldoli e la autorevole tradizione avellanita.

Conclusivamente, merita riflettere sul modo in cui il legame tra la dimensione di *locus amoenus* e il mito fondativo di Camaldoli finisca per contaminare anche la tradizione avellanita e specificamente damianea. Nel racconto di Pier Damiani, così attento alle collocazioni strategiche dei nodi narrativi[28], l'atten-

27 LER cap. 46, 68. Trad. Licciardello (io tuttavia, correggendo, traduco il titolo *De adiuratione quiescentium* con: Come scongiurano coloro che vivono nella pace). Testo latino: *«Adiuro vos» inquit «per capreas cervosque camporum, ne suscitetis dilectam, quoad ipsa velit». Adiuratio hec, quanto absurdior est in litterali superficie, tanto gloriosior in spiritali significatione; deformem habet corticem, sed medullam iocundissimam. Capree quidem egregiam habent naturam agilitate currendi, acumine videndi, pastu sublimiori; cervi quoque nichilominus velocissimi sunt, et ammirabilem habent efficaciam: nam serpentes interimunt, mutua sustentant onera, haustu aquarum venena mortifera vincunt. His ergo duorum animantium generibus duo beatorum spirituum figurantur ordines, angelici et humani. Hii enim tante celeritatis sunt, ut absque difficultate vel mora per opposita transeant, tante perspicacitatis ut Deum videant, tam excelsi pastus ut celesti cibo fruantur, gustantes et videntes quam suavis est Deus. Angues dissipant infernales, aliene subveniunt indigentie, aqua sapientie salutaris vitiorum virus expellunt. Quid ergo mirum, si pia et quieta contemplantis anima nolit eorum fraudari aspectu, quorum utitur contubernio? Dignum est enim ut per eorum nos adiuret auctoritatem, quorum societatem diligit, imitatur naturam, contemplatur gratiam, gustat suavitatem, desiderat utique potius in eorum meditatione quiescere quam habitare in tabernaculis peccatorum.*

28 Cf. il mio studio: «La "grammatica di Cristo" di Pier Damiani agiografo. Per uno studio della struttura letteraria della *Vita Romualdi*», *Benedictina* 54 (2007), 195-216. Un'altra

zione di Romualdo fin dagli esordi (siamo al capitolo I) sembra quella di collocare all'interno di un *locus amoenus* la sua idea di un eremo confacente alla sue aspirazioni, per quanto ancora non ben definite:

> ovunque gli capitava di trovare un luogo ameno tra i boschi, subito il suo animo s'infiammava del desiderio dell'eremo, esclamando tra sé: Oh, quanto starebbero bene degli eremiti in questi recessi silvestri, quanto qui potrebbero trovare pace da tutti i turbamenti del frastuono mondano![29]

E certo la visione di Apollinare al capitolo II non è pensabile senza porre davanti agli occhi il mosaico dell'abside basilica di Classe, in cui il santo è collocato proprio in quel giardino stilizzato nel modo unico e irripetibile che tutti conosciamo e ammiriamo.

Ma soprattutto nella seconda parte della *Vita Romualdi* il santo è rappresentato non solo come asceta estremo, ma anche come fondatore di eremi in mezzo a radure e a selve. In particolare l'amata Valdicastro sembra lasciare intravvedere un paesaggio con tratti propri del *locus amoenus*:

> Fu trovato, alla fine, tra i loro possedimenti, un luogo abbastanza adatto alla vita eremitica, completamente attorniato da monti e boschi. Al centro stava una vasta pianura, idonea a produrre messi, ma anche ricca di limpide acque di fonte.[30]

Ma anche potremmo osservare che quei luoghi appaiono lavorati da discepoli boscaioli e falegnami, e in controluce compare che in essi, pur nei limiti

---

lettura diversamente attenta alle rispondenze e simmetrie tematiche, proprio incentrata sul tema paradisiaco (in questo caso non configurata figurativamente sull'immagine del giardino, ma sull'evocazione del canto angelico) quella di G.I. Gargano, «Il ritorno di Romualdo fra i camaldolesi», in *San Romualdo. Storia, agiografia e spiritualità. Atti del XXIII Convegno del Centro Studi Avellaniti. Fonte Avellana 23-26 agosto 2000*, S. Pietro in Cariano VR 2002, 131-174.

29 Cf VR I, 14: *ubicumque per silvas amenum locum reperire poterat, mox se ad heremi desiderium eius animus accendebat, dicens intra se: «O quam bene poterant heremitae in his nemorum recessibus habitare, quam congrue possent hic ab omni secularis strepitus perturbatione quiescere!» Et ita mens eius coelitus inspirata iam divinabatur in amore quod impleturus erat postmodum opere*. È l'unica occorrenza dell'aggettivo *amoenus* in tutta l'opera agiografica, su 11 in totale in Pier Damiani.

30 Cf. VR XXV, 74: *Postremo repertus est in eorum possessione locus heremiticae conversationi satis congruus, montibus undique vallatus et silvis. In medio vero ampla quaedam planities non solum proferendis frugibus apta, sed perspicuis etiam fontium aquis irrigua.*

dell'ascesi, si tratta di mangiare, nutrirsi per affrontare spostamenti e lavori di bonifica di rilievo[31].

Forse già questo potrebbe essere di qualche interesse, alla luce della dialettica tra rispecchiamento e alterità che è caratteristica della relazione tra santo e agiografo: niente del genere si può ricavare negli altri ritratti di eremiti descritti spesso qua e là da Pier Damiani. E quando la tradizione agiografica camaldolese porrà mano ad adattare il racconto della *Vita Romualdi* proprio per suffragare il proprio mito fondativo, inventando una testimonianza damianea della fondazione di Camaldoli, ecco che l'aggiunta sarà posta proprio nel quadro di un contesto silvestre: appunto a Camaldoli si contestualizzerà il miracolo del faggio raccontato nel cap. XLVII, con quella interpolazione di cui merita guardare con attenzione i termini, che proprio al *campus Maldoli speciosus et amabilis* evocato dal LER sembrano fare riferimento: «*Dum in quadam heremo speciosissima et egregia, cui nomen est Camaldulensis, quam ipse edificaverat, in cella resideret...*»[32].

4. UNO SGUARDO RAPIDO A MILLE ANNI DI TRADIZIONE EREMITICA

Anche se possiamo ritrovare qualche traccia non priva di interesse per noi lettori moderni, dobbiamo insomma rilevare che, alle origini stesse della tradizione romualdino-camaldolese, il *campus amabilis*, il giardino posto nella radura di una foresta, non sembra aver prodotto nella autocoscienza eremitica particolari modulazioni in cui coniugare l'ascetismo eremitico, il quale è rappresentato piuttosto come fatto essenzialmente di digiuni e di pratiche di devozione che dovrebbero realizzare il più possibile l'anelito alla preghiera continua, quasi fosse indifferente il luogo in cui esso viene vissuto, e il lavoro che quel luogo comporta e/o rende possibile. Del resto questa prospettiva ben si colloca nella rappresentazione degli *ordines* su cui si fonda la *societas christiana* altomedievale[33]: gli *oratores* ben poco dovrebbero avere da spartire con i condizionamenti posti dal contesto naturale e lavorativo in cui sono posti i *laboratores*. Questo sembra essere un marchio fortemente identitario in tutta la successiva tradizione normativa camaldolese nelle sue varie declinazioni, tenendo oltretutto conto della

31 Cf. per es. VR XLVII.

32 Cf. VR XLVII 89 (nota 1); Caby, cit. 180-183. Si ricordi che la donazione del terreno di Camaldoli da parte del vescovo Tedaldo del 1027 suona così: *Ille locus qui dicitur campo Malduli, campus speciosus et amabilis, ubi septem purissimi fontes et amoena virecta*. Il testo è edito in Vedovato, cit. 126-128.

33 Cf. G. Duby. *Lo specchio del feudalesimo. Sacerdoti, guerrieri e lavoratori*, Bari 1998.

persistente tensione esistente tra gli eremi, inclusi quelli urbani, e i monasteri che pure rapidamente si integrano nella congregazione camaldolese, ma almeno in teoria originariamente in supporto agli eremi stessi, per preservarne la natura di luoghi unicamente o specialmente dediti alla contemplazione.

Va detto in aggiunta che la stessa antica legislazione camaldolese riservata più specificamente ai cenobiti, attestata per la prima volta in modo organico dai *Libri tres de moribus* di Martino III priore di Camaldoli del 1253 e recentemente editi[34], parla in questo caso del lavoro con un capitolo specifico, in evidente diversità rispetto alle costituzioni eremitiche, e lo descrive come attività che si direbbe regolare, presentandola come antidoto all'ozio in ottemperanza al dettato della Regola di San Benedetto, sostanzialmente parafrasato[35]. Peraltro non è senza interesse, nel contesto di indicazioni di per sé sostanzialmente topiche, trovare un tratto più originale laddove si denuncia la preoccupazione di tener conto della diversità tra i monasteri grandi e quelli piccoli, tra quelli più o meno isolati nel contado e quelli in città, la quale impone di necessità modulazioni diverse nelle possibilità e nelle condizioni di lavoro; ma è difficile intravvedere una tipologia di attività possibili, salvo la precisazione che per qualcuno il lavoro può essere quello di copiatura di manoscritti[36]. Anche qui comunque si confina il lavoro manuale e l'integrazione nell'ambiente a un ruolo decisamente marginale. Non che il problema non si ponesse da un punto di vista pratico: sono note e studiate le normative accurate nel secolare utilizzo della foresta come fonte di reddito economico[37], ma sembrano dimensioni estranee alla coscienza identitaria del semianacorestismo camaldolese.

Fa spicco l'eccezione delle pur rapide indicazioni contenute nelle costituzioni di Gerardo del 1278, in cui pure compaiono alcune notazioni descrittive che ci prospettano forme più articolate di lavoro[38]. In esse per la prima volta si prevede che qualcuno sia preposto alla sorveglianza dell'operaio che si occupa degli abeti circostanti l'eremo: un primo cenno all'ambiente particolare in cui l'eremo di Camaldoli si pone. Ma ben poco si ricava del lavoro concreto degli eremiti, a

---

34 Martino III priore di Camaldoli, *Libri tres de morbus*, ed. P. Licciardello, Firenze, Sismel-Ed. del Galluzzo, 2013.

35 Cf. *Libri tres*, III,5, 258-261.

36 Cf. *Libri tres*, III,5, 258-261.

37 Cf. *Il codice forestale camaldolese*, cit.

38 La Costituzioni sono poste in appendice al VI volume degli *Annales Camaldelenses,* edd. B. Mittarelli-A. Costadoni, Venetiis 1761. Cf .cap VII (*Qualiter debeant manualia opera exerceri,* 217) Cap. XXIV(*De officio operarii*, 228) Cap. XXIX *(De portario eremi et abietibus*, 230-231).

parte la definizione del ruolo del camerlengo (economo del sottostante cenobio di Fontebuono?), responsabile della cura della foresta con l'eventuale aiuto di un eremita. Il lavoro materiale è tuttavia demandato agli operai e ai conversi, e vige la consueta precisazione del particolare *status* eremitico, che impone di prescrivere per i solitari un regime alquanto ridotto.

Il sondaggio che stiamo proponendo potrebbe trovare un altro nodo importante su cui riflettere tra cinque e seicento, anche a motivo di tutto il processo di ripensamento che ha implicato la divisione tra la Congregazione camaldolese e quella di Monte Corona dopo il tentativo di riforma ad opera del Giustiniani. Tanto più che proprio le *Regole della vita eremitica*, redatte dal Giustiniani nel 1516[39], dunque prima della separazione da Camaldoli e pensate per Camaldoli, con ben maggior consapevolezza sembrano porre a tema un rapporto consapevole tra l'eremo e la foresta che lo circonda in termini che si accostano alla prospettiva cui si accennava *in limine* a questo studio, e non solo perché si mette esplicitamente in chiaro che si deve preservare la corona di abeti che fa da *claustrum* all'eremo, e che si deve curare che il patrimonio forestale non venga impoverito mediante oculate operazioni di rimboschimento[40], o perché lo si fa con una serie di norme che si sono volute definire «codice forestale»[41].

In effetti è rilevante il fatto che nel cap 4 («Della solitudine dell'Eremo et sequestrazione delle Celle») l'Eremo è collocato in un paesaggio dove mito del giardino e realtà ambientale concreta si fondono:

> [Romualdo] per mostrare al secolo la perfetta istituzione della vita solitaria, per instituire cotal vita più perfettamente si elesse, nei confini della Toscana e in sulla più alta cima dell'Appennino, donde si può vedere l'un mare e l'altro, un

39 Non esiste ancora una edizione a stampa del testo latino. Le citazioni saranno tratte dalla traduzione cinquecentesca *Regola della vita eremitica stata data dal beato Romualdo à i suoi Camaldolensi eremiti. Overo le Constituzioni Camaldolensi*, tradotte nuovamente dalla lingua latina nella toscana dal padre don Silvano Razzi in Fiorenza appresso Bartolomeo Sermartelli, 1575. Una scelta della *Regola* (che non comprende tutti i passi citati), già a suo tempo edita dal Lassus (Beato Paolo Giustiniani, *Regola della vita eremitica*, Eremo di Monte Rua 1984) si trova ora anche in *Elogio della vita eremitica. Scritti del beato Paolo Giustiniani*, Frascati 2005.

40 «Le cose o vero beni dell'Eremo stabili non si possano similmente mai, senza il consenso di detto capitolo, né vendere, né alienare, né permutare, né concedere in emfiteosi, eziandio che altre volte fussero state concedute, né parimente si possano tagliare abeti, senza il consenso del capitolo» (cap. 45, Dell'uso del capitolo, et delle cose, che in esso deono farsi), *Regola*, 204-205. Cf. ancora i capitoli 4 e 44.

41 Cf. nota 2.

luogo tutto cinto e circondato intorno da grandi e folte selve d'altissimi abeti e irrigato continuamente da sette lucidissimi e chiarissimi fonti. Il quale luogo, come ne fanno fede molte e antiche scritture, era chiamato Campo amabile, dal quale nome, corrotto poi il vocabolo, come nel più delle cose suole avvenire, ovvero dal nome di colui di cui si dice che era prima il campo (che Maldolo dicono si chiamava) prese il suo nome l'eremo Camaldolense[42].

Di fatto proprio il Giustiniani, nelle sue *Regole*, già di per sé scritte in una forma certamente più distesa rispetto alle Costituzioni tradizionali, dedica uno spazio di un certo rilievo al senso e alla misura del lavoro, che dovrebbe avere un rilievo non minore, anzi maggiore rispetto ai cenobiti. Così al cap. 35 (*Dell'opera necessaria delle mani*):

> L'operare con le mani, tenendo il silenzio, secondo l'ammonizione dell'Apostolo, se non ad acquistare il vitto, a fuggire l'ociosità, che alla salute delle anime è nemica, e a conservare l'umiltà, che è radice di tutte le virtù, quanto sia a tutti i Monaci, e particolarmente agli Eremiti, i quali si sono appresi a più stretto proposito di vita, non utile solamente, ma necessario, ce l'insegna e la Regola del beato Padre Benedetto, e ne ammaestra l'autorità del santissimo dottore Agostino (155).

Il tempo da utilizzare in questa attività non cambia sostanzialmente rispetto alla tradizione: si prevede che si lavori tutti i giorni non di astinenza e digiuno o di festa per tre ore o più nel pomeriggio in orari che variano secondo le stagioni, con possibile estensione del tempo da dedicare se si tratta di raccogliere il fieno o di altre incombenze periodiche. Sia pure con l'avvertenza:

> qualunque cosa, o dentro o fuori operino con le loro mani, ciò sempre accompagnino o con la meditazione della legge del Signore, o con la modulazione de' cantici divini, quasi per un certo sollevamento della fatica. Ma neanche alcuna cosa impedisce che infra queste cose non si possa orare, né è del tutto inutile. Anzi più presto è esaudita un'orazione fatta di uno che operi e si affatichi con libero animo e lieto volto, che diecimila per ociosità e negligenza di chi non vuole alcuna cosa con esse mani operare[43].

---

42 *Regola*, 22.

43 *Regola*, 155. Tuttavia è proibito «scrivere libri, ovvero fare quale altra si voglia cosa per prezzo».

Ma il discorso diventa particolarmente interessante e innovativo quando si descrivono i lavori necessari a tenere ordinati i giardini e i viali delle celle, al mantenimento degli orti. Si fa poi cenno alla scrittura, alla miniatura, alla rilegatura, a tessere cistelle, panieri, sporte e alla fabbricazione di piccoli oggetti di devozione, ma si dice anche che tutti devono saper cucire, ed esercitare le abilità proprie di ciascuno:

> fare lo scarpellino, murare, lavorare di legname e far finestre di vetro. E chi non sa nessuna di queste arti, serva a coloro che le fanno e esercitano, e si occupino in portar pesi, quando di ciò fa bisogno[44].

Di più, anche quelli che vengono all'eremo da famiglia ricca, se sani e di buona costituzione, devono fare di buon animo questi lavori umili e pesanti:

> In tutte le cose nelle quali possono essi Eremiti operare con le mani, tanto quei che sono venuti all'eremo essendo nobili, quanto quelli che vi sono venuti da più bassa e humile vita sarà cosa lodevolissima .... Che non conducano altri operarii, ma essi stessi, se possono a certe ore prescritte, e giorni, operino e lavorino[45].

Insomma una serie di attività che, sia pure in tempi ristretti, dovrebbero consentire agli eremiti di vivere una sostanziale autonomia economica e senza un eccessivo ricorso a conversi o a operai esterni. Se ne deduce una concezione del lavoro che assume un valore economico e umano, e non si riduce più a puro antidoto all'ozio. Da dove venisse questa idea al Giustiniani, segnato come è dalla sua matrice elitaria e intellettuale, meriterebbe uno studio *ad hoc*: almeno una spia viene dalla sua citazione esplicita non solo della *Regula Benedicti*, ma anche del *De opere monachorum* di Agostino. Potrebbe essere cioè un frutto del suo programmatico ritorno alle fonti patristiche della spiritualità monastica. Ma forse si potrebbero individuare altri spunti nell'*humus* dell'umanesimo rinascimentale.

Quando tuttavia passiamo in rassegna le Costituzioni successive, sia camaldolesi sia coronesi[46] (con ben poche differenze tra loro al riguardo), riscontriamo che, nel loro impianto complessivo e nel loro dettato, secondo la impostazione già disposta

44 *Regola*, 159.

45 *Regola*, 159.

46 Ciò vale già per le costituzioni coronesi del 1524, per cui si veda P. LUGANO, *La congregazione camaldolese di Monte Corona*, Frascati 1908, 152-153.

tra tre e quattrocento, restano a questo riguardo in termini alquanto più riduttivi sostanzialmente immutate, fino al secolo scorso, e tra loro con ben poche differenze.

Nelle cinquecentesche *Dichiarazioni alla Regola e Costituzioni dei Padri Camaldolesi* il rilievo va dato non al ruolo primario del lavoro per mantenere ordinato ed efficiente l'eremo (orti, giardini e costruzioni incluse), e la foresta che all'eremo fa da corona. quanto piuttosto al criterio di attualizzazione e adattamento espresso nella premessa alle dichiarazioni al cap. 48 della *Regula Benedicti*, e che rimane sostanzialmente immutato nella formulazione nelle varie Costituzioni che caratterizzano le varie Congregazioni camaldolesi che si vengono a costituire nella prima età moderna:

> considerando che ciò che s'ordina nella santa Regola non si può adempiere, overo osservare per le continue occupazioni degli Offitij, e Messe, s'ordina che gli Eremiti non passino senza un'ora almeno di esercitio corporale ogni giorno, che impedito non sia da Festa di precetto, o da mal tempo, o da gravi caldi d'Estate, cioè nel Sol Leone[47].

Si prevede, è vero, un lavoro da compiere privatamente nella cella. Quanto alla tipologia, vige una certa libertà di scelta sia pure in obbedienza al priore, ma l'elenco proposto è piuttosto scarno, a parte la confezione del pane a turno, che esenta da ogni altro lavoro.

> In oltre possono, anzi devono tutti nelle loro celle, o altrove privatamente (il che come cosa laudabile è stato permesso) far qualche opera, come è scrivere, legar libri, far Paternostri e Avemarie, per corone, far cocchiari, sporte, store di giunco, e cose simili. Ma far qualsivoglia altra cosa per servitio secolare e profano, non solo non è loro lecito, ma espressamente vietato.

L'idea della cella eremitica come luogo in cui stare come in paradiso, non consente particolari attenzioni in prima persona a ciò che sta o avviene al di fuori del recinto di mura (che ormai nel Cinquecento chiude l'insieme delle celle), se non per brevi passeggiate fino alle tre croci poco distanti; ma tantomeno non recepisce la ricchezza di lavori, manuali e no, contemplate dalle *Regole* del Giustiniani, le quali restano insomma in questo ambito un masso erratico dimenticato: forse troppo legato alla specifica situazione di Camaldoli il suo

47 Cito nella versione italiana edita in *La Regola di San Benedetto con le Costituzione delli Eremiti di S. Romualdo dell'ordine Camaldolese*, In Venetia 1595, 172-173.

dettato, e per questo difficile da assumere *in toto* per i Coronesi; e per altro verso troppo legato alla dolorosa frattura tra il Giustiniani e l'Eremo di Camaldoli per i Camaldolesi di Toscana, in una sorta di *damnatio memoriae*. Forse uno dei tanti esempi dell'esaurirsi dell'anelito riformatore dell'evangelismo cristiano del primo cinquecento nel clima di ritorno all'ordine nella chiesa tridentina.

L'impostazione delle Costituzioni al riguardo rimane di fatto sostanzialmente invariata per quattro secoli, fino a quelle del 1930. Solo in quelle del 1943[48] cambia la premessa sopra citata, ed è significativo di una diversa sensibilità che si fa strada, forse anche grazie alla nuova denominazione della congregazione a seguito della controversa unificazione degli Eremiti di Toscana con i Cenobiti avvenuta nel 1935, diventata quella di «Monaci eremiti camaldolesi dell'ordine di S. Benedetto», che riconduceva più esplicitamente alla tradizione benedettina anche la peculiare esperienza eremitica di Camaldoli: sintomaticamente sembra mettersi in sordina il privilegio eremitico di una riduzione del lavoro quasi soltanto ad antidoto contro il rischio dell'ozio:

> Secondo la venerabile tradizione monastica tutti i religiosi devono attendere al lavoro manuale sia in privato che in comune secondo che disporrà il Superiore, il quale avrà la massima cura di assegnare il lavoro secondo le attitudini di ognuno e della famiglia in generale, ordinandolo a uno scopo unico di comune utilità. (n. 138, 102).

Soprattutto va notato che non viene dato un limite temporale all'esercizio manuale. Ma ancora l'elenco dei lavori da fare privatamente nella cella è sostanzialmente immutato: «dipingere, scolpire, scrivere, legar libri, far corone del Signore e della Madonna e cose simili».

Nelle costituzioni del 1957[49] si riprende la formulazione del 1930, ma con una integrazione significativa di natura più generale:

> deve essere impegno dell'ordine organizzare il lavoro nelle varie comunità, preparando i singoli religiosi, procurando gli strumenti necessari, tenendo aggiornate le biblioteche ecc. e collegando il lavoro tra le famiglie e ordinandolo a uno scopo di comune utilità. (n. 230, 208).

48 *Regola di S. Benedetto con le Dichiarazioni e Costituzioni dei Monaci Eremiti Camaldolesi*, Subiaco 1043.

49 *Regola di S. Benedetto con le Dichiarazioni e Costituzioni dei Monaci Eremiti Camaldolesi*, Roma 1947.

Di rilievo soprattutto che per la prima volta si precisa un tempo che non è più ristretto: nel cenobio circa sette ore al giorno devono essere dedicate al lavoro della mente o delle mani; nell'eremo il lavoro manuale è più limitato, con la precisazione che tendenzialmente il lavoro è personale (n.° 231, 208). Insomma, a uno sguardo complessivo si fa più pronunciata la omologazione del monachesimo camaldolese al canone dell'*ora et labora* benedettino. Anche se al n. 236 l'elenco dei lavori da fare privatamente in cella è sempre lo stesso, molto riduttivo: «dipingere, scolpire, scrivere, legar libri, far corone del Signore e della Madonna e cose simili».

Nel quadro di questa tradizione, nella sostanza immutata nel corso dei secoli, certo fa spicco nella sua novità di contenuti e di equilibri quanto fu rielaborato nelle ultime costituzioni camaldolesi (redatte *ad experimentum* nel 1968, approvate nel 1972; rielaborate in forma definitiva nel 1984 e approvate formalmente nel 1985), frutto del ripensamento post conciliare e del più che cinquantennale e travagliato dibattito interno tra le varie anime della tradizione camaldolese[50]. Il lavoro non è più una attività marginale, ma strutturale della vita monastica anche dell'eremita:

> 4. Tanto nell'eremo che nel monastero si attende soprattutto alla vita contemplativa. Pertanto ciascuno, impegnato nel quotidiano lavoro come richiede la sua condizione di cristiano e di monaco (RB, 48; GS, 67) nell'esercizio della cristiana mortificazione e dell'ardente orazione, apra il suo cuore all'ascolto vigile e alla meditazione della Divina Parola, sostegno della fede, cibo dell'anima, sorgente pura e perenne della vita spirituale (cf. DV, 2 l-26).
> 108. Il lavoro è il mezzo normale del quale la comunità vive. Il S.P.Bennedetto vuole i monaci impegnati nel lavoro quotidiano (RB, 48); e la tradizione più autentica che si rifà al suo insegnamento ci mostra il lavoro come elemento fondamentale del vivere monastico in un equilibrio saggio e delicato con l'attività spirituale contemplativa[51].

50 Si rimanda alla più recente edizione: Congregazione Camaldolese dell'Ordine di San Benedetto, *Regola di San Benedetto, Costituzioni e Dichiarazioni*, Camaldoli, 2004.

51 Cf. ancora al n.° 112: «Nel predisporre l'orario giornaliero della comunità, si ricerchi un giusto equilibrio tra il lavoro ed il tempo in cui i monaci possano attendere con serenità e calma allo studio, alla *lectio divina* e alla preghiera, tenendo sapientemente presente le esigenze delle singole persone. Si provveda anche alle convenienti pause per il naturale riposo e la giusta distensione fisica e psichica dei fratelli, nella giornata e lungo il corso dell'anno. Nel monastero, le ore dedicate giornalmente al lavoro siano circa sette. Nell'eremo il lavoro è più limitato e di preferenza a carattere individuale, ma se le circostanze lo

5. LE SFIDE DELL'OGGI

La beata solitudine eremitica nella tradizione camaldolese nella sua idealizzazione si è venuta configurando come esperienza da vivere in un giardino armonicamente ricomposto che vorrebbe essere specchio di un giardino dell'anima, in un conversare con Dio idealmente ritrovato quasi a monte del peccato. Ma qual è il lavoro che questo giardino implica per chi lo abita? Ormai più di dieci anni orsono in altra sede ebbi occasione di analizzare il difficile farsi strada in ambito camaldolese di una sensibilità per il lavoro a partire dal Concilio Vaticano secondo[52]; soprattutto la fatica a pensare a un lavoro monastico possibile nell'oggi. Si potrebbe osservare che il problema non è solo del monachesimo camaldolese, ma, almeno per il *back ground* eremitico che lo caratterizza, si può forse individuare un tratto sotterraneo non certo privo di conseguenze: una sorta di deriva encratistica che accompagna l'autocoscienza eremitica, nel nome di un primato della contemplazione. Deriva peraltro che si è visto essere inopinatamente assente proprio nel più ideologico teorizzatore del primato dell'eremo, cioè il Giustiniani. Ma forse oggi siamo a un tornante storico che può consentire un ripensamento e nuovi paradigmi. Non rientra nelle mie competenze specifiche discuterne in modo organico, ma evidentemente non posso sentirmi esistenzialmente estraneo dalla percezione che, se non vogliamo finire come gli ultimi dei mohicani in una riserva, magari non più sicura e esente da rischi, non si può solo attendere l'evolversi degli eventi. Mi limito ad indicare telegraficamente tre riflessioni conclusive:

- Il peso di una società post cristiana è ormai un fatto ineludibile, anche ma non solo nella concreta dimensione economica: se l'eremo non si pone più al centro del mondo, che per di più non ha più un centro riconoscibile, di fatto in prospettiva ci si avvia, anche a breve termine, a una progressiva marginalizzazione che non consentirà più di vivere in un regime di protezione e di sostegno da parte dell'ambiente circostante. Che ne è allora nella nostra interpretazione di un primato della contemplazione, quale che sia il modo in cui la si vuole intendere?
- Il ruolo del lavoro per mantenersi, non solo o prevalentemente come antidoto all'ozio, si avvia a diventare più impellente. Risulta sempre più difficile anche per i monasteri storici vivere di rendite e di beneficenze: nell'obiettivo

richiedono, può essere anche collettivo, perché in armonia con la quiete eremitica».

52 «Un "lavoro monastico"? Appunti e materiali per una discussione», *Vita Monastica* 58 (2004) 9-28.

stato di necessità questo dovrebbe riproporre nuove modulazioni dell'*ora et labora*. Se siamo onesti, dobbiamo riconoscere che la vita monastica nel suo ideale più o meno mitico difficilmente si integra con i ritmi concreti dell'ambiente in cui oggi si vive; ma l'ambiente non può essere ignorato, se è vero che qualsiasi *fuga mundi* è fatta in relazione a un mondo reale, che comunque interagisce e condiziona. Questo non vale però solo riguardo alle condizioni di un lavoro economicamente redditizio, ma anche rispetto alle sensibilità oggi più diffuse di una salvaguardia del territorio e dell'ambiente naturale.

- Ne consegue una piccola, ma non irrilevante osservazione, alla luce anche della *Laudato si'* di papa Francesco che ha ispirato questo convegno: forse la tensione a conservare la bellezza e l'armonia dei «campi amabili» (tali perché così li abbiamo ereditati o perché ci è stato dato di crearli) in cui si vive potrebbe diventare (o è già?) un lavoro serio a servizio anche del mondo che ci circonda: un lavoro di custodia e di invenzione di modalità per un riuso intelligente. Probabilmente è lavoro da solo insufficiente a garantire un mantenimento e un senso al *labora* proprio del monaco e dell'eremita, ma certamente bisognoso di professionalità e di lungimiranza, se si vuole coniugare la antica sapienza e la odierna sensibilità ecologica.

Abstract

A partire dalla particolare collocazione dell'Eremo di Camaldoli, *campus amabilis* nel cuore della foresta casentinese, si discute in che misura storicamente le Costituzioni eremitiche vengono ad attestare sia il la coscienza della rilevanza del contesto naturale, sia la percezione di un possibile ruolo del lavoro volto alla cura dell'ambiente e quanto questo valga, più in generale, a definire una concezione del lavoro come valore monastico. Il quadro complessivo sembrerebbe mettere in evidenza una «deriva encratista» che ha accompagnato l'autocoscienza eremitica nel nome di un primato della contemplazione; ma almeno nell'oggi, nel venir meno dell'idea della centralità ecclesiologica e sociale del monachesimo, sembrerebbe importante assumere nuovi paradigmi.

CISTERCIAN RUINS: AN ARCHAEOLOGICAL APPROACH TO THE STUDY OF WORK AND POVERTY

Alba SERINO

The aim of the symposium "Monasticism and the Economy" was to examine economic themes in a monastic key, focusing in particular on economy and its relationship with spirituality. Considerations were made of economy as a *locus* of human interaction in society, and on monasticism, as a reconciliation between economic and religious values in modern times. This relationship appears quite complex: in recent decades, for instance, the rule of Saint Benedict has proven excellent for people of business, but where do the Benedictine values of poverty and simplicity stand within this relationship between economy and spirituality? The present paper aims at analysing this dichotomy in the medieval period. I believe that studying the complex relationship between work, religious belief and poverty in the past can constitute a useful starting point for our reflection on these topics today and contribute to a better understanding of our relationship with these aspects and its implications in the present. As an archaeologist, I will focus, in particular, on the physical evidence left by monasticism in the past and in particular by the monks of the medieval monastic order known as Cistercian[1]. By looking at specific case studies in Italy, the monasteries in Tiglieto and San Martino al Cimino, and specific choices made by Cistercian monks, the use of granges and of pre-existing structures, I will highlight how the intertwining between spirituality and economy was already relevant in the medieval period and how its study can contribute to our reflections in the present.

Alba Serino, archeologist, historian of art and architecture, lecturer at University of Tuscia.

1 The paper is based on part of the research conducted for my doctoral dissertation in Medieval Archaeology *Identity and Territory: Cistercian monasteries and the transformation of the French-Italian landscape in the Middle Ages*, tutors C. Corsi-S. Bonde, 2014/2015, University of L'Aquila (Italy).

1. WHY THE CISTERCIAN ORDER?

The Cistercian Order is an ideal example of the complex relationship between work and poverty in the past. This was a monastic order founded officially in 1098 by Robert of Molesme, with the mission to recover what he took to be the forgotten values of simplicity and sacrifice of the Rule of Saint Benedict, in response to the corruption and splendour that had developed within the widely spread Cluniac Order. From the first five "mother-abbeys" in the French region of Burgundy, Cistercian monks founded new monasteries across the whole of Europe and gradually created a large monastic network, which continued to expand until the fifteenth century. Despite the mission of these monks to recover what they took to be the forgotten values of simplicity and sacrifice of the Benedictine Rule, Cistercian monasteries could be rarely associated with poverty. On the contrary, through their adoption of advanced agricultural and engineering techniques across their extensive estates in Europe, Cistercians have been identified by scholars of Medieval Studies as the main authors of the agricultural revolution and, also, of the significant reshaping of the medieval European landscape[2].

2 For only a part of the extensive scholarship on the Cistercian Order and also its role in the transformation of the medieval landscape see A.L. FROTHINGHAM, «Introduction of gothic architecture into Italy by the french cistercian monks: I. The monastery of Fossanova; II. The monastery of San Martino al Cimino near Viterbo ; III. Chiaravalle di Castagnola; IV. Monastery of Arbona» *American Journal of Archaeology* 6 (1890); J.B. MAHN, *L'Ordre Cistercien et son gouvernement: Des origines au milieu du XIIIeme siècle, 1089-1265*, Paris 1945; L. JANAUSCHEK, *Originum Cisterciensium. Tomus I (solus editus)*, Ridgewood 1964; G. DUBY, *San Bernardo e l'arte cistercense*, Torino 1982, R. COMBA, «I cistercensi fra citta' e campagne nei secoli XII e XIII. Una sintesi mutevole di orientamenti economici e culturali nell'italia nord-occidentale» *Studi Storici* 26/2: *Economia monastica: I cistercensi e le campagne* (1985) 237-261; M. RIGHETTI TOSTI-CROCE, *Architettura per il lavoro. Dal caso cistercense a un caso cistercense: Chiaravalle di Fiastra*, Rome 1993; L. PRESSOUYRE, *L'Espace Cistercien*, Paris 1994; P. OTTONELLO, *L'Esordio Cistercense in Italia. Il mito del deserto, fra poteri feudali e nuove istituzioni comunali (1120-1250)*, Genova 1999; A.M. RAPETTI, *La formazione di una comunità cistercense. Istituzioni e strutture organizzative di Chiaravalle della Colomba tra XII e XIII secolo*, Rome 1999; G. PICCINNI, «El Modelo Cisterciense en su aplicacion italiana centro-septentrional: algunas ideas desde la historiografia» *Cistercium. Revista Cisterciense* 242-243 (2006) 45-61; T.N. KINDER *Cistercian Europe: architecture of contemplation*, Michigan 2002; J.M.M. CIVANTOS, «Il territorio stratificato: proposte dall'archaeologia del paesaggio», in *IV Congresso Nazionale di Archaeologia Medievale, San Galgano Abbey (September 26-30, 2006)*, Firenze 2006 3-7; K. ADDISON, "Changing places: the

2. THE FIRST CISTERCIANS IN THE ITALIAN TERRITORY: SS. MARIA E CROCE IN TIGLIETO

Considerations on the relationship between work and spirituality should start by looking at the earliest foundations of the Cistercian order. In this context the first monasteries, the mother-abbeys of the Burgundy region in France, were not considered, in order to focus instead on the Italian territory. The monastery identified by most scholars as the very first Cistercian foundation in the territory of Italy is the monastery of Tiglieto dedicated to Mary and St. Croce in the Liguria region[3]. Located in the middle of the Orba valley, this monastery appears at first as the perfect example of isolation and renovation of land professed by the Cistercian order. It was founded between 1120 and 1127 by a community coming from the mother abbey of La Ferté[4]. As a very early foundation, one would expect the Tiglieto monastery to adhere strictly to the rules of the recently established monastic order. However, archaeological and architectural evidence demonstrates a much more complex

---

Cistercian settlement and rapid climate change in England", in *Locating Medieval Landscapes*, edd. A.C. Lees-G.L. Overing, Pennsylvania 2006, 212-238.

3 On the foundation date of this monastery see for example P. Pistilli, «Il monastero di Tiglieto: cenni storici» *Rivista Cistercense* 5/2 (1988) 128-155; Ottonello, *L'Esordio Cistercense in Italia*, 2; P. Ottonello, *I cistercensi di Tiglieto. Mille anni di storia e di culto in valle d'Orba*, Genova 2008 14-15.

4 Scholars are divided on the identification of the precise date of arrival: most authors (especially of the seventeenth and eighteenth centuries), including Janauschek and Comba, suggest the date of 1120, Gioffredo proposes the date 1121 while other authors, such as Moriondo, Semeria, Campora, Cappelletti and Kehr believe in a later arrival of the monks in 1131 (B. Campora, *Capriata d'Orba. Documenti e Notizie*, vol.1, Tipografia editrice Torino, Torino 1909, 27-28; Janauschek *Originum Cisterciensium*, 9; Pistilli «Il monastero di Tiglieto», 129-130; G. Spinelli, «Il Monachesimo nella Diocesi di Acqui dalle Origini al Secolo XII», *Rivista di Storia, Arte, Archeologia per le Province di Alessandria e Asti*, 102/1[1994] 99-100; V. Polonio, «I Cistercensi in Liguria [secoli XII-XIV]» in *Monasteria Nova: Storia e architettura dei Cistercensi in Liguria [sec. XII-XIV]*, edd. C.B. Dufour, A. Dagnino, Genova 1998, 3-4; R. Comba, «Sulla prima irradiazione cistercense nell'Italia occidentale», *Studi Storici* 40/2 [1999] 343-344; Ottonello, *I cistercensi di Tiglieto?*, 6). This last hypothesis can be however excluded thanks to a document of 1127, describing a donation of land made to the monks, a sign that the Cistercian community of St. Maria and Croce in Civitacula had by then established in Tiglieto (F. Guasco-F. Gabotto, A. Pesce, «Carte inedite e sparse del monastero di Tiglieto, 1127-1341» *Biblioteca della Società Storica Subalpina* 69 [1923] 229). The majority of scholars believes however in the arrival of the Cistercians in 1120, identifying, as previously mentioned, the monastery as the very first Cistercian foundation in the Italian territory and outside of the French region of Burgundy, followed only a few years later by the foundation of the monastery of Lucedio in 1123-1124 (*cfr. supra*).

situation: it is true that the Tiglieto monastery was constructed in a deserted landscape, as dictated by the Rule, but this natural isolation did not coincide with the building activity of its monks and their involvement in the political dynamics of the region. The monks used brick as a building material for their monastic architectural complex, as well as for other secondary buildings in the landscape[5]. Brick was the typical building material of the region (and it is still today) and not one used by the French Cistercian communities. This means that rather than strictly adhering to the building model of the mother abbey and limiting all contacts with local inhabitants, the monks of Tiglieto adapted to local traditions and most likely involved a local workforce, skilled in the use of the building materials of the region, for the construction of their properties. And this was not the only sign of strong interaction with their territory of establishment: their building activity extended well beyond their monastic precinct, and gradually constituted what can be considered Cistercian signatures in the landscape, such as the Orba Bridge or the Cascina San Leonardo in Castellazzo Bormida (former grange of San Leonardo in Gamondio)[6]. In addition, a strong connection to local secular and religious powers emerges from documentary sources, since the very first establishment of the monks in the Orba valley. The development of their estates was, for example, highly influenced by the patronage of the marquises of Bosco and Monferrato and also after the conversion of the monastery into a commendary, the Raggi family kept an active role in the conservation of the monastery's patrimony[7]. It is interesting to note, that the monastic complex and part of the medieval properties of Tiglieto (such as the lands in Campale) belong to this family still today.

The monastery of Tiglieto suggests, therefore, that since the very first monastic foundations in Italy, a complicated relationship already existed between a strict adherence to spiritual values and the strong involvement in economic and political dynamics of the territory of establishment. After all the manual labour prescribed by the Rule implicated an inevitable impact of the monks on the area inhabited. One other interesting example of the role of Cistercian monks in reshaping the medieval landscape through their intense work and agricultural activity is the monastery of San Martino al Cimino, today part of the city of Viterbo in the Lazio region.

5 See image Appendix.

6 See image Appendix.

7 PISTILLI, «Il monastero di Tiglieto»; POLONIO, «I Cistercensi in Liguria [secoli XII-XIV]»; OTTONELLO, *I Cistercensi di Tiglieto*; R. PAVONI, «La valle degli antichi liguri alla conquista genovese» in *La Valle dell'Orba dalle Origini alla Nascita degli Stati Regionali*, edd. R. Pavoni-E. Podestà (Storia dell'Ovadese 1), Ovada 2008, 1-171.

3. THE CASE OF SAN MARTINO AL CIMINO IN THE LAZIO REGION

We can find a certain complexity in the relationship between the values of poverty and work also in San Martino Abbey. Already a Benedictine property of the monastery of Farfa since the half of the ninth century, this monastery radically grew in wealth and extension of estates with the substitution of the previous Benedictine community with a Cistercian one, coming from the mother abbey of Pontigny (between 1145 and 1150). It is significant that the documentary sources describe this choice of substitution as the solution to the economic crisis that had struck the Benedictine community. The Cistercian monks were transferred to San Martino by Pope Eugene III on purpose, to recover the loss of wealth of the monastery and thanks to the Cistercian community, the estates of this monastery arrived to extend largely across the northern area of the Lazio region. The richness of this monastic foundation brought to its entitlement as *nullius diocesis* (the identification as an independent diocese)[8].

The intense agricultural and architectural activity brought about the transformation of the landscape surrounding this monastery as well. The transformation came to constitute an actual signature of San Martino Abbey in the region, surviving still today in both the rural and urban contexts. In the rural context, we can admire along the portion of Via Cassia from Viterbo to Vetralla the series of dovecotes possessed by the monks for farming activity[9]. Here doves and/or pigeons were raised. In contrast with the erroneous identification as ancient Roman catacombs, these dovecotes can be dated to the second half of the thirteenth century thanks to a comparative study of the niches with other examples in the region[10].

---

8 On the history of the monastery and its relationship with the surrounding landscape see P. Egidi, *L'abbazia di S. Martino al Cimino presso Viterbo*, Rome 1907; E. Bentivoglio-S. Valtieri, *San Martino al Cimino: l'abbazia, il paese e un'ipotesi per il futuro*, Azienda Autonoma di Cura, Soggiorno e Turismo, Viterbo 1973; G. Petrucci *San Martino al Cimino (Viterbo III)*, Roma 1987; E. Bentivoglio, *San Martino al Cimino*, Viterbo 1991; C. Bastianelli, *San Martino al Cimino*, Viterbo 1997; A. Serino, «San Martino al Cimino presso Viterbo: l'evoluzione di un monastero in borgo», in *Storia della Città VII 2011-2012*, Roma 2014, 293-314.

9 See image Appendix.

10 Among the extensive studies on the chronology and functions of medieval cave settlements in the Tuscia region is the work of scholars such as Elisabetta De Minicis, Paolo Dalmiglio, Dina Moscioni, Vincenzo Desiderio and Giancarlo Pastura (E. De Minicis, *Insediamenti rupestri della Tuscia*, Roma 2003; Id., *Insediamenti rupestri di età medievale:*

With regard to the urban context, besides possessing several properties within the historical centre of Viterbo, including mills, vineyards, hospitals and houses, the signature of San Martino Abbey can be found in the architectural decorations of several secular and religious buildings, such as Palazzo Gatti, Palazzo dell'Abate next to Porta San Pietro and Palazzo dei Papi[11]. This type of signature supports the theory advanced by scholars, such as Enlart, that Cistercians were the main promoters of the Gothic style of architecture in Italy[12].

The monasteries of Tiglieto and San Martino highlighted the complexity of the relationship between Cistercian spirituality and the economy. The historical and geographic context of their territories definitely influenced the settlement choices of their monks, however it would be incorrect to believe that these were the exclusive factors determining their choices. The same complexity persists in all Cistercian foundations, as evident by analyzing one particular structure type used by the monks: the grange.

4. CISTERCIAN GRANGES: SECULAR OR RELIGIOUS BUILDINGS?

Granges were structures created originally for the storage of agricultural products. These buildings were positioned at regular distances from the Cistercian monastery and could be used as a node of the network of estates, to manage the entire properties of the monastery. With their peculiar triangular façade, granges distinguished themselves as an autonomous architectural type and constituted therefore a sign of the Cistercian presence in the agricultural landscape. These buildings gained a series of other surrounding secondary buildings across time and could often develop into actual farms and grow to gain autonomy and be recognized as a Cistercian monastery itself[13].

The grange of Warnavillers is for example located today in the centre of a plain in the Picardy region of France, between Estrées-Saint-Denis and Gour-

abitazioni e strutture produttive: Italia centrale e meridionale: atti del Convegno di studio, Grottaferrata, 27-29 ottobre 2005, vol. 2, Spoleto 2008).

11 On the estates of St. Martino al Cimino within the city of Viterbo see especially Egidi, *L'abbazia di S. Martino al Cimino presso Viterbo*, and Serino, «San Martino al Cimino presso Viterbo».

12 C. Enlart, *Origines françaises de l'architecture gothique en Italie*, vol. 66, Paris 1894.

13 On the Cistercan grange and its importance in Cistercian economy and spirituality see for example Righetti Tosti-Croce, *Architettura per il lavoro*; G. Coppack, «The Outer Courts of Fountains and Rievaulx Abbeys. The Interface between Estate and Monastery», in *L'Espace Cistercien*, ed. L. Pressouyre, Paris 1994.

nay-sur-Aronde. It was a grange of the Cistercian monastery of Chiry-Ourscamp, founded by a community coming from the mother abbey of Clairvaux in 1129. The monastery of Notre-Dame d'Ourscamp had developed massive estates, extending for approximately 12.000 square kilometers and its grange in Warnavillers was one of the central nodes for the control of this large territory. This building was used at least since 1156 for the collection of tithes. Some medieval structures of the grange still survive, more precisely in part of the precinct wall and the barn, the *petite grange* of 14 meters height (against the 18 m of the larger barn, built after 1156 for the necessity of more space and destroyed in a fire in the seventeenth century). This structure is one of the very few examples with the original medieval circular pillars surviving[14].

Also here the application of the rule *Ora et Labora* turns into a complex relationship between economic activities and spirituality. An extreme theoretical interpretation of these granges can be found in the views of the neo-marxist archaeologist Norman Yoffee[15]. According to Yoffee, in his study on the formation of primary states, he recognizes three different means to achieve political power: the control of economic resources, the control of knowledge, ceremonies and symbols and the control of armed forces. Granges could fit into the first category, the control of economic resources[16]. I will push this concept even further by suggesting that the evident and peculiar architectural connotation of these granges could be interpreted as the intention to actually display the control of these economic resources. It is evident that this interpretation assumes a strong distance from the religious dimension. It does however demonstrate, once again, the complexity of the economic theme within the Cistercian order in the past.

So far, the complexity of the work/poverty dichotomy has emerged under the economic point of view, through the analysis of architectural evidence con-

14 Little information on the grange of Warnavillers can be found in A. Peigné-Delacourt, *Histoire de l'abbaye de Notre- Dame d'Ourscamp*, Impr. Amienoise A. Denillet et cie, Amiens 1876; L.M. Nazart, "Le temporel et les constructions de l'abbaye d'Ourscamp jusqu'à la fin du Moyen Âge", Thèses d'École de Chartes, 1970. A study on the estates of the grange were also shared by myself together with Sheila Bonde and Clark Maines at the 88th annual meeting of the Medieval Academy of America on April 5, 2013 ("Monasteries and/in their Region: comparative analysis of Monastic Domains", in press).

15 N. Yoffee, *Myths of the Archaic State: Evolution of the Earliest Cities, States and Civilizations*, Cambridge 2005.

16 Yoffee, *Myths of the Archaic State*, 35-38.

nected to the farming activity of Cistercian monks. There is one further aspect that I would like to consider, connected to the possession of a particular kind of property: ancient ruins.

5. FOSSANOVA: ARCHITECTURAL REUSE IN THE CISTERCIAN ORDER

Archaeological research has demonstrated that medieval Cistercian foundations often re-used pre-existing structures, not only medieval ones, such as abandoned Benedictine monasteries, but also Lombard and ancient Roman ruins[17]. I have already mentioned for instance that the Cistercian community of San Martino al Cimino established into a pre-existing Benedictine monastery.

I believe that the choice of re-use is part of a complex interpretation as well. It is true that re-using a pre-existing structure to build a monastic complex was especially a matter of economic convenience, given the saving of time and cost of building material, respecting in this way the principles of poverty promoted by the Order. This habit can however be seen also under a spiritual point of view, especially in the case of the recovery of a Benedictine ruin: just like the Cistercians aimed at restoring what they took to be the forgotten values of the rule of Saint Benedict, they restored the ruined buildings of the Benedictine monastic order. But there is one further concept that appears in this dialogue between poverty and spirituality: the cultural appropriation of the past[18].

A Cistercian foundation showing a very strong connection with the ancient past is in the southern area of the Lazio region: the monastery of Maria and St. Stefano of Fossanova (province of Frosinone). The history of the monastery starts well before the arrival of the Cistercian monks from Clairvaux in 1135. Excavations revealed in fact the ruins of a Roman villa beneath the abbey. More precisely, the ruins of a *criptoporticus* (passageway) and of a peristyle (courtyard) dated to the second century BC were found beneath the refectory during the 1994-1996 excavations. Also a bath house connected to this villa and located not

---

17 On the reuse of preexisting structures in Cistercian foundations A. Serino, «Il caso cistercense: approcci teoretici allo studio del paesaggio monastico nel Basso Medioevo», *VII Congresso Nazionale di Archeologia Medievale* 1 (2015) 94-97.

18 On the concept of "cultural appropriation" see K. Ashley-V.Plesch, «The cultural processes of 'appropriation'» in *Journal of Medieval and Early Modern Studies* 32 (2002) 1-15; Nelson, R. (2003). «Appropriation» in *Critical terms of Art History*, eds. Nelson, R., Shiff E.R., Chicago, 160-173; on the application of the concept of cultural appropriation to the study of Cistercian monasticism see Serino, «Il caso cistercense».

far from the monastic church was found. The villa was reconstructed between the fourth and ninth centuries AD, proving that the site was inhabited also during this period. The structures of the Roman villa appeared then to be occupied by a first monastic community, considered by most scholars Benedictine[19].

The monks of Fossanova established in a territory with a quite strong connection to the past, as suggested by the presence of the Appian Way, by several archaeological finds in the territory and especially by the ancient ruins over which the monastery itself was built[20]. In addition, the community settled in a territory with a significantly long tradition of reclamations (as evident from the toponym *Fossa Nova*, in English "new pit"), an activity in which Cistercians excelled[21]. It is obvious that the settlement at Fossanova was highly conditioned by the pope's will and depended mostly on the strategic position of the pre-existing monastery along the southern borders of the Vatican reign. However, the intentionality of the monks to approach the memory of the past in their settlement can be considered in their construction choices at the monastery. First of all, by re-using the space of the Roman peristyle and then Benedictine cloister, the monks appear to have intentionally appropriated a space with a strong connection to the past. Factors of intentionality can be identified in the choice to reinsert the Benedictine architectural elements into the new enlarged cloister after demolishing the southern arcade[22]. This choice should be seen not only as

19 For an exhaustive description of the history and the monastic complex of Fossanova see S. Coccia-A.G. Fabiani, «Abbazia di Fossanova», in *Archeologia Medievale*, vol. 24, Firenze 1997, 55-86; G.M. De Rossi, *La Riscoperta di Fossanova*, Priverno 2002; B. Ciarrocchi, «Il materiale archeologico dell'abbazia di Fossanova: nuovi apporti alla conoscenza dell'insediamento monastico» *Rivista Cistercense* 2 (2005) 153-180; F. Ceci-G.M. De Rossi, *L'Abbazia, il museo medievale, Fossanova*, Roma 2006; G.M. De Rossi, *Fossanova e San Tommaso. Sulle orme di San Tommaso d'Aquino a Fossanova: un percorso tra agiografia e topografia*, Roma 2013.

20 Coccia-Fabiani, «Abbazia di Fossanova»; M. Cancellieri, «La media e bassa valle del"Amaseno, la via Appia e Terracina», *Bollettino dell'Istituto di Storia e di Arte del Lazio Meridionale* 12 (1987) 41-104; F. Ventre, «From the Pontine Plain to Benevento», in *The Appian Way. From its Foundation to the Middle Ages*, ed. I. Della Portella, Los Angeles 2003. 106-143; Ciarrocchi, «Il materiale archeologico dell'abbazia di Fossanova»; M.T. Caciorgna, *Una città di frontiera: Terracina nei secoli XI-XIV*, Rome 2008, 25-31.

21 One of the most studied factors of the alteration of the landscape operated by rural monasteries has been water management, especially on Cistercian monasteries: Righetti Tosti-Croce, *Architettura per il lavoro*; S. Bonde-C. Maines, «The Archaeology of Monasticism: a Survey of Recent Work in France, 1970-1987» *Speculum* 4 (1988) 804.

22 De Rossi, *La Riscoperta di Fossanova*, 50-51.

derived from the economic convenience of building over pre-existing structures, saving in this way time and building material. It should also be seen in a more symbolic manner: just like Cistercians adopted the rule of Saint Benedict and re-shaped it into a stricter legislation, these monks appropriated a Benedictine building and re-shaped it for their own use.

The construction over the peristyle should also be seen as an appropriation of the symbolic power of ancient Rome. The concept of memory returns also in the re-use of the ruins of the Roman bath house located in front of the monastic church, for a building used for farming activities. The position of the ruins facing the church and englobed into Cistercian architecture suggest the intention to acquire further legitimacy on the site through the appropriation of the ancient past. Under a theoretical point of view, the Roman bath house should be identified as both a symbolic and physical interface between the medieval monastic community and the ancient past.

The re-use of the ancient past in medieval religious buildings has been widely studied by scholars, who believe in both the economic and symbolic function of this phenomenon and in the attempt to legitimize the religious identity of these medieval sites through the appropriation of the values of early Christianity[23]. Yet, the appropriation of the past in the monastery of Fossanova appears to go beyond the mission to recover artistic and ideological values of the ancient world. Here, we do not have a simple use of *spolia*, single fragments of the ancient past. It is the appropriation of entire structures and sites of a secular past, rather than of ancient religious values[24].

---

23 Apart from Gisella Cantino Wataghin, who gives a simple economic explanation of the reuse of *spolia* in medieval ecclesiastic buildings (G. CANTINO WATAGHIN, «... ut haec aedes Christo Domino in Ecclesiam consecretur. Il riuso cristiano di edifici antichi tra tarda antichità e alto medioevo», *Ideologie e Pratiche del Reimpiego nell'Alto Medioevo, tomo primo*, Centro di Studi Italiano sull'Alto Medioevo Spoleto 1999), see L. DE LACHENAL, *Spolia. Uso e reimpiego dell'antico dal III al XIV secolo*, Milano 1995; A. ESCH, «Reimpiego dell'antico nel Medioevo: la prospettiva dell'archeologo, la prospettiva Dello storico», in *Ideologie e Pratiche del Reimpiego nell'Alto Medioevo*, vol. 1, Spoleto 1999, 73-108; L. ERMINI PANI, «Il recupero dell'altura nell'Alto Medioevo», in *Ideologie e Pratiche del Reimpiego nell'Alto Medioevo, tomo primo*, Spoleto 1999, 613-664; E. DE MINICIS, *Insediamenti rupestri di età medievale: abitazioni e strutture produttive: Italia centrale e meridionale: atti del Convegno di studio, Grottaferrata, 27-29 ottobre 2005*, vol. 2, Spoleto 2008.

24 For further considerations on the appropriation of the past in Cistercian monasteries see SERINO, «Il caso cistercense».

CONCLUSIONS

By looking at the themes of spirituality and work as an economic factor in the four medieval Cistercian foundations of Tiglieto, San Martino al Cimino, Chiry-Ourscamp and Fossanova, a significant complexity has emerged. The dialogue between poverty and spirituality in the Cistercian order was complicated by several other factors, such as the influence of the local historical and political context: the monastery of Tiglieto adapted to local building traditions in its adoption of the principles of Saint Benedict and did not conform to most of his rules from the very first foundation of the Cistercian order; the agricultural activity of monasteries such as the ones of Chiry-Ourscamp and San Martino al Cimino implied an economic situation far away from poverty; the architectural reuse of pre-existing ruins in Fossanova can be associated to principles that go beyond the simple economic convenience of saving time and building materials.

My research has underlined the continuity of life of the structures analysed up to this day. I would like to suggest that the physical structures of Cistercian economy are not the only aspects that we inherited from the Middle Ages: the intertwining between spirituality and economy appears to be relevant today just as it was in the medieval period. Cistercian culture caused a significant transformation of the medieval European landscape thanks to its complex spirituality, divided equally between work and prayer. By analysing and interpreting this phenomenon in the past, we can find a useful starting point for our reflection on our continued interaction with these topics today and perhaps a direction towards finding the perfect balance between the two.

Abstract

The Cistercian Order, founded towards the end of the twelfth century, was recognised by historians as one of the main authors of the agricultural revolution of the Middle Ages. Through their adoption of the Benedictine principles of work and prayer, these monks were capable of re-shaping the European landscape. This was possible thanks to the introduction of their advanced engineering and agricultural skills across their extensive estates. It is important to underline that, despite the mission of this monastic order to recover what the monks took to be the forgotten values of simplicity and sacrifice, Cistercian monasteries can be rarely associated with poverty. Studying this complex relationship between work, religious belief, poverty and the physical landscape in the past can contribute to a better understanding of our relationship with work and poverty and its implications today. The paper offers an overview of the approaches used in archaeology for the study of these topics in medieval monasticism. More specifically the application of some of these approaches to the physical traces left in the present will bw explained by four different case studies: the Italian foundations of Tiglieto (Liguria), Fossanova and San Martino al Cimino (Lazio) and the French monastery of Chiry-Ourscamp (Picardy). The Cistercian architecture will be considered in a wider context which includes also the economic and religious dimension: granges, hospitals, bridges, mills, dovecotes can give us different information on the concepts of work and poverty possessed by the monks in the past, both of an economic and a religious nature. Analysing the past through its physical evidence, and understanding how the complex relationship between work and poverty was perceived, can constitute a useful starting point for our reflection on our continued interaction with these topics today.

ECONOMY AND QUALITY OF MONASTIC COMMUNITY LIFE CHALLENGED BY SOCIETAL TRANSITIONS. AN ETHNOGRAPHIC CASE-STUDY OF THE TRAPPIST COMMUNITY OF THE ABBEY OF SINT-SIXTUS

Wim VANDEWIELE

1. CONTEXT

The religious landscape of present-day Western-European society is characterized on the one hand by a high level of secularization and on the other by an increased religious plurality[1]. The values intrinsic to a religiously oriented life in community are often diametrically opposed to the dominant Western-European thinking patterns such as individualism, utilitarianism and scientism. It is in this context no longer self-evident to consciously choose monastic life and it is moreover difficult to remain committed as a monk or a nun to a life characterized by a quasi-linear continuity and by exceptional obligations and limitations[2]. In addition, the rapidly ageing population in Western-Europe increasingly challenges the quality of both religious life and community life within monastic communities[3].

Wim Vandewiele, Assistant Professor at KU Leuven

1 P. BERGER, «Reflections on the Sociology of Religion Today» *Sociology of Religion* 62/4 (2001) 443-454; K. DOBBELAERE, «Towards an Integrated Perspective of the Processes Related to the Descriptive Concept of Secularization», *Sociology of Religion* 60 3 (1999) 229-247.

2 J.A. MERKLE, *Committed by Choice. Religious Life Today*, The Liturgical Press, Collegeville 1992; L. MOULIN, *De levende wereld der religieuzen: Dominicanen, Jezuïeten, Benedictijnen*, Brugge 1966; L. Strahan, *Out of the Silence. A Study of a Religious Community for Women*, Oxford 1988.

3 W. VANDEWIELE, *Contemplatieve abdijgemeenschappen in de 21ste eeuw. Een etnografische studie naar het hedendaagse contemplatieve gemeenschapsleven*, Leuven 2014; W. VANDEWIELE, «Toekomst abdijgemeenschappen onder druk? Rol en kwaliteit van het monastieke gemeenschapsleven uitgedaagd door maatschappelijke transitiebeweging», *Religie en Samenleving* 10 (2015) 25-43.

Within Roman Catholic monastic orders, a distinction is made between active and contemplative orders[4]. Outside of prayer, monastics of an active order devote their time to the fulfillment of a specific task in society, for example in the fields of education, healthcare and special youth care. A contemplative order, however, focuses almost solely on prayer, worship and contemplation. The life of the religious is in this case dedicated to community prayer and not in the first place to the fulfillment of a specific task in society.

The social services provided by active orders might be preferred in a dominant thinking pattern like utilitarianism. In Western-European society, a paradoxical attitude is adopted toward contemplative orders in particular. On the one hand they come up against a wall of societal incomprehension, on the other hand the high level of visitor participation indicates an increased interest in the mystique and spirituality of abbeys[5]. The image society creates of the social environment of contemplative orders relates to this paradoxical attitude.

This image is marked by a very persistent and conservative representation of the 'medieval' monk. As such, this 'medieval' representation is being both reproduced and enforced in e.g. commercials for beer and cheese products connected with abbey life[6].

The abovementioned social context was the starting point for the ethnographic PhD research "*Contemplative monasteries in the 21st century. An ethnographic study of present-day contemplative community life*" (2014) conducted by Vandewiele in the Abbey of Sint-Sixtus in Westvleteren (Belgium)[7]. The first part of this conference paper will focus briefly on this ethnographic study that aims to contribute to the creation of a more objective image of contemplative orders in today's society of the 21st century. The empirical fieldwork suggests that the quality of monastic community life is seriously challenged by the lower number of young monks in the past decade that entered the community and stayed on. Consequently, the second part of this paper will further examine the question whether or not the weakened attachments formed by a younger group of monks become exclusively apparent in the Abbey of Sint-Sixtus. Shouldn't the cause partly be sought within the abbey walls themselves?

4 H. Wortelboer, *Het Instituut Rooms-Katholieke Kerk*, Delft 2008.

5 Vandewiele, *Contemplatieve abdijgemeenschappen in de 21ste eeuw.*

6 A.M. Toevlucht, ... *Broeders te wezen...*, Zundert 2000.

7 Vandewiele, *Contemplatieve abdijgemeenschappen in de 21ste eeuw.*

2. ADDED VALUE OF THE ETHNOGRAPHIC STUDY

Scientific literature has also played its part in the simplification of the image of contemplative orders. Someone like Ervin Goffman, for instance, placed the monastic in his frequently cited work *'Total Institutions'* (1961) in a specific psycho-physiological framework, without basing this on empirically acquired data[8]. In his view, the monastic is a psychological weakling, seeking solace and a safe haven to shield himself from a turbulent society he cannot deal with[9]. Since the '70s, however, the focus within the social sciences has shifted towards the study of new religious movements, secularization and religious plurality[10].

Ever since, literature on Catholic monastic orders is mainly characterized by a subjective or at the most journalistic approach. A good example of this subjective perspective is Henri Nouwen's work 'Vreemdeling in het paradijs. Zeven maanden in een trappistenklooster' (1983)[11]. Specific anthropological and sociological scientific literature on monastic community life is virtually non-existent, this in stark contrast to the many works written from a spiritual, theological and esoteric point of view. The need for a more contemporary image of the way of life of contemplative communities comes to mind, both societally and scientifically.
In one of the rare ethnographic works, *'The Monastery. A Study in Freedom, Love and Community'* (1992), Hillery describes his research into a specific and anonymized Trappist community in the United States through participant observation in the guest house, individual conversations with monks and several surveys that were conducted in the enclosed community[12]. This study consists of three sub-studies on the monks' perception of freedom, power and love. Because Hillery's central focus is on these sub-studies, the reader gets but a very general description of their environment and their life in community. Moreover, his focus remains limited to an observation that starts from the

8 E. Goffman, *Over de Kenmerken van Totale Instituties*, Rotterdam 1975.

9 W. Vandewiele-W. Weyns, *Eindrapport leeronderzoek 'Totale Instituties Herbekeken. Een Participatieve Observatie'*, Antwerpen 2006.

10 Berger, «Reflections on the Sociology of Religion Today».

11 H. Nouwen, *Vreemdeling in het paradijs. Zeven maanden in een trappistenklooster*, Bossum-Tielt 1983.

12 G. Hillery, *The Monastery. A Study in Freedom, Love and Community*, Westport 1992.

perspective of the guest house and not from the environment of the enclosed community[13].

Compared to Hillery, the added value of the ethnographic study conducted by Vandewiele lies in the opportunity the researcher received to live together with the monks inside the enclosure of the non-anonymized Abbey of Sint-Sixtus in Westvleteren, thereby focusing his attention on the study of the day-to-day operations of the enclosed community as such[14]. Although this approach is less specific and has a wider focus, the observation time during the participant observation phase was used maximally for the study of the world of the enclosed community and the exploration of its external relation with the wider community.

The data acquired from the field observation translated into a detailed ethnographic description, which constituted the main focus of the PhD study. The ethnography aims to give the reader 'an' image of present-day contemplative community life, admittedly limited to a certain time and place. Furthermore, this view is also coloured by the extent to which the researcher got field access to the different facets of monastic community life.

3. ETHNOGRAPHIC RESEARCH IN ABBEY OF SINT-SIXTUS IN WESTVLETEREN

3.1. Method

The empirical and ethnographic[15] exploration of the field is more than imperative, as there is little valid social-scientific information available on monastic

13 C. Dudley-G. Hillery, «Freedom and Monastery Life», *Journal for the Scientific Study of Religion* 18 (1979) 18-28; R.L. Della Fave-G. A. Hillery, «Status Inequality in a Religious Community: the case of a Trappist Monastery» *Social Forces* 59 (1980) 62-84.

14 Vandewiele, «Toekomst abdijgemeenschappen onder druk?».

15 The central aim of the ethnographic study was to contribute to the creation of a more objective image of contemplative orders in today's society. A first subsidiary goal was to introduce the reader to the life of the monks by treading in the footsteps of the postulant, paying maximum attention to the detailed description of both the physical architecture in which the monks are living, praying and working together and the social architecture of the community with the different key role players the postulant encounters in those places. A second subsidiary goal was to broaden the ethnographic description of the physical and social architecture by using a central reading key. Erving Goffman's work «Totale Instituties» (1975) was chosen as a reading key. Within the framework of this study, the central reading key offered on the one hand the possibility to address some neglected aspects of community life, and on the other hand to enrich

life. If we are to obtain a more accurate picture of this religious form of living together, we had best study monastic community life on-site. Within the field of anthropology, a connection was found with the ethnographic tradition, more specifically with Karen O'Reilly's critical definition of what she considers to be 'ethnography':

> Ethnography is a practice that: evolves in design as the study progresses; involves direct and sustained contact with human beings, in the context of their daily lives, over a prolonged period of time; draws on a family of methods, usually including participant observation and conversation; respects the complexity of the social world; and therefore tells rich, sensitive and credible stories[16].

O'Reilly builds her critical definition of ethnography from the eclectic approach adopted by Paul Willis and Mats Trondman[17]. Willis and Trondman argue that ethnography should on the one hand be based on methods that have a direct and lasting relation to social contact with representatives of the host culture, and on the other hand that the ethnography should be theoretically founded[18]. This critical approach to ethnography was also adopted in this research study, more specifically in the study of monks in the context of their every-day life over a longer period of time. In the ethnographic account, we report on the daily life of the enclosed community within the abbey walls. The choice of participant observation is prompted by the possibility this technique offers to provide a better description of the details, dynamics and nuances of monastic life[19]. Apart from participant observation, many conversations took place in the field and several in-depth interviews with monks were conducted.

3.2. Case study Abbey of Sint-Sixtus

The field observations were made in the Abbey of Sint-Sixtus in Westvleteren (Belgium), this in the period between end 2005 and beginning 2008. The Trappist community consisted of some twenty-five monks at the time, of whom the

---

the description with a more analytical and critical reading of the acquired data.

16 K. O'Reilly, *Ethnographic Methods – Second Edition*, London 2012.

17 P. Willis-M. Trondman, «Manifesto for ethnography» *Ethnography* 1 (2000) 5-16.

18 O'Reilly, *Ethnographic Methods*.

19 R.M. Emerson, e.a., *Writing Ethnographic Fieldnotes*, Chicago 1995; H. F. Wolcott, *Ethnography a Way of Seeing*, Walnut Creek 1999.

age varied between 30 and 96 years old. The process of getting access to the abbey for research purposes has taken one year, this through active mediation of a contact person enjoying the confidence of the monastic community and of the abbot in particular. In the phase before the actual observation period in the abbey, two preliminary studies[20] were carried out.

In the actual observation period in the Abbey of Sint-Sixtus, 180 observation days were spent in the enclosure of the abbey, spread over a period of two years. This actual observation period resulted in the collection of diverse data: field notes, exclusive photo and video material, ten in-depth interviews, secondary internal source material (for example, travel diaries of the Abbot General) and legislation (Rule of St. Benedict, Canon Law, Constitutions and Statutes of the Order of Strict Observance et cetera). All data were digitalized and processed with NVivo[21].

4. QUALITY OF MONASTIC COMMUNITY LIFE CHALLENGED

During the field research, some elements were pointing to an internal rigidity that could possibly put a brake on the future-oriented dynamism within the monastic community of the Abbey of Sint-Sixtus. In the past decade, there have been fewer young monks that entered the community and stayed on. A singular answer to the question why a monk leaves may uncover some causes, but is in any case difficult to determine and remains very person-specific. After all, it doesn't answer the wider question of why it is mainly a younger group of monks that decides to leave the community prematurely.

---

20 In a first phase before the actual observation period in the Abbey of Sint-Sixtus, two small preliminary studies were carried out. The first was an explorative study of the topical value of Erving Goffman's theoretical framework in «Total Institutions» (1963). This preliminary study was titled 'Totale Instituties Herbekeken. Een Participatieve Observatie' (2006)/('*Total Institutions Revised. A Participant Observation*'). In a second preliminary study, an observation period of four weeks was spent in the Benedictine Abbey of Sint-Andries in Loppem (Belgium). This study showed on the one hand that the initial premise to make a comparative study between two abbeys of the same Benedictine family would bring little added value from a spiritual and theological point of view, and on the other hand that the limited amount of observation time would have to be distributed between the two monastic communities, which would immediately imply a loss of depth and added value. As a result, the actual observation time was used to make an in-depth study of only one monastic community.

21 D. MORTELMANS, *Kwalitatieve analyse met NVIVO*, Leuven 2011; L. RICHARDS, *Handling Qualitative Data. A Practical Guide*, London 2006.

In the older group, there may also be some monks that have played or still play with the thought of leaving, but practical and future-oriented impediments might have played or might still play a role in preventing them from proverbially throwing in the towel. The younger monks are not unlikely to see more chances to easily reintegrate themselves into society: finding a job, building a financially stable future, finding housing and perhaps starting a family. Obviously, the weaker attachment of the younger group of monks places heavy demands on the future dynamism or even continued existence of the Trappist community in Westvleteren.

> I asked brother H. if he wasn't worried about the future of the monastic community in Westvleteren, because there had been quite some fellow brothers that had left the community lately. He told me that he would of course regret it if the monastery ceased to exist in this particular place, but that he is heartened by the knowledge that their way of life continues in other places in the world. With a smile, he told me that there are even Third World Trappist monasteries where they have to refuse candidate monks[22].

4.1. Transition in ideological thought and action

This second part deals with the question whether we should seek the cause of the weaker attachment of a younger group of monks inside or outside the walls of the monastery, and whether this problem exists exclusively in the abbey of Westvleteren.

The cause can only partially be sought inside the monastery walls, and is rather situated in a wide societal development which goes far beyond specific elements inside the abbey walls. Clearly, the nature of the cause is cultural and is connected to the societal phenomenon of the rigid inter- and intra-ideological discourse in Flanders.

4.2. Framework of analysis of the cohort model

The cause of this rigidity may be found in the rapid societal changes that Flanders has been undergoing since the second half of the twentieth century. The unique and extremely fast evolution in the ideological field in Flanders

22 Fieldnotes on 16/11/2006.

results today in the distinction of three ideological cohorts[23]. Flanders has evolved in seventy years' time from a monistic Roman Catholic society, over a conflict between Roman Catholicism and organized Freemasonry, into a religiously pluralist society. From a socio-religious perspective, this paper will look further into the specific phasing of this transition, and will distinguish three ideological cohorts. Elaborating shortly on this, the analysis will be tested against the presence of internal dynamism in a monastic community.

4.2.1. Mass church cohort

Until the end of the '60s of the twentieth century, Flanders was ideologically characterized by an almost omnipresence of Roman Catholicism, which kept, despite the division of Church and State, a firm influence on society through the Roman Catholic pillar. Apart from this Roman Catholic pillar, socio-religious compartmentalized society is also comprised of a socialist and a smaller liberal pillar. This 'pillarization' created a homogenous and efficiently structured society. It meant that you were born inside a denominational or ideological group or 'pillar', were raised in it, shared joys and sorrows in it and eventually also died in it. The influence of such a pillar worked within almost all aspects of life and society. The choice of your school, the hospital when you were ill, the home for the elderly in your old age and even the organizations you voluntarily spent your free time in: all of them were largely predestined[24].

Before and just after the Second World War, parish life around the many church towers in Flanders was flourishing. Church participation and church attendance were massive and did not only have a religious but also a strong social function. The parish priests often fulfilled the role of provost in many local organizations. Consequently, the moral authority of the Church was not limited to weekly and Sunday services. The cultural blueprint that people within this cohort not only consciously, but also unconsciously received through birth, upbringing and habits is denominated 'mass church cohort'.

23 G. Marshall, *Dictionary of Sociology*, Oxford 1998; W. Vandewiele, «Gedoemd tot inter- en intralevensbeschouwelijk divers samenleven», *De Gids op Maatschappelijk Gebied*, October (2012) 25-29; Vandewiele, *Contemplatieve abdijgemeenschappen in de 21ste eeuw*.

24 G. Davie, *The Sociology of Religion. A Critical Agenda*, London 2013; G. Dierickx, *De buitenkant van de religie*, Antwerpen 2007; K. Dobbelaere-L. Laeyendecker, *Godsdienst, kerk en samenleving*, Rotterdam-Antwerpen 1974.

Ideologically, this cohort is characterized by a strong normative framework with regard to rituals, liturgical calendar, symbolism and conception of God. The strictly normative framework was rarely questioned and the socialization was facilitated by the Roman Catholic pillar with its many organizations that literally and figuratively speaking embraced the life and interactions of people. Freedom was therefore regarded as something belonging to the collective rather than to the individual[25]. Economical production was local, limited in volume and the leadership style was paternalistic and authoritarian, both in the abbeys and society. Abbeys were mostly able to be self-sufficient, because of sustainable farming and the vast availability of monastic human resources: lay-brothers and choir-brothers.

4.2.2. Baby boom cohort

At the end of the 1960s, a major turning point in the context of society and ideology was reached. Authors such as Van De Pol and Inglehart pointed at the time already to the growing shift in the conception of conventional Christianity and of the Western set of values between people born before the Second World War and what Inglehart calls the 'post-war cohorts'. Later on, Inglehart empirically confirmed that the transformation of values between these cohorts had taken place in the political culture of the industrially advanced societies, and moreover, that this shift is not a merely Western European phenomenon. With respect to religion and ideology in particular, smaller and larger shifts between both cohorts are also supported by findings from the larger European Values Study[26].

The struggle for emancipation and the resulting movement in the 1960s sparked a revolution in which, among other things, the strictly normative

25 VANDEWIELE, «Gedoemd tot inter- en intralevensbeschouwelijk divers samenleven».

26 DAVIE, *The Sociology of Religion. A Critical Agenda*; K. DOBBELAERE-L. VOYE, «Religie en kerkbetrokkenheid: ambivalentie en vervreemding», in *Verloren zekerheid. De Belgen en hun waarden, overtuigingen en houdingen*, edd. K. Dobbelaere-M. Elchardus-J. Kerkhofs-L. Voyé *et al.*, Tielt 2000, 117-152; K. Dobbelaere, «Trends in de katholieke godsdienstigheid eind 20ste eeuw: België vergeleken met West- en Centraal- Europese landen», *Tijdschrift voor sociologie* 24 (2003) 9-36; L. HALMANS-V. DRAULANS, «How Secular is Europe?» *The British Journal of Sociology* 57/2 (2006) 263-288; A. SINGELTON, *Religion, culture and society. A global approach*, London 2014; D. VOAS-S. DOEBLER, «Secularization in Europe: Religious Change between and within Birth Cohorts» *Religion and Society in Central and Eastern Europe* 4 (2011) 39-62.

framework of institutions such as Church and State were questioned and tested against the underlying values. This created new and alternative dynamics, movements and factions that did not automatically seek to join the classical pillars and acted more autonomously: the 'baby boom cohort'[27].

Ideologically, this period is characterized in Belgium by a sharp divide between Roman Catholics and organized Freemasonry. In this context, the baby boom cohort particularly questions the normative character of the rites, symbols and conception of God. It marked the time in which the Church wished to read the signs of the times and laid down new guidelines to bring liturgy closer to the people again. There were quite some experiments to redefine faith in the light of new individual and collective expectations, bringing about the birth of alternative religious communities. Economy became now more global and leadership democratized. The baby boom cohort experienced freedom in the constant questioning of the tension between the individual and the collective.

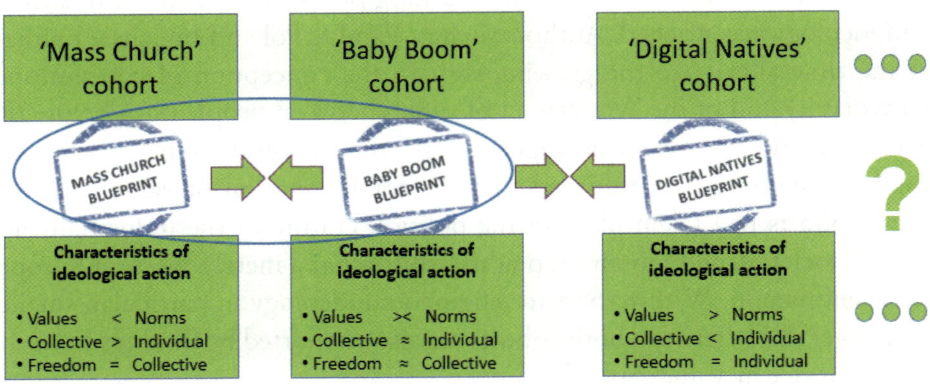

Fig 1: Ideological Cohort Model

4.2.3. Digital natives cohort

In the margin of this tension between the mass church cohort and the baby boom cohort, the newest cohort gradually emerged: the 'digital natives' cohort[28]. This cohort adopted the blueprint of an individualized society and saw

27 D. F. ALWIN, «Cohort Replacement and Changes in Parental Socialization Values» *Journal of Marriage and Family* 52/2 (1990) 347-360.

28 G. O'BANNON, «Managing our future: The generation X factor», *Public Personnel Management* 30 (2001) 95-109; J. SANCHEZ, e.a., «Does the New Digital Generation of Learners Exist? A Qualitative Study» *British Journal of Educational Technology* 42 (2011) 543-556.

the emergence of a digital world, constantly using the perspective of the individual, also in the field of ideology. The cohort of 'digital natives' goes shopping in the ideological supermarket and fills trolleys of their own with what gives them meaning, describing this in various terms such as 'God, energy or something', in which they entirely or partially – either temporarily or permanently – believe. Therefore, this cohort grows up ideologically in a religiously pluralist society. For this cohort economy is globalized and works in liquid networks, and is highly linked with individual preferences and self-development. The cohort of digital natives is used here as a catch-all term for the entire youngest cohort in Flanders, but may in fact be more diversified. Unfortunately, no sufficient empirical research data are available to refine this youngest cohort[29].

4.3. Cohort model and monastic community

Let us return here to the original question and focus again on the monastic community of Westvleteren. The reason for the weaker attachment of a younger group of monks is connected to the nature of the different cohorts that also cause the rigid inter- and intra-ideological discourse in Flanders.

The entire monastic community of the Abbey of Sint-Sixtus consisted during the observation period mainly of representatives of the first two cohorts, indicating the absence of the cohort of digital natives apart from two exceptions. In 2014, there were no representatives of the digital natives left. The cohort model can really be applied here, because the period after Vatican II marked a 'revival' in the Abbey of Sint-Sixtus. In this context, there was a peer effect that attracted young baby boomers to the liturgical renewal started by a group of young monks. They distanced themselves from the old liturgy at the time and also attached more importance to community formation within the monastery. One of the pioneers from that time reminisces about those years:

> I entered the community a few years after Vatican II. At the time, there were quite some younger fellow brothers. We distanced ourselves from the older generation and introduced some changes, especially liturgically. We also wanted more focus on community formation. Actually, when I come to think of it, today's younger generation could in fact find fault with the way we do things as well, because we've become the older generation now and we're stuck in our way of thinking[30].

29 Vandewiele, *Contemplatieve abdijgemeenschappen*

30 Fieldnotes on 04-02-2007.

New forms of liturgy were experimented with, questioning the then very normative and stringent old liturgy and symbolism and testing it against the underlying values. Additionally, more importance was attached to the internal group dynamics within the monastic community, which led to the continued use of a dorm instead of individual bedrooms. Many monastic communities did make the switch, Westvleteren didn't until 2007.

Compared to the other two cohorts, the digital natives grew up in a completely different societal context, that put more stress on the personal development of the individual than on the collective needs of the community. This is not unimportant, since the effort that monks from the digital natives cohort have to make to adapt to the group dynamics and economy of Westvleteren is very great. They have to compromise substantially on their room for self-development. The quotation below illustrates the high price they pay to adapt.

> Today I had a conversation with Father Abbot in his office. The conversation turned to the plans for the new monastery buildings that could be consulted by the brothers in the scriptorium. I told him that the change from a dorm to individual bedrooms was a huge step. He agreed and hoped it might have a positive influence both on the monks and on the community. I said with a smile that the younger brothers must certainly have been happy to be able to sleep in a bedroom of their own again. I was amazed to hear Father Abbot claiming otherwise. It had been the younger monks that resisted somewhat, since they had paid a higher price for entering the monastery by having to change over from an individual bedroom in their home environment to a dorm in the monastery. They were not used to that! Conversely, most of the older brothers, Father Abbot told me, had never known anything different. He gave the example of his own situation: in his childhood home he used to share one bedroom, this was also the case afterwards in boarding school and eventually in the monastery as well. The change the younger brothers had to make was big[31].

The digital natives' room for development is also restricted in other fields. The individual capacities or 'human resources' are being addressed less frequently, because the community takes priority over the individual.

A monk that left the Abbey of Sint-Sixtus indicates it has been very heavy on him personally that he couldn't develop his own talents anymore, because he

31 Fieldnotes on 06-02-2007.

had to devote himself entirely to the chores of the community and he thought there was little room for innovation.

> I couldn't use my talents to the full anymore. This makes me especially vulnerable now that I have left the community, because I haven't updated my skills. I have often asked permission to do so, but I first had to share in the tasks of the community. How unfortunate! It hurt, because there is another monastic community in Flanders that makes the most of the individual talents of its members for the development of its own economy. This, of course, results in making them more attractive for young people, because they still use people's talents there, apart from asking them to do the normal community chores that every member has to do. They've already had to expand their building twice to accommodate the amount of candidates. I had hoped to see this happening here as well[32].

The above quotation mentions that another Flemish monastic community of Trappists does take greater account of the room for self-development that is important to the cohort of digital natives. Considering the fact that the grass for this former monk may have looked a little too green on the other side, this does serve to remind us, however, of the fact that other interpretations of monastic community life and the attraction of candidates from the digital natives cohort are definitely possible.

4.4. Future challenges drawn from the cohort model

By applying the framework of analysis of the cohort model to the ethnographic description, a threefold challenge can be deduced for monastic community life in the near future, within what Habermas calls post-secular society. Habermas argues that religion and, by extension, more specifically also religious movements and monastic communities, has indeed lost some societal influence because of secularization, but that, in his view, this doesn't mean that religion has lost its meaning[33].

32 Interview with X, 08/02/2007.

33 J. Habermas, «Een postseculiere samenleving: Wat betekent dat?», in *Europees humanisme in fragmenten: grammatica van een ongesproken taal (Nexus 50)*, ed. R. Riemen, Tilburg 2008, 279-291; P. Loobuyck, «Het (post)seculiere perspectief van Jürgen Habermas», in *Radicale Secularisatie? Tien hedendaagse filosofen over religie en moderniteit*, edd. S. Latré-G. Vanheeswijck, Kalmthout 2013, 197-211; W. Vandewiele (2010), «Catacombenkerk in Stad Antwerpen: naar een vitale kerkelijke presentie in de binnen-

4.4.1. Monastic baby boomers

Based on the ethnographic description, we first of all conclude that in the past decade, the influx in the Abbey of Sint-Sixtus has been limited to monks from the baby boom cohort. This can be attributed to the current trend of men and women choosing more and more often to enter a monastic community later in life.

Consequently, they now have a solid basis to rely on that was built in the outside world. This base of experience is not infrequently religiously rooted in a different active congregation or in being a priest dedicated to parish life or to education. As indicated by most monks in the in-depth interviews, this base of experience is essential for the maturity that is required today to engage in life as a cenobitic monk in the 21st century[34].

This base of experience serves as a touchstone, as it were, for the choice of an exclusive orientation of religiousness on the life of prayer in community, but acts moreover as a facilitator to maintain the psychosocial balance when disruptions occur in times of crisis and the monk seriously questions his choice of monastic life, dwelling on the opportunities (for example, starting a family, perception of sexuality et cetera) he misses out on. The question that arises with the influx of monks from the baby boom cohort is whether this base of experience offers a sufficient guarantee that it can function as a lifelong touchstone and facilitator. After all, human lifespan continues to lengthen and the base of experience from the outside world is limited to the time before one entered the community. Will that base be sufficiently flexible to keep adapting to future intra-monastic, ecclesiastical and rapid societal changes?

4.4.2. Quality of religious (community) life

Another question is whether it isn't a form of palliative sedation of a community when the active contingent of a monastic community is limited to monks from the baby boom cohort? 'Après nous le deluge?'. To put it differently: isn't a monastic community dozing off in the comforting knowledge that the limited influx of baby boomers effectively helps the aged community to survive, all the while sensing that this is but a temporary and artificial prolongation of com-

stad», in *Op zoek naar Gemeenschap in een Godvergeten tijd*, edd. J. Bastiaens-G. Van Langendonck, Antwerpen 2010, 85-104.

34 Toevlucht, ... *Broeders te wezen...* .

munity life? It is a disconcerting and challenging question, but it incorporates a major concern for the quality of religious (community) life.

An influx of new monks from the digital natives cohort may not be possible anymore for every community, but in any case, the demand for quality remains crucial for those that are still part of the monastic community. Every monk follows his own individual vocation and consciously and radically chooses a life in community in which prayer is central. By doing so, the monk abandons certain acquired rights in the outside world and excludes a substantial number of potential opportunities, but instead he expects an environment in which this conscious and radical choice of monastic life can take shape fully and in which the discrepancy between monastic life and other life choices in the outside world is considerable. That is, however, where the proverbial shoe pinches.

In the monastic communities that are 'poor in digital natives', a lot of management and care tasks today end up with the remaining group of baby boomers. The full range of operational tasks that are necessary to run a monastic community and the increased care needs of the aged fellow brothers create an increasing pressure on a decreasing number of shoulders to rest the burden on. From the observation of and contacts with other abbeys showed that time for a qualitative religious life and religious life in community is rather limited.

As a result, the above question concerning the flexibility of the baby boomers' base of experience becomes more pertinent. How much could and would a monk be willing to compromise on the quality of his individual expectations of religious life in community and how flexible is his maturity in offering resistance to the increasing pressure? Even though mainly younger monks from the digital natives cohort leave the abbey, in recent years there still have been monks from the baby boom cohort that left the Abbey of Sint-Sixtus and that had nevertheless acquired a great monastic and religious maturity.

4.4.3. Monastic digital natives

In the Abbey of Sint-Sixtus, the influx of candidate monks from the cohort of 'digital natives' has been extremely small during the past two decades. Most of the ones that still entered the community, have eventually left it. They did not infrequently do so at the moment they had to decide whether or not to take solemn vows, when the community expects them to profess their final commitment.

If the remaining group of active baby boomers is already a serious cause for concern with respect to their coping ability and their expectations regarding the quality of religious life and community life, then that is all the more valid for the digital natives, so to say. Compared to the baby boomers, the cultural discrepancy between digital natives and the aged group of monks from the mass church cohort is even bigger. The baby boomers, after all, have consciously and actively rebelled against the mass church cohort in their younger years, which gave them greater knowledge of that cohort. For baby boomers, the connection to not only the worldview and self-image of the mass church cohort, but also to their thinking and way of life is bigger than for monastic digital natives.

As illustrated earlier by the cohort model, we are at a juncture where representatives of the three cohorts live together anyhow, but have - due to their different cultural blueprint - at the same time different expectations regarding themselves, economy, society and the outside world. In a closed community, it can be expected that these differences are more striking, because monks in an enclosure rely more on each other and have fewer chances to avoid one another.

4.5. Synthesis: challenges offering opportunities for the future

A monastic community faces some significant challenges nowadays. Monastic communities cannot shirk from societal developments: they, too, are confronted with the fact that living together with the three cohorts is not optional; it is a definite challenge for the future.

These challenges, however, could be translated positively into a course that offers monastic communities opportunities for the future. Monastic communities are to be considered, due to their closed character, as a microcosmos, lab or practice zone[35] in which living together in community or – as Saint Benedict of Nursia puts it – in the 'School of love', is reflected more clearly[36]. As such, interactions – both conflictual and non-conflictual – between monks in a an enclosed community are not only to be explained in terms of the individual or the character, but also societally, due to the different blueprint that monks received. Hence, monasteries are interesting labs or practice zones in which living together in community is being practiced intensively. Herein lies a potential external societal challenge for monastic communities with regard

35 P. Sloterdijk, *You Must Change Your Life*, Cambridge 2013.

36 P. Baud, e.a., *La vie cistercienne: hier et aujourd'hui*, Paris 1998; A. Louf, *De Cisterciënzerweg*, Berkel-Elschot 1996; A. Louf, *Met Gods genade. Een ontmoeting*, Tielt 2003; B. Rollin, *De Regel van Benedictus Beleven*, Lannoo, Tielt 2008; M. van Hecke, *De Sint-Sixtusabdij van Westvleteren. Spiritualiteit*, Leuven 2012.

to their future: in the unique cultural position they occupy in society and on that account, the signalling function they fulfill in it.

If we regard monastic communities as a lab with its own character or as a microcosmos in which living together is being practised as a latent function of monastic community life, then both the virtually absent influx of monastic digital natives and the quality of religious life and community life constitute a significant internal challenge for their lab function and eventual survival.

Abstract

The religious landscape of present-day Western-European society is characterized on the one hand by a high level of secularization and on the other by an increased religious plurality. The values intrinsic to a religiously oriented life in community are often diametrically opposed to the dominant Western-European thinking patterns such as individualism, utilitarianism and scientism. It is in this context not self-evident to consciously choose monastic life and it is moreover difficult to remain committed as a monk or a nun to a life characterized by a quasi-linear continuity and by exceptional obligations and limitations.

This article starts out by focusing briefly on an ethnographic study describing the physical and social environment of a specific contemplative Trappist community, the Abbey of Sint-Sixtus in Westvleteren (Belgium), thus contributing to the creation of a more objective image of contemplative orders in today's society. In the second part of the article focuses on the specific challenge of societal transitions for the relation between the monastic economy and the quality of monastic community life.

BENEDICTINE MONASTICISM

MONACHESIMO ED ECONOMIA: LE DIPENDENZE MONASTICHE DI SANTA MARIA DI FARFA E DEI SS. BENEDETTO E SCOLASTICA DI SUBIACO (LAZIO)

Giorgia Maria ANNOSCIA – Chiara CARLONI – Giulia MAGGIORE

Questo contributo è volto all'approfondimento del tema della gestione del territorio e delle risorse da esso provenienti da parte di due grandi cenobi dell'Italia centrale, San Benedetto di Subiaco e Santa Maria di Farfa[1].

L'intento è quello di far luce maggiormente, tramite un approccio storico-topografico, sulle modalità di gestione dei grandi patrimoni fondiari riferibili a questi ultimi, soprattutto nei secoli della loro formazione e definizione, tra l'VIII e l'XI. L'interesse è stato rivolto, quindi, alle dipendenze dislocate soprattutto in ambito laziale, che si è scelta come area campione, almeno nel caso di Farfa, chiarendo in questo modo il loro comportamento politico-economico sia in ambito locale sia al livello più ampio.

1. FARFA E SUBIACO

Per quanto riguarda il caso di Farfa la ricerca ha preso avvio dall'esame della documentazione edita riguardante il cenobio e riportata nel *Regesto Farfense*, nel

Giorgia Maria Annoscia, archeologist, researcher at the University Sapienza in Rome; Chiara Carloni, archeologist, archeologist operator and academic teacher at the University Sapienza in Rome; Giulia Maggiore, specialist in medieval archeology at the University Sapienza in Rome; GMA = Giorgia Maria Annoscia; CC = Chiara Carloni; GM = Giulia Maggiore.

1 I risultati preliminari della ricerca sui monasteri di Farfa e Subiaco sono editi nel volume L. ERMINI PANI, ed., *Teoria e pratica del lavoro nel monachesimo altomedievale.* Atti del Convegno Internazionale (Roma – Subiaco, 7-9 giugno 2013), Spoleto 2015. In particolare: F.R. STASOLLA, «Celle e dipendenze per l'organizzazione del lavoro monastico in area laziale», 141-161; C. CARLONI, «Celle e dipendenze del monastero di Farfa in area laziale», 163-189; G. MAGGIORE, «Celle e dipendenze del monastero del San Salvatore al Monte Amiata in area laziale», 213-230. P. ROSATI, «Celle e dipendenze del monastero di S.S. Scolastica e Benedetto in area laziale», 191-211.

Fig. 1 - I territorai analizzati: la Sabina (A) e la Valle Sublacense (B)

Liber Largitorius e nel *Chronicon farfense*[2]. I dati raccolti sono stati organizzati in un database che ha permesso di registrare, oltre alle informazioni base, quali la definizione e la localizzazione delle dipendenze, anche le varie attività produttive e i riferimenti a quelle agricole e silvo-pastorali rintracciabili. L'esigenza di realizzare questo database è stata funzionale all'impostazione di un GIS, che ha permesso, dove possibile, di organizzare le informazioni riguardo la posizione di tali celle, anche dal punto di vista materiale, di stabilire se queste strutture avessero avuto un'area di pertinenza soggetta alla loro diretta amministrazione, e di comprenderne gli sviluppi e le dinamiche insediative sia nelle campagne che nei centri urbani.

Il cenobio di Farfa, che secondo la tradizione viene fondato nella seconda metà del VI secolo, si sviluppa in breve tempo grazie alla sua posizione privilegiata, a confine tra il ducato di Spoleto e quello romano, attirando l'interesse prima dei duchi longobardi e successivamente dei sovrani franchi.

2 *Il Regesto di Farfa compilato da Gregorio di Catino* [d'ora in poi *RF*], eds. I. Giorgi e U. Balzani, Roma 1879-1914, I-V; *Liber Largitorius vel notarius monasterii pharphensis* [d'ora in poi *LL*], ed. G. Zucchetti, Istituto Storico Italiano, Roma 1913-1932, I-II.; *Il Chronicon Farfense di Gregorio di Catino* [d'ora in poi *ChF*], a cura di U. Balzani, Roma 1903, I-II.

Tra l'VIII e il IX secolo il monastero si arricchisce notevolmente grazie alle strategie politico-amministrative intraprese dagli abati, fino a raggiungere, durante la prima metà del IX secolo, il periodo più fiorente[3].

L'esame delle fonti raccolte ha permesso di evidenziare alcuni elementi significativi della gestione e dell'amministrazione delle proprietà e delle dipendenze da parte della comunità monastica.

CC

Il secondo caso di studio è quello del monastero benedettino di Subiaco e dei suoi possedimenti nella Valle Sublacense[4], un'area posta una sessantina di km a Est di Roma e oggetto di attività di ricerca coordinata dapprima da Letizia Ermini Pani e poi da Francesca Romana Stasolla ("Sapienza" Università di Roma)[5]. Il territorio, compreso tra Tivoli e Subiaco, è articolato in due distinti bacini oro-idrografici (due tratti dell'Aniene), cinti su tre lati da catene montuose calcaree (dei Ruffi a Ovest, dei Simbruini a Est, dei Sabini a Nord) e da terreni pianeggianti di tufo e pozzolana a Sud: l'area si contraddistingue come crocevia di comunicazioni tra l'Agro Romano e l'Abruzzo e tra la Sabina e il Lazio meridionale, il che addita il ruolo strategico che essa rivestì fin dall'epoca antica, vista anche la presenza di quattro acquedotti che rifornivano l'Urbe in epoca romana (l'*Anio Vetus*, *l'Aqua Marcia*, l'*Aqua Claudia* e l'*Anio Novus*), uno dei quali, l'*aqua Claudia*, era ancora attivo in epoca medievale[6].

---

3 In ultimo *Farfa, abbazia imperiale. Atti del Convegno (Farfa 2003)*, ed. R. Dondarini, Verona 2006. La ricostruzione delle vicende dell'abbazia in I. SCHUSTER O.S.B., *L'imperiale abbazia di Farfa*, Roma 1987.

4 IGM, Foglio 145, III SO, *Arsoli*; Foglio 151, IV NO, *Gerano*.

5 L. ERMINI PANI *et al.*, «La Valle Sublacense nel Medioevo: il caso di Cervara di Roma», *Temporis Signa*, II (2007) 1-39; G.M. ANNOSCIA, «Le forme e i modi dell'incastellamento nella Valle Sublacense», in L. ERMINI PANI, ed., *Le valli dei monaci*. Atti del Convegno Internazionale *De Re Monastica III* (Roma-Subiaco, 17-19 maggio 2010), Spoleto 2012, 359-395; F.R. STASOLLA, «Origine e sviluppo del Patrimonium Sanctae Scolasticae», in ERMINI PANI, ed., *Le valli dei monaci. De Re Monastica III*, 271-307; G.M. ANNOSCIA – F.R. STASOLLA, eds., *Monaci e castelli nella Valle Sublacense* (Miscellanea della Società Romana di Storia Patria, LXV), Spoleto 2016.

6 Nella Valle Sublacense venivano captati quattro dei principali acquedotti attivi in età romana (l'*Anio Vetus*, l'*Aqua Marcia*, l'*Aqua Claudia* e l'*Anio Novus*): di questi grande rilevanza ha avuto l'*aqua* Claudia, in uso almeno fino al terremoto che colpì Subiaco nel 1305. Nel 1051 (*Il Regesto Sublacense del secolo XI*, eds. L. ALLODI – G. LEVI, Reale Società Romana di Storia Patria, Roma 1885, da ora in avanti *Reg. Subl.*) papa Leone IX confermò i beni all'Abbazia e diede in concessione al monastero sublacense l'intero percorso dell'acquedotto Claudio (*Reg. Subl.*, n. 21), rafforzando di fatto una politica messa in atto dal

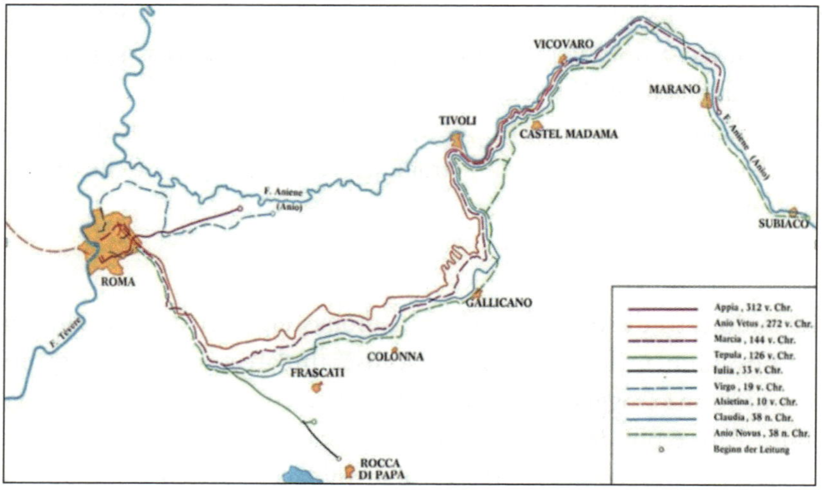

Fig. 2 - Gli acquedotti nella Valle Sublacense

Tra IX e XI secolo questa entità geografica venne istituzionalizzata in entità geopolitica sotto il controllo dell'Abbazia[7].

Fig. 3 - La piattaforma GIS della Valle Sublacense (elaborata da Lorenzo De Lellis)

monastero stesso fin dal 926 (privilegio di Giovanni X, *Reg. Subl.*, n. 9). Su questa tematica si veda P. Rosati, «I confini dei possessi del monastero sublacense nel medioevo (secoli X- XIII)», *Archivio della Società Romana di Storia Patria*, 135 (2012) 31-62.

7 P. Delogu-L. Travaini, «Aspetti degli abitati medievali nella regione sublacense», *Archivio della Società Romana di Storia Patria*, CI (1978) 17-34; L. Travaini, «Rocche, castelli e viabilità tra Subiaco e Tivoli intorno ai confini territoriali dell'Abbazia sublacense (X-XII secolo)», *Atti e Memorie della Società Tiburtina di Storia e d'Arte*, LII (1979) 65-97; P. Delogu, «Problemi di castelli nel Lazio», in *Castelli. Storia e archeologia*, edd. R. Comba-A.A. Settia, Cuneo 1984, 105-114.

In virtù dei diritti acquisiti, il patrimonio sublacense, da alcuni fondi ubicati nell'esigua entità amministrativa della *pontificia massa Jubenziana* ricavata *ex corpore patrimonium Tiburtinum*, si ampliò fino a pervenire a un assetto territoriale i cui confini lineari coincisero con quelli geografici di un'area omogenea, quella del medio bacino dell'Aniene compreso tra i monti Simbruini e i Ruffi. Questo *territorium* si andò costantemente arricchendo di undici concessioni pontificie susseguitesi dal 926 al 1051[8], fino a pervenire, assommando anche le terre dotate di immunità, a un assetto territoriale più allargato[9].

Sulla falsa riga di quanto enucleato per Farfa, la ricerca, che utilizza il metodo regressivo proposto con successo da Jean Coste per la Campagna Romana[10], è partita dallo spoglio della documentazione scritta (Regesti e Cronache monastiche)[11], che copre un lasso cronologico che va dall'VIII al XII secolo, e dall'analisi della cartografia storica e moderna. L'approccio metodologico è volto quindi alla ricomposizione della maglia insediativa e dell'assetto fondiario in epoca tardoantica, ricomposizione finalizzata a valutare l'impatto "colonizzatore" del cenobio sul limitrofo territorio.

Per quel che concerne l'uso del suolo, di particolare rilevanza e accuratezza sono i dati forniti dal *Catasto Gregoriano* (del 1816) con l'indicazione della destinazione d'uso e la giacitura (monte, piano, mista) delle singole particelle censite ai fini fiscali. Il quadro d'insieme restituisce un'immagine analitica della realtà agraria dell'epoca e consente, data la sua elevata specificità, una ricostruzione accurata delle colture nonché delle proprietà individuali, familiari e dei vari enti coinvolti, permettendo, oltre all'individuazione della localizzazione

8 *Reg. Subl.*, nn. 9, 10, 12, 13, 14, 15, 16, 17, 19, 21, 185.

9 Per i criteri di definizione del *territorium* sublacense, si rimanda a P. Rosati, «Le terre immuni del monastero sublacense: lettura archeologica dei confini», in Ermini Pani, ed., *Le valli dei monaci. De Re Monastica III*, 413-440. Per la formazione del *patrimonium* di S. Scolastica si veda F.R. Stasolla, «Origine e sviluppo del patrimonium Sanctae Scolasticae», in *Le valli dei monaci. De Re Monastica III*, ed. Ermini Pani, 271-308.

10 J. Coste, «Il metodo regressivo», in C. Carbonetti *et al.*, *Scritti di topografia medievale: problemi di metodo e ricerche sul Lazio*, Istituto storico italiano per il Medio Evo, Roma 1996, 17-23. Inoltre, J. Coste, «Un insediamento nel Tiburtino: Empiglione», *Atti e memorie della società tiburtina di storia e di arte*, LXI (1988) 147-188; J. Coste, «Un insediamento nel Tiburtino: Empiglione (continuazione e fine)», in *Atti e memorie della società tiburtina di storia e di arte*, LXII (1989) 145-185.

11 *Reg. Subl.*; Guglielmo Capisacchi da Narni, *Chronicon Sacri Monasterii Sublaci (anno 1573)*, ed. L. Branciani, Subiaco 2005; Cherubino Mirzio, *Chronicon Sublacense (1628-1630)*, ed. L. Branciani, Subiaco 2014; *Regesto della Chiesa di Tivoli*, ed. L. Bruzza, Roma 1880; P. Egidi *et al.*, *I monasteri di Subiaco*, Roma 1904.

delle particelle anche la perimetrazione quasi dettagliata delle pertinenze monastiche e delle colture praticate[12].

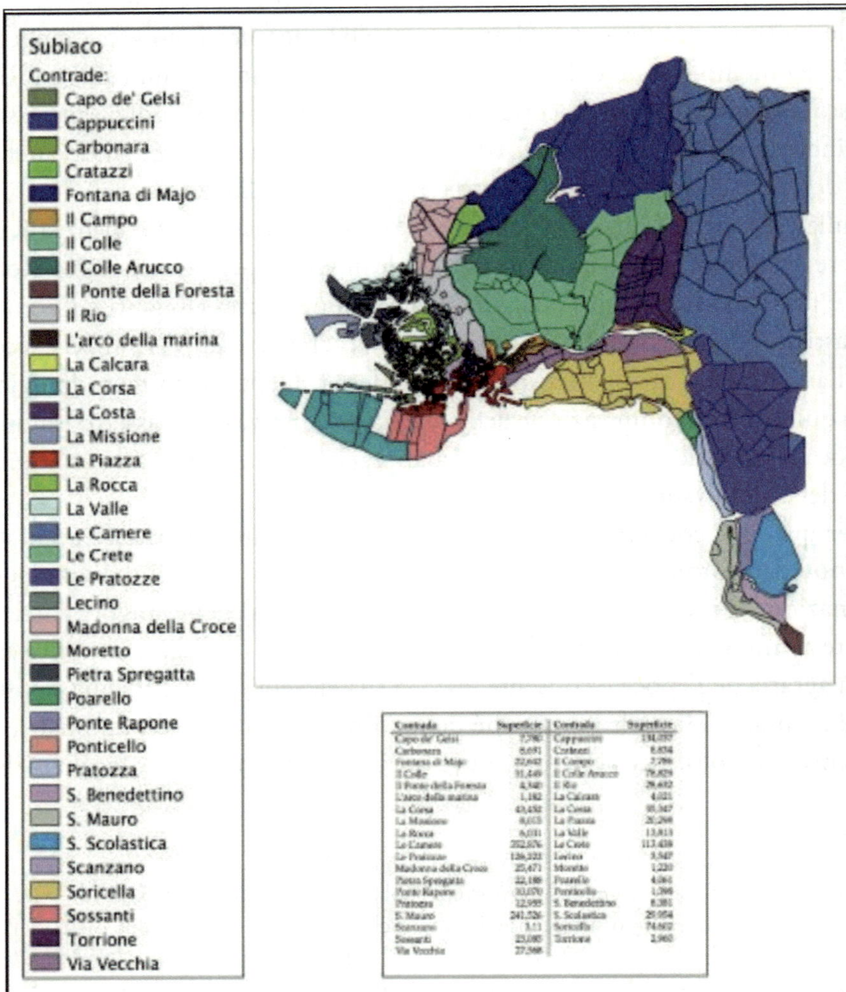

Fig. 4 - Subiaco: contrade ricavate dall'analisi del *Catasto Gregoriano* del 1816 (elaborazione di Lorenzo De Lellis)

12 Per una trattazione più ampia e dettagliata dei risultati si vedano i contributi di L. De Lellis, «Il monastero sublacense e le sue terre: un'analisi territoriale», in *Le valli dei monaci. De Re Monastica III*, ed. Ermini Pani, 1-16; L. De Lellis, «Lo sfruttamento agricolo della massa Iubenzana nel medioevo», in *Lazio e Sabina, 8. Ottavo Incontro di Studi sul Lazio e la Sabina* (Roma, 30-31 marzo, 1 aprile 2011), Roma 2012, 115-120.

In una seconda fase si è proceduto alla costruzione di una banca dati informatizzata nella quale sono confluite tutte le menzioni relative agli usi agricoli e alle strutture accessorie citate nei documenti. Si è comunque ritenuto prioritario sottolinearne le relazioni con il piano geografico-spaziale, al fine di poterne approntare una lettura che non fosse pura enumerazione quantitativa, utilizzando modelli cartografici vettoriali (GIS) e procedendo alla tridimensionalizzazione del suolo.

Abbiamo anche provato ad applicare metodologie meno usuali in archeologia, sviluppatesi invece nell'ambito dei progetti di programmazione agricola della FAO, come la *land evaluation potenziale*[13], per stimare il potenziale agricolo dei territori esaminati di modo da poter ricostruire l'uso dei suoli diacronicamente. Sul modello digitale del terreno della Valle è stata applicata una carta che prevede l'ammontare dell'esposizione solare sui versanti collinari per un periodo annuale, con intervalli di 10 giorni, così da poter verificare quali fossero le aree adatte alle varie colture, confrontando l'uso del suolo attuale con quello emerso dal Catasto Gregoriano, che più si avvicina alla situazione medievale.

I dati emersi dal confronto dei valori medi di esposizione solare e di altitudine dimostrano che la distribuzione dei valori relativi al Catasto Gregoriano sia più ristretta per l'altitudine e abbia una gamma più ampia per i valori dell'esposizione solare. La situazione attuale è esattamente opposta ed è l'esito da un lato dei progressi della meccanizzazione agricola che hanno consentito lo sfruttamento di terre poste a quote o a pendenze difficilmente lavorabili nel XIX secolo, dall'altro dell'ottimizzazione dello sfruttamento agricolo nei terreni a più alta produttività.

GMA

13 La *land evaluation* è nata in ambito agronomico per la progettazione dello sviluppo agricolo ed è stata successivamente adottata anche in archeologia (la *land evaulation potenziale*) quale strumento utile alla valutazione del potenziale agricolo di un determinato territorio. Cfr. E. van Joolen, «Potential Land Evaluation in Archaeology», in P. Attema *et al.*, eds., *New Developments in Italian Landscape Archaeology. Theory and methodology of field survey, land evaluation and landscape perception, pottery production and distribution*. Proceedings of three-day conference held at the University of Gronigen (April 13-15, 2000), Oxford 2002 (BAR Int. Ser. 1091), 185-226; A. Arnoldus-Huyzendveld-E. Pozzuto, «Il castello nel contesto territoriale. Una lettura storica del paesaggio attuale: il territorio di Castel di Pietra tra Antichità e Medioevo», in *Dieci anni di ricerche a Castel di Pietra. Edizione degli scavi. 1997-2007*, ed. C. Citter, Firenze 2009, 17-41.

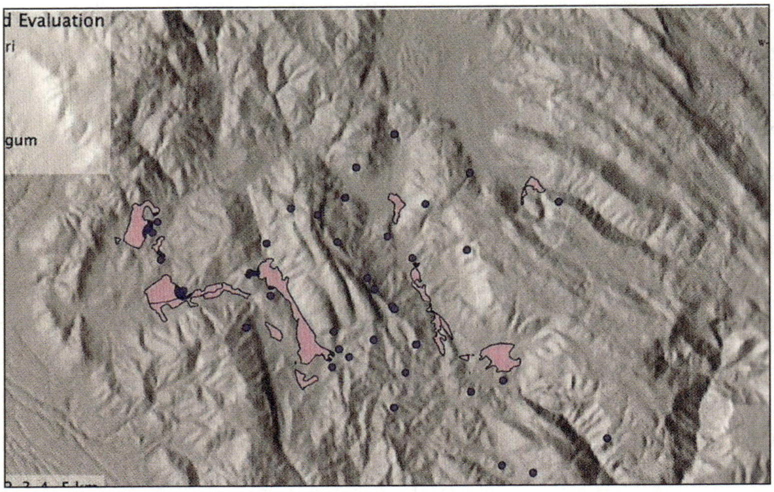

Fig. 5 - Valle Sublacense: *land evaluation* (carta elaborata da Lorenzo De Lellis)

2. DISTRIBUZIONE DELLE DIPENDENZE

È stato appurato come, per il cenobio farfense, alle varie tipologie insediative delle dipendenze, corrispondano diverse funzioni: nello specifico le *ecclesiae* e gli oratori svolgono per conto della casa madre un ruolo pastorale, mentre alle celle e ai monasteri compete una funzione prevalentemente amministrativa. Il controllo del territorio da parte di questi ultimi, viene evidenziato, fin dai primi secoli, da alcune scelte insediative economicamente funzionali, leggibile ad esempio nella posizione lungo i percorsi viari e fluviali, in prossimità di bacini lacustri e a controllo degli sbocchi sulla costa[14].

La prima area a essere interessata, a partire dalla prima metà dell'VIII secolo è la zona prossima al territorio maniale, vale a dire la fascia lungo la riva sinistra del fiume Tevere. Durante questo periodo l'abbazia si appropria di altre porzioni fondiarie, poste nel Cicolano e nel territorio della Sabina. Segue, dalla seconda metà dell'VIII secolo l'acquisizione di terreni situati nell'alta valle Sabina, nel territorio reatino, in quello amiternino, viterbese e tuscanese[15].

14 F. MARAZZI, «San Vincenzo al Volturno tra VIII e IX secolo: il percorso della grande crescita. Una indagine comparativa con le altre grandi fondazioni benedettine italiane», in *San Vincenzo al Volturno. Cultura istituzioni ed economia*, edd. F. Marazzi-P. Delogu, Cassino 1996, 71.

15 Per gli studi sull'area Sabina: E. MIGLIARIO, *Strutture della proprietà agraria in Sabina dall'età imperiale all'alto Medioevo*, Firenze 1988; A. BARONI, *Ricerche sulle strutture*

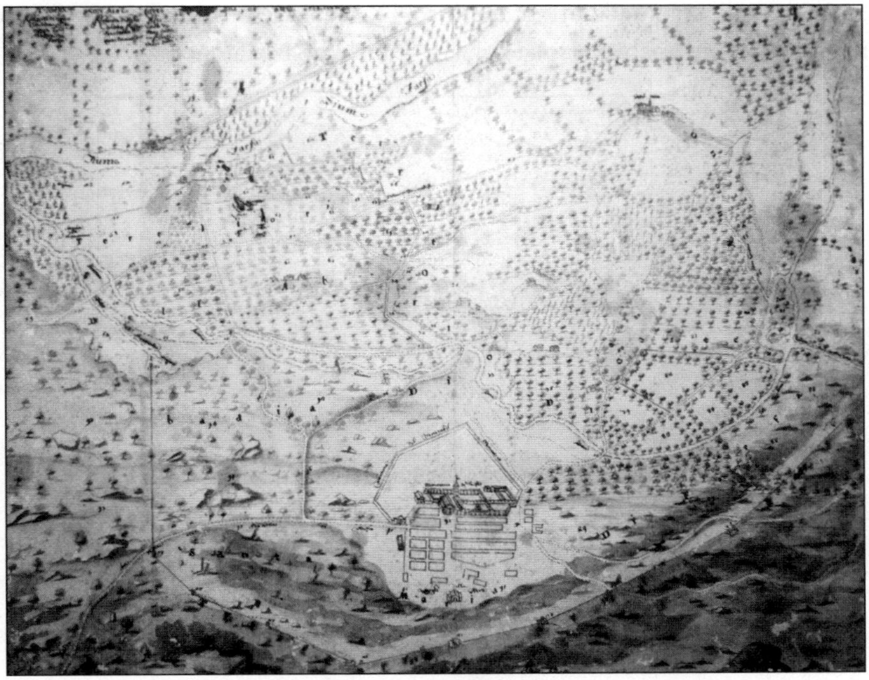

Fig. 6 - Particolare della carta storica *Pianta e delineazione del Tevere del Ven. Monastero dei monaci di S. Maria di Farfa con i suoi confini et altre adiacenze*, secoli XVII-XVIII (in Archivio del Monastero di Farfa, Racc. Cart. 7)

Già in possesso di pertinenze e proprietà nella Pianura Padana, a partire dalla seconda metà dell'VIII secolo, nell'ultimo quarto dello stesso, Farfa rivolge i suoi interessi anche alla Tuscia e, a cavallo tra la fine dell'VIII e gli inizi del IX secolo arriva a insediarsi anche in Umbria, acquisendo proprietà a Spoleto e nelle Mar-

agrarie dell'Alta Sabina tra Tardo Antico e Alto Medio Evo, Pisa 2002; M.L. Mancinelli, *Il registrum omnium ecclesiarum diocesis sabinensis (1343): una fonte per la conoscenza della topografia ecclesiastica della Sabina medievale*, Roma 2007. Per il territorio viterbese: G. Paolucci, «Le strutture agrarie dell'Alto Lazio nei secoli VIII-XI (Tuscanica, Viterbo, Corneto)», *Archivio della Società Romana di Storia Patria*, 103 (1980) 117-187. Per le valli del Turano, del Salto e del Cicolano: E. Migliario, *Uomini, terre e strade: aspetti dell'Italia centroappenninica fra antichità e alto Medioevo*, Bari 1995; A.R. Staffa, «L'assetto territoriale della valle del Salto fra la tarda antichità ed il Medioevo», *Xenia*, 13 (1987) 45-84; E. Migliario, «Per una storia delle strutture agrarie e territoriali nella valle del Turano tra Antichità e alto Medioevo: alcune riflessioni sulla massa Nautona e la massa Turana», in É. Hubert, ed., *Une Région frontalière au Moyen Âge. Les vallées du Turano et du Salto entre Sabine et Abruzzes*, Roma 2000, 53-65.

che meridionali; solo nella prima metà del IX secolo le proprietà in area marchigiana si estendono anche verso la zona di Camerino e Matelica[16].

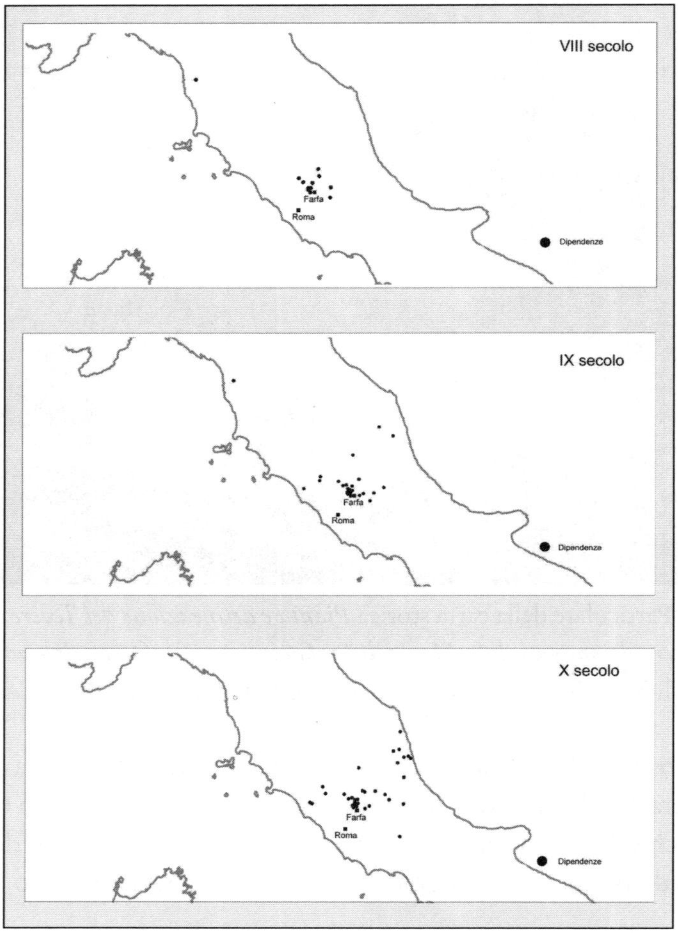

Fig. 7 - Carta della distribuzione delle dipendenze del monastero di Santa Maria di Farfa dall'VIII al X secolo

Nello stesso periodo l'abbazia risulta coinvolta nell'acquisizione di terre presso l'Abruzzo meridionale. È in questo momento che Farfa cerca di imporsi anche in territori già soggetti al controllo degli altri due cenobi operanti in quest'area vale a dire San Vincenzo al Volturno e Montecassino.

16 F. Marazzi, «San Vincenzo al Volturno tra VIII e IX secolo: il percorso della grande crescita. Una indagine comparativa con le altre grandi fondazioni benedettine italiane», in *San Vincenzo al Volturno*, edd. Marazzi-Delogu, 46-51.

Prosegue intanto, nella prima metà del secolo, l'espansione delle proprietà verso Ovest. Un importante snodo è rappresentato, nel Lazio settentrionale, dalla zona di Viterbo, già a partire dalla prima parte del IX secolo. Gli interessi dell'abbazia si spingono così anche verso le aree costiere del Tirreno, dove l'amministrazione dei beni viene assegnata alla dipendenza di Santa Maria del Mignone presso l'attuale Tarquinia[17].

In generale è osservabile come il monastero si muova lungo le direttrici delle principali vie di comunicazione che interessano il centro della penisola, coinvolgendo gli interi sistemi riferibili a queste arterie, tra le quali vanno ricordate la via Salaria, l'Aurelia, la Cassia, la Clodia, ma non dimenticando anche i percorsi fluviali, *in primis* il fiume Tevere.

GM

Per quanto riguarda il monastero di Subiaco, si constata che i possessi sono costituiti da una cella, un *monasterium* e almeno una *ecclesia* esclusivamente in area laziale (Fig. 8), a differenza di quanto abbiamo visto per l'abbazia di Farfa.

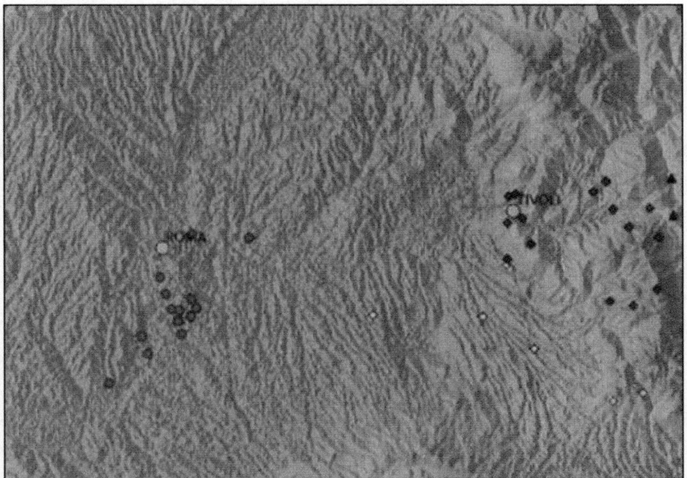

Fig. 8 - Carta della distribuzione delle dipendenze del monastero dei SS. Benedetto e Scolastica di Subiaco

17 Per una raccolta delle fonti a essa relativa: S. Del Lungo, «S. Maria del Mignone», *Archivio della Società Romana di Storia Patria* 117 (1994) 5-95. Per una differente proposta di localizzazione: E. Benelli-B. Vitali Rosati, «Contributo alla topografia dei Monti della Tolfa: S. Maria al Mignone e S. Arcangelo», in *Il Lazio tra antichità e medioevo: studi in onore di Jean Coste*, in Z. Mari-M.T. Petrara-M. Sperandio, Roma 1999, 125-129.

Sono stati individuati quattro nuclei principali dei possedimenti monastici[18]: Tivoli e Subiaco[19] e, in misura minore, Roma e Albano. Il nucleo dei beni posti nel tiburtino è affiancato dai possessi nell'area a sud di Tivoli, mentre nella Valle Sublacense si rilevano due macro-aree, una intorno a Subiaco, l'altra tra lo spartiacque dei Monti Ruffi e i centri di Anticoli, Arsoli e Cervara.

Sulla modalità di acquisizione dei beni, esemplificativo sembra essere il repentino incremento dei fondi (da uno a quattordici) posti tra porta Neola a Gallicano[20] tra IX e XI secolo. La strategia sottesa è quella di occupare progressivamente il territorio fino a includere il tratto aereo dell'acquedotto *Anio Novus*, che passava nei pressi di Gallicano per poi dirigersi a Roma, dove il monastero si premurò di acquisire la cella di Sant'Erasmo al Celio[21].

Con le stesse modalità il monastero sublacense si appropriò di alcune dipendenze nei pressi delle sorgenti della forma Antoniana, presso il "pantanello" dell'antica Gabii, e di quelle della Tepula presso Marino e Grotta Ferrata, sui Colli Albani.

GMA

3. GESTIONE DEL TERRITORIO

Sulla gestione del territorio, particolare rilevanza assumono sia l'impatto che la fondazione di un monastero ha avuto sull'area, sia i comportamenti che l'ente ha messo in atto nei confronti del comprensorio che lo ospita. Il contesto

---

18 L'analisi dei rapporti economici dell'abbazia sublacense e della crescita esponenziale delle sue ricchezze è stata analizzata da tempo, come ad esempio in R. Morghen, «Le relazioni del monastero Sublacense col papato, la feudalità e il comune nell'alto medioevo», *Archivio della Società Romana di Storia Patria*, 51 (1928) 188-211.

19 A. Appetecchia, «Subiaco nel Medioevo: aspetti di topografia urbana e di edilizia», *Temporis Signa* 4 (2009) 13-52.

20 F. Giuliani Cairoli, «I possedimenti dell'abbazia di Subiaco da porta Neola a Gallicano tra il IX e l'XI secolo», in *Il Lazio tra Antichità e Medioevo. Studi in memoria di Jean Coste*, edd. Mari-Petrara-Sperandio, 377-389.

21 Il ben strutturato monastero di Sant'Erasmo a Roma, dotato di strutture sia gestionali che amministrative autonome, viene nel 938 inglobato nel patrimonio sublacense (*Reg. Subl.*, n. 24) assieme a tutte le sue pertinenze che inizia a gestire come emancipazione diretta del suo potere. Infatti poco dopo la struttura di S. Erasmo viene indicata nel Regesto come semplice cella, dequalificata quindi sotto il profilo giuridico, come ricordato nel privilegio di Gregorio V del 997 (*Reg. Subl.*, n. 13) e in una concessione livellaria di terreni del monastero di S. Erasmo fatta all'abate nel 1024 (*Reg. Subl.*, n. 106).

nonantolano[22] ha mostrato, con efficacia metodologica, come l'ente si inserisca in un'area ancora prevalentemente a coltivo e come la fondazione del cenobio mantenga gli assetti insediativi precedenti: ne è chiara dimostrazione la marcata sussistenza, ben documentata anche dalla cartografia di età moderna, della maglia centuriale romana (nell'ambito, ovviamente, di sistemi di conduzione e gestione delle terre profondamente mutati).

In questa stessa direzione i processi di formazione, sviluppo e gestione dei patrimoni monastici di Subiaco e di Farfa sono stati analizzati in una prospettiva più ampia che ha tenuto conto dell'inevitabile flusso biunivoco[23] tra monasteri e territorio ovvero dell'azione progressiva di occupazione da un punto di vista strategico ed economico, cercando di stabilire se questa abbia risposto a caratteri di casualità o a un preciso piano di conquista dell'area.

GMA

Per l'esempio farfense, nell'area prossima al cenobio, al momento della sua acquisizione, le terre già presentano una loro fisionomia amministrativa e catastale: suddivisa in fondi e casali compresi in *curtes*, masse e gualdi, queste vengono destinate a diverse funzioni, che spaziano dallo sfruttamento agricolo, in particolare la coltura della vite, dell'ulivo e del frumento, al pascolo e al rifornimento di legname[24]. L'azione del monastero, soprattutto nel territorio prossimo alla casa madre, consiste nell'accentramento di queste risorse in entità organizzate e strutturate, quali possono essere le *curtes*.

---

22 V. Carrara, ed., *Reti monastiche nell'Italia padana. Le chiese di San Silvestro di Nonantola tra Pavia, Piacenza e Cremona; secc. IX-XIII*, Modena 1998; S. Gelichi, «*Costruire territori. Il monastero di Nonantola e le sue terre nell'altomedioevo*», *Hortus Artium Medievalium*, 14 (2008) 65-79; S. Gelichi, «*Il monastero di Nonantola e le sue terre. Controllo del territorio e organizzazione dell'insediamento nel medioevo*», in *Committenza, scelte insediative e organizzazione patrimoniale nel medioevo*. Atti del Convegno di Studio *De Re Monastica I* (Tergu, 15-17 settembre 2006), ed. L. Ermini Pani, Spoleto 2007, 325-356.

23 *L. Lagazzi*, *Segni sulla terra*: *determinazione dei confini e percezione dello spazio nell'alto medioevo*, CLUEB, Bologna 1991; E. Destefanis, *Il monastero di Bobbio in età altomedievale*, Firenze 2002; E. Destefanis, «Archeologia dei monasteri altomedievali tra acquisizioni raggiunte e nuove prospettive di ricerca», *Post Classical Archaeologies*, 1 (2011) 349-382; *La diocesi di Bobbio. Formazione e sviluppi di un'istituzione millenaria*, edd. E. Destefanis-P. Guglielmotti, Firenze 2015.

24 Si rimanda a Migliario, *Strutture della proprietà agraria in Sabina*; Baroni, *Ricerche sulle strutture agrarie dell'Alta Sabina*; Mancinelli, *Il registrum omnium ecclesiarum diocesis sabinensis (1343)*.

Tra le corti si può ricordare, ad esempio, quella di San Getulio in Sabina, citata nelle conferme pontificie e imperiali tra il IX e la fine del X secolo, e in un'ampia descrizione del primo quarto dell'XI secolo, all'interno della quale ne vengono descritti i confini, vale a dire il Tevere, il torrente Farfa, la via Britta e il *rivus Ponticulum*[25]. Questa, che doveva trovarsi nel fondo Fornicata presso la località di ponte Sfondato lungo la via Salaria ternana, doveva essere dotata anche di un traghetto sul fiume Tevere probabilmente connesso a un approdo per il trasporto delle derrate dalla Sabina a Roma.

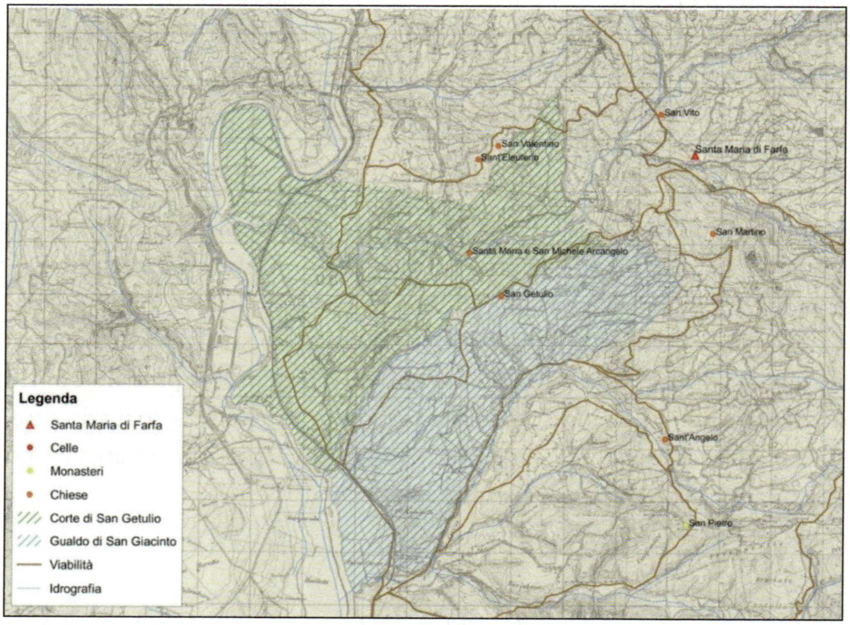

Fig. 9 - Ricostruzione dell'estensione territoriale del gualdo di San Getulio

Il patrimonio monastico era gestito, oltre che da *curtes*, da celle, tra le quali si può ricordare ad esempio quella di San Benedetto in Petrignano[26] citata per la prima volta nell'876[27], e individuata nel comune di Pescorocchiano[28], posta in

25 *RF*, II, doc. 5, 26-27; *RF*, II, doc. 15, 124; *RF*, II, doc. 224, 183; *RF*, II, doc. 282, 235; *RF*, III, doc. 413, 124.

26 Migliario, *Uomini, terre e strade*, 38-40; A.R. Staffa, «L'assetto territoriale della valle del Salto fra la tarda antichità ed il Medioevo», *Xenia*, XIII (1987) 67-68.

27 *LL*, I, doc. 52.

28 A.R. Staffa, «L'assetto territoriale della valle del Salto fra la tarda antichità ed il Medioevo», *Xenia* XIII (1987) 67-68.

una posizione strategica rispetto all'intero territorio e rispetto alla via di comunicazione tra i territori del Cicolano e la piana di Amiterno[29].

I cartulari farfensi attestano in Sabina, come in altre aree del territorio laziale, la presenza di numerosi gualdi che costituiscono un insieme di beni fiscali quali appezzamenti di terreni, generalmente boschivi e destinati a pratiche silvo-pastorali, come l'allevamento di ovini, bovini, suini e cavalli, attività incentivate dall'esenzione del pagamento di dazi e di censi, concessa dalle autorità imperiali. Questi sono principalmente dislocati in Sabina, ma sono rintracciabili anche presso la costa, ad esempio il gualdo a ridosso del fiume Mignone controllato dalla cella di Santa Maria.

In quest'ottica è leggibile la volontà dell'abbazia sia di disporre di terre utili allo svolgimento delle attività silvo-pastorali sia di porsi a controllo dei percorsi, come già sottolineato, che attraversano l'Italia centrale da est a ovest, alcuni dei quali importanti vie di transumanza.

All'area sabina è possibile mettere a confronto l'organizzazione fondiaria nella quale lo stesso monastero si trova a operare in altri territori, ad esempio in quello viterbese ma anche in quello prossimo alla costa, sempre rimanendo all'interno del panorama laziale[30].

Qui le forme di insediamento maggiormente attestate dalle fonti farfensi sono i *vici* e i *casalia*. Fino all'XI secolo sono documentati grandi nuclei fondiari composti da un centro gestionale, *cella* o *curtis*, e una serie di appezzamenti terrieri anche non connessi tra loro fisicamente, legati, almeno nei primi due secoli di gestione, da concessioni livellarie. La ricerca è stata rivolta, recentemente, all'esame delle tipologie di colture praticate dalle dipendenze del monastero e documentate nelle fonti prendendo in considerazione anche i centri più distanti dalla casa madre. Da una prima analisi dei dati raccolti per i secoli VIII-IX, si registra una maggiore diffusione della coltivazione del frumento e dell'ulivo, un aspetto che potrebbe indicare una certa continuità con i secoli precedenti; mentre tra il X e l'XI secolo si registra in contemporanea con la diffusione di aree incolte, un incremento della viticoltura in linea con quanto già documentato negli studi.

GM

29 Migliario, *Uomini, terre e strade*, 82-83.

30 G. Maggiore, «Celle e dipendenze del monastero del San Salvatore al Monte Amiata in area laziale», in L. Ermini Pani, ed., *Teoria e pratica del lavoro nel monachesimo altomedievale*, Convegno Internazionale *De Re Monastica VI* (Roma-Subiaco 2013), Spoleto 2015, 213-230.

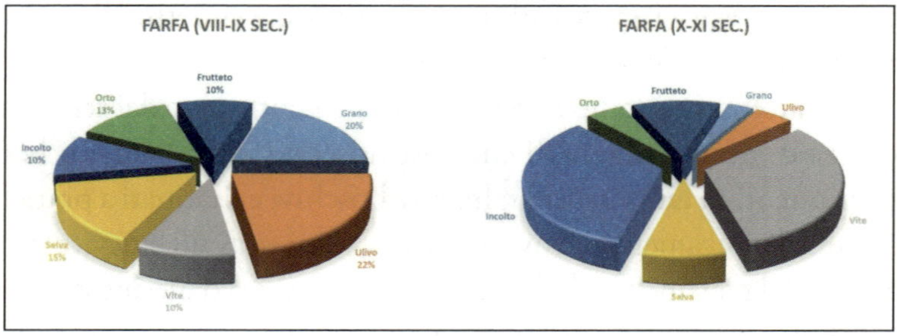

Fig. 10 - Grafici delle tipologie di colture dell'abazia di Farfa nei secoli VIII-IX e X-XI

Per il caso sublacense, il paesaggio agricolo era composto da piccole cellule, *fundi* o *praedia*, raggruppate in vaste proprietà terriere, le *massae*: i coloni coltivavano terre fertili delimitate da *silvae*, paludi (pantani) e *incoltum*. Un territorio con una gerarchizzazione delle particelle che non ha conosciuto variazioni strutturali rispetto alla tardo antichità, quanto piuttosto una semplificazione delle componenti costitutive[31].

Come già accennato, le dipendenze sono costituite da una cella, un *monasterium* e almeno una *ecclesia*. Il termine *cella* è polivalente e variegato: da centro gestionale di un'azienda agricola a centro dell'economia agricola dell'area financo a luogo di raccolta della produzione agricola o della quota di essa che spetta alla casa madre. Le *cellae* sembrano correlate al lavoro e alla trasformazione dei beni agricoli per la produzione di generi alimentari più complessi (molitura, panificazione, vinificazione). Per contro i *monasteria* rivestono un ruolo di raccordo con la casa madre nella gestione delle rendite fondiarie e della forza lavoro impiegata nei *fundi* e nelle *cellae*.

Non è ancora chiaro se i monasteri includessero tra le loro dipendenze terre a gestione diretta, il che sembrerebbe ipotizzabile per Subiaco visto che nei documenti non viene citata alcuna cella entro il perimetro delle terre immuni.

La realtà monastica fu dunque un elemento di rottura? Una consolidata tradizione storiografica ha insistito sul ruolo di primaria importanza rivestito dal monastero sublacense (casa-madre)[32] nel quadro di una rilevante e subitanea

31 F.R. Stasolla, «Celle e dipendenze per l'organizzazione del lavoro monastico in area laziale» e P. Rosati, «Celle e dipendenze del monastero dei SS. Scolastica e Benedetto in area laziale», in Ermini Pani, *Teoria e pratica del lavoro nel monachesimo altomedievale*, rispettivamente 141-161 e 191-212.

32 Nei pressi dello speco dell'*Anio Vetus* sorge una delle strutture più imponenti nella caratterizzazione del territorio, la villa di Nerone, per la quale la documentazione archeologica ha

trasformazione territoriale e nella razionalizzazione della gestione della risorsa "territorio". L'azione riformatrice si sarebbe esplicata nell'immediato accentramento intorno alla casa-madre, mediante la stipula di contratti a lunga durata, mirato a una progressiva occupazione dei *deserta loca* di gregoriana memoria in cui l'unico centro di una qualche consistenza era rappresentato da *Sublaqueum* e dalla scarsa popolazione residente.

GMA

4. ATTIVITÀ PRODUTTIVE E MERCATI

L'analisi del territorio sublacense ha restituito molti dati sull'uso del suolo, in particolare sul rapporto tra popolamento agrario e maglia di distribuzione delle 26 chiese rurali[33] presenti dalla tarda antichità nel territorio fra Tivoli e Subiaco, strutture che sino al X secolo svolsero certamente una funzione agglutinante per la popolazione delle campagne.

L'approccio metodologico è stato quello di determinare areali di cinque chilometri attorno a ciascuna chiesa[34]. La distanza di cinque chilometri è stata scelta in quanto rappresenta la distanza media percorribile a piedi in un'ora su un terreno di media pendenza. Tradizionalmente adottata negli studi relativi alla *site catchment analysis*[35], è stata eletta a rappresentare un parametro medio per ipotizzare una

---

ormai chiarito la presenza di forme di continuità di vita dall'età romana, pur con variazioni funzionali. Come in molti altri siti, alcuni ambienti della villa furono probabilmente occupati da eremiti, e la tradizione vuole che sia stato proprio Benedetto, nella sua prima fase di vita ascetica solitaria, a prenderne possesso. Cfr. L. Pani Ermini, «Subiaco all'epoca di S. Benedetto. Nota di topografia», *Benedectina*, 28, 1-2 (1981) 69-80; M.G. Fiore Cavaliere, ed., *Sublaqueum – Subiaco. Tra Nerone e Benedetto*, Roma 1994. Per la possibilità di identificare le strutture del primo impianto benedettino: F.R. Stasolla, «Il monachesimo in Italia dalle origini a Gregorio Magno: modalità insediative, architetture, organizzazione topografica e spaziale», in *Monachesimi d'Oriente e d'Occidente nell'Alto Medioevo*. Atti della LXIV Settimana CISAM (Spoleto, 31 marzo – 6 aprile 2016), in corso di stampa. Si rimanda da ultimo ad A. Appetecchia, *I monasteri benedettini di Subiaco e le loro dipendenze nel Medioevo*, tesi di Dottorato di ricerca in Archeologia – curriculum di Archeologia e Antichità post-classiche, Sapienza Università di Roma, discussa nel dicembre 2010.

33 P. Delogu-L. Travaini, «Aspetti degli abitati medievali nella regione sublacense», *Archivio della Società Romana di Storia Patria*, CI (1978) 17-34.

34 G. Macchi Jánica, *Geografia dell'incastellamento: analisi spaziale della maglia dei villaggi fortificati medievali in Toscana (XI-XIV sec.)*, Firenze 2007.

35 Cf. J. Conolly-M. Lake, *Geographical Information System in Archaeology*, Cambridge University press, Cambridge 2006; D. Wheatley-M. Gillings, *Spatial Technology and Archaeology. The Archaeological Applications of GIS*, New York 2002.

distribuzione del popolamento agrario in relazione ai punti focali del paesaggio quali le chiese rurali. Suddetti areali di cinque chilometri attorno a ciascuna delle 26 chiese rurali vengono a comprendere porzioni di territorio che racchiudono la maggior parte delle terre abbaziali poste nella Valle Sublacense[36].

La comparazione tra i dati del *Catasto Gregoriano* e quelli della contrattualistica agraria tardo–medievale[37] conferma l'applicabilità dello schema teorico di von Thünen[38], un modello di sfruttamento dei suoli agricoli a intensità decrescente dal centro (chiesa rurale o seriore centro fortificato) al suo esterno (orto, *farragum*, seminativo e incolto)[39]: sulla base di una carta delle aree destinabili a coltivo si è riscontrato come una buona parte di queste disti meno di due chilometri dalle chiese rurali[40].

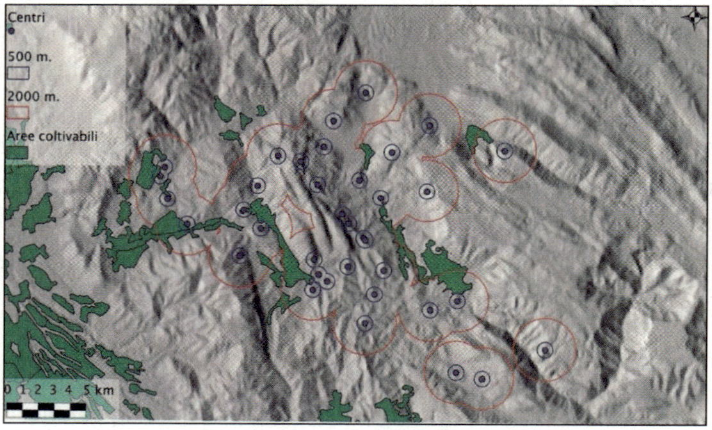

Fig. 11 - Determinazione delle aree destinate a coltivo in relazione ai centri della Valle Sublacense (pianta elaborata da Lorenzo De Lellis)

36 L. De Lellis, «Lo sfruttamento agricolo della massa Iubenzana nel medioevo», in *Lazio e Sabina, 8*, 115-120.

37 A. Pagani, «Patti agrari e gestione della terra: appunti per una storia delle campagne sublacensi nel basso medioevo», in *Terra e lavoro nel Lazio meridionale: la testimonianza dei contratti agrari (secoli XII-XV)*, edd. A. Cortonesi-G. Giammaria, Bari 1999, 100-114.

38 J.H. von Thünen, *Der Isolierte Staat in Beziehung auf Landwirtschaft und Nationalökonomie*, Hamburg 1826.

39 P. Toubert, *Les structures du Latium Médiéval. Le Latium méridional et la Sabine du IXe siècle à la fin du XIIe siècle*, Roma 1973, 336-337; S. Passigli, *Contratti agrari e paesaggio vegetale nel Lazio meridionale (secoli XIII-XV)*, in *Terra e lavoro nel Lazio Meridionale*, edd. Cortonesi-Giammaria, 115-145.

40 L. De Lellis, «Il monastero sublacense e le sue terre: un'analisi territoriale», in *Le valli dei monaci. De Re Monastica III*, ed. Ermini Pani, 1-16.

La collazione dei dati sulle essenze arboree ha restituito un quadro ampio: sfruttamento dell'incolto e delle risorse boschive, seminativo e colture più specializzate. Agli orti limitrofi ai centri seguono i *farraginalia* e le canapaie, queste ultime spesso in prossimità dei corsi d'acqua per facilitare la fase successiva della "marcita" della canapa. A differenza dei terreni più prossimi agli abitati, in quest'area sembra quasi del tutto assente l'associazione con l'arboricoltura.

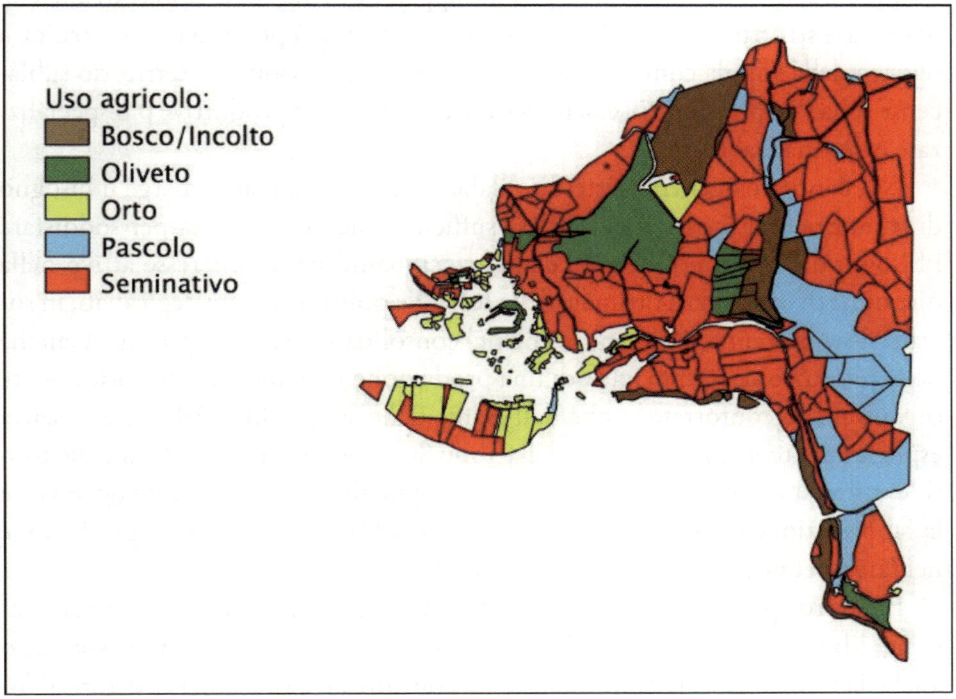

Fig. 12 - Subiaco: carta riassuntiva delle classi agricole ricavate dal *Catasto Gregoriano* del 1816 (carta elaborata da Lorenzo De Lellis)

Nella fascia successiva trovava spazio la cerealicoltura estensiva, spesso in accoppiata all'arboricoltura secca (olivi, castagni ed essenze legnose) e alla vite "sospesa", tipica soprattutto del paesaggio della piantata tosco-umbra-marchigiana. La cerealicoltura estensiva interessava sia i terreni di recente dissodamento sia i terreni a essa tradizionalmente deputati.

L'ultima fascia, per posizione geografica e per intensità del suo sfruttamento, era quella occupata dai boschi e dai pascoli, spesso uniti nella forma del pascolo boscato diffuso praticamente in tutta l'Europa medievale.

Tra le colture specializzate si annoverano la vite, il frutteto, l'orto e probabilmente una minima parte di oliveto, maritato con la vite o accoppiato con essenze orticole. La medesima considerazione vale in misura ancor maggior per la quantificazione del ruolo delle risorse dell'incolto, della selva e del pascolo.

La vite è la coltura più attestata dalle fonti. Particolarmente interessante appare il panorama relativo ai possedimenti destinati alla viticoltura nell'area romana, distribuiti prevalentemente nell'area extramuranea sud-orientale tra porta San Sebastiano e porta Portuense e lungo i patrimoni dell'Appia. Questi fondi, affidati in conduzione a privati, appaiono nelle fonti dotati di tutte le necessarie strutture accessorie, compresi i *calcatoria* già presenti o da costruirsi a seguito della stipula contrattuale. Rispetto alle attestazioni nel territorio sublacense si ha l'impressione di essere di fronte a delle unità produttive più specializzate e destinate al mercato.

Nel panorama generale attestato dalle fonti, se da un lato emerge il bisogno di garantire una produzione di base sufficientemente completa per soddisfare i bisogni del consumo interno, dall'altro si manifesta un interesse attivo nella direzione di un utilizzo ottimale delle terre. La politica terriera degli abati, in sostanza, sembra intervenire, oltre che nel consolidamento della proprietà, anche nelle produzioni. L'immagine di una produzione vitivinicola sistematicamente organizzata è confortata anche dall'esame delle attestazioni del salice, essenza esplicitamente diffusa nell'area della Valle Sublacense e del tiburtino dalle fonti, e utilizzata tradizionalmente nei lavori agricoli, quali la legatura delle viti e la fabbricazione di contenitori da trasporto in fibra vegetale, la cui produzione nell'area è continuata sino in tempi recenti.

L'oliveto appare in percentuali relativamente basse e si attesta principalmente nel tiburtino, nei dintorni di Roma e nella zona di Subiaco. In questo senso anche la vicinanza della Valle Sublacense con altre aree tipicamente dedite all'olivicoltura, quali la Sabina e il Lazio Meridionale, potrebbe essere una concausa della modesta presenza dell'olivo.

Una spia per l'approvvigionamento dell'olio pensiamo possa essere costituita dal traffico commerciale con l'area sabina, dove la produzione olearia era ben nota e fortemente radicata, traffico testimoniato dalla presenza di ceramiche invetriate di produzione sabina nello scavo di Cervara di Roma[41].

41 F.R. Stasolla, «Lo scavo di Cervara di Roma», in Ermini Pani, ed., *Le valli dei monaci. De Re Monastica III*, 461-477; G.M. Annoscia, «La Rocca di Cervara di Roma e la sua coquina», *Temporis Signa*, VIII (2013) 93-124; G.M. Annoscia, «Le ceramiche della rocca di Cervara di Roma», in *Le ceramiche di Roma e del Lazio in età medievale e moderna VII*. Atti del VII Convegno di studi *La polifunzionalità nella ceramica medievale*, edd. F.R. Stasolla-G.M. Annoscia (Roma – Tolfa, 18-20 maggio 2009), Roma 2015, 269-295.

La politica agraria del monastero di Subiaco ha privilegiato coltivazioni intensive, nello specifico la vite, utilizzando le altre colture per scopi di autosostentamento: un'economia combinata di tipo silvo-pastorale e agricola, unita allo sfruttamento sapiente delle risorse in un costante adattamento a quanto il territorio stesso offriva. Si rimarcano, quindi, articolati meccanismi gestionali messi in atto dal cenobio al fine di valorizzare le potenzialità differenziate dei singoli territori, in una logica di complementarietà e di integrazione.

GMA

Per quanto riguarda l'esempio farfense, l'esame condotto finora permette di sostenere che le celle, i monasteri e probabilmente anche alcune chiese, gestivano le attività produttive e la forza lavoro all'interno dei fondi, gualdi e casali e che solo alcune erano anche abilitate all'incameramento dei prodotti e dei censi.

Un interessante spunto per la nostra ricerca è, infatti, costituito dall'indagine sulla fase successiva lo sfruttamento agricolo del territorio, vale a dire quella riguardante la lavorazione dei prodotti, funzionale sia al fabbisogno locale sia a un'eventuale immissione sul mercato dei prodotti finiti, il che apre un altro filone di ricerca, vale a dire quello costituito dal ruolo svolto da grandi cenobi nella circolazione delle merci sia a piccolo che ad ampio raggio[42].

Per l'esempio farfense, uno dei principali materiali oggetto di sfruttamento sarebbe stato, cosa non nuova, proprio il legname, come indica la frequente citazione nelle fonti di selve (*silvae*) che appaiono molto spesso tra le pertinenze di *vici* e *casalia*, di solito affiancate ad altre colture[43].

Uno degli aspetti principali della produzione è però sicuramente rappresentato dalla gestione degli impianti molitori, sia in connessione con la casa madre sia con le dipendenze dislocate nel territorio. Dall'analisi delle informazioni raccolte emerge come il monastero poteva gestire sia singole strutture molitorie sia veri e propri sistemi organizzati di opifici afferenti a uno stesso bacino fluviale[44].

---

42 F. Marazzi, «Portus Monasterii: scali portuali monastici lungo il corso del Volturno (IX-X secolo)», *Annuario Associazione Storica del Medio Volturno*, 2 (2014) 209.

43 G. Paolucci, «Le strutture agrarie dell'Alto Lazio nei secoli VIII-XI (Tuscanica, Viterbo, Corneto)», *Archivio della Società Romana di Storia Patria*, 103 (1980) 141.

44 Per una panoramica sulla molitura ad acqua in area laziale si rimanda a D. De Francesco, *La molitura ad acqua nel Lazio nei secoli III-XII: dal controllo imperiale al patrimonio ecclesiastico*, Edizioni Quasar, Roma 2009. Sull'amministrazione e gestione dei mulini da parte dei monasteri si rimanda al recente contributo di P. Galletti, «I mulini monastici tra IX e XI secolo: tecnologia e organizzazione del lavoro e della produzione», in Ermi-

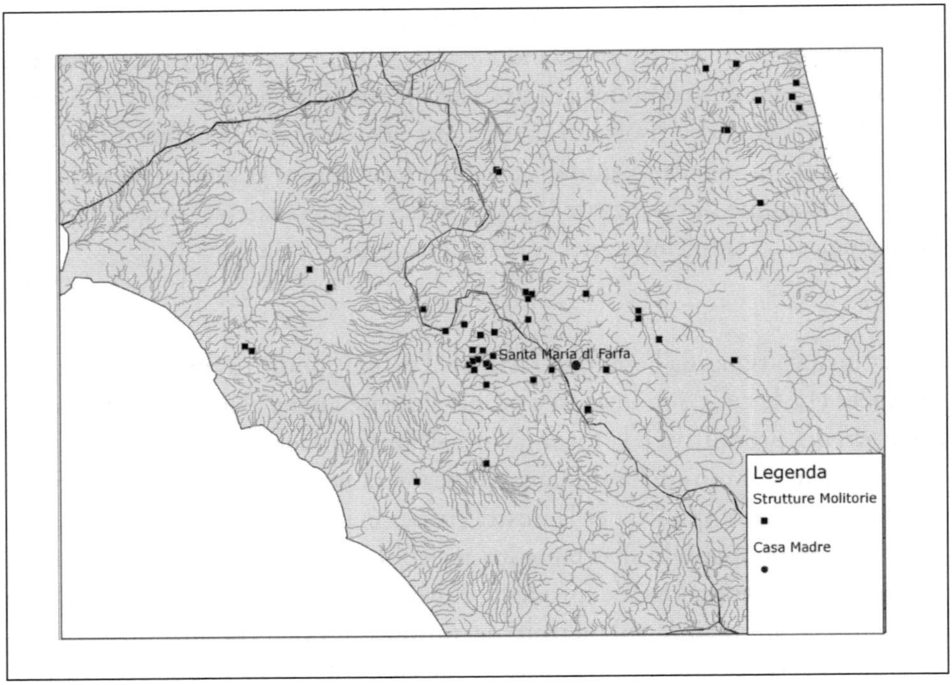

Fig. 13 - Gli opifici idraulici del monastero di Santa Maria di Farfa (secoli VIII- XI)

Nei cartulari farfensi le citazioni riguardanti i mulini sono relativamente scarse per i secoli VIII-X, mentre aumentano a partire dall'XI, sia nel territorio prossimo alla casa madre che in quello più distante, ad esempio, rimanendo in ambito laziale, nell'area viterbese, tuscanese e cornetana[45].

La difficoltà è stata, ovviamente, tenere conto delle differenze territoriali, ma soprattutto della diversa evoluzione di tali territori, che quindi sono stati trattati parallelamente, cercando di cogliere il diverso o comune atteggiamento assunto dal cenobio a fronte dei sistemi nei quali si andava a inserire.

NI PANI, ed., *Teoria e pratica del lavoro nel monachesimo altomedievale, De Re Monastica VI*, 267-291.

45 Un approfondimento è stato condotto sulla valle fluviale del Farfa dove è stato riscontrato come i mulini entrino a far parte della proprietà monastica, almeno in un primo momento, attraverso donazioni, e come rari siano gli esempi di vendite da parte di privati. Sono stati riconosciuti 32 impianti, tra i quali 22 funzionali alla macinazione del grano, o meglio di cereali panificabili; 9 per la molitura delle olive; uno per la gualcatura della lana. E. SANTINI, «Opifici idraulici medievali nel bacino del fiume Farfa», *Temporis Signa*, 1 (2006) 157-186.

In generale, ampliando lo sguardo ad altri esempi in area laziale, è stato osservato come nei primi secoli di vita del cenobio rari siano i casi di mulini assegnati alle dipendenze della casa madre, quindi gestiti direttamente da celle.

Questi ultimi sono menzionati nelle fonti più comunemente come *molino*, ma in pochi casi anche come *aquimolis* e *aquimolo molente* (in riferimento ai mulini natanti del Tevere) e risultano distribuiti lungo il percorso dei fiumi Tevere, Velino, Cantaro, Mignone, Turano, oltre che del Farfa, ma anche nei pressi dei loro affluenti.

Diversi riferimenti riguardano il centro di Rieti che sembrerebbe rappresentare un caso unico tra quelli documentati nel Lazio, anche per la distribuzione di tali impianti lungo le vie di accesso all'insediamento, in prossimità delle porte[46].

Gli interessi dell'abbazia si estendono, già nell'VIII secolo, anche in altre aree del Lazio, ad esempio nella massa Turana; nell'area viterbese, dove sono attive le celle di San Valentino e Santa Maria e nel territorio tuscanense in riferimento alla cella di San Mamiliano, dove l'abbazia ottiene tutti i diritti di gestione dei corsi d'acqua e delle connesse attività di produzione.

A queste testimonianze si aggiunge l'area posta presso la bassa valle del Mignone, affidata alla cella di Santa Maria del Mignone, citata a partire dagli anni 857-859, che avrebbe gestito, lungo il corso del fiume omonimo, diversi mulini, delle peschiere e anche un porto[47].

CC

Il controllo delle acque in area sublacense, che si esplica attraverso i diritti d'uso di corsi d'acqua maggiori e minori, delle mole ad acqua e degli allevamenti ittici è ben evidente a livello documentario, ma colpisce nella sua complessità topografica.

Il monastero acquisisce sistematicamente tutti i terreni a ridosso dell'*acqua Claudia*, tutelando il suo percorso fino a Roma con la creazione di *ecclesiae*, *monasteria* e *cellae*: il cenobio sorge nei pressi delle sorgenti dell'*aqua* stessa, sul *lacus Neronianus*, e si premura di acquisire una cella interna alle mura, quella di S. Erasmo, nel luogo in cui l'acquedotto entra a Roma. In sostanza, alla fine

46 L'argomento è stato affrontato da L. SALADINO-M. C. SOMMA, «Elementi per una topografia di Rieti in età tardoantica ed altomedievale», *Mélanges de l'École française de Rome – Moyen Âge* 105 (1993) 23-122.

47 *RF*, III, doc. 300, 1-7; *ChF*, I, 216.

dell'alto medioevo il monastero aveva raggiunto il pieno controllo dell'acqua nell'intero comprensorio della media Valle dell'Aniene[48].

Per quanto riguarda i mulini, essi si attestano prevalentemente nell'area tra il tiburtino e il sublacense[49] e sono ubicati sempre in stretto rapporto con la viabilità. La quasi totalità delle strutture molitorie dell'area, infatti, viene a trovarsi nelle immediate vicinanze di percorsi viari, siano essi riferibili a epoca medievale o ereditati dall'età romana. Tale constatazione esplica senz'altro la presenza di una progettualità nella scelta dei luoghi ove impiantare i mulini, in funzione sia delle risorse idriche che della facilità di accesso e di movimentazione della materia prima e del risultante prodotto finito. Infatti con il termine *molendinum* vanno intese tutte le forme di molitura, vista la presenza di macine da cereali e di torchi da olio e da vino.

Dalla lettura delle fonti emerge lo stretto controllo esercitato dal potere abbaziale sulle strutture molitorie, che appaiono sempre attribuite in maniera esclusiva al cenobio sublacense, essendone vietata ai terzi la realizzazione o la vendita in assenza dell'esplicito consenso dell'abate. Un simile rapporto di esclusività risulta in essere anche per le peschiere, localizzate lungo il corso del fiume Aniene nei pressi di Subiaco e nella parte settentrionale della Valle.

GMA

Uno sguardo più approfondito merita la distribuzione di tali impianti molitori anche all'interno dell'Urbe, dove parte del frumento che proveniva dall'area Sabina, era macinato presso le mole natanti del Tevere. Nel Regesto Farfense sono ricordate donazioni di alcuni opifici idraulici natanti posti all'altezza della posterula Episcopio, localizzata nell'area dell'attuale lungotevere Sangallo e presso la località *Captum Seccuta*, coincidente con la stessa area prima indicata[50].

---

48 Z. Mari, «Note sugli acquedotti della valle dell'Aniene», *Atti e memorie della società tiburtina di storia e arte*, LXXII (1986) 31-45; C. Roncaioli Lamberti, «La Marcia e la Claudia nella gola di S. Cosimato», in *Il trionfo dell'acqua. Acque e acquedotti a Roma*, Roma 1986, 89-91; M.G. Fiore Cavaliere-Z. Mari, «Acquisizioni lungo il tracciato degli acquedotti aniensi», *Quaderni del Centro di studio per l'archeologia etrusco-italica*, XII, 2 (1995) 470-472; G. Cappa-A. Felici, «Acquedotti romani, cisterne, cavità artificiali e naturali nella rupe di S. Cosimato a Vicovaro», *Atti e memorie della società tiburtina di storia e arte*, LXXI (2008) 65-85.

49 La presenza omogenea di mulini sulla base delle sole fonti documentarie è stata rilevata da Daniela De Francesco (De Francesco, *La molitura ad acqua nel Lazio*).

50 *RF,* III, doc. 665-666, 65-68.

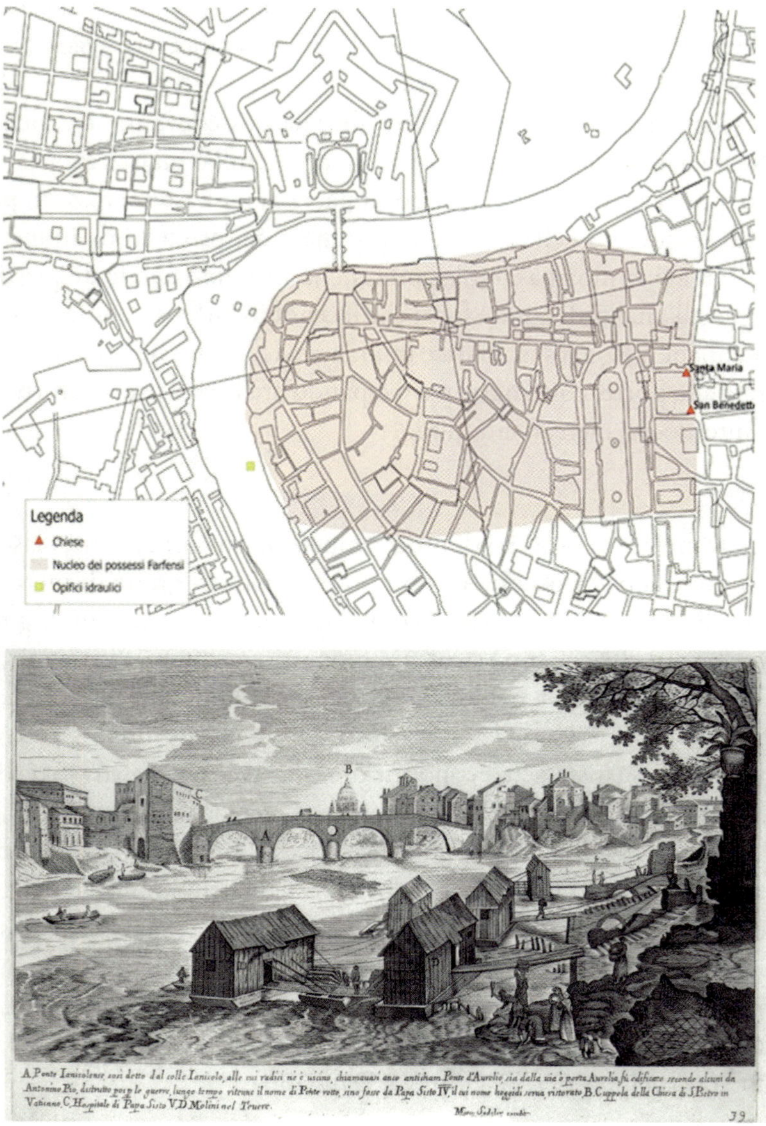

Fig. 14 - Le dipendenze di Farfa nella città di Roma e i mulini natanti del Tevere (*Veduta del Tevere con ponte Gianicolense e mulini sulla sponda del fiume,* di E. Sadeler)

È probabile che il monastero possedesse anche le aree di attracco e le posterule di accesso presenti lungo il tratto di mura che costeggiava il fiume, controllando il commercio dei prodotti. Le strutture produttive erano amministrate da una serie di celle poste in prossimità del settore occidentale delle Terme Alessandrine, nell'area del *Campum Agonis* e del Pantheon, due chiese dedicate a Santa Maria (divenuta nel 1478 la chiesa di San Luigi dei Francesi) e a San Benedetto, e un oratorio intitolato al San Salvatore[51].

Nella seconda metà dell'XI secolo l'abbazia possedeva inoltre, nell'area di Piazza Navona, diversi stabili, sia abitazioni che fienili o magazzini.

Si può ipotizzare che l'ampia area occupata dal monastero, fosse in parte destinata allo stoccaggio delle derrate importate e dei prodotti da immettere sul mercato, immaginando una circolazione anche ad ampio raggio di questi ultimi.

Emerge dall'analisi di queste fonti che il cenobio farfense, come nel centro di Rieti, così anche a Roma si stabilisce in un'area della città ben precisa, prossima alle mura e alle porte, comunque partecipando attivamente con un ruolo di rilievo all'interno dei mercati cittadini.

CC

Successivamente ai processi di produzione e di trasformazione, ciascun monastero si preoccupa di occupare con i propri prodotti quote di mercato sulle piazze cittadine e di promuoverne il commercio spesso anche a lunga gittata. La quota di mercato che ciascuna struttura monastica acquisisce varia in relazione all'area di espansione e alla potenza economica e commerciale.

Il quadro che emerge dall'osservazione topografica è interessante e rivela molto bene come sussistessero economie di scala diversa nello stesso territorio[52]: il monastero sublacense mira alla conquista del mercato romano, convogliando i suoi sforzi nel controllo delle acque, dei processi di trasformazione e della vie di comunicazione verso Roma. Il cenobio possiede beni immobili nella città di Roma, con una netta predilezione per le aree suburbane, spesso concessi a enfiteusi a lungo periodo. I possessi sublacensi sono posti sul Celio (il monastero di S. Erasmo), a Porta Maggiore (la chiesa di S. Teodoro), nell'area tra il Laterano e S. Maria Maggiore, nei pressi della chiesa di S. Vito (la cella di S. Scolastica) e della via Lata (la chiesa dei SS. Cosma e Damiano).

---

51 *RF,* Appendice II, V, 330. I. Lori Sanfilippo, «I possessi romani di Farfa, Montecassino e Subiaco - secoli IX-XII», *Archivio della Società Romana di Storia Patria* 103 (1980) 21.

52 Per l'analisi anche metodologica dell'economia di rete del monastero si rinvia a F.R. Stasolla, «Monastic archaeology: integrating sources and methods to reconstruct Mediterranean landscapes», in 22nd *Annual Meeting of the EEA* (Vilnius, 31st August - 4th September 2016), in corso di stampa.

Forse tali complessi hanno funzionato anche da postazioni destinate all'immagazzinamento del *surplus* dei prodotti della Valle, come ad esempio nelle celle vinarie del monastero di S. Erasmo, *surplus* da vendere sul mercato romano secondo un modello economico che prevedeva la presenza stabile di strutture di vendita dei più importanti monasteri sui mercati urbani, fino a determinarne l'andamento dei prezzi, sul tipo di quelli noti per il monastero di Nonantola a Pavia e per il monastero di S. Ambrogio per il mercato di Milano. In effetti, il vino era un alimento necessario all'economia romana, che si approvvigionava di grano dal Lazio settentrionale, di olio dalla Sabina e di vino dai vigneti suburbani, cui potremmo aggiungere l'area sublacense. Non a caso il patrimonio immobiliare del monastero nella città di Tivoli[53], unico centro lungo la via per Roma, è costituito soprattutto da strutture molitorie per la trasformazione dei prodotti da inviare verso il più vicino mercato, appunto quello romano.

GMA

Così come sottolineato prima da Toubert, poi da Marazzi, tali monasteri avrebbero assunto *in primis* la funzione di "forzieri di rendite", ma in seguito avrebbero esercitato il loro spirito imprenditoriale, esigenza alla quale rispondeva anche la voluta acquisizione di beni fondiari con vocazione differente[54].

Questo dinamismo interno sarebbe stato influenzato da un'accelerazione dei movimenti commerciali determinatasi nei decenni iniziali del IX secolo, e, all'interno dei patrimoni fondiari monastici, sarebbe stato diretto sia dalle proprietà e pertinenze verso la casa madre, sia anche dall'abbazia a luoghi dove specifici prodotti potevano essere oggetto di mercato[55]. Nel caso di Farfa, perlopiù si tratta di scali e non di porti, per sottolineare come questi assumano solo la funzione di punti di smistamento e non diano vita a insediamenti stabili di sorta[56].

---

53 A titolo esemplificativo si veda il caso della cella sublacense di S. Barbara, detta anche S. Barbara e Anastasio a Tivoli: strategicamente posta a Tivoli presso l'imbocco dei possessi verso Roma, gestisce l'attività molitoria non solo per il monastero ma anche per i fondi tiburtini. La cella è citata più volte nei documenti dal 936 al 1051 (*Reg. Subl.*, nn. 3, 12, 13, 14, 15, 17, 21, 138, 166).

54 F. Marazzi, «San Vincenzo al Volturno tra VIII e IX secolo: il percorso della grande crescita. Una indagine comparativa con le altre grandi fondazioni benedettine italiane», in Marazzi-Delogu, *San Vincenzo al Volturno. Cultura istituzioni ed economia*, 69.

55 Marazzi, «San Vincenzo al Volturno tra VIII e IX secolo», 70.

56 Marazzi, «San Vincenzo al Volturno tra VIII e IX secolo», 72.

Fig. 15 - Localizzazione delle saline e dei porti fluviali e marittimi controllati dal monastero farfense

Interessante è notare ancora una volta l'importanza fondamentale delle vie d'acqua, sia per lo sfruttamento della risorsa idrica stessa, sia in relazione alla navigabilità a piccolo cabotaggio, sia anche come via di penetrazione dalla costa verso l'interno e viceversa.

Allo sfruttamento delle risorse idriche da parte del monastero va collegata anche la pratica dell'itticoltura, esercitata da Farfa almeno dalla seconda metà dell'VIII secolo, grazie anche alle elargizioni dei sovrani[57].

Esempi di *piscarie* sono attestati a Rieti e nel territorio a essa afferente, con il controllo dei laghi Maggiore e Lungo, ma anche presso Tivoli, dove la chiesa di Sant'Adriano gestiva beni immobili e terreni e possedeva anche delle paludi[58]. Un altro settore produttivo è rappresentato dalla gestione delle saline, in particolare quelle poste nel territorio di Porto e Ostia, presso la foce del Tevere, dove l'attività di estrazione del sale, per il cenobio farfense, è documentata per la prima volta all'inizio dell'XI secolo[59].

57 T. Leggio, *Pesca ed acque nel medioevo reatino*, Rieti 2007.

58 Si rimanda a *RF*, II, doc. 81, 76-77; *RF*, II, doc. 223, 182; *RF*, III, doc. 420, 130-131; *LL*, I, doc. 170, 120 e doc. 197, 133.

59 S. Pannuzi, «La laguna di Ostia: produzione del sale e trasformazione del paesaggio dall'età antica all'età moderna», *Mélanges de l'École française de Rome – Moyen Âge*, 125/2 (2013), http://mefrm.revues.org/1507, [accesso: 05-01-2018].

Fig. 16 - Localizzazione delle peschiere amministrate dall'abazia di Farfa

È ravvisabile nelle fonti come anche le saline, così come evidenziato per i mulini, vengano affidate dal monastero a privati mediante contratti di livello.

Non avendo notizie di celle presenti nell'area di Porto e Ostia è probabile che l'abbazia gestisse direttamente questi impianti.

Inoltre, è interessante rilevare la ripartizione della gestione delle saline di Porto da parte dei monasteri di Farfa e di San Benedetto di Subiaco, ciò fa presupporre che queste costituissero una fonte di rendita notevole per gli enti monastici[60].

GM

Nel quadro dell'approvvigionamento del complesso monastico sublacense, un ruolo economico non secondario per garantirsi uno sbocco a mare o comunque alle vie d'acqua dovettero svolgerlo anche le saline attestate in relazione a tre toponimi (*Burdunaria*, *Pedica vetere* e *Serpentaria*) riconducibili alla zona di Campo Maiore, situata sulla costa tirrenica nei pressi di Roma, tra Porto e Maccarese[61]. Le saline sono citate in documenti di metà X-metà XI secolo che ricordano la loro cessione a livellari in seguito all'incameramento nei beni ab-

60 Le saline sono ricordate in *LL, I*, doc. 60, 61. S. Nardi Combescure, «L'Étrurie Méridionale entre l'Antiquité Tardive et le Haut Moyen Âge. Vieux problémes et nouvelles pistes de recherche», *Mélanges de l'École française de Rome – Moyen Âge* 114/2 (2002) 924-925.

61 M.T. Maggi Bei, «Sulla produzione del sale nell'alto medioevo in zona romana», *Archivio della Società Romana di Storia Patria*, CI (1978) 354-366.

baziali per mezzo di donazioni. L'adozione del contratto livellare – a fronte di un'eventuale prima entratura corrisposta in denaro – garantiva in seguito il versamento annuale di un canone in natura, assicurando in tal modo al cenobio sublacense la disponibilità di un prodotto altrimenti vincolato a specifiche zone di produzione.

Il monastero sublacense si preoccupa quindi di occupare con i propri prodotti quote di mercato sulle piazze cittadine e di promuoverne il commercio anche a lunga gittata garantendosi uno sbocco a mare o alle vie d'acqua. In questa direzione l'abbazia di Subiaco controlla Ostia con le sue saline, ma anche l'area che dai Colli Albani dà verso la Campania fino a Sabaudia, il territorio terracinese[62] e quello del lago di Fogliano[63].

GMA

Nonostante l'assenza di dati certi sullo sfruttamento di altre saline in area laziale da parte di Farfa, di notevole rilevanza è la vicinanza delle saline alla cella di Santa Maria sul Mignone, nell'area tarquiniese, che potrebbe essere messa in connessione con la zona destinata al pascolo nei pressi della cella, così come già proposto in passato da Sara Nardi Combescure, a sua volta connessa al *gualdus* citato nelle fonti, che avrebbe offerto la possibilità al monastero di stabilire un possibile asse di transumanza tra i pascoli interni e quelli costieri.

L'indagine fin qui presentata nei due *territoria* monastici di Farfa e di Subiaco racchiude potenzialità notevoli in ordine anche al confronto con il *topos* agiografico – e in parte, almeno nei decenni passati, storiografico – della fondazione del monastero in un *desertum* di selve, con una connotazione di isolamento dal mondo che, sia sul fronte storico che su quello archeologico, gli studi recenti tendono fortemente a ridimensionare, sottolineando piuttosto, nel caso in cui l'incolto costituisca effettivamente la nota dominante nel paesaggio altomedievale in cui un monastero si inserisce, il ben noto valore di questo tipo di ambiente come risorsa economica.

GM

62 I signori di Terracina, facendo fede a un atto documentario, devono consentire ai monaci l'accesso in città per l'uso del porto di fondo (M.T. Caciorgna, *Una città di frontiera. Terracina nei secoli XI-XIV*, Roma 2008).

63 Nello specifico la chiesa di S. Donato (*Reg. Subl.*, n. 51) presso il lago di Fogliano (LT), una torre vicina ai laghi, la cella oggi santuario di S. Maria di Sorrisco di Sabaudia (*Reg. Subl.*, nn. 3, 21, 183, 203, 216) e ogni terra fino al mare. Tutti questi possedimenti si affacciavano sulla laguna che univa il promontorio di Anzio al Circeo e consentivano così di controllare il traffico di cabotaggio di navi di passaggio tra Roma e il Sud Italia.

Abstract

One of the research themes carried out by the Department of Medieval Archaeology, Sapienza University of Rome (prof. Francesca Romana Stasolla) is about the monastic dependencies (cells, *Ecclesiae* and monasteries) of two Benedictine monasteries of Lazio, Santa Maria of Farfa and SS. Benedict and Scholastica of Subiaco. This communication focuses on the first results emerged from a comparison of written sources (published and unpublished related chronological horizon of VIII - XI century) and topographic analysis of these monastic cells using a regressive method. The collected data were organized in a GIS platform which enabled to geolocalize the dependencies and to identify its territories, resulting from precise strategies of monastic patrimony management. In this direction, the cells and the ecclesiae placed next to the mother house, many of them pre-existent, seem to have played an important role since the formation of the abbeys' land endowment. Unlike the cells farthest from the Abbey would seem to have had more pronounced fiscal and economic functions.

The analysis also revealed the different productive and economic value of the dependencies of the two monasteries (especially regarding the use of water and agricultural and forestry-pastoral resources), as well as common elements in the management of these.

A THEOLOGICAL APPROACH TO THE BENEDICTINE CONCEPT OF POVERTY

Izsák Baán

Most of our contemporaries, both inside and outside the Church, derive their view of religious life from the so called «classic» triple vows of poverty, chastity and obedience. This picture is often based on personal or literary experiences either about St. Francis of Assisi, or about his one-time or now living followers. People who approach our monasteries with this picture in mind are often surprised or even disappointed when looking for Benedictine poverty. In most countries of Europe, the sons of St. Benedict have huge properties, imposing, antique buildings, and lately, because of the difficult economic situation, they are engaged in new enterprises, ranging from web- designing to organic farming; from water power stations to wine production.

To the disapproving questioners, we often give a stereotypical response, namely, that Benedictine monasteries can have possessions, but the monks need to use them in a spirit of poverty. The paradoxical nature of this statement, however, is more discouraging than comforting for those who are scandalized at Benedictines engaged in business enterprises involving «luxury» items. For this reason, it is probably beneficial that we do not resort to this oversimplified answer but, instead, look to the Rule of St. Benedict and the monastic tradition for guidelines to understand more deeply the relationship between monasticism and possessions. Let's look for signposts on the path of the Rule that help us to navigate this complex area of monastic life. Nowadays, such signposts are clearly needed, as our communities currently face discouraging crossroads, unforeseeable curves, slippery and swampy places, as well as various kinds of stumbling blocks, in dealing with worldly possessions whilst on the path of following Christ.

Izsák Baán, Hungarian Benedictine monk of Bakonybél Priory, theologian, specialist in monastic history and literature in late Antiquity.

1. THE POVERTY OF THE POOR (*PAUPERTAS PAUPERUM*)

The ideal of «holy poverty» is unknown for Benedict. The word poverty (*paupertas*) appears in the Rule only once, and it is not used to describe a monastic ideal, but points rather to an unfortunate reality. In Chapter 48 we read that monks must not be sad if «local conditions or their poverty should force them to do the harvesting themselves» (RB 47,7)[1]. The lack of material resources here is an exceptional situation which, should it occur, must be accepted with peace. It is not an ideal program to be implemented, but a practical solution to solving a problem.

Although «poverty» in and of itself, does not appear as a value for the community, the importance of dealing with the poor is clearly emphasized in the Rule. Amongst those who knock on the door of the monastery, special attention has to be paid to people in need, «in adoration of Christ, who indeed is received in their persons» (RB 53,7). This conviction comes from the Gospel of Matthew, Chapter 25, and appears several times in the Rule as an important pillar of Benedictine Christology. The cellarer has to treat the poor with special care (RB 31.9). Anticipating their needs, he is to put aside for their use the monks' used items of clothing (RB 55,9). «Relieving the lot of the poor» is an important instrument of good works (RB 4,14). Furthermore, the monks are instructed to give thanks for the poor who present themselves at the monastery gates even at inconvenient times (RB 66,3).

The belief that the poor have a key role on the stage of The Great Theatre of the World according to Calderon, and that on the day of Judgement we have to give account of what we did to the «least of these» (Matt 25,45), has defined the relationship of Benedictine communities to various forms of human need for centuries, and has become the foundation of all their social activities. In the Rule of St. Benedict, however, the adjective «poor» (*pauper*) is never used for the monks. The poor are outside[2]. If we want to learn more about the monks' relationship to possessions, we have to continue our study by shifting our focus onto different semantic fields.

---

1 *The Rule of St. Benedict*, ed. T. Fry, Collegeville 1981. (Cited in the main text: RB.)

2 According to A. Böckmann the standards of living of the monks in Benedict's monastery was the same as that of the poor (*pauperes*) in general in the 6th century. She thinks that the Rule avoids the use of the word either because of prudency, or because it wants to make a difference between the suffocating experience of poverty and poverty willingly chosen. Cf. «Akzentuierungen der neutestamentlichen Armut nach der *Regula Benedicti*», in *Regulae Benedicti Studia* 5 (1976) 141.

2. THE PURE FORM OF POSSESSION (*PROPRIUM PROPRIUM*)

The title of Benedict's chapter which directly relates to our topic, Chapter 33, begins with the question «whether the monks ought to have anything of their own (*Si quid debeant monachi proprium habere*)». The question is not about possessing (*habere*) in general, but whether monks can keep things as their «own (*proprium*)». The adjective «*proprius*» appears in the Rule quite often, and each time it is a useful indicator of the Benedictine way with respect to possessions. From now on, we are going to examine this word, and the domains of meaning surrounding it. However, in order to shed light on the deeper roots of the «Benedictine private ownership» theme, we have to start our discussion literally with Adam and Eve.

The opening lines of the Prologue of The Rule interpret the path of the monk as a return to the One from whom man had departed because of his disobedience (RB Prol 2). The exercises of the monastic life, according to early monastic tradition, were meant to restore the original state of man as ordered by God. The ideal monastery is to be a «*Paradisum claustralis*».

If we read the Jahwist's creation account, looking for just how the man in Paradise «owned» the created world, we have to make the following statements. The inspired author portrays Adam as someone infinitely rich, yet, at one and the same time, completely poor. He does not even have his own clothing, but, in a perfect openness to the Creating God, he possesses everything together with God. His desire, which, «before and above all other possible goals is directed to happiness, is the ideal state of freedom»[3], and has only one object: God.

In the text of the Bible, Adam does not make any requests. It is God, for example, who realises and puts into words the man's desire for a mate (Gen 2,18). Only God is capable of purely possessing, since in Him possessing and possessed coincide. As Deridda says, he is the absolute presence of selfness, the logocentric, fundamental structure. And this absolute identity, realised in eternal presence, is not made impure by any difference[4].

God, who possesses everything, entrusts the Garden to the man placed in Paradise «to cultivate and tend it» (Gen 2,15). Everything serves the purpose of man so that he can become more and more who he was destined to be, thereby fulfilling

3 P. SEQUERI, *Il Dio affidabile*, Brescia 1996, 400.

4 J. DERRIDA, *Limited Inc. Signature événement contexte*, Paris 1990, 18. Deridda's statement is based on the double meaning of the Latin word *proprius* (French *propre*). It means at the same time «private, own» and «pure, clear».

his vocation. He can never, however, renounce the unique foundation of his existence, that of being possessed by God. Man's very existence, according to Saint Thomas, is «*simplex et completum sed non subsistens* (complete and simple, but not subsistent)».[5] The constellation arising from this truth is in elliptical form, which cannot be transformed into a circle. Possessing together with the purely possessing God is only possible if man accepts his place in this «elliptical field» which is the mirror image of the life of the Holy Trinity. The desire of man can only remain as it was designed by God, only if the distinctiveness of the focal points is kept, only if the ontological difference between God and man is respected. The object of man's desire, the focus of his attention is the «more than», the Other. If he chooses to usurp it, making it his own possession, he must then leave behind that place properly his in the divine order of things, thus distorting that elliptical field and denying the otherness of the Other. There is only one way to reconcile this paradox: God's gratuitous giving. In his love, God wants to give everything to man. According to the Book of Revelation, He even wanted to bestow knowledge and life, originally reserved only for God («To him that overcomes, I will give to eat of the tree of life, which is in the midst of the paradise of God» Rev 2,7). Man, however, can only receive this as a gift, it is not something he can usurp as his own possession.

3. INAPPROPRIATE POSSESSION (*PROPRIUM INPROPRIUM*)

We know that man did not remain in this elliptical field, completely open to God. According to the creation account, he tried to usurp something that he could only have had as a gift. He tried to dissolve the ontological distance, wanting to «be like God» (Gen 3,5). Eating the fruit of the tree of knowledge symbolizes a new modality of knowing and possessing. Until this point, Adam gave a name to the animals and to his wife, being aware that they were gifts, respecting the difference and the distance that distinguished him from God. Now he eats of the forbidden fruit and thereby destroys the object of his desire. When the original relationship between man and God is broken, the finitude embedded in infinity up until this point by this relationship, appears in its (literally) naked reality. Refusing the in-

5 THOMAS AQUINAS, *De potentia* 1, 1 ad 1. This sentence (which pithily expresses a consistent doctrine in Thomas) touches the mystery of created being as love. Being is wealth, unity, plenitude, light, life, goodness: pure, simple act (*completum et simplex*). Nevertheless, *as such* it is always given away radically. In this sense, it can be thought of as poverty, refusal to cling to self, expropriatedness, emptiness (the emptiness of love). Cf. S. OSTER, «Thinking Love at the Heart of Things. The Metaphysics of Being as Love in the Work of Ferdinand Ulrich», *Communio* 37 (2010) 671-672.

finite horizon closes the man within the walls of his own finitude, which is called death (Rom 5,12). Instead of gazing at the world with awe and wonder, he now experiences fear for his very life. Now his desire, closed to infinity, tries to usurp every object that offers happiness. «Fixation chases away, makes the object remote, and the object of desire is not any more the truth of the subject he wanted to own. Desire, in this way, degrades his own purpose and object into a dead fetish»[6]. We know from the divine sanction addressed to the woman, that her object of desire, the man, will now begin to rule over her (Gen 3,16).

This sinful modality of possessing is in the mind of Benedict when he opens Chapter 33 with one of the most severe sentences of the Rule: «This most wicked vice especially is to be cut out of the monastery by the roots (*radicitus amputandum est*)» (RB 33,1). The author of the Rule is aware of the fact that this kind of *proprium* is sinful, because it is based on illusion, because man thinks that he can possess something as solely and exclusively his, although it is really the object of his desire that possesses him.

In the monastic tradition, greed (*avaritia*) appears as a dangerous passion, because the desire implanted in man, originally directed to infinity, is insatiable and will always find a new object for itself. Cassian, the source for Benedict on this topic, writes: «If it is disregarded and once allowed to gain entrance into the heart, is most dangerous to everyone, and can be expelled only with great difficulty. It becomes the root of all evils and gives rise to a multiplicity of incitements to sin»[7]. Without any doubt, the source of the theory concerning these «thoughts» is Evagrius, who elaborates on the metaphor used by the Apostle, according to which «the love of money is the root of all evil» (1 Tim. 6:10) Evagrius writes: «One who wishes to cut off the passions should cut out their root; for while avarice remains, there is no benefit in trimming the branches: whenever they are cut off they will immediately sprout again»[8]. Benedict himself warns his monks about greed twice, with particular reference to those who are charged with handling the «goods» of the monastery: the cellarer (RB 31,12) and the artisans of the monastery (RB 57,7).

The first step in getting rid of the desire to possess, of returning to the «elliptical field» is to take some distance from things. This is why the novice is

6 E. Salmann, «Felicità o salvezza?», in *Presenza di spirito*, Padova 2000, 157. «La fissazione allontana, fa fuggire l'oggetto – e l'oggetto del desiderio non è più la verità del soggetto che si voleva possedere. Il desiderio riduce il suo obiettivo e oggetto in un feticcio morto».

7 Johannes Cassianus, *De institutis coenobiorum* VII, 2.

8 Evagrius, Oct. sp. 3,2. R.E. Sinkewicz, *Evagrius of Pontus. The Greek Ascetic Corpus*, Oxford 2003, 78.

required to «take off his own things» (RB 58,26 *exuatur rebus propriis*), he has to give up power over his own body (RB 58,25 *potestas proprii corporis*), and he has to accept that the community itself takes some distance from the «goods» of food by the practice of fasting (RB 49). The freedom from things also manifests itself in Benedict's provision that when the Superior orders something (RB 5,7-8), or the bell calls them for prayer (RB 43,1), the monks have to stop what they are doing or put down what is in their hands.

However, distancing from material objects or from the body, in itself, does not satisfy Benedict. The key to returning to God, for man who has strayed from God, is obedience. Benedict right in the opening paragraph of the Prologue addresses those, who «are willing to give up even their free will» (RB Prol 3 *abrenuntians propriis voluntatibus*). This «self-will (*voluntas propria*)», separated from the obedience of faith, is the most dangerous of possessions for Benedict. It is an obstacle on the path of the monk toward God. This is why monks must not follow their own hearts' desire in the monastery (RB 3,8). In this context, it is understandable that amongst the instruments of good works, he exhorts his disciples «to hate one's own will» (RB 4,60 *voluntatem propriam odire*). Giving up this self-will, which Gyrovagues are not capable of doing, appears – supported by Bible verses – both in the first and second degrees of humility (RB 7,12.19.31).

4. THE GRATUITOUS GIFT AND COMMON POSSESSION (*PROPRIUM DONATUM ET COMMUNE*)

Looking at Chapter 33 again, we discover that after Benedict enjoins the monks with increasing vehemence to look at neither objects, nor their bodies, nor their will as their own, he then approaches the question from a positive point of view. He does not stop at the bare requirement of renunciation and of dispossession. Instead he shows the disciples a method of «possessing» that is in harmony with what we have learned about the pure form of possession, that is, the gratuitous gift and the common possession.

As the man in Paradise possessed everything as a gift from the Creator, so must the monks «for their needs look to the Father of the monastery (*omnia necessaria a patre sperare monasterii*)» (RB 33,5). Calling the abbot «Father» by Benedict here is probably not only to ease the harsh tone of the chapter[9], but we can also discern in reliance on the abbot for needs, a form of possession

9 Cf. A. Borias, «Le Chiasme dans la Règle bénédictine», *Revue bénédictine* 95 (1985) 30-32.

that is characteristic of gifts gratefully accepted from the Creator, and possessed together with Him. This assumption is further strengthened if we look at those places in the Rule, where the adjective *proprius* is used in a positive context. Two such references can be found in Chapter 40, which deals with the measure of drink. «Everyone has his own gift from God (*unusquisque proprium habet donum ex Deo*)» (RB 40,1). Benedict cites St. Paul 1 Cor 7,7. So the gratuitous gift from God can be considered a *proprium* of sorts, personally owned, just as the reward everyone will get for their renunciation (*«propriam se habituros mercedem sciant»*) (RB 40,4). Chapter 54 can also be cited in which the author of the Rule considers gifts arriving from outside the monastery that the monk can only accept from the hand of the abbot. Possessing gifts received from God and the abbot, gives birth to a special attitude which characterizes Benedictine culture all over the world. The awareness that our possessions are gratuitous gifts results in respectful handling and treating the objects of the monastery with special care, ordinarily reserved for the sacred vessels of the altar (RB 32). It also underlies the fact that Benedictine communities have lived, sometimes for centuries, in the places chosen by their founders and have consequently tried to preserve the buildings as well as the natural environment for future generations.

Returning to Chapter 33, we see that Benedict is in strong opposition to private ownership, putting greater emphasis on the common possession of goods. «All things should be the common possession of all, as it is written (Acts 4,32), so that no one presumes to call anything his own» (RB 33,6). In this foundational verse, we see the model of the Early Church of Jerusalem, in which, according to Acts «the multitude of them that believed were of one heart and of one soul: and no one claimed that any of his possessions was his own, but they had everything in common» (Acts 4,32). The effect of this text on early monasticism is remarkable. According to Athanasius, Saint Antony is meditating on this verse when he enters the church at the beginning of his conversion[10]. Cassian derives cenobitic monasticism directly from this community of the Apostles[11]. Moreover, Augustine resorts to this verse about community in Christ, united in one heart and one soul, when he is explaining the origin of the word: «monk (*monachus*)»[12]. In early monasticism the basis for the common possession of goods, deemed important even for hermits living alone, was the «koinonia» of the

10 ATHANASIUS, *Vita Antonii*, 2.

11 JOHANNES CASSIANUS, *Conlationes patrum*, XVIII, 5.

12 AUGUSTINUS, Exp. in Ps. 132,6. St. AURELIUS AUGUSTINE, *Exposition on the Psalms*, Digital Psalms version 2007 (public domain), 1078.

Church, the community with one another and God rooted in the Holy Trinity. Common possession is a form of «owning» that preserves the distance between the possessed object and the possessor. It does not allow the horizon, open to the «other», to be closed by usurpation (*expropriatio*), or the possessed object to take away human freedom.

In Chapter 33, Benedict emphasizes that everything must be common («*omniaque omnibus sint communia*») (RB 33,6), but in this «everything», common meals have a distinguished and symbolic place (RB 43,15: *mensa communis*), because in connection with eating, the danger of losing distance, of the distorted desire of covetousness, or of indulging in the vice of gluttony, is even greater. In opposition to self-will, then, there is the conviction that monks, separated from God because of disobedience, do not return to Him on their own individual paths, but they follow Christ, who wants to lead them to eternal life all together (RB 72,12: «omnes *pariter ad vitam aeternam perducat*»), by means of a common rule of life (RB 7,55: «*communis monasterii regula*»).

5. POSSESSION IN CHRIST (*PROPRIUM CHRISTI*)

As we have seen, Benedict contrasts the vice of private ownership with two alternative forms: the gratuitous gift and common possession. However, we can only understand Chapter 33 in depth, with its requirement of giving up private ownership, if we read it in the context of the whole Rule, keeping in mind the Benedictine approach to Christology. Benedict takes the title of this chapter from the Rules of Saint Basil translated by Rufinus, where we can read after the title: «Since Christ gave his life for us, how can we consider our own that which is much less personal than our life?»[13]. Based on this, the final reason for the Benedictine attitude towards possessions required by the Rule is the following of Christ itself. «Just as Christ gave his life for the community, and the monk gives his very self to Christ and the community, so should he symbolise and concretise this self-gift by dispossession»[14]. Christ, who «was rich, yet for your sakes became poor, that you, through his poverty, might be rich» (2 Cor 8,9) is kept before the eyes of the monk, who uses the objects of this world, but who does not possess them. The *monachus*, who is climbing the ladder of humility,

13 Basilius, Reg. fus. tr., 29. A.M. Silvas, *The Rule of St Basil in Latin and English. A Revised Critical Edition*, Collegeville 2013, 102.

14 J. Gribomont, «The commentaries of Adalbert de Vogüé and the Great Monastic Tradition», *The American Benedictine Review* 36/3 (1985) 254.

and is willing to renounce his own will, follows Christ, who has come not to do his own will, but the will of Him who sent Him (John 6,38, RB 7,32).

The poverty of the monk, however, is not only imitating the poor Christ as a role model, it is more than mere «*imitatio*», but extends to «*participatio*». The personal relationship with the Son, who was made flesh, who died and rose again, creates an opportunity for the monk, that «through Him, with Him and in Him», on the path toward the Father, the monk might experience something of that original and pure form of possession, intended by God from the beginning. In this experience, rooted in the mystery of Easter, attainable only through the cross and the stages of renunciation, we can encounter something purely possessed (*proprium proprium*), all within the matrix of the resurrection which restores the original right relationships among God, self, others and material goods. The monk, who prefers nothing whatever to Christ (RB 72,11), who holds nothing dearer to himself than Him (RB 5,2), who looks for Him in the psalms, in *Lectio Divina*, in the abbot, the brother, the sick and the poor, can slowly experience that through his monastic consecration he becomes a possession of Christ instead of the possessor, «entering Christology from anthropology»[15].

According to Saint Bernard, man receives Christ from the Father in compensation for the lost unity of Paradise («*Pro paradiso quem perdidimus, restitutus est nobis Christus Salvator*»)[16]. In this way he can «possess» Him as a gift from God (Rom 8,32). At the same time, however, according to the logic of Paul, the monk himself and with him the community in which he lives in this relationship, becomes the possession of Christ (1Cor 3,23, 2Cor 10,7, Gal 3,29, etc.). In unity with Christ, the monk becomes a co-heir (Rom 8,17), so that he can possess everything. Possessor and possessed, the Son and redeemed humanity – due to the hypostatic union of Christ's human and divine natures – are in complete unity, although still distinguishable from each other in Christ. The monk, who gives himself to Christ, can be part of this experience in Him. The prayer that is offered for the monk taking his vows in the *Regula Magistri*, and with which we conclude our sequence of thoughts expresses this transition beautifully in the following passage:

> Behold, Lord, whatever you have given me I am returning to you, offering it together with my soul and in my poverty, and I want my possessions to be there where my heart and my soul are, but in the power of the monastery and of the

15 Cf. H. U. von Balthasar, «Johannine Themes in the Rule of St. Benedict and their Meaning Today», *Cistercian Studies Quarterly* 11 (1976) 11-24.

16 Saint Bernard of Clairvaux, *Sermones de diversis* 96,1.

abbot whom you, Lord, are setting over me. (...) Consequently, because through him you keep our needs in mind, we ought to have nothing of our own, for you are our surety for everything and in all things you alone suffice[17].

CONCLUSION

We can state that the Rule gives little guidance about exactly how poor monasteries should be to those who are discouraged by looking at our enterprises. Benedict urges that monasteries shall have everything that is necessary (RB 66,6), but this is not his primary concern. He gives a much more detailed teaching about the inner attitude monks must have in relation to temporal goods. It is without any doubt that monks must possess (*habere*) tools in order to be able to do their everyday tasks, but their spiritual disposition while doing so, matters more. We tried to demonstrate that instead of the «most wicked vice of private ownership» (RB 33,7), that separates the monk from God, Benedict encourages his monks to take some distance from material goods by means of renunciation, to be aware that these are gifts, and to avoid the sin of greed by practicing the common possession of goods. However, giving up private possessions, paying special attention to the gifts of God and of the abbot, and common possession as characteristic of Benedictines, are difficult to understand in depth without viewing them from the perspective of Christology. The genuine «*proprium benedictinum*» is the path leading back to the Father, upon which the monk sets out, with the help of the exercises of monastic life, the abbot and his brethren. He strives to be in a living relationship with God, and meanwhile himself becomes the possession of Christ. This is what Benedict has before his eyes when he makes provisions concerning material goods. The wealth or poverty of the monastery is only important to the extent to which it promotes or hinders progress on this Christ-centered and Christ-accompanied path.

Abstract

L'ideale della "santa povertà" è sconosciuta nei primi secoli del monachesimo, nella RB "povertà", lungi da essere un ideale, è la scomoda realtà della mancanza di risorse. Se invece cambiamo campo semantico e studiamo quello che Ben-

17 *Regula Magistri* 89, 18-23. L. Eberle (trad.), *The Rule of the Master* (Cistercian Studies 6), Kalamazoo 1977, 259.

edetto insegna su ciò che è “proprio” del monaco, si apre un sentiero ricco di significati.

Chiamando in aiuto l’antropologia teologica prima di tutto dobbiamo capire la natura del possedere nella sua forma pura (*proprium proprium* – giocando sul doppio significato della parola latina), voluta da Dio. Partecipare alla ricchezza del creato rimanendo in unione col Dio – che è l’unico a possedere in modo puro in quanto in lui “proprietario” e “proprietà” coincidono –, presuppone l’accettazione della natura paradossale del desiderio. Rispettare lo stato creaturale significa una proprietà ricevuta come dono ed aperta ad un altro.

Il peccato marca una rottura in questo campo ed introduce una forma impropria di proprietà (*proprium inproprium*). L’aspetto concreto materiale (proprietà privata e avarizia con essa legata) e l’aspetto spirituale (volontà propria) di questa forma peccaminosa di possedere si presentano come grandi ostacoli nel cammino del cristiano e come temi importanti in tutta la tradizione monastica compresa la RB. La presa di distanza dalle cose, la sottomissione ad un superiore in obbedienza e la proprietà comune appaiono come rimedi ed aprono una strada di ritorno alla vera libertà creaturale (*proprium donatum et comune*).

In fine l’aspetto mistico della vita monastica rende possibile l’esperienza di appartenere a Cristo in modo tale da diventare sua proprietà (*proprium Christi*) e possedere in e con lui tutto nella più perfetta povertà.

Lo studio propone un cammino teologico-spirituale nel mondo della povertà monastica partendo da un analisi lessicale della Regola di Benedetto arricchendo il campo con altri testi della tradizione a lui anteriore.

MONASTICISM AND ECONOMY IN THE HORIZON OF A POOR CHURCH AND THE CHURCH OF THE POOR: SOME GUIDELINES TAKEN FROM THE RULE OF ST. BENEDICT, CH. 31 (CELLARER)

Aquinata Böckmann

My purpose is to elaborate some relevant lines of thought in regard to the main theme, examining important passages of RB 31 on the cellarer, and looking at them in the light of our present situation and more specifically of the encyclical letter of Pope Francis "Laudato si"[1].

Since this chapter 31 deals directly with the administration of material goods, what comes to our mind today, might be: political scandals due to lack of accountability, worldwide corruption, different facets of the poor, wars and financial scandals, crisis of the environment and climate. We are more aware than before that the administration of goods involves not only material things and the reality of creation but also service to people, especially to the poor, as Pope Francis clarified[2].

Monasteries develop alternative models of responsible administration of goods, both inside and beyond the community. The person of the cellarer is crucial to all these questions. In the following reflections, I retain the word "cellarer" according to the Rule of St. Benedict (RB). It is easy to translate it as economist, administrator, manager, and to see in him also a model for all our communities of different kinds, or even societies today.

In Benedict's time, and especially during the wars of the Ostrogoths (6th century), religious communities may have been chiefly concerned about guaranteeing the essentials for surviving. Monastic administration in general was oriented

Aquinata Böckmann, Missionary Benedictine Sister of Tutzing, ex-professor of the Monastic Institute at Pontifical Athenaeum S.Anselm, specialist in the Rule of Saint Benedict, author of important exegetic books on this theme.

1 Franciscus, *Laudato si*, Vatican 2015.

2 Franciscus, *Laudato si*, § 48; 117.

to a just distribution of goods inside the community, where the goods are common to all, and to the protection of the needy outside. Through their stability the monasteries were stewards of creation in their surroundings, farther away and in the future.

The concrete situation of RB shows that the community itself was poor. Only once poverty is explicitly mentioned. Benedict talks about the situation of "poverty" (48,7), which has as a consequence that all brothers have to help together working in the harvest, a work looked at as a hard one. Benedict does not explicitly call the individual brothers "poor", as it was the custom in other Rules, but he talks about the "poor" outside[3]. In a time of war, the monastery was a support for many poor and strangers, refugees and people in want.

As for the cellarer, the pre-benedictine community rules mention that common goods are cared for by certain persons and distributed according to the needs of the brothers who gave up their proper ownership. The cellarer is not to act according to preferences. His role is seen as a service, and the common things as consecrated tools[4]. The qualities of this cellarer are strongly stressed in RB 31. He has to be disciplined in food and drink, to serve everyone without murmuring and not be negligent[5]. Benedict differs considerably from his immediate source (Rule of the Master: RM). He places the many (!) desired qualities right at the beginning, and he stresses the fraternal relationships. [6]

In my reflections, I will point to some orientations which seem relevant in our situation today in regard to the theme of a poor Church and the Church of the poor. Even though the whole chapter can offer us interesting guidelines, I want to focus on three situations in RB 31, where we find explicitly the concept of brothers, or "little ones" as their description (31,6.13.16), and the least inside or beyond the community for which he should have the most solicitous care (31,9f) and respect. At the same time, all things are to be looked at as sacred vessels of the altar.

We can put all of this into a bigger context: challenges and demands by persons, collective entities or regions in our world today.

---

3 *RB* 4,14; 53,15; 55,9; 58,24; 59 T; 66,3 .

4 Basil, *Regula*, CSEL 86: 103f; 111f; Rule of the Four Fathers 3,21-30 (ed. Early Monastic Rules, Collegeville 1981, 26f); Oriental Rule 25 (*ibid.*, 72f).

5 Caesarius, *Rule for Virgins*, 30; 32.2 (ed.: SC 345, 208f; 212f).

6 Exegesis of *RB* 31: Cf. A. Böckmann, *Geeint in Christus*, St. Ottilien 2011, 227-269, bes. 242-245; 247-251; 256-258; 260-262.

1. 31,7
   "If any brother happens to make some unreasonable demand of him, he should not annoy him with disdain, but reasonably and humbly deny the improper request."

1.1. There is an unreasonable demand or claim (inrationabiliter postulat). May be the request is for extraordinary things, for too much, in a too short time or just for the personal comfort. Such an "improper request" can easily happen in community, where on the one hand everything is in common, and on the other hand the brothers may ask the necessary things from the responsible person (cf 33,5).

It is not ideal that the brother asks unreasonably, he should have learned to live a simple and unpretentious life, he should see the whole picture of his community, the broader surrounding and time; today, we would add the responsibility for the environment.

1.2. Benedict states first that the cellarer will not reject the request with contempt and disdain and in this way irritate the brother, or literally: make him sad, depress him. We can imagine such an answer, like: "A good brother will not claim these things", or "You are not aware that you renounced all these things", or "Your monastic formation should tell you not to demand". This would irritate the brother, and not be helpful to him at all. He could be depressed, and maybe no more have the courage to ask for anything, or be dejected, tempted to procure the necessary things from elsewhere, or even despair of his monastic vocation and run away (as Benedict mentions several times, cf 48,24; 64,19, Prol 48). In his resentment, he might begin to murmur, which has an effect on the whole surroundings. This occurs easily if someone does not understand why a request was denied.

1.3 The cellarer listens to the improper request. But it becomes clear to him that he has to say "No". The consequences of granting the request will be harmful for the community, for the situation, the environment and for the brother himself, who might be tempted to ask more and more things. Saying "no" can bring about the danger that this refusal looks and feels like undervaluing or ignoring the person who requests. Benedict's cellarer avoids personal rejection and aims at strengthening the individual even at this difficult moment. The person deserves a reason[7].

7 K. Dollard-A. Marrett-Crosby-T. Wright, *Doing business, The Rule of Benedict and Business Management; A Conversation*, London 2002, 100-102.

1.4 The cellarer gives an answer qualified by "reasonably and humbly". At first Benedict mentions "reasonably", then "humbly" (cf 65,14)[8]. This sequence is typical for him. The monk on the eleventh degree of humility does not speak few and *holy* words (as it is stated in RM – the immediate source of RB), but few and *reasonable* words (7,60). Since the cellarer is to answer reasonably, he must be wise (31,1) as it was said before. It is not with emotions, but with objective reasons, why a "No" is said. After listening in depth, even to an improper request, the cellarer looks into reality: What are the reasons that he cannot give, or that it is not good for the other? Explaining this, he helps the demanding brother to be realistic and aware of his vocation, of his community and of environment. It seems that Benedict himself was such a reasonable, experienced and wise man, firmly in contact with reality, using his good common sense. This is the human base on which Christian and monastic values can build.

The answer is further qualified by: "with humility". Some verses later it is said of the cellarer: "Humility – he must have above all things" (31,13). Humility has to do with "humus": earth and soil. Here he is firmly rooted, and answers as the "earth", the community and its environment require it. A humble answer can also entail a distance from one's own opinion, which does not need to be defended (cf also 3,4). The cellarer does not raise himself above the unreasonable petitioner. This procedure can help us even today when we must deny a request to do it without offending the demanding persons.

1.5 This is in agreement with RB 66,4 where the porter gives an answer "in the gentleness of the fear of God, ... in the warmth of love". He listened to the needs of the arriving people, especially the poor; and now the answer can be a "Yes" or a "No". Whether "Yes" or "No", in any case it is a qualified answer, which is concerned about "what is useful for the other" (72,7 – in the chapter of the good zeal). And it entails a "Yes" to the person.

Coming back to our chapter: surely it would not be good for the demanding brother that all his wishes were fulfilled. But with tactful love, the cellarer in all humility tells him some reasons, why he cannot or should not fulfill the request. So the other one can learn, take some steps (together with the cellarer) to live his vocation more authentically. The individual learns to ask without demanding. It is an "educational challenge"[9]. He learns to take responsibility for himself and

---

8 The same happens if an outsider expresses a criticism "reasonably with the humility of love" (rationabiliter cum humilitate caritatis"; then the superior should prudently consider whether the Lord sent him for that very purpose (61,4).

9 Cf. *Laudato si*, 209, 213.

his community, maybe confronting himself with the real poor of his time. - One of Benedict's keywords in regard to food and clothes is "sufficit". What is necessary "to make, to put under" a huge or a little building, like pillars in the ground? These pillars are necessary, but what is "superfluous" has to be removed[10]. The whole monastery has a frugal life-style, which has to be discerned always anew.

1.6 Today we think of claims coming from poor or well-to-do people who demand and demand according to the mentality of our affluent society: "The emptier a person's heart is, the more he or she needs things ... It becomes impossible to accept limits"[11]. We are confronted with very many "unreasonable demands" – sometimes egoistic, only concerned about one's own progress, and well-being. It is not just the others who have to learn, it is also we – ourselves, who have to cut down on "unreasonable demands" which arise in us, seeing "our common home", as Pope Francis calls it[12], becoming more reasonable, earth-bound and humble, taking into account the concrete and global situation and considering not only the present situation but also the one of the coming generations. We are ever anew challenged to give a reasonable and humble answer in our present and future environment and to concretize it in daily actions[13].

2. 31,13 OF HUMILITY

> he must have above all things, and to the person to whom he has nothing material to give, let him offer a good word as answer, for it is written: "A good word is better than the best gift"

2.1. Once again the cellarer must say a "No", but this time he does not have what others need. In this context Benedict uses a strong introduction: "Before all he must have humility". It becomes clear that the whole of chapter 7 on humility serves as basic guidelines for this person, his attitudes and actions: fear of God (31,1), obedience (31,4ff.12.15), patience in difficulties (31,7.13), awareness of his own limitations (31,1), solidarity with the others (31,2.6), silence and reasonable speech (31,7.13). As mentioned, the word "humility" derives from humus, - soil, earth. At the end of chapter 7 we see the monk bowed down, looking down at the earth, wherever he is, not only in the oratory, but also in the garden, on the way, and on the fields (7,63). The whole space becomes sacred. In this

10 *RB* 55,11; Cf. 55,4.10.15; *RB* 39,1.3.4; 40,3.

11 Cf. *Laudato si*, 213, 204.

12 See subtitle of the encyclical letter.

13 FRANCISCUS, *Laudato si*, 217, Cf. 222, 147, 208, 211.

way, the cellarer should always be in contact with the dust, the soil, the concrete reality, and treat it with reverence. This will have consequences in regard to human relations as well as to the whole cosmos.

2.2. In 31,13f humility is concretely connected with a situation where the cellarer cannot give what is requested, even something necessary. "He has nothing material to give" (31,13). This situation can be a consequence of the wars in Benedict's time (cf 48,7). The unpleasant situation can also show the cellarer's limitations, and make him vulnerable to the brothers. He cannot generously reach out and give what others need. Common ownership does not entail that all the time everybody receives everything he needs. The monastery itself can be "poor" (cf 48,7) and not have the necessary resources, which normally would be available. A spontaneous reaction of the cellarer to the petitioner could be: "Your problem is to desire too many things. It is necessary now to cut down on your needs and live a simple life. You are not thinking of our community and the situation of our society now." Happily, the recommended answer in RB 31 is different.

2.3. Benedict admonishes the cellarer to offer a kind word. *The good word* (31,14) is not simply a pious, edifying sentence, but is characterised as a "responsio" (an answer) and presupposes having listened to the other (see also 66,1-4). It presupposes humility in accepting one's own limitation (and that of the community). The good word can be as manifold as the different people are. It shows humility and understanding and is of real benefit, of "usefulness" to the other (cf RB 72,7). And this word seems even to be better than material goods. Humaneness and understanding are given. The scarcity of goods makes room for a deeper personal relationship. Those who cannot get the necessary things are respected in their dignity. The two sides are present to each other in concern and understanding[14]. Where there is mutual trust, it is easier to accept that something is lacking and to accept more willingly a simple life-style.

2.4. All our organisations have specific limitations; and humility would entail also to respect this "earth" and to accept it. It could bring us closer to one another. - In our global situation, we must count with the fact that needed supplies are not always available, that even the communities and organisations may be in need. If this is balanced by friendly human and Christian relations, then need and privations unite the members firmly with one another. It is not the ideal situation, but everyone tries to make the best out of it. In our situation today, we will not be always those who give. It is a two-way relationship of giving and receiving. And we might think of what we receive from very poor regions,

14 Cf. *Laudato si*, 223-231.

maybe in terms of personnel, of hope, of joy, of quality of life in spite of their poverty[15]. We too have to accept our vulnerability and sometimes our incapacity and should not cover it up with many nice words.

3. 31,16

   To the brothers he shall offer the regular allowance without any arrogance or delay so that they be not scandalised, remembering the divine word what the person deserves, who scandalises one of the little ones.

3.1. The offering of things to the dependent persons is given without "tyfum", concretely without incense, wanting to be incensed (also translated with arrogance). This would be the contrast to humility, and others feel their dependence, being in a lower position. The cellarer should grant requests without delay, with attentiveness to the needs of the brothers (cf also 66,1-4). The common renunciation of private ownership puts more responsibility on those who distribute. The verse builds on the equality of everybody; no side feels superior.

3.2. The brothers are called "little" ones (pusilli). Jesus admonishes the disciples not to scandalise the little ones (Mt 18,6), putting a stone on their way so that they will stumble and fall. It would be better that a person who does this, be drowned in the depth of the sea with a great millstone round his neck. The brothers through their giving up of property and privileges become "pusilli" (little ones), fragile and easily vulnerable[16]. Each one depends on the other. The mediation of money is lacking, so the personal relationship becomes the more important. As a consequence, the brothers can live in deep solidarity with the little and least ones in society and might understand them better, as they also depend on the good will of those who distribute.

3.3. The cellarer should be understanding, seeing himself in the same situation of poverty (cf 31,13). He wants to walk with all the brothers, together on the way, and not putting stones on their path, so that the weak persons could fall. Not even <u>one</u> of them should be scandalised, but on the contrary, respected and appreciated. Comprehension of the little ones inside – and further: outside! This will also promote an atmosphere of kindness amongst each other (cf RB 34) and peace, avoiding destructive murmuring. No-one - or all of the brothers - are worthy of incense!

15 Franciscus, *Laudato si*, 226-231; 158.

16 Cf. A. de Vogüé, *La Règle de Saint Benoît, Commentaire doctrinal et spirituel*, Paris 1977, 228f.

3.4. For today it seems particularly important, that those who on the superficial level are the givers and helpers, do not want to be "incensed", and by this humiliating those who receive. We are more aware that we have to exceed the category of "giving alms" as former centuries and also Benedict in his time said in some texts (4,14; 58,24; 55,9). But he adds to his immediate source some expressions like in 31,9 "with greatest care and solicitude" (cf 53,15), and giving an "answer"(cf 66,1-4), and this means much more than giving. Today as concerns our "preferential option" for the poor, we clarify that it is about solidarity with them. "Laudato si" says in the context of common ownership: "This option entails recognising the implications of the universal destination of the world's goods ... it demands before all else an appreciation of the immense dignity of the poor...". [17]

This brings us to the middle of the chapter 31.

4. 31,9

Of the sick, the children, the guests and the poor he must take care with total commitment, knowing without doubt that he will have to render an account for all these on the day of judgement

4.1 The utmost care for sick, children, guests and poor is formulated in a very strong way. As Benedict will state in 53,15: In the strangers and poor Christ is more particularly received. Also, RB 36 speaks of the greatest care for the sick "before and above all" (36,1). Loving concern for the least members is one of Benedict's chief admonitions to the abbot and officials[18]. It is linked here and in other texts with the responsibility before God[19]. The weak are easily neglected, since they hold no positions of power and cannot easily get a hearing. If someone is caring precisely for these persons, he must have accepted his own dark and weak aspects. Presumably, he only can treat these groups with true compassion if he has experienced himself some poverty, sickness and being a stranger.

4.2 The verse mentions four categories: sick, children, guests and poor. In all these persons, Christ comes to meet the community and its officials in a special way. Benedict says so specifically concerning the sick (36,2-3), strangers and poor (53,15). The cellarer is thus united with Christ; he serves Christ whom he encounters in these persons, and he imitates Christ in his service. Christ is on

17 Franciscus, *Laudato si*, 158.

18 Cf. *RB* 27,1.5.8-9; 36,1-2.6.10; 37,1; 48,24 etc.

19 Cf. *RB* 2,37f; 3,11; 63,3; 64,7; 65,22.

both sides[20]. In this verse also the children are added, probably alluding to the word of Jesus: "Anyone who welcomes one little child like this in my name welcomes me" (Mt 18,5). With this category, the vision to the coming generation is alluded to. Looking at other texts in RB (4,14-16; 66,3-4) we may say that one need not necessarily give them something material every time.

4.3 For all the categories it holds that they will not or cannot follow the timetable, when the cellarer has scheduled hours for receiving requests. They interrupt settled routines and plans. The care for them, and being available to them is a proof, if the cellarer really puts persons first[21]. Unlike his immediate source, Benedict speaks not only about giving things, but about the concern which involves the heart, about the care which arises from love. This attitude can be concretized in as many forms as there are people. It is a consequence of listening and being present, as we see it in the chapter of the doorkeeper (66,1-2). And it can also entail receiving a blessing from the other side (66,3; 53,24).

4.4 This concords with "Laudato si" which talks often about the weak and least in our societies. In our throwaway culture, what is fragile, defenseless, is in danger[22]. Therefore especially all these people need reverence and have to be respected in their basic human dignity. We think also concretely of those who do not respect our schedules, disciplinary methods, or cannot fill out the complicated written request-forms.

In 31,9 Benedict speaks of the weak "vessels" inside and beyond the community. It is logical that he goes on to talk about the material vessels of the monastery.

5. 31,10

of All the utensils of the monastery and the entire property he will regard as sacred vessels of the altar. Nothing he should think to be neglected.

5.1. The cellarer takes care that the vessels, the utensils of the monastery and all the possessions are handled with cleanliness and reverence and are not to be neglected. For today we include Computers, means of communication and tools of the different specialised services, but also our land and our environment. The goods of the monastery could be lacking, although they are given over to qualified persons on whom the abbot can rely (32,1). An insert (2,35f) of the chapter

20 All this Benedict has newly developed in contrast to the RM, which had mentioned the relationship in almsgiving only (16.32-37).

21 Doing business, 145, 211.

22 Nn. 22, 48, 56, 94.

on the abbot lets us see the actual situation in which also RB 31 was written. In order not to be disquieted, if the monastery's possessions are scanty, the abbot "may not plead lack of resources as an excuse", but should recall the word of Scripture: "Seek first the reign of God and his justice, and all else shall be added besides." This passage indicates that the possessions of Benedict's monastery must have been indeed not enough from time to time. With this a new light is shed on 31,10. It is not a matter of sacralising goods by accumulating money and wealth. But in this concrete situation of lacking resources, one should not overlook the faith vision and providence of God, who will grant us the necessary if we set our priorities according to the Gospel (poor and weak), if we act according to the Christian values with the preferential option for the poor (including children, sick, strangers and poor as v. 9 said).

5.2. This is reinforced by the term that follows: *sacred vessels of the altar*. The altar is placed at the heart of the profession in RB 58, and oblation in RB 59. None of the sources of the RB 31 spoke of vessels of the *altar*. When Benedict uses this expression, he points to chalice and paten. They contain the bread and wine which will become Christ's flesh and blood; they will contain the mysterious presence of Christ! The consequence: all things can become recipients of Christ's presence! It is a powerful statement and touches the core of Benedictine spirituality, its Christ-centeredness, and it effects on the whole of creation. Thus, administering the goods is a priestly service, a liturgy. All of us are a holy priesthood (1 Pt 2,9). As stated in Zech 14,20, in the last age, all things will be holy. So also, the entire creation will shine in God's light. The sentence "so that in all things God maybe glorified" is said in the context of selling the monastic products, and it is a core statement of the Benedictine spirituality (57,9). Such orientations are eminently significant in our time.

5.3. Coming back to our chapter (31,9-11), one can certainly say: As at the altar bread and wine, body and blood of Christ, are shared, so the items of daily life should become a bond of love, forming communion among all the members, and especially becoming a bond of love to the sick, the poor, the least who are the special vessels of the Lord. The altar is the centre of this unity. Here new members, brothers of the community are born by their total dedication to Christ, and to the way of life (the term of "brother" is used the first time in this context, - 58,23). Here also, the wider unity of the members of Christ is formed with the poor and guests, the children and the sick. In RB 58 the movement goes from the altar of profession to the feet of the brothers (58,23). It is a gesture, among others, which symbolises the building up of a community by service in the spirit of the washing someone's feet (a very lowly service still in the 6th century).

5.4. As it becomes very clear in the RB, the adoration of Christ in the oratory ("orare" in RB 52,3f) is followed by adoring Christ in the poor (RB 53,7: "Christ be adored"). In this sentence of 31,10 the two dimensions – vertical and horizontal – have their roots so to say in the altar: the vertical towards God, and the horizontal towards creation, towards the brothers and sisters, especially to the poor.

5.5. As usual in the monastic sources, the idea of sacred vessels evokes the prohibition against neglect. Nothing, not even the least item! Everything belonging to God is great. The consequence is clear in this context: things are to be used according to the intention of the Creator. In the entire chapter one senses a responsibility in the care for things and persons before God. In those days it was certainly very necessary to train the monks in cleanliness, order and respect for the common goods. But for Benedict this is not enough, and this verse is closely tied to verse 31,9: to the care for the little ones. As he pays attention to things, to creation, he also does to persons, mainly the least ones. All this is certainly related to the fear of God and wisdom mentioned in 31,1-2.

5.6. In the endangered environment of today, attention is drawn to all the small steps for preserving creation, and sustainability. How imperative is reverent treatment of things, without carelessness! We are responsible for our world now and the coming generations. Benedict wants to educate us to reverence before the seemingly insignificant things and actions of daily life and before the least of the people. Sometimes we neglect this while awaiting great things. "Our way of dealing with the monastic goods reveals our attitude. A violent handling of items expresses the inner disposition of a person. Whoever is attentive to his soul will also show reverence for objects."[23] Equally important is the awareness that everything should benefit the people, especially the weak!

5.7. *House of God* (domus Dei) in 31,19 is not just the monastery church, but the entire monastery area. It belongs to God, God should reign here, one should be able to encounter God. It is characteristic of Benedict that this idea is linked to brotherly love, to peace, joy, tranquility, and especially mutual love and attentiveness, which should radiate to the neighborhood. "Laudato si" speaks of the global "common home" already in its subtitle. The encyclical letter also stresses

23 A. Grün, *Schöpfungsspiritualität*, Münsterschwarzach 1996, 25; see 22f. J. Chittister, *The Rule of Benedict*, New York 1992, 105; B. McGinn, «St. Benedict as the Steward of Creation», *The American Benedictine Review* 39 (1988) 173f.

that the Eucharist is "a source of light and motivation for our concerns for the environment, directing us to be stewards of all creation"[24].

5.8. In the admonition not to neglect anything, to have the greatest care for children ... and poor we could see the concern of sustainability expressed. The monks of today have to live in a way which meets the needs of the present and future generations. They have a special interest in the long term viability of the land and the local ecosystem, especially in the use of local resources, "using ... what is needed, sharing resources with the poor and living a simple lifestyle"[25]. This entails honest discernments of needs and moving toward greater simplicity – seen as greater freedom. Living in this specific place enables a deep relationship to grow with the land. The "humans learn through listening, waiting, acting, they gradually adapt to the rhythm with the seasons of the land"[26]. Their decisions will be made with an understanding of their consequences. I think, this attitude is deeply linked to humility, being "earthed", and to reverence to creation in the sense, that everything can reveal the presence of Christ.

CONCLUSION

Safeguarding the order of creation is closely linked to love of neighbour and the option for the poor.

This chapter RB 31 viewed superficially, would seem to be dealing primarily with material goods, but turns out to be one of the most spiritual chapters of the Rule of Benedict. On the basis of a "poor" monastery, it deals with the poor, the least in the community and all the needy around. – Some guidelines:

- Emphasis on the responsible and reverent use of things
- Simplicity of life style
- Attention to the function of material goods to serve the weak persons in and beyond the community
- Care, responsibility for a just distribution, considering human needs
- A humane and Christian atmosphere in regard to giving and requesting, marked by reverence
- Awareness that all things can mediate God's and Christ's presence

24 FRANCISCUS, *Laudato si*, 236.

25 Cf. A. MCCARTHY: «A Humble Stance: Benedict's Gift to the Cosmos», *The American Benedictine Review* 56 (2005) 63.

26 MCCARTHY: «A Humble Stance: Benedict's Gift to the Cosmos», 65.

- Connection between humility and love to all, especially to the weak and least ones.

If monasteries are in the heart of the Church, then their behaviour will have an influence on a "poor Church" and "the Church of the poor".

Abstract

The purpose of this paper is to elaborate some relevant lines of thought in regard to the main theme, seeing three important situations in chapter 31 on the cellerar, and looking at them in the light of our present situation and more specifically of the encyclical letter of Pope Francis "Laudato si". The administration of goods involves not only material things and creation but also service to people and especially to the least ones. Monasteries develop alternative models of responsible administration of goods, both inside the community and in their environments. The person of the cellarer is crucial to all these questions.

The paper focuses on five main points:

- What will be the answer to unreasonable requests, as they arise in our times?
- What is our answer today if there are reasonable demands, which in our situation we cannot gratify?
- How can one grant help, care, solidarity without asking to be "incensed"?
- How to put into action the utmost care for sick, children, guests and poor? To place people before things?

And what could it entail for us to treat all items of our "common home" (subtitle of "Laudato si) as sacred vessels of the altar? And to be responsible for this "common home" before God?

GRENZZIEHUNG UND GRENZÜBERSCHREITUNG. DIE *REGULA BENEDICTI* IM ANGESICHT DES ÖKONOMISMUS

Manuela Scheiba

EINLEITUNG

Benediktinisches Mönchtum ist nicht jenseits von ökonomischen Gegebenheiten, Erfordernissen und Überlegungen, anvertrauten Gütern, wirtschaftlicher Tätigkeit und «kluger Haushaltung»[1] angesiedelt[2]. Viele Regelpassagen und ihre spezifische Terminologie verdeutlichen das. Die Brüder sind erst dann «wirklich Mönche, wenn sie von der Arbeit ihrer Hände leben»[3], konstatiert Benedikt. Auch vom Verkauf handwerklicher Produkte, von Werkstätten, Mühle und Garten, von Preisgestaltung, Nutznießung, Handel sowie preisgünstigem Einkauf ist in seiner Regel die Rede[4]. Die monastische Gemeinschaft akzeptiert das Vermögen, das ein Mönch vor seiner Profeß oder das die Eltern eines darge-

---

Manuela Scheiba, Benedictine nun in Alexanderdorf (Berlin), professor at the Pontifical Athenaeum St. Anselmo in Rome, specialist in the Rule of St. Benedict.

1 Der Begriff «Ökonomie» geht zurück auf die Regeln, das Gesetz, die Lebensordnung (νόμος) eines Hauses (οἶκος). Er steht für die geordnete Einrichtung und Verwaltung von Haus- und Landwirtschaft, Aufwendungen und Erträgen, die den Unterhalt des Menschen sichern. In der Theologie ist «Ökonomie» (lat. *dispositio*; auch: *dispensatio*) ein heilsgeschichtlicher Grundbegriff. Cf. J. Baumgarten, «Wirtschaft/Wirtschaftsethik IV. 1. zum Begriff der Ökonomie», in *Theologische Realenzyklopädie*, vol. 36, Berlin 2004, 144-145; H. Rabe-U. Dierse, «Ökonomie», in *Historisches Wörterbuch der Philosophie*, vol. 6, Basel 1984, 1149-1162; F. Kambartel, «Ökonomie», in *Enzyklopädie Philosophie und Wissenschaftstheorie*, vol. 2, ed. J. Mittelstraß, Mannheim-Wien-Zürich 1984, 1073-1074.

2 Zu Ökonomie und Mönchtum cf. H.M. Biedermann, «Economia monastica orientale», in *Dizionario degli Istituti di Perfezione*, vol. 3, Edizioni Paoline, Roma 1976, 1012-1020; J. Leclercq, «Economia monastica occidentale», in *ibid.*, 1020-1027; E. Werner, »Visione marxista dell'economia monastica", in *ibid.*, 1027-1031.

3 *RB* 48,8.

4 Cf. *RB* 55,7; 57,4.7; 59,5; 66,6.

brachten Kindes dem Kloster in einer Schenkung (*donatio*) vermachen[5]. Beim Umgang mit Geräten, Werkzeugen, Kleidern und der gesamten Habe (*substantia, res*) des Klosters achtet man auf Ordnung, Sauberkeit, Sorgfalt und Sparsamkeit[6]. Benedikt legt Wert darauf, daß «das Haus Gottes [...] von Weisen und weise verwaltet (*amministrare*)»[7] wird. Der Abt wird darin als «würdiger Verwalter (*dispensator*)»[8] bestellt, nach dessen Anweisung (*dispensatio*) die Mönche mit dem Lebensnotwendigen versorgt werden[9]. Da ihm viel anvertraut (*conmittere*) wird[10], muß der Obere Rechenschaft über seine Verwaltung (*uilicatio*) ablegen[11]. Nach guter Verwaltung (*bene ministrare*) kann der Abt aus dem Mund des Herrn die Verheißung an den guten Knecht im Evangelium hören, daß er ihn zum Verwalter seines ganzen Vermögens machen wird[12]. Im ökonomischen Spannungsfeld von Arbeit, Verdienst des Lebensunterhalts, Besitz, ausreichender Versorgung, Gastfreundschaft und dem Dienst an den Armen und Kranken[13] macht die Benediktsregel die Notwendigkeit einer guten Haushaltung deutlich, die auch in der Bibel eine Rolle spielt[14]. Dabei eröffnet das monastische Programm der Gottsuche einen weiten Horizont, der bis in unsere Gegenwart hinein Distanz, kluge Unterscheidung und Kritik ermöglicht durch einen anderen Blick auf Mensch, Gesellschaft, Wirtschaft und Kultur.

1. ÖKONOMISIERUNG DER HEUTIGEN GESELLSCHAFT

1.1. Ökonomismus als Weltanschauung

Sozialwissenschaftler weisen auf eine zunehmende Ökonomisierung nicht-ökonomischer Teilbereiche in der modernen Gesellschaft hin[15]. Ökonomie

---

5 Cf. *RB* 58,24; 59,5.

6 Cf. *RB* 2,35; 31,10.12-13; 32; 35,8-11; 39,1.3-6; 46,2; 55,9.12-14; 57,6.

7 *RB* 53,22; siehe auch *RB* 53,18.

8 Cf. *RB* 64,5.

9 Cf. *RB* 22,2; 33,5; 41,5; 55,18.

10 Cf. *RB* 2,30.32-33; Lk 12,38.

11 Cf. *RB* 64,7.

12 Cf. *RB* 64,21-22; Mt 24,47. Auch der Cellerar des Klosters, dem im Rahmen seines Amtes die Sorge für Personen und materielle Dinge im Kloster anvertraut ist, wird in ähnlicher Weise an seine Rechenschaftspflicht erinnert und zu einem guten Dienst ermahnt. Cf. *RB* 31,3.8-9.17; 1 Tim 3,13.

13 Cf. *RB* 31,9; 36,10; 53; 55,9; 66,3.

14 Cf. 1 Kor 4,1f; Tit 1,7; 1 Petr 4,10.

15 Cf. U. Schimank-U. Volkmann, «Ökonomisierung der Gesellschaft», in *Handbuch*

bemächtigt sich gewissermaßen des Lebens. Ein «Ökonomismus»[16], der «Ökonomisierung [...] zum Prinzip der praktischen Vernunft erhebt»[17], macht sich breit. Die Organisationslogik des Wirtschaftlichen, die Verabsolutierung der «ökonomische(n) Rationalität (Effizienz) zum obersten Wertgesichtspunkt» führt zu «einer nahezu grenzenlosen Ökonomisierung unserer Lebensformen, der Gesellschaft und der Politik»[18]. Im Rahmen dieser Allgegenwart der Ökonomie, der erdrückenden Übermacht wirtschaftlicher Rationalität und der damit verbundenen «Dominanz ökonomischer Indikatoren in der Selbstwahrnehmung von Gesellschaften»[19] werden Welt und Mensch vor allem aus der Perspektive von Wirtschaft und ökonomischer Verwertbarkeit in den Blick genommen. Betriebswirtschaftliche Zugänge, Wettbewerbs- und Profitlogik, Begriffe wie Wachstum, unternehmerisches Kalkül, Kompetenz, Effizienz oder Performance gewinnen im Zuge der ökonomischen (Um-)Interpretation der gesellschaftlichen Beziehungen und der menschlichen Existenz immer mehr an Gewicht. In diesem ökonomisch verzeichneten Denken wird der Mensch letztlich auf eine Art Konglomerat von Bedürfnissen reduziert, die steuer- und befriedigbar sind. Menschliche Reflexe und sozialen Beziehungen

---

der Wirtschaftssoziologie, ed. A. Maurer, Wiesbaden 2008, 382-393; *Gouvernementalität der Gegenwart. Studien zur Ökonomisierung des Sozialen*, edd. U. Bröckling-S. Krasmann-T. Lemke, Frankfurt am Main 2000; H. ROSA, *Weltbeziehungen im Zeitalter der Beschleunigung. Umrisse einer neuen Gesellschaftskritik*, Berlin 2012, 151-268; P. ULRICH, *Integrative Wirtschaftsethik. Grundlagen einer lebensdienlichen Ökonomie*, Bern-Stuttgart-Wien [4]2008, 101-220.

16 Cf. G. KIRCHGÄSSNER, «Auf der Suche nach dem Gespenst des Ökonomismus. Einige Bemerkungen über Tausch, Märkte und die Ökonomisierung der Lebensverhältnisse», *Analyse und Kritik* 19 (1997) 127-152. Im Zuge einer einseitigen Akzentuierung wirtschaftlicher Faktoren in gesellschaftlichen Entwicklungstheorien – wie beispielsweise im Marxismus als «historischem Ökonomismus» (Antonio Labriola) – werden ökonomische Modelle auf andere gesellschaftswissenschaftliche Bereiche übertragen; cf. S. CREMASCHI, «Economicismo», in *Enciclopedia Filosofica*, vol. 4, Milano 2006, 3208-3209.

17 U. THIELEMANN, «Integrative Wirtschaftsethik als Reflexionsbemühung im Zeitalter der Ökonomisierung», in *Reflexionsfelder integrativer Wirtschaftsethik*, edd. D. Mieth-O.J. Schumann-P. Ulrich (Ethik in den Wissenschaften 16), Tübingen-Basel 2004, 69-102, hier: 96.

18 P. ULRICH, *Zivilisierte Marktwirtschaft. Eine wirtschaftsethische Orientierung*, Bern-Stuttgart-Wien 2010, 34.

19 F. HEIDENREICH, «Ökonomismus – eine Selbstgefährung der Demokratie? Über Legitimation durch Wohlstand», in *Bedrohungen der Demokratie*, edd. A. Brodocz-M. Llanque-G.S. Schaal, Wiesbaden 2008, 370-384, hier: 380; cf. G. KIRCHGÄSSNER, *Homo Oeconomicus*, Mohr Siebeck, Tübingen 1991.

werden in ein ökonomisches Verwertungsmodell überführt, wobei Medien, Moden, Milieus und der jeweils zur allgemeinen Norm hochstilisierte gesellschaftliche *mainstream* eine wichtige Rolle spielen. Diese Tendenz zur ideologischen Verwirtschaftlichung menschlichen Lebens und all seiner Beziehungen in heutigen westlichen Gesellschaften verlockt durch die in Aussicht gestellte Steigerung von Autonomie- und Authentizitätschancen und die Verheißung von Selbstverwirklichung durch materiellen Wohlstand. Nicht wenige Menschen übernehmen heute unkritisch die mit der Durchökonomisierung des ganzen Lebens verbundene ideologische Fremdbestimmung und ökonomistisch verengte Vision menschlicher Existenz.

1.2. Ökonomie und Religion

Christliche (und somit auch monastische) Existenz vollzieht sich nicht indifferent gegenüber den sozial-politischen, wirtschaftlichen und kulturellen Entwicklungen der jeweiligen Zeit. Die Kirche als Ganze ist deshalb herausgefordert, wenn Profitdenken, Wirtschaftssprache, ökonomisches Kalkül und Machbarkeitswahn auf immer mehr Bereiche menschlichen und gesellschaftlichen, ja auch kirchlichen Lebens überzugreifen drohen[20]. In Kirche, Pfarrgemeinden, Ordensgemeinschaften und im Leben des einzelnen Christen kann – wie in anderen Bereichen der Gesellschaft – alles schnell zum «Betrieb» werden. Authentisches christliches Leben hat es jedoch wesentlich mit organischem Wachsen und Reifen zu tun, nicht zuerst mit Planen, Konstruieren, Optimieren

20 Deutliche Worte fand Prof. em. Jürgen Moltmann in seinem Festvortrag zum Auftakt des Studientages der vier kirchenleitenden Organe der ELKB am 31. Mai 2014 im Landeskirchlichen Archiv der ELKB in Nürnberg: «Heute ist wohl an die Stelle der Politisierung aller Verhältnisse durch den totalen Staat die Ökonomisierung aller Verhältnisse durch den totalen Markt getreten. Müssen wir also in den Kirchen effiziente Unternehmensstrukturen aufbauen? [...] Es droht uns nicht eine ideologische Politisierung der Kirche wie durch die Nazis und die Deutschen Christen damals. Es droht uns aber eine nicht minder gefährliche ideologische Ökonomisierung der Kirchen, wie wir sie auch an den deutschen Universitäten erleben. Wie kann Kirche „effektiver" gemacht werden? Wie kann die Zahl der Taufen, Konfirmationen und kirchlichen Amtshandlungen erhöht werden? Wie kann die Kirche auf ihr „Kerngeschäft" verschlankt werden? Wie kann die „Kirche im Angebot" attraktiver werden? Der religiöse „Service" der Kirche an ihren „Kunden" muss verbessert werden. Damit entmündigt man die aktiven Brüder und Schwestern zu passiven „Kunden" und macht aus selbstständigen Gemeinden betreutes Leben in den Kirchen.» Cf. J. Moltmann, *Die Barmer Theologische Erklärung – Ein Bekenntnis?*, http://wort-meldungen.de/?p=7347 (2014), [abgerufen: 17-02-2016].

und Management. Kirche, Christen und Klöster als «Kirche im Kleinen» sind nicht zuletzt deshalb in eine besondere Verantwortung und auf den Prüfstand gerufen, weil Ökonomie und Religion in der Geschichte immer in einem engen Verhältnis zueinander gestanden haben. J. Hörisch wies in seiner Monographie über «Die Theologie der Märkte» treffend darauf hin, daß die «Münzprägung in Tempeln» begonnen habe, noch heute «der Marktplatz neben [...] der Kirche» liege und «Begriffe wie Messe, Erlös, Kredit, Schuldner, Gläubiger, Pekuniäres, Obolos, Moneten, Testament und Offenbarungseid einen ökonomisch-religiösen Doppelsinn» besäßen.[21] Die Frage richtigen oder falschen Wirtschaftens stellt ein wichtiges Thema in biblischen Erzählungen dar[22]. Zeitlichkeit und Schuld sind zentrale Motive sowohl christlichen Handelns als auch der Finanzwirtschaft. Blinder Glaube kann wie irrationale Hoffnung Charakteristikum ökonomischen Handelns sein. Kulturhistorisch gesehen hat der Kapitalismus Denkmuster aus dem Christentum übernommen. Karl Marx sprach einst vom «Fetischcharakter» und den «theologischen Mucken»[23] der Ware. Max Weber untersuchte kausalhistorisch die Genese des westlichen Kapitalismus aus dem Geist der protestantischen Askese[24]. Walter Benjamin entwickelte die These vom «Kapitalismus als Religion»[25]. Das Verhältnis von kapitalistischem Wirtschaftssystem und religiöser Praxis wurde engagiert in der lateinamerikanischen Befreiungstheologie thematisiert[26]. Einige antikapitalistische Bewegungen sowie kommunistisch-diktatorische Regimes treten bis in unsere Zeit mit dem quasi-religiösen Anspruch auf, ein Reich der wirtschaftlich-politischen Gerechtigkeit und des Friedens auf Erden zu errichten.

---

21 J. Hörisch, *Man muss dran glauben. Die Theologie der Märkte*, Wilhelm Fink Verlag, München 2013, 13; cf. *ibid.* auch zum folgenden in diesem Abschnitt.

22 Cf. z.B. Jakob und Joseph (Gen 30,25-31,1; 41,48-57), Händler und Geldwechsler im Tempel (Joh 2,13-16), Weinbergspächter (Mk 12,1-9), anvertraute Talente (Mt 25,14–30) bzw. Minen (Lk 19,12–27), Arbeiter im Weinberg (Mt 20,1-16).

23 K. Marx, *Das Kapital. Kritik der politischen Ökonomie*, vol. 1, Verlag Otto Meissner, Hamburg 1867, 47.

24 Cf. M. Weber, *Die protestantische Ethik und der Geist des Kapitalismus*, Tübingen 1934.

25 Cf. W. Benjamin, «Kapitalismus als Religion [Fragment]», *Walter Benjamin. Gesammelte Schriften*, vol. 6, edd. R. Tiedemann-H. Schweppenhäuser, Frankfurt am Main 1991, 100-102.

26 Cf. G. Collet, «Befreiungstheologie I/II (Historische, geographische, politische Wurzeln/Systematisch-theologisch)», in *Lexikon für Theologie und Kirche*, vol. 2, ed. W. Kasper, Freiburg i. Br. 1994, 130-134; T. Hausmanniger, «Befreiungstheologie III (Theologisch-ethisch)», in *ibid.*, 134-135.

2. WERT ODER WÜRDE DES MENSCHEN?

2.1. ÖKONOMISIERUNG DES HUMANEN

Das «immanenzaffine Credo»[27] heute um sich greifenden ökonomistischen Denkens, ein nicht auf «Erlösung», sondern auf «Erlös»[28] ausgerichtetes Glaubensbekenntnis zum Irdischen, hat Folgen für die Sicht des Menschen und die Konzeption menschlichen Lebens überhaupt. Im Ökonomismus werden zentrale menschliche Werte einer ökonomischen Uminterpretation unterzogen. K.P. Liessmann hat im Zusammenhang mit Überlegungen zum Wert des Menschen darauf hingewiesen, daß der erst seit Mitte des 19. Jahrhunderts in Ethik und Politik gebräuchliche Begriff «Wert» ursprünglich aus dem Bereich der Volkswirtschaftslehre stammt[29]. Er steht zunächst dafür, was Dinge oder Produkte auf dem Markt wert sind, welchen Preis, welchen Geldwert sie besitzen. Der Wertbegriff beinhaltet sowohl ein Moment der Verdinglichung als auch der Subjektivierung. Jeder Wert läßt sich in einem materiellen Äquivalent ausdrücken, und alles, das einen Wert besitzt, kann diesen – in Abhängigkeit vom Markt – ebenso verlieren. Auch der Mensch hat in diesem System einen «Wert», insofern er «Humankapital», Objekt der Wünsche und Interessen anderer ist[30]. Moderne Formen der Sklaverei sowie Kriminalität (z.B. im Kontext von Armutsmigration, Organtransplantation oder Leihmutterschaft) zeugen in besonderer Schärfe von Tendenzen in Richtung auf eine «Ökonomisierung und Kalkülisierung des Humanen», eine «schleichende Diskreditierung des Menschlichen»[31] in unserer Zeit. Im Gegensatz dazu betont die christliche Anthropologie auf der Grundlage der Lehre von der Gottebenbildlichkeit des Menschen (Gen 1,26f; 5,3; 9,6)[32] die unantastbare Würde und die daraus folgende fundamentale Gleichheit aller Menschen[33]. Jeder Mensch besitzt unab-

---

27 SWR2 Essay «Man muss dran glauben. Ein ökonomisch-theologischer Essay. Von Jochen Hörisch, gesendet am 24.09.2012, https://www.swr.de/-/id=10205564/property=download/nid=659852/u9wiwl/swr2-essay-20120924.pdf [abgerufen: 17-02-2016].

28 Cf. Hörisch, *Man muß dran glauben*, 14.

29 Cf. K.P. Liessmann, *Lob der Grenze. Kritik der politischen Unterscheidungskraft*, Wien 2012, 60-73, hier: 63.

30 Cf. Liessmann, *Lob der Grenze*, 61-65.

31 Liessmann, *Lob der Grenze*, 61.

32 Cf. J. Jervell-H. Crouzel, «Bild Gottes I-II», in *Theologische Realenzyklopädie*, vol. 6, edd. G. Krause-G. Müller, Berlin-New York 1980, 491-502.

33 Cf. W. Huber, «Menschenrechte/Menschenwürde», in *Theologische Realenzyklopädie*,

hängig von Geschlecht, Alter oder Herkunft einen absoluten Wert, der nicht an ökonomische Berechnungen oder Marktinteressen gebunden ist – einen Wert, der durch Schwäche, Krankheit, Versagen oder Scheitern, durch die Erfahrung von Grenzen, die wesentlicher Bestandteil menschlicher Existenz sind, nicht gemindert werden kann.

2.2. Zwang zur Selbstoptimierung

Aus der Perspektive der Ökonomismus gesehen, erzeugt die Macht des Marktmechanismus ein Menschenbild im Zeichen grenzenloser Selbstoptimierung. In diesem Zusammenhang gelten die Devise «Selbsterhalt durch Selbststeigerung»[34] sowie der Imperativ des «unternehmerischen Selbst»[35]. Die Unternehmenslogik, sich auf dem Markt zu behaupten, bestimmt vor allem in westlichen Ländern und von dort übergreifend auf andere Staaten immer mehr Bereiche menschlicher Lebensführung[36]. A. Kreutzer hat in seiner «theologische(n) Kritik der überzogenen Leistungsgesellschaft»[37] darauf hingewiesen, daß sich heute nicht wenige Menschen dazu gedrängt fühlen, sich als «Unternehmer und Unternehmerinnen ihrer selbst»[38] zu verstehen und sich nicht nur im Kontext des Berufslebens, sondern in *jeder* Lebenssituation als «unverwechselbar» und «authentisch» zu «vermarkten»[39]. Da der Grad an Unverwechselbarkeit und der Marktwert im gesellschaftlichen Leben immer noch steigerbar sind, beugen sich diese Menschen dem heute oft zu vernehmenden Appell zu Selbstoptimierung und der ständigen Anspannung, «sich nie genug (zu) sein»[40]. In Analo-

vol. 22, ed. G. Müller, Berlin-New York 1992, 577-602.

34 Cf. W. Post, «Finanzkrise», *Orientierung* 73/10 (2009) 109-112, hier: 112.

35 Cf. U. Bröckling, *Das unternehmerische Selbst. Soziologie einer Subjektivierungsform*, Suhrkamp, Frankfurt am Main 2007; Id., «Diktat des Komparativs. Zur Anthropologie des „unternehmerischen Selbst"», in *Anthropologie der Arbeit*, edd. U. Bröckling-E. Horn, Tübingen 2002, 157-173.

36 Die Bezeichnung des Menschen als «Ich-AG» wurde von der «Sprachkritischen Aktion Unwort des Jahres» 2002 zum «Unwort» gekürt, weil es eine «Herabstufung von menschlichen Schicksalen auf ein sprachliches Börsenniveau» impliziere. Cf. http://www.unwortdesjahres.net/index.php?id=34, [abgerufen: 20-02-2016].

37 A. Kreutzer, «Gnade für das „unternehmerische Selbst". Eine theologische Kritik der überzogenen Leistungsgesellschaft», *Stimmen der Zeit* 232/8 (2014) 547-557.

38 Kreutzer, «Gnade für das „unternehmerische Selbst"», 548 [unter Bezugnahme auf U. Bröckling (Anm. 35)].

39 Kreutzer, «Gnade für das „unternehmerische Selbst"», 549.

40 Kreutzer, «Gnade für das „unternehmerische Selbst"».

gie zu den «Marktmechanismen der Präsentation» und den «Grundlagen der Werbestrategie» preisen Menschen ihr «Hochglanz-Ich [...] auf dem Markt des Lebens»[41] an. Sie verbergen oder verleugnen oft jedoch Grenzen und Aspekte ihres Lebens oder ihrer Person, die solchen Optimierungszwängen nicht entsprechen. Der Leistungs- und Wettbewerbsdruck der äußeren Verhältnisse, das Diktat des sogenannten gesellschaftlichen *mainstream*, die Angst vor dem Nicht-mithalten-Können und dem beruflichen oder privatem Scheitern verführen nicht wenige Menschen zur Selbstausbeutung und zur «Überdehnung des menschlichen Maßes»[42]. Selbstmanagement- und Ratgeberliteratur boomen.

2.3. Bildung als Markt

Im Zuge der Ökonomisierung unterschiedlicher Bereiche menschlichen Lebens wird heute mitunter – und durchaus verräterisch! – von «Bildungsmarkt» bzw. «Wissenschaftsbetrieb» gesprochen. Der Bildungssektor selbst versteht sich gewissermaßen als Markt[43]. Oberste Priorität hat in einer solchen Logik die ökonomische Verwertbarkeit von Bildung[44]. Es gibt heute Universitäten, die auf das betriebswirtschaftliche Effizienzprinzip getrimmt werden und Gefahr laufen, zumeist Schmalspur-Absolventen für den Arbeitsmarkt zu «produzieren». Viele Studenten sind im Gegenzug dazu angehalten, ihr Studium möglichst schnell abzuschließen. Schulische und universitäre Wissensaneignung ähnelt mitunter einer Art «Lernstoff-Bulimie (Reinwürgen – Rauskotzen – Vergessen)»[45]. Wenige haben die Zeit, Lehrveranstaltungen zu besuchen, die das eigene Fach nur am Rande betreffen. Aufgrund von Leistungsdruck und Prüfungsstreß geben nicht wenige Studierende an, mit Medikamenten sowohl physische als auch psychische Grenzen hinauszuschieben und ihrer Konzentrationsfähigkeit nachzuhelfen[46].

---

41 Kreutzer, «Gnade für das „unternehmerische Selbst"», 550; cf. auch zum folgenden.

42 Cf. Liessmann, *Lob der Grenze*, 53.

43 Cf. J. Krautz, *Ware Bildung. Schule und Universität unter dem Diktat der Ökonomie*, Kreuzlingen-München 2007; T. Philipp, «Bildung und Menschenbild», *Stimmen der Zeit* 233/6 (2015) 375-384.

44 Cf. T. Höhne, «Ökonomisierung von Bildung», in *Handbuch Bildungs- und Erziehungssoziologie*, edd. U. Bauer-U.H. Bittlingmayer-A. Scherr, Wiesbaden 2012, 797-812; G. Kruip, «In der Menschenwürde begründet», *Herder Korrespondenz* 63/3 (2009) 145-149.

45 E. Hurth, «Auf dem Weg zur Verblödung?», *Herder Korrespondenz* 64/1 (2010) 43-48, hier: 48; cf. S. Orth, «Lernziel Bildung», *Herder Korrespondenz* 62/3 (2008) 109-111.

46 Cf. S. Becker-J. Gerding-M. Popp, «Generation Ich», *Der Spiegel* 44 (2014) 44-46.

An einigen Universitäten haben sich sogenannte «Karriere Center» etabliert, die auf ihre Weise deutlich machen, daß Bildung[47] heute oft nicht zweckfrei ist, sondern sich in den engen Grenzen ökonomisch begründeter Vorgaben bewegt[48]. Sie vermag auf diese Weise kaum noch, den Menschen als Ganzen zu formen und in ihm «Sinn und Geschmack fürs Unendliche»[49] zu wecken.

2.4. Mediatisierung von Lebensformen oder Ökonomie der Aufmerksamkeit

Eine vom Ökonomismus geprägte Sicht des Menschen und seiner Lebenswelt hat auch Auswirkungen auf die Beziehungen von Menschen zueinander. Auf dem Hintergrund eines Wettbewerbs um das begehrte, aber als begrenzt angesehene Gut von Aufmerksamkeit und Anerkennung[50], prägen Casting-Kultur und ein sensationistisch deformierter Medienbetrieb mehr und mehr Bereiche heutiger Gesellschaften. E. Hurth[51] hat in diesem Zusammenhang deutlich gemacht, daß in der modernen Leistungsgesellschaft mediales Ansehen nicht nur bei Menschen, die erwerbsunfähig oder auf Sozialleistungen angewiesen sind, als reale Möglichkeit zur «Identitätsvergewisserung»[52] und zur Aufwertung des eigenen Selbst gilt. Mediale Beachtung stellt gewissermaßen einen Kapitalfaktor dar: Wer in den Medien ist, kann aus der so gewonnenen Aufmerksamkeit bares Geld schlagen. Die mediale Selbstdarstellung unterliegt jedoch den «Gesetzen von Show-Inszenierungen»[53]. So kann es vorkommen, daß sich Menschen plötzlich vor dem «Tribunal der Medien» wiederfinden und «im Haifischbecken ihre Haut bestmöglich präsentieren und vermarkten» müssen.

---

47 Zur Weite des Bildungsbegriffs in Geschichte und Gegenwart cf. R. Lennert *et al.*, «Bildung», in *Theologische Realenzyklopädie*, vol. 6, edd. G. Krause-G. Müller, Berlin-New York 1980, 569-635.

48 Cf. J. Overhoff, *Vom Glück, lernen zu dürfen. Für eine zweckfreie Bildung*, Stuttgart 2009, 9-19.

49 Cf. F.D.E. Schleiermacher, «*Über die Religion. Reden an die Gebildeten unter ihren Verächtern (1799)*», *Kritische Gesamtausgabe*, vol.1/2: *Schriften aus der Berliner Zeit* 1769-1799, ed. G. Meckenstock, Berlin-New York 1999, 212.

50 Cf. G. Franck, Ökonomie der Aufmerksamkeit. Ein Entwurf, Carl Hanser Verlag, München 1998; J. Bernardy, *Aufmerksamkeit als Kapital. Formen des mentalen Kapitalismus*, Marburg 2014.

51 Cf. zum folgenden in diesem Abschnitt: E. Hurth, «Träume vom Ruhm. Was hinter Casting-Shows steckt», *Herder Korrespondenz* 67/4 (2013) 209-213.

52 Hurth, «Träume vom Ruhm», 210.

53 Hurth, «Träume vom Ruhm», 211; auch die folgenden Zitate.

In der heute stark von Individualismus, Anonymisierung und Bindungslosigkeit gekennzeichneten Gesellschaft verwischen sich somit die «Grenzen zwischen Privatem und Öffentlichem». Menschen tauschen auf dem medialen Markt der Möglichkeiten «Intimität gegen Publizität». «Der gecastete Mensch gehört zur Produktpalette einer schier endlosen Wertschöpfungskette, in der sich Wert des Menschen an dem bemißt, was man von ihm verwerten kann»[54].

2.5. Selbstbehauptung und Selbstdurchsetzung

Ein im Zuge des Ökonomismus verengter Blick auf den Menschen und die menschliche Gesellschaft knüpft häufig an den menschlichen Urinstinkt zur Selbstbehauptung und Selbstdurchsetzung an[55]. Es gehört nicht erst zur Unternehmens- und Marktlogik, sondern bereits zu den anthropologischen Grundkonstanten, daß sich der Mensch beständig Fremdes (z.B. Nahrung, Kleidung) aneignen muß, anderes Leben braucht, um selbst existieren zu können. Schon in der biblischen Paradieserzählung sind damit der Verdacht und die Angst verbunden, zu kurz zu kommen[56]. Nahrungs- und Kopulationskonkurrenz prägen somit die Entwicklungsgeschichte der Menschheit. Entwicklungspsychologen haben herausgefunden, daß bereits bei spielenden Kindern die menschliche Neigung sichtbar wird, die Sphäre der eigenen Selbstbehauptung immer weiter auszudehnen, das eigene «Ich» auf Kosten des «Du» durchzusetzen[57]. K.P. Liessmann[58] hat darauf hingewiesen, daß im gesamtgesellschaftlichen Rahmen jedoch Recht und Gesetz einer schrankenlosen menschlichen Selbstbehauptung und -durchsetzung in verschiedenen Bereichen des Lebens Grenzen setzen. Menschlichen Handlungsoptionen werden eingeschränkt, um die Lebensmöglichkeiten anderer Menschen zu schützen. Politische, ökonomische und moralische Grenzen besaßen und besitzen noch immer eine unentbehrliche humane Schutzfunktion. Deshalb mußten sie in der Geschichte nicht nur markiert und

---

54 Hurth, «Träume vom Ruhm», 506.

55 Cf. auch zum folgenden: H.-B. Gerl-Falkowitz, *Verzeihung des Unverzeihlichen? Ausflüge in Landschaften der Schuld und der Vergebung*, Wien-Graz-Klagenfurt 2008, 74-76.

56 Cf. Gen 3.

57 Cf. H. Mayer-P. Heim-H. Scheithauer, *Papilio – Ein Programm für Kindergärten zur Primärprävention von Verhaltensproblemen und zur Förderung sozial-emotionaler Kompetenz. Ein Beitrag zur Sucht- und Gewaltprävention. Theorie und Grundlagen*, Augsburg [3]2012.

58 Cf. zum folgenden: Liessmann, *Lob der Grenze*, 38-39.

festgelegt, sondern oft auch erkämpft und ausgehandelt werden. Gerade schwache Menschen, Minderheiten, Machtlose sind es, die Grenzen brauchen.

2.6. Nie genug?!

Menschen, die sich dem Ökonomismus-Diktat eines «Immer mehr», «Immer schneller», «Immer raffinierter»[59] beugen – sei es bezüglich «konsumierter Güter, genutzter Medien [oder] wahrgenommener Termine»[60] – laufen Gefahr, die Fähigkeit zu verlieren, Grenzen wahrzunehmen, zu setzen und zu akzeptieren. Im Gegenzug dazu mehren sich jedoch in heutigen Gesellschaften Stimmen, die auf die Notwendigkeit einer «Kultur der Genügsamkeit» und einer «Ökonomie des „Genug für alle"»[61] hinweisen und in Wirtschaft, Politik sowie im sozialen Miteinander das Bewußtsein stärken, das dem «Genug» dient.

2.7. Arbeit als Lebensausdruck schlechthin

Die Betrachtung des gesellschaftlichen Lebens unter vornehmlich ökonomischen Gesichtspunkten verleitet zur Preisgabe einer wichtigen Errungenschaft der Moderne: Die Grenzziehung zwischen Arbeits- und Freizeit wird aufgegeben. Es gibt Menschen, die nicht nur immer mehr arbeiten; Arbeit wird für sie geradezu zum «Ausdruck für Lebenstätigkeit schlechthin»[62], zum Wertmaßstab und zum Rechtfertigungskriterium aller menschlichen Tätigkeiten. In der Logik des Ökonomismus gilt als sinnvoll nur das, was Menschen vor sich oder anderen als «Arbeit» deklarieren können: nicht nur Erwerbstätigkeit, sondern beispielsweise auch Beziehungs-, Erziehungs-, Bildungs-, Betreuungs-, Versorgungs-, Erinnerungs-, Körper-, Regenerationsarbeit etc. Muße oder auch anderes menschliches Tun, das sich nicht als «Arbeit» ausweisen läßt, erscheinen leicht als suspekt oder erzeugen ein schlechtes Gewissen. Ein ökonomisch verengter Blick auf verschiedene Bereiche der menschlichen Gesellschaft kann zu Grenzverschiebungen und -verletzungen führen, die nicht lebensdienlich, sondern inhuman sind und Menschen physisch und psychisch krank machen können.

---

59 A. Riedlsperger, «Für eine Kultur der Genügsamkeit», *Stimmen der Zeit* 231/8 (2013) 505-506, hier: 505.

60 Riedlsperger, «Für eine Kultur der Genügsamkeit».

61 Riedlsperger, «Für eine Kultur der Genügsamkeit».

62 Cf. auch zum folgenden: Liessmann, *Lob der Grenze*, 161-168.

2.8. Arme unter Generalverdacht

Wo immer Menschen meinen, sich über ihre «Arbeit» definieren zu müssen, werden Geld und (beruflicher) Erfolg gewissermaßen zu «Sakramenten» gelingenden Lebens. Armut wird im Kontext einer erwerbsarbeitszentrierten Gesellschaftslogik zum Stigma[63]. Es gibt Fälle von Eltern und Kindern, die bereits im Schulalter ihr Nicht-Mithalten, Sich-nicht-Leistenkönnen schamhaft vor Nachbarn und Mitschülern verbergen[64]. Wo Erfolg einzig der ureigenen, persönlichen Leistung des Menschen zugeschrieben wird, stehen Arme leicht unter Generalverdacht. Menschen, die am Leistungsideal scheitern, einen sogenannten «Migrationshintergrund» haben, krank, alt oder «behindert» sind, ihren Arbeitsplatz verlieren etc., gelten in einer vom Ökonomismus geprägten Sicht des Menschen gleichsam als nicht mehr oder nicht voll gesellschaftsfähig. Sie erfahren Formen von Ausgrenzung und Teilhabeverweigerung auf verschiedenen Ebenen des gesellschaftlichen Lebens[65].

2.9. Plädoyer für Endlichkeit und Vollendung – Lob der Grenze

2.9.1. Grenze als Gestaltungsprinzip

Das Gestaltungsprinzip der Grenzsetzung und die Fähigkeit, mit Grenzen umgehen zu können, sind wesentliche Bestandteile aller menschlich-schöpferischen Lebensvollzüge. Menschen müssen unterscheiden, bestimmen, festlegen, ausschließen etc. Das erfordert nicht nur den Mut zur Form, sondern auch die Einsicht, daß Grenzen notwendig und lebensfördernd sind[66]. Charakteristisch für die Ideologie des Ökonomismus sind die Furcht vor Grenzen, vor allem Begrenzten sowie der starke Impuls, Grenzen zu ignorieren, aufzuheben, zu beseitigen, zu überschreiten oder zumindest hinauszuschieben. «Turbokapi-

63 Cf. S.U. Neumann, «Anstößige Armut», *Christ in der Gegenwart* 66/42 (2014) 475.

64 Cf. *Meine Familie ist arm. Wie Kinder im Grundschulalter Armut erleben und bewältigen*, ed. K.A. Chassé-M. Zander-K. Rasch, Wiesbaden ³2007.

65 Cf. S. Sittenthaler-E. Jonas, «Der Schmerz der sozialen Ausgrenzung», in *Armut und Wissen. Reproduktion und Linderung von Armut in Schule und Wissenschaft*, edd. H.P. Gaisbauer-E. Kapferer-A. Koch-C. Sedmak, VS Springer, Wiesbaden 2013, 271-288; U. Becker, *Die Inklusionslüge. Behinderung im flexiblen Kapitalismus*, Bielefeld 2015, 69-81.86-119. *Handbuch Armut und Soziale Ausgrenzung*, edd. E.-U. Huster-J. Boeckh-H. Mogge-Grotjahn, Wiesbaden ²2012.

66 Cf. O.-P. Hessel, «Endlich leben», *Christ in der Gegenwart* 57/27 (2005) 221-222.

talismus», «Turboschulen», «Enhancement» (die physische und psychische «Verbesserung» des Menschen) und der «Verlust von Grenzkontrollen»[67] im weitesten Sinn sind Fälle von «schlechter Unendlichkeit» in Teilen der heutigen Gesellschaft. K.P. Liessmann weist zu Recht darauf hin, daß «überall dort, wo Grenzen verschwinden, [...] neue, andere Grenzen, die über Inklusion und Exklusion entscheiden»[68], entstehen.

2.9.2. Befreiende Grenzöffnung angesichts von Tendenzen zu einer gnadenlosen Leistungsgesellschaft

Eine vom Ökonomismus geprägte Konzeption des Menschen und des menschlichen Lebens insgesamt mündet in die «Pathologien»[69] einer überfordernden, letztlich lebensmindernden Leistungsgesellschaft sowie in die Ideologien der Machbarkeit mit ihrem Diktat der Selbstermächtigung, Selbstschöpfung und Selbstoptimierung. Das «Identitätsangebot christlicher Anthropologie»[70] und das ihm innwohnende Humanisierungspotential stellt ein wichtiges Korrektiv angesichts solcher Tendenzen in der heutigen Gesellschaft dar. Das christliche Menschenbild hält modernen Selbstüberforderungszwängen und Versagensängsten, in denen nicht wenige Zeitgenossen gefangen sind, die unantastbare menschliche Würde entgegen, die der nach Gottes Bild geschaffene Mensch besitzt, sowie die damit ebenfalls verbundene geschöpfliche Grenze. In der christlichen Selbstdeutung als von Gott geschaffenes, geliebtes, «begnadetes» Geschöpf nimmt der Mensch seine Identität vor allem im Kontext von Gabe, Be-Gabung und Geschenk wahr. Das alte christliche Leitwort «Gnade» für die Beziehung zwischen Gott, dem Schöpfer, und dem Menschen als sein Geschöpf impliziert den Vorrang eines «geschenkten Selbst» und einer freien, liebenden Zuwendung und Bejahung. Das humanisierende Potential der christlichen Gnadentheologie besteht in einem alternativen Identitätskonzept: im Bewußtsein eines vorgängigen, vorrangigen und bleibenden Angenommen-Seins des Menschen durch Gott. Im Glauben an dieses vorbehaltlose Akzeptiertsein können Menschen lernen, ihre eigenen Grenzen anzunehmen, ohne jedoch auf diese sklavisch festgelegt zu sein.

---

67 Liessmann, *Lob der Grenze*, 36.

68 Liessmann, *Lob der Grenze*.

69 Kreutzer, «Gnade für das „unternehmerische Selbst"», 547 [unter Bezugnahme auf *Pathologien des Sozialen. Die Aufgaben der Sozialphilosophie*, ed. A. Honneth (Philosophie der Gegenwart, vol. 12247), Frankfurt am Main 1994].

70 Kreutzer, «Gnade für das „unternehmerische Selbst"», 552; cf. zum folgenden: *ibid.*, 552-554.

3. ZUM HUMANISIERUNGSPOTENTIAL DER *REGULA BENEDICTI* (RB) – EINIGE IMPULSE

Die Benediktsregel weist auf dem sie prägenden Hintergrund christlicher Taufspiritualität einen Weg zu erfülltem, vollendetem Menschsein jenseits ökonomistisch verengter Lebensauffassungen. Dabei kommt es sowohl zu Grenzziehungen als auch zu Grenzüberschreitungen.

3.1. Leben unter Führung des Evangeliums – Die Benediktsregel als Grenzziehung

Der Begriff «Regel/*regula*» bezeichnet eine Festlegung, Richtlinie, Richtschnur, eine Vorgabe. Er steht für eine Ordnung, eine Norm, eine Schiene, die ein Abweichen ausschließen möchte[71]. In antiken Wurfmaschinen meint *regula* das Leitsystem, das die Geschosse, die beim Start eine Grundorientierung bekommen haben, auf der Zielbahn halten soll[72].

Eine *regula* ist so immer auch Grenzziehung, ein Hinweis auf Differenzen, Unterschiede zum Umfeld. Das Unterscheidende eines Lebens nach der *Regula Benedicti* ist, daß es ein «Leben unter der Führung des Evangeliums»[73] sein will. Menschen grenzen sich von dem ab, was «man», was der sogenannte gesellschaftliche «*mainstream*», macht, weil sie die Wege gehen wollen, die der Herr ihnen zeigt[74].

Zudem weist das Leben «im Kloster [...] unter Regel und Abt»[75] allen Bereichen menschlichen Lebens Grenzen zu. Tagesablauf, Usanzen, hausinterne Festlegungen und Traditionen begrenzen und bestimmen über Raum, Zeit sowie Art und Weise des Ablaufs vieler alltäglicher Lebensvollzüge, z.B. Arbeit, Ruhe, Gespräch und Austausch, Mahlzeiten, die Ausübung von Autorität und Verantwortung[76].

---

71 Cf. «Regel», in *Etymologisches Wörterbuch des Deutschen Q-Z*, ed. W. Pfeifer *et al.*, Berlin 1989, 1393-1394; «regula», in *Ausführliches lateinisch-deutsches Handwörterbuch*, vol. 2, ed. K.E. Georges, Darmstadt 1995, 2285.

72 Cf. M. Casey, «In Eintracht Gott dienen. Ordnung im Verständnis des heiligen Benedikt», *Erbe und Auftrag* 85 (2009) 126-142, hier: 135.

73 *RB* Prol 21.

74 Cf. *RB* Prol 20.

75 *RB* 1,2.

76 Cf. M.-G. Lepori, «Die modernen Kommunikationsmittel und das monastische Leben», *Cistercienser Chronik* 118/2 (2011) 204-213, hier: 208.

3.2. Die Grenzziehung des Anfangs

Der *nouiter ueniens*[77], der an die Klosterpforte klopft, ist auf Distanz zu seiner bisherigen Lebensweise gegangen. Er hat – in der Antwort auf einen Ruf[78] – die Initiative ergriffen und möchte einen neuen Anfang, ein *initium,* wagen. Er stellt mit dieser Ent-scheidung das Eigene gegen das Vorgegebene, Vorangegangene, setzt nicht nur einfach fort, was seine Vorfahren begonnen haben, sondern geht auf Distanz, um selbst etwas zu beginnen, sich neu zu de-finieren[79]. Wer immer einen Unterschied macht, zieht eine Grenze. Der Anfang im klösterlichen Leben setzt eine Grenze. Jetzt ist es nicht mehr so, wie es vorher war. Das kategoriale Ziehen einer Grenze bedeutet noch keine Wertung[80]. Auf der anderen Seite jedoch setzt ein Klostereintritt einen Grundsatz frühchristlicher Taufspiritualität um[81]: «Sich dem Treiben der Welt entziehen (*saeculi actibus se facere alienum*)»[82]. Dahinter steht keine Miß- oder Verachtung der Welt, wohl aber ein Wahrnehmen der Differenz zwischen der eigenen Taufverpflichtung und dem, was «man» tut, was Menschen in einer Gesellschaft umtreibt, die den Bezug zur Transzendenz und zu Gott weithin verloren hat. Der Mönch möchte einer selbstreferentiellen, innerweltlichen Betriebsamkeit Widerstand leisten, Nein-Sagen lernen (Max Scheler)[83]. Dieses Sich-fremd-Machen (*se facere alienum*) meint ein Loslassen, ein Verzichten[84]. Dabei entsagt der Mönch wie jeder Getaufte nicht der Welt als guter Schöpfung Gottes, sondern den *saecularia desideria*, durch die Menschen versucht sein können, sich mehr oder weniger auf ein Bündel von (ökonomisch befriedigbaren) Bedürfnissen zu reduzieren. Christen, die nach der Benediktsregel leben, wollen sich – biblisch gesprochen – «von der Gottlosigkeit und den irdischen Begierden lossagen und besonnen, gerecht und fromm in dieser Welt leben»[85]. Diese Lossagung knüpft an

77 *RB* 58,1.
78 Cf. *RB* Prol 1-3.15-16.
79 Cf. Liessmann, *Lob der Grenze*, 17-18.
80 Cf. Liessmann, *Lob der Grenze*, 29f.
81 Cf. zum folgenden: M. Puzicha, «Klausur und Internet. Über die Grenzziehung zwischen Kloster und Welt», *Monastische Informationen* 147 (2011) 9-14, hier: 10.
82 *RB* 4,20.
83 Cf. M. Scheler, «Die Stellung des Menschen im Kosmos» [zuerst 1928], *Gesammelte Werke*, vol. 9, ed. M.S. Frings, Bern-München 1976, 7-71, v.a. 44-45.
84 Im Sinne von Lk 14,33: «Darum kann keiner von euch mein Jünger sein, wenn er nicht auf seinen ganzen Besitz *verzichtet*» (Hervorhebung von mir).
85 Cf. Tit 2,12.

das monastische Programmwort «Fliehe» der Wüstenväter[86] an, das in seiner entschiedenen Grenzziehung paradoxerweise einen neuen Freiraum eröffnete[87].

3.3. Die Grenzziehung durch Klausur und Sammlung

Der Anfang im klösterlichen Leben als Grenzziehung und Zeichen der Differenz hat eine räumliche Komponente – es ist die Grenze selbst: wer ein Kloster betritt, weiß, daß sich nun ein anderer Raum mit anderen Gesetzen auftut[88]. Der Klausurmauer, die seit den Anfängen des Mönchtums Teil seines Selbstverständnisses ist, kommt nicht nur eine Schutzfunktion zu. Sie markiert auch eine ideelle Grenze, einen Ort der Transzendenz inmitten der profanen Welt, einen Lebensraum, in dem himmlisches Leben im Irdischen aufscheint[89]. Im Unterschied zur *Regula Magistri*[90] geht es Benedikt jedoch nicht um die Schaffung einer in sich geschlossenen, selbstgenügsamen «Parallelgesellschaft». Die Klausurmauer ist und bleibt durchlässig. Die ständige Präsenz des Pförtners[91], der den ankommenden Menschen (das im Kloster offenbar nicht «ökonomisch» begrenzte Gut der) Aufmerksamkeit schenkt, ihnen jederzeit öffnet, zuhört und antwortet, ist Programm. Auch wenn die *Regula Benedicti* damit rechnet, daß ein Armer vor den Toren des Klosters «schreit»[92], muß man in der Regel nicht lärmen[93] – oder in heute vertrauten Kategorien: Marktgeschrei, Medienrummel oder wirkungsvolle Selbstinszenierung betreiben –, um in Benedikts Kloster Gehör und Aufmerksamkeit zu finden[94]. Die klösterliche Atmosphäre gesammelten Schweigens fördert nicht nur das Gebet und vertieft

---

86 Cf. AP Arsenios 2.

87 Cf. M. Puzicha, «*Sich dem Treiben der Welt entziehen* (*RB* 4,20)», *Monastische Informationen* 79 (1994) 14-18.

88 Cf. Liessmann, *Lob der Grenze*, 25.

89 Cf. Puzicha, «Klausur und Internet», 9.

90 Cf. die Sicht der Gemeinschaft am Ende der Regel: RM 95,22-23.

91 Cf. *RB* 66,2.4.

92 *RB* 66,3: *pauper clamauerit*.

93 Für jeden Mönch gilt: *non sit clamosus in uoce* (*RB* 7,60). Zu Lärm als einer Art «Herrschaftsanspruch» cf. Liessmann, *Lob der Grenze*, 150-159.

94 Diese Haltung des Hörens und der gesammelten Aufmerksamkeit muß jedoch von Mönchen und Nonnen stets neu eingeübt werden. Sie ist keine einmal erworbene und dann unverlierbare Haltung. Benedikt erinnert seine Mönche daran, täglich den Ruf Gottes zu hören, seinen Anspruch durch das Wort der Hl. Schrift zu vernehmen, das eigene Herz nicht zu verhärten, sondern sich Gott zur Verfügung zu stellen (cf. *RB* Prol 9f.14; *RB* 7,1).

die Gottesbeziehung der Mönche. Sie ermöglicht zugleich Rücksichtnahme[95] und aufmerksame Sorge[96] füreinander[97]. Diese innerklösterliche Grundhaltung hat dann auch Auswirkungen auf den Umgang mit den Menschen jenseits der Klausurgrenzen, die mit ihren unterschiedlichen Anliegen zum Kloster kommen. Benedikts Mönche nehmen sich Zeit für den Gast, kommen ihm entgegen, laden ihn zum Gebet ein. Anschließend widmet sich ihm der Obere oder ein beauftragter Bruder und schenkt ihm Aufmerksamkeit[98]. Gäste können an wesentlichen Lebensvollzügen (Gebet und Mahl) innerhalb der Klausurmauern teilhaben[99]. Dennoch bleibt eine nichtmaterielle Grenzziehung bestehen, die sich aus dem monastischen Proprium und der Priorität der monastischen *conuersatio morum*[100] ergibt: Schweigen, rechtes Wort, Antwort geben können, ohne geschwätzig zu werden, verantwortungsvolle Gestaltung von Außenkontakten, Widerstand gegen Ablenkung und Neugier, Beibehaltung des einfachen monastischen Lebensstiles, Vorrang des Gottesdienstes[101].

In bezug auf die Mönche selbst zielt der begrenzte klösterliche Lebensraum mit seinen sichtbaren und unsichtbaren Klausurmarkierungen nicht auf eine Einengung ihres menschlichen Lebens. Monastische Klausur[102] erschöpft sich nicht in kirchenrechtlichen Bestimmungen oder der Aufforderung, «nicht draußen herumzulaufen»[103]. Sie ermöglicht und fördert Konzentration und Intensität menschlichen Lebens angesichts der Versuchung zum *foris uagare*, zu einem Sich-Treiben-Lassen, das auf vielen Ebenen menschlicher Existenz durchbrechen kann. Benediktinische Mönche und Nonnen, die sich vorbehaltlos dazu entschieden haben, «in den Hürden des Herrn eingeschlossen»[104] zu sein, bejahen im Gehorsam die diesen Hürden eigenen Grenzen, die sich von ihren persönlichen Grenzvorstellungen unterscheiden können. Das Ja zu den

95 Cf. *RB* 48,5; 52,2-3.

96 Cf. *RB* 38,6-7; 53,6f.

97 Cf. A. Böckmann, *Geeint in Christus. Exegetischer Kommentar zur Regel Benedikts, Teil 2: Kapitel 8 bis 51*, St. Ottilien 2013, 441f; M. Scheiba, «„Prinzip Sorgfalt". Ein Grundsatz Benedikts für den Umgang mit sich selbst, den Mitmenschen und den Gütern», *Erbe und Auftrag* 88/1 (2012) 7-17, hier: 10f.14.

98 Cf. *RB* 53,8.

99 Cf. z.B. *RB* 53,8-14.24; *RB* 56.

100 *RB* 58,17.

101 Cf. *RB* 4,51-53; 7,56.60; 43,1-3; 48,18; 53,11.23-24; 66,1; 67,4; Puzicha, «Klausur und Internet», 12.

102 Cf. zum folgenden: Puzicha, «Klausur und Internet», 10f.

103 *RB* 66,7.

104 *RB* 1,8.

claustra monasterii und zur Beständigkeit in der *congregatio*[105] erfordert eine entschiedene Absage an eine unverbindliche, jederzeit aufkündbare Betriebsamkeit, ein von wechselnden Launen Getriebensein, ein Nicht-bleiben-Können, das sich alle irdischen Möglichkeiten offenzuhalten sucht[106]. In der gesammelten Konzentration des monastischen Lebens, jenseits von oberflächlicher Ablenkung und Zerstreuung, kann wieder der «Geschmack am Unendlichen» hervorbrechen, der keinem immanenzaffinen Credo verpflichtet ist, sondern in Menschen die Sehnsucht weckt, das zu erlangen, was innerweltlich vergeblich gesucht wird, nämlich «was kein Auge gesehen und kein Ohr gehört hat, was aber Gott denen bereitet hat, die ihn lieben»[107].

3.4. Grundpfeiler benediktinischen Gemeinschaftslebens: Gebet – Arbeit – lectio

3.4.1. Strukturierung des Tages als Grenzziehung

Klöster sind keine Nicht-Orte[108], keine vereinheitlichten Räume, die sich als Markenzeichen des Ökonomismus in vielen Teilen der Welt gleichen. Anders als in den homogenen Zeit-Räumen einer ökonomisierten Gesellschaft zeigt der klösterliche Raum keine Tendenz zur Vereinheitlichung. Er birgt heilige Räume und Zeiten: Eingeräumtes, Be- und Abgegrenztes, Geheimnis, Anfang und Ende, Tag und Nacht, Alltag und Fest[109], Schweigen und Wort, Arbeit und Ruhe, Einsamkeit und Gemeinschaft. Bestimmten Zeiten sind bestimmte Räume zugeordnet – Oratorium, Refektorium, Dormitorium, Zelle der Novizen, Garten und Werkstätten, Küche, Pforte und Gästehaus. Die klösterliche Tagesordnung mit ihrem Wechsel von Arbeit, *lectio* und Stundenliturgie[110] ist gewissermaßen ein «Freund des Mönchs». Sie hilft ihm, heilsame Grenzen zu ziehen, sich ständig in Raum und Zeit von allem zu lösen, was in seinem Leben zum Gegenstand von Abhängigkeit und (Selbst-)Ausbeutung werden könnte[111]. Die Benediktsregel legt Wert darauf, daß die Mönche vor dem nächtlichen Gebet genügend

105 Cf. *RB* 4,78.

106 Cf. *RB* 1,11; 4,20.78; 67,7.

107 1 Kor 2,9; *RB* 4,77.

108 Cf. M. Scheiba, «Virtuelle Welten und Bodenständigkeit. Eine benediktinische Standortbestimmung», *Erbe und Auftrag* 90/2 (2014) 142-151.

109 Cf. M. Scheiba, «Alltag und Fest. Zum Umgang mit der Zeit in der Benediktsregel», *Erbe und Auftrag* 85/2 (2009) 143-152.

110 Cf. *RB* 48.

111 Cf. Lepori, «Die modernen Kommunikationsmittel», 208.

Zeit zur Ruhe und Verdauung (des Abendessens) haben[112]. Die Zeit für die Erledigung der notwendigen Arbeit ist begrenzt durch Zeiten für Lesung, Gebet/Liturgie, gemeinsame Mahlzeiten und Schlaf. Arbeit ist für Benedikts Mönche nicht Lebensausdruck schlechthin. Sie wird jedoch wertgeschätzt, erhält einen privilegierten Platz im Tagesplan und findet zu den für die Brüder günstigsten Zeiten statt: im Sommer in den kühleren Morgen- und Abendstunden, im Winter zu den helleren und wärmen Stunden um die Mittagszeit, beginnend am späteren Vormittag[113]. Wenn das Zeichen zum Stundengebet ertönt, bricht jedoch jeder sofort seine Arbeit ab[114]. Dem Gottesdienst (*opus dei*) soll nichts vorgezogen werden[115]. Die Strukturierung des Tages geschieht – bei aller klugen Berücksichtigung der notwendigen Arbeit sowie der erforderlichen Zeiten und Bedingungen für sie – vom Gottesdienst her. Der Abt selbst trägt Sorge (eventuell durch die Beauftragung eines zuverlässigen Mönches) für das pünktliche Anzeigen der Gebetszeiten am Tag und bei Nacht[116].

Die Strukturierung der Tage in der RB basiert auf einer Grenzziehung, die durch die kosmisch-natürlichen Rhythmen von Tag und Nacht, den Wechsel der Jahreszeiten und das Kirchenjahr gegeben ist[117]. Der Mönch schwingt in den natürlichen, kosmischen Rhythmus ein. Die Nacht wird nicht zum Tag gemacht: Abendgebet und Abendmahlzeit sollen stets noch bei Tageslicht stattfinden[118]. Eine Mittagsruhe gleicht den aufgrund der kürzeren Sommernächte reduzierten Nachtschlaf aus; im Winter mit seinen langen Nächten ist dies nicht nötig. Auch in der Gewährung anderer Pausen[119] untertags beachtet die Tagesstruktur menschliche Bedürfnisse und Grenzen und verhindert eine Überdehnung des menschlichen Maßes. Es gibt ein «Genug».

---

112 Cf. *RB* 8,2.

113 Cf. *RB* 48,4.6.10-11.14.

114 Cf. *RB* 43,1; 48,12.

115 Cf. *RB* 43,3.

116 Cf. *RB* 47,1.

117 Die Benediktsregel folgt noch der antiken Zeitbemessung, bei der die Nacht (Zeitspanne vom Untergang bis zum Aufgang der Sonne) und der Tag (von Sonnenaufgang bis Sonnenuntergang) in je 12 Stunden eingeteilt waren. Je nach Jahreszeit mit ihren längeren oder kürzeren Tagen und Nächten konnte eine Stunde zwischen 40 und 80 Minuten lang sein. Cf. P. Engelbert, «Die *Zeit in der Regel* des hl. *Benedikt*», in *Denken im Raum des Heiligen* (FS A. Paus), ed. H. Bürkle, St. Ottilien 2007, 215-229; Scheiba, «Alltag und Fest», 144f.

118 Cf. *RB* 41,8f.

119 Cf. *RB* 8,4; 42,5; 48,5.12.

3.4.2. Lectioni uacare

Eine wichtige Grenzziehung in der benediktinischen Tagesstruktur sind die Zeiten für die geistliche Lesung, die *lectio diuina*. Das Studieren, betende Lesen, Vor-sich-Hersagen, Auswendiglernen, Verinnerlichen der Heiligen Schrift stellt ein wichtiges Strukturelement christlicher Lebensgestaltung in der Alten Kirche und im Frühen Mönchtum dar[120]. Benedikt legt Wert auf ein Freisein (*uacare*)[121] der Mönche für diese *lectio*, auf eine im Tagesablauf ausgesparte und zugesicherte Zeit – ungestört durch andere Arbeiten, Aufgaben, Dienste oder Verpflichtungen[122]. Die Brüder unterbrechen ihre tägliche Arbeit jedoch nicht, um sich – gleichsam ohne schlechtes Gewissen – innerhalb der *lectio* lediglich einer anderen Form von Arbeit zu widmen, nämlich der Ausbildung im Sinne einer Befähigung zu liturgischen Diensten, zum Tischleser, zur Noviziatsbetreuung oder Gästeunterweisung[123]. Dem Erwerben dieser notwendigen Kenntnisse und Fähigkeiten mißt die RB durchaus große Bedeutung bei[124]. In der Tat stellt die tägliche *lectio diuina* – genauso wie die Begegnung mit Gottes Wort in der Stundenliturgie und bei der Tischlesung einen wichtigen Bildungsfaktor dar. Doch «Bildung» meint in der RB mehr als nur Ausbildung. Das «Vakuum» der täglichen *lectio* stellt eine Provokation dar. Es fordert die Mönche heraus, sich leer zu machen von sich selbst[125], um ganz frei zu werden für Gott, für die innerliche Prägung, Formung, Bildung und Umgestaltung durch sein Wort, durch die Begegnung mit Christus selbst[126]. «Bildung» ist gemäß der RB ein lebenslanger und ganzheitlicher Prozeß[127]. Benediktinische Mönche und Nonnen reifen «unter der Führung

---

120 Cf. M. Puzicha, «Lectio divina – Ort der Gottesbegegnung», *Erbe und Auftrag* 87/3 (2011) 245-263, hier: 245.

121 Cf. *RB* 48,4.10.13.17.22.

122 Cf. M. Puzicha, *Die Heilige Schrift in der Regel Benedikts* (Weisungen der Väter 7), Beuron 2009, 73.

123 Cf. A. Southey, «Weihnachtsrundbrief ,78: Lectio Divina», *Cistercienser Chronik* 120/3 (2013) 443-448, hier: 445; Puzicha, *Die Heilige Schrift*, 70.

124 Cf. *RB* 8,3; 58,5. Benedikt legt auch Wert auf einen fehlerfreien Vortrag von Psalmen, Lesungen, Responsorien und Antiphonen im Oratorium (cf. *RB* 45,1) oder bei Tisch und auf den Aspekt der Auferbauung der Gemeinschaft (cf. *RB* 38,1.12; 47,3).

125 Cf. E. Bianchi, *Wir sind nicht besser. Das Ordensleben in der Kirche und inmitten der Menschen*, EOS Verlag, St. Ottilien 2011, 217.

126 Cf. A. Böckmann, *Christus hören. Exegetischer Kommentar zur Regel Benedikts. Teil 1: Prolog bis Kapitel 7*, St. Ottilien 2011, 41-46; Puzicha, «Lectio divina», 248-250.254-255.

127 Cf. Puzicha, *Die Heilige Schrift*, 72.75.92-93; Ead., «Lectio divina», 261-263.

des Evangeliums»[128] am Du Gottes und in der Bewährung im Dienst innerhalb der Gemeinschaft. Die radikale Zuwendung zum Herrn erfordert ein immer neues Verlassen seiner selbst und das Vertrauen, sich in der täglichen *lectio* der Leere, dem Nichts-leisten-Müssen und dem nicht unmittelbar oder nachweisbar Zweckdienlichen überlassen zu dürfen[129]. Zugleich stellt dies hohe Ansprüche an Disziplin und Eigenverantwortung benediktinischer Mönche und Nonnen. Benedikt wußte um damit verbundene Gefährdungen, um die Versuchung des Ausweichens durch ein oben schon erwähntes Sich-Herumtreiben[130], ein *uacare fabulis*[131], ein Sich-Zeitnehmen für belangloses Geschwätz. Die RB sieht deshalb den Schutz des Freiraums der *lectio* in der monastischen Gemeinschaft vor und läßt speziell beauftragte Brüder darüber wachen[132].

3.4.3. Vorrang der Person vor ökonomischer Effizienz

Die Grenzziehung im benediktinischen Tagesablauf machte bereits deutlich, daß Arbeit keinen absoluten Wert darstellt und durch Zeiten für Stundenliturgie, *lectio*, gemeinsame Mahlzeiten, Pausen oder Schlaf in die Schranken gewiesen wird.

Neben dem Aspekt der Vermeidung von Überarbeitung oder der Versuchung zur Selbstausbeutung liegt das Humanisierungspotential der RB auch darin, daß der konkreten menschlichen Person Vorrang gegenüber dem Streben nach ökonomischer Effizienz eingeräumt wird. Kranken, schwachen oder weniger belastbaren Konventsmitgliedern[133] wird eine Arbeit oder Tätigkeit zugewiesen, die sie nicht überfordert, erdrückt oder zum Verlassen des Klosters veranlaßt[134]. An Sonntagen werden nur die notwendigen Dienste getan. Die übrige Zeit steht (neben den Zeiten für das gemeinsame Gebet) allen Mönchen für die *lectio* zur Verfügung. Wenn einzelnen Brüdern auch in dieser Zeit eine Tätigkeit zugewiesen wird, dann geschieht dies nicht, um deren Arbeitskraft voller auszuschöpfen oder dem Kloster zusätzliche Erwerbsquellen zu erschließen, sondern aus einem geistlichen und gewissermaßen therapeutischen Beweggrund heraus. Einzelnen

---

128 Damit ist die gesamte Hl. Schrift angesprochen. Auch die zu ihr hinführende oder sie auslegende Literatur ist für die *lectio* bedeutsam (vgl. *RB* 9,8; 73,2-5). Cf. PUZICHA, «Lectio divina», 247.253-255.

129 Cf. PUZICHA, «Lectio divina», 248.

130 Cf. *RB* 66,1.7.

131 *RB* 48,18.

132 Cf. *RB* 48,17-20.

133 Cf. M. PUZICHA, «Wer sind die „fratres delicati"? (48,24). Das Zeugnis der monastischen Literatur», *Monastische Informationen* 126 (2006) 11-16.

134 Cf. *RB* 48,24-25.

Mönchen oder Nonnen, die sich aus bestimmten persönlichen Gründen zeitweise nicht der geistlichen Lesung widmen können oder wollen, kann durch die Zuweisung einer geeigneten Aufgabe geholfen werden, nicht in fruchtlosem Nichtstun, Orientierungslosigkeit oder Entmutigung zu versinken bzw. andere zu stören[135]. Benedikt weiß mit der patristisch-monastischen Tradition vor ihm um die Ambivalenz von Muße (*otium*)[136], um das destruktive Potential von Müßiggang (*otiositas*)[137], lähmender Langeweile, Sinn- und Ruhelosigkeit (*acedia*)[138] im Leben des einzelnen sowie der Gemeinschaft[139].

Der Vorrang der menschlichen Person vor jedem wirtschaftlichem Kalkül zeigt sich exemplarisch in RB 31 über den Cellerar. Er ist in besonderer Weise für die ökonomischen Belange der Gemeinschaft zuständig und trägt Verantwortung sowohl für die materiellen Güter des Klosters als auch für die Versorgung und das Wohl der Brüder (insbesondere der Kranken)[140] sowie der Kinder, der Gäste und der Armen[141]. Weil der Cellerar der ganzen Gemeinschaft wie ein Vater sein[142] und für alle und alles Sorge tragen soll[143], ist er von dem sehr einfordernden Küchendienst befreit, bei dem sich die Brüder normalerweise abwechseln[144]. Wie andere Mönche, die entweder arbeitsmäßig stark beansprucht oder aber weniger leistungsfähig sind (Küchendiener, Pförtner, Brüder, die in der Gästeküche tätig sind), soll er Hilfe zur Erfüllung seiner vielen Aufgaben bekommen[145]. Das Ziel der gegenseitigen Unterstützung im Kloster ist nicht primär der ungehinderte und effektive Ablauf der einzelnen Arbeitsprozesse. Es geht vielmehr um die konkreten Menschen selbst, die diese Arbeiten bewältigen müssen. Der Cellerar soll seinen umfangreichen Dienst *aequo animo* verrichten können, d.h. nicht aufgrund von Überforderung Schaden an seiner Seele nehmen[146]. Statt Selbstausbeu-

135 Cf. *RB* 48,23.

136 Cf. *RB* 48,18.

137 Cf. *RB* 6,8; 47,4; 48,1.24 (*otiositas, otiose, otiosus*).

138 *RB* 48,17: *frater acediosus*.

139 Cf. M.B. Meeuws, «„Ora et Labora": devise bénédictine?», *Collectanea Cisterciensia* 54 (1992) 193-214.

140 Cf. *RB* 36,10.

141 Cf. *RB* 31,9.

142 Cf. *RB* 31,2.

143 Cf. *RB* 31,3.

144 Cf. *RB* 35,1.5.

145 Cf. *RB* 31,17; 35,3-4; 53,18-20; 66,5. Bezeichnenderweise verwendet die *RB* in diesem Zusammenhang den Begriff *solatium*, der nicht nur tatkräftige Unterstützung, sondern auch Trost für die aufgewühlte Seele der Überlasteten impliziert.

146 Cf. *RB* 31,17.

tung empfiehlt Benedikt dem Cellerar, auf seine Seele zu achten[147]. Der Mensch in der Sicht der RB ist mehr als seine Arbeitskraft und seine Leistung. Er besteht aus Leib und Seele; und auf die Bedürfnisse beider ist gleichermaßen zu achten[148].

Der Vorrang der menschlichen Person vor ökonomischer Effizienz tritt auch im Kapitel 57 über die Handwerker des Klosters zutage[149]. Für Benedikt zählt keineswegs nur das Können eines begabten Handwerkers oder Künstlers im Kloster, dessen Arbeit der Gemeinschaft ökonomischen Gewinn bringt. In der Sicht der RB ist es vorrangig, daß Mönche oder Nonnen sich nicht über ihre Arbeit und Leistung definieren müssen. Vielmehr sind auf dem Hintergrund der Taufe alle Glieder der monastischen Gemeinschaft «einer in Christus» und haben unabhängig von Herkunft, Ausbildung oder Können die gleiche Würde[150]. Diese Sicht des Menschen ist für die RB so zentral, daß das Kloster sogar wirtschaftliche Einbußen in Kauf nimmt, ein Glied der Gemeinschaft zeitweilig aus seinem Arbeitsbereich entfernt[151], wenn es sich in einem ökonomisch verkürzten, leistungsorientierten Selbstbild verfangen hat und so Schaden an seiner Seele nimmt.

3.4.4. Arbeit und soziale Verantwortung

a) Leben im Angesicht von Armut

Benedikt und seine Mönchsgemeinschaft kannten Armut aus eigener Erfahrung. Von 535-553 verheerten die Ostgotenkriege das Land. Zerstörung der wirtschaftlichen Grundlage und Infrastruktur, Hunger, Krankheiten, Plünderungen, Flüchtlingsströme waren die Folgen. Montecassino lag an einem strategisch wichtigen Knotenpunkt und an einer Nord-Süd-Verbindungslinie des Landes. Hier erlangt ein wichtiges Grundprinzip der Benediktsregel große Bedeutung: Alle Gäste, die zum Kloster kommen, sollen wie Christus aufgenommen werden. Größte Sorge (*maxime susceptioni cura sollicite*) soll dabei Armen und Pilgern geschenkt werden[152]. Auch der Klosterpförtner ist gehalten, unverzüglich Antwort

147 Cf. *RB* 31,8.

148 Cf. *RB* 2,31.34.37; 7,9; 27,6; 41,5.

149 Hier ist der Vergleich mit RM 85, das inhaltlich *RB* 57 nahekommt, aufschlußreich. Bereits im Titel von *RB* 57, «Von den Handwerkern des Klosters», wird deutlich, daß es nicht allein um wirtschaftliche Belange geht, sondern vor allem um die Menschen, die diese Tätigkeit ausüben. Der Titel in RM lautet bezeichnenderweise: «Wie und zu welchem Preis Handwerkserzeugnisse, die im Kloster hergestellt wurden, verkauft werden sollen».

150 Cf. *RB* 2,20.

151 Cf. *RB* 57,2-3.

152 Cf. *RB* 53,1.15.

geben, sobald jemand klopft oder ein Armer ruft[153]. Der Cellerar sorgt gewissenhaft (*cum omni sollicitudine curam*) für Kranke, Kinder, Gäste und Arme[154]. Wenn ein Mönch neue Kleider erhält, werden die alten in der Kleiderkammer aufbewahrt, um sie an Arme weitergeben zu können[155]. Ein Mönch, der Profeß machen möchte, soll sein Vermögen vorher an die Armen verteilen oder es in einer feierlichen Schenkung dem Kloster vermachen[156]. Eltern, die ihr Kind dem Kloster darbringen wollen, wird nahegelegt, ein eventuell vorhandenes Vermögen nicht für das Kind aufzusparen, sondern dem Kloster als Almosen (*elemosina*) zu schenken. Arme, die gar nichts besitzen, können ihr Kind auch ohne eine solche Schenkung dem Kloster übergeben[157]. Auch wenn die RB von anderen als den «Armen» spricht, war Benedikts Kloster offenbar ebenfalls arm[158] und der Almosen bedürftig – obwohl die Mönche selbst arbeiteten und gegebenenfalls auch ihre Ernte ohne die Hilfe anderer einbringen mußten[159]. Dennoch legt die Regel Wert darauf, daß Klostererzeugnisse immer etwas (*aliquantulum*) billiger verkauft werden, als es andere Produzenten tun[160]. Das Motiv dafür ist wiederum die Sorge für Arme und weniger Kaufkräftige, nicht jedoch das Unterbieten und Vernichten anderer Anbieter auf dem Markt[161]. Eine Kultur der Genügsamkeit[162], des «Genug für alle», ein einfacher Lebensstil sowie ein selbstverständliches Teilen und Teilhabenlassen von armen, bedürftigen Menschen ist kennzeichnend für die konkrete Art, wie die RB dem allgegenwärtigen Phänomen der Armut in ihren unterschiedlichen Erscheinungsformen inner- und außerhalb der Klausurgrenzen ohne Schuldzuweisungen und Stigmatisierungen begegnet.

b) Ehrlichkeit

Trotz konkreter Armutserfahrung in politisch und ökonomisch schwieriger Zeit besteht die RB auf einen redlichen Umgang mit dem Klostergut. Der Cellerar wird gemahnt, nichts nachlässig, sondern alles wie heiliges Altargerät

153 Cf. *RB* 66,3.
154 Cf. *RB* 31,9.
155 Cf. *RB* 55,9.
156 Cf. *RB* 58,24.
157 Cf. *RB* 59T.4-5.8.
158 Cf. 31,13; 40,8.
159 Cf. *RB* 48,7.
160 Cf. *RB* 57,8. Die Magisterregel macht in diesem Zusammenhang die Einschränkung «ein wenig» nicht; cf. RM 85,2.
161 Cf. A. Böckmann, *Mit Christus zum Ziel. Exegetischer Kommentar zur Regel Benedikts, Teil 3: Kapitel 53 bis 73*, EOS Verlag, Sankt Ottilien 2015, 96.
162 Siehe dazu Punkt 3.6.1.

zu behandeln. Auch soll er weder in Geiz noch in Verschwendungssucht verfallen[163]. Er muß ein Vorbild sein für alle Brüder, die mit den Werkzeugen, Kleidern oder sonstiger Habe des Klosters pfleglich umgehen sollen[164]. Wer etwas zerbricht oder verliert, muß es unverzüglich ehrlich bekennen und Genugtuung leisten[165].

Ehrlichkeit ist auch das Prinzip beim Verkauf der Klosterprodukte. Brüder, die den Handel abschließen, dürfen nicht betrügen bzw. verheimlichen, wieviel Geld sie eingenommen haben. Die Regel verweist hier auf das negative biblische Beispiel von Hananias und Saphira, die aufgrund ihrer Unlauterkeit und des Verstoßes gegen die Gütergemeinschaft der jungen christlichen Gemeinde starben[166]. Benedikt weist mit dieser Stelle aus der Hl. Schrift auf das Problem eines geistlichen Todes hin, der sich aus Habsucht, Geiz und Gier ergibt. Diese Haltungen sind weder mit einem christlichen noch einem monastischen Leben vereinbar und würden es von Grund auf korrumpieren. Der einzelne Mensch zählt – unabhängig von den von ihm angehäuften materiellen Gütern. Er muß kein falsches Selbstbild präsentieren.

3.5. Askese und sozialer Impuls

3.5.1. Maß und Genügsamkeit

Daß Erfahrungen mit Armut inner- und außerhalb des Klosters im Hintergrund der Benediktsregel stehen, ist bereits deutlich geworden[167]. Armut ist für Benedikt ein anzutreffendes Faktum, kein Ideal. Benediktinisches Leben ist wesentlich ein maßvolles, genügsames Leben. «Maß» und «maßvoll» sind entscheidende Schlüsselworte und Grenzziehungen in der *Regula Benedicti*[168]. Eine weitere Grenzmarkierung stellt das Verb «*sufficere*» (genügen) dar. Es wird bezeichnenderweise dreimal im Kapitel über das «Maß der Speise» gebraucht, neben dem Hinweis auf die Sparsamkeit (*parcitas*), sowie einmal im Kapitel über das «Maß des Getränks»[169]. Auch im Kapitel über die Kleidung und das Schuhwerk der Mönche, in dem auch auf andere Dinge des persönlichen Gebrauchs Bezug genommen wird, findet das be-

163 Cf. *RB* 31,10-12.
164 Cf. *RB* 32,4.
165 Cf. *RB* 46,1-4.
166 Cf. Apg 5,1-11.
167 Siehe oben Pkt. 3.5.4.
168 Cf. M. Scheiba, «“Sed omnia mensurate faciat” (*RB* 31,12) – Eine Wortstudie», *Regulae Benedicti Studia* 20 (2001) 141-164.
169 Cf. *RB* 39,1.3.4; *RB* 39,10; *RB* 40,3.

zeichnende Verb *sufficere* dreimal Verwendung[170]. Zudem wird in der RB das rechte Maß (*mensura*) der Kleidung, die «passen» (*mensurata*) soll, betont[171]. Darin äußert sich auch der Respekt vor der Einzigartigkeit jedes Bruders. Alles Überflüssige soll in Benedikts Kloster vermieden, das Notwendige jedoch zur Verfügung gestellt werden, und zwar in dem unterschiedlichen Maß, wie es jeder einzelne nötig hat[172].

Im Rahmen der benediktinischen Gastfreundschaft sind im Gästebereich genügend Betten bereitzustellen[173]. Für die Gäste gibt es zudem eine eigene Küche. Ihnen zuliebe bricht der Abt, außer im Falle eines streng gebotenen Fasttages, das Fasten; die Brüder jedoch behalten ihr übliches Fasten und ihren gewohnten genügsamen Lebensstil bei[174].

Diese Grenzziehungen markieren ein einfaches, maßvolles – ein asketisches – Leben, dem ein «nie genug» fremd ist.

3.5.2. Dynamik der Askese

Der Begriff «Askese» kommt in der RB nicht vor. Ihr Inhalt ist jedoch präsent, wenn auch die Regel von ihrem literarischen Genus her keine geschlossene Lehre zu diesem Thema bietet. Im griechischen Verb *askéo* klingt das Sich-Mühen an, etwas sorgfältig zu bearbeiten, herauszuarbeiten, auszubilden, einzuüben. Christliche Askese zielt auf die Herausbildung einer reifen christlichen Persönlichkeit. Das erfordert eine leib-seelische Anstrengung, Zucht von Körper und Geist, Mäßigung, Verzicht. Wie bei einer Statue werden die Konturen, Züge, ja das Bild der Figur erst sichtbar im Verlauf des Herausmeißelns, Abschlagens, Wegschneidens aus dem Rohmaterial[175].

In der *Regula Benedicti* wird dieser Prozeß des Herausbildens u.a. mit Begriffen wie *continentia, abstinentia, abrenuntio, mortificatio* verdeutlicht[176]. Sie reflektieren einen wichtigen Teilaspekt der monastischen *conuersatio morum*, die jedoch nicht (negativ) in Zucht, Maß oder Grenzziehung aufgeht, sondern (positiv) auch ein bewußtes Formen, Wachsenlassen und Voranschreiten bein-

---

170 Cf. *RB* 55, 4.10.15.

171 Cf. *RB* 55,8.

172 Cf. *RB* 55,11.18; *RB* 33,5; 34T.1.3-4.

173 Cf. *RB* 53,22.

174 Cf. *RB* 53,10-11.16.

175 Cf. H.U.v. BALTHASAR, «Askese. Vortrag vom 18.2.1964 im Auditorium Maximum der Universität Freiburg i. Br.», *Communio* 29 (2000) 50-62, hier: 50-52.

176 Cf. M. PFEIFER, «Führt Verzicht wirklich zur Freiheit? Systematische Überlegungen zur Askese in der RB», *Regulae Benedicti Studia* 20 (2001) 59-81, hier: 62f.

haltet (*cura, solicitudo, proficere, perficere*). Schon im griechischen Begriff «*askesis*» geht es um einen Verzicht eines positiven Zieles wegen[177].

3.5.3. Solidarisch leben

Das asketische Bemühen in der RB ist nicht Selbstzweck, sondern impliziert eine beständige Grenzüberschreitung: heraus aus dem Gefängnis egoistischen Eigenwillens in die Weite des Herzens, des entschiedenen Altruismus, in die Freiheit der Liebe zu Gott und dem Nächsten. Eine solche Liebe ist in gewisser Weise selbst strengste Askese, denn sie erfordert von Seiten der Mönche und Nonnen u.a. Selbstlosigkeit, Freundlichkeit, Dienstbereitschaft, Gastfreundschaft[178]. Askese ist in der monastischen Tradition wie auch in der RB ein wichtiger sozialer Impuls[179]. Sie führt zu einer Haltung, die jedes Tauschverhalten oder ökonomische Kalkül sprengt. Sie macht fähig zu einer Solidarität jenseits gesellschaftlicher Stigmatisierungen oder Ausgrenzungen. Neben der oben angesprochenen vorurteilsfreien Sorge für die Armen wird dies auf bezeichnende Weise im Kapitel 4 über die Instrumente der guten Werke deutlich: Unmittelbar nach einer Liste von Werkzeugen, mit denen der Mönch der Fixierung auf sein eigenes Ich absagt, um Christus nachzufolgen, und sich in der Zucht des Leibes sowie im Verzicht übt, schließen sich die Werke der Barmherzigkeit an[180]. Diese Aufeinanderfolge bewahrt vor dem Mißverständnis einer «Askese», bei der Menschen lediglich auf andere, vielleicht subtilere Weise um sich selbst und ihren vermeintlichen geistlich-menschlichen Fortschritt kreisen.

3.6. Ne quid nimis – *Zum Umgang mit Alter, Krankheit, menschlicher Schwäche und Versagen*

3.6.1. Schützende Grenzziehung

Im 64. Kapitel der RB, das eine Art zweiten «Abtsspiegel» enthält[181], wird der Obere darauf hingewiesen, daß er bei notwendigen Zurechtweisungen von Mön-

177 Cf. J. Bergmann *et al.*, «Askese», in *Theologische Realenzyklopädie*, vol. 4, edd. G. Krause-G. Müller, De Gruyter, Berlin-New York 1979, 195–259; U. Bianchi *et al.*, «Askese», in *Lexikon für Theologie und Kirche*, vol. 1, ed. W. Kasper, Freiburg i. Br. [3]1993, 1074-1083.

178 Cf. Balthasar, «Askese», 61-62.

179 Cf. weiterführend: R. Nürnberg, *Askese als sozialer Impuls. Monastisch-asketische Spiritualität als Wurzel und Triebfeder sozialer Ideen und Aktivitäten der Kirche in Südgallien im 5. Jahrhundert*, (Hereditas 2), Bonn 1988.

180 Cf. *RB* 4,10-13.14-19.

181 *RB* 64, das in VV 1-6 gemäß der Überschrift *De ordinando abbate* von der Wahl des Abtes

chen klug handeln und «nicht zu weit gehen» solle (*ne quid nimis*), damit das Gefäß nicht zerbreche, wenn er den Rost allzu heftig auszukratzen versuche[182]. Benedikts Mahnung «Nichts zu sehr, nichts zu viel» fordert kein laues Mittelmaß, sondern hat mit dem Wahrnehmen und Beachten von menschlichen Grenzen zu tun. Der Abt in seiner Verantwortung für jedes Glied der Gemeinschaft darf nicht maßlos (*non sit nimius*)[183] sein, sondern muß die Fähigkeit zur *discretio*, d.h. zu kluger Unterscheidung, besitzen[184]. Er darf die Brüder herausfordern, aber nicht überfordern, ermutigen, aber nicht beschämen. Die Starken in der Gemeinschaft sollen – jenseits von Selbstoptimierungsdruck und der Versuchung zur Selbstausbeutung – das finden, was sie suchen. Die Schwachen jedoch sollen nicht im Gefühl des Nicht-mithalten-Könnens oder Scheiterns davonlaufen.

Ein oft auch vorausschauendes[185] Wahrnehmen und Akzeptieren von menschlichen Grenzen zieht sich wie ein roter Faden durch die gesamte Regel[186].

---

handelt, bietet in VV 7-22 eine Art Abtsdirektorium, das eine Ergänzung zu *RB* 2 (*Qualis debeat esse abbas*) darstellt.

182 Cf. *RB* 64,12.

183 *RB* 64,16

184 Cf. *RB* 64,12.16-19.

185 Der Abt sei in all seinen Anordnungen umsichtig (*prouidus*) und überlegt (*consideratus*); cf. *RB* 64,17.

186 Jenseits von Leistungsdruck und Pensumdenken sind Kürzungen des monastischen Offiziums möglich (cf. *RB* 18,24f.). Der Abt muß die Grenzen der Auffassungsgabe der einzelnen Brüder beachten und deshalb seiner Gemeinschaft in zweifacher Weise als Lehrer vorstehen (cf. *RB* 2,12): durch sein Wort (für die Verständigen) und durch sein praktisches Lebensbeispiel (für weniger Gelehrige). Zudem bedürfen Alte und Kinder in der Gemeinschaft besonderer Rücksicht und einer angemessenen Behandlung, z.B. bezüglich der Mahlzeiten oder in Fragen der Korrektur (cf. *RB* 30,2; 37; 39,10). Alle Brüder werden aufgerufen, Krankheiten und charakterliche Schwächen mit größter Geduld an einander zu ertragen (cf. *RB* 36,5; 72,5). Wahrnehmung menschlicher Grenzen zeigt sich auch in der Berücksichtigung von Fällen, in denen ein Bruder sich nicht in der Lage sieht, einen Auftrag zu erfüllen, weil er das Maß seiner Kräfte zu übersteigen scheint (*excedere*). Hier ist ein offenes Gespräch mit dem Abt möglich, in dem beide Dialogpartner sich in der Suche nach dem Willen Gottes in dieser Situation unterstützen; cf. A. Böckmann, «Wenn einem Bruder Unmögliches aufgetragen wird (*RB* 68)», *Erbe und Auftrag* 68 (1992) 5-21. Umgang mit menschlichen Grenzen ist auch bei der Zuteilung des Notwendigen in der Klostergemeinschaft gefordert. Die Regel Benedikts verzichtet hier auf starre, einheitliche Vorgaben für alle. Sie folgt vielmehr dem Grundsatz der Jerusalemer «Urgemeinde», daß jedem zugeteilt werde, was er nötig hat. (Cf. *RB* 34,1; Apg 4,32. Auch Augustinus, *Praeceptum* 5,4-5, folgt dieser Leitvorstellung). Das Notwendige wird nicht einfach vom Abt bestimmt und zugewiesen, sondern entspricht dem, was von den Mönchen erbeten wird. Jedes Glied der Gemeinschaft darf und muß selbst

3.6.2. Grenzen der Toleranz

Grenzen schützen nicht zuletzt Form und Gestalt des monastischen Lebens selbst. Sie fordern Mönche und Nonnen zur Konfrontation ihres eigenen Verhaltens mit den vereinbarten Grundsätzen, Festlegungen sowie Toleranzgrenzen der Gemeinschaft heraus und machen Exzesse und Übertretungen bewußt. Benedikt weiß um die Gefahr, daß festgelegte Grenzen in der Gemeinschaft nicht immer respektiert werden[187] und trifft in seiner Regel Vorkehrungen dagegen. Um das hohe Gut der Gütergemeinschaft vor der Aushöhlung durch heimlichen Sonderbesitz zu schützen, schreckt er z.B. vor Kontrollen nicht zurück[188]. Der stark beanspruchte Cellerar wird vor Brüdern geschützt, die zu Unzeiten mit ihren Wünschen an ihn herantreten wollen[189]. Mönche in verantwortungsvollen Positionen werden mehrfach an ihre Rechenschaftspflicht vor Gott erinnert, damit sie die mit ihrem Amt verbundenen Vollmachten nicht überschreiten oder mißbrauchen[190]. Die Grundhaltungen von Schweigen und Sammlung werden angesichts von Mönchen betont, die zuviel Unnützes reden[191] oder zu viele Kontakte haben[192]. Auch in heutigen Gemeinschaften bleiben solche Grenzmarkierungen notwendig, damit das monastische Leben sein klares Profil behält und sich nicht einfach dem gesellschaftlichen «*mainstream*» anpaßt[193].

3.6.3. Umgang mit Grenzverletzungen innerhalb der Gemeinschaft

Die Benediktsregel spricht – nicht im (wirtschafts-)kriminologischen oder strafrechtlichen Sinn – von «Delinquenten»[194], von Regelübertretern, Normverlet-

entscheiden, was er/sie benötigt. Die Regel rechnet mit unterschiedlichen Bedürfnissen, mit Mönchen/Nonnen, die mehr oder weniger als andere brauchen (cf. *RB* 34,2ff; 40,4). Das Erbetene muß sich jedoch in jedem Fall innerhalb gewisser Grenzen bewegen, d.h. es muß im Rahmen der Möglichkeiten der Gemeinschaft liegen (cf. *RB* 31,13) und mit den Grundprinzipien monastischen Lebens vereinbar sein; cf. PUZICHA, «Klausur und Internet», 14. Benedikt zieht hier eine Grenze, die Achtung vor der Individualität der einzelnen Mönche zum Ausdruck bringt und diese zugleich schützt.

187 Cf. LEPORI, «Die modernen Kommunikationsmittel», 209.

188 Cf. *RB* 55,16.

189 Cf. *RB* 31,18.

190 Cf. *RB* 2,34.37.38; 3,11; 31,9; 63,3; 65,22.

191 Cf. *RB* 4,52; 6,2-4; 7,56-58.60-61; 43,8; 48,18-21; 53,23-24; 67,4-5.

192 Cf. *RB* 53,23-24; 66,1.7; 67,7.

193 Auch in heutigen Gemeinschaften gibt es Mönche und Nonnen, die zuviel arbeiten, zuviel reden, Begegnungen mit Gästen unnötig ausdehnen, sich definieren über Gespräche, Kontakte, Termine, Kurse, Publikationen etc. Cf. LEPORI, «Die modernen Kommunikationsmittel», 209; PUZICHA, «Klausur und Internet», 12.

194 *RB* 2,26: *peccata delinquentium*.

zern, Schuldigen. In seiner Verantwortung für die ganze Gemeinschaft darf der Abt über Fehlverhalten, durch das Brüder sich selbst und anderen schaden, nicht hinwegsehen, sondern muß es gleich beim Entstehen mit der Wurzel zu beseitigen suchen[195]. Die RB motiviert nicht dazu, anderen ein makelloses «Hochglanz-Ich» zu präsentieren, sondern Brüder, die Fehler begehen, etwas versäumen, verschulden, zerbrechen oder sich sonst irgendwie verfehlen (*excesserit*), werden aufgefordert, von selbst ihre Schuld vor Abt und Gemeinschaft bekennen[196].

Ausgrenzung von Menschen, Ausschluß von Gliedern der Gemeinschaft und Teilhabeverweigerung liegen jenseits der Zielvorstellungen der *Regula Benedicti*. Dennoch nimmt sie die Realität von Brüdern in den Blick, die sich durch ihr Grundsätze und Toleranzgrenzen verletzendes Verhalten[197] letztlich selbst außerhalb die Gemeinschaft gestellt haben[198]. Der Abt muß für alle Brüder, die sich verfehlt haben[199], und insbesondere für diese Ausgeschlossenen besondere Sorge tragen. Weil jede *excommunicatio* dem betreffenden Gemeinschaftsglied die eigene Situation verdeutlichen soll, muß die Art der Ausschließung der tatsächlichen Schwere der Verfehlung entsprechen[200]. Auch darf kein Bruder eigenmächtig einen anderen aus der Gemeinschaft ausgrenzen[201]. Wer mit einem Ausgeschlossenen ohne Erlaubnis verkehrt, überschreitet eine Grenze. Er verhindert den Prozeß der Bewußtwerdung im schuldig gewordenen Bruder, schadet folglich ihm und der ganzen Gemeinschaft und muß deshalb ebenfalls ausgeschlossen werden[202]. Der nur relative Wert der Ausschließung wird in der RB jedoch unmißverständlich verdeutlicht: Brüder, die sich verfehlen, das «Brenn-

195 Auf den Oberen selbst fällt auch jedes Versäumnis, jedes nachlässige Schuldigbleiben seitens des Cellerars oder der Pfleger gegenüber den Kranken zurück (cf. *RB* 36,10).

196 Cf. *RB* 7,47; 45,2; 46T.1-3. Von einer Reise ins Kloster zurückkehrende Brüder bitten alle im Oratorium um das Gebet wegen der Fehler (*excessos*), die sie vielleicht unterwegs begangen haben (cf. *RB* 67,4).

197 *RB* 23 nennt als die Gemeinschaft schädigendes Verhalten, das deshalb zur *excommunicatio* führt: widerspenstiges, ungehorsames, stolzes Auftreten, sich widersetzend, *contrarius* zur Regel oder den Vorschrift der Oberen, Murren, Zum-Verächter-Werden.

198 Dieser «Selbstausschluß» wird dem betreffenden Bruder durch die *ex-communicatio* von den zwei Grundvollzügen benediktinisch-kommunitären Lebens klargemacht: der Ausschließung vom Gemeinschaft stiftenden und ausdrückenden Mahl (cf. in diesem Zusammenhang auch *RB* 51,3) und der Ausschließung vom gemeinsamen Gebet (cf. *RB* 24T; 44,1) bzw. der Möglichkeit, die Gemeinschaft im Chor zur repräsentieren (durch Psalmenvortrag oder eine andere Gebetsform).

199 *RB* 27,1: *delinquentes fratres*.

200 Cf. *RB* 24,1.

201 Cf. *RB* 70,2.

202 Cf. *RB* 26T.1-2.

mittel»[203] der Ausschließung aber nicht verstehen[204], sollen auf andere Weise so zurechtgewiesen werden, daß sie geheilt werden[205]. Wer trotz Ausschließung und öfterer Zurechtweisung in seiner Haltung verharrt und sich nicht heilen lassen will, darf auch äußerlich nicht mehr Glied der Gemeinschaft sein, sondern muß sie verlassen[206].

Bei Grenzüberschreitungen, die keinen endgültigen Ausschluß aus der Gemeinschaft nach sich ziehen, verlangt die Benediktsregel Satisfaktion und Besserung von Seiten des Delinquenten[207]. Die Brüder sollen erkennen, daß sie Gott[208], dem Abt und der Gemeinschaft[209] oder einem Bruder[210] etwas schuldig geblieben sind: Gehorsam[211], Ehrfurcht, Aufmerksamkeit[212], Sorgfalt[213] o. ä. Deshalb sollen sie Genüge tun, sich ent-schuldigen, Wiedergutmachung leisten[214]. Die so erlangte Vergebung geht in der RB jedoch über jede Ökonomie von Schuld und Wiedergutmachung hinaus. Das «Sufficit»[215] des Abtes, der Segensspruch von Abt oder Älteren[216], der Schuldenerlaß[217] und die erlangte Verzeihung[218] stehen im Kontext eines nichtökonomischen Überschusses, des *ut sanentur*[219], der Heilung. Ein Mönch, der zur 12. Demutsstufe fortgeschritten ist und auf dem Boden (*humus*) der Wirklichkeit steht, sieht sich dennoch als Schuldiger (*reus*) vor Gott gestellt[220]. Er weiß um sein andauerndes Schuldig-

203 *RB* 28,3.
204 Cf. *RB* 23,4; 30,2.
205 Cf. *RB* 30,3.
206 Cf. *RB* 28,1.5-6.
207 Cf. *RB* 27,3; 44T.
208 Cf. *RB* 11,13.
209 Cf. *RB* 24,4.7; 44,3.8.9; 46,3.
210 Cf. *RB* 71,8,
211 Cf. *RB* 5,19.
212 Cf. *RB* 45,1.
213 Cf. *RB* 43,6.11-12.16.
214 Cf. *satisfacere* – lat. *satis* (genug) und *facere* (tun, machen, betreiben): Zufriedenstellung, Genugtuung, Wiedergutmachung, Entschädigung, Entschuldigung leisten; *RB* 43,12: ein Schuldiger (*reus*) muß Genugtuung leisten.
215 *RB* 44,10.
216 Cf. *RB* 44,10; 71,8.
217 In der Ökonomie bedeutet der Schuldenerlaß, d.h. der Vertrag zwischen Gläubiger und Schuldner, der zum teilweisen oder ganzen Erlöschen der betroffenen Schulden führt, die radikalste Sanierungsmaßnahme für Schuldner in der Krise.
218 Cf. *RB* 7,48 (Ps 31,5); 24,7; 43,11.
219 *RB* 30,3.
220 Cf. *RB* 7,64.

bleiben, auch um Schaden, den Menschen selbst nicht mehr gutmachen können. So hofft er auf eine *absolutio*, eine Ablösung, die es nur im Absoluten geben kann[221]: bei Gott. Er ist letztlich der Heilende, der dort alles vermag[222], wo Menschen unweigerlich an ihre Grenzen stoßen.

3.7. Demut als Grundhaltung

3.7.1. Umgang mit eigenen Grenzen

Die Hoffnung (*spes*) auf Gott[223] bewahrt den Mönch vor Extremen, die einen authentischen menschlichen Fortschritt blockieren: vor einer Verzweiflung (*de-speratio*)[224], die zu Resignation und Rückzug[225] oder zu Vermessenheit[226] und wahnwitzigen Grenzüberschreitungen verleitet.

Die Benediktsregel lädt den Mönch ein, im Vertrauen auf Gott[227] gewissermaßen an «die Ränder (zu) gehen»[228], zunächst an die eigenen Ränder, die Grenzen eigener Kraft[229], des eigenen Charakters, an die dunklen Stellen der eigenen Gedankenwelt und des falschen Tuns[230].

221 *RB* 2,9: Der Abt als Hirt wird im Gericht des Herrn freigesprochen (*absolutus*), wenn er alle Hirtensorge für die ihm von Gott anvertrauten Menschen aufgewandt hat.

222 Cf. *RB* 28,5.

223 *RB* 4,41: *Spem suam Deo committere.*

224 *RB* 4,74: *Et de Dei misericordia numquam desperare.*

225 Siehe dazu auch: C.S. Lewis, *The Problem of Pain* (first published 1940), Samizdat University Press, Québec 2016, 81: «the doors of hell are locked on the *inside*».

226 Für Benedikt ist die *praesumptio* bzw. die Haltung des *praesumere* (cf. *RB* 3,4.9.10; 20,1; 26,1; 31,15; 33,2.6; 38,8; 43,11.18; 44,6; 47,3; 49,9; 51,1; 54,2.5; 57,4; 60,5; 62,3.8; 63,16; 67,5-7; 69T.1.3; 70T.1.6) ein gefährliches Hindernis auf dem Weg des Menschen zu Gott und damit zur Vollendung menschlichen Lebens. Cf. P. Miquel, «Praesumere – praesumptio dans l'ancienne littérature monastique», *Revue Bénédictine* 79 (1969) 424-436; B. Zorzi, «Vivere limiti e talenti in relazione. Glosse sull'uso del verbo "praesumere" nella Regola di san Benedetto», *Inter Fratres* 57 (2007) 165-187.

227 Cf. *RB* 68,5.

228 Cf. *Apostolisches Schreiben EVANGELII GAUDIUM des Heiligen Vaters Papst Franziskus an die Bischöfe, an die Priester und Diakone, an die Personen geweihten Lebens und an die christgläubigen Laien über die Verkündigung des Evangeliums in der Welt von heute*, ed. Sekretariat der Deutschen Bischofskonferenz (Verlautbarungen des Apostolischen Stuhls 194), Bonn 2013, 21: «den Mut zu haben, alle Randgebiete zu erreichen, die das Licht des Evangeliums brauchen» (EG 20).

229 Cf. *RB* 68T: Wenn einem Bruder Unmögliches aufgetragen wird.

230 Cf. *RB* 7,44-48.

Für Benedikt ist das Bemühen um die eigene Besserung (*emendatio*) nicht nur im Kontext von monastischen Grenzüberschreitungen[231] angesiedelt. Sie ist vielmehr eine Lebensaufgabe des Mönchs[232] und setzt die Bereitschaft zur Selbsterkenntnis und Selbstannahme sowie Lernfähigkeit voraus[233]. Die Benediktsregel propagiert hier jedoch weder ein «Sich-selbst-nie-genug-Sein» noch ein Programm asketisch-moralischer «Selbstoptimierung». Sie ermutigt den Mönch vielmehr, aus einem «Leben im Falschen»[234] herausfinden, um Gott und dem Nächsten näherzukommen, gemeinschafts- und gottfähiger und so letztlich «heil» zu werden. Auf diesem Weg zum Heil kommt der Mönch an der Erkenntnis der eigenen Geschöpflichkeit und ihrer Grenzen, die sich im Angesicht des Schöpfers vollzieht, nicht vorbei[235].

3.7.2. Demut als Lebensstil

Auf dem Weg der Demut, zu dem die Benediktsregel einlädt, können Menschen lernen, sich der eigenen Wirklichkeit zu stellen und – selbst inmitten von Phänomenen einer «Casting-Kultur» – eigener oder fremder Überbewertung zu widerstehen[236]. Sie beginnen, sich dem gesellschaftlichen Anreiz zu *performance* und Selbstvermarktung nicht unkritisch zu beugen. Statt sich primär über die eigene Arbeit, Erfolg, Ämter, Positionen bzw. Befugnisse zu definieren[237], lassen sich Mönche und Nonnen auf einen Lebensstil ein, der

231 Cf. Besserung der Murrer (*RB* 5,19), der häufig Zurechtgewiesenen (*RB* 28T.1), des von Stolz aufgeblähten Dekans (*RB* 21,5), des rebellischen Priesters (62,10), des stolzen, überheblichen, die Regel verachtenden Priors (*RB* 65,19), des widerspenstigen, ungehorsamen, hochmütigen Mönchs (*RB* 23,3), des Ausgetretenen (*RB* 29,1), dessen, der die Sachen des Klosters nicht in Ordnung hält (*RB* 32,5), der sich am Laster des Privateigentums erfreut (*RB* 33,8), der zu Tisch zu spät kommt (*RB* 43,15f), der vom Oberen Angebotenes ausschlägt (*RB* 43,19), der die Zeit der *lectio* schwatzend vergeudet (*RB* 48,20), dessen Schuld/Versäumnis durch andere bekannt wird (*RB* 46,4).

232 Cf. *RB* Prol 36.47; *RB* 2,40; 4,58.

233 Cf. M. Puzicha, «Nicht eine Tugend, sondern Lebensstil. Demut bei Benedikt», *Erbe und Auftrag* 91/4 (2015) 366-378, hier: 368.370.

234 Cf. «*mendum*», «*mendus*», «*mendosus*», «*mendositas*», in *Dictionnaire latin-français des auteurs chrétiens*, ed. A. Blaise, Brepols, Turnhout 1954, 525; «*emendo*», ebd. 306. Vom Substantiv *mendum* (= Fehler) leiten sich *e-mendare*, *ex mendo* ab: aus einer Fehlhaltung herauskommen; cf. Puzicha, «Nicht eine Tugend», 368, Anm. 4. Weiterführend auch: «Es gibt kein richtiges Leben im falschen», in: T. Adorno, *Minima Moralia. Reflexionen aus dem beschädigten Leben*, Frankfurt am Main 2001, 59.

235 Cf. Puzicha, «Nicht eine Tugend», 373.

236 Cf. Puzicha, «Nicht eine Tugend», 374.

237 Cf. *RB* 31,16; 57,1-3; 65,2. Dem Cellerar, der in Benedikts Kloster eine Art Prototyp für

in gegenseitigem Hören, Liebe und Dienstbereitschaft zur Wahrnehmung der eigenen Gaben und Grenzen Raum gewährt und zum unspektakulären Einbringen der jeweiligen Fähigkeiten, Kräfte, Kenntnisse und Ideen ermutigt. Frei vom selbstauferlegten Zwang zur Selbstdarstellung lernen Mönche und Nonnen auf der Basis der Benediktsregel, ihr Talent zum Singen oder Lesen zum Lob Gottes und zur Auferbauung der Gemeinschaft einzusetzen[238]. In Übereinstimmung mit Benedikts Grundsätzen im dritten Regelkapitel bemühen sich Mönche und Nonnen bei gemeinsamen Beratungen darum, ihre Sicht des Sachverhalts, die immer begrenzt sein wird, ohne Rechthaberei und besserwisserische Hartnäckigkeit vorzutragen sowie rhetorische Begabung nicht im Sinne von Manipulation und Dominanz zu mißbrauchen, die das Erwägen anderer Argumente zu verhindern sucht[239]. Der Weg der Demut, zu dem die *Regula Benedicti* einlädt, befähigt Menschen auch zu wahrer Loyalität, zur Anerkennung der Autorität anderer aus einer Haltung aufrichtigen Gehorsams heraus, die berechtigte Kritik einschließt[240].

3.8. Primat der Gnade

3.8.1. Gnade in RB

Die *Regula Benedicti* ermutigt Menschen zur Wahrnehmung der eigenen Fähigkeiten und Begabungen[241], ohne dabei eigenen Grenzen und Schwächen auszuweichen. Die Benediktsregel macht in verschiedenen Passagen immer wieder das menschliche Angewiesensein auf Gott deutlich und lädt die Brüder dazu ein, in jeder Lebenssituation ihre Hoffnung auf ihn[242] zu setzen. Dem literarischen Genus einer monastischen *Regula* entsprechend, entwickelt Benedikt keine eigentliche Gnadentheologie. Doch bereits im Prolog, der wie eine Ouvertüre zentrale Anliegen des monastischen Lebens vorstellt, ruft er dazu auf, Gott zu bitten, daß er vollende, was man Gutes zu tun beginne[243]. Dies ist die charakteristische Grundhaltung der Mönche sowohl bei ihrem liturgischen als auch praktischen

---

alle ist, die im Kloster in besonderer Weise Verantwortung tragen, wird bezeichnenderweise gesagt: *Humilitatem ante omnia habeat* (*RB* 31,13)!

238 Cf. *RB* 38,12; 47,3; 53,8-9.

239 Cf. *RB* 3,4.9.

240 Cf. *RB* 3,5.7-9; 21,2; 31,15; 41,5; 65,16f.

241 Cf. *RB* Prol 6.

242 Cf. *RB* 4,41.

243 Cf. *RB* Prol 4.

Dienst in der Gemeinschaft[244]. Sie rechnen mit Gott, mit seiner Gnade, seiner ungeschuldeten, liebenden, helfenden Zuwendung gerade dort, wo sie an ihre Grenzen stoßen, etwas aus eigener Kraft nicht zustande bringen[245]. Sie nehmen das Gute in sich und all ihre Möglichkeiten wahr, sehen diese aber in ihrer Verbindung zur Quelle alles Guten, zu Gott, dem Schöpfer der Welt[246]. Im Wissen, daß das Gute in ihnen nicht nur Ergebnis eigener Leistung, sondern Gabe Gottes ist, preisen sie Gott, der in ihnen wirkt.[247] In der Sicht Benedikts ist der Mensch nicht gnadenlos auf sich selbst geworfen oder sich selbst überlassen, sondern lebt durch die Taufe[248] in Gott, in jener Beziehung und Bezogenheit auf Gott, die theologisch «Gnade»[249] genannt wird. Wo Menschen bewußt aus dem Sich-Verdanken und Empfangen leben, ist mangelnder Selbstachtung, verzweifelter Selbstausbeutung und Selbstüberforderung der Boden entzogen. Die Benediktsregel sieht den Menschen als einen, «der das Leben liebt», der seine Lebenszeit zu nutzen weiß, der eilt und das tut, was bleibt, was ihm «für die Ewigkeit nützt»[250], der letztendlich aber die Führung in seinem Leben vertrauensvoll Christus übergibt[251].

3.8.2. Radikaler Altruismus

Gnade ist eine Beziehungskategorie, ein personaler Begegnungsvorgang, der auch die Beziehungen der Menschen untereinander befreien kann von gnadenloser Selbstbehauptung, Selbstdurchsetzung und ökonomischem Kalkül. Monastisches Leben nach der *Regula Benedicti* bedeutet das Eintreten in die «Schule für den Dienst des Herrn»[252], in der Mönche und Nonnen lernen, dem

244 Cf. *RB* 18,1; 35,17. Vgl. Böckmann, *Christus hören*, 8.

245 Cf. *RB* Prol 41; *RB* 68,5; 73,8-9.

246 Cf. *RB* 16,5.

247 Cf. *RB* Prol 29-30; *RB* 4,42.

248 Zum Taufhintergrund der *RB* cf. Böckmann, *Christus hören*, 11.209; E. Manning, «Une catechèse baptismale devient Prologue de la Règle du Maître», *Revue Mabillon* 52 (1962) 61-73; M. Puzicha, «Leitworte altkirchlicher Taufspiritualität im Prolog der Benediktusregel», *Monastische Informationen* 98 (1998) 19-24.

249 Cf. H.G. Reventlow *et al.*, «Gnade», in *Theologische Realenzyklopädie*, vol. 13, ed. G. Müller, De Gruyter, Berlin-New York 1984, 459-511; E.-M. Faber, «Gnade. VI. Systematisch-theologisch», in *Lexikon für Theologie und Kirche*, vol. 4, ed. W. Kasper, Freiburg i. Br. 1995, 779-785.

250 Cf. *RB* Prol 15.43-44.

251 Cf. *RB* Prol 20-21; *RB* 72,12.

252 *RB* Prol 45.

Herrn zu dienen und seine Gegenwart in anderen Menschen zu erkennen[253] sowie so zu dienen, wie der Herr selbst es tut[254]. Sie treten damit in eine Dynamik der Dienstbereitschaft[255] ein, in die Entschiedenheit, das zu tun, was dem anderen nützt[256]. Ein solcher Altruismus impliziert beständige Grenzüberschreitung. Das Gefangenbleiben in den engen Hürden egoistischen Eigenwillens[257] ist damit unvereinbar und würde das zönobitische Leben von Grund auf korrumpieren[258]. Die Benediktsregel lädt die Brüder vielmehr dazu ein, den Weg der Gebote Gottes «mit weitem Herzen» in der Freude der Liebe zu laufen[259]. Auf diesem Weg «unter der Führung des Evangeliums»[260] lernen Menschen, frei zu werden von der lähmenden Angst, zu kurz zu kommen, falls sie das eigene «Ich» nicht beständig auf Kosten des «Du» durchzusetzen suchen. An die Stelle gnadenloser Selbstbehauptung und Selbstdurchsetzung kann das Über-sich-Hinausschreiten (Transzendieren) treten, das den anderen zum Zentrum macht. Als eine Art «praktisches Testament» Benedikts[261] ist diese Haltung zugleich das entscheidende Kriterium für *alles*, was Mönche und Nonnen tun – für ihr asketisches Bemühen, ihr Gebet, ihr Schweigen und Reden, ihre Arbeit usw. Nur in einer Haltung des Altruismus sind Menschen tatsächlich gemeinsam unterwegs auf dem Weg zu Gott.

3.8.3. Verdienst und Lohn

Auf dem Weg zur Erlangung der Grundhaltung des Altruismus klammert die Regel den – bereits biblisch verankerten – Gedanken an «Verdienst» und «Lohn» für das Tun des Guten nicht aus. Benedikt spricht fünfzehnmal von

253 Cf. *RB* 2,2; 36,1-3; 53,1.7.15.

254 Cf. A. Böckmann, *Perspektiven der Regula Benedicti. Ein Kommentar zum Prolog und den Kapiteln* 53, 58, 72, 73, Münsterschwarzach 1986, 44-48; Böckmann, *Christus hören*, 74.

255 Cf. *RB* 1,2; 35. Siehe auch Böckmann, *Perspektiven der Regula Benedicti*, 33-36.

256 Cf. *RB* 48,17-21; 72,7.

257 Cf. *RB* 1,8-9.

258 Das Gefangenbleiben der einzelnen in der Selbstsucht macht das Leben in der Gemeinschaft mühevoll. Es engt den Lebensraum ein. Augustinus, «Sermo 69,1», *Sermones in Matthaeum I*, edd. P.-P. Verbraken *et al.* (CCL 41 Aa), Turnhout 2008, 460: «*Quare enim omnes laboramus, nisi quia sumus homines mortales, fragiles, infirmi, lutea uasa portantes, quae faciunt inuicem angustias? Sed, si angustantur uasa carnis, dilatentur spatia caritatis*».

259 Cf. *RB* Prol 49.

260 *RB* Prol 21.

261 Cf. Böckmann, *Mit Christus zum Ziel*, 350.

«Verdienst/verdienen» (*meritum/mereor*) oder «Lohn» (*merx*)[262], wobei er diese Begriffe in einem analogen Sinn verwendet[263]. Es geht ihm nicht um Leistung, Selbstvermarktung oder wirtschaftliches Kalkül. In Übereinstimmung mit biblischer Erfahrung und in Anlehnung an die liturgische Gebetssprache der Kirche[264] knüpft die RB vielmehr an die anthropologische Grundgegebenheit an, daß die Hoffnung auf bleibenden Lohn, Menschen in ihrem Mühen um das Gute motiviert, ja über sich hinauswachsen läßt[265]. Der Lohn- und Verdienstgedanke steht in der *Regula Benedicti* zudem in enger Verbindung mit dem Gemeinschaftsleben[266] sowie dem Aspekt der Öffentlichkeitsrelevanz eigenen und kommunitären Handelns. Daraus ergibt sich für alle eine eigene Verantwortung vor Gott, vor einander und vor Außenstehenden[267]. Verdienst steht in der RB nicht im Kontext von Selbstdarstellung oder der Anhäufung bestimmter Dinge oder Leistungen, sondern hat mit lebensfördernden Beziehungen zwischen Personen zu tun. Auch der in der *Regula* erwähnte Lohn ist keine Sache, sondern Gott selbst, das Leben in enger Gemeinschaft mit ihm[268]. Der in der Benedikts-

262 Cf. T. Kardong, «Merit and Reward in Benedict's Rule», in *Regulae Benedicti Studia*, vol. 19, ed. M. Hebler, EOS Verlag, St. Ottilien 1997, 115-131.

263 Christlich-monastisches Leben wurzelt letztlich nicht in wie auch immer gearteten eigenen «Verdiensten», sondern im Handeln Gottes am Menschen und dem menschlichen Mitwirken, dem Miteinander von Gott und Mensch im Raum der Gnade (cf. oben, Pkt. 3.9.1.).

264 Cf. die Formulierung *mereamur* in *RB* Prol 21.50. Siehe weiterführend: E. Kasch, *Das liturgische Vokabular der frühen lateinischen Mönchsregeln* (Regulae Benedicti Studia Supplementa 1), Hildesheim 1974.

265 Cf. *RB* 40,4. Asketischer Übereifer jedoch wird mit dem Hinweis auf die fehlende Anrechnung als «Verdienst» unterbunden (vgl. *RB* 49,9).

266 Dienste, die mit besonderen Anforderungen verbunden sind (z.B. Küchen- oder Krankendienst), ist ein motivierender Lohn verheißen (cf. *RB* 35,2; 36,5). Die vorbildliche Lebensführung von Mönchen, die sich bewährt haben, findet Anerkennung zur Auferbauung aller. Cf. *RB* 2,22; M. Puzicha, «Achtung, Würde und Ehrfurcht. Ein Grundthema der Benediktusregel», *Monastische Informationen* 95 (1998) 14-20, hier: 16. Pädagogisch motiviert ist auch, daß in der *Regula Benedicti* ein «verdienstvolles Leben» sowohl Kriterium für die Rangfolge (cf. *RB* 63,1) als auch für die Beauftragung mit einem verantwortungsvollen Dienst in der Gemeinschaft ist. Dekane werden *secundum vitae meritum* ausgewählt (cf. *RB* 21,4). Dasselbe Kriterium gilt für die Wahl eines Abtes (*RB* 64,2).

267 Mönche, die sich aus reiner Absicht und Eifer für Gott für die Wahl eines würdigen Abtes einsetzen und so in der Diözese einen Skandal verhindern, wird Lohn verheißen (cf. *RB* 64,5-6).

268 Cf. *RB* 4,75-78

regel zum Ausdruck kommende Lohn- bzw. Verdienstgedanke[269] unterstreicht den Wert menschlichen Bemühens im Kontext der gnadenhaften Zuwendung Gottes und hebt andererseits auch den Aspekt der Verantwortung des Einzelnen vor Gott und den Menschen hervor[270].

3.9. Leben im Horizont von Endlichkeit und Vollendung

Benediktinische Mönche und Nonnen üben sich darin, den «Tod täglich vor Augen»[271] zu haben. Die eschatologische Ausrichtung im benediktinischen Mönchtum weicht der Grenze zwischen Leben und Tod nicht aus, sondern hat sie in einer Grundhaltung der Verantwortung vor Gott und den Menschen im Blick. Die kaufkraftgestützte Todesverdrängung in der vom Ökonomismus geprägten Lebensanschauung und die Gier, so viel Welt zu konsumieren wie nur möglich, stehen in starkem Kontrast zu dieser christlich-monastischen Haltung. Die Benediktsregel lädt Menschen ein, die Augen vor der ganzen Wirklichkeit menschlicher Existenz nicht zu verschließen, sondern wachsam zu sein[272], ihre eigene Schwachheit[273], ihr Denken und Tun im Aufschauen zu Gott[274] kritisch in den Blick zu nehmen. Nach der Benediktsregel lebende Mönche und Nonnen, die Leidenschaft für das Leben haben, es lieben und «gute Tage sehen»[275] wollen, sind sich dessen bewußt, daß der Tod den Menschen nicht erst am Ende des Lebens begegnet. Boten und Vorboten des Todes (Grenzerfahrungen,

---

269 Die Verdienstlehre ist theologisch ambivalent und hat im Verlauf der Geschichte zu Mißverständnissen geführt. Weil Jesus Christus ein für allemal die Erlösung der Menschheit bewirkt hat, kann von «Verdiensten» des Geschöpfes Mensch nur im analogen Sinne gesprochen werden. Der Mensch kann und muß sich sein Heil letztlich nicht selbst verdienen. Cf. W. Molinski, «Verdienst», in *Sacramentum Mundi*, vol. 4, Herder, Freiburg i. Br. 1969, 1159-1165; P. Fransen, «Gnade und Verdienst», in *Mysterium Salutis*, vol. 4/2, edd. J. Feiner-M. Löhrer, Einsiedeln 1973, 977-982.

270 Die enge Verbindung menschlichen Bemühens und gnadenhafter Ermöglichung durch Gott kommt z. B. in *RB* 4,42; 40,4; 49,9 zum Ausdruck. Der Aspekt menschlicher Verantwortung wird z.B. deutlich in *RB* 5,17-19; 64,6.

271 *RB* 4,47: *mortem cottidie ante oculos suspectam habere.*

272 Cf. auch die unmittelbar folgenden Werkzeuge (*RB* 4,48-51) und die 1. Stufe der Demut (*RB* 7,10-30) sowie Jesu Mahnung zur Wachsamkeit (Mk 13,33-37; Mt 24,42).

273 Die Mahnung *suamque fragilitatem semper suspectus sit* (*RB* 64,13) gilt insbesondere dem Abt in seiner Verantwortung für die Gemeinschaft, ist jedoch im Licht des Demutsweges (cf. *RB* 7) für alle Mönche gültig.

274 *Suspicere* wird in der Vulgata im Sinn des Nach-oben-Blickens (Dan 13,35; Jes 22,11; Gen 15,5; Mk 7,34) gebraucht; cf. Böckmann, *Christus hören*, 258-259.

275 Cf. *RB* Prol 15.

Scheitern, Schuld etc.) begleiten vielmehr das Leben des Menschen von Anfang an. Sie verbergen sich in jeder menschlichen Geschichte und zwingen dazu, abschiedlich zu leben[276]. Die monastische *conuersatio morum* schließt immer auch harte Wegstrecken[277] ein und die Bereitschaft umzukehren[278], sich vom Herrn wieder neu den Weg zum Leben zeigen[279] zu lassen. Die Grenze, die das Leben vom Tod trennt, wandelt ihre Gestalt Laufe des Lebens. Auch Mönche oder Nonnen können sich durch eine schwere, dauernde Pflege erfordernde Krankheit oder Siechtum über Jahre hinweg auf dieser Grenze bewegen. Selbst wenn für Benedikt die Sorge für Kranke und Schwache oberste Priorität hat[280] und das Leben gerade in und durch seine Endlichkeit kostbar und gut zu nutzen ist[281], muß die Todesgrenze nicht quälend hinausgeschoben werden. Sie bedeutet nicht das Ende, sondern birgt ein Hoffnungspotential in sich, das jeder Grenze innewohnt: «daß es drüben weitergeht, daß es überhaupt ein Drüben gibt»[282]. Benedikt nennt dieses «Drüben» das «himmlische Vaterland»[283], das «ewige Leben», das der Mönch «mit allem geistlichen Begehren ersehen»[284] soll. Der Tod kann das menschliche Leben nicht rückwirkend entwerten, weil er gewissermaßen kein Punkt, sondern ein «Doppelpunkt»[285] ist. Er verleitet den Mönch jedoch nicht dazu, gleichsam selbstbestimmt «mit dem Kopf durch die Wand» des Daseins zu wollen, wo es ihm als beschädigtes, verweigertes, behindertes oder verhindertes Leben begegnet. Er nimmt vielmehr aus Liebe zu seinem Schöpfer[286], den die Leidenschaft für das Leben in die Zonen des Todes gezogen hat, «in Geduld an den Leiden Christi»[287] teil und hält in schwierigen Situationen standhaft aus[288]. Im Unterschied zu einer heute diagnostizierten

---

276 Menschen machen die Erfahrung, daß ihre eigene Lebensgeschichte oder die anderer immer wieder an Grenzen stößt, neu gefügt werden muß, auch wenn sie zeitweise scheinbar keinen Sinn mehr erkennen läßt.

277 Cf. *RB* Prol 48; *RB* 58,8.

278 Cf. Böckmann, *Mit Christus zum Ziel*, 134, Anm. 75-76; zu Handschriftenvarianten bei *conuersatio/conuersio* cf. *Benedicti Regula*, ed. R. Hanslik (CSEL 75), Wien 1977, 149.

279 Cf. *RB* Prol 20f; *RB* 72,12.

280 Cf. *RB* 36-37; 48,24f.

281 Cf. *RB* Prol 43-44.

282 Liessmann, *Lob der Grenze*, 176; cf. *ibid.*, 176-197.

283 *RB* 73,8

284 Cf. *RB* 4,46.

285 Cf. H. Zahrnt, *Glauben unter leerem Himmel*, München 2000, 254.

286 *RB* 73,4.

287 *RB* Prol 50.

288 Cf. z.B. *RB* 7,35-43.

«Geschwätzigkeit des Todes»[289], die sich in einer exzessiven Selbstsorge äußern kann, als übertriebene Sorge um den eigenen Körper, seine Leistungsfähigkeit oder Jugendlichkeit[290], lädt die Benediktsregel Menschen ein, den Blick nicht zu verlieren auf das gute Leben in seiner Fülle. Erst wo der Tod dem Leben Form gibt, wird aus dem *bíos* eine Biographie[291], ein Leben, das unter Führung des Evangeliums und Christi zur Vollendung gelangt.

SCHLUSSBEMERKUNG

A. Stock wies in einem Beitrag zur Frage des theologischen Umgangs mit dem Phänomen der Kultur darauf hin, daß der Begriff «Kultur» seinen lateinischen Ursprüngen nach aus dem Bereich des Landbaus, der «Bearbeitung und Pflege des Ackers», der mit mühevoller Arbeit und Umsicht verbundenen «Bestellung des Bodens» stammt[292]. Diese Tätigkeit, die für die Existenz des Menschen auf dieser Erde grundlegend ist, wurde später auf «die ganze darauf aufbauende menschliche Lebensgestaltung, Lebensart und Lebensform übertragen, auf ihre Aus- und Weiterbildung, die Sitten und Gebräuche des Lebens, ihre Pflege und Entwicklung»[293].

Benediktinisch-monastisches Leben basiert wie Kultur insgesamt auf Entscheidungen. Damit sind Grenzziehungen, die Wahrnehmung und/oder der bewußte Vollzug von Grenzüberschreitungen verbunden. Jede Lebenskultur verlangt jedoch nicht nur einmalig, sondern immer wieder, klare Entscheidungen auf der Basis kluger Abwägung und Unterscheidung (*discretio*)[294]. Davon zeugt bis in die heutige Zeit die Regel Benedikts.

«Barbarei» ist, wie J. Manemann in einem Plädoyer für «Theologie als Kulturwissenschaft» dargelegt hat, in allen Geschichtsepochen nicht einfach Gegenstück zur Kultur, sondern dieser auch immanent[295]. Sie motiviert somit zur

289 Cf. A. NASSEHI, «Die Geschwätzigkeit des Todes. Oder: Der Tod als Parabel auf Offenheit durch Geschlossenheit», in ID., *Geschlossenheit und Offenheit, Studien zur Theorie der modernen Gesellschaft*, Frankfurt am Main 2003, 287-309.

290 Cf. A. HILT, «Die Praxis der *ars moriendi* oder die Erfahrung, leben zu lernen und sterben zu können», *Philosophische Rundschau* 55 (2008) 307-331, hier 307.

291 Cf. HILT, «Die Praxis der *ars moriendi* oder die Erfahrung», 308.

292 Cf. zum folgenden: A. STOCK, «Sensibilität ist gefragt. Wie soll Theologie mit Kultur umgehen?», *Herder Korrespondenz Spezial* 66 (2012) 25-29.

293 STOCK, «Sensibilität ist gefragt».

294 Cf. weiterführend J. GRIBOMONT-J. LECLERCQ, «Cultura monastica», in *Dizionario degli Istituti di Perfezione*, vol. 3, Roma 1976, 332-339.

295 Cf. J. MANEMANN, «Theologie als Kulturwissenschaft. Ein Plädoyer», Orientierung 70

Kulturkritik. Der Begriff «Kultur» ist in der heutigen Gesellschaft vielfach und facettenreich präsent. Aber auch Erscheinungsformen von Unkulturen müssen in der Gegenwart beim Namen genannt werden – aus der Verantwortung für diese Erde und die Menschen, die auf ihr leben. Kulturhermeneutik und -kritik können nicht nur Aufgabe der modernen Kulturwissenschaft sein. Es ist ein Terrain, das ebenso nicht allein Politikern, Ökonomen, Soziologen oder anderen Gesellschaftswissenschaftlern überlassen werden kann. Es braucht vielmehr auch einen theologischen Umgang mit Kultur. Theologen können und müssen sich vom christlichen Menschenbild und der christlichen Soziallehre her hier konstruktiv und horizonterweiternd zu Wort melden. Doch nicht allein die Theologie, auch die Kirche als Ganze und in ihr das Mönchtum sind herausgefordert, sich nicht erst angesichts von spezifischen gesellschaftlichen Tendenzen und Formen von Unkulturen in ihrer jeweiligen Zeit aus christlicher Verantwortung einzubringen. Das benediktinische Mönchtum war in der Geschichte ein wichtiger Kulturträger. Die Benediktsregel ist auch heute, angesichts von Entwicklungen in Richtung auf eine «Ökonomisierung» wichtiger Bereiche menschlichen Lebens, ein nicht zu unterschätzender Stimulator einer verantwortungsvollen Kulturkritik, weil sie deutlich macht, daß der Wert des Menschen und der Sinn seines Lebens nicht an der Meßlatte der Ökonomie abgelesen werden können.

Abstract

According to sociological research, current society today is characterized by tendencies towards a growing economic outlook. According to it, the human being, the world, various social or cultural facts are merely reduced to economic dimensions. There are even tendencies today to interpret the whole sum of human life in terms of the production, acquisition, and distribution of wealth. According to the moral and social philosophy of *economism*, that gains some influence in current society, the human being is continually forced to self-improvement and even self-exploitation in order to meet the economic standards proclaimed by omnipresent mass media. Wherever a unilateral economic outlook prevails, society is tempted to degenerate into a «casting society» where extreme individualism, assertiveness, and ego-marketing are paramount. Economism leads people to describe themselves in terms of their work as it is promoted life's ultimate task and justification. In the range of «academic business», there are

(2006) 38-43, hier: 38-39, zitiert in: STOCK, «Sensibilität ist gefragt», 28.

tendencies to give economic usability of education top priority today. When the predominant logic in society is centred on gainful employment, the poor and poverty raise a general suspicion. Whoever fails due to the omnipresent performance standards, whoever is of foreign or migration background, who is ill or handicapped, who lost his work etc. may easily face social marginalization.

In the face of certain dehumanizing tendencies that are necessarily connected with a unilateral economic approach to mankind and society, the paper emphasizes some of the humanizing potential of Benedict's Rule. It shows, that the Rule itself is essentially a creative and critical fixing of boundaries in order to facilitate and to foster life «with the Gospel for our guide» (RB Prol 21). It is a Rule «written for beginners» who have the courage to cross obsolete boundaries and to set out (RB 73,8). Monastic enclosure, far from the intention to create a kind of «parallel society», aims at the concentration and intensification of human life. The monastic concept of silence and listening is opposed to today's hype and market clamour. The 3 fundamental columns (prayer, work, *lectio divina*) in RB are fixing boundaries in the daily time-table in order to avoid being overwhelmed by work and destructive private ambition (RB 48). The Rule stresses the priority of the single person in contrast to economic efficiency (RB 57) and puts emphasis on the aspect of social responsibility in the context of work, asceticism and poverty (RB 57; 4; 31; 53; 55; 66). Under the motto «*ne quid nimis*» (RB 64,12), the paper considers Benedict's treatment of weaknesses, old age, sickness, and faults in the monastic community and underlines the priority of grace – not of performance or achievement – even though RB also mentions «merit» and «reward». Last but not least, the paper presents Christian-monastic altruism (RB 72,7) as a radical border crossing and human life in the light of finiteness and perfection (RB 4).

Just as Benedictine monasticism was an important culture-bearer in history, the RB is still today a stimulator for a well-grounded culture critique and offers wise and experienced Christian and monastic guidelines for people in today's world.

NON-CHRISTIAN MONASTICISM

EURASIAN MONASTICISM: MEDIEVAL MONASTERIES IN A GLOBAL CONTEXT

Anthony John Lappin

When considering monasticism, above all Western monasticism, scholarly emphasis has recently fallen on the structures of monastic communities following on from Giorgio Agamben's delineation of the *forma-di-vita* as instantiated by monastic *regulae*. These structures are both internal to and, in the sources used, idealize those same monastic communities which they regulate; and these ideal monastic communities are in turn understood as embodying a rejection of the *operosità* which dominates normal, worldly civilization; such *forme-di-vita*, however, go further, and provide a negation of the sub-human field of nature[1]. I wish, however, to look in a different direction, away from the metaphysical supremacy often claimed for monasticism, to consider, rather, the impact that monasticism — or, rather, individual monasteries, families and alliances of monastic houses — had on their surroundings: the ecology of their interraction and survival within an economic and social world; the influences that they brought to bear and had brought to bear upon them; the *raison d'être* of their perdurance as communal institutions. This analysis is not, in spirit, a comparative exercise: that is, not a means of eliciting similarities and differences between Benedictine monasticism and Theravada Buddhist monasticism as Friedrich-Silber did in her now classic study[2]. Still less is it a simple observation that there were monasteries and temples dotted here and there, stretching across the Eurasian continental landmass and its contiguous islands, from Japan to Iceland, from Gotland to Sri Lanka. It is, rather, a means of looking at medieval society — which may be defined, for our pur-

---

Anthony John Lappin, philologist and historian, research professor at Maynooth University, Ireland.

1 G. Agamben, *Altissima povertà*, Neri Pozza, Vicenza, 2011, and *L'usi del corpo*, Vicenza, 2014.

2 I. Friedrich Silber, *Virtuosity, Charisma, and Social Order: a comparative sociological study of monasticism in Theravada Buddhism and medieval Catholicism*, Cambridge, 1995.

poses, as a society in which monasteries occupied a dominant position within the social and economic landscape. We may thus talk of a characteristic type of interraction with the world outside the monastic walls, a recurring set of interests and influences irrespective of religion, or rule, or founder: monasteries providing a crucial, and at times formative, impulse to trade, determining or altering patterns of landholding, contributing to the exploitation of land (and rivers, lakes and seas), spurring on cultural production (artisanal and intellectual), and offering a central channel for the expression of religious devotion. Local differences count for something; but not everything.

1. MONASTERIES AS FOUNDATIONAL STRUCTURES

The existence of monasteries throughout Eurasia is not an accidental quality of the three world religions of Buddhism, Christianity and Hinduism; but, rather, an essential means by which those religions themselves spread and were implanted within societies. The case of Buddhism is paradigmatic: spreading from a first eremitic community beside a major trade-route, it implanted itself through, in the main, monasteries. The rise of monasticism in Christianity is placed in the wastes of Egypt during the third century (and desert monasticism continued to have an undeniable cachet for long afterwards); nevertheless well-established city-dwelling communities were also to be found towards the end of fourth century[3], and prior existence of regulated communities of urban presbyters (whose identity was later that of «canons») cannot but be surmised. Hinduism (as distinct from Brahmanism) sees its very foundation in the monastic establishments created by Śaṅkara in the early eight century[4]; and whilst Islam did not itself officially provide permanent monastic settlements[5], Christian monasticism flourished into the second

3 At, for example, Milan and Rome: see P. Brown, *Augustine of Hippo: a biography*, University of California Press, Berkeley (CA) 1967, 136–37.

4 G. Chandra Pande, *Life and Thought of Śaṅkarācārya*, Motilal Banarsidass Publishers Pvt. Ltd., New Delhi, 1994, 337; D.N. Lorenzen, *Who Invented Hinduism? Essays on religion and history*, New Delhi 2006; N. Isaeva, *Shankara and Indian Philosophy*, Albany (NY) 1993, 81; F. Whaling, «Śaṅkara and Buddhism», *Indian Journal of Philosophy* 7 (1979) 1-42, at 30.

5 On Sufi monasteries formed specifically at the shrines of holy men and subsisting through donations, see J. Abbink, «Muslim monasteries? Some aspects of religious culture in northern Ethiopia», *Aethiopica* 11 (2008) 117-33, at 121-22; in general, Idries Shah, *The Sufis*, London ²1977, 291.

millenium AD, spreading with the opportunities opened by conquest[6]: one must conclude, at the very least, that there was a symbiotic relationship. Even Zoroastrianism provides evidence for monastic forms of life around temples, and there were even significant enough numbers for them to be mentioned in a Chinese imperial edict of suppression in the mid-ninth century[7].

The medieval Eurasian world, then, from the eighth into the eleventh or twelfth century was characterized by the omnipresence of monastic establishments, belonging to different religions and affecting allegiance to various groupings within those religions; yet all characterized by a structured, communal life; an emphasis upon celibacy as part of an ascetic programme; the institutional holding of property; and a consistent engagement with the outside world. Characterizations of monasteries and nunneries as «cut off from the world» misunderstand how an individual's ascetic removal took place within the greater economic and institutional structures with their informal, accompanying webs of support, all of which allowed this *ascesis* in the first place. It would be tempting, then, to claim that this study makes the skilled administrators, the *oeconomos* or bursar, into the most important figure in the monastery, rather than the spiritual master; and our unit of measurement when one calculates what a «monastery» is, therefore, must not be limited to the cloister and church, the prayer-hall and dormitory, the hallowed space within the coenobitic walls — rather the «monastery» must be considered as an economic system joining monks or nuns or both to the monastic servants, labourers, serfs and temporarily corvéed peasants (in short, and in good Latin, the monastic *familia*), interracting within a landscape of territories held under varying conditions of lordship, and necessitating constant relations with other monastic and secular lordships and with multiple other forms of economic and social interests[8]. Nevertheless, it is important not to over-egg the econo-

6 In general on the *dhimmitude* of Christians, see S. Griffith, *The Church in the Shadow of the Mosque: Christians and Muslims in the world of Islam*, Princeton University Press, Princeton 2009, and *Christians and Others in the Umayyad State*, ed. A. Borrut-F.M. Donner, Chicago 2016; on the diffusion of monasteries in the Church of the East, W. Baum, «The Age of the Arabs (650-1258)», in *The Church of the East: a concise history*, ed. W. Baum-D.W. Winkler, London 2003, 44-50.

7 T. Daryaee, *Sasanian Persia: the rise and fall of an empire*, I.B. Tauris, London 2009, 147; L.E. Browne, *The Eclipse of Christianity in Asia: from the time of Muhammad till the fourteenth century*, Cambridge 1933, 97.

8 For the Carolingians: W. Horn-E. Born, *The Plan of St Gall: a study of the architecture and economy of, and life in, a paradigmatic Carolingian monastery*, Berkeley (CA), 1979, I:341; for the Irish church: C. Doherty, «Some aspects of hagiography as a source for

mic pudding as a utilitarian be-all-and-end-all: one of the key elements of any monastery's development and survival was its ability to convert material suport into spiritual merit; and it was its basic ability to effect this transformative exchange which guaranteed its importance. As was formalized within Buddhism, but which may stand for all monastic traditions:

> The traditional logic for monastic distance from the laity was that, through their strict adherence to the norms of monastic codes, monks made themselves into repositories of merit. As such, the monks, isolated from ordinary secular community life, nevertheless provided an indirect service by offering the laity an opportunity to generate merit through donations. The symbiotic relationship functioned through the logic of donation, purity, and merit[9].

2. MONASTERIES AND THE SELF

The central core of a monastery was the ascetic individuals who created and continued its existence, establishing and developing an institutionalized means of existence and which offered them all a structure of support and a focus of vital interest from conversion to grave. Crucial in this aspect was the expectation of celibacy – or, rather, the renunciation of any claim made by the individual's progeny. Here, monastic *milieux* offered a direct contrast to the aristocratic societies that surrounded them, where the privileges and duties of birth weighed heavily upon subsequent generations, and «life chances» (if we may call them that) were determined almost exclusively by the alignment, not of the stars, but of acknowledged parenthood. Yet this definition of the monastery as a «counter-culture» may obscure other aspects of the monastery's attraction, such as

Irish economic history», *Peritia* 1 (1982) 300-28, at 313-15.

9 J.A. Silk, *Managing Monks: administrators and administrative rules in Indian Buddhist Monasteries*, Oxford 2008, 6. As a conscious evolution from the very start of Buddhism: A.S. Amar, «The *Buddhakṣetra* of Bodhgaya: sangha, exchanges and trade networks», in *Religions and Trade: religious formation, transformation and cross-cultural exchange between East and West*, edd. P. Wick-V. Rabens, Leiden 2014, 134. In a similar vein, J. Van Engen, «The crisis of cenobitism revisited: Benedictine monasticism in the years 1050–1150», *Speculum* 61 (1986) 269-304; I. Friedrich Silber, «Monasticism and the "Protestant ethic": asceticism, rationality and wealth in the medieval west», *British Journal of Sociology* 44 (1993) 103-123. With regard to Hinduism, J.C. Oman, *The Mystics, Ascetics, and Saints of India: a study of the Sadhusim, with an account of the Yogis, Sanyasis, Bairagis, and other strange Hindu sectarians*, London 1905, 249-250.

providing a pressure-valve for the societies in which they found themselves and which they also formed, by providing individuals a means of escape from some aspects of their own networks of dependency. So the monastery offered not so much a counter-culture, more a parallel and interracting sub-culture.

Such a stepping-aside from the requirements of providing their families with descendents freed the institution's substance from division through inheritance or unmanageable expansion. It also guaranteed that the individual's primary commitment was to the institution itself, and the institution's own interrelations with the world outside. The *monachos* was thereby provided with an anchor and responsibility which was not held by the bureaucrat, the *litteratus*, the lawyer or the secular or temple priest, whose career advancement was linked to much closer individual worldly interraction: within an imperial, royal or episcopal *curia*; within the law courts; or within merchant guilds and markets. As such, the monastery provided a crucial element in constructing a sense of corporate belonging, and a possibility for the creation of independent cultural expression: part of this, of course, is through liturgy, whose importance, in allocentric societies, cannot be emphasised enough. And part, through more speculative, literary and theological endeavours which were allowed by the accumulation of wealth, a obligatory foundation for the *otium* necessary for any setting of questioning quill to invitingly blank leaves, and for the formation of the essential audience, possessed of a relevant education which would allow appreciation and diffusion of such intellectual work. The creation and consumption of monastic literature, then, played a crucial role in forming a coenobitized individual.

Monasteries tended to form greater structures, as federations or through the scattering of daughter-houses, and here we see the transfer of knowledge and personel over sometimes large distances, correspondingly bringing an awareness of cultural variations by and to those who were moved around. Thus in China we find stagnation avoided by the constant renewal of the leaders of monasteries either internally through rotation[10]; or by the state control of abbatial appointments through an examination system; or the systematic opening out of family monasteries as public monasteries; the inclusion of monasteries whose abbatial appointments were internal (a succeeding abbot appointed by the previous one) into a wider network by converting them into public monasteries whose abbots necessarily were apponted by the state; or, finally, the conscious creation of monastic federations and families through

10 O. Moore, «The Ceremony of Gratitude», in *State and Court Ritual in China*, ed. J.P. McDermott, Cambridge 1999, 197-236, at 218.

their allegiance to united doctrinal systems, whose fortunes waxed and waned with imperial favour through succeeding dynasties[11]. In India in the eleventh and twelfth centuries, philosophico-theological currents institutionalized themselves in sub-continent-wide monastic lineages which preserved and propagated individual's teachings[12]. The basic religious ideology embodied by the monastery consistently spread to the laity, wherever these monasteries were founded; such contagion might be at the level of doctrine, of social *mores*, or even in the more advanced elements of state-formation[13].

Full involvement in the monstery required an apprenticeship in deportment, a learning of suitable behaviour in the mind, and with the body: monastic discipline had education at its heart[14]. Apart from the formation of the monk or nun, it soon also offered education to those who would remain outside the walls of the monastery, often exerting a definitive influence over secular educational systems: so the preparation of candidates for state examinations was often carried out by Buddhist monasteries during the eighth century in China, their methods modelled by secular masters, and influencing even the conduct of examinations and the celebration of success[15]. The famous Buddhist university of Nalanda was built around monasteries, indeed was a monastery of monasteries, catering for religious and secular students[16]; and Hindu monasteries or *maths* busied themselves with offering a strong

11 S. Weinstein, *Buddhism under the T'ang*, Cambridge 1987; Chi-Chiang Huang, «Elite Clergy in Northern Sung Hang-chou: a convergence of interest» in *Buddhism and the Sung*, edd. P.N. Gregory-D.A. Getz, Honolulu (HI) 1999, 295–239.

12 M. Clark, *The Dasanami-Samnyasis: the integration of ascetic lineages into an order*, Brill, Leiden 2006; *An Introductory Dictionary of Religious Studies*, edd. O.O. Espin-J.B. Nicholoff, Collegeville (MN) 2007, 894, with particular reference to Ramanuja (from the early eleventh century) and Nimbarka (mid-twelfth century).

13 W.M. Bodiford, «The Medieval Period: eleventh to sixteenth centuries», in *Nanzan Guide to Japanese Religions*, edd. P.L. Swanson-C. Chilson, Honolulu (HI) 2005, 167; J.R. Goodwin, *Alms and Vagabonds: Buddhist temples and popular patronage in medieval Japan*, Honolulu (HI) 1994, 2.

14 For example, J. Leclerq, *L'Amour des lettres et le désir de Dieu*, Paris 1957; and for a view of the flux within that period, *Medieval Monastic Education*, edd. G. Ferzoco-C. Muessig, London 2000.

15 L.A. Walton, *Academies and Society in Southern Sung China*, Honolulu (HI) 1999, 12; B.A. Elman, *Civil Examinations and Meritocracy in Late Imperial China*, Cambridge (MA) 2013, 227.

16 F.M. Asher, *Nalanda: situating the Great Monastery*, Marg, Mumbai, 2015; Le Huu Phuoc, *Buddhist Architecture*, New York 2010, 58-62; B.N. Misra, *Nalanda*, 3 voll., Delhi 1998, I:261.

intellectual competition to the Buddhists' coenobitic universities[17]. At a lower level, but still concerned with the transmission of knowledge (primarily of ritual practice), are the Daoist monastic traditions which coalesced between the fourth and sixth century AD[18].

3. MONASTERIES AND THE ENVIRONMENT

When a group practising a revolutionary form of religious life reached Paris from the heretic-ridden Midi towards the end of the second decade of the thirteenth century, with the intention of living off the alms of the citizens and dedicating themselves to preaching, they were upraided by one of the more important burghers: "It would be good for you to have lands and vines and servants, so that you might keep yourselves"[19]. In the main, monasticism demanded significant land-holding and servant-holding to function, with such possessions gained through the transfer of land from aristocracy to coenobium. As perhaps might be expected from a predominantly rural society, significant monastic possessions of land could only come about through the favour of the ruling elite. As an example, we might take the mountain-passes through the Ghats to the western coast of India, a part of the Western Deccan, where rock-cut monasteries refer to sometimes large grants of coconut-groves: one inscription, from Nasik, mentioned the bestowal of an expanse comprising thirty-two thousand trees[20], equalling about one hundred and fifty hectares of prime coastal strip[21]. The Buddhist monasteries in this area were dependent for their prosperity between the first century BC and the fourth AD upon a non-Buddhist elite, even though a majority of their donations came from much more humble devotees[22]. From the point of view of rulers,

---

17 R. Collins, *The Sociology of Philosophies: a global theory of intellectual change*, Cambridge (MA) 1998, 250. For western Europe, J.D. Lowrie, *The Medieval University, 1200-400*, London 1961, 6-17.

18 L. Kohn, *Monastic Life in Medieval Daoism: a cross-cultural perspective*, Honolulu (HI) 2003, 40-42.

19 R.E. Lerner, «Philip the Chancellor greets the early Dominicans in Paris», *Archivum Fratrum Praedicatorum* 72 (2007) 5-17, at 12.

20 E. Senart, «Inscriptions in the caves at Nasik», in *Epigraphica indica*, 42 voll., Delhi, 1892-1978, 8:78-80.

21 The optimal density in India is around 175 trees per hectare; maximum density in gardens is 250: K.G. Tejwani, *Agroforestry in India*, New Delhi 1994, 67.

22 K.D. Morrison, «Trade, urbanism, and agricultural expansion: Buddhist monastic institutions and the State in the early historic Western Deccan», *World Archaeology*

monasteries offered an opportunity for conspicuous display of gift-giving, but also a stable personnel that could monumentalize and memorialize the rulers themselves[23]. Dynastic memorialization is perhaps an unsurprising constant, with the spiritual welfare of the donor and deceased family taken over by the monastic community itself[24].

The amassing of surplus at the monastery and its other holdings may not have been solely in aid of the powerful: the surplus is time and again called on to alleviate famine in all traditions[25]. Yet it would be unthinkable for monks to work such large landholdings so distant from the monastery, whether manual work was specifically embraced (as in Benedictine monasticism) or wholly rejected (as in most forms of Buddhism)[26]. And so the gift of land also implied or necessitated the gift of the workers on the land, be they slaves, serfs, bonded peasants or tenant farmers[27]. Care should be taken at this point not

---

27 (1995) 203-21, at 210. For the beginnings of Buddhist monasteries towards the beginning of the first century AD, see J. Bronkhorst, *Buddhism in the Shadow of Brahmanism*, Leiden 2011, 18.

23 For example, the Srivijaya's domination of trade routes during the last centuries of the first millenium saw numerous monasteries founded at a distance from their centre of power: L.N. Shaffer, *Maritime Southeast Asia to 1500*, Armont (NY) 1996, 49. Massive foundation of monasteries as an expression of control of the empire in China in the early seventh century: J. Robson, «Buddhism and the Chinese Marchmount System», in *Religion and Chinese Society. A centenial conference of the École Française d'Extrême-Orient*, vol. 1: *Ancient and medieval China*, ed. J. Lagerwey, Hong Kong 2004, 341-384.

24 O.G. Oexle, «Memoria und Memorialüberlieferung im früheren Mittelalter», *Frümittelalterliche Studien* 10 (1976) 70-95; M. Lawers, *La Mémoire des ancêtres, le souci des morts: morts, rites et sociétés au moyen âge (Diocèse de Liège, XIe–XIIe siècles)*, Paris 1997; I. Friedrich Silber, «Gift-giving in the great traditions: the case of donations to monasteries in the medieval west», *Archives européennes de sociologie* 36 (1995) 209-243.

25 For the importance of the tithe-barn to the medieval European economy: M. Arnoux, «Pour une économie historique de la dîme», in *La Dîme dans l'Europe médiévale et moderne. Actes des XIIIes Journées Internationales d'Histoire de l'Abbaye de Flaran 3 et 4 octobre 2008*, ed. R. Viader, Toulouse, 2010, 145-160, at 156-157.

26 *An Introductory Dictionary*, edd. Espin-Nickoloff, 896.

27 G. Schopen, «The monastic ownership of servants or slaves: local and legal factors in the redactional history of two vinayas», *Journal of the International Association of Buddhist Studies* 17 (1994) 145-174. Rights and dues were not necessarily simple: for the *corvée* of peasants (*vishti* in Sanskrit), see M.K.V. Narayan, *Flipside of Hindu Symbolism: sociological and scientific linkages in Hinduism*, New Delhi, 2007, 158-159. For monastic investment in agricultural improvements and use of tenants, see N. Karashima, «The land donation to Hindu temples in medieval south India», *Journal of Asian*

to simply assume that success of monasteries depends «upon an expanding and growing economy and a sophisticated political system capable of extracting and channelling surplus»[28]; rather, groups of significant landholders were able to divest themselves for certain periods of large areas of land and of the peasantry which also depended upon that territory, under conditions which are often opaque.

These grants of land and other privileges — such as tax free status, rights to hold (and tax) markets — were also a means by which the spiritual power of the monastery was wedded to the dynastic concerns of the donor: co-opted by the obligation of showing gratitude in the form of the performance of rituals for the protection of the rulers, monasteries (be they in India, China, Japan or the Holy Roman Empire) turned into semi-independent departments of the state. They were not, on the whole, autonomous, self-governing institutions which was, and still remains, the ideal to which it is felt that these establishments should have conformed[29]: political reality consistently produced a different outcome. Intimate financial relations which guaranteed permanence to the institution would also lead to ideological co-option[30], and consequently serious difficulties, acute crisis and occasionally extinction when régimes lost the Mandate of Heaven. The attraction of such consolidation was a freeing from dependence upon donations from individuals to keep the monastery going from day to day[31], whilst, at the same time, allowing these increasingly powerful monasteries to become important political players in their own right, both in regional significance and in their influence over individual officials and rulers[32].

Such inter-dependence might, however, involve not just the liturgical transmogrification of base gold into spiritual treasure, but a conscious exchange of goods: German imperial monasteries, for example, received lavish largesse since they offered way-stations during the emperors' circulation of their realms[33]. The

---

and African Studies 2 (1969) 29-65, and summary in *Anthropos* 65 (1970) 283.

28 Collins, *Sociology*, 207.

29 See Bronkhorst, *Buddhism*, 238; P.N. Gregory, «The Vitality of Buddhism in the Sung», in *Buddhism in the Sung*, edd. P.N. Gregory-D.A. Getz, Honolulu (HI) 1999, 5; Bodiford, «The Medieval Period».

30 G. Schopen, *Bones, Stones, and Buddhist Monks*, Honolulu (HI) 2005, 61.

31 As pointed out for Buddhist monasteries in Sri Lanka: J. Neelis, «Localizing the Buddha's presence», in *Religions and Trade: religious formation, transformation and cross-cultural exchange between East and West*, edd. P. Wick-V. Rabens, Leiden 2014, 45-64, at 48.

32 Huang, «Elite Clergy».

33 J.W. Bernhardt, *Itinerant Kingship and Royal Monasteries in Early Medieval Germany*, Cambridge 1993, 149, 153-55. Christian monasteries were also used as way-stations

sources usually depict these large grants as instances of exemplary generosity; yet what motivated them was the more important reciprocal generosity of the monastery over time. Demands, such as the imperial visitations mentioned (added to those basic and institutional demands created by a stable population of monks or nuns, of laybrothers, servants, slaves and artisans), would spur any administrator to look for extra territories which might be rendered productive; given the vagaries of the weather and its effect on local harvests, these would be chosen ideally at some distance from the mother house[34].

Monastic federations or families consistently appear, and, as has been used to describe Japanese monasteries, could be "miniature states within a state, with their own politics, privileged classes of clerics [...] peasants and craftsmen, commercial enterprises, and militias"[35]. Describing these federations as *states*, however, could focus (wrongly) on the compact, continuous and unified extension of a modern state, when monasteries in fact offered pockets (in varying sizes) of jurisdictional alterity throughout the kingdom or empire, and often beyond the limits of any one secular polity, straddling borders and political situations.

Yet, often, the crucial economic and legal relationships that allowed the monastery to function over time tend to be absent from the sources which are traditionally thought of as purely "monastic": thus, our relatively good information on multiple supramundane or abstract aspects of the Indian Buddhist world of thought is mirrored by our comparative ignorance about the mundane details of the day to day life of Indian Buddhist monasticism (not to mention the life of nonmonastic Buddhists)[36].

The absence from spiritual writing did not mean that no thought went into such a crucial matter, and monastic groupings can be seen as responsive to the social, political and economic contexts in which they were placed[37]. The collection of legal material into cartularies by western monastic establishments, and their function as a *lieu de mémoire* encapsulated both the monks' or nuns'

---

and rural retreats by Umayyad and Abbasid rulers: G.D. Anderson, *The Islamic Villa in Early Medieval Iberia: architecture and court culture in Umayyad Córdoba*, Farnham 2003, 124-125.

34 For the heavy weight of hospitality borne by monasteries in the middle ages, and their responses to it (particularly in ensuring that there was enough wine to cope with sudden influxes of fighting men and retainers), see S. Rose, *The Wine Trade in Medieval Europe 1000-1500*, London 2011, 39.

35 Bodiford, «The Medieval Period», 165.

36 Silk, *Managing Monks*, 13.

37 Schopen, «The Monastic Ownership», 145.

possessions and rights, but also the relationships of mutual dependence owed by and to the laity that cared for the monastery's lands, or acted for the monastery by way of trade. The rise in status and attractiveness of the lay brother in a range of monastic orders during the twelfth and into the thirteenth century, particularly with the Cistercians, the Grandmontines, the Dominicans and the Franciscans, does show an attempt to come to terms with the role of the monastic *familia* within the broad umbrella of the monastic vocation. This even went as far as handing over the running of the instution to the lay brothers in the case of the Grandmontines[38], and the theological reflexion on their treatment in the Cistercian segment of the mid-thirteenth-century *De doctrina cordis*[39], spurred doubtless by the difficulties caused by a well-appreciated disparity between the lay-brothers' important economic role and yet highly subordinate position within the Cistercians, and which chafed enough for the discontent to flare up repeatedly through episodes of disobedience, riots, and even the kidnapping of abbots[40].

4. MONASTERIES AND THE MARKET(S)

A corollary of the insistance that monasticism implies «otherworldliness» is the reticence – and at times vehement hostility – frequently shown to the financial, indeed commercial, aspect of monastic sustenance. This has its roots, as Friedrich-Silber suggested with regard to Weber's distinct bias against monasticism, in the hostility of Reformed theology towards these institutions[41]; and, more precisely, in the hostility of Reformed theologians towards religious institutions seeking a means of financial independence rather than latching on as tightly as possible to funding by the state. Financial independence, of course, could also produce the twin vices of political and ideological independence combined with allegiances which escaped from the increasing emphasis upon the centrality (in economics, philosophy and morality) of the State.

38 S. Tugwell, «Notes on the life of St. Dominic», *Archivum Fratrum Praedicatorum* 65 (1995) 5-96, 66 (1996) 5-200, 57 (1997) 27-59, 68 (1998) 5-116, 73 (2003) 1-141, at 66: 64.

39 N. Palmer, «The authorship of the *De doctrina cordis*» in *A Companion to The Doctrine of the Hert: the Middle English translation and its Latin and European contexts*, edd. C. Whitehead-D. Reveney, Exeter 2010, 19-56.

40 B. Noell, «Expectation and unrest among Cistercian lay brothers in the twelfth and thirteenth centuries», *Journal of Medieval History* 32 (2006) 253-274.

41 Friedrich Silber, *Virtuosity*, 10.

No matter what post-Protestant distate might be forthcoming from the observation, it must be emphasised that monasteries were deeply embedded in trade networks; perhaps most paradigmatically, as recipients of merchants' donations. We might take the Buddhist legend of the caravan merchants, Trapusa and Bhallika, whose early encounter with the Buddha led them to be both lay disciples and founders of the earliest stupas where the Buddha's relics (comprising strands of hair) would be venerated — now, of course, claimed by a number of sites[42]; or we might consider the donation of a monastery to the Buddha and his followers by the wealthy Anathapindika[43]. Buddhist monasteries thrived along trade routes, and possibly — in the earliest period, where states were small and incapable of investment in roads, markets or way-stations — provided a minimal economic infrastructure[44]. The same may be noted in the early medieval west.

Trade flowed through monasteries as they were consumers of goods in their own right, relying upon their own wealth through produce and donation; thus it has been suggested that Buddhist demand for the high-value "seven jewels" (gold, silver, chrystal, lapis lazuli, carnelian, coral, pearls) significantly stimulated ancient trade from China westwards; the expansion of trade and of Buddhist monasticism went hand-in-hand[45]. Direct purchase by the monastery, or direct purchase by benefactors to give directly to the monastery, was but one element of the monastic impact on trade. Thus donations should be seen not only as an important catalyst for trade, but also as part of the means by which trade itself was supported: donations were motivated not simply by individual generosity, but comprised a public action that bound the giver to a cultic centre, around which a tradition of conspicuous gift-giving for the benefit of the wider community (both monks and merchants) could be established; the monastery was thus enabled to act as a focal point for a necessarily diasporized trading community[46].

42 J.M. Rosenfield, *The Dynastic Arts of the Kushans*, University of California Press, Berkeley (CA) 1967, 221.

43 J. Neelis, *Early Buddhist Transmission and Trade Networks: mobility and exchange within and beyon the northwestern borderlands of South Asia*, Leiden 2011, 30-34, 46.

44 M.L. Smith, «The role of ordinary goods in pre-modern exchange», *Journal of Archaeological Method and Theory* 6 (1999) 109-135, at 120-121.

45 Xinru Liu, *Ancient India and Ancient China: trade and religious exchanges AD 1–600*, Delhi, 1997; idem, *The Silk Road: overland trade and cultural interactions in Eurasia*, Washington D.C. 1998, 10-11.

46 For a modern anthropological study of just this form of relationship, see P. Ratanapruck, «Kinship and religious practices as institutionalization of trade networks: Manangi trade communities in south and southeast Asia», *Journal of the Economic and*

Support for trade may have taken on a much more practical aspect, with quartering for merchants and beasts of burden on the Silk Road[47]; with offering secure banking and accommodation for merchants in Chinese or Byzantine cities[48]; with providing a crucial focus for all things commercial, social and spiritual amongst nomadic pastoralists[49]; or with the almost ubiquitous coincidence of markets beside monastic settlements[50]. Royal grants to hold markets may have simply regularized a situation which was already ongoing, as traders took advantage of a monastery's location in a landscape without major towns; its potential to supply arbitration; diffuse connexions between monastery-markets within the region or through long-distance monastic federations; exclusion from taxes; and, crucially for a market, the monastery's gravitational effect upon the local (and often wider) population on major feast-days. The coenobitic imput in maintaining bridges and roads – often presented as a religious injunction – should not be overlooked as part of the maintenance or creation of a suitable infrastructure for trade[51].

Direct involvement in trade (as seller rather than buyer) is sometimes rather more difficult to establish, but was still common. Certainly early Egyptian Christian monasticism adopted simple production techniques and market sales to provide the wherewithall for basic survival in a desert environment[52]. Larger, later monasteries in the same region, however, show an incipient spe-

---

Social History of the Orient 50 (2007) 325-346; M. Puett, «Economies of ghosts, gods, and goods: the history and anthropology of Chinese temple networks», in *Radical Egalitarianism: local realities, global relations*, edd. F. Aulino-M. Goheen-S.J. Tambiah, New York 2013, 91-100.

47 For example, the now-abandoned Selime Monastery in the Cappadocian section of the Silk Road, which lived on for a time as a caravanserai. For stabling, see J.E. Cooper-M.J. Decker, *Life and Society in Byzantine Cappadocia*, 80; L. Rodley, *Cave Monasteries of Byzantine Cappadocia*, Basingstoke 2012, 71-85.

48 W. Eberhard, *A History of China*, Berkeley (CA) [4]1977, 126, referring to Buddhist monasteries of the fourth century AD. For the Venetian use of monasteries as «clearing houses, banks and sometimes goods-depositories» in cities with which they traded, see S. Ogilvie, *Institutions and European Trade: merchant guilds, 1000-1800*, Cambridge 2011, 10.

49 O. Bruun, *Precious Steppe: Mongolian nomadic pastoralists in pursuit of the Market*, Lexington Books, Lanham (MD) 2006, 121: the monastery «organized markets, housed trade representations, received trade caravans, engaged in money-lending, and offered a range of spiritual services».

50 Bernhardt, *Itinerant Kingship*, 149.

51 For example, Goodwin, *Alms and Vagabonds*, 2.

52 E. Agaiby, *Manual Labor in Early Egyptian Monasticism: from late third to mid-fifth century*, St Cyril Society Press, Virginia 2015.

cialization in pottery production, possibly dividing their production into market-orientated and monastic wares, with a corresponding division of producers into lay artisans outside the monastery's walls for the former, and monks within for the latter[53]. Pre-Islamic Palestinian monasteries supplied agricultural products on a commercial scale to local towns, constructing industrial wine- and olive-presses within their environs; they continued to do so in centuries following the conquests[54]. The production of material directly for sale in the market is witnessed most acutely in houses of nuns; thus the Poor Claires were enjoined to live from alms and the work of their own hands when they were founded in the thirteenth century[55]; and Taoist nuns in family-founded convents in Puyuan were expected to survive from the proceeds of silkworm-farming and silk production[56]. Generally, medieval European nunneries produced textiles and embroidery — often to extremely high standards — as a means of guaranteeing an income in an economy in which textile production was the near-exclusive domain of women[57]. At least some of this output would have been for liturgical or other sacral use, parallelling the monastic painting, and subsequent circulation, of icons in Byzantium[58]. In these cases, monastic production came with a particularly high social capital for the possessor; this may also have stretched to more mundane monastic products, since, as Gottdiener avers, «Objects involved in the everyday life of social groups are used because they perform some practical function [...] their use values can also be transformed by users into sign vehicles that signify a second-order function»[59].

53 I. Dvoržak Schrunk, «Spiritual economy and spiritual craft: monastic pottery production and trade», in *Living for Eternity: the White Monastery and its neighbourhood. Proceedings of a symposium at the University of Minnesota, Minneapolis, March 6–9, 2003*, ed. P. Sellew, Minneapolis 2009, 83–96.

54 G. Avni, *The Byzantine-Islamic Transition in Palestine: an archaeological approach*, Oxford 2014, 201-202.

55 B.M. Bolton, «Mulieres sanctae», in *Women in Medieval Society*, edd. B. Bolton-S. Mosher Stuard, Philadelphia (PA) 1993, 148-149.

56 R. Van Glahn, «The sociology of local religion in the Lake Tai Basin», in *Religion and Chinese Society. A centenial conference of the École Française d'Extrême-Orient*, vol. 1: *Ancient and medieval China*, ed. J. Lagerwey, Hong Kong 2004, 773-816.

57 T. Ó Carragáin, «Is there an archaeology of lay people at early Irish monasteries», *Bucema: Bulletin du Centre d'Études Médiévales d'Auxerre*, hors série 8 (2015) at §23, cem.revues.org/13620.

58 B. Crostini, in this volume.

59 M. Gottdiener, *Postmodern Semiotics: material culture and forms of postmodern life*,

Besides nunneries and their concentration on woven goods, full-scale specialization was the trade-related response of many monasteries; this may be found in early medieval Ireland, for grain production[60]; or in Byzantium, at the monastery of Ganos near Constantinople which was wholly dedicated not simply to the production of wine, but to all aspects of its preparation and distribution[61]. Cistercian monasteries in France and Spain specialized in wine-production; their English confrères in wool[62]. Donations might already forsee the marketability of crops: thus the large coconut groves of the Western Ghats were presented to a monastery well-positioned on trade-routes through mountain passes to take advantage of a valuable commodity[63]. Produce from far-flung holdings might be transported to the monastery at fixed period through the year (perhaps even with an element of ritual, but certainly with a consistent attempt to be freed from onerous tolls)[64], but, as markets became more commonplace, economic rationality imposed the local sale of produce and the transfer of money to the mother house, which then depended increasingly upon the markets of the towns closer to it[65].

Monastic holdings might stretch beyond country estates that generated produce to physical properties in market towns where the surplus or commercial produce of the monastery could be sold, as was the case with the Benedictine priory of St-Pierre-de-Juziers (Yvelines), until the town council of Mantes-la-Jolie tired of the competition from the monkish products of the vineyard and reclaimed the townhouse they maintained towards the end of the thirteenth century[66]. This was, simply, a commercial outpost, for a priory that, since the

Oxford, 1995, 181.

60 A. O'Sullivan-F. McCormick-T. Kerr-L. Harney, *Early Medieval Ireland: archaeological investigations 1930–2004*, Dublin-Belfast 2008, 154.

61 N. Günsenin, «Ganos wine and its circulation in the eleventh century», in *Byzantine Trade, 4th–12th Centuries: the archaeology of local, regional and international exchange. Papers of the thirty-eighth Spring Symposium of Byzantine Studies, St John's College, University of Oxford, March 2004*, ed. M. Mundell Mango, Farnham 2009, 145-56.

62 Rose, *The Wine Trade*, 40

63 H. Prabha Ray, *Monastery and Guild: commerce under the Sātavāhanas,* Oxford 1986, 207; Morrison, «Trade», 212.

64 For the system of *mesagium* (monthly supply from different manors), and the gradual movement towards money transfers, see G. Duby, *L'Économie rurale de la vie des campagnes dans l'occident médiéval,* Paris 1962, 389-392.

65 Duby, *L'Économie*, 231.

66 Duby, *L'Économie*, 230. In the mid-thirteenth century, the abbey of Buckfast purchased access to a sub-set of the nearby Totnes guild's activites for the princely sum of

tenth century, had been the direct possession of Saint-Père-de-Chartres (Eure et Loire). As major traders in bulk, the monasteries could also act as middle-men for smaller producers, such as in the wool trade: this highly profitable activity of the English Cistercian houses was notable enough to cause concern to the order as a whole at the beginning of the thirteenth century[67]. Despite their confrères worries, this activity certainly eased access to the wool-market for numerous small producers. The Cistercians, too, buoyed by their commercial income, could even take out mortgages and loans with the purpose of improving their buildings[68]. The technological innovations, through capital, manpower and communications, which were brought about by both Cistercians in the west and Buddhist monasteries in the east, is in no doubt[69].

Donations of more movable materials could also be recycled through trading relationships. Money might be used as loans or reinvested in trade through the involvement of lay middlemen[70]. Or local conditions might also produce an excess of offerings in one species (such as cloth), which would then be traded for more useful goods[71].

In conclusion, then, the self-contained "monastic city" of the Carolingian age, producing and consuming from its own artesanal and agricultural production, often held up as the ideal for all ages, to which each monastery should have aspired, may well be an exception within monasticism, thrown up by a stagnant economy[72] or at least the monasteries' having been sidelined

22 pence (or thirty grams of silver) per annum: see C. Gross, *The Gild Merchants: a contribution to British municipal history,* vol. 1, Oxford 1890, 40.

67 D. Knowles, *The Monastic Order in England: a history of its development from the times of St Dunstan to the Fourth Lateran Council,* Cambridge ²1963, 351-353. For a monastic role as intermediaries in the pearl trade of pre-Islamic monasteries in south Arabia, see P. Hellyer, «Nestorian Christianity in pre-Islamic UAE and South-Eastern Arabia», *Journal of Social Affairs* 18 (2001) 79-99, at 97.

68 Knowles, *The Monastic Order*, 354.

69 K. Pletcher, «Political disunity between the Tang and Song Dynasties», in *The History of China*, Britannica Educational Publishing, New York 2001, 130-137, at 134.

70 Neelis, «Localizing the Buddha's presence at wayside shrines in northern Pakistan», 47.

71 J. Neelis, *Early Buddhist Transmission and Trade Networks: mobility and exchange within and beyond the northwestern borderlands of South Asia*, Leiden 2011, 37.

72 J. Henning, «Early European towns: the way of the economy in the Frankish area between dynamism and deceleration 500-1000 AD», in *Post-Roman Towns, Trade and Settlement in Europe and Byzantium*, vol. 1: *The Heirs of the Roman West*, ed. J. Henning, Berlin 2007, at 20, 27. Henning argues, further, that the "monastic city" kept the economy stagnant; this would, however, not seem to be the case regarding most monastic outposts in other areas.

from the major revenue-streams of the Carolingian state (perhaps for good reason, if these were based primarily on raiding for slaves and pillage).

5. MONASTERIES AND THE SACRED

Monasteries assured the continuity of the institutional entity and stability of the monks through the marshalling of those elements of the *familia*, local aristocracy, representatives of central government, and networks of trade; and the stability ensured a cultural production that offered significance to the monastic vocation and provided various levels of integration to the laity that drew near to, or were employed by, the coenobium[73]. This rather brutal and reductivist characterization of the monastery as, simply, the *coenobium oeconomicus*, though, omits the transcendental element around which monasteries were able to channel both the monks' and nuns' asceticism and the laity's devotions. Whilst there is a consistent emphasis upon a spiritual ideal in the monastic vocation, a means of self-transcendence for the individual monk or nun, it should be emphasised in turn that monasteries were in general built around, and for, relics[74]. In Buddhism, the monks remained the custodians of the *stūpa* that (ideally) contained the relics of the Buddha (or his disciples), and relic-worship may have been the most prevalent expression of Buddhism itself[75]. Relics were both paraded and enclosed[76], with the enclosure – the *stūpa* – itself being seen as both symbol of the Buddha's enlightenment and, more importantly and concretely, as a representation and actualization of the Buddha's presence itself[77]. To this being or deity donations could made, and

73 For example, J. Kieschnick, *The Impact of Buddhism on Chinese Material Culture*, Princeton 2003, 53-54.

74 J. Bronkhorst, «Les reliques dans les religions de l'Inde», in *Indische Kultur im Kontext: Rituale, Texte und Ideen aus Indien und der Welt. Festschrift für Klaus Mylius*, ed. L. Göhler, Harrasowitz, Wiesbaden 2005, 49-85, at 59.

75 Bronkhorst, *Buddhism*, 208; Ś. Bianji, *The Great Tang Dynasty Record of the Western Regions, Translated by the Tripitaka-Master Xuanzang under Imperial Order*, trans. Li Rongxi, Berkeley 1996, 149-151; P. Skilling, «Cutting Across Categories: the ideology of relics in Buddhism», *Annual Report of the International Research Institute for Advanced Buddhology at Soka University for the Academic Year 2004*, Tokyo 2004, 269-310, at 302: «Since the early spread of Buddhism was also a spread of relics and stupas, there was a constant need for relics, and for an ideology that explained their significance.»

76 In Japan, for example, state-sponsored relic processions were an important part of statecraft: Ruppert, *The Jewel in the Ashes*, 40.

77 For the liturgical veneration of the *stūpa*, see A. Bareau, «La construction et le culte des

it was the stūpa-Buddha which possessed those gifts in rather more than the sense of a legal fiction. And it was from such donations, for example, that (commercial) loans could be made[78].

In Hinduism, a number of *math* were built around the founder's tomb, which became the focus of the monastery, integrated within its symbolic language and liturgy, and the means by which monastic lineages might guarantee and express their legitimacy[79]. The case of Śaṅkara, whose bodily remains are disputed between his main monastic foundations, indicates an early importance granted to the relic of the founder[80]. Although it is usually affirmed that relic-veneration has no part in Hinduism, this is not, nor has it ever been, the case[81]. When we turn to Christian monasticism, the role of relics is well-established, although perhaps the written record — specializing in accounts of miracles associated with relic-bearing shrines — rather occludes the institutional importance of relics as modes of authenticity (uniting the monastery with the past as well as the titular saint), of representation (the saint both standing for and being represented by the monastery), and of authority (in the possession of lands, donated to and held by the saint through the relics, and administered by the eponymous community)[82].

Relics, then, were not an adjunct to the serious business of either ascetism or providing a proto-capitalist boost to the economy; they were the very heart of the monastic endeavour. The relics were not simply prized as a draw upon the laity's generosity, but the saint's *praesentia* in them was expressed through the coenobium. The monks or nuns venerated the relics; but they could, in their turn, represent the relics–the Buddha–the saint–the holy man. The boundaries of the manifestation of the *praesentia* were necessarily blurred.

---

stūpa d'après les Vinayapiṭaka», *Bulletin de l'École Française d'Extrême-Orient* 50 (1962) 229-274, at 242-247. For symbolism: A. Foucher, *Les bas-reliefs gréco-bouddhiques du Gandhāra*, Paris, 1905, 49-62; Bronkhorst, «Les Reliques», 56; Ruppert, *The Jewel in the Ashes*, 14.

78 Ruppert, *The Jewel in the Ashes*, 31.

79 Véronique Bouillier, cited by Bronkhorst, *Buddhism*, 211, and Id., «Les Reliques».

80 Pande, *The Life and Thought*, 359.

81 S. Sarma, *The Neo-Vaiṣṇavite Movement and the Satra Institution of Assam*, Gauhati 1966, 125-126.

82 On the latter point, see Friedrich Silber, «Monasticism». For a comparison of western and eastern relic cults, see R.H. Sharf, «On the allure of Buddhist relics», *Representations* 66 (1999) 75-99.

CONCLUSION

I have outlined a four-fold definition of monasticism, in which the usual characteristics of the submission to a particular type of rule or spiritual ideal have taken a background importance. In its stead, I have argued for the central role of the generation of a surplus (through production and donation), and consquent involvement in trade, as a characteristic feature of monasteries, independent of religious or doctrinal affiliation. Such integration shows monasticism not as withdrawal from society but as a fundamental contributor to the social world; legislation regarding monks and nuns' taking part in markets, travelling with merchants, buying and selling, should not be seized on as evidence of decline but rather thoughtful engagement with what could be the limits of the monastic lived-out *vita*, rather than its essentialization into a *forma*. Furthermore, a relationship (liturgical, devotional, emotional, intellectual) with the relics at the centre of the community was the means by which the coenobium coalesced and defined itself, as monks and nuns firstly, and then, subsequently, in unity and in contact with the surrounding laity. The injunction of celibacy ensures the development of institutional loyalty which can be set against familial and political claims, but also the potential to create a culture independent to some degree of the surrounding socio-economic conditions. Evidently, to allow the development of such a social structure, communal effort and communal relation to the sacred must play a role equal or greater than the individual's own charisma, and belief-systems must be both tolerant of celibacy and of the principle that the holy dead bring no ritual contamination — indeed, these two concepts may ultimately be intrinsically linked. Monasticism throughout Eurasia may thus be considered as a unity, as a similar set of responses within different religious traditions.

Abstract

The paper proposes to consider, from a comparative perspective, monasteries as centres for commercial exchange and as nodes within trading networks, taking in the contemporary practice of Chinese Buddhist, early Hindu and early medieval western monasticism during 800–1200. First of all, the circulation of goods within the local economy through practices of gift-giving and construction and embellishment of the monastery is discussed; then the well-attested functions of trading guilds in the East, which functioned both as financial representatives of the monastery and – through monastic families – as cogs within intercontinal trade routes. Further, these networks as offering a means of self-determination for the monastery, contrasting with the centripetal pull of attempted government control is considered, subsequently, these results are applied to early medieval monasticism in Europe and the rise of monastic towns as an economic function of the monastery is outlined and the common feature of lay supervision of monastic lands with trading guilds is compared. Thus, the centrality of monastic culture for the development of medieval trade, and conversely for trade as a central element in the development of monasticism, is argued for.

ELOGIO DEL LAVORO INUTILE. OSSERVAZIONI SULLA DIALETTICA AZIONE-CONTEMPLAZIONE TRA MONACHESIMO CRISTIANO E MONACHESIMO INDU-BUDDHISTA

Paolo Trianni

Non vuol essere provocatorio associare il lavoro all'inutilità, né tantomeno il farne un elogio. Se viene sollevato tale aspetto è perché una riflessione spirituale e teologico-filosofica sull'attività lavorativa umana – soprattutto se considerata dal punto di vista monastico – solleva delle paradossalità sulle quali è opportuno soffermarsi con degli approfondimenti specifici.

In prima istanza, elogiare il lavoro "inutile" significa mettere in evidenza una dimensione antitetica al costume attuale, incline a leggere l'attività umana prevalentemente come "utilitarismo" declinato ad un consumismo che ha molto spesso un carattere ossessivo. Il lavoro monastico, soprattutto se confrontato con tali scenari, ha una natura profetica che va controcorrente rispetto a come viene vissuto nelle società postmoderne assuefatte alla tecnocrazia e all'ideologia neoliberista. È emblematico che un teologo come Enzo Bianchi – e lo mettiamo in evidenza non per svilire la figura del monaco ma per valorizzare una delle sue qualità antropologiche precipue – abbia affermato che il monaco "non serve a nulla". Il priore di Bose, con questa sua "provocazione" voleva infatti sottolineare una dimensione essenziale della vita monastica: quella di essere radicata sulla contemplazione anziché sull'azione e sull'utilità intesa come vantaggio personale.

Un secondo punto che è necessario prendere in esame, strettamente connesso a quello precedente, è la differenza che da sempre contraddistingue le due tendenze spirituali dell'incarnazionismo e dell'escatologismo. Queste categorie tradizionali della storia della teologia spirituale indicano due atteggiamenti diversi di fronte al mondo, e suggeriscono quindi anche due modi assai differenti di vivere ed orientarsi verso il lavoro. Il modo incarnazionista lo vive in maniera più attiva e fattiva, il modo escatologista è invece maggiormente distaccato, e non si lascia coinvolgere nelle di-

Paolo Trianni, theologian and philosopher, expert in interreligious dialogue, professor at the Monastic Institute at the Pontifical Athenaeum S.Anselmo.

namiche intramondane, rispetto alle quali conserva anzi una pregiudiziale critica. Alla luce di questa distinzione, è chiaro che la maniera monastica di vivere il lavoro non può che essere ricondotta all'escatologismo, ed è interessante dare sottolineatura di come questa dimensione la si possa ritrovare anche nella sensibilità monastica di altre religioni e in uno dei principali testi sacri dell'India come la *Bhagavad Gita*.

Un terzo punto da approfondire, complementare a quello appena esposto, è la dinamica che intercorre tra contemplazione ed azione. La tensione tra questi due poli – il primo riconducibile all'escatologismo il secondo all'incarnazionismo – è presente in tutte le grandi tradizioni spirituali, soprattutto quelle orientali, ed è parimenti presente anche nel pensiero filosofico greco. Sono due le problematiche che si aprano quando si analizza questa tensione: la prima è se sia veramente armonizzabile una vita autenticamente contemplativa con l'azione laboriosa e gli impegni mondani; la seconda è se sia possibile un'attività lavorativa capace di conservare uno stato interiore contemplativo, disinteressato, altruistico. Papa Bergoglio, nella sua enciclica *Laudato si'* – che dedica al lavoro i numeri dal 124 al 129 – invita esattamente a ricercare un modo di lavorare che non smarrisca tali caratteristiche, perché, come scrive, «quando nell'essere umano si perde la capacità di contemplare e di rispettare, si creano le condizioni perché il senso del lavoro venga stravolto (LS 127).

Un quarto punto che ci sembra opportuno articolare in maniera più estesa è come le contrapposizioni menzionate tra azione e contemplazione, tra incarnazionismo ed escatologismo, tra utilità ed inutilità, le si ritrovino, sia pure con un linguaggio diverso, anche in altre tradizioni monastiche, specialmente quelle del buddhismo e dell'induismo.

In generale, ad ogni modo, la tesi di fondo che vorremmo argomentare è che oggi il lavoro ha perso spessore spirituale anche perché non è vissuto con quello spirito escatologistico con il quale, per l'appunto, è praticato quotidianamente nelle regole monastiche. In conseguenza di ciò, è possibile dare dimostrazione di come i monaci – in questo mondo globalizzato dominato dalla finanzia, dal consumismo, dall'arrivismo, dal disinteresse ecologico – possono insegnare agli uomini del nostro tempo a vivere in maniera più spirituale il valore del lavoro.

1. IL LAVORO COME INUTILITÀ

Non è semplice individuare una definizione esatta ed universalmente condivisa di lavoro[1]. Questa fondamentale attività umana ha subito troppe variazioni storiche, e, soprattutto l'avvento della tecnica, dell'industrializzazione e del capitalismo li-

1 Cf. E. Chiavacci, *Teologia morale,* vol. 2, Assisi 1990, 192.

berista, hanno snaturato il carattere ed il senso che il lavoro aveva nelle società passate. Anche papa Francesco, nella sua recente enciclica, ha voluto mettere l'accento su questo specifico punto: «Siamo chiamati al lavoro fin dalla nostra creazione. Non si deve cercare di sostituire sempre più il lavoro umano con il progresso tecnologico: così facendo l'umanità danneggerebbe sé stessa» (LS 128).

Già la filosofia novecentesca aveva molto riflettuto sulle trasformazioni che esso ha subito con l'avvento della modernità, è sufficiente ricordare gli studi di H. Bergson, B. Russel, M. Heidegger, S. Weil o la Scuola di Francoforte. Negli anni Settanta, in Germania, proprio in virtù della centralità esistenziale che aveva assunto questa attività umana emerse quella che è stata definita "riabilitazione della filosofia pratica"[2]. Una filosofa che ha riflettuto con particolare vigore su questo tema è stata poi quella di Hanna Arendt, la quale ha sviluppato una riflessione critica sulla tecnica soffermandosi proprio sulla rivoluzione che essa aveva apportato alla realtà del lavoro[3].

La teologia, che sempre fa da specchio alla presa di posizione delle varie correnti filosofiche, ha fatto una certa fatica a riflettere su questo tema. Il lavoro come è vissuto nelle società industriali moderne, infatti, non è presente nella Bibbia, e questo ha sollevato vari problemi di metodo. La teologia del lavoro, cioè, come tutte le altre "realtà terrestri" tipiche del nostro tempo, era inizialmente mancante di un suo metodo appropriato[4]. Anche in assenza di esso, però, il magistero ecclesiale aveva iniziato ad interessarsi al tema sin dalla *Rerum novarum* di Leone XIII, e i successivi interventi di Giovanni Paolo II, come la *Laborem exercens* e la *Centesimus annus*, che hanno impostato una riflessione sul lavoro assai articolata.

2 L'espressione *Rehabilitierung der praktischen Philosophie* è stata coniata da Karl-Heinz Ilting ed è stata poi ripresa da Manfred Riedel attraverso una voluminosa antologia in due volume da lui curata (cf M. Riedel, *Rehabilitierung der praktischen Philosophie*, Rombaci, Freiburg 1972-1974). Strettamente connesso ad essa, fu il dibattito che si sviluppò tra "neoaristotelici" e "postkantiani", che ha condotto a guardare in modo nuovo alla *praxis* e quindi anche al lavoro.

3 Secondo il pensiero della Arendt la modernità coincide con l'*homo faber* di cui aveva parlato Marx. A suo avviso, a causa della tecnica, esso ha finito col perdere il suo carattere di ciclicità mutandosi così in un'attività produttiva di tipo "progressivo" che ha modificato radicalmente la società contemporanea (cf. H. Arendt, *Vita activa: la condizione umana,* Milano 2004).

4 Per riflettere sul lavoro, o quantomeno su talune attività lavorative non presenti nella Bibbia, è stato necessario fare ricorso al metodo della comprensione oggettiva che muove induttivamente dalla realtà per poi risalire alla Scrittura (cf. Z. Alszeghy-M. Flick, *Metodologia per una teologia dello sviluppo*, Brescia 1970).

Le grandi e molteplici questioni legate alle varie attività lavorative, però, rimangono aperte. Senza addentrarci in speculazioni di carattere filosofico, è indubbio che oggi il concetto stesso di lavoro sia andato in crisi. Quella contemporanea, per esempio, è stata definita un'età del Non Lavoro[5]. Giordano Frosini, teologo pistoiese da sempre attento a queste tematiche, notava che «All'ideologia del lavoro si sta sostituendo, già da tempo, l'ideologia del rifiuto del lavoro»[6]. Su un piano etico-spirituale oggi si parla diffusamente anche di peccato del lavoro o di antiteologia del lavoro[7]. È possibile che una delle varie cause che hanno contributo a questa situazione attuale dipenda dal fatto che quando in ambito teologico è nata una teologia del lavoro, con autori del calibro di M.-D. Chenu, J. Maritain, E. Mounier, G. Thils, Y.M.-J. Congar, la si è da subito collocata nell'orizzonte dell'incarnazionismo. Tale approccio, sia pure involontariamente, potrebbe aver finito per "mondanizzare" il lavoro anche all'interno dell'orizzonte cristiano. Per meglio dire, certe derive consumistiche o antiecologiche tipiche del mondo moderno non sono state provocate dal cristianesimo, ma indubbiamente sono state operate anche da dei cristiani a causa di una insufficiente teologia del lavoro[8].

Come dimostrano anche i numeri di *Laudato si'* menzionati in precedenza, la crisi attuale dell'attività lavorativa, almeno sul piano etico, sembra legata all'avanzata della tecnica e al consumismo, ambiti che l'enciclica stessa lega intimamente, proprio perché la prima si è oggi messa al servizio del secondo. Anche in ambito teologico, però, il rapporto tra tecnica e lavoro non è certamente un tema nuovo. Già Chenu sosteneva che il «Il passaggio dall'utensile alla macchina non solo ha aperto una nuova fase della vita economica, ha inaugurato una nuova era dell'umanità»[9]. Lefranc, da parte sua, affermava che «la storia del lavoro non conosce che due grandi epoche: l'età dell'utensile e l'età della macchina»[10]. La tecnica ha appunto cambiato l'approccio ed il giudizio che la teologia dava e dà al lavoro.

---

5 Su questo tema: "Monachesimo nell'Età del Non Lavoro" è stato organizzato un convegno il 4 e 5 novembre 2011 nel monastero camaldolese di Bardolino. Il simposio si metteva in continuità con una precedente riflessione della comunità monastica camaldolese sul tema del lavoro i cui atti sono stati pubblicati in *Vita Monastica* (229) 2004.

6 G. Frosini, *L'attività umana. Per una teologia del lavoro*, Cinisello Balsamo (MI) 1994, 30.

7 Cf. Frosini, *L'attività umana*, 184.

8 Frosini fa rientrare la teologia dell'ecologia all'interno della teologia del lavoro: «L'ecologia è oggi un nuovo capitolo della teologia del lavoro», in Id., *L'attività umana*, 203.

9 M.-D. Chenu, *Per una teologia del lavoro*, Torino 1964 (edizione originale 1955) 30ss.

10 G. Lefranc, *Storia del lavoro e dei lavoratori*, Milano 1978, 4.

Gli escatologisti, per esempio, hanno sempre letto con sospetto il predominio che essa sta assumendo in questa attività umana, gli incarnazioni, invece, l'hanno in molti casi salutata con entusiasmo. Il summenzionato Giordano Frosini si rivela tendenzialmente incarnazionista quando afferma che «Non bisogna credere che Dio si trovi più facilmente nel lavoro a contatto con la natura che nel lavoro tecnico. Evidentemente questa convinzione deriva da una concezione che privilegia il lavoro agricolo per il semplice fatto che non si è ancora assimilata a sufficienza una cultura di tipo industriale. Tutto il lavoro, quello industriale forse più di quello agricolo, è capace di avvicinare l'uomo a Dio, se egli sa riguardare l'opera delle sue mani con lo sguardo profondo della fede»[11].

Se sul lavoro sia maggiormente opportuno avere uno sguardo escatologistico anziché incarnazionistico, è una questione su cui torneremo a riflettere nel paragrafo successivo, sta di fatto, però, che da un punto di vista cristiano occorre riscoprire un modo "ecologico" di lavorare, leggendo l'ecologia in quel senso "integrale" a cui sollecita il pontefice. Non c'è dubbio, ad ogni modo, che l'attuale crisi morale del lavoro sia legata allo spirito con cui esso è sempre più diffusamente vissuto. Nel modo in cui esso è vissuto nel nostro tempo assistiamo infatti ad un "utilitarismo" dilagante, ad uno smarrimento totale della sua originaria dimensione ascetica, ad una assuefazione consumista, ad un arrivismo egoistico, ad un carrierismo egocentrico che ne oscurano il valore spirituale. Soprattutto, però, il decadimento etico dell'attività lavorativa poggia sul fatto che essa è sempre e solo finalizzata ad un guadagno relativo e mediato, e mai ad una verità assoluta.

Per riflettere teologicamente e spiritualmente su questo decadimento del lavoro, è utile fare riferimento ad una distinzione presente nel pensiero di Aristotele tra scienza filosofica "teorica" dedicata alla contemplazione della verità, e scienza "pratica" mirata all'opera (*ergon*). Secondo lo stagirita i filosofi "pratici" non si occupano della verità, perché quest'ultima è necessariamente "teorica", mentre essi si occupano di cause relative, rimanendo così impigliati in un orizzonte condizionato[12]. Nel *Protrettico* Aristotele scrive: «Il cercare che da ogni scienza derivi qualche cosa di diverso e che essa debba essere utile, è proprio di uno che ignora completamente quanto distinto sia da principio le cose buone e quelle necessarie: essa in

11 G. FROSINI, *L'attività umana. Per una teologia del lavoro*, Cinisiello Balsamo (MI) 1994, 173.

12 Scriveva Aristotele: «È giusto anche chiamare la filosofia (*philosophian*) scienza della verità, poiché di quella teoretica è fine la verità, mentre di quella pratica è fine l'opera (*ergon*); se anche infatti i (filosofi) pratici indagano come stanno le cose, essi non considerano la causa per sé, ma in relazione a qualcosa ed ora» (ARISTOTELE, *Metafisica*, II, 1, 993 b 19-23).

realtà, differiscono al massimo. Quelle infatti, tra le cose senza di cui è impossibile vivere, che sono amate per causa di altro, devono essere dette cose necessarie e concause, mentre quelle che sono amate per se stesse, anche qualora non ne derivi nulla di diverso, devono essere propriamente buone [...]. Sarebbe dunque del tutto ridicolo cercare da ogni cosa un vantaggio diverso dalla cosa stessa e domandare: "quale vantaggio dunque ne deriva a noi?" o "quale utilità"»[13].

Volendo attualizzare queste considerazioni aristoteliche, potremmo concludere che lo spaesamento attuale che vive questa fondamentale compito umano è legata al suo sradicamento dalla verità teorica, dal suo distacco da un senso ultimo, da una premessa contemplativa, da una mancanza di indipendenza dall'interesse e dal vantaggio personale. Di conseguenza, la critica spirituale che può essere rivolta all'"utilità" è quella di essere legata alla trascuratezza di un significato superiore dell'attività lavorativa, che non è solo "utile" a qualcosa di altro, ma rimanda ad un valore e ad una verità in sé e per sé. Letta in quest'ottica, l'utilità rivela la sua natura di utilitarismo, perché il lavoro risulta "schiavo" del guadagno, della strumentalità, della relatività, del beneficio sensibile, di obiettivi meramente ed esclusivamente materialistici.

Da questo punto di vista, il senso del lavoro monastico e la sua spiritualità del lavoro riverberano le radici aristoteliche di cui sopra. Per il monaco, infatti, il lavoro non è necessario, è buono. Nell'orizzonte dell'esistenza monastica il lavoro è "in-utile" perché non è relativo, perché non declinato ad un secondo fine, non finalizzato ad altro. Secondo la tradizione monastica, cioè, questa attività non è funzionale a qualcosa o utile a qualcuno, è buona in sé. È questo il motivo per il quale, anche nel campo specifico del lavoro, i monaci svolgono una funzione di testimonianza profetica. Essi insegnano e sono chiamati ad insegnare all'uomo moderno una spiritualità del lavoro maggiormente libera e disinteressata. All'interno della quotidianità monastica il lavoro non perde la sua natura contemplativa originaria proprio perché "in-utile". Tra coloro che si riconoscono nella Regola di Benedetto, esso è vissuto come valore in sé, senza la partecipazione contaminante di un ego interessato e senza la ricerca di beni o vantaggi consumistici. Il lavoro monastico è "ecologico" per eccellenza, e, soprattutto, è spirituale e contemplativo. Esso, infatti, è legato alla verità – così come la concepiva Aristotele – proprio perché essenzialmente "teorico".

Come dicevamo, e come approfondiremo nei paragrafi successivi, è compito del monachesimo insegnare una spiritualità del lavoro "teorica" ed "escatologistica". Nelle loro microsocietà i monaci sono chiamati a testimoniare con coerenza

13 ARISTOTELE, *Protrettico*, fr. 12 Ross = 42-44 Düring.

un modello esemplare che può e deve essere un riferimento per la società più ampia. Le organizzazioni statali devono imitare il modo monastico di vivere il lavoro all'insegna della generosità, della comunione, dell'organizzazione senza arrivismi, del distacco dall'utile come dallo spreco. Da questo punto di vista, è quindi possibile fare un elogio del lavoro "in-utile" tipico del monaco, perché tale aggettivo diviene sinonimo di un'attività umana vissuta in totale libertà. Si capisce, inoltre, come esso rappresenti un momento strutturale della santificazione monastica. Il fare per il fare, infatti, è parte integrante della spersonalizzazione e dell'umiltà del monaco, ed è un esempio della sua separazione dal mondo e da quelle tendenze egoiche e strumentali che sono tipiche dello spirito mondano. Egli si libera da quei vincoli ed insegna agli uomini il modo di liberarsene.

2. LA TENSIONE CLASSICA TRA ESCATOLOGISMO ED INCARNAZIONISMO

La spiritualità cristiana può essere distinta in due grandi correnti di pensiero che l'hanno accompagnata sin dai suoi albori: quella dell'escatologismo[14] e quella dell'incarnazionismo[15]. Sebbene presenti da sempre nella tradizione cristiana, negli Quaranta hanno preso la forma di vere e proprie scuole teologiche che, ponendosi il problema dell'atteggiamento che era necessario assumere rispetto al mondo moderno, si sono inevitabilmente occupate anche della questione del lavoro. I teologi cercavano di capire se vi sia una continuità o una rottura drastica fra l'attività umana e il progresso del Regno di Dio, fra la storia e l'eternità, fra liberazioni umane e salvezza cristiana. Per la continuità si schieravano gli incarnazionisti, per la discontinuità gli escatologisti, sebbene, in entrambe le scuole, con sfumature varie ed accenti diversi. In uno scenario nel quale l'avanzata della tecnica e del progresso scientifico aveva fatto entrare l'umanità in un'era di ri-

14 Il manifesto dell'escatologismo è costituito da un articolo di L. Bouyer pubblicato nel 1948. Il movimento si è successivamente organizzato intorno alla rivista *Dieu Vivant*. Ad esso sono riconducibili anche H. de Lubac e J. Daniélou, sia pure in senso mitigato. L'escatologismo, in estrema sintesi, è il riconoscimento dell'elemento trascendente e metastorico che è alla base della fede e della speranza cristiana. Per i suoi autori «La potenza del male è talmente rimarcata che il mondo è inevitabilmente condannato alla distruzione con tutti i valori terrestri, i cosiddetti valori della civiltà umana» (G. FROSINI, *La fede e le opere. Le teologie della prassi,* Cinisello Balsamo [Mi] 1992, 57).

15 L'incarnazionismo è legato al nome di Y.M-J Congar, fin da quando, nel 1935, sulla rivista *La vie intellectuelle* ne coniò il termine. Vi fecero parte anche M.D. Chenu e P. Telhard de Chardin. All'interno di questa corrente prese poi vita la teologia delle realtà terrestri di G. Thils. Esso coincide con l'attenzione alla storia, e alle dell'attività umana.

schio per le sorti dell'intero pianeta, le due correnti assunsero un atteggiamento opposto nei riguardi della terra, della storia e del progresso umano. Gli incarnazionisti propendevano per l'impegno e l'ottimismo, all'opposto, gli escatologisti, per il distacco critico e il pessimismo. In generale, comunque, il vero punto discriminante che distingueva queste due correnti era quello della continuità/discontinuità fra la natura e la soprannatura, fra la storia profana e la storia sacra.

In questo quadro il lavoro ed il suo senso assumevano una grande centralità. Secondo gli escatologisti il modo di lavorare del nostro tempo era ed è tacciabile di "sadduceismo cattolico", ovverosia di eccessiva preoccupazione per i cosiddetti valori terrestri ed umani. Uno dei teologi spirituali che, anche nel post Concilio, ha continuato ad avere un atteggiamento sostanzialmente escatologista è stato il domenicano direttore della «Rivista di ascetica e mistica» Innocenzo Colosio. A suo avviso la spiritualità cristiana correva il rischio di diventare troppo incarnazionista, ed era convinto che le molte attività in cui è coinvolto il cristiano nella società contemporanea lo portassero ad assecondare eccessivamente il mondano. Colosio denunciava infatti come uno dei pericoli spirituali della modernità fosse il «primato dell'azione e deprezzamento della contemplazione»[16]. Naturalmente gli autori escatologistici critici dell'evoluzione subita dal lavoro con l'avvento della modernità e della tecnica sarebbero diversi. Tra i molti pensatori che si potrebbero citare, scegliamo di menzionare Lanza del Vasto, teologo interprete cristiano del messaggio di Gandhi, che si è particolarmente distinto nelle sue critiche alle attività umane che si svolgono nella società attuale. Il pensatore italiano, in particolare, non soltanto sviliva molti lavori moderni associandoli al gioco, ma in taluni casi li ha persino demonizzati[17]. Del resto, fra gli argomenti che più platealmente fanno collocare Lanza del Vasto all'interno dell'escatologismo, c'è il suo legare il lavoro al peccato originale[18]. Egli, per essere più precisi, sebbene sottolineasse che esso era presente anche nella gioia del paradiso, lo considerava una sostanziale purificazione dalla colpa originale: «il lavoro è il castigo del peccato, ma la ragione del castigo è la purificazione. Il lavoro ha due volti: lavorare è, da una parte, tendere al profitto e subire le conseguenze della colpa e, dall'altra, obbedire al Creatore e in certo

16 I. Colosio, «Le caratteristiche positive e negative della Spiritualità odierna», *Rivista di ascetica e mistica* 45 (1965) 328.

17 Lanza del Vasto intitolò il secondo capitolo de *I quattro flagelli*, "Il diavolo nel gioco", riconducendo non a lavori ma a giochi attività quali la politica, il commercio e la finanza (cf. G. Lanza del vasto, *I quattro flagelli*, Torino 1996, 59-120).

18 Lanza del Vasto, riconduce il peccato originale all'acquisizione della conoscenza del bene e del male, scriveva: «La conoscenza del bene e del male ha fatto del lavoro dell'uomo un castigo», in Id., *I quattro flagelli*, 23.

modo collaborare con lui, dominarsi, mettersi alla prova, esercitarsi, perfezionarsi, esprimersi; in ultima analisi, servire la famiglia umana nel bisogno comune»[19]. Delle molte dimensioni che può avere il lavoro, cioè, Lanza del Vasto accentuava quella religiosa e quella legata al sacrificio. Soprattutto, però, esaltava il lavoro artigianale e denigrava quello condizionato dalla civiltà industriale: «Tra tutti i danni provocati dallo straripamento della tecnica, uno dei più funesti è forse lo svilimento del lavoro umano»[20]. È questa, appunto, una posizione tipicamente escatologistica sulla quale ha argomentato ripetutamente: «Il lavoro che la macchina non può sopprimere, lo domina con tutta la sua irrefrenabile forza, lo cancella e lo incatena. Così l'uomo è ridotto a servire le macchine, a diventare una sottomacchina. Il suo lavoro cessa di essere faticoso per diventare spossante, tormentoso per la ripetitività, opprimente per la monotonia. Il lavoro esige dall'uomo sempre meno forza, sempre meno abilità e intelligenza»[21]. Le critiche lanzavastiane, in definitiva, erano rivolte al lavoro industriale e all'implicito sistema economico che lo sottende: «Questo processo di decomposizione e, infine, di eliminazione del lavoro dell'uomo, avviene attraverso la macchina e si chiama industria»[22].

Il filosofo pugliese, sotto la doppia spinta dell'insegnamento gandhiano e della tradizione biblica, fondò e promosse delle comunità fondate sul lavoro agricolo ed artigianale. Quest'ultime, che pur essendo composte da gruppi di famiglie hanno un'impronta monastica di fondo, come dimostra l'obbedienza ad una regola comune, sono un esempio di come la sensibilità escatologistica tipica del monachesimo possa essere estesa a vari altri modelli sociali.

3. CONTEMPLAZIONE O AZIONE?

La tensione tra escatologismo e incarnazionismo è parallela a quella tra contemplazione e azione. All'interno della spiritualità cristiana tra questi due orizzonti c'è sempre stata una distinzione netta, anche se l'epoca conciliare ha cercato di riavvicinarli. Un esempio che possiamo trarre dalla storia della spiritualità che rimane paradigmatico è la figura di Isacco di Ninive, il quale rinunciò alla dignità episcopale per ritornare nella sua grotta eremitica. A suo avviso, non era assolutamente possibile conciliare la vita solitaria con quella operosa nel mondo, e, secondo lui, anche la testimonianza di Paolo – tra i pochi santi che sono riusciti

19 Lanza del Vasto, *I quattro flagelli*, 30.
20 Lanza del Vasto, *I quattro flagelli*, 100.
21 Lanza del Vasto, *I quattro flagelli*, 103.
22 Lanza del Vasto, *I quattro flagelli*, 101.

a sintetizzare la vocazione apostolica con quella contemplativa – non poteva essere presa ad esempio perché egli era unico in ogni cosa[23]. Nei secoli, la tensione tra queste due esigenze dell'esistenza cristiana è andata di pari passo allo sviluppo dell'annuncio evangelico. Essa è sempre stata un tema dibattuto fino ai giorni nostri, e, di fatto, ha puntellato la nascita e la strutturazione della teologia spirituale moderna. Il padre conciliare Henri de Lubac sosteneva al riguardo che ci sono sempre due rischi: quello di incarnare troppo il cristianesimo, e quello di dare un'eccessiva importanza all'azione[24]. Non è un caso che uno dei maggiori interrogativi che da sempre si è posta la teologia spirituale è se sia superiore la vita contemplativa o quella attiva. Tommaso, che ha riflettuto anche su questo tema, propendeva per la superiorità della vita contemplativa[25].

In definitiva, queste due modalità di rispondere all'annuncio di Cristo appaiono distinte e difficilmente coniugabili. Assumendo tale differenziazione, potremmo appunto descrivere il monaco come colui che, in via preliminare, non crede nell'armonizzazione possibile tra azione e contemplazione, e, con la propria scelta di vita, attesta la sua fede nel primato esclusivo della via spirituale contemplativa. Tuttavia, fermo restando che il monachesimo è per eccellenza la via dell'escatologismo e non dell'incarnazionismo, se andiamo ad analizzare in profondità la radice greca del concetto di contemplazione emergono significati ulteriori che consentono di leggere il monaco ed il monachesimo in una chiave che attribuisce sensi nuovi, e meno astorici, alla scelta contemplativa monastica.

---

23 Scriveva Isacco: «Ora, se tu vuoi tenere la vita solitaria, sii come un cherubino, che non si cura di nessuna cosa della terra [...] Se poi qualcuno osa portare l'esempio di Paolo – poiché anche Paolo lavorava e faceva elemosine -, a costui rispondiamo, riguardo a Paolo, che Paolo era unico e abile in ogni cosa. Un altro Paolo non sappiamo se sia mai esistito» (Isacco di Ninive, *Discorsi ascetici/1*, Roma 1984, 192). Nella stessa pagina approfondiva: «Se tu sei uno che vive nel mondo, conduciti come i buoni secolari; se invece sei un solitario, sii eccellente nelle fatiche nelle quali eccellono i solitari. Perché, se tu volessi praticarle entrambe, falliresti in entrambe» (*ib.*, 191)

24 Annotava de Lubac: «Volendo incarnare il cristianesimo si finisce col disincarnarlo, svuotandolo di se stesso» (H. de Lubac, *Paradoxes*, Paris 1946, 74). Con toni escatologistici aggiungeva il padre conciliare: «Che bel piano di cristianesimo incarnato Satana presentò a Gesù nel deserto» (*ibidem*, 75).

25 Precisava l'aquinate: «la vita contemplativa ha un riferimento immediato e diretto all'amore di Dio...ma la vita attiva è destinata più direttamente all'amore del prossimo.. perciò per sua natura la vita contemplativa ha meriti più grandi rispetto a quella attiva... tuttavia può accadere che una persona avrà più merito nelle opere della vita attiva che un'altra in quelle della vita contemplativa: per esempio, se per abbondanza dell'amore divino una persona consente di essere separata dalle dolcezze della contemplazione divina, per un certo periodo, onde poter eseguire la volontà di Dio a gloria sua» (Tommaso, *Summa*, II-II, q. 182, a. 2).

Nella cultura occidentale il concetto di contemplazione ha delle basi platonico-plotiniane, ed allude, in generale, ad una sorta di metarazionalità che sola consente di arrivare al Vero. Il termine usato è quello di *theoria*, lemma che nel mondo greco non corrisponde ad un semplice assistere, ma ad un autentico patire (*pathos*). Per essere più precisi, infatti, con essa si intende un essere rapiti dalla e nella contemplazione.

Può apparire sorprendente, al riguardo, che questa dimensione risulti presente in modo trasversale nelle culture religiose e nella mistica di varie religioni. Alla *theoria* del mondo greco – a prescindere da eventuali fecondazioni e diretti collegamenti storici che non si possono escludere – corrisponde quasi esattamente il *dhikr* islamico e il *dhyana* indù e buddhista. D'altro canto, persino un teologo come Balthasar riconosceva che la *theoria* plotiniana proveniva dall'India[26].

Solo apparentemente, però, la contemplazione greca è disgiunta dall'azione e dalle responsabilità storiche. Alcuni studi, infatti, hanno dimostrato come la *theoria* sia condizionata e dipendente da un agire morale. Gadamer, per esempio, scriveva che «Il "*theorein*" greco non è un astratto pensare, ma un pensare che incide profondamente sulla vita etico-politica»[27]. Ciò è del tutto coerente con le linee fondamentali del pensiero greco. Per essi, infatti, filosofare implicava un preciso atteggiamento morale ed uno stile di vita[28]. In sostanza, quindi, possiamo affermare che «la greca contemplazione implica un preciso atteggiamento pratico nei confronti della vita»[29]. Contemplazione, infatti, significa confrontarsi con l'intero e con l'assoluto, e ciò comporta un atteggiamento libero e distaccato: «il confrontarsi con l'assoluto e con l'intero comporta un distacco dalle cose che gli uomini hanno comunemente in massimo pregio – come per esempio la ricchezza, gli onore, il potere e simili -, e dunque comporta una vita di tipo, per così dire "ascetico"[30]. Viene sottolineato, per esempio, che contemplando l'intero mutuano le usuali prospettive, muta il significato della vita dell'uomo e si impone una nuova gerarchia di valori[31]. Una tale lettura della *theoria* implica che contemplazione e politica, che per i moderni appaiono antitetici, nel mondo greco erano invece

26 Cf. M. Buioni, «Il cristianesimo e le altre religioni in Hans Urs von Balthasar», *La Sapienza della Croce* 1 (2004) 21.

27 G. Reale, *Storia della filosofia greca e romana*, vol. 9: *Assi portanti del pensiero antico*, Milano 2004, 21.

28 Cf. H.G. Gadamer, *Verità e metodo*, Milano 2000, 271-273.

29 Reale, *Storia della filosofia greca e romana*, vol. 9, 21.

30 Reale, *Storia della filosofia greca e romana*, vol. 9, 22.

31 Reale, *Storia della filosofia greca e romana*, vol. 9.

pacificamente connessi tra loro. Il vero filosofo nella cultura greca è sempre stato colui che si è rivelato capace di realizzare un'autentica coerenza tra vita e pensiero.

Alla luce di queste articolazioni sulla *theoria* e sulla natura ultima del filosofo, potremmo fare dei collegamenti con la vita monastica, e dare dimostrazione di come il monaco, con il suo orientamento esistenziale verso la contemplazione, corrisponda al vero filosofo del mondo greco. Il monaco è per eccellenza il contemplatore dell'"intero", e proprio perché consapevole "dell'intero" egli sintetizza in maniera ideale pensiero e vita. Considerando questa coerenza essenziale della sua vocazione, nell'esistenza monastica non c'è alcuna antitesi tra contemplazione ed azione. Per meglio dire il monachesimo – e forse solo esso – rende possibile la convivenza di queste due dimensioni dell'esistere altrimenti inconciliabili. La scelta di vita monastica esprime una raggiunta saggezza, una coscienza dell'"intero" che, pur separandosi dal mondo, ne ha compreso la natura ultima. A suo modo, il monaco cerca "attivamente" di trasformare la realtà mondana, e dà testimonianza viva e concreta di valori alternativi. Questo si ripercuote direttamente anche nel suo modo di concepire il lavoro che sintetizza contemplazione ed azione. Il lavoro monastico, infatti, è un'azione contemplativa ed una contemplazione attiva. Esso è contemplativo perché "in-utile", ed è attivo perché testimonianza dell'"intero", della consapevolezza del senso ultimo dell'esistenza terrena. Da questo punto di vista, la vita monastica, sebbene escatologistica e separata, non è totalmente disincarnata o astorica. Con la sua testimonianza, il monaco svolge un servizio essenziale per gli uomini del proprio del tempo: quello della profezia, e la profezia è sempre contemplazione ed azione. Essa, infatti, è escatologistica, ma anche pienamente incarnata nelle necessità e nei bisogni spirituali dell'epoca storica nella quale è vocata ad esprimersi. Il "lavoro" del monaco produce sempre degli effetti storici, ed è comunque, anche nella solitudine di una cella, un servizio alla storia. Esso è "in-utile" e proprio per questo utilissimo, ed anzi necessario ed indispensabile, affinché i cristiani di ogni tempo possano comprendere quale deve essere il significato escatologico del loro agire nel mondo.

4. IL LAVORO NELLE CULTURE MONASTICHE DELL'ORIENTE

Le dinamiche oppositive tra azione e contemplazione, tra escatologismo e incarnazionismo, tra utilità ed in-utilità, le si ritrovano anche in altre religioni, soprattutto quelle del mondo monastico indiano indù e buddhista.

Nel contesto asiatico, per esempio, il concetto di in-utilità trova delle vere e proprie premesse metafisiche nell'acosmismo della *maya*, cioè dell'illusione cosmica. Sia nell'induismo che nel buddhismo è infatti presente un relativismo totale per quanto riguarda l'ontologia del mondo e per quanto concerne la sussistenza dell'essere personale. Questa convinzione ha delle conseguenze dirette sul piano della spiritualità orientale, la quale è notoriamente priva di una sensibilità, potremmo dire, "incarnazionista". Essa, cioè, è totalmente disinteressata alla storia e al mondo, ed è invece concentrata sulla sola vita interiore. È questo il carattere fondamentale del misticismo indiano, sebbene non manchino eccezioni, a partire dalla testimonianza di Gandhi.

In generale, comunque, sono diverse le condizioni che rendono disincarnata, ed anzi acosmica, la spiritualità orientale. Nel mondo religioso indù, ad esempio, Dio non ha bisogno dell'uomo, e si crede che abbia creato il mondo senza uno scopo perché non ha alcun bisogno di prefiggersi un fine e non tende ad un fine al di fuori di sé. All'interno del Vedanta, che è la principale filosofia indiana, il primato esclusivo della contemplazione acosmica e disincarnata è persino ovvio, nella misura in cui l'azione non è considerata un mezzo di salvezza dal momento che nasce da una falsa identificazione del Sé più profondo con l'io empirico[32]. Nell'induismo, pertanto, la contemplazione è considerata superiore all'azione. Quest'ultima, anzi, è ritenuta persino "peccaminosa", nella misura in cui è legata ai "frutti", cioè all'utilità, e quindi generatrice di altro *karma*, ovvero di azioni future che innescano una catena senza di fine di cause ed effetti. A grandi linee, questo è appunto l'insegnamento di Shankara, che, per il contributo che ha dato allo sviluppo del monachesimo e del pensiero indù, è spesso paragonato a san Benedetto e a san Tommaso. La sua visione negativa dell'azione, però, ha sollevato uno dei massimi problemi della filosofia indiana che è stato risolto soltanto con la *Bhagavad Gita*. Quest'ultimo testo, infatti, insegna come agire in modo non peccaminoso, cioè senza creare *karma*[33]. A partire da tale testo, la religiosità indù ha così iniziato a parlare di *swadharma* e di *karma yoga*, ovverosia di azione compiuta entro i dettami della propria casta di origine e di azione disinteressata. Percorrendo questa ipotesi risolutiva, il pensiero indiano si è così emancipato dall'ambiguità fondamentale dell'azione, e l'ha anzi rivalutata, perché Gandhi,

32 Cf. Sankaracarya, *Viveva-Cuda-Mani (Il gran gioiello della discriminazione)*, Roma 1972.

33 Si legge nel testo sacro indiano: «colui che vede nell'agire il non-agire e l'agire nel non-agire, quegli è saggio fra gli uomini, quegli è uno che ha realizzato l'unione e che ha portato del tutto a compimento l'opera sua. Colui le cui imprese sono tutte esenti dall'atto di volizione che procede dal desiderio, colui le cui opere sono bruciate al fuoco del conoscere, questo, appunto, i sapienti chiamano uomo di sapere. Avendo dismesso l'attaccamento al frutto dell'opera, sempre soddisfatto, senza doversi appoggiare ad alcunché, egli non fa nulla, sebbene sia sempre occupato ad agire» *(Bhagavad-Gita* IV, 18-20).

per esempio, ha insegnato esattamente il *karma yoga*, cioè un impegno storico che, siccome compiuto nel disinteresse personale e senza ego, diventa via di santificazione. Da questi principi della spiritualità indù possiamo quindi ricavare che anche in Oriente un'azione, per essere virtuosa, deve essere in-utile, cioè non mirare al vantaggio personale e ai frutti egoistici che se ne possono ricavare.

In generale, però, l'induismo ha una visione dell'esistenza la cui struttura è piramidalmente orientata verso il monachesimo, ovvero verso il disimpegno delle responsabilità familiari e mondane che devono riguardare sono la prima fase della vita. Almeno per le caste elevate, infatti, ancora oggi l'esistenza di un indù è scandita in quattro fasi: quella del *brahmacharya* (studente); quella del *grihasta* (capofamiglia); quella del *vanaprastha* (eremita); e quella del *samnyasa* (monaco itinerante). Il lavoro in senso stretto riguarda soltanto la seconda fase della vita, esso, però, come affermano le *Leggi di Manu* e le *Upanishad* della rinuncia, viene dichiarato incompatibile con la vita del *samnyasin*, cioè del monaco[34]. Naturalmente il bimillenario e variegato mondo monastico indiano non manca di eccezioni rispetto a questa consuetudine, e, per esempio, nella scuola Lingayats è proibito mendicare ed è richiesto ai monaci di lavorare anche per il beneficio dei poveri e degli indigenti[35].

La cultura del lavoro, però, è di sicuro maggiormente sviluppata nel mondo buddhista anziché in quello indù. Se nel *Vinaya pitaka* – la regola monastica di questa religione – era previsto che i monaci buddhisti, come i *samnyasin* indù, praticassero la mendicità, con lo sviluppo dei monasteri hanno sviluppato un'articolata spiritualità del lavoro. Soprattutto nella tradizione buddhista zen il lavoro ha assunto un'importanza centrale. Non è un caso, per esempio, che all'interno di una delle sue scuole sia diffuso un principio assai prossimo alla sensibilità paolina: "Un giorno senza lavoro è un giorno senza cibo"[36]. L'attività lavorativa, nel mondo zen, è strettamente associata alla pratica contemplativa. Nel buddhismo theravada, invece, il lavoro manuale è particolarmente raccomandato solo ai monaci all'inizio del loro cammino, o a quelli che praticano con grande assiduità la meditazione. In generale, comunque, nel buddhismo il lavoro – o almeno certi lavori – sono visti con un certo sospetto se comportano l'uccisione di animali (ad esempio l'agricoltura) o un'esaltazione dell'ego. In generale, nel

---

34 Per un approfondimento sul tema si prenda in esame il capitolo unidicesimo di M. de Dreuille, *Uno sguardo ad Oriente*, Praglia 2013, 304-342).

35 Cf. D.M. Sadasivaiah, *A comparative study of two virasaiva monasteries*, Bangalore 1967, 91-113.

36 Cf. H. Dumoulin, *A history of Zen Buddhism*, London 1963, 103.

quadro di questa religione, così come per il mondo greco, vale il principio di fondo che il lavoro non è preliminarmente in antitesi con la contemplazione, se vissuto con un distacco dall'io e dai frutti dell'azione. Questa categoria, che abbiamo definito dell'inutilità, è dunque trasversale, ed è indubbiamente uno dei temi principali su cui può confrontarsi il dialogo esperienziale del DIM/MID[37].

CONCLUSIONI

Alla luce di questa veloce rassegna attraverso il monachesimo cristiano, la filosofia greca e le tradizioni orientali, possiamo concludere che contemplazione e lavoro non sono tra loro in antitesi, a patto che quest'ultimo sia vissuto con libertà interiore. Gaetano Favaro scriveva che «nell'esperienza cristiana – e potremmo aggiungere in misura maggiore nel monachesimo – contemplazione e azione si intrecciano e si completano non tanto dall'esterno, ma all'interno del mistero trinitario di Dio nel cuore dell'uomo. La contemplazione è il fondamento dell'azione»[38]. Il monachesimo, quindi – ma sarebbe meglio dire i monachesimi di tutte le religioni -, promuovono una comprensione del lavoro escatologistica assai distante se non antitetica a come la società contemporanea vive questa fondamentale attività umana. L'attuale maniera distorta di viverlo, quella che è stata definita antiteologia del lavoro, deriva anche da un incarnazionismo distorto e mal compreso. In generale, pertanto, la testimonianza dei monachesimi può essere un richiamo ed un modello per la società contemporanea. Se quest'ultima, nelle sue molteplici attività lavorative, cerca l'utilità, il monaco rimane invece aperto alla contemplazione disinteressata, perché è colui che riproduce la teologia del sabato. Il lavoro, infatti, anche secondo la tradizione ebraica, dovrebbe rimanere aperto al sabato, la cui celebrazione è sempre vista in prospettiva escatologica[39]. Il monaco, in virtù dello spirito con cui vive il lavoro, è dunque un esempio di contemplativo-attivo, e come tale deve essere un modello esemplare per tutti i cristiani. Egli *è colui che educa alla spiritualità e al senso profondo dell'attività umana nel mondo.* È compito del monaco, quindi, ri-insegnare all'uomo e al cristiano di oggi a lavorare.

---

37 Il DIM è il Dialogo Interreligioso Monastico, organizzazione benedettina internazionale che porta avanti il dialogo dell'esperienza religiosa. Per un approfondimento si consideri la rivista on line «Dilatato Corde».

38 Cf. G. Favaro, *La dialettica contemplazione-azione nel dialogo interreligioso*, in *Monachesimo cristiano e non cristiano*, ed. Centro interreligioso Henri Le Saux (Quaderni del Centro Interreligioso Henri Le Saux 7), Milano 1990, 139.

39 Si consideri: Gen 2,2; Es 20,8-11; Deut 5,15; Deutero Isaia 5,6, 1-7.

Abstract

Il fondatore di Bose Enzo Bianchi affermava provocatoriamente che il monaco "non serve a nulla". Con questa aggettivazione, però, coglieva un aspetto essenziale della vita monastica: il suo orientamento radicale alla contemplazione. È lecito interrogarsi, infatti, su quale sia il senso spirituale dell'azione – ed in particolare il lavoro – per un cristiano e, nello specifico, per un monaco. Il lavoro, dopo la svolta incarnazionista del Concilio Vaticano II, si è aperto alla modernità, alla tecnica, al sistema economico liberista e alle politiche industriali, stravolgendone così, almeno in parte, la sua costitutiva dimensione ascetico-soteriologica. La questione verrà analizzata anche facendo un confronto con il mondo monastico indù e buddhista dove il tema ha una rilevanza primaria. Nel mondo indiano, infatti, la contemplazione, è in primo luogo un'azione disinteressata compiuta senza ego e senza un secondo fine. Tale atteggiamento è presente anche nell'ambito della spiritualità cristiana del lavoro, specie quella escatologistica del monaco, che è sempre orientata alla teologia del sabato. Lo spirito con il quale il lavoro viene vissuto nel mondo monastico deve quindi fare da modello per tutti i cristiani, ed è auspicabile che si diffonda sempre più nella società moderna, dove troppo spesso è declinato al consumo, al carrierismo e al vantaggio personale.

MONASTIC INSPIRATIONS

DALLA REGOLA DI SAN BENEDETTO ALLA QUALITÀ TOTALE: ALLA RICERCA DELLE ORIGINI CULTURALI DEI PIÙ MODERNI ED EFFICACI MODELLI DI GESTIONE DELLE ORGANIZZAZIONI

Sergio Bini

PREMESSE

Quindici secoli fa Benedetto da Norcia, un giovane monaco italiano, pose le basi per un particolare "sistema monastico cenobitico" che nel tempo ha consentito la costruzione ed il governo del processo di trasformazione e di sviluppo della civiltà occidentale; questo silenzioso, continuo e straordinario lavoro ha avuto il suo fondamento nella Regola Benedettina: un piccolo e prezioso libro scritto a Montecassino dall' «uomo di Dio» e universalmente noto come *Regula Benedicti* [RB].

"Ausculta", *"humilitas"*, *"humanitas"*, *"discretio"*, *"stabilitas"*, *"de taciturnitate"*, *"statio"*, *"ora, lege et labora"*, sono solo alcune tra le più significative parole-chiave sulle quali poggiano i paradigmi innovativi della *leadership* benedettina e del modello cenobitico delle comunità organizzate proprio sulla base dei principi della *Regula Benedicti*. I contenuti di questa «regola caratterizzata da una singolare discrezione ed esposta in chiarissima forma»[1] sono da quasi 1.500 anni permanentemente attuali anche per la gestione efficace e sostenibile delle organizzazioni.

Sergio Bini, insegna «Gestione delle risorse umane e del benessere organizzativo» presso il Corso di Laurea magistrale in Programmazione e gestione delle politiche e dei servizi sociali dell'Università LUMSA di Roma (Italia) – s.bini@lumsa.it;
ingegnere, già dirigente d'azienda; *past president* dell'Associazione Italiana Cultura per la Qualità centro-insulare AICQ-CI di Roma;
confratello della Venerabile Arciconfraternita dei Santi Benedetto e Scolastica dei Nursini in Roma [http://www.nursini.org];
componente del Gruppo di ricerca internazionale "Cultura e Pastorale dell'Amministrazione del Monastero e dei Beni Ecclesiastici" presso il Pontificio Ateneo di Sant'Anselmo di Roma. [ing.sergiobini@yahoo.it]

1 San Gregorio Magno, *Vita di San Benedetto e la Regola* (Libro dei Dialoghi – volume II, paragrafo 36), Roma 1975, 102.

Per gli studiosi di Organizzazione aziendale, di Gestione delle organizzazioni, di Teorie e tecniche della Qualità, di *Business Administration* e di Benessere organizzativo, la *Regula Benedicti* può essere considerata la "madre" dei Sistemi di Gestione per la Qualità[2], della Qualità Totale (internazionalmente conosciuta come *Total Quality Management*) e dei più moderni modelli per conseguire l'Eccellenza sostenibile. Infatti, la *Regula Benedicti* (se opportunamente interpretata, compresa, interiorizzata, declinata ed applicata) costituisce una solida guida di sapienza per l'uomo di sempre. L'adozione diviene, cioè, utile per poter:

- comprendere meglio sia la persona (come entità e come singolo), sia il gruppo (nel suo insieme);
- costruire un processo virtuoso nel gruppo, cioè un miglioramento continuo dei singoli, della comunità, dell'organizzazione e di tutte le attività che vengono svolte al suo interno.

Nel presente contributo si intendono evidenziare ed illustrare sinteticamente solo alcuni degli aspetti più salienti della *Regula Bendicti* che è possibile rintracciare anche nei modelli più avanzati per i sistemi di gestione per la Qualità approfonditi nella letteratura tecnica internazionale e nell'esperienza delle migliori organizzazioni:

- la "*leadership* umile", basata sui concetti cristiani dell'umiltà e dell'attenzione alla persona intesa come patrimonio da valorizzare (la «*pietra che i costruttori hanno scartata è diventata testata d'angolo*»[3] e/o «*la pietra angolare*»[4]; oppure, ancora, come la «*pecorella smarrita*» che il buon pastore ricerca paternamente, dopo aver lasciato le altre al sicuro nell'ovile[5]);
- l'organizzazione, intesa prima di tutto come comunità che ascolta e che pone solidamente la persona (che nel linguaggio della Qualità diventa – di volta in volta – il cliente interno e/o il cliente esterno) al centro dell'attenzione di tutti;

---

2 I "requisiti" dei Sistemi di Gestione per la Qualità sono stati formalmente definiti a livello internazionale dall'International Organization for Standardization (ISO) solo a partire dal 1987 attraverso gli standard ISO della serie 9001, periodicamente aggiornati e rivisti. L'ultima versione è stata emanata a settembre 2015 come standard ISO 9001:2015. I "principi di gestione per la Qualità" sono diventati: 1) la focalizzazione sul cliente; 2) la leadership; 3) la partecipazione attiva delle persone; 4) l'approccio per processi; 5) il miglioramento; 6) il processo decisionale basato sulle evidenze; 7) la gestione delle relazioni. (Cf. UNI EN ISO 9001:2015 – *Sistemi di gestione per la qualità. Requisiti*, settembre 2015).

3 Vangelo secondo Matteo 21, 42.

4 Salmo 118, 22

5 Cf. Vangelo secondo Matteo 18, 12-14.

- la costruzione della comunità a partire dal reclutamento e dalla selezione delle persone; con il successivo processo di formazione continua; di maturazione e di crescita di ciascuno, singolarmente e come parte della comunità: perché «*è l'organizzazione che crea la comunità*»[6];
- come cambia il valore ed il ruolo del lavoro per tutte le persone e l'importanza che assume il singolo;
- il miglioramento continuo[7] lungimirante che traguarda verso l'eternità, basato su metodologie che risultano anticipatrici del ciclo PDCA[8], del *self-assessment* (autovalutazione ed autocontrollo), del *benchmarking* (confronto con i migliori) e del *problem finding/problem solving* (ricerca delle cause/motivazioni che generano gli errori e/o il mancato raggiungimento dei risultati attesi; quindi, sviluppo di metodiche per rimuovere i problemi e le cause, senza farsi tentare da più sbrigativi interventi limitati agli effetti e/o ai "responsabili" dell'errore);
- un modello culturale che aiuta a riscoprire un nuovo futuro riuscendo a gestire saggiamente il tempo-*kayròs*, senza farsi travolgere e schiacciare dal tempo-*chrònos* (che oggi si potrebbe declinare in concetti come "fretta", ansia, "*multitasking*", efficientismo a prescindere dall'efficacia del proprio agire, e così via).

1. SAN BENEDETTO DA NORCIA ED IL MONACHESIMO OCCIDENTALE

È universalmente noto che grazie a Benedetto da Norcia[9] nasce il monachesimo cenobitico. Non tutti, però, hanno elaborato una adeguata consapevolezza che

6 Cf. S. Bini, «La "Regola Benedettina": uno strumento sempre attuale per una gestione efficace delle organizzazioni», *L'Amministrazione Ferroviaria* 1 (2012) 23-42.

7 Cf. S. Bini, *Il miglioramento continuo e la Vision 2000,* in *Conoscere le ISO 9000:2000 – cambiamento, cliente, processi e miglioramento continuo*, Milano 2001, 105-195.

8 PDCA è l'acronimo di *Plan-Do-Check-Act* che rappresentano le quattro fasi del Ciclo di Deming che costituisce la base metodologica del miglioramento continuo della Qualità: pianificare – realizzare – misurare/monitorare – agire di conseguenza.

9 San Benedetto nasce a Norcia (Umbria) attorno al 480; dopo una breve permanenza a Roma per seguire gli studi letterari e giuridici, si ritira in una grotta a Subiaco; abbraccia la vita monastica e crea delle comunità religiose basandosi sulle regole tratte dalle Sacre Scritture. Dopo aver fondato 12 monasteri a Subiaco, con un gruppo di monaci si reca a Montecassino e fonda l'imponente Monastero nel 529, inteso come opera del Signore ed una *Dominici Schola servitii.* A partire dal 530 circa mette mano alla redazione della immortale *Regula.* Vive a Montecassino sino alla morte (che sarebbe avvenuta il 21 marzo 547).

Fig. 1 Benedetto da Norcia, il Santo del lavoro [copertina dell'omonimo libro di Vincenzina BATTISTELLI, edito dall'Istituto Miss. Pia Società San Paolo, Roma 1942; l'immagine è tratta dall'esemplare appartenente a Sergio Bini]

nei successivi quindici secoli – grazie al "Suo" modello organizzativo, spirituale e culturale particolarmente strutturato – i numerosissimi monaci appartenenti alla grande famiglia benedettina hanno assicurato un eccezionale sviluppo culturale, architettonico, economico, produttivo che ha consentito di plasmare sia la nostra civiltà, sia i capisaldi della inarrivabile cultura occidentale.

Al riguardo, il grande sociologo e scrittore belga Léo Moulin [1906-1996] – benché non credente – in ogni occasione enfatizzava che:

> i monaci sono all'origine, inconsapevole ed involontaria, di un movimento economico e sociale così profondo, così diverso e vasto che l'evoluzione del Medio Evo sarebbe difficilmente spiegabile senza la loro presenza e la loro azione.
> In questo senso, san Benedetto e con lui i benedettini sono i "padri dell'Europa" nel senso pieno del termine, sia da un punto di vista storico che sociologico [...][10].

10 L. Moulin, *La vita quotidiana secondo San Benedetto*, Milano 2008, 59.

Anche se Benedetto definisce la "Sua" *Regula Benedicti* solo una «*piccolissima Regola* da principianti [...]» con la quale risulta possibile «finalmente raggiungere, con l'aiuto di Dio, quelle più alte vette di dottrina e di virtù [...] ricordate» [RB, cap. LXXIII], sono moltissime le "lezioni" in essa contenute che si ritrovano nei modelli di gestione più avanzati ed evoluti delle migliori organizzazioni. Concretamente la *Regula Benedicti* costituisce da sempre, pertanto, una guida di sapienza perennemente utile per le comunità stabilmente organizzate e strutturate, che si sono dotate di una visione sistemica, che fissano obiettivi di lungo termine e che operano con elevatissimo contenuto valoriale/etico. Si tratta di una metodologia lungimirante che – efficacemente interiorizzata e declinata quotidianamente in forma attualizzata (ai tempi, ai luoghi ed alle situazioni) da generazioni di monaci – ha consentito di avviare ed alimentare silenziosamente innumerevoli serie di inesorabili ed efficaci circoli virtuosi in tutti i settori possibili; questa azione continuativa ha favorito il cambiamento del corso della storia, della società, della cultura, della solidarietà e in particolare ha operato concretamente per assicurare dignità e qualità al lavoro.

Il Pontificio Consiglio della Giustizia e della Pace, ne dà merito ed esplicita testimonianza nel paragrafo 266 del capitolo VI del Compendio della Dottrina Sociale della Chiesa, dedicato proprio al «lavoro umano»[11]. Il modello virtuoso entrò, purtroppo, in crisi solo in quei periodi in cui la Chiesa decise di commissariare Abbazie e Monasteri "nominando" degli "Abati Commendatari"; l'Abate, cioè, in questi periodi e situazioni, non veniva "eletto dalla comunità" tra i monaci esperenziati e dotati degli specifici requisiti fissati dal capitolo LXIV della *Regula*[12]. Risultò questa un'esperienza estremamente negativa, in quanto venne sottovalutato l'effetto dirompente nei confronti del "gregge", quando questo subisce un "pastore esterno" che non conosce né le "pecore" affidate, né le abitudini locali, né l'ambiente, né le regole della "casa".

---

11 Pontificio Consiglio Giustizia e Pace, *Compendio della Dottrina sociale della Chiesa*, Città del Vaticano 2005, 149.

12 «L'autorità passava quindi ad un estraneo, non eletto dai monaci ed ignaro dell'ideale monastico, spesso altero, più spesso avido delle rendite abbaziali, per nulla curante del bene dei monaci, sempre più immiseriti ed angariati dai suoi esattori insaziabili. Con l'andar del tempo questa Commenda divenne ereditaria in alcune grandi famiglie, di modo che le abbazie vennero a var parte del loro patrimonio [...]» [da E. Onori, *Farfa*, Castelli e Rocche (anno IX, n. 35), Viterbo 2011, 26].
La soluzione italiana di affidare "*in commendam*" organizzazioni complesse a personaggi esterni alle stesse (che costituisce una forma di surrettizio "commisariamento") non sembrerebbe, purtroppo, essersi mai interrotta fino ai giorni nostri.

Il 24 ottobre 1964, in occasione della riconsacrazione dell'Abbazia di Montecassino (sostanzialmente rasa al suolo nel 1944 – durante l'ultimo conflitto mondiale – a seguito di prolungati, incredibili e devastanti bombardamenti da parte degli aerei "alleati"), il Pontefice Paolo VI con lettera apostolica *"Pacis Nuntius"* proclamava san Benedetto Abate "patrono principale dell'intera Europa", sottolineandone la figura come:

> messaggero di pace, realizzatore di unione, maestro di civiltà, e soprattutto araldo della religione di Cristo e fondatore della vita monastica in Occidente: questi i giusti titoli dell'esaltazione di san Benedetto Abate. [...] principalmente lui e i suoi figli portarono con la croce, con il libro e con l'aratro il progresso cristiano alle popolazioni sparse dal Mediterraneo alla Scandinavia, dall'Irlanda alle pianure della Polonia.
> Con la croce, cioè con la legge di Cristo, diede consistenza e sviluppo agli ordinamenti della vita pubblica e privata. Egli insegnò all'umanità il primato del culto divino per mezzo della preghiera liturgica e rituale.
> Con il libro, ossia con la cultura, lo stesso san Benedetto, da cui tanti monasteri attinsero denominazioni e vigore, salvò con provvidenziale sollecitudine, nel momento in cui il patrimonio umanistico stava disperdendosi, la tradizione classica degli antichi, trasmettendola intatta ai posteri e restaurando il culto del sapere.
> Con l'aratro, infine, con la coltivazione dei campi e con altre iniziative analoghe che riuscì a trasformare terre deserte e inselvatichite in campi fertilissimi e in graziosi giardini; e unendo la preghiera al lavoro materiale, secondo il suo famoso motto *ora et labora*, nobilitò ed elevò la fatica umana [...][13].

In occasione del grande giubileo di san Benedetto, anche il Pontefice Giovanni Paolo II volle ricordare la portata lungimirante della Lettera Apostolica di Paolo VI sottolineando, in particolare, che:

> san Benedetto da Norcia è divenuto patrono spirituale dell'Europa perché, come il profeta, egli ha fatto del Vangelo il suo nutrimento, e ne ha gustato in una volta la dolcezza e l'amarezza.
> Il Vangelo costituisce infatti la totalità della verità sull'uomo: è insieme la gioiosa novella e nello stesso tempo la parole della croce.

---

13 Cf. PAULUS VI, «Litterae Apostolicae *Pacis Nuntius* (29 decembris 1964)», *AAS* 56 (1964) 965. È la Lettera Apostolica con la quale il Pontefice Paolo VI proclamò san Benedetto Abate patrono principale dell'intera Europa.

La stessa decisione presa dal cardinale Joseph Ratzinger di scegliere il "nome" di Benedetto (XVI) per svolgere il proprio magistero, come successore di Pietro, sembrerebbe essere stata molto di più di una semplice coincidenza. Di conseguenza, la stessa preziosa Lettera Enciclica *"Caritas in veritate"* andrebbe considerata come una sorta di "Regola Benedettina del terzo millennio"; coerentemente con tale linea, in occasione dell'udienza generale del 9 aprile 2008 Benedetto XVI nel soffermarsi ad illustrare la grande figura del padre del monachesimo occidentale ritenne opportuno sottolineare che:

> in contrasto con una autorealizzazione facile ed egocentrica, oggi spesso esaltata, l'impegno primo e irrinunciabile del discepolo di san Benedetto è la sincera ricerca di Dio sulla via tracciata dal Cristo umile ed obbediente, all'amore del quale egli non deve anteporre alcunché e proprio così, nel servizio dell'altro, diventa uomo del servizio e della pace.
> [...] in questo modo l'uomo diventa sempre più conforme a Cristo e raggiunge la vera autorealizzazione come creatura ad immagine e somiglianza di Dio.

Figura 2 - «Ora, lege et labora» nel chiostro di un monastero benedettino.
«"I Benedettini al lavoro: chi scolpisce una bella statua, chi prepara disegni e modelli, chi dipinge un quadro [...]" Storia della Chiesa – parte II – pag. 28 – Ediz. U.G.C.»
[copia della cartolina realizzata dal Provveditorato
Cattolico di Roma, 1931; della collezione di Sergio Bini]

Dalla lettura data da Benedetto XVI si potrebbe sintetizzare che il messaggio spirituale consegnato dal Santo di Norcia alla Chiesa ed all'umanità sia focalizzato fondamentalmente attorno a due elementi centrali:

- la perenne ricerca di Dio: la *Regula* ricorda di «cercare veramente Dio» [RB, cap. LVIII] nella sollecitudine alla preghiera, nell'obbedienza e nell'accettazione delle contrarietà. San Benedetto traccia con energia l'invito a cercare Dio con assiduità, a permettere che Dio sia la presenza che orienta la vita dell'uomo, perché senza questa presenza l'uomo perde inesorabilmente il senso profondo della vita e dimentica il proprio autentico e unico valore di creatura amata da Dio in Cristo. Senza l'orientamento a Dio, l'uomo, inevitabilmente, trasforma se stesso in idolo, perdendo la libertà proprio quando si illude di conquistarla con le proprie forze, anziché accoglierla come dono del Creatore.
- L'amore di Cristo: la *Regula* ricorda che «non si deve anteporre nulla all'amore di Cristo» [RB, cap. IV e cap. LXXII]. I discendenti di san Benedetto sono chiamati a realizzare concretamente questo invito, nel vedere e amare Cristo nel proprio abate [RB, cap. II e cap. LXIII], negli infermi [RB, cap. XXXVI], negli ospiti (che avrebbero potuto trovare ospitalità solo dopo aver pregato insieme ed aver "condiviso" i principi della *Regula Benedicti*) [RB, cap. LIII][14], nei poveri e nei pellegrini [RB, cap. LIII]. Il comandamento dell'amore verso Dio e verso il prossimo (in cui si deve riconoscere Cristo), allora, diventa la sintesi intramontabile del messaggio benedettino, che è il nucleo stesso del Vangelo da praticare e diffondere (attraverso un'intensa attività evangelizzatrice grazie a comportamenti esemplari, una preghiera intensa, una liturgia coinvolgente e con azioni decise e prive di tentennamenti[15]).

2. LA *REGULA BENEDICTI* È PRESENTE ANCHE NELLA NOSTRA VITA QUOTIDIANA

La perenne attualità della lezione lasciataci dal grande Benedetto da Norcia nelle bellissime pagine della sua *Regula Benedicti* deriva – secondo chi scrive – dalla circostanza che il Patrono d'Europa «non era un sognatore, ma un umile realista», che aveva la sensibilità e la capacità di vedere in prospettiva, vivendo

14 S. Bini, «Alla riscoperta della Regola Benedettina – L'"ospitalità benedettina": strumento per l'evangelizzazione misericordiosa», *NURSINI – Notiziario dell'Arciconfraternita dei Santi Benedetto e Scolastica all'Argentina* 1 (2016) 12-15.

15 Si consiglia la lettura di Bernardo da Chiaravalle, *De Laude novae militiae ad Milites Templi*, (scritta tra o 1128-1136), traduzione a cura di G. Brogi, Edizioni Argonautiche, 2010.

in prima persona la "parola di Dio". La freschezza e la contemporaneità della *Regula Benedicti* – e, quindi, della lezione benedettina – emergono da una nutrita serie di segnali, di evidenze e di coincidenze; a partire dalla situazione caotica che la società sta vivendo che, per molti versi, risulta confrontabile con quella dell'epoca di san Benedetto (crollo dell'Impero; grandi invasioni da parte di popolazioni straniere; stato di abbandono nel controllo del territorio; diffusi fenomeni di banalizzazione dei valori e di relativizzazione delle verità; infragilimento dei caratteri e decadenza dei costumi; e così via).

Dallo studio della *Regula Benedicti* (i cui concreti effetti innovativi sono percepibili ancora oggi, a partire dalla valorizzazione del territorio con la rete di abbazie, monasteri, priorati, cattedrali, pievi, piccole chiese rurali, infrastrutture legate alla concreta attuazione territoriale della "economia curtense", e così via) emerge che il modello "originario" di continente europeo costituisce una sorta di filiazione del disegno tracciato da san Benedetto:

- concetti-base della vita delle organizzazioni: parlamento, elezioni, scrutinio, ballottaggio, rappresentanza, arbitrato, cooperative, fondazioni, imprese a rete, *franchising*, *brainstorming*, *outsourcing*, assistenza sanitaria e strutture ospedaliere, *welfare*, servizi per la terza età e ostelli, e così via;
- parole e forme: "avere voce in capitolo", "tutti i Salmi finiscono in Gloria", "l'ozio è il padre dei vizi", "dare il tempo al tempo", "il lavoro nobilita l'uomo", "è l'abito che fa il monaco", "avere il senso della misura"; dall'esperienza della vita monastica benedettina sono stati tramandati anche termini nuovi come: rubrica, scomunica, colazione, *breakfast*, biscotto, indispensabile, pietanza, e così via;
- invenzioni e soluzioni tecnologiche: i vari tipi di mulino (ad acqua; a vento); bussola; aratro; organizzazione tecnica dell'agricoltura, della silvicoltura, dell'apicoltura, della pescicoltura, della frutticoltura; stampa; ferratura dei cavalli; orologio (lo "svegliarino"); altoforno; tecniche di costruzione delle cattedrali e dei monasteri; logistica per l'organizzazione dei cantieri; insieme con una moltitudine di prodotti innovativi e di tante altre "cose nuove". Anche per questo, nel 1957 Pio XII proclamò san Benedetto da Norcia "patrono degli ingegneri e degli architetti italiani"[16].

16 Cf. S. BINI, *S. Benedetto da Norcia patrono degli ingegneri: dalla Regula Benedicti ai sistemi integrati per la gestione efficace delle organizzazioni*, atti del seminario presso l'Ordine degli Ingegneri della provincia di Roma, Roma, 15 dicembre 2014; in: https://www.ording.roma.it/archivio/14304-binisergio(aicq-cieordineingegneriroma)sbenedettoeingegneri-20141215.pdf [accesso: 05-05-2016].

La *Regula* di san Benedetto va, quindi, ben oltre la prioritaria dimensione "religiosa"; essa da secoli costituisce, indiscutibilmente, una guida metodologica che mette ordine nella vita delle persone e delle comunità (organizzazioni; aziende; imprese; reti di imprese; gruppi; e via di seguito). Dagli USA, Skrabec junior conferma che grazie alla Regola di san Benedetto:

> le comunità benedettine furono la dinamo economica della loro epoca.
> Erano centri agricoli, di produzione e di conoscenza [...] all'inizio la loro attività fu agricola, ma ben presto seguirono la strada [...] per raggiungere l'indipendenza economica, ottenendo i loro primi successi nella pesca, nella lavorazione della lana, nella macinazione del grano e nell'allevamento dei cavalli. Le comunità monastiche erano organizzazioni culturali nelle quali venivano promossi studi ed esperimenti nel campo della manifattura di beni.
> Nel XV secolo, ormai i monasteri [...] gestivano attività come la fabbricazione della birra, l'estrazione dei minerali, la molitura del grano, la produzione del ferro e la lavorazione del vetro [...] Queste comunità "industriali" ed i loro monopoli controllavano l'Europa attraverso dipendenze ("masserie") [...] L'efficienza organizzativa è l'eredità che esse hanno lasciato al nostro secolo, alla cui base troviamo alcuni principi benedettini: armonia, lavoro di gruppo e stabilità[17].

Ancora oggi, i principi della *Regula Benedicti* regolano la vita e le relazioni all'interno delle imprese; in particolare in quelle di «piccole» dimensioni e quelle artigiane (soprattutto italiane) che hanno una guida "paterna" del proprietario/artigiano/imprenditore; spesso al loro interno vengono gestiti "familiarmente" non solo orari, riti, attività, ruoli, compiti e responsabilità di ciascun protagonista, ma anche i processi di crescita personale e relazionale dei singoli. La visione metodologica è confermata dal pensiero di Bernardo di Chartres sintetizzato nella seguente metafora:

> siamo nani sulle spalle di giganti: la nostra ragione potrà essere tanto più potente e lungimirante, quanto più ci saremo impadroniti del pensiero dei "giganti", cioè dei classici: solo a partire dalle loro altezze, da quanto essi hanno conquistato con il loro ingegno, potremo lanciare uno sguardo su orizzonti più lontani[18].

---

17 Q.R. Skrabec jr, *La Regola di San Benedetto per il successo negli affari*, Roma 2007, 55-56.
18 G. Cuccato, *San Benedetto: un uomo che desidera la vita*, Genova-Milano 2005, 75.

Ancora oggi vengono "raccolti" i risultati del duro ed assiduo lavoro di generazioni di monaci[19] che hanno operato silenziosamente per «coltivare ed avere cura del giardino (la Terra) [...]»[20] come inutilmente richiesto da Dio ai nostri progenitori Adamo ed Eva. Per il grande architetto francese – cui va il merito di aver mirabilmente recuperato e restaurato Notre-Dame di Parigi – Eugène Viollet-le-Duc [1814-1879]:

> la Regola di san Benedetto è forse il più grande fatto storico, anche considerato dal solo punto di vista filosofico. Il «coro benedettino» ha giocato il ruolo più determinante nella strutturazione delle forme liturgiche e del gregoriano, condizionando gli sviluppi successivi della musica, così da poter affermare con buona approssimazione di verità che senza i Benedettini, oggi non avremmo neppure un Johann. Sebastian Bach così com'è[21].

3. DALLA COSTRUZIONE DI SANTE COMUNITÀ CENOBITICHE ALL'ORGANIZZAZIONE DI REALTÀ EFFICACI

Esaminando – con particolare attenzione, sensibilità, competenza ed una lunga esperienza manageriale – le fresche pagine della *Regula Benedicti*, tra le righe si colgono moltissimi elementi significativi che nei secoli hanno trovato spazio nelle teorie e nelle metodiche gestionali per la Qualità e per l'innovazione; ad esempio:

- eliminazione delle negatività nella vita quotidiana;
- gestione e valorizzazione delle persone (le cosiddette "risorse umane") attraverso personalizzati processi di selezione, formazione permanente, condivisione ed assimilazione delle "regole", utilizzazione proficua, azioni esemplari per creare motivazione e senso di appartenenza. Ma anche efficaci misure disciplinari;
- ottimizzazione del lavoro di squadra per la condivisione delle conoscenze e delle competenze;

---

19 Il "monaco" concretizza il concetto di "unità"; viene dal latino *"monachus"* e dal greco *"monachos"* (da *"monos"*: «uno solo») e perché vuole realizzare l'aspirazione di essere "uno" per Dio "solo" [Cf. G. COGONI, *Il monachesimo dalle origini a Benedetto da Norcia*, Cagliari 2016, 12-13].

20 Genesi 2, 15.

21 A. STENDARDI, «Introduzione», in GREGORIO MAGNO, *Vita di San Benedetto e la Regola*, Roma 1995, 43.

- capacità di integrare nel lavoro le dimensioni materiali (tangibili) con quelle spirituali (intangibili);
- finalizzazione – sia individuale che collettiva – dei comportamenti e delle azioni della comunità monastica al raggiungimento dell'autorealizzazione (posta al vertice della piramide dei bisogni di Abraham H. Maslow, del 1954). La soddisfazione, infatti, deve riguardare indistintamente tutte le persone che vivono ed operano all'interno di un ambito territoriale di influenza del Monastero/Abbazia; oggi la si chiamerebbe *Stakeholders Satisfaction*, ovvero la "soddisfazione bilanciata di tutte le parti interessate";
- codici di condotta, codici etici, *dress code* (come vestirsi per essere riconoscibili), modelli organizzativi, comportamenti che prediligono l'approccio olistico delle problematiche proprie della vita quotidiana;
- sviluppo di un'organizzazione capace di creare – coralmente e con continuità incrementale – conoscenze, competenze, metodologie e soluzioni innovative.

La *Regula Benedicti* sintetizzata nel motto «*ora et labora*» – anche se più correttamente andrebbe utilizzata la formula più estesa: «*ora, lege et labora*»[22] – costituisce, quindi, un progetto di vita, un insieme di principi chiaramente più vicino al significato originario della parola latina «*regula*»[23], o guida, piuttosto che al termine «*lex*» o legge. Essa costituisce una guida che aiuta a costruire progressivamente uno stile di vita; un insieme di peculiarità che la rendono uno strumento sempre vivo e attuale per i singoli e per le organizzazioni che hanno al centro realmente e concretamente la persona.

Grazie all'adozione sistematica e sistemica di questi insegnamenti si possono costruire le condizioni favorevoli per ottenere il miglioramento continuo dei singoli, del gruppo, della comunità e dell'insieme delle attività comunque svolte.

---

22 All'epoca, la società si divideva in uno schema gerarchico che prevedeva tre *"ordines"*: gli uomini di preghiera (gli *"oratores"*); gli uomini della guerra (i *"bellatores"*); gli uomini del lavoro dei campi (i *"laboratores"*). I monaci era i "migliori" perché riuscivano a coniugare gli aspetti legati alla preghiera con gli aspetti legati al lavoro che all'epoca era essenzialmente agricolo; durante la giornata il tempo era dedicato per *"orare"* e per *"laborare"* ("arare, lavorare la terra" e non, semplicemente l'attuale lavorare).
[Cf. A. Davril-E. Palazzo, *La vita dei monaci al tempo delle grandi abbazie*, riedizione il Giornale – BMilano 2006, 21].

23 «Regula» – oggi tradotta con il termine "regola" – nell'accezione originaria significava, invece, "indicatore stradale", "ringhiera"; cioè, qualcosa a cui aggrapparsi e sorreggersi nel buio o nei momenti di stanchezza. Qualcosa che indica la strada e aiuta ad andare avanti verso una determinata (corretta) direzione, nel "deserto della vita" quotidiana [Cf. J. Chittister, *Fermati e ascolta il tuo cuore: vivere oggi la Regola di San Benedetto*, Cantalupa 1999, 13].

SELF-ACTUALISATION	Spirituality; harmony; excellence.
SELF-ESTEEM	Common destiny; humbleness; "lectio divina".
SOCIAL NEEDS [BELONGING]	Communities/organization; daily-meeting (*"consilium"*); team-working.
SAFETY	Self-sufficiency; obedience to the "Rule" (*"Regula Benedicti"*); stability (*"stabilitas"*).
PHYSIOLOGICAL NEEDS	Meals and regular rest; job involvement.

Figura 3 - La *Regula Bendicti* e la Piramide dei bisogni di Abraham H. Maslow[24]

La "sapienza benedettina" consente di penetrare nei significati delle cose e delle azioni umane, di conoscere l'uomo in tutte le sue manifestazioni evidenti (parole e azioni) e le sue dimensioni più nascoste. Le tre principali virtù della *Regula Benedicti* per il miglioramento si identificano con:

- l'"obbedienza", cioè mettersi in ascolto vicendevole in piedi *(ob-audire)* per essere pronti ad agire secondo saggezza, conoscenza e competenza [RB, cap. V];
- il "silenzio", che non è un vuoto mentale o assenza di proposte, ma il modo che le fa maturare. Sobrietà e proprietà del linguaggio sono funzionali al silenzio [RB, cap. VI];
- l'"umiltà", che è un sentirsi sempre vicini alla terra *(humus)*, cioè prossimi ai problemi ed attenti alle realtà quotidiane, per avere sempre la percezione della fallibilità e della fragilità [RB, cap. VII].

Per la *Regula Benedici* «unico è il monastero, unico l'abate, unico è il legislatore. Non vi è più dispersione [...]»[25]; il voto di stabilità *(stabilitas loci)* è la madre dell'affidabilità e costituisce un concetto sempre attuale che rientra nel macro-indicatore "miglioramento di innovazione ed apprendimento" del mo-

24 Rielaborazione dell'A. sulla base delle argomentazioni formulate da Skrabec, *La Regola di San Benedetto per il successo negli affari*.

25 Stendardi, «Introduzione», 18.

dello di *Balanced Scorecard* di Kaplan e Norton[26] (modello che valuta negativamente quelle organizzazioni che registrano un elevato *turn over* del personale).

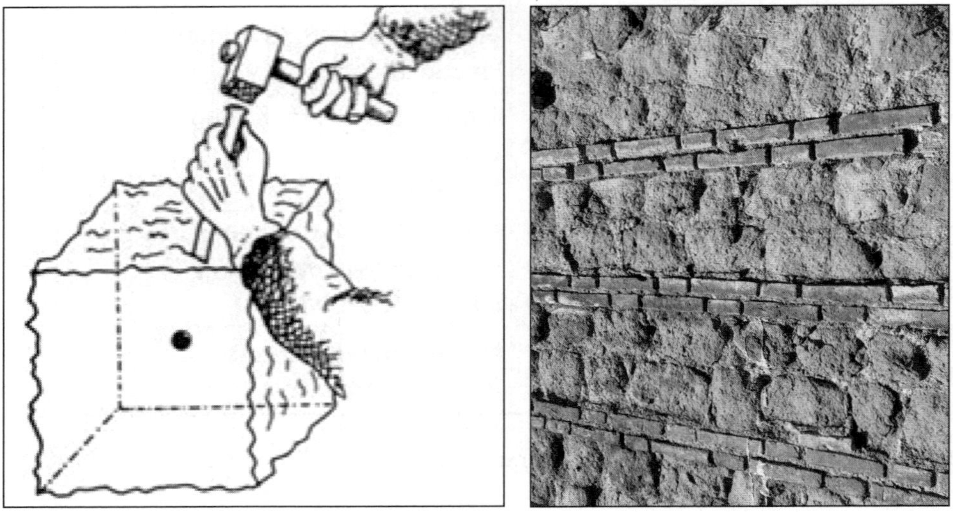

Figura 4 - L'«Opus Dei» è anche lavorare sulle persone in quanto «pietre vive» [Cf. la 1^ lettera di Pietro apostolo, 2-4]. La logica seguita è confrontabile con le tecniche utilizzate nell'antica Roma per la realizzazione di murature in *"opus incertum"*; occorreva, cioè, lavorare tutte le singole pietre (ognuna diversa dall'altra, a differenza dei mattoni) per poter ottenere una puntuale e reciproca giustapposizione. La costruzione veniva irrobustita grazie all'inserimento di ricorsi di laterizio (dei "regoli" di mattoni) e/o di testate d'angolo in pietra squadrata.

Un'attenzione particolare lo merita l'inizio del "prologo":

ASCOLTA, figlio, i precetti del maestro,
PORGI attento il tuo cuore,
RICEVI di buon animo i consigli di un padre che ti vuole bene
e METTILI risolutamente in pratica,
per RITORNARE con la fatica dell'obbedienza a Colui dal quale ti eri allontanato [...].
[RB, prologo]

26 Cf. Robert S. Kaplan-David P. Norton, *Balanced Scorecard – tradurre le strategie in azione*, Torino 2007.

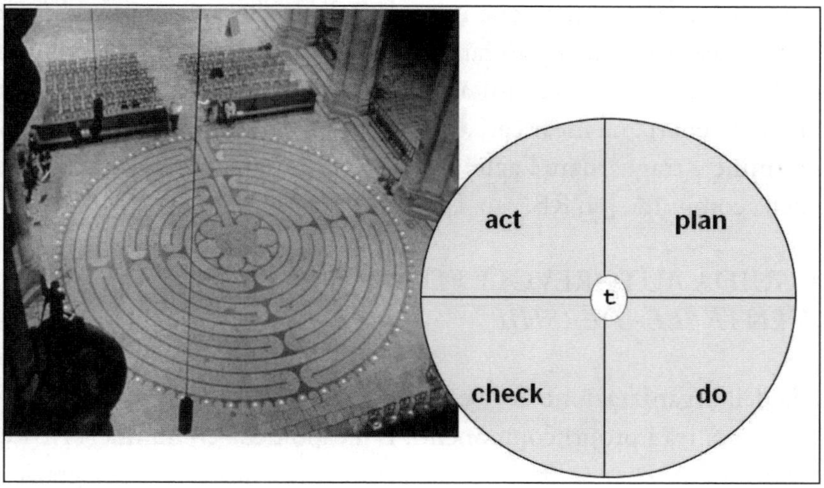

Figura 5 - Il miglioramento continuo: da Chartres, al ciclo di Deming P.D.C.A.

Dalla lettura approfondita di queste righe, traspaiono con chiarezza (anche se in filigrana) le fasi *plan – do – check – act* del ciclo PDCA di Deming che costituisce la base del miglioramento continuo[27].

È una ulteriore conferma che dalla *Regula Bendicti* si possono estrarre diversi paradigmi metodologici che costituiscono le fondamenta comportamentali per la stabilità e la sostenibilità delle organizzazioni.

Come noto, la *Regula Benedicti* è composta da un prologo e da 73 capitoli. In particolare, il Prologo definisce i principi della vita stabilmente cenobitica e paragona il monastero[28] ad una *"scuola"* che insegna la scienza della salvezza per i monaci; costituisce, quindi, una sorta di solida *"vision"* metodologica generale della vita della comunità cenobitica che riesce a legare tutti i suoi componenti.

---

27 La logica del "ciclo di Deming" per la gestione delle attività strumentali al miglioramento continuo è ampiamente riportata nelle norme internazionali ISO della serie 9000 relative ai «Sistemi di Gestione per la Qualità». Vedere anche le NOTE 2, 7 e 8.

28 Monastero deriva dal verbo greco «monàzein» ("vivere da solo") designava il complesso di edifici che consentiva alla comunità dei monaci di vivere stabilmente ed autarchicamente quasi esclusivamente con i frutti del proprio lavoro.
Quando con Francesco d'Assisi e Domenico di Guzmán, nascono gli "ordini mendicanti" (Francescani e Domenicani) i frati "inventano" il Convento, che deriva dal termine latino «conventum» ("adunanza, convegno"); soluzione coerente con il modello di vita itinerante (come superamento della stabilità monastica) e l'acquisizione di risorse provenienti dall'elemosina (come superamento del principio monastico dell'autonomia della comunità, ottenuta solo grazie al lavoro di tutti i membri).

Il voto di *"stabilitas"* distingue i cenobiti dagli altri monaci perché – come viene sottolineato – non si può fare affidamento su persone svolazzanti da un luogo all'altro e/o da una comunità all'altra e/o da un lavoro all'altro. Non servono né "mercenari", né incaricati a tempo; tutti devono pensare all'unisono, a lungo termine e traguardare l'agire e la vita quotidiana coralmente al bene comune della comunità. [cf. RB, cap. I]

4. LA GUIDA AUTOREVOLE ED AMOREVOLE DIVENTA *"LEADERSHIP"*

La guida dell'organizzazione deve essere affidata alla *leadership* di uomini scelti dalla comunità tra i propri componenti. È il capo della comunità (l'Abate) che *«deve riuscire a costruire la comunità per mezzo dell'organizzazione»* grazie a particolari doti/caratteristiche umane ed attraverso coerenti comportamenti esemplari. È indispensabile, quindi, che l'Abate *«detesti i vizi, ma ami i fratelli ...»* [RB, cap. LXIV] e nel correggere agisca con prudenza e senza eccessi, perché volendo raschiare troppo la ruggine, non gli capiti di rompere il vaso; abbia sempre presente la sua fragilità e si ricordi che "non si deve spezzare la canna incrinata".

La *Regula* ricorda all'Abate che deve operare cercando di *«essere amato più che temuto»* [RB, cap. LXIII];

> l'Abate si ricordi sempre di quello che è e di come viene chiamato, e sappia che a chi fu dato molto, molto sarà richiesto. Sia inoltre consapevole della difficoltà e della delicatezza del compito che si è assunto di governare le anime, adattandosi ai diversi temperamenti, che richiedono alcuni la dolcezza, altri il rimprovero, alti ancora la persuasione; sappia adattarsi e conformarsi a tutti, secondo l'indole e l'intelligenza di ciascuno, così da non subire perdite nel gregge affidatogli, rallegrandosi invece per il suo incremento [RB, cap. II].

L'Abate si deve liberare dall'orgoglio di dirigere una comunità (spesso importante) prestando la massima attenzione al singolo che deve essere rispettato con tutte le sue debolezze (comportandosi sempre come il "buon pastore"). In questo modo, mentre segue il singolo potrà conoscere meglio anche le proprie debolezze e troverà il modo per vincerle.

Per garantire la gestione efficace della comunità, la *Regula Benedicti* prevede la presenza di altre figure di supporto confrontabili con altri ruoli (omologhi) presenti nelle attuali organizzazioni: Priore (direttore generale); Cellerario (direttore amministrativo e direttore approvvigionamenti); Decani (dirigenti);

Circatores (*Internal auditing*); *Armarius* (responsabile formazione e cultura d'impresa); e così via.

L'Abate è tenuto a consultare quotidianamente i monaci per pianificare le attività e per adottare le scelte importanti:

> ogni volta che in monastero si devono trattare cose d'importanza, l'Abate raduni tutta la comunità ed esponga egli stesso di che si tratta. E, udito il parere dei fratelli, consideri dentro di sé la cosa, e faccia quello che gli sembrerà più utile. Abbiamo detto di chiamare tutti a consiglio, perché spesso il Signore ispira al più giovane il partito migliore. [...] consigliati in tutto ciò che fai e dopo non avrai a pentirtene [RB, cap. III][29].

5. LA QUALITÀ DI UNA COMUNITÀ DIPENDE DALLA QUALITÀ DELLE PERSONE E DAI VALORI CONDIVISI

Come già detto, con la *Regula* cambia il valore, il ruolo, la qualità e la dignità del lavoro. Merita di essere evidenziato che il quarantottesimo capitolo – dedicato al "lavoro manuale quotidiano" – si apre con un lapidario «l'ozio è nemico dell'anima: perciò i fratelli, in tempi stabiliti, devono attendere al lavoro manuale; in altre ore, pure assegnate, alla sacra lettura» e che «sono veramente monaci quando vivono del lavoro delle proprie mani, come hanno fatto i padri e gli apostoli» [RB, cap. XLVIII].

All'interno dell'organizzazione monastica, pertanto, il lavoro va eseguito bene, con serenità, senza tristezza e, soprattutto, senza mormorazione – cioè senza recriminazioni – nella gioia di lavorare a fianco degli altri monaci[30]. Grazie ai monaci benedettini, il lavoro viene nobilitato perché diventa un modo di pregare Dio e di contribuire alla realizzazione della Sua gloria, mentre all'epoca il lavoro era un'attività quasi esclusivamente attribuita agli schiavi[31].

---

29 La metodologia è sostanzialmente riconducibile al *"brainstorming"* messo a punto nel 1963 da A.F. Osborn.

30 L. Moulin, *La vita quotidiana secondo San Benedetto*, Milano 2008, 109.

31 Anche il "lavoro" sta tornando ad essere qualcosa di confrontabile con la situazione esistente al tempo di san Benedetto. Ovviamente si tratta di una versione attualizzata che è un misto tra precarietà, flessibilità, mercificazione, globalizzazione, delocalizzazioni, esternalizzazioni, è così via. Sostanzialmente il mercato del lavoro è governato solo dalla ricerca del guadagno ottenuto attraverso il perseguimento della cosiddetta produttività – a qualsiasi costo – che porta all'ingrossamento della schiera dei "senza lavoro", dei lavoratori occasionali, alla progressiva perdita dei diritti ed alla sublimazione della qualità del lavoro.

La qualità del «lavoro» e la dignità del lavoratore risultano essere tra le più grandi innovazioni introdotte da san Benedetto nella cultura occidentale; prima, infatti, i "non lavoratori" erano al vertice della piramide sociale. Questa rivoluzione avviatasi nelle Abbazie si propagò progressivamente estendendosi anche all'interno delle città; il notissimo motto «ora et labora» – grazie alla congiunzione *"et"* – esprime la stringente reciprocità dei due termini, che costituiscono aspetti inscindibili, ognuno dei quali finisce per dare il vero senso all'altro. Entrambe le attività hanno la stessa dignità e tutte devono ricevere la medesima dedizione. Ogni attività prepara e conduce all'altra, e tutti vi sono impegnati, in quanto ognuno ha il dovere di sostenere la comunità; il lavoro manuale si alterna alla preghiera e si vive in preghiera. Non c'è una attività più importante delle altre, ma tutte sono necessarie per edificare la "città di Dio": *«il messaggio è di sorprendente attualità. Infatti non viene messo il lavoro sopra di tutto, ma neanche si vive fuori dalla realtà e dell'impegno sociale:* san Benedetto tenta, con la sua Regola, di trovare un punto di equilibrio tra attività e contemplazione»[32]. Il senso di «comunità» viene vissuto come una potente spinta verso la Qualità Totale.

La comunità attribuisce grande importanza all'orgoglio del lavoro, risultato corale ottenibile solo grazie all'impegno del gruppo, perché le sue radici sono più profonde: è la fierezza di appartenere ad una collettività e quindi di ricercare insieme il «bene comune»! È questo senso di dignità che porta i componenti dell'organizzazione a proclamare al mondo esterno dove lavorano; la motivazione benedettina per la qualità collettiva è nell'affermazione delle capacità personali, rafforzata dalla disciplina della *Regula Benedicti*.

La chiave della qualità benedettina è rendere lo sforzo individuale parte integrante della comunità. I monaci eseguivano splendide copie artistiche di libri, che richiedevano anni di lavoro; il riconoscimento per quest'opera scrupolosa andava al valore complessivo dell'attività comunitaria, quindi, al monastero. La qualità benedettina era rivolta anche ai servizi, infatti, i concetti di ospitalità e di assistenza sanitaria e sociale fondano le loro basi su principi cristiani. Ma i viaggiatori portavano anche idee, recavano notizie e spesso informazioni (l'attuale *benchmarking*).

Per una migliore comprensione dei fenomeni legati all'attuale precarietà nel mondo del lavoro si rinvia al libro dell'autorevole sociologo del lavoro: L. GALLINO, *Vite rinviate. Lo scandalo del lavoro precario*, Roma-Bari 2014.

32 L. BRUNI-A. SMERILLI, *Benedetta economia: Benedetto da Norcia e Francesco d'Assisi nella storia economica europea*, Roma 2010, 56.

Con l'applicazione della *Regula Benedicti* non si pretende che un lavoro venga compiuto sempre alla perfezione, ma viene richiesto che gli errori si debbano obbligatoriamente auto-denunciare subito al "capo della comunità": l'Abate. Erano previste, infatti, sanzioni severe per chi non informava tempestivamente l'Abate riportandogli gli errori che aveva commesso:

> se, mentre è impegnato in un qualsiasi lavoro in cucina, in dispensa, nel proprio servizio, nel forno, nell'orto, in qualche attività o si trova in un altro luogo qualunque, un monaco commette uno sbaglio, rompe o perde un oggetto o incorre comunque in una mancanza e non si presenta subito all'abate ed alla comunità per riparare e confessare la propria colpa, sarà sottoposto ad una punizione più severa, quando il fatto verrà reso noto dagli altri [RB, cap. XLVI].

Ma questo è proprio uno dei principi-base del *just in time* che va sotto il nome di *Jidoka*[33].

La *Regula Bendicti* prevede anche l'entrata in gioco di "mentori" o di tutori per assicurare e/o per rafforzare le condizioni necessarie per garantire il corretto trasferimento delle conoscenze utili per creare l'eccellenza e l'innovazione nelle arti e nei mestieri. Se si leggesse questa modalità di relazione della conoscenza monastica utilizzando il lessico della letteratura scientifica si dovrebbe utilizzare il concetto di «*knowledge management*» (la gestione delle conoscenze) sviluppato da Ikujiro Nonaka[34] (nel 1991) oppure il modello di «*Learning Organization*» (una organizzazione che apprende) introdotto da Peter Senge (nel 1992) per definire quegli ambienti organizzativi che favoriscono la fertilizzazione, lo sviluppo e la trasmissione delle conoscenze e delle esperienze accumulate[35].

6. DALLA *REGULA BENEDICTI* UNA LEZIONE ANTICIPATRICE ANCHE DELLA SOSTENIBILITÀ AMBIENTALE!

Per illustrare il ruolo concretamente avuto dalle generazioni di monaci benedettini nell'abbellimento dell'ambiente che circonda Monasteri ed Abbazie, il sociologo Léo Moulin nei suoi scritti evidenziava che:

---

33 Cf. T. OHNO, *Lo spirito Toyota*, Torino 1993.

34 I. NONAKA, *The knowledge creating company*, in Harvard Business Review 69 (6): 96-104, 1991.

35 P. SENGE, *La Quinta disciplina*, Milano 1992.

> la prima questione che si poneva era quella del posto della nuova fondazione [del Monastero]: "perché i monaci andavano a spendersi in luoghi così lontani, inospitali, spesso in condizioni climatiche che ponevano dei problemi tremendi?"
> Essi cercavano anzitutto la solitudine, lontano dalla corruzione e dal frastuono della città.
> Ancora, essi dovevano trovare i mezzi per sopravvivere. Per questo essi dovevano avere delle terre, dei pascoli, dell'acqua e una foresta. Delle terre rese coltivabili tramite prosciugamento e irrigazione, dissodamento, bonifica. Pascoli per gli animali, acqua per la cucina, la pulizia dei locali e specialmente dei *necessaria* (servizi igienici), la cura del corpo, l'irrigazione dei giardini, i vivai, la fabbricazione della birra, i mulini, che all'epoca rappresentavano uno dei punti avanzanti della tecnologia e il cui impiego era allora molteplice.
> ... il loro lavoro secolare ha profondamente umanizzato il paesaggio.
> La bellezza è in buona parte opera degli uomini[36].

Al riguardo merita di essere ricordato, in particolare, san Romualdo – riformatore in senso eremitico del monachesimo benedettino – che fondò tra il 1012 ed il 1024 la Congregazione Camaldolese negli omonimi boschi del Casentino: «quanto potrebbero, gli eremiti, abitare felici in queste boscose solitudini; quanto vi potrebbero vivere pacificati, salvati dal chiasso che distrae!». Successivamente, nel 1080 Rodolfo, il quarto Priore dell'Eremo, codifica per la prima volta le consuetudini di vita della comunità: *"Liber eremiticae regulae aditae a Rodulpho eximio doctore"*. Al capitolo 49, nel testo si cantano sui sette alberi elencati nel libro di Isaia quali segno della fertilità della terra rifondata da Dio [Is 41, 19] e, contemplandone le proprietà, vi scopre l'indicazione di quelle virtù che ogni monaco deve possedere.

Nel testo viene affermato anche che ogni monaco deve diventare quegli alberi:

> tu dunque sarai:
> un Cedro per la nobiltà della tua sincerità e della tua dignità;
> un Biancospino per lo stimolo alla correzione ed alla conversione;
> un Mirto per la discreta sobrietà e temperanza;
> un Olivo per la fecondità di opere di letizia, di pace e di misericordia;
> un Abete per elevata meditazione e sapienza;
> un Olmo per le opere di sostegno e pazienza;
> un Bosso perché informato di umiltà e perseveranza[37].

---

36 L. Moulin, *La vita quotidiana secondo San Benedetto*, Milano 1980, 15 e ss.

37 Francesco d'Assisi *et al.*, *La Regola, via di conoscenza e amore*, Verona 2007, 58 e ss.

Nei secoli successivi, questi santi monaci bianchi hanno utilizzato con grandissima lungimiranza e con differenti metodologie (progressivamente più raffinate) le foreste; inizialmente l'approccio alla gestione delle risorse forestali era solamente dettato da "esigenze spirituali", con il passare del tempo si è arricchito e adattato alle necessità delle popolazioni locali ed alle esigenze economiche che il periodo storico richiedeva.

La gestione dei boschi, in partenza trasmessa oralmente, rientra ufficialmente nelle regole della vita quotidiana dei monaci con le prime norme scritte a tutela dell'integrità della foresta già nel XIII secolo, fino ad essere incorporata ne "La regola della vita eremitica" di Paolo Giustiniani del 1520, comunemente conosciuta come il "Codice forestale Camaldolese". In questo "Codice" tornano con grande insistenza le parole "custodire" e "coltivare" azioni che risultano utili per realizzare il compito assegnato dal Creatore all'uomo quando gli affida la Terra [Genesi 2, 15], «facendo riemergere la dimensione biblica del progetto divino da realizzare in armonia con tutta la Creazione»[38]. Grazie a queste "regole" i monaci Camaldolesi hanno gestito saggiamente le risorse naturali del territorio dal 1027 fino al 1866.

In merito sembrano opportuno riportare le interessanti parole di Padre Bernard Sawicki osb contenute nella sua puntuale glossa alla lettera Enciclica *Laudato Si'* di Papa Francesco[39].

> La sensibilità monastica, con la sua capacità di integrare le varie dimensioni del discorso teologico, risulta proprio da un certo tipo di ecologia della vita dei primi monaci. Basta leggere i primi testi che la descrivono [...] il luogo naturale e privilegiato dei monaci era il deserto, con tutta specificità e severità della natura che lo formava e circondava. Questo deserto non serviva solo come una fuga dal mondo. Al contrario [...] i primi monaci percepivano il mondo proprio attraverso le categorie della natura. Erano proprio la sensibilità e il linguaggio del Vangelo: forse un po' più radicale e diretto.
>
> La forza "ecologica" della tradizione benedettina sta nella virtù che oggi ci manca tanto: la *discretio* cioè il discernimento e, in altre parole, la capacità (o l'arte) di trovare sempre una misura giusta – sia nel nostro rapporto con il mondo, sia

38 R. Romano, *Il Codice forestale camaldolese: le radici della sostenibilità*, in http://agriregionieuropa.univpm.it/il(content/article/31/21/il-codice-forestale-camaldolese/ [accesso: 01-04-2016].

39 Franciscus, *laudato si' – Enciclica sulla cura della casa comune*, Città del Vaticano 2015.

> nelle nostre relazioni con gli altri e con noi stessi. Proprio ne risulta un equilibrio che è la base di qualunque preoccupazione ecologica.
> In virtù di questo equilibrio la cultura monastica [...] si diffondeva in Europa. [...] È particolarmente impressionante e allo stesso tempo affascinante vedere come i monaci potevano inscrivere i loro monasteri nei paesaggi circostanti. Creavano una sintonia tra la forma del terreno, il gioco della luce ma anche il potenziale agricolturale dell'ambiente.
> Per questo la cultura monastica medievale può servire come un modello di una vita veramente ecologica, cioè realmente sincronizzata con la natura[40].

Questo modello è ancora oggi attuale e valido per realizzare un futuro che sia realmente e concretamente sostenibile, cioè durevole.

7. STUDIARE, APPROFONDIRE E DIFFONDERE LA CULTURA BENEDETTINA: UN PATRIMONIO DELL'UMANITÀ!

Con la preoccupazione che si possa realizzare l'aforisma profetico di George Orwell: «chi controlla il passato controlla il futuro; chi controlla il presente controlla il passato» (che, in forza di una normale esperienza maturata, potrebbe essere aggiornato in: "chi si appropria del nostro passato, si appropria del nostro futuro") si è voluto porre mano alla attivazione di un "cantiere culturale" per la riproposizione metodologica della lezione del monachesimo benedettino, nonché delle "regole" e della cultura della *Regula Benedicti*. È nata, così, l'idea di dare vita ad un «Centro Studi sulla Qualità Benedettina», (appoggiandosi inizialmente presso l'Associazione Italiana Cultura per la Qualità Centro-Insulare AICQ-CI di Roma).

L'azione ha visto anche il coinvolgimento della Venerabile Arciconfraternita dei Santi Benedetto e Scolastica dei Nursini di Roma; infatti a partire dal 2012 ogni numero del Notiziario "NURSINI" dell'Arciconfraternita ospita degli approfondimenti finalizzati alla "riscoperta della Regola Benedettina" per assicurare una maggiore diffusione possibile degli aspetti principali della cultura benedettina.

Si è inoltre posto mano ad una serie di iniziative (eventi, pubblicazioni, seminari, conferenze, presenze sul web, e così via) strumentali per ampliare al concreta promozione dello studio, dell'approfondimento, della rivitalizzazione e della diffusione della cultura benedettina.

---

40 B. SAWICKI, «Una glossa monastica alla Lettera Enciclica "Laudato si'" del Papa Francesco», *Studia Monastica* 57 (2015) 449-460.

Al riguardo, merita di essere ricordato uno degli eventi più significativi: «COENOBIA: il festival della cultura benedettina». È stata una iniziativa avvincente sperimentata nel borgo medievale di Orvinio (Rieti), a metà strada del "Cammino di S. Benedetto"[41] (percorso progettato per i pellegrini che collega in 16 tappe Norcia con Montecassino, passando per Subiaco); il paese ospita la preziosa Abbazia di S. Maria del Piano[42], di epoca carolingia, i cui ruderi continuano a resistere nonostante l'incuria del tempo. Il 12 luglio 2014 si è tenuta l'edizione "zero" che ha registrato una grande partecipazione di persone rimaste affascinate da questa lezione millenaria che appartiene al patrimonio culturale non solo italiano ma dell'intera umanità.

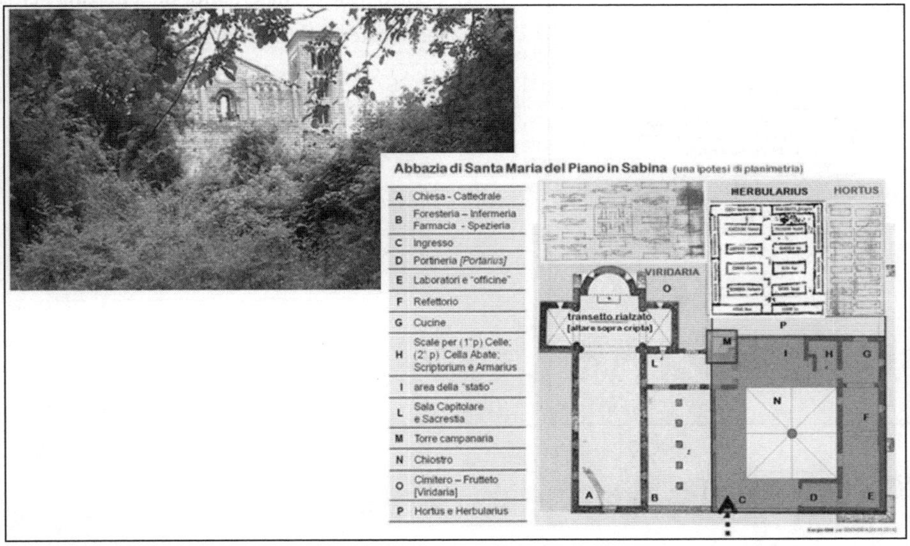

Figura 6 - L'antica Abbazia di Santa Maria del Piano di Orvinio (Rieti)
[la foto e la ricostruzione della planimetria dell'Abbazia sono di Sergio Bini]

41 Cf. il sito del "Cammino di San Benedetto": www.camminodibenedetto.it [accesso: 05-05-2016].

42 Una leggenda vuole che l'Abbazia di Santa Maria del Piano in Sabina fosse stata fatta realizzare proprio per volere di Carlo Magno, come una sorta di ex-voto, nel luogo in cui aveva sconfitto i Saraceni dopo una lunga, dura e sanguinosa battaglia; risulterebbe stata aperta al culto nell'817, nello stesso anno dell'importantissimo – soprattutto per la *Regula Benedicti* – Sinodo di Aquisgrana voluto da Ludovico I detto il Pio (figlio di Carlo Magno e imperatore dell'Impero carolingio dall'814 all'840).
Ludovico il Pio ebbe come consigliere particolare san Benedetto di Aniane [n. 750 circa - m. 12.02.821], riscopritore/rielaboratore della *Regula Benedicti* e artefice del rilancio del monachesimo benedettino.

Dagli approfondimenti sviluppati e dallo studio della letteratura disponibile, emerge chiaramente che "la lezione e l'esperienza benedettina", scaturenti dalla *Regula Benedicti* in quindici secoli di vita, andrebbero salvaguardate come "patrimonio dell'umanità" e riconosciute, pertanto, tra i principali "siti immateriali e culturali" mondiali da porre sotto la tutela [forse anche dell'UNESCO].

Questo sì che rimane un grande sogno accarezzato da tempo da parte dell'autore e che sarebbe auspicabile che tutto il movimento benedettino facesse proprio!

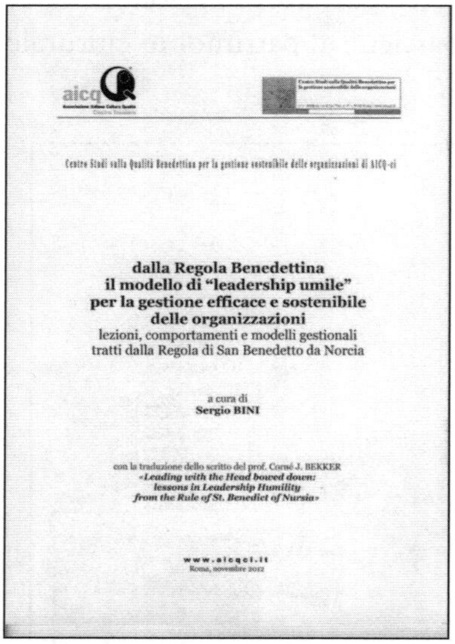

Centro Studi sulla Qualità Benedettina per la gestione sostenibile delle organizzazioni di AICQ-ci

dalla Regola Benedettina il modello di "leadership umile" per la gestione efficace e sostenibile delle organizzazioni
lezioni, comportamenti e modelli gestionali tratti dalla Regola di San Benedetto da Norcia

a cura di
Sergio BINI

con la traduzione dello scritto del prof. Corné J. BEKKER
«Leading with the Head bowed down: lessons in Leadership Humility from the Rule of St. Benedict of Nursia»

www.aicqci.it
Roma, novembre 2012

Figura 7 - La prima pubblicazione sul modello di "leadership umile" secondo la Regola Benedettina del Centro Studi sulla Qualità Benedettina per la gestione sostenibile delle organizzazioni [editata da AICQ-CI, Roma 2012].

CONCLUSIONI

L'uomo di ogni epoca ha avuto sempre bisogno di un armonioso ordine quotidiano, di un intenso clima familiare da costruire anche nell'ordine politico, sociale e giuridico, perché la vita di ogni singola persona e di ogni comunità si riflette poi nella vita di un popolo e, quindi, di un intero continente.

Anche l'uomo del terzo millennio, quindi, avrebbe bisogno del silenzio, della stabilità e dell'armonia.

Per sopravvivere spiritualmente dovrebbe poter ordinare lo spazio ed il tempo in cui vive, dovrebbe sottoporre le attività culturali e politiche a verità fondamentali, quali il rispetto di ogni persona ed il valore del lavoro umano. E, all'interno di questo quadro di riferimento, il continente europea del terzo millennio o sarà benedettino oppure sparirà come realtà culturale, valoriale e spirituale, rimanendo luogo di (illusorie) ricchezze materiali e di (concrete) povertà spirituali, una penisola dell'Asia e/o un partner economico e militare di qualche grande potenza (di turno). In estrema sintesi, la vita di ciascuno di noi potrebbe essere paragonata ad un percorso nel deserto sulle tracce dell'esperienza di Gesù.

Dom Jacques Dupont, Priore della Certosa di Serra San Bruno, ricorda che il deserto è:

> un luogo senza strade e senza sentieri, senza segnaletica e senza punti di riferimento, ma è proprio lì che Dio conduce l'uomo ed il suo popolo perché vivano forti esperienze di fede, perché imparino ad affidarsi totalmente a Lui laddove non c'è nessun appiglio umano e terrestre.
> Il deserto è un luogo senza vie, ma paradossalmente è attraverso di esso che passa l'unico cammino che deve percorrere chi cerca il Signore[43].

Allora c'è proprio bisogno di un *Regula*, cioè di una guida o di un "mancorrente spirituale", che possa fornire un metodo per aiutare tutti a superare i momenti più difficili e a saper distinguere i miraggi, dai veri punti di riferimento, in quanto *«ci sono delle vie che alcuni chiamano giuste e che alla fine precipitano nell'inferno»* [RB, cap. VII].

Per concludere, quindi, piace riportare le parole del monaco benedettino tedesco Anselm Grün che dà una sua lettura della *Regula Benedicti*, a partire dal prologo:

> *è evidente che il cammino spirituale di trasformazione di questo mondo secondo lo Spirito di Gesù è frutto di duro lavoro.*
> Secondo Benedetto la spiritualità non è un lusso per uomini che avrebbero altrimenti già tutto.
> La spiritualità è piuttosto duro lavoro, fatica, sincera lotta con se stessi, contrasto ai propri vecchi modelli di vita, per farsi sempre più impregnare dello Spirito di Gesù [...]
> perché i problemi del mondo non sono da compiangere, ma da risolvere!
> Fai quello che puoi. Costruisci intorno a te una comunità che se ne faccia carico!
> Può essere la tua famiglia, la tua cerchia di amici, la tua ditta, la tua parrocchia.
> Se, dovunque tu viva, crei una cultura di vita cristiana, sarà tanto lievito per questo mondo[44].

---

43 Cf. L. Accattoli-J. Dupont, *Solo dinanzi all'Unico*, Soveria Mannelli (CZ) 2011.

44 A. Grün, *Benedetto da Norcia: la Regola per l'uomo d'oggi*, Cinisello Balsamo (MI) 2006, 104-105.

È questo l'impegno che ciascuno di noi dovrebbe mettere in atto quotidianamente, per potersi comportare effettivamente da buon cristiano e per poter dare una testimonianza esemplare alle persone che si incontrano nella vita quotidiana (anche lavorativa) sempre più frettolosa e sempre più devalorializzata da un crescente relativismo amorale, a partire dalle organizzazioni aziendali e dagli ambienti lavorativi.

Abstract

Fifteen centuries ago, Benedict of Nursia – a young Italian monk – founded the monastic system, that has built and lead the western civilization. This discreet and, at the same time, extraordinary work is based on the Benedictine Rule: a little and interesting book, called *Regula Benedicti.*

Ausculta, humilitas, humanitas, discretio, stabilitas, ora, studia et labora are some of the most important keywords, on which the paradigm of leadership and the Benedictine model rest. Cenobitic organized communities, based on the Benedictine Rule, are significant and topical examples of the effective, efficient and sustainable management of organizations.

The *Regula Benedicti* represents the "mother" of the Quality Management System, until the Total Quality Management and the modern sustainable Excellence.

The *Regula Benedicti* is a precious guide to the human wisdom. It is always useful for:

– a better understanding of both, the person (as an entity and a human being) and the group (as a community and an organization);
– the creation and implementation of a "virtuous circle" in the group. This element is essential for a «continuous improvement» of every person, the community, the organization and all the activities in general.

We can find some of the most salient aspects of *Regula Benedicti* in the most advanced models of Quality Management. In effect, in the technical literature as well as in the experience of the best organizations, it is possible to find examples of:

– *"humble leadership"*, based on the Christian concepts of humility and attention to the people, considered as an asset to be enhanced (the *"stone which the builders rejected has become the corner stone ..."* or as the *"lost little sheep"*);
– organization – primarily intended as a community – that listens and considers people [internal and external customers] as the center of everyon's attention;
– «continuous improvement» towards eternity, based on Plan-Do-Check-Act cycle, self-assessment and problem solving;

- creation of the community from the choice, the education and the individual growth (because *“it’s the organization that creates community”*);
- change of the value and the role of “work” by the *Regula Benedicti*;
- cultural model oriented to discover a new future, developing the ability to manage time-*kairòs*, without being crushed by the time-*chrònos*.

CORPORATE GOVERNANCE AND LEADERSHIP FROM A MONASTIC PERSPECTIVE. A LITERATURE REVIEW

Ksenia Keplinger – Birgit Feldbauer-Durstmüller

INTRODUCTION

Ethical scandals, corruption, and falsified financial statements have shown very clearly that current corporate governance practice is not able to prevent the abuse of power, manipulation of incentives, and excessive risk taking[1]. To regain control and restore trust in the economic system[2], it is necessary to look at leadership and governance issues from a different point of view. Benedictine monasteries seem to offer a model of leadership and governance that has been successfully used for almost 1,500 years in different economic, social, and political settings. Having established basic governance instruments

---

This paper is a shortened version from Keplinger/Feldbauer-Durstmüller (2016). Earlier versions of this paper, "Corporate Governance and Leadership from a Monastic Perspective: A Literature Review", were presented at the 10th International Conference of the International Society for Third-Sector Research (theme: "Democratization, Marketization, and the Third Sector") in July 2012 in Siena, Italy, at the 73rd Annual Meeting of the Academy of Management (theme: "Capitalism in Question") in August 2013 in Lake Buena Vista, USA, and at the IABE-2016 Washington DC – Summer Conference (theme: "Global Business and Economics Issues: The Future of the European Union, United States and Emerging a Markets") in April 2016 in Washington, DC, USA. The contribution is published in the *International Journal of Strategic Management.* Cf. K. Keplinger-B. Feldbauer-Durstmüller, «Monastic approach to governance and leadership: A literature review», *International Journal of Strategic Management* 16/1 (2016) 39-60.

Birgit Feldbauer-Durstmüller, full Professor and Head of Institute for Management Control & Consulting at the Johannes Kepler University Linz Austria, Ksenia Keplinger, postdoctoral researcher in Organizational Leadership and Information Analytics at the University of Colorado Boulder, USA.

1 Cf. K. Rost-E. Inauen-M. Osterloh-B.S. Frey, «The corporate governance of Benedictine abbeys», *Journal of Management History* 16/1 (2010) 90-115.

2 Cf. M. Pirson-S. Turnbull, «Toward a more humanistic governance model: Network governance structures», *Journal of Business Ethics* 99/1 (2011) 101-114.

very early, Benedictine monasteries were able to survive over centuries and had an essential impact on the development in many European countries[3].

The 1,500-year legacy of the RB[4] as well as the wide variety of Benedictine organisations (e.g., schools, hospitals, universities, publishing houses, etc.) illustrate the relevance of the RB to many types of organisations, not just religious ones[5]. A considerable part of the RB is devoted to leadership issues such as cultivating a consultative climate and encouraging the virtues of humility, obedience, justice, discretion, prudence, and discernment[6]. Consequently, the RB offers a useful time-tested model for organisational development and re-instilling ethical leadership[7]. Leadership from a monastic perspective is an alternative concept that could provide promising solutions for some management problems in modern companies and organisations. Therefore, it is essential to understand the state of the art of this emerging field and predict the likely directions of its development in the future[8]. Although similar reviews have been published in different fields of management, we could not find any studies that review the literature on monastic governance and leadership. Even recent literature reviews on corporate governance[9] and leadership issues[10] do not consider the ideas and experience of the Benedictines to address agency problems and enhance leadership.

---

3 Cf. E. Inauen-K. Rost-M. Osterloh-B.S. Frey, «Back to the future – A monastic perspective on corporate governance», *Management Revue* 21/1 (2010) 38-59.

4 Cf. T.G. Kardong, *Benedict's Rule: A translation and commentary*, Collegeville (MN) 1996.

5 Cf. C.C.A. Chan-K. McBey-B. Scott-Ladd, «Ethical leadership in modern employment relationships: Lessons from St. Benedict», *Journal of Business Ethics* 100/2 (2011) 221-228.

6 Cf. Chan-McBey, Scott-Ladd, «Ethical leadership in modern employment relationships: Lessons from St. Benedict», 221-228.

7 Cf. Chan-McBey, Scott-Ladd, «Ethical leadership in modern employment relationships: Lessons from St. Benedict», 221-228; D.A. Tredget, «"The Rule of Benedict" and its relevance to the world of work», *Journal of Managerial Psychology* 17/3 (2002) 219-229.

8 Cf. J.J. Chrisman-F.W. Kellermanns-K.C. Chan-K. Liano, «Intellectual foundations of current research in family business: An identification and review of 25 influential articles», *Family Business Review* 23/1 (2010) 9-26.

9 Cf. L.A. Bebchuk-M.S. Weisbach, «The state of corporate governance research», *Review of Financial Studies* 23/3 (2010) 939-961; P. Brown-W. Beekes-P. Verhoeven, «Corporate governance, accounting and finance: A review», *Accounting and Finance* 51/1 (2011) 96-172; L.V. Ryan-A.K. Buchholtz-R.W. Kolb, «New directions in corporate governance and finance: Implications for business ethics research», *Business Ethics Quarterly* 20/4 (2010) 673-694.

10 Cf. M.E. Brown-M.S. Mitchell, «Ethical and unethical leadership: Exploring new avenues for future research», *Business Ethics Quarterly* 20/4 (2010) 583-616; D.V.

The motivation for this study is to provide a comprehensive interdisciplinary overview of governance and leadership research from the monastic perspective, to identify gaps within existing research, and to outline areas for further investigation. In addition, we wish to discuss the relevance of the monastic leadership and governance principles for non-religious organisations. Our review consists of the following parts. The next section describes a methodological approach for collecting and analysing the data. After this, we present the results of the content and citation analysis of the publications reviewed. The content analysis identifies the existing methodological and thematic priorities of the field of monastic leadership and governance. With the help of the citation analysis we evaluate the influence of particular works, authors, and journals as well as the importance of certain topics in this area of study. The final part contains a brief summary of the most important findings and ideas for future research.

1. RESEARCH METHODS

In order to conduct a systematic review of leadership and governance research with regard to monastic aspects, we followed a three-step approach. The first step was to identify relevant articles published in peer-reviewed academic journals between 1991 and 2014. Book chapters, book reviews, working papers, and conference papers were not included in the study. The articles were selected by conducting a keyword search in nine databases: Business Source Complete (EBSCO), Emerald, Web of Science, JSTOR, SAGE, ScienceDirect, SSRN, SpringerLink, and Wiley Online Library. To find appropriate articles, we used various combinations of the terms "St. Benedict," "Benedictine monastery," "Benedictine abbey," "monastic leadership," "religious leadership," "monastic governance," and "religious governance." In addition, we conducted a manual search of leadership journals (13), corporate governance journals (7), historical journals (29), sociological journals (8), and journals focused on religious studies (12). To ensure thorough coverage, we also included business journals (60) that deal with governance and leadership issues in our study. The selection of journals was based on different rankings of

Day-J.W. Fleenor-L.E. Atwater-R.E. Sturm-R.A. McKee, «Advances in leader and leadership development: A review of 25 years of research and theory», *The Leadership Quarterly* 25/1 (2014) 63-82; S.A. Eisenbeiss, «Re-thinking ethical leadership: An interdisciplinary integrative approach», *The Leadership Quarterly* 23/5 (2012) 791-808; S. Finley, «Servant leadership: a literature review», *Review of Management Innovation and Creativity* 5/14 (2012) 135-144.

peer-reviewed academic journals. All papers (52) that met our search criteria were added to our database and reviewed carefully. We eliminated eight articles from the dataset because they either contained only a brief description of monastic leadership and governance or were published in non peer-reviewed journals. Finally, the database of 44 articles was accepted for further analysis. Secondly, we employed a framework offered by *Reichers* and *Schneider*[11] in 1990 to determine the stage of development in monastic leadership research.

The third step was to conduct a content analysis of the articles to identify the topics covered, the methods of data collection, and the theoretical frameworks applied. Using content analysis allows researchers to choose measures that best fit the purpose of their study[12]. After reading the articles multiple times, we coded them for author names, institutional affiliation, discipline, location, country of study, type of research, and year of publication. In addition, we coded how the authors view the principles of monastic leadership and governance, how they evaluate the relevance of the monastic approach to other organisations, and what ideas they have for future research. After completing the coding by two independent researchers, we performed reliability checks of the data. Finally, a citation analysis was performed to identify the most influential authors, articles, and journals in the field of monastic leadership and governance. Citations are considered to be reliable indications of scientific interaction between researchers[13] and of the significance of published statements[14]. Thus, the frequently cited articles are generally agreed to provide the most important findings and thus have an essential influence on works that follow[15]. Consequently, a citation analysis can be used as a measure

11 Cf. A.E. Reichers-B. Schneider, «Climate and culture: An evolution of constructs?», in *Organizational climate and culture*, ed. B. Schneider, San Francisco (CA) 1990, 5-39.

12 Cf. C. Marshall-G.B. Rossmann, *Designing qualitative research*, Newbury Park (CA) [5]2011.

13 Cf. K. Gundolf-M. Filser, «Management research and religion: A citation analysis», *Journal of Business Ethics* 112/1 (2013) 177-185.

14 Cf. S. Roth-M. Gmür, «Strukturen und Entwicklungslinien der Marketingforschung. Ergebnisse einer Zitations- und Kozitationsanalyse nordamerikanischer Marketing-Journals 1987-2001», *Marketing Zeitschrift für Forschung und Praxis* 26/2 (2004) 141-158.

15 Cf. F.A. Badua-G.J. Previts-M.A. Vasarhelyi, «Tracing the development of accounting thought by analyzing content, communication, and quality in accounting research over time», *Accounting Historians Journal* 38/1 (2011) 31-56; U. Schäffer-C. Binder-M. Gmür, «Struktur und Entwicklung der Controllingforschung: Eine Zitations- und Kozitationsanalyse von Controllingbeiträgen in deutschsprachigen wissenschaftlichen Zeitschriften von 1970 bis 2003», *Zeitschrift für Betriebswirtschaft* 76/4 (2006) 395-440.

to evaluate the impact of an article, author, and journal on the development of the field[16]. The results of the study are presented in the following sections.

	1991	1992	1993	1994	1996	1999	2002	2005	2006	2007	2008	2009	2010	2011	2012	2013	2014	Total
Business and Management				**1**			**2**	**1**		**1**	**1**	**1**	**5**	**1**	**3**	**2**	**3**	**21**
Accounting, Auditing & Accountability J											1							1
American Review of Public Administration													1					1
Culture and Organization							1											1
Economics Bulletin															1			1
Enterprise & Society													1					1
European J of Management															1			1
J of Business Ethics														1				1
J of Global Responsibility													1					1
J of International Management																	1	1
J of Leadership, Accountability and Ethics															1			1
J of Management & Governance																	1	1
J of Management Development													2					2
J of Managerial Psychology							1											1
Management Revue												1						1
Managerial and Decision Economics																1		1
Nonprofit Management & Leadership				1														1
Organization								1										1
Qualitative Research in Accounting & Management																1		1
Qualitative Research in Organizations and Management										1								1
Society and Business Review																	1	1
Historical Studies						**1**		**1**	**1**	**1**	**1**		**1**		**1**			**7**
Accounting History									1									1
Accounting, Business & Financial History											1							1
English Historical Review															1			1
J of Management History						1				1			1					3
J of Medieval History								1										1
Religious Studies	**1**	**2**		**1**	**1**				**2**	**2**	**1**	**2**	**1**		**1**	**1**		**15**
American Benedictine Review	1	2		1	1				2			2			1	1		11
Cistercian Studies Quarterly										1	1							2
International J for the Study of the Christian Church										1								1
Religion Compass													1					1
Sociological Studies			**1**															**1**
British J of Sociology			1															1
Total	**1**	**2**	**1**	**2**	**1**	**1**	**2**	**2**	**3**	**4**	**3**	**3**	**7**	**1**	**5**	**3**	**3**	**44**

Table 1: Articles by journal, journal type, and year of publication[17]

16 Cf. Badua-Previts-Vasarhelyi, «Tracing the development of accounting thought by analyzing content, communication, and quality in accounting research over time», 31-56.

17 Source: Own illustration.

2. PRELIMINARY RESULTS

2.1. Sources of the articles reviewed

The articles accepted for the final analysis (N = 44) were published in 30 different academic journals between 1991 and 2014. Table 1 provides an overview of the number of articles by journal, journal type, and year of publication. It shows a rapid increase in the number of publications dealing with the monastic approach to leadership and governance within the last five years. Almost half of the publications (19 out of 44) appeared between 2010 and 2014, and the peak of interest was in 2010, with seven published articles. One possible explanation for it might be an intensive scholarly search for alternative models and ideas for advancing governance quality and reinforcing ethical leadership after the financial crisis in 2008. Our findings indicate a remarkably growing interest in monastic leadership and governance, especially on the part of business scholars.

2.2. Stage of development in research on monastic leadership and government

To evaluate the state of the art in research on monastic governance and leadership, we employ a framework developed by *Reichers* and *Schneider*[18]. According to their model, the evolution of scientific ideas consists of three stages. The first stage (introduction and elaboration) includes attempts to legitimise the new concept. Publications discuss the definition and the importance of the construct as well as provide preliminary findings as evidence that a phenomenon described by the concept is genuine. The second stage (evaluation and augmentation) is characterised by the appearance of the first critical reviews that raise concerns about the inadequate operationalisation and the ambiguity of empirical results. During the third stage (concept consolidation and accommodation), generally accepted definitions are developed and meta-analytic studies are conducted. Moreover, the concept is used as a moderator and mediator in more general models within the field[19].

The analysis of the articles shows clearly that research on ethical leadership in the monastic context is in the nascent stage of development. The vast majority of the articles (25 out of 44) analyse the main theoretical framework (RB) and

18 Cf. Reichers-Schneider, «Climate and culture: An evolution of constructs?», 5-39.

19 Cf. Reichers-Schneider, «Climate and culture: An evolution of constructs?», 5-39.

present ways to extend and transfer this knowledge to modern life. Empirical results are often used to prove that the phenomenon of monastic governance and leadership really exists[20]. However, the emergence of some critical publications[21] indicates a first step toward the second stage of the construct development.

3. QUALITATIVE CONTENT ANALYSIS OF ARTICLES

3.1. Overview of main topics

To learn more about the development of research on monastic leadership and governance across time, we coded all articles for topics covered. By defining the codes, we followed a step model of deductive category development formulated by *Mayring*[22]. At the beginning, we derived the selection criteria from our research question that included the principles of monastic leadership, governance instruments, and organisational structure. Additional categories (e.g. relevance for other organisations) were derived from multiple readings of the articles. Finally, we revised and adjusted the categories.

An analysis of the development of main topics across time shows that the principles of monastic leadership have been the favourite topic in the last 23 years (see Table 1). Remarkably, a strong interest in studying the relevance of monastic leadership to other organisations emerged only within the last 12 years. During these years, a number of scandals related to fraudulent book-keeping, inflated manager compensation, and millionaire severance packages for executives ruined the illusion of ethical leadership and good corporate governance[23]. The search for enhancing ethical leadership and finding alternative models of

20 Cf. Inauen-Rost-Osterloh-Frey, «Back to the future – A monastic perspective on corporate governance», 38-59; E. Inauen-K. Rost-B.S. Frey-F. Homberg-M. Osterloh, «Monastic governance: Forgotten prospects for public institutions», *The American Review of Public Administration* 40/6 (2010) 631-653; B. Kleymann-H. Malloch, «The rule of Saint Benedict and corporate management: employing the whole person», *Journal of Global Responsibility* 1/2 (2010) 207-224; Rost-Inauen-Osterloh-Frey, «The corporate governance of Benedictine abbeys», 90-115.

21 Cf. B. Feldbauer-Durstmüller-S. Sandberger-M. Neulinger, «Sustainability for centuries – monastic governance of Austrian Benedictine abbeys», *European Journal of Management* 12/3 (2012) 24-34.

22 See Mayring (2014).

23 Cf. W. Bratton, «Enron and the dark side of shareholder value», *Tulane Law Review* 76/4 (2002) 1275-1361; Inauen-Rost-Osterloh-Frey, «Back to the future – A monastic perspective on corporate governance», 38-59.

governance that would be able to reduce agency problems resulted also in an increased interest in the instruments of monastic governance and the organisational structure of monastic communities (see Figure 1).

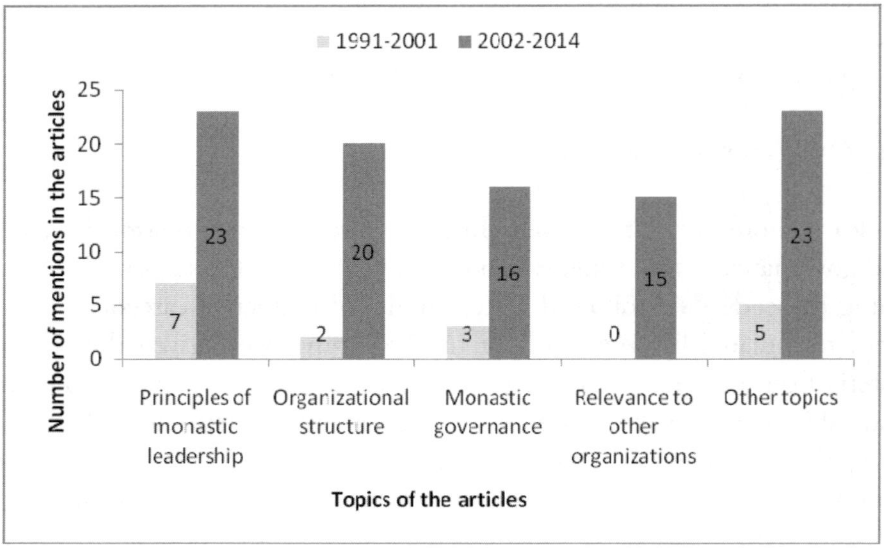

Figure 1: Development of topics across time[24]

3.2. Principles of ethical leadership in the monastic context

The RB, supplemented by the statutes, traditions, history, and experience of each community, forms the basis for the monastic way of living and has enormous influence on the daily life of a monastery[25]. According to the RB, the community is guided by non-economic goals such as the vision of monastic fulfillment and Christian salvation[26]. Being a spiritual leader, the abbot is the steward of this shared vision[27], which is extremely important both for the present and for the future of monastic life[28]. Vision is not only the ability to

24 Source: Own illustration.

25 Cf. Feldbauer-Durstmüller, Sandberger-Neulinger, «Sustainability for centuries – monastic governance of Austrian Benedictine abbeys», 24-34.

26 Cf. T.G. Kardong, «The abbot as leader», *The American Benedictine Review* 42/1 (1991) 53-72.

27 Cf. T.G. Kardong, «The abbot as leader», 53-72.

28 Cf. J.J.O. Gerry, «Abbatial leadership», *The American Benedictine Review* 43/1 (1992) 29-46.

conceive a clear and attractive goal but also the ability to communicate this goal to the community and make it powerful in their lives[29].

Benedictine monasteries refer to a common value system that goes far beyond "codes of best practice"[30] and cements the attitudes, behaviour, and actions of a monk in his daily routine[31]. In other words, monks develop emotional identification with the community and place where they live[32]. The process of stringent selection and rigorous socialisation helps the Benedictines to implement the core values in the community[33] and create collective identity[34].

A clearly defined division of labour and a strict hierarchy, in which everyone knows his place within the monastic community[35], helps to reduce conflicts and facilitate coordination. Typically, the hierarchical structure of a monastic organisation involves four main levels, namely abbot, posts of responsibility (e.g., prior, cellarer), seniors, and juniors[36]. Despite the hierarchy, decision-making is based on a consultative and participative approach as every member of the community has equal input[37]. In this case, the leader has an opportunity to listen to the advice of others without delegating his responsibility to make a decision[38]. According to the study of Rippinger, the

29 Cf. J.J.O. Gerry, «Abbatial leadership», 29-46.

30 Cf. Inauen-Rost-Osterloh-Frey, «Back to the future – A monastic perspective on corporate governance», 38-59; Inauen-Rost-Frey-Homberg-Osterloh, «Monastic governance: Forgotten prospects for public institutions», 631-653; Rost-Inauen-Osterloh-Frey, «The corporate governance of Benedictine abbeys», 90-115.

31 Cf. RB, «Rule of St. Benedict, Chapter 4», (2016), http://www.osb.org/rb/text/rbejms2.html#4, [accessed: 09-05-2016].

32 Cf. T. Janotík, «Benedictine monasteries from the point of view of happiness economics», *Economics Bulletin* 32/2 (2012) 1215-1225.

33 Cf. Inauen-Rost-Osterloh-Frey, «Back to the future – A monastic perspective on corporate governance», 38-59; Inauen-Rost-Frey-Homberg-Osterloh, «Monastic governance: Forgotten prospects for public institutions», 631-653; Rost-Inauen-Osterloh-Frey, «The corporate governance of Benedictine abbeys», 90-115.

34 Cf. Janotík, «Benedictine monasteries from the point of view of happiness economics», 1215-1225; L.R. Whatley-A.B. Popa-H. Kliewer, «Community and leadership: The role of humility, rhythm, and experiential learning», *Journal of Leadership, Accountability, and Ethics* 9/4 (2012) 113-143.

35 Cf. Tredget, «"The Rule of Benedict" and its relevance to the world of work», 219-229.

36 Cf. P. McGrath, «Thinking differently about knowledge-intensive firms: Insights from early medieval Irish monasticism», *Organization* 12/4 (2005) 549-566.

37 Cf. Chan-McBey, Scott-Ladd, «Ethical leadership in modern employment relationships: Lessons from St. Benedict», 221-228.

38 Cf. D.A. Tredget, «Practical wisdom and the Rule of Benedict», *Journal of Management Development* 29/7-8 (2010) 716-723.

abbots perceive collaborative decision-making as a genuine aid in arriving at a final decision[39].

The RB contains descriptions of the qualities and functions of a leader that are often related to the concept of servant and/or ethical leadership[40]. Thus, the leadership function of an abbot involves challenging the strong and caring for the weak in order to encourage the broad participation and personal development of community members[41]. The abbot entrusted with directing souls is expected to behave like a father in order to shape the behaviours of the individuals[42]. To be authentic, the abbot is expected to teach by example and live in accordance with the vision that he proposes[43]. Consequently, the abbot occupies a leadership position in order to serve the whole monastic community and any other communities the monks feel responsible for[44].

The last guiding principle of Benedictines is economic and social sustainability. The monastic economy aims to provide continuous income for living a frugal life and securing resources for future generations[45]. Sustainability from the social perspective is described in several passages of the RB, requiring the abbot to prevent his monastic brothers from having an overload of work and to encourage their personal development[46]. Community members are also encouraged to not just simply obey the commands of the abbot but

39 Cf. J. Rippinger, «A monastic questionnaire: Reflections of retired abbots», *The American Benedictine Review* 43/4 (1992) 429-437.

40 Cf. Chan-McBey, Scott-Ladd, «Ethical leadership in modern employment relationships: Lessons from St. Benedict», 221-228; Tredget, «"The Rule of Benedict" and its relevance to the world of work», 219-229.

41 Cf. Kardong, «The abbot as leader», 53-72.

42 Cf. A. Böckmann, «Qualifications of the monastery cellarer – (RB 31): Part I», *The American Benedictine Review* 57/1 (2006) 18-40; A. Böckmann, «Qualifications of the monastery cellarer – (RB 31): Part II», *The American Benedictine Review* 57/2 (2006) 186-211.

43 Cf. Gerry, «Abbatial leadership», 29-46; Tredget, «"The Rule of Benedict" and its relevance to the world of work», 219-229.

44 Cf. Chan-McBey, Scott-Ladd, «Ethical leadership in modern employment relationships: Lessons from St. Benedict», 221-228.

45 Cf. Feldbauer-Durstmüller, Sandberger-Neulinger, «Sustainability for centuries – monastic governance of Austrian Benedictine abbeys», 24-34; F.M. Mannion, «Benedictine economics and the challenge of modernity», *The American Benedictine Review* 47/1 (1996) 14-36.

46 Cf. RB, «Rule of St. Benedict, Chapter 64», (2016), http://www.osb.org/rb/text/rbeaad2.html#64, [accessed: 10-05-2016].

to be sensitive, ready to tolerate deficiencies, and respond to the needs of each other before they are spoken[47].

3.3. Organisational structure

A democratically elected abbot, or prior as his representative, is in charge of governing the autonomous monastic communities. This position is somewhat similar to CEO in modern companies. The abbot nominates officials who are responsible for specific matters, such as economy, education, pastoral care, and others. Their counterpart in modern organisations would be "executive board." All monks with solemn profession form the convent that participates in making decisions in important affairs. On many other issues, the abbot and his officials are advised by a council consisting of members elected by the convent and members appointed by the abbot[48]. The role of the council could be compared to the role of the advisory board in a private company. Based on the strong participation right of Benedictines, it is possible to say that all decisions about the monastic community and its future development are the result of internal democracy[49]. To sum up, the monks possess both the instrument of democratic vote and the instrument of monitoring. Moreover, they have created a unique organisational structure where important issues are solved in open discussions and people have the intrinsic motivation to fully invest their potential in the long-term future of the community[50].

3.4. Monastic governance instruments

Internal governance instruments of the Benedictines include accountability of community members concerning various matters to the abbot, monitoring and advising the abbot and his officials through the council, annual obliga-

47 Cf. J. Kodell, «Mutual Obedience: My brother's need is the voice of God», *The American Benedictine Review* 64/4 (2013) 404-411.

48 Cf. Inauen-Rost-Osterloh-Frey, «Back to the future – A monastic perspective on corporate governance», 38-59; Inauen-Rost-Frey-Homberg-Osterloh, «Monastic governance: Forgotten prospects for public institutions», 631-653; Rost-Inauen-Osterloh-Frey, «The corporate governance of Benedictine abbeys», 90-115.

49 Cf. Janotík, «Benedictine monasteries from the point of view of happiness economics», 1215-1225.

50 Cf. Janotík, «Benedictine monasteries from the point of view of happiness economics», 1215-1225.

tions of the abbot to report on the financial situation of a monastery and participation of the entire convent in the decision-making process[51]. Participative decision-making not only provides monks with a medium for sharing everyday problems and openly discussing important issues but also cultivates shared affective states in the long term[52]. It directly contributes to the process of socialisation and might even prevent agency problems that are typical for modern corporations (divergence of interests of managers/owners/employees of a company). The fact that every member identifies himself with the community and knows that his or her voice is heard encourages crucial organisation-specific investment necessary for a long-term economic success[53]. Moreover, a common understanding of values, goals and principles of action provides additional internal incentives for appropriate behaviour[54]. Similar instruments are implemented at each organisational level of the Benedictine Order[55].

As for the external governance mechanisms, they contain a need for approval of certain transactions by the Holy See, annual financial and personnel reports, as well as visitations of communities by abbots or monks from other communities[56]. Considering not only the current economic situation of a monastery but also the spiritual condition and personal relationships between community members, these visitations aim to conduct supportive control

51 Cf. Inauen-Rost-Osterloh-Frey, «Back to the future – A monastic perspective on corporate governance», 38-59; Inauen-Rost-Frey-Homberg-Osterloh, «Monastic governance: Forgotten prospects for public institutions», 631-653; Mannion, «Benedictine economics and the challenge of modernity», 14-36; Rost-Inauen-Osterloh-Frey, «The corporate governance of Benedictine abbeys», 90-115; Tredget, «"The Rule of Benedict" and its relevance to the world of work», 219-229.

52 Cf. Janotík, «Benedictine monasteries from the point of view of happiness economics», 1215-1225.

53 Cf. Janotík, «Benedictine monasteries from the point of view of happiness economics», 1215-1225.

54 Cf. Inauen-Rost-Osterloh-Frey, «Back to the future – A monastic perspective on corporate governance», 38-59.

55 Cf. Feldbauer-Durstmüller, Sandberger-Neulinger, «Sustainability for centuries – monastic governance of Austrian Benedictine abbeys», 24-34.

56 Cf. Feldbauer-Durstmüller, Sandberger-Neulinger, «Sustainability for centuries – monastic governance of Austrian Benedictine abbeys», 24-34; Inauen-Rost-Osterloh-Frey, «Back to the future – A monastic perspective on corporate governance», 38-59; Inauen-Rost-Frey-Homberg-Osterloh, «Monastic governance: Forgotten prospects for public institutions», 631-653; Rost-Inauen-Osterloh-Frey, «The corporate governance of Benedictine abbeys», 90-115.

and induce reflection[57]. The monastic visitations are always announced in advance, which gives community members an opportunity to prepare properly. The results and recommendations are first discussed with the abbot and later presented to the whole community. However, the monitoring of the implementation of the measures is often not a high priority[58].

3.5. IMPLICATIONS FOR OTHER ORGANISATIONS AND AREAS

Monastic communities and modern businesses can benefit from each other's wisdom and experience[59]. Thus, monastic leadership and governance principles could be used as a framework for addressing certain issues in leadership and organisational control in other types of organisations. Several papers published between 2002 and 2014 investigate the relevance of those principles to knowledge-intensive firms[60], public institutions[61], modern-day religious institutions[62], stock corporations[63], and other types of organisations[64]. Furthermore, the applicability of the RB to modern employment relationships[65]

57 Cf. E. INAUEN-M. OSTERLOH-B.S. FREY-F. HOMBERG, «How a multiple orientation of control reduces governance failures: A focus on monastic auditing», *Journal of Management and Governance* 19/4 (2015) 763-796; ROST-INAUEN-OSTERLOH-FREY, «The corporate governance of Benedictine abbeys», 90-115.

58 Cf. INAUEN-OSTERLOH-FREY-HOMBERG, «How a multiple orientation of control reduces governance failures: A focus on monastic auditing», 763-796.

59 Cf. C. SCHÜTZ, «To serve life: The Rule of Benedict as a guide for a Benedictine school», *The American Benedictine Review* 60/2 (2009) 154-167.

60 Cf. MCGRATH, «Thinking differently about knowledge-intensive firms: Insights from early medieval Irish monasticism», 549-566.

61 Cf. INAUEN-ROST-FREY-HOMBERG-OSTERLOH, «Monastic governance: Forgotten prospects for public institutions», 631-653.

62 Cf. B. PRIETO-L. MATÉ-J. TUA, «The accounting records of the monastery of Silos throughout the eighteenth century: The accumulation and management of its patrimony in the light of its accounts books», *Accounting History* 11/2 (2006) 221-256.

63 Cf. ROST-INAUEN-OSTERLOH-FREY, «The corporate governance of Benedictine abbeys», 90-115.

64 Cf. G. HOLZHERR, «The hidden treasure: the relevance of Regula Benedicti», *The American Benedictine Review* 60/2 (2009) 168-182; INAUEN-ROST-OSTERLOH-FREY, «Back to the future – A monastic perspective on corporate governance», 38-59; KLEYMANN-MALLOCH, «The rule of Saint Benedict and corporate management: employing the whole person», 207-224; P. MCGRATH, «Early medieval Irish monastic communities: A premodern model with post-modern resonances», *Culture and Organization* 8/3 (2002) 195-208.

65 Cf. CHAN-MCBEY, SCOTT-LADD, «Ethical leadership in modern employment relation-

and management education[66] has been thoroughly explored. *Hiebl* and *Feldbauer-Durstmüller* examined the role of a Benedictine cellarer and described the aspects (e.g., stewardship behaviour, long-term orientation) that could be reasonably transferred to the corporate world[67]. In their recent work, *Inauen* and his colleagues argued that the extension of auditing and monitoring procedures by including measures to strengthen the sense of community and support individual members is worth considering toward better governance beyond religious organisations[68]. According to *Rost* and *Grätzer*, governance by rules implemented by the Catholic Orders would also be a superior governance mechanism for multinational organisations as it would help them to better cope with organisational and environmental complexity and uncertainty[69]. The ways that the Benedictines develop and maintain a healthy community might also be of interest for contemporary organisations[70].

It is common knowledge that the modern business world is characterised by information overload, instant communication, and complexity[71]. This means that leaders have to make prudent decisions quickly in order to live a morally good life in relationship to other individuals and stakeholders[72]. The principles of monastic leadership offer a daily framework for acquiring practical wisdom, which enables people to make prudent judgments and take actions guided by values and morals[73]. When leaders are able to create space for flourishing practical wisdom and cultivate such tacit knowledge, they are able to make enlightened decisions[74]. This ability is of great importance for leaders of any

---

ships: Lessons from St. Benedict», 221-228; Tredget, «"The Rule of Benedict" and its relevance to the world of work», 219-229.

66 Cf. Tredget, «Practical wisdom and the Rule of Benedict», 716-723.

67 Cf. M.R.W. Hiebl-B. Feldbauer-Durstmüller, «What can the corporate world learn from the cellarer?», *Society and Business Review* 9/1 (2014) 51-73.

68 Cf. Inauen-Osterloh-Frey-Homberg, «How a multiple orientation of control reduces governance failures: A focus on monastic auditing», 763-796.

69 Cf. K. Rost-G. Grätzer, «Multinational organizations as rule-following bureaucracies - the example of catholic orders», *Journal of International Management* 20/3 (2014) 290-311.

70 Cf. Whatley-Popa-Kliewer, «Community and leadership: The role of humility, rhythm, and experiential learning», 113-143.

71 Cf. Tredget, «Practical wisdom and the Rule of Benedict», 716-723.

72 Cf. Tredget, «Practical wisdom and the Rule of Benedict», 716-723.

73 Cf. M.K. Leavy, «The meaning of monastic stewardship», *The American Benedictine Review* 45/3 (1994) 229-248; I. Nonaka-H. Takeuchi, «The wise leader», *Harvard Business Review* 89/5 (2011) 58-67.

74 Cf. Z.A.S. Udani-C.F. Lorenzo-Molo, «When servant becomes leader: The Corazon

organisation, irrespective of its size and activity. While profit-oriented organisations aim at financial goals, the Benedictines focus on non-economic goals and place the "human-being" and his search for God at the centre of attention.

3.6. Other topics

Other topics discussed in the articles include Weber's perception of the monastic economy[75], the relationships between nuns and their male supervisors[76], spiritual crisis in society[77], practical wisdom in the RB and Catholic social teachings[78], the history of Flemish monasticism[79], and location of decision rights in Catholic religious orders[80]. *Bargiela-Chiappini* suggested liminal ethnography as a new approach for conducting research in segregated organisations, such as monasteries[81]. The role of hospitality in monastic practice was investigated by *Mannion*[82] and *Tredget*[83]. *Fassler* argued that the way the experience of singing chants shaped monastic thought and life could be a subject worth studying[84]. The question of burnout amongst abbots and the ways a former leader can serve his community were addressed by Rip-

C. Aquino success story as a beacon for business leaders», *Journal of Business Ethics* 116/2 (2013) 373-391.

75 Cf. I.F. Silber, «Monasticism and the protestant etic: Asceticism, rationality and wealth in the medieval West», *The British Journal of Sociology* 44/1 (1993) 103-123.

76 Cf. M. Herder, «Substitute or subordinate? The role of a male procurator at a Benedictine women's monastery», *Journal of Medieval History* 31/3 (2005) 231-242.

77 Cf. Holzherr, «The hidden treasure: the relevance of Regula Benedicti», 168-182.

78 Cf. E. Cornuel-A. Habisch-P. Kletz, «The practical wisdom of the Catholic social teachings», *Journal of Management Development* 29/7 (2010) 747-754; Tredget, «Practical wisdom and the Rule of Benedict», 716-723.

79 Cf. S. Vanderputten, «Crises of cenobitism: Abbatial leadership and monastic competition in late eleventh-century Flanders», *English Historical Review* 127/525 (2012) 259-284.

80 Cf. T. Ehrmann-K. Rost-E. Inauen, «Location of decision rights in Catholic religious orders», *Managerial and Decision Economics* 34/1 (2013) 29-39.

81 Cf. F. Bargiela-Chiappini, «Liminal ethnography: Understanding segregated organizations», *Qualitative Research in Organizations and Management: An International Journal* 2/2 (2007) 126-143.

82 Cf. Mannion, «Benedictine economics and the challenge of modernity», 14-36.

83 Cf. Tredget, «"The Rule of Benedict" and its relevance to the world of work», 219-229.

84 Cf. M. Fassler, «Filming the nuns of Regina Laudis: Old and new evidence for monastic studies», *Religion Compass* 4/6 (2010) 340-352.

pinger[85]. *Janotík* examined the Benedictine way of life from the perspective of happiness economics. He argued that social interaction and personal identification of monks with their communities are crucial for the successful historical performance of monasteries[86]. In their recent work, *Payer-Langthaler* and *Hiebl* analysed what the term "performance" means in the monastic context[87].

3.7. Theoretical foundations, purposes, and research methods employed in the articles

One of the categories we coded in our dataset was a theoretical foundation underlying each publication. As the use of theoretical frameworks and research methods varies widely across different disciplines, we grouped all the articles into four categories: business and management (21), history (7), religion (15), and sociology (1). The results of the analysis are presented in Table 2. Most articles reviewed (25 out of 44) employed the RB and/or appropriate statutes of communities as a primary theoretical framework. Remarkably, the RB formed the basis not only for the religious publications but also for the historical and business articles. Furthermore, the framework of organisational theories (especially a premodern organisational approach) has also been frequently used in the articles reviewed.

The main idea of premodern organisational theory is that looking back can often improve flexibility and bring new insights into contemporary developments[88]. More than half of the historical articles and three business publications employed this framework. Four out of 21 publications from the area of business and management studies as well as one historical article, were based upon the agency theory. Agency theory suggests that both a principal and an agent are utility-maximizers and are driven by self-interest. Information asymmetry and divergent interests of the principal and the agent cause agency problems[89].

85 Cf. J. Rippinger, «A monastic questionnaire: Reflections of retired abbots», *The American Benedictine Review* 43/4 (1992) 429-437.

86 Cf. Janotík, «Benedictine monasteries from the point of view of happiness economics», 1215-1225..

87 Cf. S. Payer-Langthaler-M.R.W. Hiebl, «Towards a definition of performance for religious organizations and beyond: A case of Benedictine abbeys», *Qualitative Research in Accounting and Management* 10/3-4 (2013) 213-233.

88 Cf. P. McGrath, «Knowledge management in monastic communities of the medieval Irish Celtic church», *Journal of Management History* 13/2 (2007) 211-223.

89 Cf. K.M. Eisenhardt, «Agency theory: An assessment and review», *Academy of Management Review* 14/1 (1989) 57-74.

Research area	Business and Management	History	Religion	Sociology
Theoretical framework				
Rule of St. Benedict and/or Statutes	8	2	14	1
Organizational theories	3	4		
Agency theory	4	1		
Leadership theories	3		1	
Embeddedness theory	3			
Political economics	3			
Psychological economics	3			
Control theory/framework	2	1		
Knowledge management	1	1		
Catholic social thought	1			
Concept of community	1			
Concept of liminality				1
Experiential learning theory	1			
Henri Fayol's Principles of Management	1			
Human resource management theory	1			

Research area	Business and Management	History	Religion	Sociology
Mutual correspondence of sentiments	1			
Protestant ethic				1
Sociology of gender		1		
Research methods				
Research design and methods of data collection				
Case study	6	5	2	
Interview/group discussion	9	1		
Participant observation	3	1		
Questionnaire	2		1	
Expert panel	1			
Research design and methods of data analysis				
Documentary research methods	5	10	3	
Hermeneutics	5		12	
Content analysis	6		1	
Comparative analysis	2	2	1	1
Regression analysis	2			

RESEARCH AREA	BUSINESS AND MANAGEMENT	HISTORY	RELIGION	SOCIOLOGY
Ethnography	2			
Exploratory analysis	1			
Factor analysis	1			

Table 2: Theoretical frameworks and research methods in publications reviewed[90]

Leadership theories have been used as a theoretical framework for one religious article and three business publications. Considering monastic leadership as a journey or a dream where the abbot and community members raise one another to higher motivation and morality, *Kardong* presents a transformational view of leadership[91]. The next article represents the trait approach to leadership and tries to find the main characteristics that define outstanding religious leaders[92]. In the third article modern leadership theories, such as stewardship, ethical leadership, and servant leadership are examined in the Benedictine context[93]. Finally, the fourth publication explores leadership as a collective practice and builds upon such leadership theories as distributed collaborative, shared, and collective leadership[94]. Embeddedness theory, political economics, and psychological economics were further theoretical frameworks applied by the authors of business publications (see Table 2).

According to the results of the content analysis, a case study approach was especially favoured in our sample. Not only business and management researchers but also scholars in history chose to do case studies with monasteries and/or companies managed by the Benedictines (see Table 3). In addition, conducting open-ended and semi-structured interviews with monks, nuns, and lay workers and/or organising group discussions was the preferred data collection method in the articles reviewed. As for the methods of data analysis, most publications

90 Source: Own illustration.

91 Cf. KARDONG, «The abbot as leader», 53-72.

92 Cf. D.J. NYGREN-M.D. UKERITIS-D.C. MCCLELLAND-J.L. HICKMAN, «Outstanding leadership in nonprofit organizations: Leadership competencies in Roman Catholic religious orders», *Nonprofit management and leadership* 4/4 (1994) 375-391.

93 Cf. CHAN-MCBEY, SCOTT-LADD, «Ethical leadership in modern employment relationships: Lessons from St. Benedict», 221-228.

94 Cf. WHATLEY-POPA-KLIEWER, «Community and leadership: The role of humility, rhythm, and experiential learning», 113-143.

relied on qualitative methods such as a hermeneutic approach and documentary research (see Table 3). Documentary research methods are associated with the analysis of primary, secondary, and tertiary documents that contain information about the phenomenon a researcher is interested in[95]. These techniques have often been considered the sole domain of professional historians and librarians[96]. Thus, all historical articles in our dataset apply this method of data analysis. However, documentary research can be also adopted by researchers from other areas, as reflected in our findings in Table 3.

Hermeneutics deals with identifying the meaning of the external objectifications of the human mind, such as texts and works of art[97]. Having been traditionally applied as a method to understand religious writings, hermeneutics is nowadays used for interpreting human practices, events, and situations[98]. The vast majority of religious articles in our dataset (12 out of 15) and 23.8% of business publications use the hermeneutics approach to analyse the data. Furthermore, frequently used research methods in all disciplines include a content analysis and a comparative analysis.

As shown in Table 3, the main purpose of most articles reviewed is to extend/transfer theory to modern organisations (27 out of 44) or to analyse the theoretical frameworks (11 out of 44). Naturally, half of the historical articles focus on tracing the historical development of monastic leadership and governance. In contrast, business scholars are particularly interested in implementing the existing knowledge about monastic governance and leadership in different types of contemporary organisations (see Table 3). As far as the type of research is concerned, 84% of all studies are qualitative because of the nascent nature of research on leadership and governance from a monastic perspective. However, the number of quantitative studies grew rapidly in the last three years. Particularly interesting is that almost two thirds of the publications are written by single authors. Whilst business and management scholars prefer to collaborate with each other, all religious studies and five out of seven historical studies are conducted single-handedly (see Table 3).

---

95 Cf. K. Bailey, *Methods of social research*, The Free Press, New York (NY) [4]1994.

96 Cf. M. Mogalakwe, «The use of documentary research methods in social research», *African Sociological Review* 10/1 (2006) 221-230.

97 Cf. R.E. Palmer, *Hermeneutics*, Evanston 1969.

98 Cf. M. Crotty, *The foundations of social science research*, St. Leonards 1998.

	Business	Religion	Sociology	History	Total
Type of research					
Qualitative research	15	15	1	6	37
Quantitative research	6			1	7
Authorship					
Single author	8	15	1	5	29
Multiple authors	13			2	15
Purpose					
Analyze theory	2	9			11
Extend/Transfer theory	18	5	1	3	27
Trace hist. development	1	1		4	6
Total	21	15	1	7	44

Table 3: Purpose, research area and type of research articles[99]

In addition, we coded all articles for country of study in order to learn more about the geographical regions researchers were most interested in. Figure 2 demonstrates that scholars focused mostly on the European countries, in particular on Switzerland, Austria, UK, Ireland, Germany, and Spain. This can be easily explained by the long history and strong traditions of Benedictines in these countries, as well as by their enormous influence on the cultural and historic development of Europe in the past.

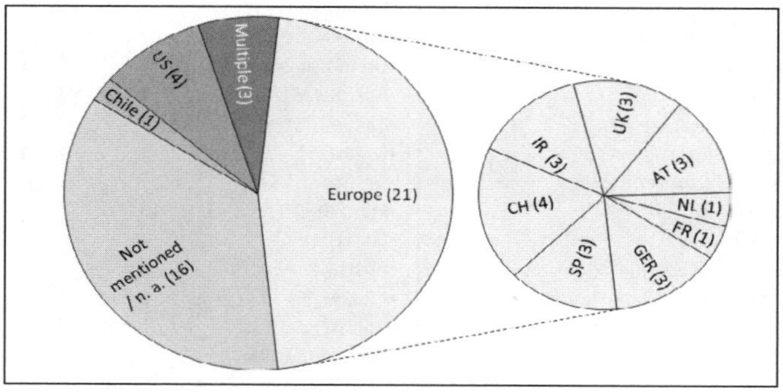

Figure 2: Country of study[100]

99 Source: Own illustration.
100 Source: Own illustration.

3.8. Information about the authors

As leadership in the monastic context is an emerging field of study, it seems appropriate to learn more about the authors whose research interests include this field. For this reason, we coded the publications for author type (academic, practitioner, O.S.B.), gender, discipline, and country of affiliation. The most interesting results are presented in Figure 3. Our analysis shows that the 44 articles reviewed were written by 53 authors. This number reflects the number of unique authors, as researchers, who published more than one article were counted only once.

Although the 43.2% female authors still represent a minority, this share is not negligible. Most authors have academic affiliations (35 out of 53) or combine research with an occupation outside science (2 out of 53). They come from a variety of disciplines, including organizational studies (9), accounting and business history (6), human resource management (4), and leadership studies (4). As we focused on the monastic view of leadership, a relatively high percentage (28.3%) of the authors coming from the Benedictine Order is not surprising (see Figure 3). According to the Benedictine census of 2005, there were nearly twice as many Benedictine women as men[101]. Despite this, our dataset contains only one female Benedictine author compared to 14 male authors from the OSB. More than half of the authors reside in Europe (32; 60.4%), followed by North American scholars (19; 35.8%).

Disciplines	Country of affiliation	
•Accounting and business history	•United States (US):	15
•Organizational studies	•Switzerland (CH):	07
•Human resource management	•United Kingdom (UK):	07
•Psychology	•Austria (AT):	04
•Sociological theory	•Canada (CA):	04
•Christian social ethics	•Spain (ES):	04
•Music history and liturgy	•Germany (DE):	03
•Economics	•France (FR):	03
•Leadership	•Israel (IL):	02
•Business communication/discourse	•Australia (AU):	01
•Medieval and early modern history	•Ireland (IE):	01
•Management control and consulting	•Italy (IT):	01
•Strategy and business policy	•Netherlands (NL):	01
	•Czech Republic (CZ):	01

101 Cf. T. Wright, «The Benedictine life: Decline, growth and innovation», *International Journal for the Study of the Christian Church* 7/3 (2007) 179-193.

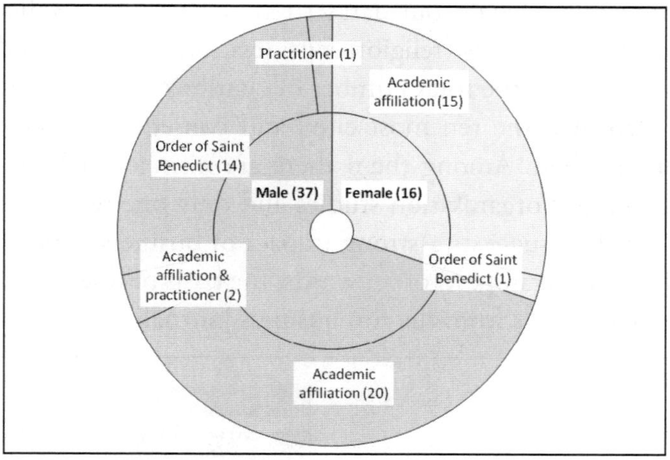

Figure 3: Information about authors[102]

4. CITATION ANALYSIS OF THE ARTICLES

With the help of a citation analysis, we aim to identify the most cited publications, authors, and journals within our original dataset. The dataset included 44 articles and cited 2,193 scientific publications. The number of citations per article varied from 1 to 159. The authors of the articles used mainly books/book chapters (44.46%) and journal articles (44.60%) as sources for their works. Working papers, conference papers, reports, and dissertations were cited 240 times (10.94% of all citations). The sources used are represented in Figure 4.

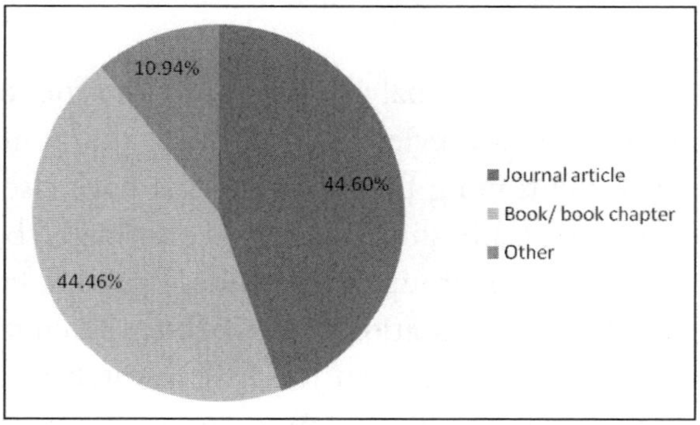

Figure 4: Sources of scientific works cited[103]

102 Source: Own illustration.

103 Source: Own illustration.

As for the cited journals, our dataset referred to 229 specific publication outlets from different areas (religion, business, organization studies, history, sociology, etc.). Using the total number of citations received as the main criterion, we identified the ten most cited and consequently most influential journals for this field. Among them there are nine journals from the areas of management and organisation studies and only one religious journal (see Figure 5). This fact suggests a strong impact of business studies on research about monastic leadership. In other words, the basis of research in this field is formed by the citations from the top business journals.

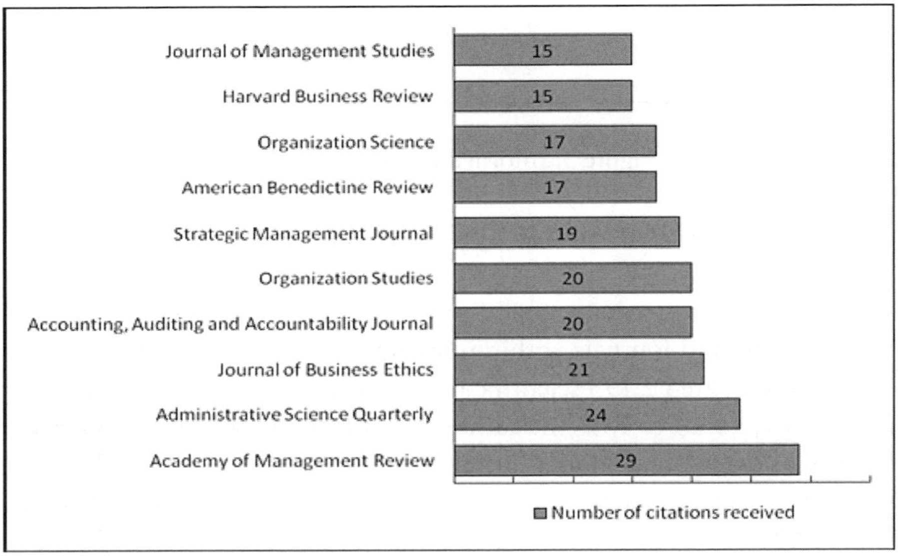

Figure 5: Most cited journals[104]

The next step of our citation analysis was to identify the top ten frequently cited authors in the articles reviewed in terms of the number of citations received. It is worth mentioning that self-citations have also been counted. Remarkably, the monastic leadership literature is dominated by research originating from the Swiss research group that includes Bruno S. Frey (53 citations received), Margit Osterloh (42 citations), Katja Rost (22 citations), and Emil Inauen (20 citations). They have been the first researchers to actively look for new models of governance and offer monasteries as a possible alternative. Although the works of Michael C. Jensen and Alfred Kieser have been cited pretty frequently (31 citations and 15 citations, respectively), these authors

104 Source: Own illustration.

did not study leadership in the monastic context. Jensen's agency theory[105] and Kieser's organisation theory[106] have been cited in many articles reviewed because they served as theoretical frameworks. Although the majority of the top cited authors come from the business area, the list also includes representatives of other disciplines such as religion or psychology. For example, Adalbert de Vogüe (16 citations received) and Terrence Kardong (12 citations) are well-known and respected religious scholars and interpreters of the RB.

Further results of the citation analysis show clearly that the field of monastic leadership is a very new area of research. There is almost no collaboration and networking between the scholars working on these topics. Remarkably, there is also very little interdisciplinary research. Although the topic of monastic leadership requires an interdisciplinary approach to take into consideration the historical, theological, and economic aspects, our dataset contains only four articles written by an interdisciplinary team. As researchers from different fields use various research methods and techniques, they could benefit from interdisciplinary discourse between business scholars, historians, religious writers, and psychologists. Consequently, an interdisciplinary approach should be encouraged in order to foster the development of this research area.

To sum everything up, the results of our study show clearly that monastic leadership is an interesting topic for scholars from different areas of expertise that can be published in various scientific journals. However, a comprehensive view on this topic is missing. Scholars working in the field use the literature and research methods usually applied in their area of study and tend to neglect the value of historical or religious sources. Yet an understanding of the historical and religious context is extremely important to avoid misinterpretations of the Benedictine way of living. In addition, the existing literature mostly aims to study the RB and does not pay much attention to the statutes of monasteries that could be a useful source for doing economical or sociological research.

CONCLUSION AND OUTLOOK

Our study contributes to current knowledge in three ways. Firstly, it provides the first interdisciplinary literature overview about monastic leadership, de-

105 Cf. M.C. Jensen-W.H. Meckling, «Theory of the firm: Managerial behavior, agency costs, and ownership structure», *Journal of Financial Economics* 3/4 (1976) 305-360.

106 Cf. A. Kieser, «From asceticism to administration of wealth. Medieval monasteries and the pitfalls of rationalization», *Organization Studies* 8/2 (1987) 103-123.

scribes the development of this field from 1991 to 2014, and gives a brief summary of the most important findings and intellectual contributions. This is useful for scholars because it improves the understanding of the interdependencies between past and present research[107]. To take into consideration the historical, theological, and economic aspects of this topic and avoid misinterpretations of the Benedictine way of life, the interdisciplinary approach should be encouraged. Secondly, our study contributes to a better understanding of monastic organisations and raises awareness of the international audience for the phenomenon of leadership in the monastic context. Consequently, it can serve as a facilitating tool to enter this emerging research field. Thirdly, the study reveals existing research gaps and presents promising areas for future advances in knowledge.

The results of the content analysis show that research on monastic leadership is still in its infancy. A significant portion of the articles reviewed conduct a qualitative analysis of the RB and demonstrate possibilities for transferring this knowledge to modern life. Empirical findings are often used to prove that the phenomenon of monastic leadership really exists[108]. Remarkably, the principles of monastic leadership are a topic of interest for scholars from many different disciplines including human resource management, history, organisational studies, religious studies, sociology, and psychology.

The articles reviewed deal with a number of different themes. One of the most popular topics is the principles of monastic leadership, which include having a shared vision, common goals, and values; choosing new community members with the help of a long-lasting selection and socialisation process; defining a clear hierarchy; having a participative approach to decision-making; encouraging the personal development of individuals; and ensuring economic and social sustainability of a monastery. An authentic leader is expected to teach by example and serve the whole monastic community.

Due to scandals connected with falsified financial statements and inflated manager compensations, interest in analysing alternative models of leadership

---

107 Cf. Chrisman-Kellermanns-Chan-Liano, «Intellectual foundations of current research in family business: An identification and review of 25 influential articles», 9-26.

108 Cf. Inauen-Rost-Osterloh-Frey, «Back to the future – A monastic perspective on corporate governance», 38-59; Inauen-Rost-Frey-Homberg-Osterloh, «Monastic governance: Forgotten prospects for public institutions», 631-653; Kleymann-Malloch, «The rule of Saint Benedict and corporate management: employing the whole person», 207-224; Rost-Inauen-Osterloh-Frey, «The corporate governance of Benedictine abbeys», 90-115.

and governance has increased considerably. Some researchers even argue that the main reason for the recent scandalous outcomes is "broken character and not broken systems"[109]. Consequently, scholars should shift their attention to the individual level of the business world, inside the consciences of leaders[110]. The centerpiece of Benedictine governance is an individual and his/her search for God. For this reason, the instruments of monastic governance can be seen as a suitable source of new ideas for governance models. Accountability of community members to the abbot concerning financial matters, participation in the decision-making process, monitoring and advising the abbot through the council, annual reporting obligations of the abbot, authorisation of certain transactions by the Holy See, and visitations of communities are integrative parts of monastic governance.

Several authors tried to apply monastic leadership principles beyond the monastic sector and transfer them to knowledge-intensive firms, public institutions, modern-day religious institutions, stock corporations, and other types of organisations[111]. As monasteries and modern organisations demonstrate fundamental differences in the basic ideas, the leadership principles cannot be transferred directly. Whereas private organisations mostly implement a function-oriented view of persons and focus on the financial goals, the Benedictines concentrate on non-economic goals and place the "human-being" at the centre of attention. Obviously, the issue of transferability requires further investigation and also demands an interdisciplinary approach.

With the help of a citation analysis we identified the most influential journals and authors in the field of monastic leadership. We also showed that

109 Cf. Udani, Lorenzo-Molo, «When servant becomes leader: The Corazon C. Aquino success story as a beacon for business leaders», 388.

110 Cf. G. Bragues, «The ancients against the moderns: Focusing on the character of corporate leaders», *Journal of Business Ethics* 78/3 (2008) 373-387.

111 Cf. Holzherr, «The hidden treasure: the relevance of Regula Benedicti», 168-182; Inauen-Rost-Frey-Homberg-Osterloh, «Monastic governance: Forgotten prospects for public institutions», 631-653; Kleymann-Malloch, «The rule of Saint Benedict and corporate management: employing the whole person», 207-224; McGrath, «Early medieval Irish monastic communities: A premodern model with post-modern resonances», 195-208; McGrath, «Thinking differently about knowledge-intensive firms: Insights from early medieval Irish monasticism», 549-566; Prieto-Maté-Tua, «The accounting records of the monastery of Silos throughout the eighteenth century: The accumulation and management of its patrimony in the light of its accounts books», 221-256; Rost-Inauen-Osterloh-Frey, «The corporate governance of Benedictine abbeys», 90-115.

there is a lack of interaction between the researchers in this interdisciplinary area. Thus, scholars tend to see everything from the perspective of their own discipline and use mostly secondary sources. In addition, the development of the RB in the historical context is often disregarded and the modern interpretations of the RB are rarely used. Consequently, a common foundation for research on monastic leadership has yet to be developed.

In terms of future research, it might be interesting to extend the literature review by including books and commentaries of the RB. As humanities scholars publish more in books and not in journals, these scientific works are more difficult to find and analyze. *Böckmann*, *Puzicha*, and *Casey*[112] are examples of Benedictine authors dealing with the modern interpretation of the RB and considering the historical roots of the RB (i.e., Rule of Master, Rule of St. Pachomius). An in-depth analysis of such scientific work might bring new valuable insights. The influence of cultural differences on the interpretation of the RB and specific leadership structures in monastic organisations is another research question worth studying.

It would also be fruitful to find out what aspects of monastic leadership and governance could be transferred to modern organisations and how this could be done. A further research opportunity might be conducting an analysis of the economic role and importance of Benedictines in different countries, as they are one of the largest monastic groups within the Catholic Church. Previous studies mostly focused on certain regions and particular historical factors[113]. At the macro level, there is a need to widen the regional focus of re-

112 Cf. A. Böckmann, *Perspectives on the Rule of Saint Benedict: Expanding our hearts in Christ*, Collegeville (MN) 2005; M. Casey, *Fremd in der Stadt: Glaube und Werte in der Regel des Heiligen Benedikt*, EOS Verlag, Sankt Ottilien 2009; M. Casey, *Einführung in die Benediktusregel*, EOS Verlag, Sankt Ottilien 2010; M. Puzicha, *Kommentar zur Benediktusregel*, Sankt Ottilien 2002.

113 Cf. A. Dobie, «The development of financial management and control in monastic houses and estates in England c. 1200–1540», *Accounting, Business & Financial History* 18/2 (2008) 141-159; Fassler, «Filming the nuns of Regina Laudis: Old and new evidence for monastic studies», 340-352; Herder, «Substitute or subordinate? The role of a male procurator at a Benedictine women's monastery», 231-242; Inauen-Rost-Osterloh-Frey, «Back to the future – A monastic perspective on corporate governance», 38-59; Inauen-Rost-Frey-Homberg-Osterloh, «Monastic governance: Forgotten prospects for public institutions», 631-653;McGrath, «Early medieval Irish monastic communities: A premodern model with post-modern resonances», 195-208; McGrath, «Thinking differently about knowledge-intensive firms: Insights from early medieval Irish monasticism», 549-566; Prieto-Maté-Tua,

search and incorporate, verify, and complement the results of detailed studies that have been conducted on individual monasteries.

Abstract

In this paper, the first interdisciplinary overview of governance and leadership research from the monastic perspective is conducted, following a three-step approach in order to conduct a systematic review of governance and leadership research with regard to monastic aspects.

- The first step was to identify relevant articles published in peer-reviewed academic journals between 1990 and 2014. The selection of journals was based on different rankings of peer-reviewed academic journals. All papers (44) that met our search criteria were added to our database and reviewed carefully.
- Secondly, a content analysis of the articles is done to identify the topics covered, the methods to gather data and the theoretical frameworks applied. In addition, a framework offered by Reichers and Schneider is also used in order to determine the stage of development in research on monastic governance and leadership.
- Thirdly, a citation analysis was carried out to identify the most influential authors, articles and journals in the field of monastic governance and leadership.

This study contributes to current knowledge in three ways. Firstly, it provides a better understanding of monastic organisations and acknowledges the importance of monasteries in economic history. Secondly, it describes the development of an alternative approach to corporate governance and leadership in the last 20 years and provides a brief summary of the most important findings and intellectual contributions to this field. Thirdly, the study reveals existing research gaps and presents promising areas for future advances in knowledge.

«The accounting records of the monastery of Silos throughout the eighteenth century: The accumulation and management of its patrimony in the light of its accounts books», 221-256; J.F. Roca, «Monks and businessmen in Catalonia: The Benedictines of Montserrat (1900-1936)», *Enterprise & Society* 11/2 (2010) 242-274; Rost-Inauen-Osterloh-Frey, «The corporate governance of Benedictine abbeys», 90-115.

TOWARDS SEMANTIC SECULARISATION? REFLECTIONS ON ECONOMY AND MONASTICISM

Marcin JEWDOKIMOW

INTRODUCTION

This paper[1] touches upon an issue of economisation processes in reference to monasticism. Basing on field researches conducted in Poland, in towns where Cistercian monasteries are located, I propose a concept of semantic secularisation, understood as a process of attaching secular meanings to religious objects and phenomena, such as a monastery. This attachment facilitates different, non-religious actions towards religious objects and phenomena, such as treating a monastery as a local resource or a tourist asset. It is not an exterior process, since also monks apply secular language to depict monasteries.

1. ECONOMY AND MONASTICISM – OVERVIEW

Economy has been and is a challenge for monasticism. Isabelle Jonveaux stresses that

> From the very beginning of monasticism, work and economy generated deep tensions within religious life [...] the tension between work or economy and prayer life did not disappear with the redaction of rules or institutionalisation of communities in defined monasteries but continues throughout the whole history of monasticism. More particularly, this question has often been the cause of reforms or creations of new monastic movements[2].

Marcin Jewdokimow is Assistant Professor in the Institute of Classical and Cultural Studies, Faculty of Humanities, Cardinal Stefan Wyszyński University (UKSW, Warsaw), researcher

1 The article was funded by National Science Centre (Poland) – UMO-2013/09/D/HS6/03019.

2 I. JONVEAUX, «Redefinition of the Role of Monks in Modern Society: Economy as Monastic Opportunity», *Annual Review of the Sociology of Religion* 5 (2014) 71-86, 72.

This tension between otherworldly orientation and economic efficiency was highlighted by Max Weber:

> The ascetic monk has fled from the world by denying himself individual property; his existence has rested entirely upon his own work; and, above all, his needs have been correspondingly restricted to what was absolutely indispensable. The paradox of all rational asceticism, which in an identical manner has made all ages stumble, is that rational asceticism itself has created the very wealth it rejected. Temples and monasteries have everywhere become the very loci of rational economies[3].

Hence, there is a clear link between monasticism, asceticism and rationality, the uncovering of which pushed Weber to state: «In fact, the whole history of monasticism is in a certain sense, the history of a continual struggle with the problem of the secularising influence of wealth»[4]. Max Weber in «Protestant Ethics and the Spirit of Capitalism» claims that medieval monasticism was an important ancestor of protestant ethics, hence, an important contribution to economic expansion and the rationalisation process. As one can read in footnotes to the book: «a fundamental postulate of my whole thesis: the Reformation took rational Christian asceticism and its methodical habits out of the monasteries and placed them in the service of active life in the world»[5]. Differently speaking, catholic monasticism is the very source of Puritan asceticism, and so of modern capitalism[6]. Paul-André Turcotte concludes (commenting on Weber):

> Overall, and in synthesis, asceticism, as a method of rational self-control and development of organic life, is revealed at the heart of the deployment of religious virtuosity of monasticism and its relationship with the world and the Church, in an ambivalent relationship of protest or criticism or attestation, that according to their periods of life, from the institution of the beginning of integrative institutionalisation, in agreement with situational factors and the degree of submission to the control of ecclesiastical or civil authorities[7].

---

3 M. WEBER, *Essays in Sociology*, London 1948, 334.

4 M. WEBER, *The Protestant Ethic and the Spirit of Capitalism*. London-New York 1992 (repr. 2005), 118.

5 WEBER, *The Protestant Ethic* (cf. nt. 4), 196, footnote 79.

6 Compare F. SILBER 2001. «Monasticism and the Protestant "Ethic": ascetism, rationality and wealth in Medieval West», *British Journal of Sociology* 44 (2001) 103-123.

7 P-A. TURCOTTE, «Monasticism and Society in Max Weber and Ernst Troeltsch», *Annual Review of the Sociology of Religion* 5 (2014) 261-276, 266.

Contemporary monasteries have decreased in terms of economic power; the economic context in which they operate has also changed. Hence, the relationship between monasticism and economy is to be rethought. As Jonveaux stresses «In most European countries today economic activities have become a first necessity for monasteries that have lost their traditional sources of incomes»[8] and as a result «a large part of monastic communities today live thanks to the direct work of monks»[9]. Jonveaux puts it very well: «The most relevant questions for monks and nuns today is indeed to find an economic activity that can be productive for the community but which also can be integrated into a coherent religious system»[10] and «ideally monks would like to insert their economic activities in the religious utopia in order not to disturb religious coherence, but they come up against the necessity to find markets in order to sell their products»[11]. And if monks and nuns are more and more engaged in markets and market logics, may they still be understood as communities devoted to otherworldly goals or a form of radical protest[12]. Consumption logics, promotion and brand approach do their job... As a result, monasteries adapt to new cultural and economic conditions by the use of contemporary means such as tourist offers, promotion and production of «monastic» products, etc. Scholars unveil processes of commercialisation of monastic products, commercialisation of monastic traditions, and the space of monasteries[13]. Economy had been and is today one of the major factors influencing monasteries. This issue has not been yet addressed in the Polish context (and Jonveaux's studies are an international exception).

Today, not only economical logics but also new media and tourism influence patterns of *fuga mundi*[14]. For instance, Jewdokimow showed that monastic

8 Jonveaux, «Redefinition of the Role of Monks» (cf. nt. 2), 73.

9 Jonveaux, «Redefinition of the Role of Monks» (cf. nt. 2), 74.

10 Jonveaux, «Redefinition of the Role of Monks» (cf. nt. 2), 74.

11 Jonveaux, «Redefinition of the Role of Monks» (cf. nt. 2), 78.

12 J. Seguy, «A Sociology of Imagined Societies: Monasticism and Utopia», *Annual Review of the Sociology of Religion* 5 (2014) 284-320.

13 Compare Jonveaux, «Redefinition of the Role of Monks» (cf. nt. 2), M. Jewdokimow, «From the secular to the post-secular. The place of religion in the local public sphere in the context of monasteries in Poland – a case study», *Journal of Religious Studies, History, and Society/ Revista Ciências da Religião-História e Sociedade* 13/1 (2015) 226-240.

14 Compare M. Jewdokimow, «Monasteries in the Internet. A Case Study of Polish Websites», *Journal of Religious Studies, History, and Society/ Revista Ciências da Religião-História e Sociedade* 12/1 (2014) 288-298, Jewdokimow, «From the secular to the post-secular» (cf. nt. 10), E. Bosgraaf, «Ascetism in transition: exploring the con-

communities (Cistercians) eagerly display their everyday life on the Internet, previously hidden to an outside viewing[15] open up their space to tourists and, hence, commercialisation processes[16]. Hence, inner organisation devoted to seeking God and *fuga mundi* is being challenged not only by the economy but also broader cultural and social changes (including new media and tourism). Economy is one of the factors which influence monasticism today.

2. ECONOMIC LANGUAGE AND ECONOMIC PRACTICES – CASE STUDY OF CISTERCIAN MONASTERIES IN POLAND

The issue of interrelationship between monasticism and economy today may be approached from different angles. For instance, if a monastery is being understood as an institution, one aims at uncovering how it reacts to these new economic conditions, how it adapts to them or how these new conditions influence its organisation. Within my studies, I propose to change the point of view and the scope of interest – from focusing on inner transformations taking place within monasteries and scrutinising a monastery as an institution to focus on a context in which monasteries operate. And within this very context to concentrate on relevant factors related to the economy of monasteries or – speaking more precisely – to economisation processes related to monasteries. By economisation processes, I mean processes that are related to economy, mostly: production, consumption and commercialisation, which influence monasteries today. These processes operate in two interconnected registers: of language and of practices, of how a monastery is being described, what meanings are being attached to it and of what kind of actions have been taken towards it or are planned/desired to be taken?

In a further analysis, I base on findings from my field research which I have conducted in Poland since 2012 in selected towns where Cistercians monasteries are placed – Wąchock[17], Jędrzejów, Szczyrzyc and Sulejów. I carried out

cepts of memory, performance and ambiguity in twentieth-century Dutch monastic life», *Numen* 55 (2008) 536-60, I. Jonveaux, *Le monastère au travail: le royaume de Dieu au défi de l'économie*, Paris 2011, Id., «Redefinition of the Role of Monks» (cf. nt. 2).

15 Jewdokimow, «Monasteries in the Internet. A Case Study of Polish Websites», (cf. nt. 14). M. Jewdokimow, « Prezentacje klasztorów i autoprezentacje mnichów na cysterskich stronach WWW – w stronę sekularyzacji semantycznej?», *Przegląd Socjologii Jakościowej* 13/1 (2017) 110-126.

16 Jewdokimow, «From the secular to the post-secular. The place of religion in the local public sphere in the context of monasteries in Poland – a case study» (cf. nt. 13).

17 The field studies in Wąchock was conducted as a part of the following project: *Cultural*

30 semi-structured in-depth interviews with local actors (representatives of local government and its institutions such as local centres of culture or libraries, NGOs and monks), analysis of local web-sites and publications (such as tourist brochures) which I collected in the field.

In local brochures, albums, on websites, and by my informants a monastery is being described as: a relic, a monument, a place to visit, a cultural heritage, a tourist asset, a local resource, a lever of development of a local community. The first five descriptions may be grouped, since they refer to the cultural value of a monastery which is being understood as an attraction for a tourist. As it was stated by informant no. 3.:

> Most of the residents – I think I do not exaggerate – think that [this monastery] <u>is the most important relic</u> in [a town – MJ]... If one asks them, I think that everyone would say that a Cistercian monastery is <u>our pearl</u>.

This manner of description is almost omnipresent in local tourist publications such as brochures and albums, and in informants' narratives. For instance, one of the monastery is an «attraction» because of its «outstanding» architecture and amenities, including church organs. Other informants underline that «the monastery is beautiful inside, a chapel is beautiful, a refectory is beautiful, mostly for visitors who say that inside there you eat differently and sit differently. You have totally different experiences» (informant no. 1.). This monastery attracts both tourists and pilgrims but also «ordinary people»: «Ordinary people are enchanted when they see the monastery» (informant no. 2.).

Understanding a monastery as a relic, as an attraction allows redefining it as a tourist asset and opens up space for non-religious actions towards it.

> It is a place that really gave rise to ... [a town – MJ], the pearl in the crown of Jędrzejów. A powerful monument. One of the few such powerful monuments of Romanesque architecture in Kielce. There are even fragments of the pre-Cistercian church from the turn of the eleventh and twelfth centuries .... But this means that it draws a lot of tourists to ... [the town – MJ], winds kind of prosperity but also indicates the needs that lie ahead for the authorities, right? We

heritage of dissolved monasteries on the territory of former Poland and in Silesia in the 18th and 19th centuries: fate, significance, cataloguing is carried out within the framework of the Ministry of Science and Higher Education's "National Programme for the Development of Humanities" for 2012–2016.

> are at the moment when we try to do something together with the monastery in terms of accommodation rooms (informant no. 4.).

A representative of a local government claims that it is necessary that a monastery will act as a tourist asset. According to him it is its contemporary faith.

> Therefore, the only chance that we [a town] ever existed in the public space in Poland, is tourism, is the development of tourism. And without the development of tourism in the arch-abbey we simply cannot do it. Tourism will not move. Now we are just in the process of establishing the life a local tourist organisation, we have already held several meetings on the subject. And if everything rests virtually on monastery, on the museum ..., several other monuments here in ...[the town – MJ] ...But it [the monastery] is the centre, it is the heart of it all (informant no. 5.).

Its faith is also a promotion of the town countrywide.

> And as I said, the Cistercians it is not only religion, but also what is happening around the abbey. A jewel in the crown and a good ... good promotion of [our town – MJ] (informant no. 2.).

One may see that in the register of language a monastery is being transformed into a consumable good. Hence, language is a vital factor in terms of economy – it redefines a monastery as an object ready-to-economise and, hence, facilitates or even permits to act upon it in terms of economy. Hence, for instance it is obvious that one has to invest in a monastery because it will profit back in terms of community development or levering tourist ratio.

Conducted studies show also concrete practices of economisation. Here I will outline most relevant instances from the places I have studied. Local governments dedicate money for both conservation and modernization; monasteries are included in local developmental strategies; local business establishes joint ventures with monks (monasteries provide infrastructure or legitimate a brand's name). In 2015 in Szczyrzyc a brewery has been relaunched (relaunched because – as it is said – it is a continuation of work of brewery from 1623[18]) as a joint venture of an abbey and a local business. An abbey in Wąchock opened

18 Http://www.browarszczyrzyc.pl/s1-historia-browaru-szczyrzyckiego.html [access: 11-11-2018].

a restaurant inside it walls. In buildings historically belonging to a monastery in Sulejów a restaurant is placed (since 70s).

3. TOWARDS SEMANTIC SECULARISATION?

To my mind, presented analysis develops thesis on secularising influence of wealth on monasticism which I introduced in the very beginning of this paper. Secularisation is not only the result of wealth surplus but it also operates on a semantic register. But may one understand this economisation processes in the register of language and practices as secularizing ones? This thesis is clearly backed by Max Weber's findings which I presented earlier. I would add to it that what we see here it is not only secularisation in terms of how an institution operates but also in terms of language – how institution's actions (and an institution as such) is being named – a kind of semantic secularisation[19]. By semantic secularisation I mean the process of attaching secular meanings to religious objects and phenomena, such as a monastery. This attachment facilitates different, non-religious actions towards religious objects and phenomena, such as treating a monastery as a local resource.

One may ask whether this process of semantic secularisation is exterior or interior. Conducted interviews show that is both. For monks to whom I talked, a monastery is a religious institution, yet it traditionally engages in the public sphere by different activities (running a hospital and organising healthcare actions, providing education services to schools or organising cultural activities). Monks want to develop non-religious activities such as ecological agriculture, tourism activities, healthcare actions – they understand it as a return to tradition which is not in conflict with an ideal of retreat from the world. These engagements are inspired by religious content and goals. Here religion and culture merge. Yet, a monk to whom I talked does not understand it as a means of conversion – rather as presentation, as an offer which it is to be taken or not, depending on an individual will:

19 I have intorduced this concept in refenrence to visual communication conducted by monks in: JEWDOKIMOW, «Prezentacje klasztorów i autoprezentacje mnichów na cysterskich stronach WWW – w stronę sekularyzacji semantycznej?» (cf. nt. 15). In another article I have discussed this concept in reference to local discourse – in: M. JEWDOKIMOW, «*Klasztor w lokalnym dyskursie społecznym – studium przypadku klasztorów cysterskich*», in *Kościoły – Religie – Kultury. Współczesne wymiary reprezentacji i partycypacji*, edd. M. Sroczyńska-S. Zaręba, Warszawa 2017, 129-144.

> But it is not [so] that we will present something, and the very goal – to convert – will be hidden. No! Not at all. We will present how Cistercians lived, present without any subtext, without any intention to convince someone to convert ... A free man he should have the greatest knowledge of the culture both material and spiritual, then he has a greater ability to make choices. But it must be present without any hidden agendas, the most objectively (informant no. 3.).

A monastery wants to «present» itself in order to attract both believers and non-believers and by doing so to present an alternative to the contemporary philosophy of life. According to monks, the monastery wants to develop in terms of economy in relation to tourism. It is a way to present Cistercian spirituality and lifestyle but also to help the town to overcome social and economic issues, to provide work and – broadly speaking – to develop:

> Terrible unemployment, all young people want to flee, unfortunately ... And chance is tourism, we also operate under such terms. Because it's not just that we have something we want, but we also want to do something for the people – provide jobs related to keeping a pilgrimage house running or producing souvenirs (informant no. 3.).

> According to the monk after Aggiornamento: «we may understand *labora* in this way, that today to work means something else. It means to work for people, for the community, for the presentation of culture» (informant no. 3.).

This redefinition of what to work means abolishes alleged contradiction between activities in the public sphere and religious, otherworldly goals. A monk reaches his religious goals by the work for the community. Hence, if there is no tension between this kind of work and religious goals, then the project may be further developed:

> Some businessmen once came and told me: 'listen, if you have here something like that for a few days, to stop, to be silent, to cut off from everything,' We wanted the pilgrim house to be such a place. And so out of the tourist season, which is 4 months only, all the rest of it would be the stays precisely, any such retreat, such cut off, maybe a physical work? It would be a complete detachment from everything that these people do. And if it is combined with a healthy kitchen, with old traditional stuff, I think it would be a great thing for the people. «I myself would have gladly gone somewhere in a place like this ... », (informant no. 3.)

CONCLUSIONS

The secularisation thesis is today under critique[20], which unveils its limits and assumptions – mainly that religion is to be annihilated in and by modernity. In 1994, José Casanova asked «who still believes in the *myth* of secularisation?»[21] and showed that the disappearance of religion in selected Western countries is not the case. Rather, religion in modern societies undergoes a paradox process of both privatisation and de-privatisation[22]. «The modern walls of separations between church and state keep developing kinds of cracks through which both are able to penetrate each other»[23]. Studies on the relationship between monasticism and economy show that there are other «walls» that are being gradually forced – those of economy and religion. Historical studies conducted for instance by Max Weber uncovered a secularising influence of wealth on monastic orders; contemporary studies clearly show that economy is still a challenge for monasticism. However, the very nature of this challenge seems to be changed because both economic systems and the economic power of monasteries had shifted. Presented paper discussed a term «semantic secularisation» which seeks to grasp one of many aspects of these shifts. Semantic secularisation highlights that the influence of economy on religion affects language by which one describes and perceives the world and that secular, i.a. economy-driven meanings are being attached to religious objects and phenomena (such as a monastery) which facilities different actions towards them. Hence, perhaps it is a point to reconsider post-secular claims about «returning» of religion – religion «returns» but in an altered habit.

Abstract

The aim of the proposed paper is to reflect on economisation processes which affect monasteries in local contexts today. As shown by researchers (for instance Isabelle Jonveaux, Stafania Palmisano) monasteries today undergo transformations which are related to broader cultural shifts (such as spreading of consumption culture). This paper proposes to focus on outside factors of economisation

20 For instance T. Asad, *Formations of the secular. Christianity, Islam, modernity*, California 2003; J. Casanova, *Public religions in the modern world*, Chicago 1994 (repr. 2012).

21 Casanova, *Public religions* (cf. nt. 18) 11.

22 Casanova, *Public religions* (cf. nt. 18) 41.

23 Casanova, *Public religions* (cf. nt. 18) 41.

processes affecting monasteries not an inner economic logic of monasteries or monastic economy which is a main topic of the symposium. The author assumes that contemporary rediscovery of monastic economy relates to processes of monasteries' economisation; they overlap.

The perspective applied in the paper is both anthropological and sociological which results in studying monasteries as institutions facing local and global trends by the use of qualitative methods (in-depth interviews, observation, text analysis). Based on the field research being conducted in Poland (five Cistercian monasteries) by the author from 2012 until today the paper reflects on the main features of the processes under scrutiny. Analysis of collected data shows that one may distinguish different aspects of the processes that relate to both narrative and practical dimensions. As for narrative dimension, denominating a monastery in narratives of cultural heritage, tourist asset, and local resource facilitates economisation processes. As a result, imposing these secular narratives on a monastery enables concrete practices affecting it, for instance (1) local governments dedicate money for both conservation and modernisation, (2) monasteries are included in local developmental strategies, or (3) local business establishes joint ventures with monks (monasteries provide infrastructure or legitimate a brand's name).

WHAT CONTEMPORARY MANAGERS CAN LEARN FROM BENEDICTINE MONKS?

Ryszard Kołodziej

INTRODUCTION

There is a saying between philosophers that everything in later philosophy are only glosses on Plato. The author of this article will attempt to prove that almost everything in contemporary management theories and practice are only glosses on St. Benedict's Rule. The only difference is that the first ones (philosophers) know Plato well, whereas the managers do not know St. Benedict. We will explain why this is a shame.

In contemporary management and leadership concepts there is a focus on effectiveness and efficiency aspects of managing organisations and people. Also, the strategic approach is of concern. Not setting these aspects explicitly as goals or as a basis for the organisation survival and development, Benedictine monasteries all over Europe and the Globe proved to be strategically driven, vital and well (which means effectively and efficiently) managed. We will explain what made the Benedictine organisation so successful that it has survived for fifteen centuries of difficult times.

We will focus on key characteristics of the Benedictine organisation and on the Benedictine leadership model and explain how these concepts can be successfully applied in contemporary organisations. The value driven management together with a concept of an organisation as a community will be discussed. Also, other aspects important for continuous improvement and development such as learning, quality oriented and flexible organisation will be analysed. We will show how the "ground rules" or principles of Benedictine communities represented by Benedictine vows of *stabilitas*, *conversatio morum* and *obedientia* created good conditions for sustainable growth.

In the leadership dimension of management, we will focus on the model of leadership represented by the abbot and analyse it in terms of contemporary

Ryszard Kołodziej, PhD, MBA, manager, consultant, free researcher, Benedictine oblate.

leadership models. We will compare it also with the concepts of "situational leadership" and "servant leadership".

1. KEY CHARACTERISTICS OF CONTEMPORARY MANAGEMENT VERSUS MANAGEMENT IN THE BENEDICTINE ORGANISATION

We will compare contemporary management theories and practices with those presented in *The Rule of St. Benedict* (RB)[1] and represented by common practices of Benedictine monasteries. Although St. Benedict did not make any theoretical statements on the management model for the monastery, he described in the Rule series of principles and good management practices that may be interpreted as such a model and represent specific management or leadership style.

There are plenty of management theories, models and trends present and discussed in the literature. This summary of key characteristics of contemporary management theories and practices is based on over two decades of studies and practice in management and business or organisational consultancy, performed by the author for over thirty business and non-profit organisations, including a Benedictine abbey.

Key characteristics of contemporary management include: strategic approach, focus on effectiveness and efficiency, learning and innovation, quality orientation, flexibility or agility and relationship management as a basis for development. We will discuss the listed aspects of management of today and compare them with Benedictine practices.

Before we do that let's clarify one very important distinction: between management and leadership. Management[2] is an art and practice of using available resources to achieve assigned goals, objectives and results. In the management paradigm everything used to achieve results is treated as a resource. That means also people are treated as resources, what can be noticed in management language. Human Resources ("HR"), Human Resource Manager ("HR Manager") etc. are usual names used in almost every company and at almost every Univer-

---

1 The author will use in this text the abbreviations " the Rule" or "RB" for The Rule of St. Benedict. All citations are taken from: *The Rule of St. Benedict in English*, ed. T. Fry, The Liturgical Press, Collegeville 1982 and are referred to in the following way: (*RB* Chapter,Sentence_Range) e.g. (*RB* 4,8-10)

2 This is a definition of the author. Other definitions focus on management functions, e.g.: Management - The act, manner, or practice of managing; handling, supervision, or control. (http://www.thefreedictionary.com/management [access: 20-03-2016])

sity with management curriculum, including those of Christian origin. Additionally, from the management point of view resource is anything that generates costs[3]. So we as human beings have been treated for decades this way until now by business and management theories and practice[4].

This is in total opposition to the philosophical concepts of Christian personalism of Karol Wojtyła, stating that persons are not to be used, but to be respected and loved[5], followed by the social teaching of John Paul II[6]. So, this is a big challenge to Christian thinkers and management authorities to change that present paradigm or mindset although there are some symptoms of change in a right direction that can be observed in changing leadership paradigms, especially in modern high technology companies. We will discuss that later in this article.

On the other hand, "leadership" is an art and competence to lead other people[7]. So, the leadership dimension of managing organisations will be most important for understanding the human aspect of that reality. So, further we will apply the word "management" to different aspects of arranging and developing business and non-profit organisations whereas "leadership" will be used for addressing interpersonal aspects of management.

Some reflection on the Catholic leadership model based on the official teaching of the Catholic Church one can find in the document of the Pontifical Council for Justice and Peace[8] but also that document is burdened with the contemporary management language.

3 Dictionary definition: Resources: The total means available to a company for increasing production or profit, including plant, labor,and raw material (http://www.thefreedictionary.com/resource [access: 20-03-2016])

4 There is need for indepth study of the process of evolving the concept of «human resources", first formulated in the work of J.R. Commons,*The Distribution of Wealth*, Macmillan, New York 1893 and developed in its modern form by E.Wight Bakke, *The Human Resources Function*, Yale Labor and Management Center, 1958

5 The sentence is a summary of so called "personalistic norm", see: Karol Wojtyła, *Love and Responsibility*, San Francisco 1981, 41 (first published in Polish in 1960)

6 Ioannes Paulus II, «Litterae Encyclicae *Laborem Exercens* (5 novembris 1981)», *AAS* 73 (1981) 577-647; Id., «Litterae Encyclicae *Sollicitudo Rei Socialis* (7 maii 1988)» *AAS* 80 (1988) 525-540, Id., «Litterae Encyclicae *Centesimus Annus* (9 octobris 1991)», *AAS* 83 (1991) 793-867.

7 Dictionary definition: Leadership: the position or function of a leader (http://www.thefreedictionary.com/leadership [access: 20-03-2016])

8 *Vocation of the Business Leader. A Reflexion*. Pontifical Council for Justice and Peace (Iustitia et Pax), Rome 2012

Coming back to the main course of our reflection we will comment on one of the key characteristics of contemporary management which is strategic approach.

1.1. Strategic Approach

Strategic approach means having vision, a sense of mission and long term goals and strategies. Strategic approach is about thinking to the future in a proactive way and taking into account the changing environment. That means also strategic flexibility that may result in business model adaptation or change. At the same time, social aspects of strategic thinking lead to questions about what constitutes so called "corporate culture" which means common value system and resulting rules and principles of behaviour between the organisation members and to external stakeholders[9]. At the strategic level of organisational thinking there are also the CSR (Corporate Social Responsibility) policies.

Benedictine organisation described in the Rule is a community. Community means possessing and following common goals, values and principles. It means also having common vision of the future and a common sense of mission. This is of course a different vision and mission from that formulated in a business organisation but from the management point of view it does not really matter. The strong "culture" of the Benedictine monastery is based on values and principles presented in the Rule and preserved for centuries. We will not discuss here these values in detail because they are common to all Christian communities as they originate in the Gospel but we will comment shortly on the specific principles of common life represented by the Benedictine vows[10] of *stabilitas (*stability), *conversatio morum* (fidelity to monastic life[11]), and *obedientia* (obedience). Discussing the sense and different dimensions and meanings of every vow exceeds the framework of this article but the important thing is that every community member is obliged to declare before the whole community that he will follow

9 Stakeholder, def.: A person or organization with a legitimate interest in a given enterprise, organization or in a project. Stakeholders may influence and may be influenced by it. Internal stakeholders include different groups of organization members. External stakeholders may include customers, suppliers or other partners but also local communities or local government.

10 See: *RB* 58,17

11 *"Conversatio morum"* is translated by some authors differently as "conversion of manners" which focuses more on a change than on following the existing rules

those principles in his (monastic) life. The Benedictine vows play, in fact, very similar role to the marriage vows, but applied to a wider community.

Who can represent more inspiring and profound vision than a community looking forward to the Eternity? This is also true for a strong sense of mission of a lively Christian community.

For the purpose of this chapter, it is important that Benedictine organisations apply strategic, long term thinking, based on vision, mission, common values and principles that constitute a strong organisational culture. Social responsibility of Benedictine monasteries is mainly based on the rule of hospitality[12] which made those monasteries the first well organised medical treatment system in Europe and a basis for development of several "industries" such as agriculture, education and others.

1.2. Focus on effectiveness and efficiency

The contemporary world tends to expect us to produce or do as much as possible in the most cost effective way[13]. This is probably the most important difference between the modern management paradigm and the Rule. The questions of the goal and the sense stand as a very important reference point to thinking about work and its results or better – its fruits. Work has in the Benedictine thinking a spiritual sense. Although there is no place in the Rule where one could find the statement "*Ora et Labora*"[14], prayer and labour is the essence of Benedictine life and both have direct spiritual meaning. Benedict starts Chapter 48 of the Rule on "The Daily Manual Labour" with the sound statement: "Idleness is the enemy of the soul". And then: "Therefore the brothers should have specified periods for manual labour as well as for prayerful reading"[15]. In the next sentences of the same chapter one can read: "When they live by the labour of their hands, as our fathers and the apostles did, then they are really monks. Yet, all things are to be done with moderation on account of the faint-hearted"[16]. This means that labour is important for the monks but also that there should be a balance be-

12 «All guest who present themselves are to be welcomed as Christ [...] Proper honor must be shown to all, especially to those who share our faith and to pilgrims» (*RB* 53.1-2)

13 This led to development of such management concepts as Management by Objective (MBO), Key Performance Indicators (KPIs) or Lean Manufacturing.

14 Latin: «Pray and work» known as a popular motto of Benedictines, formulated many centuries after the Rule was written.

15 *RB* 48,1-2

16 *RB* 48,8-9

tween work and other important activities. This kind of balance would make a difference to contemporary unbalanced world of business. So even if we use the words "effectiveness" and "efficiency" to Benedictine life, they have quite different meaning. Instead of "efficiency" or productivity the more adequate word would be probably "diligence" which presents focus on engagement and motivation. This in turn is more consistent with the most modern trends in thinking about well managed, productive organisations than economic thinking of the last several decades. That shows again the power and topicality of the value and principle driven management paradigm of the Benedict Rule.

1.3. Learning organisation

Learning organisation[17] and knowledge based organisations[18] are other important concepts of modern management. In Benedictine practice those concepts are present in two areas: learning as a duty of every community member, developed by the practice of "Lectio divina"[19] and learning of the organisation itself. The "holy reading" should be practiced by every monk on a regular basis; as general attitude[20], every day[21], especially every Sunday[22] and additionally in specified seasons[23]. This shows the importance of learning, in only few modern organisations so precisely defined and arranged.

Learning of the whole organisation is secured by the attitude of listening, being a norm for all brothers and especially for the decision makers, and translated to organisational practices. A good example is the decision making process described in the Chapter 3. "Summoning the Brothers for Counsel", starting with the statement: "As often as anything important is to be done in the monastery,

---

17 P.M. Senge, *The Fifth Discipline.* Century Business, London 1990. M. Pedler-J. Burgogyne-T. and Boydell, *The Learning Company: A strategy for sustainable development*, London [2]1997.

18 N.D. Jatinder-S. Gupta-K. Sharma, *Creating Knowledge Based Organizations*, Idea Group, 2004.

19 Latin: «holy reading»

20 «Listen readily to holy reading, [...] These, then, are the tools of the spiritual craft» (*RB* 4,55 [...] 4,75) .

21 «Therefore the brothers should have specified periods for manual labour as well as for prayerful reading» (*RB* 48.1-2).

22 «On Sunday all are to be engaged in reading except those who have been assigned various duties» (*RB* 48.22).

23 «During this time of Lent each one is to receive a book from the library, and is to read thew hole of it straight htrough» (*RB* 48,15).

the abbot shall call the whole community together and himself explain what the business is; and after hearing of advice of the brothers, let him ponder it and follow what he judges the wiser course"[24]. Just after that, Benedict explains why all brothers should be called for counsel and the reason is that "the Lord often reveals what is better to the younger"[25]. This attitude of listening to the next generations could be a benchmark for many present organisations.

Learning organisation means also developing competencies of the community members by changing on a regular basis responsibilities in the monastery. This applies to all main functions of key decision makers like the abbot or the cellarer but also current responsibilities for daily tasks, necessary for living, changed on weekly basis. This enabled exchanging experience between those more advanced with the younger and developing good organisational practices for centuries.

1.4. Quality orientation

Focus on quality of products and processes as a basis for business and organisational success is one of the most important characteristics of management thinking of the last decades. The main reason for that, was a rising level of competition in most industries. This challenge lead to development of such quality management concepts as TQM (Total Quality Management)[26], Six Sigma[27] or quality management standards and norms governed by international or national standard organizations like ISO[28] or ANSI[29].

According to the ISO 9000:2005 norm, quality is a "Degree to which a set of inherent characteristics fulfills requirements"[30]. This standard defines requirement as need or expectation.

Benedict was not a quality assurance manager but it is clear that the Rule was written to standardise. In fact, it established a standard for organising lives of several and then hundreds of monasteries. It established organisational rules and what we would call today "procedures" describing how things should be done

---

24 *RB* 3,1-2.

25 *RB* 3,3.

26 A.R. Martínez-Lorente-F. Dewhurst-B.G. Dale, «Total Quality Management: Origins and Evolution of the Term», *The TQM Magazine* 10 (1998) 378-386.

27 G. Tennant, *SIX SIGMA: SPC and TQM in Manufacturing and Services,* Gower, 2001.

28 ISO - International Organization for Standardization, www.iso.org.

29 ANSI - American National Standards Institute, www.ansi.org.

30 ISO 9000:2005, *Quality management systems - Fundamentals and vocabulary*, International Organization for Standardization, 2005.

well, together with what we would call with contemporary language of quality management -"quality metrics" to assess performance against assigned norms.

What is special to the St. Benedict's Quality Management System (BQM System) is focus on quality of processes and people who take responsibility of a specific role in the community. Those characteristics of individuals we would call long time ago "virtues" but nowadays we can call them just "competencies". Good illustration of that is Chapter 31. "Qualifications of the Monastery Cellarer" which first describes the virtues and competencies of a person but also says how he should deal with goods: "He will regard all utensils and goods of the monastery as sacred vessels of the altar, aware that nothing is to be neglected"[31]. The last sentences of the chapter explain why standardised rules and processes are important: "Necessary items are to be requested and given at the proper times, so that no one may be disquieted or distressed in the house of God"[32].

Although most of the Rule instructions apply to "internal stakeholders" which are community members, some other say how to deal with external "clients". In Chapter 57 on "The Artisans of the Monastery" Benedict warns the brothers: "Whenever products of these artisans are sold, those responsible for the sale must not dare to practice any fraud."[33] And then: "The evil of avarice must have no part in establishing prices, which should, therefore, always be a little lower than people outside the monastery are able to set, so that in all things God may be glorified"[34]. The last part of the sentence is in fact the real motto of Benedictines: "*Ut in omnibus glorificetur Deus*" which established very strong foundation for the BQM System, because of giving deep, spiritual reason and motivation for quality oriented living and work practices.

1.5. Flexibility or agility

Changing environment and competitive pressure makes flexibility the key strategic asset of business organisations. This applies to business models, marketing strategies, organisational and technological changes and implied new management concepts such as agile organisation[35] or agile management[36]. In the busi-

31 *RB* 31,10-11.
32 *RB* 31,18-19.
33 *RB* 57,4.
34 *RB* 57,7-9.
35 E. Leybourn, *Directing the Agile Organisation: A Lean Approach to Business Management*, IT Governance Publishing, 2013.
36 A. Moran, *Managing Agile: Strategy, Implementation, Organisation and People*, Spring-

ness and organisational context agility means the ability of an organisation to adapt rapidly to changing environment and stakeholder expectations. The main reason of being flexible or agile is to survive and be able to develop.

In the case of a Benedictine community flexibility does not mean necessarily rapid adaptation to changing environment; Benedictine monasteries are rather seen as a symbol of stability in the face of changing environment. On the other hand, there are many places in the Rule being the evidence of flexibility in thinking about the Rule and its application. Benedict stresses the fact that in specific conditions of a community, exceptions from the Rule are allowed and recommended. This may apply to "The proper amount of food"[37] or drink[38] or to the way the psalms are said[39]. Also the organisational structure of a monastery is flexible in a sense that all main functions are named and described but some are treated as optional (e.g. that of deans[40]). This is the responsibility of the abbot to apply the Rule accordingly, for common good. We will show in the next chapter that the most important aspect of flexibility in managing the organisation is the approach of its leaders to other community members. Final evidence of the Benedictine flexibility in changing environment is the fact of sustainable development of the Benedictine global organisation for fifteen centuries.

1.6. Relationship management as a basis for development

Relations are important to any business and organisation not only in the B2B[41] context but also in the B2C[42] industries. Good and long lasting relations with customers are treated as a key company asset. For a Benedictine organization, relations are everything; first with God, then with brothers in the community and then with the others. As the importance of the first two types of relations seem to be obvious for a Christian community and different from other organ-

---

er, 2015.

37 *RB* 39.

38 *RB* 40.

39 *Above all else we urge that if anyone finds this distribution of the psalms unsatisfactory, he should arrange whatever he judges better* (*RB* 18,22).

40 *RB* 21,1.

41 B2B – Business to Business relations, when partners or clients are other businesses rather than individuals.

42 B2C – Business to Customer relations, when a company offers and sells goods or services to individuals.

isations' situation, let's focus on the third type of relations, which in the Rule mainly apply to guests and foreigners.

Chapter 53 on "The reception of guests" starts with the statement: "All guests who present themselves are to be welcomed as Christ, for he himself will say: I was a stranger and you welcomed me (Matt 25:35)"[43] and then: "Great care and concern are to be shown in receiving poor people and pilgrims"[44]. It is clear that according to the Rule all people either in the community or outside it should be treated with love and respect. This kind of general attitude seems to be fruitful for any organisation also today and most companies at least pretend to think and behave that way. The reason, of course, is usually quite different because it comes from pragmatic or even egoistic motivations but no business (or other) organisation in the contemporary world could admit that good relations and respect are not important. There is also more and more visible focus in the HR or personnel management on establishing positive, friendly relations between company members and this applies not only to peers abut also to all subordinate – supervisor type relations.

2. CONTEMPORARY LEADERSHIP CONCEPTS VERSUS BENEDICTINE LEADERSHIP

Choosing from many contemporary leadership models and concepts we will present here two which seem to be important because of being popular and influential. The first one is the "Situational leadership model"[45] of Paul Hersey and Ken Blanchard and the second one is the "Servant leadership"[46] concept, developed by Robert K. Greenleaf.

Before we start to discuss those specific works, it is worth mentioning that in most curricula or workshops on leadership an important starting point is to show two main domains or dimensions with which any leader has to deal. The first one is the domain of goals and results; leadership means to lead other people somewhere – to show the direction and, in a business context, – to achieve assigned results. The second important domain is that of human relations and involves interpersonal skills such as motivating other people, negotiating, re-

43 *RB* 53,1-2.

44 *RB* 53,15

45 See: P. Hersey-K.H. Blanchard, *Management of Organizational Behavior [3rd Edition]- Utilizing Human Resources*, New Jersey/Prentice Hall 1977.

46 R. Greenleaf, *The Servant as Leader* [rev. ed.], Indianapolis 1991.

solving problems, etc. Depending on what is the main focus of a leader, we may name the core leadership styles, as presented in Fig.1. It is usual to assume that the best leaders are able to combine in a consistent way thinking about goals and results with thinking and acting which focuses on people and their needs. So, within a framework of the simple leadership style model presented in Fig.1 one could justify the thesis that the "Integrated" leadership style should be most effective in any circumstances. Nevertheless, more advanced studies lead to the conclusion that there is no single "ideal" leadership style which is always effective and not depending on circumstances and people that are led. This is, in fact, the key finding of the Situational leadership theory and model of Hersey and Blanchard. According to this theory the most successful leaders are those who can adapt their leadership style to the maturity level, called "Performance readiness", of an individual or group. Performance readiness consists of two dimensions: ability (called also "competence"[47]) and willingness (called also "commitment"[47]). The model uses a chart similar to this of Fig.1, with the same axes, to describe possible "leadership behaviours" but calls them differently as Directing, Coaching (for Integrated), Supporting (for Social) and Delegating (for Indifferent).

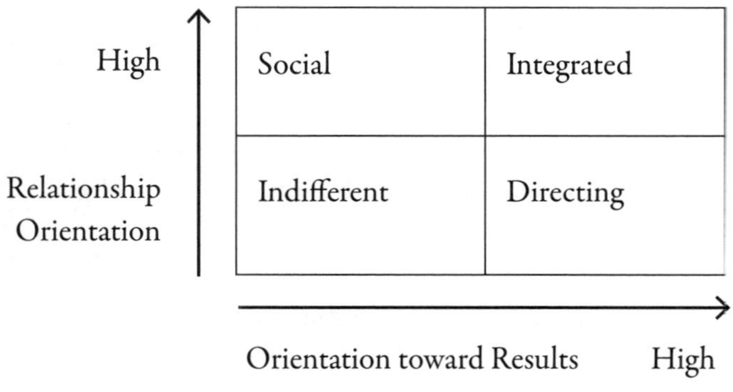

Fig.1. Core leadership styles

One should choose the leadership behaviour that would be most effective in specific circumstances depending on the performance readiness of an individual or team.

47 K.H. Blanchard-P. Zigarmi-D. Zigarmi, *Leadership and the One Minute Manager: Increasing Effectiveness through Situational Leadership*, New York 1985.

The same idea we can find already in the Rule although described with more common language and without using charts. The essence of that thinking could be summarised by the sentence of Benedict from the Chapter 2. "Qualities of the Abbot": "In his teaching the abbot should always observe the Apostle's recommendation, in which he says: *Use argument, appeal, reproof (2 Tim 4,2).* This means that he must vary with circumstances, threatening and coaxing by turn, stern as a taskmaster, devoted and tender as only a father can be."[48] We could illustrate that possible attitudes of the abbot by a chart similar to that of Fig.1 but using the language of the Rule. At the same time we can see what is a sense and "application" of two very important characteristics of Benedictine relationships[49], which are love and obedience, in what we could call a "Leadership model of the abbot". In Fig. 2 we illustrate those different leadership styles of the abbot together with their relationship base characteristics.

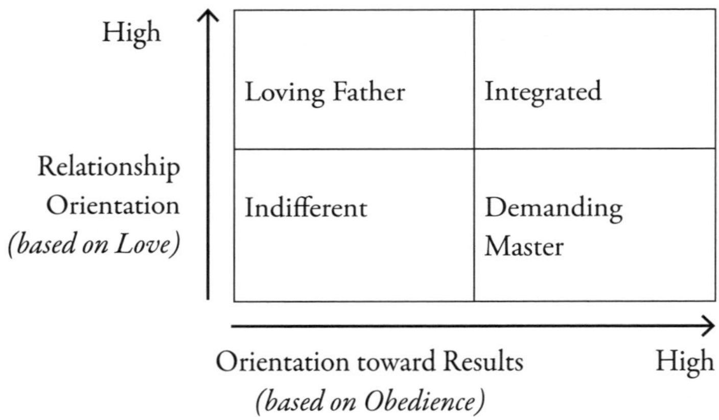

Fig. 2. Abbot's leadership model

In the sentences cited above Benedict focuses on varying circumstances as a basis for adjusting the abbot's leadership style but in other sentences of the same chapter he pays more attention to the ability and willingness of a disciple (what we called in the Situational leadership model "performance readiness"): "Furthermore, anyone who receives the name of abbot is to lead his disciples by a twofold

48 *RB* 2,23-24

49 Using the expression «Benedictine relationships" we mean relationships between members of a Benedictine community, based on directions of the Rule.

teaching: he must point out to them all that is good and holy more by examples that by words, proposing the commandments of the Lord to receptive disciples with words, but demonstrating God's instructions to the stubborn and the dull by a living example"[50]. We can illustrate with those words not only the analogy between the Abbot's leadership and the Situational leadership concepts but also another important aspect of leadership discussed widely in the literature and important for the management practice which is source of authority of a leader. Again, Benedict predicted conclusions of many contemporary management, sociological and psychological studies which have made obvious supremacy of the authority based on attitude and competence over that based on a formal position[51].

Another important leadership concept is "Servant leadership", developed in a modern form by Robert K. Greenleaf. In fact, the core concept is as old as our human civilisation, already present in thinking of Chinese ancient philosophers such as Lao-Tzu[52] or in the Bible, presenting the teaching of Jesus[53]. What is important, Robert K. Greenleaf formed a modern movement supported by many influential management authorities such as already mentioned in this article Ken Blanchard or other renowned writers like Stephen Covey and Peter Senge. Servant leadership becomes also a standard in thinking and practice in high technology sectors and is promoted by such a powerful institution as the Project Management Institute, the biggest and most influential, global project management professional association.

Robert K. Greenleaf defines the servant leadership this way: "The servant-leader is servant first... It begins with the natural feeling that one wants to serve, to serve first. Then conscious choice brings one to aspire to lead. That person is sharply different from one who is leader first."[54] Very similar words one may read in the Rule at many places like this one: "Let him who has been appointed abbot always bear in mind what a burden he has taken on himself, and to whom he will have to *give an account of his stewardship* (Luke 16, 2); and

50 *RB* 2,11-12.

51 See e.g. the concept of Charismatic authority of Max Weber, in "Politics as Vocation" 129-198, and "Discipline and Charisma" 59-72 in: M. Weber, *Rationalism and Modern Society*, edited and translated by T. Waters-D. Waters, Palgrave MacMillan 2015.

52 Lao Tzu, *Tao Teh Ching*, trans. John C.H. Wu, Boston-Massachusetts-Shambhala 2006, 35.

53 See: Mark 10, 42-45, New International Version Bible, https://www.biblegateway.com [access: 15-04-2016].

54 R. Greenleaf, *The Servant as Leader* [rev. ed.], Indianapolis 1991.

let him know that it behooves him rather to serve his brethren than to lord it over them."[55]

So, we have proven again that another important contemporary management concept is only a gloss on what St. Benedict presented in his Rule.

3. BENEDICTINE RULE FOR MANAGERS AND ORGANIZATIONS OF XXI CENTURY? (CONCLUSIONS)

We have been able to present in this article only a brief overview of key concepts of contemporary management and compare them with the teaching of St. Benedict. It becomes an amazing experience discovering the same ideas and conclusions on how to manage organisations and how to lead other people in the small book written about fifteen centuries ago by a simple although educated monk. It is a pity that this teaching gets so little attention in management curricula of business universities and in business literature. All the themes that have been only marked here need to be further developed and discussed for common profit of contemporary managers and leaders, not only those of business and non-profit organisations but also those of monastic communities. As the first ones could learn directly from the original teaching of St. Benedict, the last ones could benefit from the modern theories and concepts that being based on the same ideas, have developed their psychological and operational aspects, making them more suitable and effective in contemporary environment.

Abstract

There is a saying between philosophers that everything in later philosophy are only glosses on Plato. The author makes attempt to show that many of contemporary management theories and good practices are only glosses on Saint Benedict Rule. The only difference is that the first ones (the philosophers) know Plato whereas the managers do not know Saint Benedict. The author tries to explain why this is a shame.

In contemporary management and leadership concepts there is a focus on effectiveness and efficiency aspects of managing organisations and people. Also, strategic approach is of concern. Not setting these aspects explicitly as goals or the basis for organisation survival and development, Benedictine monasteries all over Europe and the Globe proved to be strategically driven, vital and well (which means

55 *RB* 64,7-8

effectively and efficiently) managed. It is explained what made the Benedictine organisation so successful that it survived for fifteen centuries of difficult times.

The value driven management together with a concept of an organisation as a community has been discussed. Also, other aspects important for continuous improvement and development such as learning, quality oriented and flexible organisation are analysed. It is also shown how the "ground rules" or principles of Benedictine communities represented by Benedictine vows of *stabilitas, conversatio morum* and *obedientia* created good conditions for sustainable growth.

In the leadership dimension of management, the author focuses on the model of leadership represented by the abbot and analyses it in terms of contemporary leadership style models, comparing it also with the concepts of "servant leadership" and "situational leadership".

With focus on key characteristics of Benedictine organisation and Benedictine leadership concept it has been shown that these concepts can be successfully applied in contemporary organisations.

BEYOND WORK-LIFE BALANCE: TOWARD A MONASTIC ETHIC OF TIME AND PRODUCTIVITY

Katharine MASSAM

The «struggle to juggle» paid work and the rest of life is not new, but it is confronting many Australians so starkly that the Australian Work and Life Index (AWALI) now uses the term «work-life interference» rather than «work-life balance» to describe the experiences most workers report. Both terms, «balance» on the one hand and «interference» on the other, imply «work» and «life» are equal categories[1]. The assumption behind the slippage in our language is alarming: it implies «life» is no longer an overarching category but has somehow become opposed to «work» rather than being inclusive of it. The shift is nevertheless reflected in reality with the most recent AWALI suggesting the tension is getting worse, especially for women and sole-parents in full-time work[2]. The researchers' decision to talk about «work-life interference» rather than «balance» is an effort to rehabilitate other responsibilities so that work stands as part of life alongside family and community commitments, church and social involvements, leisure, and other choices people might make about what to do with their time. Work is related to well-being. So, as well as raising political and economic issues, work is a theological question.

Theologians already know this. In 1991 Miroslav Volf's book *Work in the Spirit* put the longer tradition of vocation, and especially the reality of work in Eden as a gift before the Fall, in the context of a theology of hope and the

---

Katharine Massam is a historian whose writing focuses on the intersections of theology and wider culture, particularly in postcolonial settler societies. She teaches at the University of Divinity in Melbourne (Australia).

1 Australian Work and Life Index, http://www.unisa.edu.au/Research/Centre-for-Work-Life/Our-research/Current-Research/Australian-Work-And-Life-Index/ [access: 25-11-2016]; N. SKINNER-B. POCOCK, «Flexibility and Work-Life Interference in Australia», *Journal of Industrial Relations* 53 (2011) 65-82.

2 B. POCOCK-S. CHARLESWORTH-J. CHAPMAN, «Work-family & work-life pressures in Australia: Advancing gender equality in 'good times?», *International Journal of Sociology & Social Policy* 33 (2013) 594-612.

coming of a new creation[3]. Ecumenically these insights had been building for at least a century, from the publication in 1891 of *Rerum Novarum,* Leo XIII's encyclical on social and economic structures that affirmed ordinary working life. After the Second World War, Catholic social teaching and Thomist foundations combined when Marie-Dominique Chenu OP published his *Theology of Work*. These strands were picked up at the Second Vatican Council especially in the *Pastoral Constitution on the Church in the Modern World*, (*Gaudiem et Spes)* with its embrace of the concerns of the world for the church. More recent encyclicals, including John Paul II's 1981 letter on human work, *Laborem Exercens*, have argued for the spiritual and practical importance of work as not only instrumental, but also ontological and relational: What we produce, what we work at, also produces us, shapes us, and our relationships[4]. If how we spend our time shapes us, it follows that there is a call to reclaim time as a resource for God's life in us.

In the monastic world, there is a long history to understanding «work» and «time» as tools for engagement between God and humanity. This paper has a foundation in the monastic principles of «holy work», rest and leisure, and ancient teaching on the «sanctification of time». These principles will be familiar to many monastic readers, but less attention has been paid to the ways these principles of the use of time were applied, nuanced and adapted in particular situations. The example in a focus here offers a case study of one missionary's understanding of the place of work in his own monastic life as well as in the life of the town he founded. The Spanish Benedictine monk and bishop Rosendo Salvado (1814-1900) wrote extensively about his experience of work in nineteenth-century Australia.

***

The founder of the mission to the Yued-Noongar people at New Norcia in Western Australia did not lead a balanced life. Salvado was a formidable polymath who honoured three personal touchstones: patience, perseverance and prayer,

3 M. Volf, *Work in the Spirit:Toward a Theology of Work*, Oxford University Press, New York 1991.

4 M. Volf-G. Preece, «Work», in *The Oxford Companion to Christian Thought: Intellectual, Spiritual and Moral Horizons of Christianity*, ed. A. Hastings, Oxford University Press, Oxford 2000, 759-761; D. Savage, *The Subjective Dimension of Human Work. The Conversion of the Acting Person According to Karol Wojtyla/John Paul II and Bernard Lonergan*, Peter Lang, New York 2008.

but "balance"? No. Born in Tuy, on the Spanish side of the border between Galicia and Portugal, in March 1814 as Napolean's soldiers were being driven north by the British army, Salvado entered the Benedictine monastery of St Martin in Compostella aged 15 in 1829, the same year that the British government established a colony at the Swan River on the south-west coast of Australia. When anti-clericalism closed the Spanish monasteries in 1835, Salvado eventually followed his friend José Serra to join the Benedictine community at Cava in Italy[5]. Gradually they shared their hope for missionary work overseas, both as a fresh start for European monasticism as well as for what they could offer as evangelists, and in 1845 they set out from Rome to Western Australia with a small international band of missionaries led by the Irish bishop John Brady[6].

Aged 31 years when he arrived in Western Australia, Rosendo Salvado had many talents. He was widely appreciated in Catholic Europe and among the Protestant opinion-makers in Australia. Perceptive, adaptable, musical, highly-cultured and charming, he is remembered by the Yued-Noongar community today as a friend to Aboriginal Australians[7]. While they are critical of strands of historiography that simply celebrate the mission, New Norcia's Aboriginal Corporation takes Salvado's respectful engagement with the local people through 54 years at New Norcia as a sign of enduring commitment. For his part, Salvado regarded the *Australiani* as capable of matching and exceeding any level of education or culture Europe could present. Their capacity for intellectual work was, he said, simply like «the property of fire to heat and to burn»[8]. As we will see, Salvado's awareness of the Yued people's intelligence casts light on his understanding of the place of work and especially manual work in Christian life. His writing also reveals his own approach to wide-ranging and competing demands.

His reports to the Roman Congregation for the Propagation of the Faith in 1883 and 1900 offer particularly valuable insight into his view of work at New

---

5 The standard biography remains G. Russo, *Lord Abbot of the Wilderness. The Life and Times of Bishop Salvado*, Polding Press, Melbourne 1980. See also the indications of more recent research in J.H. Smith, *Rosendo Salvado, Commemorating Two Hundred Years, 1814-2014,* Benedictine Community, New Norcia WA 2014.

6 D.F. Bourke, *The History of the Catholic Church in Western Australia*, Archdiocese of Perth, Perth WA 1979.

7 M. Nannup-M. Drayton-P. Willaway, «A Friend of the Yued People», in *Rosendo Salvado: Commemorating 200 Years*, ed. J.H. Smith, Benedictine Community, New Norcia WA 2014, 1.

8 *Report of Rosendo Salvado to Propaganda Fide in 1883,* ed. and trans. S. Girola, Abbey Press, Northcote VIC 2015, 167.

Norcia. These documents, two of the ten accounts Salvado provided at intervals to the body responsible for overseeing Catholic missionary work, explain the mission at various stages in its history. The report of 1883 is the longest at some 100,000 words, while the last report, written 8 months before Salvado's death in December 1900, includes important reflections on the enterprise[9]. In both Salvado described a life in which he said, essentially, that there were not enough hours in the night to do his day job.

Balance remained, in one way, part of what Salvado wanted to demonstrate. In the 1883 *Report* in particular Salvado was concerned to establish for the young Domenico Jacobini, Cardinal Prefect of the Congregation, that the Australian missionary enterprise was a genuinely monastic community. While they worked, «with all our strength almost day and night, in such a way that the weeks seemed like days»[10], Salvado was aware that «the religious community has its duties...and if these were not satisfied [then] the missionary duties would be accomplished badly and for a short time»[11]. In keeping with monastic practice then, the bell would ring out over the bush near the bend in the river that the Yued people call Borragin at 2.45 in the morning, for prayers to begin at 3.00am. Salvado told the cardinal of the routine of the day, following the time-honoured pattern of prayer and work. Initially he had thought he would join the people in their nomadic life, but after a year and struggling with the diet, his plan shifted to establishing a stable monastic centre, a farming settlement on the model of the monasteries of Europe. He was proud of the community «since all the work, including the most onerous of which there is not a little, is accomplished with alacrity and good spirit, and everything progresses although slowly, without other income than that obtained by our toils»[12]. The monks worked with the people, and the people (if they chose to work with the mission) prayed with the monks in the evening. Significantly, manual work, liturgy and music (especially when directed by the Aboriginal organist Paul Piramino) were mutual points of connection across the two communities.

9 New Norcia's Abbey Press is publishing translations of these reports into English, see n. 8 above, also *Report of Rosendo Salvado to Propaganda Fide in 1900*, ed. and trans. S. Girola, Abbey Press, Northcote VIC 2016; *Aborigeno con gli Aborigeni per l'evangelizzazione in Australia: il testo della Relazione (1883) per Propaganda Fide del vescovo Rudesindo Salvado,* edd. G. Cipollone-C. Orlandi (Pontificio Comitato di Scienze Storiche, Atti e Documenti 32), Libreria Editrice Vaticana,Vatican City 2011.

10 *Salvado 1883*, 90.

11 *Salvado 1883*, 90.

12 *Salvado 1883*, 93.

During the day Salvado was everywhere: assigning jobs, directing work, standing in for workers. He was constantly on the move, and calculated that he would walk 20 miles on a normal day without leaving the Mission itself[13]. Ordinary days ended for the community at 8 o'clock in the evening, but not for Salvado. By night he did the accounts and attended to «one of the most interesting jobs»[14] of conducting an extensive correspondence. As a consequence, «not once, but many times the bell for Matins rang and I went to church after staying up all night, with no sleep at all, and without getting through all the post for Europe»[15]. He did not thrive on this. He reported fever and a racing pulse, and yet maintained a gruelling pace by necessity:

> From all of this I was in a state of constant activity and I felt as if a strong and continuous fever was burning me, so to speak, as my pulse was beating not less than ninety times a minute, and yet I did not feel sick, although many times the sun had already set and I had not sat down even for a moment throughout the whole day and without having had any other food or nourishment but a cup of tea in the morning. I am not saying these things in order to win esteem and God knows it, but in order that the life of the New Norcia missionary monks and their Superior be known at least in part by those who should know[16].

Salvado insisted he was not sick but if those charged with oversight knew their early monastic history they might have had pause for thought. His self-diagnosis of health despite it all cried out for checking against the long tradition of spiritual advice concerned not only with work but more fundamentally with the underlying relationship to «time» and awareness of «God's time» at that.

Did Rosendo Salvado's superiors have cause to wonder whether or not he was in the grip of *acedia*? This spiritual illness was famously diagnosed by Evagrius of Pontus in the 4th century as the «noon-day demon» who disrupts any sense of Godly time, with both listlessness and overwork[17]. The disease progresses

---

13 *Salvado 1883*, 93.

14 *Salvado 1883*, 93.

15 *Salvado 1883*, 90.

16 *Salvado 1883*, 94-95.

17 Evagrius Ponticus, *Praktikos: Chapters on Prayer*, trans. S. Tugwell, Faculty of Theology, Oxford 1987, 6; Cassianus, *The Conferences*, trans. B. Ramsey, Newman Press, New York 1997, 5.2, 5.10.2.; Id., *The Twelve Books of John Cassian on the Institutes of the Cenobia and the Remedies for the Eight Principal Faults*, A Select Library of Nicene and Post-Nicene Father of the Christian Church, Second Series, vol. 11, trans. P. Schaff-H.

through fatigue, isolation, and a collapse of any sense of time, followed by agitation and displacement activity. All sorts of good deeds fritter away the monk's capacity to focus. Acedia, named for a time of day, squanders the fundamental earthly resource of time to spend against vice, in virtue, and with God.

Crucially though, the tradition advises that the cure for this illness is not rest but a quiet focus on the task at hand, the work the monk is really called to do. The cure for the vice of *acedia* underlined the place of work in a healthy spirituality. Against the vice of distraction, the monastic tradition recommended the virtue of persistence, in both prayer of the psalms and in work. Thus, while it was likely to have been spiritually risky for Salvado to overwork as he did, he seems to have remained sure of his purpose and focus. He was not distracted, or avoiding other things. A monastic director would probably have been persuaded that this was not a case of *acedia*. Salvado made the case that his tasks were determined by his vocation.

Salvado's monastic commitment was shaped by the *Rule of Benedict*[18]. Benedict also had a high view of work, not as an end itself, but as a tool for spiritual growth. Benedict's chapter on «manual labour» puts work in the context of rest, and study or reading, and prayer. So, while idleness is an enemy, activity is not a weapon in itself; instead work is a spiritual discipline in an ordered pattern of life[19].

The *Rule* goes on to detail what this spiritual approach to work would look like. Benedict's monasteries were to be «schools for God's service»[20], described essentially as a «workshop» [*oficina]* for developing a holy life[21]. The self-sufficiency and hard work that became a hall–mark of monastic communities was a consequence of a shared aspiration to focus on God. Prayer interrupted the work, and work interrupted the prayer as equal partners in the ordering of the community's life. However, Benedict assumed everyone was going to sleep for something like eight hours, work for eight hours and have eight waking hours otherwise *vacare Deo*, «free for God», in prayer, reading, leisured reflection.

Overall, the work that supported the community, and the process of working itself was to be a dimension of contemplation for the members of the com-

---

Wade, William Eerdmans, Grand Rapids, MI 1982, 5.1.

18 *RB 1980: The Rule of St Benedict in English with Notes*, ed. T. Fry, Liturgical Press, Collegeville (MN) 1981.

19 A. Böckmann, «RB 48: Of the Daily Manual Labor», *The American Benedictine Review* 59 (2008) 141-166; P. Déseille, «Acedia According to the Monastic Tradition», *Cistercian Studies Quarterly* 37 (2002) 297-301.

20 «Prologue», in *RB 1980*, 45, 18.

21 *RB 1980*, 4:78, 29.

munity. In particular manual work was central as a strategy for a godly focus, not simply as an end in itself. Meaningful work provided a foundation of quiet reflection and warded off spiritual danger[22]. The cooking pots were as precious as the vessels of the altar, and if anything was prized in particular it was hard manual labour to meet life's necessities.

The monastery was also community, not a factory or a work-camp. Here is another vital nuance in the Benedictine understanding of labour. Alongside the affirmation of work without any hierarchy of tasks, Benedict also insists the members of the community need to be seen clearly as individuals, not as cogs in a machine. He pithily insists that talent has a role to play in determining tasks, that «brothers should read and sing, not according to rank, but according to their ability to benefit their hearers»[23]. Artisans with particular skills were to «practise their craft with all humility» for its own sake and the sake of their souls, not with the conceited sense of «conferring something on the monastery»[24]. Members were given particular roles according to the qualities they possessed[25].

Throughout Benedict insists the monastic leaders should pay attention to specific needs of individuals in making sure they have clothes that fit, sufficient food, appropriate tools, and also the opportunity to negotiate «impossible tasks»[26].

The watchword of the entire document is «listen» so that authority is exercised in light of the experience of the whole[27]. A Benedictine eye would see the people involved in the work, and their particular talents and needs, as well as the tasks that require attention. The *Rule* was a manifesto for clear-eyed discernment of talent and ability, as well as guidelines aimed not at the production of goods, but at bringing the community closer to God. So what did this look like in the complicated and contested space of the Benedictine mission to the Aboriginal people at New Norcia?

---

22 Cassianus, *Institutes*, 10.7.

23 *RB* 38:12.

24 *RB* 57:2

25 On the cellarer and prior *RB* 65; *RB* 31, counsellors for the wayward *RB* 27; doorkeeper *RB* 66; abbot: *RB* 2, 64.

26 On individuals having what they "need" *RB* 33,34; provision of adequate food and drink *RB* 39,40; clothes and shoes, *RB* 55; impossible tasks *RB* 68.

27 The entry for «listening» in thematic index to *RB 1980* makes the network of mutual listening clear, with the primary need for the whole community to listen for the divine voice.

***

Significantly, Salvado insisted that training for meaningful work, not education for its own sake, or literacy in or of itself, would secure the future for the Aboriginal Yued people. In his *Report* of 1900 Salvado took the Roman officials back through the history of the mission to show how both his initial aim of sharing the Aboriginal lifestyle and also the next hope of an agrarian village of workers had both been «a beautiful ideal», but impossible to achieve[28]. As it turned out, the monastic holdings could support only a limited number of families on wages of £1 a week. While the shared work of the monks and the Aborigines remained central to the town, Salvado increasingly saw New Norcia as the hub that would enable Aboriginal people to find a place in the community of European settlers. Religious instruction and education that would garner employment were the twin pillars of his approach. «The object of the missionary monks at New Norcia is then twofold, but with unity,» Salvado explained to the Prefect (this time the Polish Cardinal Halka-Ledóchowski):

> that is to say instructing the *Indigeni* in religious matters so they can become good Christians and save their souls, and at the same time instructing them in manual trades and mainly in agricultural occupations so that, by this practice, they can obtain the necessary means to live as good Christians wherever they are[29].

Proudly, Salvado noted that New Norcia's practical education offered the people more than other missions where literacy was emphasized for its own sake. Salvado insisted that however skilled the Yued-Noongar people became at bookwork, the racist context meant «they would not be employed if they could only read and write»[30]. In the minds of some commentators, Salvado's commitment to work was pragmatic, an alternative to the futile work of preaching. But the Benedictine's position was much more subtle. The interplay of Benedictine principles of prayer and work underpinned the pattern of life in the monastic mission town for the whole community not only for the monks.

In reporting on his approach, Salvado foregrounds his own monastic commitment and argues the work he undertook was essential to that commitment.

---

28 *Salvado 1900,* 50. See also K. Massam, «Introduction», in *Report of Rosendo Salvado to Propaganda Fide in 1900*, ed. and trans. S. Girola, Abbey Press, Northcote VIC 2016.

29 *Salvado 1900, 96.*

30 *Salvado 1900, 96.*

He laboured as he was able and called to do. He saw himself only as missionary and a monk, not a farmer or fundraiser, although he accepted that he had those roles and more for the sake of the mission. Equally the success of the farm and the town was not an end in itself, as the work of the people was not an end in itself. Work was an expression of his vocation. Similarly, under his influence others in town emerged in roles that both suited their capacities and fitted the purpose of the mission. Salvado's ability to see aptitude in others, combined with the conviction that gifts had a corresponding service, ran counter to any talk of work-life balance or work-life interference. It also ran counter to the racism of the colony.

Salvado detailed the achievements of Aboriginal workers to make the case that work underpinned dignity. The example of John Malley (Walley) captured the essence of his argument[31]. Malley's work in the capital as a skilled shoemaker attracted favourable press, but Salvado was more pleased by the report that reached him of the Aboriginal man refusing to take a job at the expense of another worker, explaining he would not deny someone else the bread they both needed. In this case the master cobbler employed them both. Malley's generosity was evidence for Salvado of solid Christian convictions.

In contrast to the «unfounded prejudice» they confronted, Salvado emphasised Aboriginal Australians were «capable, very capable, to achieve any education and culture whatsoever, both physical and intellectual, exactly the same as the European»[32]. The skilled work of three Aboriginal women employed as government telegraphists at New Norcia at different times in the 1870s attracted particular attention[33]. Mary Ellen Pangerian Cuper, Sarah Ninak and Carmen Ngarbak outshone their European male counterparts and astonished colonial authorities but Salvado was not surprised, «since I well knew that those Aborigines are unbeatable in these and similar operations»[34]. In the face of regular attempts to undermine and outsmart them, it was the unruffled dignity and patience of the telegraphists, even more than their skill, that Salvado pointed to as key achievements[35].

Work of other kinds was equally valuable when it supported a dignified presence. Salvado called attention to Eliza Tainan Willaway, a widow in her 40s, who

31 *Salvado 1883*, 156-157.

32 *Salvado 1900*, 84.

33 For example, *West Australian,* 29 April 1885, 3; *Freeman's Journal*, 7 November 1891,15; *Daily News*, 28 September 1891, 3.

34 *Salvado 1883*, 132.

35 *Salvado 1883*, 130-32; Salvado, *1900*, 60-67.

was an accomplished needleworker and baker and matron at the Girls' House. In 1889 she spoke on behalf of the women and girls of the mission to welcome the visiting Cardinal Moran. Felix Jackimarra, member of the prize-winning cricket team spoke on behalf of the men. These two leaders together with the champion shearers, expert ploughmen, women in various homesteads who kept in touch with each other by letter, and accomplished musicians in the string orchestra and brass band, all astounded the visitor. Salvado took the achievements in stride and posits the variety of skills as a «natural» outcome of human dignity and Christian discipleship. The Benedictine ethic at New Norcia attributed a profound relationship between work and holy living for women and for men in the mission town. That focus provided impetus for them to exercise leadership and responsibility that subverted prevailing stereotypes of both race and gender.

***

We noted at the outset of this discussion that the ontological realities of work as shaping identity are familiar to theologians. In the mid-1980s Michel Foucault directed attention to the ways in which particular philosophical schools of thought promoted disciplines of the body[36]. His work raised awareness of the bodily dimensions of the history of ideas, and of monastic history, as I have noted elsewhere[37]. Essentially the *Rule of Benedict* is not a set of beliefs that are assented to, but a way of life. Monasticism is embodied, and under its auspices so is Christian discipleship. In this way, the day to day realities of ploughing and administration, telegraphy and sewing fit Foucault's category of «technologies of the self». They are practices that create the self as a monastic person or Christian disciple. Work shapes us.

However, in response to Foucault's insight Pierre Hadot pointed to caveats in matters of faith. He argued persuasively that the endpoint of these technologies of belief is not the self, but beyond the self[38]. His clarification is that the

36 Especially M. Foucault *Histoire de la sexualité*, vol. 3: *Le souci de soi*, Gallimand, Paris 1984, in English as *The History of Sexuality*, vol 3: *The Care of the Self*, Vintage Books, New York 1986.

37 For example, see the discussion of related material in K. Massam, «Missionary Women and Holy Work», *Journal of Australian Studies* 39 (2015) 44-53.

38 P. Hadot, «Reflections on the Idea of the "Cultivation of Self"», in *Philosophy as a Way of Life: Spiritual Exercises from Socrates to Foucault*, trans. M. Chase, Blackwell, Oxford-New York 1995, 206-213. For the connections between Foucault and Hadot and their distinct views see C. Wimberly, «The Joy of Difference: Foucault and Hadot on

goal of the disciplined physical life is not discipline for its own sake. Spiritual disciplines, such as work, fasting, and modes of prayer, are practical tools but meant to reach beyond the immediate to a deeper goal. For Christian monastics the goal is holiness, salvation, God. So the physical practices of the *Rule* are not then technologies of the self, but strategies for transcending that self, for living a life that embodies values and beliefs outside and beyond the self.

At this point then, the work of the telegraph office and the kitchen and the Abbot's desk are exactly equivalent. The morse key, soup pot and letters to Rome were contrasting technologies in the reputation they had and in the remuneration they attracted, but to the monastic mind, each was an equivalent. Their purpose was not production, but that they enabled people to take their place in a community of commitment.

Reframing any particular task in this way points towards a fundamental monastic ethic that clarifies the purposes of work. If the work itself is the point we risk distorting the ethic with competition and envy. If the achievement of the person is the point the risk is pride, but if the purpose behind the work is to forge a deeper bond with our true selves and who we are in God, then we are in synch with a long tradition. The overarching focus in the monastic framework was «elsewhere», and the stock in trade of the lifestyle of the monks and so also for the people in their orbit was a commitment to technologies of holy living. Salvado's New Norcia suggests that the stark Christian question is simply: who or what does this work serve?

Abstract

The opening sentence of Chapter 48 of the *Rule of Benedict* warns that «idleness is the enemy of the soul». This has sometimes been read in contrast to the blessing of Eden. But in keeping with his reputation for balance and sanity, Benedict's full chapter on «manual labour» puts work in the context of rest, reading or study, and prayer. While idleness is an enemy activity is not a weapon in itself; instead work is a spiritual discipline in an ordered pattern of life.

This paper draws on the *Rule of Benedict* to explore the place of «work» and «leisure» in Christian life. It examines the place of work at the Benedic-

the Aesthetic and the Universal in Philosophy», *Philosophy Today* 53 (2009) 191-202; O. Irrera, «Pleasure and transcendence of the self. Notes on "A dialogue too soon interrupted between Michel Foucault and Pierre Hadot"», *Philosophy and Social Criticism* 36 (2010) 995-1017.

tine mission of New Norcia in Western Australia, both in the life of the nineteenth-century founder Rosendo Salvado and for the Yued-Noongar Australians who joined the mission, and sets the historical material in the context of Pierre Hadot's insights into the ancient «technologies of self» that aimed not so much to fashion an individual (as Michel Foucault has argued) but rather to form a disciple.

CONTEMPLATION AGAINST ECONOMIC INJUSTICE. INTER-SPIRITUAL DIALOGUE OF BENEDICTINE MONASTICISM WITH ENGAGED BUDDHISM

Thomas QUARTIER

INTRODUCTION

What is the relation between contemplation and personal and societal engagement in the face of economic injustice? In this article, the author takes as his starting point a number of field experiences in a Dutch Benedictine abbey. Here, students struggled with the dilemma of the desire to change the world, whilst at the same time feeling the need to walk the inward path[1]. Comparative dialogues were held, exploring the differences between Benedictine monasticism, the tradition of the researcher, and practitioners of Engaged Buddhism. Led by these dialogues, the method of "reciprocal illumination" enables the articulation of general thoughts regarding the horizon and the concrete steps of engaged contemplation against the notion of economic injustice. These steps are "not knowing", "bearing witness" and "loving action"; the horizon is the theological perspective of eschatology. Contemplation can in itself be a form of engagement (*actio in contemplatione*). This insight helps to reflect on the role of monastic life in a society which is often dominated by unjust economic mechanisms.

The relation between spirituality and economy is a complicated one. In recent years, spirituality has become a market of economic significance. There is also a quest for spiritual training to deal with the economic challenges people face in their professional or private lives. Monasteries are popular places where the self-affirmative way of handling the modern economy is cultivated, both to

Thomas Quartier, Benedictine monk of St. Willibrord Abbey in Doetinchem (NL), professor for Ritual and Liturgical Studies at Radboud University Nijmegen (NL) and for Monastic Spirituality at KU Leuven (BE), research fellow at Titus Brandsma Institute (NL), visiting professor at the Pontifical Athenaeum Sant'Anselmo in Rome.

1 T. QUARTIER, *Heilige Wut. Mönch sein heißt radikal sein*, Freiburg 2018, 107ff.

earn the living for the monastic community and to help visitors come to terms with their various functions in society. However, spiritual life can also offer a different perspective on economy: a more critical one when regarding economic injustice. Particularly when it comes to contemplative spirituality, such as in monasteries, it is important that we try to understand this criticism. The critical potential of monasteries is not often clearly visible to the outside world, however it is an integral part of what this spiritual form-of-life entails. Spiritual engagement is not merely confirmative, but touches and transforms existential attitudes. For the Benedictine monk Jakobus Kaffanke this transformation needs a substantial contemplative imbedding, and for him this is faith: "As a result of superficiality and the efflux of members, our societies are under stress and depleted. The only real answer to this development is radical renewal and re-affirmation of the Christian faith, a contemplative deepening of the mystery"[2]. The experience of the mystery is central in this contemplative countermovement. When today people often rely on different spiritual traditions, the basic question is how these various forms of contemplation do benefit in dealing with economic injustice.

From a religious studies point of view, it is not self-evident that the link between contemplation and societal engagement is actually made. This became particularly clear to me when some of the religious studies students of my faculty visited my abbey. They struggled with the challenge of social responsibility of our community and asked me as a monk of the abbey *and* professor at their university: "How can you spend your time in the choir stalls, when the world is suffering under economic injustice everywhere? Is it not self deceptive to focus on an inward path when a small minority (1%) of the world's population will own 99% of the economic wealth in a few years?" Obviously, monastic life gave some young students the impression of being unaware of the economic reality that cannot be neglected if you take your social responsibility seriously. The idea that opposing economic injustice requires an active role in society was self-evident to them. It is strange for contemporary individuals to consider that it can make sense to leave the world behind and live in a contemplative community in search of God – as a form of engagement against economic injustice in the world. "That might be spiritual, but contains no engagement," a student sketched the dilemma. "Why hide yourself away behind the walls of a monastery?".

2 *Das Schauen Gottes wiedererlangen: Kontemplation als Leben des inneren Menschen und als Herz des Mönchtums*, edd. L. Eibicht-J. Kaffanke-C. Schäfer (Weisungen der Väter 21), Beuron 2012, 8.

In a second experience, the visitors also felt the power of the inward path walked by the monastic community. "Could it be the ultimate critical contribution against economic injustice is to maintain a place of contemplation? Do the monks offer their prayers against injustice and suffering?" These questions point in a different direction. The idea of being critical within contemplative practice sounded counter-intuitive for many of them, but after some days in the monastery, existential questions came up. There may be a relation between contemplation and economic injustice: opposing the economic law of efficiency by rejecting it fully. This is only possible when the goal of your engagement is a spiritual one. Of course, this description is much too simplistic from a spiritual point of view, but it shows us the difficult position of contemplation in a society where even critical activity is measured according to its "economic" efficacy. In that perspective, contemplation and criticism against economic injustice do not seem to be happy bedfellows[3].

A third voice heard during my students' visit broadened the horizon in a comparative sense. "I practice zen-meditation, and I am frequently in doubt whether it is a waste of time. Is it just a way of training myself for the things I have to do in my life?" That would be a self-affirmative way of using spiritual practices. Another student had a clear opinion on this: "No, when I sit on the meditation cushion, I am aware of all the injustice in the world. And I change the world by meditating". Both repertoires, monastic and zen spirituality, are popular these days in Western societies. However, just like monasticism, Western Zen-Buddhism can quickly be perceived as a form of a comforting wellness training to ensure your capacity to handle the tasks you are confronted with in everyday life. Its potential can be a critical engagement against economic injustice and suffering in the world[4]. All three reactions of my students during their visit to the abbey encouraged me to conduct "consultative research"[5] on the question of how Benedictine spirituality – in dialogue with Buddhist Zen-practitioners – can contribute to a critique against economic injustice today. The research is consultative, because it is directly linked to my own spiritual engagement as Benedictine monk, and to the engagement of the dialogue partners from my own tradition and from Zen Buddhism who are involved.

3 T. Quartier, «Spirituality – Engagement and Reflection. Dialogical Explorations among Practitioners and Intellectuals», *Studies in Spirituality* 25 (2016) 307-330.

4 P. van der Velde, *De oude Boeddha in een nieuwe wereld. Verkenningen in de Westerse dharma*, Vantilt, Nijmegen 2015, 27.

5 R. Grimes, *Rite out of Place. Ritua, Media, and the Arts*, Oxford 2006.

The main research question is: *What does contemplation against economic injustice mean in a monastic perspective and how does this relate to engaged Buddhism?* When studying ancient and contemporary resources, I quickly found that both Buddhism and Benedictine Monasticism have some interesting perspectives to offer. To be able to illuminate my own view on the Benedictine tradition, I entered a dialogue with Engaged Buddhism, inspired by the religious studies perspective of my students. Reciprocal illumination of traditions can be a benefit for all[6]. In the first part of this article, the question will be asked, what engaged contemplation means and what a dialogue between Benedictine monasticism and Engaged Buddhism can add to its meaning (1). In the second part, I describe the two traditions (2), and in the third part the actual dialogues held for the research and the inter-spiritual perspectives that were opened (3). Finally, I return to the main question of societal engagement from within a contemplative life (4).

1. ENGAGED CONTEMPLATION IN DIALOGUE

Not only visitors experience difficulties when it comes to the question of how to relate to society where injustice today is greater than ever before in human history. This also applies to practitioners in contemplative life. One of the members of my monastic community said to a student during her stay at our guesthouse: "I would like to go to political demonstrations, protest against war and injustice directly, but my contemplative life makes that impossible." Obviously, contemporary monks can experience political relevance and their way of life as separate realities. "As I obviously cannot hold a protest vigil in front of a political building, I choose to look for my engagement here in the abbey." It seems that the relevance of a contemplative form of life is restricted to the arena of the monastery and not beyond. That puts this kind of contemplation outside society, because today the growing mobility enables people to quickly move from one spot to the other and goes against the monastic vow of stability. Therefore, not only modern society, but also contemplative life as such, from the inside, seems to question the relationship between contemplation and engagement that enables spirituality to fully take place. The preconditions in society and in contemporary monasticism seem to be rather clear in that contemplative life might be inspiring and worth living for an individual or group, but it does not engage with the course the world takes

6 A. Sharma, *Religious Studies and Comparative Methodology. The Case for Reciprocal Illumination*, New York 2006.

beyond the monastery walls and the economic injustices to be found there. However, this is a rather one-sided image. The critical function of spirituality in society is based on a complex relationship between practices of spirituality and effects. As if spiritual interventions are treatments for issues, where success depends on the solutions applied. Societal relevance in a spiritual sense can be much more indirect and implicit. Still, the question remains how it can be found among the young students and the monk in my abbey in the Netherlands.

From the perspective of spirituality studies, the relation between action and contemplation is the basis of every spiritual engagement. According to Waaijman, "A certain tension between the pure contemplative practice and everyday actions is unavoidable". But that does not mean that this tension has not led to a productive synthesis in the history of spirituality[7]. Many active religious congregations found their contemplation in their concrete everyday actions. Being with the poor, for example, is a pure act of contemplation (*contemplatio in actione*). In the twentieth century we saw an impressive amount of vocations geared in this direction, but at the same time, the crisis of the relationship between action and contemplation can be observed. Many religious people lost their space for contemplation, as they were so strongly engaged in social practices that they simply did not manage to reserve time and attentiveness for a more quiet and peaceful way of searching for God. In the midst of the economically dominated world, attention is fragile and the claim that it is possible to find God everywhere can be hard to fulfil when there are no contemplative forms available. Another synthesis of action and contemplation can be found in contemplative religious life. Here, the twentieth century has also led to significant insights. In the 1960s, Christian monks searched for their roots and found that the early monks indeed existed outside the world, but regularly returned to criticise ecclesial and political developments. They walked the streets without belonging there. Furthermore, through interreligious dialogue they found that within Eastern spirituality the link between society and monastery was very close.[8] But how can these insights be brought into your own contemplative life? Here we arrive at the need for dialogue between Buddhism and Western monasticism, which we owe to the pioneers from that period, and which enriches contemplation against economic injustice.

---

7 K. Waaijman, *Spiritualiteit. Vormen, grondslagen, methoden*, Kok, Kampen 2000, 342ff [*Spirituality. Forms, Foundations, Methods*, Leuven 2002].

8 D. Steindl-Rast, *Ich bin durch Dich so ich*, Münsterschwarzach 2016, 92.

The autobiographical writings of Brother David Steindl-Rast impressively show a witness of this movement. He acquired an increasingly critical potential from contemplative life. For example, he has become involved in an online project in recent years: "Our website is going to be revolutionary – and contemplative. We want to build a network of persons worldwide. Everything that connects people is revolutionary in our society which is dominated by hierarchical powers."[9] Brother David is clearly referring to the most famous pioneer to be mentioned here, the American Trappist monk Thomas Merton. For Merton, Christian love needs to be found within your own interior and needs to flow out to the world[10]. This brought him to political engagement in his later period. He opposed the Vietnam War and was engaged as a writer and activist, together with many representatives of the political left. To do this, he indeed rediscovered the roots of his monasticism and sought inspiration in the dialogue with Buddhist monks who had already worked on an engaged form of contemplation before that period[11]. However, the consciousness of engagement as a consequence of your contemplative vocation has quickly disappeared from many monastic agendas. Of course, today's social climate is not directed towards political engagement in general, and the voice against economic injustice from the last decades can no longer be heard particularly loudly. But another reason could also be a lack of hermeneutical dialogue among contemplatives themselves. The witness of Brother David, who is still very active in his nineties, in the footsteps of Merton and many others, urges all people who are confronted with the dilemma between action and contemplation, opposing economic injustice and the inward path, to build a network that helps to create a truly contemplative synthesis against what is wrong in the world (*actione in contemplatione*).

What is needed for the students visiting my Dutch abbey and for the monk looking for a place where social engagement can take place, is a spiritual dialogue with their own tradition and with other schools of spirituality. The experience of the 1960s era shows that the strength of contemplative traditions can be very inter-spiritually oriented. Contemplation unifies traditions. For contemporary searchers, this unifying effect needs to be socially engaged. Monks and nuns should rediscover their *actio*, similar to active religious people endeavouring to rediscover their *contemplatio*. Their specific charism in this rediscovery could be that

9 Steindl-Rast, *Ich bin durch Dich so ich*, 161-162.

10 T. Merton, *No man is an island*, HBJ Book, New York 1978.

11 B. Griffiths, *Essential Writings*, ed. Th. Matus (Modern Spiritual Masters Series), Maryknoll (NY) 2004.

they offer a dimension of engagement that is not caught up in criteria of efficiency, one which is slower than any other place in society. Contemplation as such can be a form of engagement. Our abbeys could be an inspiration for many different forms of social engagement. The hypothesis derived from these thoughts reads as follows: *the reinvention of contemplative engagement can be a source for other forms of engagement against economic injustice in contemporary society.*

Of course, this hypothesis cannot be verified or falsified, as the results of contemplative engagement cannot always be measured empirically. We can try to enter spiritual dialogues from a Benedictine perspective. What is meant by spiritual dialogues here? There is a long tradition in spiritual dialogues that result in an open model of deep communication – not primarily directed to solutions, but to insight (*collatio*). Waaijman distinguishes a few important ingredients of such a dialogue: first, it means listening to each other's voices among dialogue partners; second, it means to depart from affairs that touch all of the partners and that can be compared from each other's point of view; third, new insights can be gained that are enriching for the spiritual understanding of the affairs shared[12]. This model can be used as an instrument for spiritual research[13], as we will see with regard to the topic of engaged contemplation against economic injustice in this article. The dialogue I want to lead from my own tradition with practitioners of Engaged Buddhism needs clarification first. In the second part, I will explore these schools, Benedictine and Buddhist. After that, I will report from the actual dialogues. We will learn about contemporary experience of contemplation and share practices on a personal level regarding social order and economic injustice.

2. TRADITIONS: BENEDICTINE MONASTICISM AND ENGAGED BUDDHISM

Inspiration for engagement against economic injustice can be found both in Christian and Buddhist schools of spirituality. The first significant tradition in this regard is Christian monasticism. The inspiration relies strongly on the horizon of the engagement, which is always divine. This horizon might be an interesting ingredient in the dialogue to follow. The other dialogue partner comes from Buddhist spiritual tradition. Engagement contains concrete steps against suffering,

---

12 WAAIJMAN, *Spiritualiteit*, 777-779.

13 T. QUARTIER, «Monastisches Engagement in Kunst und Kultur. Lebensentwürfe im hermeneutischen Lehrgespräch mit dem Liedermacher Konstantin Wecker», *Studies in Spirituality* 24 (2015) 313-338.

with economic injustice as one important cause of suffering. In this way, you can relate your own contemplation of concrete situations. What could this horizon and those concrete steps mean, regarding engagement against economic injustice? It is worth exploring these ingredients before we explore the actual meeting in the next paragraph. First we listen to the voice of the origins of engaged monasticism, and secondly to the voice of the steps to be taken in engaged Buddhism.

2.1. Monasticism and engagement

Although monastic spirituality had a societal relevance from its very beginning, it often runs the risk of losing this. There is a notion that the doors of the monastery are perceived as a deep gap: they mark a one way street – you can enter, but you will never leave[14]. Saying farewell to the world implies not only independence from it, but also indifference to it. This resulted in a way of monastic life that was alienated from real life, both inside and beyond the monastery: inside in the sense of an autistic attitude – residing next to each other in the community without reciprocal engagement – and outside in the sense of neglecting economic injustice, oppression and political reality. These tendencies run parallel with the field notes in our introduction. However, the relation to the world is not necessarily one of ignorance. When Michael Casey talks about monks being "strangers to the city", this does not imply that they do not *relate* to the city. The stranger is not a part of the economic life of the city, but he still plays an important role[15].

If we want to enter a spiritual dialogue in search of a synthesis of action and contemplation, it is important not to get stuck in possible alienations, but instead to search for the original intuition of monasticism. Both tendencies of an autistic life and of alienation from the world are not in line with the early tradition of monasticism. In the life and teachings of the father of Western monasticism, St Benedict, we find two arenas of engagement: the *other* and the *world*. In his famous Rule (RB), he clearly reminds his monks of the obligation to "be the first to show respect to each other, supporting with the greatest patience one another's weaknesses of body or behaviour and earnestly competing in obedience to one another" (RB 72, 4-7)[16]. Our spiritual search is never independent of the others

14 T. Quartier, «De kunst van het loslaten. Monastieke stabiliteit in tijden van grotere flexibiliteit», *De Kovel. Monastiek tijdschrift voor Vlaanderen en Nederland* 34 (2014) 20-31.

15 M. Casey, *Strangers to the city. Reflections on the Beliefs and Values of the Rule of St Benedict*, Brewster 2005.

16 T. Fry, *The Rule of St Benedict* (Vitage Spiritual Classics), New York 1998.

living together with us, whether they are economically effective or not. Without directing our spiritual engagement towards the other (*obedience*), including the imperfect state and the dissonant impulses this might result in, contemplation would be empty. For monks, the monastic community is the first arena for contemplative engagement (*actio*). Build a just economy among yourselves!

But next to that, this community is not an island, it is relevant to and a model for the world. We find this clearly illustrated in the life of St Benedict, as described by Pope Gregory the Great. In his vita we read a passage that shows the socio-political relevance of contemplative monastic life. Benedict is visited by king Totila, who had threatened the people of Italy and brought disastrous economic injustice to the inhabitants:

> "When Totila saw him sitting far off, he did not dare to approach but prostrated himself on the ground. The man of God said two or three times "Get up!" But he did not dare to rise from the earth before him, so Benedict, servant of Jesus Christ, was kind enough to go himself to the prostrate king. He raised him from the ground and rebuked him for his deeds. Then in a few words he foretold all that would happen to him. "You are doing much evil, and you have done much evil. It is time to stop this poor behaviour! At any rate, you will enter Rome, you will cross the sea. You will reign nine years and die on the tenth". When he heard this, the king shook with terror. He begged for prayers and departed. From that time on he was less cruel. Not long afterward he did take Rome, and then crossed over to Sicily. And in the tenth year of his reign, by the judgment of God, he lost his kingdom and his life" (VB 15)[17].

We find how the life of a monk becomes a vital sign that is highly relevant to societal power. However, Benedict's engagement is not a grasping of power, but is simply letting the king participate in his contemplative space, and trying to give him insight into the true nature of his deeds of injustice. The very nature of the engagement is invisible: the king is only aware of its power when he actually enters the sacred place of contemplation. The social arena for contemplative engagement with the world is the engagement itself. Being in the monastery does not, in a Benedictine sense, mean to have no influence, rather, it means to just be there.

But what is the special character of the engagement that makes it relevant for community and societal leaders? In case of the king, it is the Divine prophecy that Benedict relates. He offers an apocalyptic scenario for the king. And in case

17 T.G. Kardong, *The Life of St Benedict by Gegory the Great*, Collegeville 2009, 63.

of the community, it is also the Divine nature of shared monastic life. Benedict is clear about that in the chapter from the RB that was quoted earlier: "Just as there is a wicked zeal of bitterness which separates from God and leads to hell, so there is a good zeal which separates from evil and leads to God and everlasting life" (RB 72, 1-3). Obviously it is not just a question of human justice, but of Divine justification. The goal of contemplative engagement is eschatological: "To their fellow monks they show the pure love of brothers; to God loving fear; to their abbot unfeigned and humble love. Let them prefer nothing whatever to Christ, and may he bring us all together to everlasting life" (RB 72, 8-12).

The monk has directed his search for God through his engaged contemplation, and that is the core of his monastic life (RB 58, 7). But why is it then that my young students visiting the abbey get the impression that there is no practical relevance to monastic life? And why does the monk quoted feel he misses an arena for engagement with the world? These kinds of questions are not so much of a principal nature but are very concrete indeed. Obviously, the concrete practice has occasionally lost its link with the engagement that is included in the origins of monasticism. The search for this link between origin and contemporary practice is one possible motivation to enter the spiritual dialogue: to share best practices and enrich your synthesis of contemplation and action.

2.2. Engaged Buddhism

How is the link between contemplation and concrete praxis laid in Engaged Buddhism? It is one of the characteristics of this type of Zen that concrete arenas of contemplative engagement are sought[18]. Retreats are no longer held in the meditation centre (*zendo*), but together with the homeless on the street. This is obviously a choice which differs from the one that the monk in my abbey makes. The relation between the outer world and the inner world of the monastery is turned on its head: contemplation does in this case not occur inside the separated contemplative space, but in unity with the suffering. Still, it is not a social project, as the perspective of being with the homeless is meditative. You are not trying to solve their problems, but to live among them. This means that contemplation is a way of engagement that is different from a practical one, although the two can surely be complementary. Of course, there are also many social projects in Engaged Buddhism. These occur at the margins of society and have an effect on the inner world. The desire is comparable to our monk: to let your contemplation be socially rel-

18 Van der Velde, *De oude Boeddha*, 260-263.

evant and engaged. This does not mean to replace contemplative exercises with political demonstrations, but to *relate* the exercises to the world – the poor who are obliged to live at the sharp end of economic injustice.

For this purpose, you can follow three steps that the Zen master Bernard Glassman distinguishes. They relate people to the suffering that surrounds them (*dukha*) in a truthful way. This is a central concept in Buddhism. First, there is the step of "*not knowing*"[19]. You relate to the suffering you meet in the world. This step is different from involved activism, but also from the apathy that can result from leaving the world fully. Openness is the most important virtue of not knowing. What sounds plausible is not self-evident at all. Quickly, the self-confirmative effect of meditative exercises closes the meaning ascribed to suffering. The openness morphs into an illusory world. The other risk is blind activism. To be so closely engaged with concrete suffering and economic injustice that you forget the ultimate perspective that enables suffering to be contemplated. This is again not an open attitude: there is a presupposition of knowing what the solution to suffering is and how it can be stopped.

This can rapidly lead to disappointments, as no one can effectively end all the suffering and economic injustice they perceive in the world. Consider the monk: for him it is essential to stick to his life, and not try to escape the state of not knowing. If he neglected this stable way of remaining in his place, and was continuously touring to demonstrate for peace, he would run the risk of claiming to have a recipe for knowledge. On the other hand, he may not forget the dimension of his responsibility for justice, because that would close his openness. The dilemma from our introduction cannot yet be resolved.

The second step of Engaged Buddhism helps contemplative persons relate to this dilemma. What can we do if we cannot end all suffering? We have to *"bear witness"* to the pain we perceive and injustice in the world. In a contemplative sense, this implies a way to deal with suffering that cannot be measured with the criterion of efficiency, where the only important result would be that something is resolved. It is important to just stand or sit (meditatively) and do justice to the suffering that one perceives exactly by standing by or sitting with the suffering persons. Together with the first step of not knowing, bearing witness forms the core of this type of Zen. But how do you bear witness to suffering?

In the end you need an ultimate truth to accept suffering in the choir stalls as our monk, or while sitting on the meditation cushion. This truth can be found in

19 B. Glassman, *Bearing Witness. A Zen-Master's Lessons in Making Peace*, New York 1998.

the inner self where every witness has its origin. The witness that our monk, as well as many other seekers, bears is contemplative truth. But, the Christian monk will of course relate to a revealed truth in the witness of Jesus Christ, which the Buddhist will not. Still, the witness as such unites the Zen-practitioner and the monk. Every witness of suffering needs patience and stability. To stand the challenge of bearing witness *is* already engagement. But is that all? In engaged Buddhism it is necessary that to witness also has practical consequence[20].

The third step is, therefore, "*loving action*". The truthfulness of contemplation makes it so that the love that is perceived in your inner self streams out and becomes a responsible action in the world. But this is, again, another form of worldliness opposed to the criterion of efficiency in a functional sense. As if it would be a better kind of love if the scope of the practical engagement were broader, more efficient. It is important that love *becomes* the way in which you contemplate the suffering in the world. This will automatically make the pain less dominant and less threatening. No one can remain fully in the stage of not-knowing. The engagement requires witnesses, but even this is not sufficient; there will always be an intrinsic motivation for loving action. It all becomes truthful in practice, but without the meditative embedding, practice is impossible.

It would be a far too narrow idea of action to reduce the complex relationship between bearing witness and loving action to merely problem solving strategies. What needs to be done in every concrete situation (what is the loving action)? Simply do what needs to be done, is the answer from the contemplative humus of Engaged Buddhism. The goal of this type of engagement is not to grasp each and every opportunity. It means to be in your place with a contemplative attitude and reduce the suffering that surrounds you by doing what is just from the witness you bear, without knowing beforehand what will be the exact message or meaning of your action. Of course we can think of the monk from my Dutch abbey: his starting point is staying in place (*stabilitas*). This is a kind of contemplative virtue for him. It can surely be seen as a concrete form of bearing witness that Engaged Buddhism tries to evoke. But let us also think about my students who react with doubts about the relevance of monastic life: from the perspective of Engaged Buddhism, you could suggest withholding quick judgments about how effective an engagement might be. It is not only the scope that is decisive, but perhaps even more it is the depth of contemplative engagement. The dilemma is still not removed, but the relation with the world becomes the

20 *Pearls of Ash and Awe. 20 Years of Bearing Witness in Auschwitz with Bernie Glassman & Zen Peacemakers*, ed. K. Battke, Berlin 2015.

starting point for concrete loving action that suits everyone's particular way of life. Engaged Buddhism demonstrates a challenging and inspiring synthesis for everyone who wants to live contemplatively. Of course, the idea of not knowing can be found in many spiritual traditions. And for monks this perspective is well known. But the dilemma we sketched shows how practitioners run the risk of losing their engagement or their contemplation by *knowing* what the right path is. The fragile synthesis needs best practices, and Engaged Buddhism can perhaps offer a mirror for every form of engaged spirituality. Not knowing is always necessary, and monasteries are just like meditation centres and everyday places of contemplation, in that they are good spots to exercise it.

Of course, there are more spiritual virtuosi[21] who are witnesses to suffering, not just in Engaged Buddhism. A distant past in schools of spirituality, pioneers of contemplative life and/or resistance against economic injustice are often cited. However, when contemplation becomes a form of bearing witness, this happens in the here and now. Only by acting here and now can you relate to everything and everyone. Basic Buddhist thought is at stake here. The unity of contemplation and action is formed by a continuously meditative life and attentive exercises that can take place on the street *and* in the refectory of the monastery. Witnesses are never far away, but the monk who wonders how he can engage is also a witness, perhaps for the students who are full of doubt. Still, the best practices remain empty if there is no concrete, practical side to the contemplative coin. Otherwise you could still ask whether these thoughts are too idealistic. Are there lived witnesses to suffering who can help the monk, the students, and anybody who is searching for engaged contemplation? It is exactly this search for lived spirituality that engaged me in an inter-spiritual dialogue with two prominent practitioners and teachers of Engaged Buddhism.

3. PERSONAL AND SOCIAL INTER-SPIRITUAL PERSPECTIVES: DIALOGUES

Engaged contemplation touches practitioners deeply into the core. Bearing witness can shake the foundations of anyone's existence. Everything you were supposed to know is different when bearing witness to suffering – often the result of economic injustice. In the choir stalls, at the meditation centre, or in everyday situations of contemplation, true suffering is present if you remain

21 M. Riesebrodt, *Cultus und Heilsversprechen. Eine Theorie der Religionen*, Munich 2007, 176.

open to it. You can learn from specific contemplative moments and contexts, and discover arenas of contemplative engagement by keeping your meditation open. This applies to every contemplative way of life, from Buddhist practitioners to the monk and the students looking for inspiration. The relevance of meditation as a form of being united with the world, not separated from it, is one of the reasons why Engaged Buddhism is relevant in inter-spiritual dialogue with Christian monastic life[22]. Bearing witness directs every person to reality, to touch its full dimensions, to the good things, but also to suffering. You can then play creatively with the relationship between action and contemplation.

The risk of becoming alienated from the world can be avoided by contemplating suffering. Sometimes you will no longer perceive suffering because you are caught up in the meditation hall or the chapel. One presupposes to already know the truth. Is this the case with the Christian monk? If he seriously takes the message of Christianity as an ultimate horizon for his practice, he can never assume to know what salvation is. St Benedict did not show a concrete treatment to king Totila. Rather, he offered an alternative perspective gained from his monastic life, and which changed the world. Monasticism can perhaps help to avoid losing the ultimate perspective, the openness of a fulfilment that we are still awaiting (eschatologically). There are no simple recipes for a better world, but there are living witnesses. One can relate to suffering in the monastery exactly by being united with all things, as St Benedict showed by directing the monastic community towards mutual love and respect. And you can do this on the street, searching for the open horizon where an end will be made to the suffering being witnessed. Everyone who is engaged contemplatively, Buddhist or Christian, can change the world and make it better. This is the starting point for the dialogues I led. For the Buddhist witnesses, I found two Zen teachers: Joan Halifax, who works with the dying on a personal transformation, and David Loy, whose engagement is directed towards societal order and a form of social revolution.

3.1. Personal transformation

If we wish to develop an attitude towards changing economic injustice, this can never be separated from personal suffering. Economic injustice is a result of an egocentric culture that does not respect human fragility and contingency.

22 K. Wecker-B. Glassman, *Die revolutionäre Kraft des Mitgefühls*, Munich 2013.

The first suffering we have to bear witness of is the individual person's burden of death. Zen teacher Joan Halifax offers spiritual care to the dying, and has been doing so for decades. Her starting point is contemplation with a strong inter-spiritual orientation[23]. In her we meet a first witness of engaged contemplation, and an engaged dialogue partner for our search of engaged resistance against injustice. In the Upaya Zen-centre which Halifax set up, the terminally ill, their loved ones, and professional care givers are welcomed into a contemplative environment. Here, the unjust situation of an economically determined healthcare system is undermined. The truthfulness of being with the dying is not a matter of buying treatments or knowledge. It rather concerns "direct experience", as Halifax stresses in our dialogue[24]. That means for her a contemplative attitude which "switches off reason". "Isn't that a bit vague?" I ask. "No," is Roshi Joan's answer, "many professional caregivers react much too strongly when they are confronted with death. The reason is that they are afraid of losing grip on a situation that cannot be grasped with mere reason. Death can be a very contemplative moment. One just needs to have the courage to really be with the dying. That transcends the boundaries of reason and creates openness." And what does it mean to bear witness at a deathbed?

> First of all, it means to bear witness of your own mortality. Being with dying makes you realise that you are going to die yourself. Then you can help people by contemplating peace with human mortality. This will give peace to the dying, as well as to their loved ones, and you can be engaged in true loving action.

That does not sound like a vague illusion. In one of her books, Halifax stresses that contemplation entails very concrete transitions: *personal transformations* of which death is the most crucial. For her, contemplation together with the dying person is a continuous transformation, in the sense of a rite of passage. You can learn to leave things behind in the face of death: "To free your mind and be really engaged with life." That is the first step of a rite of passage[25]. It creates the openness that is essential for contemplation. The second step, transformation, "does not take place in a mysterious veil of ignorance but in bearing

23 J. HALIFAX, *The Fruitful Darkness. A Journey Through Buddhist Practice and Tribal Wisdom*, New York 1993.

24 The dialogue with Roshi Joan Halifax took place on 17 December 2014. The conversation has been taped and coded. In a further step of analysis, core quotations have been selected, some of which are presented in this article.

25 A. VAN GENNEP, *The Rites of passage*, Chicago 1961.

witness to mortality in a very concrete situation – the suffering of the dying and of yourself." The third step, integration, helps the engaged persons to act by being present. "In the Zen centre a contemplative space is kept open – and that *is* loving action."[26] This is a strong statement against economic injustice in many healthcare institutions in Western society today. Leave the space open for real transformation, beyond economic categories.

How does this wisdom relate to a monastic charism? Monastically speaking, the *memento mori* found in the Rule of St Benedict is an important parallel: "Day by day remind yourself that you are going to die" (RB 4, 47). The perspective of not knowing and being open is broadened by Benedict in the sense of God's salvation, which offers a perspective for every person. This does not contradict being with the dying, on the contrary; being with the dying is an additional impulse for Christian monks not to forget the concrete situation of *memento mori*. The otherworldliness that is stressed in Christianity is, of course, not shared by Halifax. But she makes clear that "there are many ways to salvation". Perhaps the sense of an ultimate salvation can help Engaged Buddhists remember the eschatological horizon of their engagement. It is impressive to hear Roshi Joan talk about how contemplation enriches her way of thinking:

> It broadens every rational deliberation. When you meditate, you are present in the first and third person at the same time. You are engaged in contemplative exercise, and by doing so you are able to observe yourself from the outside. Meditation liberates you from the prison of your prejudices and frees your perception.

If you get the impression that meditation might become irrelevant at a particular moment and that only concrete praxis counts, Halifax immediately corrects this misunderstanding: "There are many ways, indeed, but there needs to be an explicit space for contemplative exercises, otherwise people forget their engagement and are not really present at a deathbed." If you are really engaged contemplatively, "you touch on death automatically. As soon as this happens, everyone is truthful." This also applies to monks: Benedict describes it as a central spiritual virtue to "leave your own will behind" (RB 7, 12). This does not mean to neglect your life, but to be open, not being caught up in your own will and suspicion, dominated by economic categories. To do so, you need to remain in the choir stall and be willing to help whoever needs help in the concrete sit-

26 J. Halifax, *Being with Dying. Cultivating Compassion and Fearlessness in the Presence of Death*, Boston 2009.

uation. Sometimes you will be physically present at the deathbed, and at other times "in spirit", by keeping open a space for contemplation on which the dying, the bereaved, and professionals can depend. Monasteries are such spaces– and they have a high value for a culture of dying. In this sense, hopefully every hospital, nursing home, or hospice is a something of a monastery, and not just a commercial business.

The starting point for creating a contemplative space for the dying is your own inner self. If this is taken seriously, you can discover open experiences of suffering, and bear witness to them. The wisdom from spiritual traditions like Christianity and Buddhism can, in this way, meet in the engaged contemplation of death. The inhabitants of the Upaya Zen-centre and the monastery are, in this respect, close to one another. Contemplative experience does not confuse the beliefs articulated (reincarnation or resurrection), but it functions as a shared inspiration to discover an open horizon. Different traditions help to withstand the dilemma sketched in our introduction.

3.2. Social revolution

Contemplation opens the doors of spiritual revolution for social order. This is the core message of my dialogue with Zen teacher and philosopher David Loy. Really? How can an apparently individualistic worldview like Zen lead to social change? Many societal problems find their origin in the disturbed relationship Western individuals have with their inner self. They live in dualities, as Loy puts it. Perhaps contemplative persons can also run the risk of getting stuck in dualities. The monk from my abbey seems to struggle with the duality of spiritual life and worldly action. The dilemma remains present. If you want to change the world and its social order, you need to start with the relationship with your own interior. And that is a plea for contemplation. Does Engaged Buddhism shed light on the path the Christian monk is seeking, and vice versa?

Throughout the dialogue with the teacher David, I am constantly struggling with the question of which criterion is relevant for social change. What is true? What is my real inner self and what is not?[27] How can our monk know what is the right way to relate to the world? As soon as we enter the intersubjective field of social order, the scope of truthful action seems to become less incidental. As if there may be something like an objective truth. Does that contradict the first step of "not knowing"? If we do not accept any claim of truth, how can our monk

27 The dialogue with David Loy took place on 19 November 2014. Cf. note 24.

know when it is better to stay away from demonstration, and remain ensconced in the monastery? Is it socially wrong to be focused on just one place, here and now, in the monastery or in the meditation centre? The question of truth cannot be answered by dogmatic assumptions, if we take the contemplative path seriously, but it is also difficult to leave it completely open-ended. For Loy, the answer must be "liberation from suffering", just as for Roshi Joan on a personal level (i.e. *being with the dying*). According to him there are several layers of suffering. Next to the personal suffering in the face of death, there also exists a form on the societal level, an explicit form of economic injustice: "There is a lot of structural suffering, this kind of *dukha* is what I am aiming at. The way to liberation implies that one has the courage to revolt against suffering. This is possible if you discover your inner self; being a subject beyond duality."[28] Again, you get the impression, just like in my dialogue with Joan Halifax, that this sounds rather vague. Who searches for this kind of path in an economically dominated world?

The spiritual philosopher makes a clear statement on this: "To explore the boundaries of truth does not mean that there is no truth. Contemplation does not neglect truth, but helps to find it." The monk can find the truth in what he is doing exactly by doing it. As Loy writes:

> That's why today's social order can benefit from Buddhism. The practices of contemplation are directed to knowing yourself and liberating yourself from its boundaries. Just like the modern mind struggles for freedom. Buddhism helps to give depth to that struggle and liberates our social and economic order from the many prejudices it is based on: more and more profit, more effective time management. That prohibits people from really enjoying the deep value of things. And that is the source of injustice and suffering[29].

Here we find a similarity with the position that St Benedict took in his era, and with lived spirituality in contemporary monasticism: the way to the inner self is liberated from prejudices. The lesson we can learn from monasticism is the concentration on the here and now of your place and time (*claustrum*), which does not permit vagueness. This stability guarantees again not to lose sight of the horizon of ultimate salvation. Loy's vision of Engaged Buddhism sketches a political perspective that cannot be forgotten in engaged contemplation

28 D.R. Loy, *A new Buddhist path. Enlightenment, evolution and ethics in the modern world*, Somerville 2015.

29 D.R. Loy, *Money, Sex, War, Karma. Notes for a Buddhist revolution*, Somerville 2008.

– the political and eschatological dimensions can enrich each other. "We need concrete practice and at the same time social relevance – and all of this with a spiritual horizon," and that is the shared programme in our dialogue. The truthfulness of the social revolution depends on the personal transformation, as mentioned in the last dialogue, and this comes from contemplation. This means that engagement can only be contemplative, and contemplation must be verified and deepened in engagement. How, then, can it be socially engaged if the central path runs inwards?

The place for contemplation is, according to David Loy, first and foremost a lived spiritual life. This can take place in a monastery, where you invest a great deal of time and attention on contemplative exercises, but this is not an absolute prerequisite. Contemplation within the world (and outside the monastery) is also absolutely necessary if you do not want to lose the aim of social engagement: "It is not very difficult to be enlightened in a meditation centre. But is that real transformation?" Loy asks. "Only by being engaged can the transformation be really alive." The inward as well as the outward path are both necessary for social revolution: "Monastic life has created whilst simultaneously destroying contemplation. Spiritual life was cultivated, but it lost its social relevance." Does this mean that contemplative "professionals" like our monk are not necessary? "No, they are very necessary, but they must not forget that they are engaged within the structural suffering of the world. A monastery or meditation centre must not become an island". We can sum up this insight as follows: "Engagement deepens your contemplation". It belongs to contemplation, but without contemplation, this type of social revolution is impossible. This is a counterintuitive idea that contradicts the spontaneous reactions of the young people in my abbey. But in spirituality often the counterintuitive insights bring us closer to a core of truth that different spiritual traditions share.

Still, the question remains open as to what social engagement can be in practical terms. In our dialogue, we see many possibilities. The monk, the professor, the caregiver and the students, they are all *engaged* in one way or another against economic injustice. And they are searching for contemplation. The truth that can be found in the inner self can be many different things – emptiness, God, Jesus. In every case it streams out in the form of compassionate engagement with the world[30]. This means that the decision of our monk to stay in the monastery can be an authentic form of contemplative engagement (*actio in contempatione*) that does not exclude practical social engagement with a contemplative horizon (*contemplatio in actione*). These are all forms of spirituality which enable

30 Cf. K. Armstrong, *Twelve Steps to a Compassionate Life*, New York 2010.

subjects to find personal transformation and be involved in social revolution in accordance with their particular charism.

4. ECONOMIC INJUSTICE: A CALL FOR REFLECTION

What would brother David Steindl-Rast and brother Thomas Merton feel when reading the summaries of inter-spiritual dialogues? They would probably recognise what they themselves wrote about economic injustice; that engagement for justice presupposes you are at peace with yourself. Without contemplation, it is impossible to contribute to an economically just way of treating individuals and to political activities. If this is true, contemplation becomes a universal source of revelation for all people: those who belong to your own tradition, to another tradition, or to no tradition at all[31]. And what is a possible path to follow? The experience of meeting representatives of Engaged Buddhism grounds contemplation:

- *not knowing* implies that you leave certainties behind, including social prejudices and patterns;
- *bearing witness* means that you are existentially involved, and that you make a visible statement;
- *loving action* helps engaged contemplatives transform their inspiration into reality.

This can take place in many different *places*. Of course, it is not everyone's charism to hold their retreat on the street with the homeless, and not everyone enjoys spending their time in the closed space of the monastery. But there is no good or bad, as long as the dilemma of contemplation and action is not resolved too quickly. As already indicated, you need to be careful not to eliminate the differences between spiritual traditions: the *horizons* and meaning systems can be very different. The profound reflection on the role of Christ in meditation by fr. Laurence Freeman shows the significance of theological substantial wisdom[32]. The common contemplative core – insights and practices – helps practitioners to constantly reflect on the balance they find for themselves. This is true for the monk in my abbey, who was already reflecting on this question. But it can also be a challenge for the young students. Let us conclude with the hope that the

31 T. Merton, *Contemplation in a World of Action*, Notre Dame (IN) 1999.

32 L. Freeman, *Jesus – the Teacher Within*, Continuum, London 2000.

practitioners and teachers we met from Engaged Buddhism and Benedictine life take this challenge seriously[33].

When economic injustice touches the individual, contemplation can contribute to its transformation. And if it touches groups and societies, it entails a social revolution, which might turn out to be very different from what is usually expected. The economy of the every day is in fact the space for the Holy, and for that reason it is of eminent importance that contemplation safeguards economic justice on the levels we have seen. This is a hopeful sign on the way to engaged contemplation and an important topic for every scholar working on spirituality.

Abstract

The relation between contemplation and personal and societal engagement highly determines the relevance of monastic life in the face of economic injustice. Today, many visitors of Benedictine abbeys do not automatically experience their critical function. Do monks escape the threat of economic injustice in the world by hiding behind the walls of their monastery? How does their form-of-life relate to other schools of spirituality? In an inter-spiritual perspective, we find different models of directly or indirectly being engaged with suffering in the world, for example in Engaged Buddhism. In this paper, the question is asked what contemplation against economic injustice means from a monastic perspective, in dialogue with Engaged Buddhism. In search for a fruitful relation between contemplation and engagement (*actio in contemplatione*), the author, a Benedictine monk himself, conducted inter-spiritual dialogues with two prominent representatives of Engaged Buddhism. Departing from monastic sources and fundamental model of relating to suffering in Zen-Buddhism, personal and social forms of engagement facing human suffering are related to one-another (*reciprocal illumination*). All participants, including the author, are both, practitioner and scholar. Their research perspective can be called "consultative". Personal transformation and social revolution call for a spiritual reflection. The paper tries to offer heuristic concepts for this process of reflection in a spiritual and scholarly sense.

33 T. Quartier, *Das Kloster im Leben. Monastische Spiritualität als Provokation*, Kevelaer 2016, 27.

MONASTICISM AND BRAND – A PRECARIOUS DIALOGUE. SOME OBSERVATIONS AT THE INTERFACE BETWEEN SOCIOLOGY, ECONOMY AND THEOLOGY

Bernard Sawicki

Once the Patriarch of Antioch was sitting with his bishops in the courtyard of the church of Saint Julian. Whilst they were engaged in discussion, they heard an unusual commotion in the street. At that moment a luxurious carriage was passing by outside the church. The courtesan Pelagia was proudly seated inside. The road sparkled from the brilliance of the jewels which she wore. The air was filled with the scent of her expensive perfumes. The crowd of people cheered her as though they were out of their minds. The bishops turned their heads aside in disgust, to avoid facing the satanic woman, who had led so many of the young aristocrats of the city into the mire of immorality. Only one, Bishop Nonos, followed her persistently with his gaze, until she disappeared at a turn in the road. Afterwards he turned to the other bishops and said to them with a sorrowful voice: "Woe to us, brothers in Christ. This woman puts us to great shame. Did you see how much care she takes in dressing her body in order to lure her lovers? While we lazy people-what do we do to adorn our souls to attract the love of our heavenly Bridegroom?" Saying these things, he prayed with fervour for that sinful soul. And his prayer was heard. Divine Grace restored her and Pelagia came to believe in Christ, repented her sinful life, was baptised by the holy Nonos, and came to a holy end[1].

The aim of the present paper is to have a general look at the encounter between monasticism and brand, including both its positive and negative aspects. As was mentioned in the title, this encounter is a dialogue that assumes an interaction: branding is affecting monasticism and, one can hope, vice versa. In other words:

Bernard Sawicki, Benedictine monk of Tyniec Abbey (Poland), lecturer at the Pontifical Athenaeum Sant'Anselmo in Rome.

1 *The Evergetinos: A Copmplete Text*, vol. 3, edd./transl. H. Patapios, Archbishop Chrisostomos, Bishop Auxentios, Center for Traditionalist Orthodo Studies, Etna (CA) 1998, Argument 4, 1.

monastic life, from its very beginning, may be seen in the categories of branding – even as a form of branding. Such an approach would be a particular form of religious character of branding, recently noticed and discussed by many authors[2]. Here, however, one may have doubts whether this relation is symmetrical, i.e. to what extent commercial branding is just "spying" religious (and in our case monastic) qualities, to imitate (not to say "steal" and just [ab]use) them and to what extent (if at all) religious (or monastic) standards may influence branding, i.e. its quality, activities and strategies. Another level of this dialogue are the potential profits and losses (advantages and disadvantages) of monasticism: to what extent in contact with branding is it losing its reputation and identity, how much can it gain (if at all) from this interaction (contact with society, opportunities for evangelization, financial support). The balance seems to be more than necessary, given that branding and monasticism, willy-nilly, continue their joint march and, at the same time, in social life branding is not only more present, but even more obsessive – whereas the presence of monasticism is shrinking.

1. TOWARDS AFFINITY BETWEEN BRAND AND MONASTICISM

Anthropological and even an existential understanding of brand already shows analogies with the concept of monasticism. Obviously both brand and monasticism may be defined in very different ways. They cover, each on its side, quite a wide part of reality. Even in a general definition of monasticism one can find many elements which fit to brand. If we refer to the history of brand, we can notice that when this concept was introduced into the marketing literature in the early 1900s, the central notion was that brands first of all constituted a way for customers to identify and recognize goods (and their manufacturer)[3]. Theologically speaking, monasticism has always been a special form of life, a sign by a particular, radical commitment to God – an eschatological sign, marking special people to express the importance of God. A monk – and his life – have to indicate the only purpose of our life on earth – the highest sort of goods.

Enzo Bianchi describes monasticism as a set of five oppositions: desert and world, obedience and freedom, solitude and community, work and prayer,

2 See, for example, B. Ballardini, *Gesù lava più bianco ovvero come la Chiesa inventò il marketing*, Roma, 2014; M. Lindstrom, *BRAND Sense: Build Powerful Brands though Touch, Taste, Smell, Sight and Sound*, New York 2005; L.B. Jones, *Jesus, CEO: Using Ancient Wisdom for Visionary Leaders*, New York 2005.

3 M. A. Merz-Y. He-S. L. Vargo, «The evolving brand logic: a service-dominant logic perspective», *Journal of the Academic Marketing Sciences* 37 (2009), 328-344, 330.

temptation and prophecy[4]. To some extent monasticism can also be described, under different aspects, in bipolar categories: it is unique in its character but globally present, it demands loyalty but is expression of a free creativity, it tends to be highly personalised but create community, it results from a hard work but in many cases can and should be contemplated, it may seduce but also open new horizons of experience and pleasure.

In another text Bianchi, emphasizing purely theological – or rather christological – objective of monasticism as "the conditions to increase in the knowledge (*gnosis*) of Christ and God" so everything which is included by the term "contemplation": assiduity with the word of God, the prayer in vigilance, compunction, silence, renunciation[5].

This emphasis on a life in a constant effort may seem contradictory to a general understanding of brand as a source of multifarious satisfaction. However, is not the contemplation the best way towards a final and definite existential satisfaction? If so, to achieve it some, at least minimal restrictions are necessary. In this line man can situate the short definition of monasticism, given by Adalbert De Vogüé after some monastic writings by Gregory the Great: renunciation and desire.[6] This dialectic is very present – up to a deformation – in the modern experience of brand. Brand usually plays with desires, imposing – sometimes perversely – renunciations to increase the satisfaction of desire.

In the classical definition of brand given by the most influential expert in it, Philip Kotler, we read that it *is an offering from a known source*[7]. Religious connotations of such a definition seem obvious. On the horizon appears the idea of sacrifice – so dear to monasticism. "To offer" means to give for free, not without effort. The giver himself pays the price. A known source assumes a previous relationship with the recipient and trust. They both know the source. The donor respects this knowledge, submitting its donation to the standards already known to the recipient.

This dimension of offering is also present in the etymology of the word "brand" which comes from "burn" i.e. *marking one's property with a heated iron*[8]. Brand also guarantees a value of the product. In some cases, it maybe 70% of the

4 E. Bianchi, *La vita altrimenti. Pensieri sul monachesimo*, Brescia 2006.

5 E. Bianchi, *contemplazione e vita apostolica in oriente*, in *Monachesimo, laicità e vita religiosa*, ed. G. Brunelli, Bologna 1995, 89-96, 93.

6 A. De Vogüé, *Sguardi sul monachesimo,* transl. G. Giacomelli, Bologna 2006, 113-119.

7 P. Kotler, *Marketing, Management. Millenium Edition*, Boston 2002.

8 G. Muratovski, «Icons of Popular Culture: Religious Dimensions of Branding», in *Consumer Culture Selected Essays*, ed. G. Muratovski, Bristol 2016, 1-39, 11.

product's value[9]. This value relies on "object formulations" growing and changing in a specific local social context sometimes, quite often unfortunately and unjustly reducing brand to this social context. Brand and its social aspect are tightly connected – even to such extent, that the quality of brand may be attributed to a specific social milieu[10].

Concerning the monasticism itself and its meaning, besides its "technical" description, some attempts have been made to determine the reason for monasticism. They can be divided into three types:

- those which emphasise its anthropological meaning,
- those which underline its symbolic meaning,
- those which focus on its transcendent essence[11].

So, an archetype of the Christian monk may be outlined in the following way:

1. The primacy of Kingdom of God
2. The choice of virginity as eschatological testimony
3. The constant welcome and protection of God of the Word
4. The necessity of a protective hedge (in solitude, time, space, silence)
5. The awareness of proper limits
6. Detachment from any human realisation only in natural horizons
7. The testimony of mystery[12].

According to the monks of the Subiaco Congregation monasticism may be characterised through:

1. the places of hope,
2. humility
3. life in time of hope,
4. the reciprocity of ambience of creation and ambience of symbols,
5. use of body
6. use of things
7. meditation of the Scripture in the faith

9 M. Viñarás-F. Cabezuelo-J.M. Herranz, «Filosofía corporativa y valores de marca como ejes del nuevo paradigma comunicativo», *Prisma Social* 4 (2015) 379-410, 392.

10 A. Agha, «*Tropes of Branding* in Forms of Life», *Signs and Society* 3/S1 (2015) 174-194, 191.

11 B. Sawicki, *Concept of the Absurd and Its Theological Reception in Christian Monasticism*, Lewiston 2005, 455.

12 I. Gargano, «Una riflessione sul monachesimo» in *Monachesimo, laicità e vita religiosa*, ed. G. Brunelli, Bologna 1995, 109-110, 110.

8. spiritual battle for charity and justice
9. opening for other sources of life[13].

Cynthia Bourgeault, notices the importance of stays in monasteries for peace, emphasizes the value of monastic balance "attempting only that which can really be done" and proposes "monastic" projects of living and working together[14].

For Raimon Panikkar, monasticism appears as the universal human archetype which may be presented in the following nine categories:

1. The Breakthrough of the Primordial Aspiration
2. The Primacy of Being over Doing and Having
3. Silence over Word
4. Mother Earth Prior to the Fellowship of Men
5. Overcoming Spatio-temporal Parameters
6. Transhistorical Consciousness above Historical Concern
7. The Fullness of the Person over the Individual
8. The Primacy of the Holy
9. The Memory of the Ultimate and the Presence of Its Gate[15].

These, perhaps too far going statements, only show the actuality of monasticism. As Louis Bouyer puts it

> the monk is the only authentic inheritor of the entire movement which brought our occidental humanity from the awakening of its consciousness. Only it is in the right line of its highest and deepest aspirations, as the most constant ones. Only it touches, only it realises its most intimate desires which all the existence but which, maybe, one is not clearly aware[16].

The communion and connectedness with other aspects of reality is here very important – as well as sensibility and attentiveness. As Giuseppe Dosetti writes:

> The monastic life, properly because of its detachment from every "curiosity" towards what passes, towards "chronicle", towards every-day events, is par excel-

13 G. Lafont *et al.*, *Il monachesimo all'alba del terzo*, Parma 1997, 16-28.

14 C. Bourgeault, *Future Directions and Developments of Monastic Life in the Church* in *The Continuing Quest for God. Monastic Spirituality in Tradition and Transition*, ed. W.Skudlarek, Collegville (MN) 1982, 286-296, 291-296.

15 R. Panikkar, *The Blessed Simplicity*, New York 1982, 39.

16 L. Bouyer, *Le sens de la vie monastique*, Turnhout Paris 1950, 311-312.

lence in communion not only with what is eternal, but with true, not curious history, which is the history of salvation: of all people and, above all, the history of humble, poor, small, of those who do not have "creativity" or are disturbed to express it (and surely are the major part of human beings), or are "without history"[17].

And Pierangelo Sequeri links it directly and essentially to the most normal Christian life:

> Monasticism is a special inclination of obedience to the evangelical hope. It is not a clap of thunder, or a mystical crisis, alternative to the sterility and insufficiency of the world. Christian monasticism is rather a symbol of the highest quality of the faith common to Christians[18].

This symbolical character of monasticism – as its anthropological base: self-attainment of freedom, process of perception, personal onset of the world underlines Thomas Merton, relating monasticism to importance of freedom, being together, alienation, contemplative liturgy, awareness of failure, autonomy and heteronomy[19].

Nevertheless, monasticism remains universal. Some authors note explicitly its affinity with philosophy. Hans Urs von Balthasar turns attention to *otium, kenosis, agape* and *martirion*: the monks have privilege to do nothing but searching wisdom, what is possible only through getting rid of unnecessary things, a life full of charity and open to bearing witness[20]. Here the existential dimension of monasticism passes naturally into the Gospel. Elmar Salmann speaks here about existential rooting[21].

All its universality, closeness to human affairs and yet certain aspect of transcendence, is a base of affinity between monasticism and brand. They both play

17 G. Dossetti, *Con Dio e con la storia. Una vicenda di un cristiano e di un uomo*, Marietti, Torino 1986, 31.

18 P. Sequeri, «"Beata solitudo?" Monachesimo cristiano e città postmoderna», in *"Un monastero alle porte della città". Atti del convegno per 650 anni dell'Abbazia di Viboldone*, Milano, 1999, 63-75,71-72.

19 T. Merton, *The Silent Life*, New York 1957, VII-X, 24-30.

20 G. Meiattini, *Monachesimo e teologia: la triplice prospettiva di H.U. von Balthasar*, Lugano 2012, 119-126.

21 E. Salmann, *Monachesimo e filosofia. Una piccola teoria del simbolo*, in *Presenza di Spirito*, Padova 2000, 278-305, 291.

in the delicate space between individuality and community, attraction and honesty, economy and values. They are social and economic phenomena, however open for transcendent values and able to create community among people.

2. CATEGORIES OF AFFINITY

Exploring the above- mentioned affinity, one can distinguish its different categories: sense of transcendence, narration, importance of rite, reliability, responsibility, relationships, community, intimacy. Discussing them separately, one after another will provide different platforms for more detailed inspection of interaction between monasticism and branding – exactly on one of these "levels of affinity".

2.1. Sense of transcendence

Even Noami Klein, contesting the pressure of logo and branding notices immaterial aspects of branding. The act of branding is becoming a larger and larger focus for all the companies. The real production is actually focused on the brand itself. The corporate cultures have acquired many features which make them to be a cross between fraternity house, religious cult and sanatorium[22]. The set of these references is a little bit particular but also very meaningful. Evidently brand wants to be something more than just a commercial name. Klein says here explicitly about transcendence: *the brand, and the selling of the brand acquired an extra component that can only be described as spiritual. Advertising is about hawking a product. Branding, in its truest and most advanced incarnations, is about corporate transcendence*[23].

In this sense branding evokes also special approach of people, involving them on different levels. One can say here about "enthusiasm", "zeal". People not only promote but also defend and advocate their brand. Their involvement goes towards identification with brand which they try to protect and preserve, being driven by aspects of nostalgia[24]. Such identification would bring to same be-

22 N. Klein, *No logo*, London 2000, 36.

23 Klein, *No logo*, 41.

24 J. Eighmey-S. Sar-G. Anghelcev, *Brand zealotry: what is it, and who are the zealots?*, American Academy of Advertising. Conference, 2006, http://s3.amazonaws.com/academia.edu.documents/39016849/Eighmey_Sar_Anghelcev_Brand_Zealotry.pdf?AWSAccessKeyId=AKIAIWOWYYGZ2Y53UL3A&Expires=1491684081&Signature=bEbNqD5u9mbI3BPC5MmtTBVntYE%3D&response-content-disposition=in-

haviours which might be characterised as (1) active information seeking about leading brands regardless of whether the brands are new or well-established, (2) opinion leadership and opinion-seeking relating to leading brands, (3) alertness to the latest news relating to brands of interest, and (4) identification with the core values associated with their favoured brands[25]. This "brand zealotry" becomes a sort of mission where the highest quality of brand is communicated to other people – both individuals and family, friends, associates and others[26]. About 2.5 percent of the adult populations are the brand zealots[27].

But it is not all. One says about "brand spirituality" which results from a gradual synthesis of mind-, market-, heart- and social share. Brand awareness is transformed into brand knowledge and, successively, into brand image, brand experience, brand loyalty crowned by its metamorphosis into brand spirituality[28]. Muratovski wites that in its purest form branding has religious rather than commercial origin what qualifies definition of brands as "sacred objects" or emblems a community may identify with[29].

Some brands obtained this specific, spiritual character. Steve Jobs, Apple's founder, was described as a 'technological messiah' and the 'high priest' of Apple. He just blurred the line between salesmanship and evangelism. *Like a 'religious revivalist', he was selling not just consumer commodities, but also a 'vision of life' – their article states. His preacher-like appearance and quasi-religious product launches – as the commentary continues – were part of the 'magic' that allowed the 'devotees' to ignore that the products themselves were often 'overpriced and underpowered'*[30]. It looks like the world of branding has taken refuge in the world of sacred and assumed 'religious dimensions'[31]. The identity of brand remains mysterious. Its definition develops over time by a kind of mystical *via negativa*, defining itself not so much by saying what brand is as what it is not: the product[32].

---

line%3B%20filename%3DBrand_zealotry_What_is_it_and_who_are_th.pdf, [access: 8-04-2017], 104.

25 Eighmey-Sar-Anghelcev, *Brand zealotry*, 105.

26 Eighmey-Sar-Anghelcev, *Brand zealotry*, 108.

27 Eighmey-Sar-Anghelcev, *Brand zealotry*, 111.

28 B.S. Wijayal, «Dimensions of Brand Image: A Conceptual Review from the Perspective of Brand Communication», *European Journal of .Business and Menagament* 31 (2013) https://www.academia.edu/23496391/Dimensions_of_Brand_Image_A_Conceptual_Review_from_the_Perspective_of_Brand_Communication [access: 08-04-2017], 57.

29 Muratovski, «Icons of Popular Culture», 13.

30 Muratovski, «Icons of Popular Culture», 14.

31 Muratovski, «Icons of Popular Culture», 32.

32 P. Manning, *The Semiotics of Brand*, Toronto 2010, 33-49, 36.

2.2. Narration

So, brand develops in the context of a mythology with all benefits mythology may bring. First of all, it defines and reinforces community values[33]. The community grows in and through storytelling. The stories are also very important in branding.

> Stories based on common experiences with the brand serving to invest the brand with meaning, and meaningfully link community member to community member. Communities traditionally create and retell myths about what happens to those who leave the safety of the community to venture out to the unknown world. The telling of these stories has a ritualistic character about it, and certainly represents a strong tradition within the brand communities[34].

Brand formulations typify their specific sign values which determine different social domains in which life and various persons communicate[35].

> A product brand is thus typically a point of intersection of several meta-semiotic discourses, each of which regulates the sign values of specific brand fractions—a trademark, a logo, a product line, the social personae formulated for its users—which tend to be best known to those they routinely attempt to reach and are grasped less well, or not at all, by others. And when they are grasped well, what is grasped includes the stereotypic indexical values of specific products and what they convey about their use and users[36].

Brand is connected with the indexical values, relying on variable sources and object formulations arisen and changing across participation frameworks of social life. Branding, apart from being a productive process includes also all social practices of the users in which brand works and is transformed[37]. All this complex ensemble of practices form a semiotic design, intended to organise and manage the perception of consumers. This discourse, standardised and coordinated by the producers intends to achieve, but never fully, "hegemonic control

33 A.M. Muniz jr-T.C. O'Guinn, «Brand Community», *Journal of Consumer Research* 27 (2001), 412-432, 422.
34 Muniz-O'Guinn, «Brand Community», 423.
35 Agha, «Tropes of Branding», 174.
36 Agha, «Tropes of Branding», 179.
37 Agha, «Tropes of Branding», 192.

over audiences' perception of what the brands means"[38]. There is a social distance between brand and audience, due to the rhetoric and linguistic choices used in branding. Some brands seeking to maintain an image of authority and professionalism adopt a detached and impersonal style. Others may be more personal and familiar[39]. The consumers as target audience may interpret brand messages and actualise them differently constructing in this way their self-concepts and reality[40]. As Holt notices, *marketing is a form of distorted communication in that marketers control the information that is exchanged. Marketers organise the code, and we as consumers have no choice but to participate*[41]. The "consumer religion" which has been emerging more and more evidently in our times proclaims its belief that happiness can be achieved by possession branded goods in such persuasive and convincing way because their narration is more powerful than the product themselves[42]. Approaching brands from the semiotic point of view may reveal some folk or semiotic ideologies latent in economic categories[43]. Brand narration is a complex issue but it is becoming more and more important. For brand experts it is clear that

> from an emotional-branding standpoint, brand strategists should focus on telling stories that inspire and captivate consumers. These stories must demonstrate a genuine understanding of consumers' lifestyles, dreams, and goals and compellingly represent how the brand can enrich their lives. [...] The strategic objective of emotional branding is to forge strong and meaningfully affective bonds with consumers which later become part of their life stories, memories, and an important link in their social network[44].

In this narration a historical continuity, clear and convincing reference to the past guarantee authenticity[45]. So, one can say about a marketplace mythology

---

38 «Critical Discourse Studies and Branding», in *The Routledge Handbook of Critical Discourse Analysis*, edd. J. Flowerdew-J. Richardson, London 2017, 2, 4.

39 «Critical Discourse Studies and Branding», 47.

40 Wijaya, «Dimensions of Brand Image», 56.

41 D.B. Holt, «Why Do Brands Cause Trouble? A Dialectical Theory of Consumer Culture and Branding», *Journal of Consumer Research* 29 (2002) 70-90, 71.

42 Muratovski, «Icons of Popular Culture», 13.

43 Manning, *The Semiotics of Brand*, 46.

44 C.J. Thompson-A. Rindfleisch-Z. Arsel, «Emotional Branding and the Strategic Value of the Doppelgänger Brand Image», *Journal of Marketing* 70 (2006) 50-64, 51.

45 Thompson-Rindfleisch-Arsel, «Emotional Branding», 62.

which however, generates conflicting discourses of power. Various pressures of social or institutional character create different configurations of power relationships engendering the identity positions and identity practices[46]. Brand is a space of intersection of different narrations expressing multifarious tensions between producers and critics. But only in this way, brand forges its identity which is fully possible only in a social context.

2.3. Importance of rite

Apart from narration – or rather intensifying its role – brand generates and requires rituals which imply a sort of tradition related to a brand and developed from it. Rituals and traditions remind, actualise and perpetuate the community's shared identity, history, culture and consciousness[47]. Obviously, brand communities cannot do without rituals and ritual narration. In this way, they may be socially vital, grow, be reproduced and transmit or even propagate its values. The analogy with monasticism is evident: life in a monastery (particularly a Benedictine one) is focused on liturgy regularly celebrated by and in the community.

Some authors notice a sort of competition between religious narration and rituality and new marketing narrations and rites. The declining popularity of saints (at least in the United States), for example, might be explained by the progress of medical sciences. Only the need of memory and cultural and spiritual identity survives and comes back in marketplaces and the ideological fusion of brand narration and rituality. In this fusion strangely come back various Gnostic and Romantic myths. It is very interesting to what extent the Gnostic myths has exerted a significant influence on American popular culture. As Craig Thompson notices, *despite its strong Romantic overtones, the marketplace mythology of holistic well-being is heavily steeped in this Gnostic mythos*[48]. Brand narration has become a space of ideological and spiritual competition. Holistic well-being claims to be more relevant to natural health consumers than other, more traditional and often dualistic system[49]. Romantic metaphors and myths present Nature as Maternal Power and admit a possibility of revenge of Nature.

46 C. J. Thompson, «Marketplace Mythology and Discourses of Power», *Journal of Consumer Research* 31 (2004) 162-180, 173.

47 Muniz-O'Guinn, «Brand Community», 413.

48 Thompson-Rindfleisch-Arsel, «Emotional Branding», 165.

49 Thompson-Rindfleisch-Arsel, «Emotional Branding», 166.

Gnostic metaphors and myths believe in technology as a Divine tool and as way of liberation[50].

2.4. Reliability

Any convincing and solid presence in society requires reliability. To be noticed, invited to an interaction, to influence one needs to be reliable. Our landscape and our history is marked by various places or buildings which in a concrete way give base to our identity. Such character has also the imagery of medieval monasteries, evoking a powerful, effective, and motivating message. Even today the narrative of monastic craftsmanship amazingly does hold some validity. As Julie Kappelman writes that

> monastic life freed its members from some of the stresses of medieval life such as food insecurity, pursuit of personal property, and individual obligations to reigning leaders. Ability to devote time to brewing, greater security in maintaining adequate supplies, and a subsequent higher capacity to experiment with brewing techniques and recipes made monasteries well renowned for their brews compared to those produced by their non-monastic contemporaries. Even the unreligious or the apathetically religious may reflect upon the monks as those who invested their product with devotion and care that was consistent with their preoccupation with Higher Things[51].

Perhaps this is why modern corporations every now and then make nostalgic allusions to monasteries and monastic culture, trying to gain in this way a degree of reliability. Such high, ideal standards seem to be a standard for marketing practices[52]. One can see it very well in beer branding which creates a salient image that aligns the product with quality. *The nostalgic past corresponds to a desire to be aligned with the esteemed religious figures who are depicted as knowledgeable. Mimicry and mockery manifested in beer branding asserts similar claims about society as the idealisation of the religious past*[53].

50 Thompson-Rindfleisch-Arsel, «Emotional Branding», 168.

51 J. Kappelman, «Not Just Sex That Sells: Religious Rhetoric and References in Contemporary Beer Branding» *Summer Research* (2013), http://soundideas.pugetsound.edu/summer_research/203 [access: 08-04-2017], 6

52 Kappelman, «Not Just Sex That Sells», 8.

53 Kappelman, «Not Just Sex That Sells», 14.

Of course, such practices are based on stereotypes. Analogies and similarity are almost necessary to dispatch and understand messages conveyed by the brand. The messages of spiritual or religious based on personal beliefs and faith[54], however introducing into new realities (or just "dissolving" them by branding).

However, the reliability of brand has an ambiguous character. Reliability is to convince us, but what for? As Simon Anholt provocatively notices, brand is not what we want: it is to convince us[55]. People, he adds, need hope. They like to be seduced and bewitched[56]. However, this rapport (or rather relationship) between brand and client, is not a manipulation. It is a contract based on some values. Good reputation, good name and credibility are the base of trust[57]. A good brand may be constructed only through coherence and consequence[58] which is a solid, ethical requirement. In this way the brands may oppose the logic of the consumer where culture and values become subordinated to the rules of market with bestselling as the only criterion[59].

The experts are unanimous: the new publicity should focus on generating confidence. Confidence is the final objective of advertising messages which often have emotional character. But, first of all, the values of a brand are to be transmitted. Thus, the publicity is another form of transmitting confidence through the values[60].

2.5. Responsibility

Reliability is related to responsibility. One cannot be reliable without being responsible. As a reliable discourse creates community, each community to live and grow well needs the responsibility of its members. Albert Muniz and Thomas O'Guinn write that *a sense of moral responsibility is a felt sense of duty or obli-*

54 N. Miwichian-K. Polyorat, *Temple Personality: The Application of Brand Personality Concept to Temple as a Brand* , http://wbiworldconpro.com/uploads/japan-conference-2014/marketing/1417598474_501-Thon.pdf [access: 08-04-2017], 5.

55 S. Anholt, *Sprawiedliwość marek,* Warszawa 2006 (Polish transl. of *Brand's New Justice,* Elsevier, Amsterdam 2003), 131-132, 135.

56 Anholt, Spr*awiedliwość marek,* 229.

57 Anholt, Spr*awiedliwość marek,* 34.

58 Anholt, Spr*awiedliwość marek,* 125.

59 Z. Bauman, *Płynne życie*, Kraków 2007 (Polish transl. of *Liquid life*, Cambridge University Press, York 2005), 94-96.

60 Viñarás-Cabezuelo-Herranz, «Filosofía corporativa y valores de marca», 406.

gation to the community as a whole, and to its individual members. This sense of moral responsibility is what produces, in times of threat to the community, collective action[61]. This sense also contributes to group cohesion and to social commitments, referring to a subtle and highly contextualised moral system. And this is what happens in brand communities[62].

Moral responsibility also means looking out for and helping other members of the community. Quite often this help comes without saying or thinking, just spontaneously. In a brand community it may include actions to help fellow community members to solve problems with products, what is necessary if a brand is in use through several years[63]. So, each brand has a social character, including corporative philanthropy, marketing for special benefit causes, patronage in social or a corporative volunteer service[64]. Responsibility is a binder of any community. It is a base of relationships which makes every community real and livable.

2.6. Relationships

Brand is also a mediation of body[65]. It works through body and appeals to body. Only in this way it may effectively create responsibility. Real and sound relationships create a sort of universe. Like myths, brands speak one with another. They construct and transform mutually their identity[66]. They create a substitute transcendence – a closer and more accessible one. The means for this are very natural and obvious and, again, the same as in the epoch of myths: narration, affect and passion[67].

According to Martin Lindstrom, the new branding is a social binder which will connect and unify whole generations of people[68]. Brand is playing with this natural need of bonds and its cultural and social destruction. In this way, for example, the spirituality of children is confiscated to lubricate the modes of market economy[69].

61 Muniz-O'Guinn, «Brand Community», 413.
62 Muniz-O'Guinn, «Brand Community», 424.
63 Muniz-O'Guinn, «Brand Community», 425.
64 Viñarás-Cabezuelo-Herranz, «Filosofía corporativa y valores de marca», 400.
65 Viñarás-Cabezuelo-Herranz, «Filosofía corporativa y valores de marca», 293-298.
66 Viñarás-Cabezuelo-Herranz, «Filosofía corporativa y valores de marca», 14.
67 Viñarás-Cabezuelo-Herranz, «Filosofía corporativa y valores de marca», 131-141.
68 Lindstrom, *BRAND Sense*, 13.
69 Bauman, *Płynne życie*, 18.

Noemi Klein writes that brand is an experience, a lifestyle. The brand builders conquer new spaces and so new consensus is born: the products which are more and more rather concepts than commodities[70].

Obviously, the main line on brand relationship is the rapport between producer and customer. Companies and, especially, small firms engage and develop strategies of planned activities, innovative practices to cultivate enriching relationships with their clients[71]. A good customer-brand relationship is expected to improve a firm's financial bottom-line. A competitive business environment drives firms just to build and maintain such good relations[72]. Brand is something more than a mere product or even a factor of social relationships. It is more than just a logo, name, symbol, trademark, or label attached to a product. *Brand is a mark left on the minds and hearts of consumers, which creates a specific sense of meaning and feeling*[73].

Thus, it will not be exaggerated to say that brand is just a relationship, a kind of relationship that involves trust[74]. These relations may be described as brand love relations. Some scholars define them as *the degree of passionate emotional attachment a satisfied consumer has for a particular trade name*[75]. In this sense a clear distinction is made between brand liking and brand love where the latter is described as a more enduring and deeper continuum distinctly different from the concept of liking a brand. Consumers who love a brand have usually integrated the brand into them selves and have a longer-term relationship with them. This is proposed as another difference with the concept of liking a brand[76]. Speaking more philosophically, when people try to make sense out of their surroundings and create more happiness for themselves and others by doing so, brands and products can play a part in this. There is simply no other way of completely making sense of the world than by at least, possibly even tem-

70 Klein, *No logo*, 41.

71 M. Chovancová-C.Nedu Osakwe-B.U. Ogbonna, «Building Strong Customer Relationships through Brand Orientation in Small Service Firms: An Empirical Investigation», *Croatian Economic Survey* 17 (2015) 111-138, 128.

72 Chovancová-Nedu Osakwe-Ogbonna, *Building Strong Customer*, 129, 131.

73 Wijaya, «Dimensions of Brand Image», 55.

74 Wijaya, «Dimensions of Brand Image», 55.

75 R.J.J. Voorn, *What's this thing called Love? Exploring the relationship between brand love, personality, and the propensity to anthropomorphize,* Master thesis, University of Twente 2013, 81.

76 Voorn, *What's this thing called Love?*, 14.

porarily, anthropomorphizing a part of it. And we only have our own senses and mind to do that with[77].

In this way relationship with brand is a substitute – or actualization – of relationships with human beings. Of course, it has its consequence for the role of brand in our life:

> Humanising a brand empowers it to play a more central role in the consumer's life, potentially enabling the consumer to project an aspect of his or her self that might be desirable for relationships he or she seeks [...] or possibly even give him or her a sense of comfort at having found a brand that "fits" with his or her self-concept [...][78].

This impact of brand on real human relationships is getting stronger and may even be dangerous:

> For the anxious attachment types, when the brand is associated with a personality trait that the individual considers important or relevant for maintaining relationships with others, brand attachment, purchase likelihood, and brand choice are enhanced. This occurs because these individuals use the brand as a means for signalling their ideal self-concept to potential relational partners[79].

2.7. Community

Good, responsible and reliable relationships are a natural base for a community. Living in community is not only essential for monastic life but also for society which is currently very atomised and alienated. Today many people are looking for social bonds. In this field brands offer a sense of belonging[80], where loyalty and faithfulness count so much. They guarantee our safety, providing us with a sense of predictability[81].

The community and a brand need to be animated by somebody. It is a person around which the bonds will appear and which authenticates the brand. These persons, called *celebrities*, are the priests and prophets of a brand (even if, in differ-

77 Voorn, *What's this thing called Love?*, 47.

78 V. Swaminathan-K. M. Stilley-R. Ahluwalia, «When Brand Personality Matters: The Moderating Role of Attachment Styles», *Journal of Consumer Research* 35 (2009) 985-1002, 985.

79 Swaminathan-Stilley-Ahluwalia, «When Brand Personality Matters», 996.

80 Lindstrom, BRA*ND Sense*, 218-219.

81 Lindstrom, BRA*ND Sense*, 208.

ence to priests, they promote themselves!). They bind the dispersed society of our days. They are known because of being known. Through their career and behaviour they are the main factors responsible for creation of communities – even if these communities are only imaginary, loose, fragile, transitory and ephemeral[82]. They are the objects of cult, but their cults are not exclusive[83]. However, they may also become the victims sacrificed on the altar of community to integrate its bonds.

Another important factor generating community in society is "event"[84]. The events. Such as sport games or concerts, especially of popular music – but not only! – if not create a real community, they give us an impression of it. They create some noncommittal links, offering a space of at least partial oblivion and liberation. In this way a "brand community" comes into being. It is

> a specialised, non-geographically bound community, based on a structured set of social relationships among admirers of a brand. It is specialised because at its centre is a branded good or service. Like other communities, it is marked by a shared consciousness, rituals and traditions, and a sense of moral responsibility. Each of these qualities is, however, situated within a commercial and mass-mediated ethos, and has its own particular expression. Brand communities are participants in the brand's larger social construction and play a vital role in the brand's ultimate legacy. The first and most important element of community is [...] consciousness of kind. Consciousness of kind is the intrinsic connection that members feel toward one another, and the collective sense of difference from others not in the community. Consciousness of kind is shared consciousness, a way of thinking about things that is more than shared attitudes or perceived similarity[85].

The brand communities are important first of all for the producers, because they reflect the situated embeddedness of brands in the day-to-day lives of consumers and the links created around brand: ways in which brands connect consumer to brand, and consumer to consumer. In brand community three essential markers of community, such as consciousness of kind, rituals and traditions, and moral responsibility, are apparently present. Only the differences in their expression make brand communities something significant in their own right[86].

82 BAUMAN, *Płynne życie*, 80.
83 BAUMAN, *Płynne życie*, 81.
84 BAUMAN, *Płynne życie,* 97-98.
85 MUNIZ-O'GUINN, «Brand Community», 412-413.
86 MUNIZ-O'GUINN, «Brand Community», 418.

> Brand communities are generally open social organisations in that they do not deny membership, but like most communities they do have status hierarchies. Ostensibly, anyone who is devoted to the brand can be a member of the community, regardless of ownership. However, the devotion to the brand must be sincere and for the right reasons. Differentiating between those who are true believers in the brand, and those who are merely opportunistic is a common concern voiced by brand community members. The existence of a common enemy against whom to unite makes this brand community particularly strong[87].

The ethic dimension of such communities is very interesting: *In fact, brand communities generally seem more democratic and inclusive than many traditional face-to-face communities. Perhaps this is because they are so entirely situated in a relatively laissez-faire market force ethic, or the commercial ethos*[88].

> Brand communities are largely imagined communities. Brand communities represent a form of human association situated within a consumption context. In contrast to previous marketing research, they are not homogeneous lifestyle segments [...] or consumption constellations [...]; here community is formed around one good or service, not many. They are explicitly commercial social collectives centered around a brand, not incidental contact with commercial space. It is our position that brand community is neither any more nor less real than many other forms of community, and is simply an essential form humans invariably employ in their social existence[89].
>
> Communities exert pressure on members to remain loyal to the collective and to the brand. In our view, a brand with a powerful sense of community would generally have greater value to a marketer than a brand with a weak sense of community. However, it should also be recognised that a strong brand community can be a threat to a marketer should a community collectively reject marketing efforts or product change, and then use communal communications channels to disseminate the rejection[90].
>
> At this moment in the early twenty-first century, the notion of community occupies a particularly important space. The things that community has traditionally represented are sites of considerable contestation in the postmodern world.

87 Muniz-O'Guinn, «Brand Community», 419.
88 Muniz-O'Guinn, «Brand Community», 421.
89 Muniz-O'Guinn, «Brand Community», 426.
90 Muniz-O'Guinn, «Brand Community», 427.

> At this moment we seek to understand community's existence, persistence, endurance, and constant reinvention in the postmodern consumption space where enormous changes in human communication reside. At this nexus we introduce the idea of brand community. We believe brand communities to be real, significant, and generally a good thing, a democratic thing, and evidence of the persistence of community in consumer culture[91].

To resume this important and interesting survey of communitarian aspect of brand it must be admitted that that brands are social objects and socially constructed. It means that consumers are actively involved in that creation. It further shows that brand community clearly affects brand equity[92]. So, brand just needs a community – on different levels and dimensions. Small brand communities are created by stakeholders[93]. Larger and very diversified are everywhere where brands appear.

2.8. Intimacy

The final circle of affinity between brand and monasticism is intimacy, understood as the highest and deepest form of being together, crowning all relationships. Intimate contact means involvement up to a certain identification. No wonder than that members of brand communities often feel that they have a better understanding of the brand than the manufacturer does. In fact, they also feel that the brand belongs to them as much as it does to the manufacturer[94].

Klein puts it in a very radical and meaningful way saying that the true meaning of a lifestyle brand is that you can live your whole life inside it[95]. The relationship between brand and consumer is very difficult to define. It glitters with different aspects. Klein asks whether it is an arranged marriage, a friendship or a "master/slave engagement"? She repeats, after Foumier, that this connection between consumer and brand is driven by *the deep and significant psychological and socio-cultural meanings the consumer bestows on the brand in the process of meaning creation*[96]. This relationship, as Klein continues, has transformed into something *much more invasive and profound* as just a simple, straightforward relationship. However, it is at least ambiguous. People feel both guilty and

91 Muniz-O'Guinn, «Brand Community», 428.
92 Muniz-O'Guinn, «Brand Community», 427.
93 Merz-He-Vargo, «The evolving brand logic», 10.
94 Muniz-O'Guinn, «Brand Community», 424.
95 Klein, *No logo*, 160.
96 Klein, *No logo,* 187.

connected, like fans with a celebrity: this connection is volatile, emotionally intense but shallow[97]. At the same time any design is embedded in the local context of the home country, in local-specific forms of life[98]. It seems to play with our dreams and memories, exploring and transforming the most intimate sphere of our identity. In one of the articles dedicated to businessmen launching their own brand, the following statement can be found: *Your brand is a living, breathing organism. It has a soul. It's not one thing: it is everything. It's not just a logo or a tagline or a colour, as important to your brand as those things are. You're more than two arms, two legs, a head and torso; you're more than just your clothes*[99].

So, getting through different aspects of marketing which may be referred to monasticism – and not without certain affinity – one can discover that, at the end, the central place in this affinity is taken by the human being: its needs but, perhaps more, by its deepest identity, taken into consideration, approached from different sides with a hope of responding to its most authentic aspirations.

3. THE SPACES OF MUTUAL INTERACTION

If so, given the huge amount of literature concerning branding and considerable differences between marketing and theological language, this paper can only be an attempt at drafting a general panorama of interaction between branding and monasticism, more proposing fields for future exploration than providing unequivocal explanations. Referring to a sample of publications about this issue four dimensions of this interaction will be proposed: 1) ethical challenges focusing on authenticity, contestation, discretion and respect; 2) redefinition of the idea of service; 3) issues of identity authenticity; understanding; 3) importance and interpretation of values.

3.1. Ethical challenges: between authenticity, contestation, discretion and respect

Amazingly monasticism still remains very helpful to brands. One of the articles on this subject put this rapport very clearly, naming monasticism as much attrac-

97 Klein, *No logo,* 333.

98 Agha, «Tropes of Branding», 193-194.

99 T. Taylor, «Branding: Three Thing You may Be Doing That Don't Work», *Electric Light &Power* 38 (2007) 38.

tive for brand as sex[100]. The impressive list of beers produced in North America and in Western Europe leaves no doubts about the power of monasticism – at least in this segment of the market. There are products which have nothing to do with monasticism, but willingly recall diverse monastic associations[101]. Calling a beer "Lost Abbey" increased the results of selling[102]. However, these are examples taken from commercial, non- monastic companies.

The monks themselves create and diffuse their publicity. As Jonveaux notice, it has its style: monks just should be authentic, show it and the success is sure[103]. What this authenticity, however, would mean, is not so clear. Very often monastic authenticity is inseparably connected with an evident manifestation of exotic attributes making monks more medieval and conceptual than contemporary and modern. The line between this stereotypical image of monks and their authentic values which might be attractive for the society is very delicate. To monks seen as mascots the monks living frugal, simple and harmonious life should be opposed. Here all the positive aspects of brand could and should be applied – a view on an ideal which, however, is accessible. Behind this value naturally the monks guarantee solidity, honesty and reliability.

But does not it mean that they enter into a terrible fight which goes on behind the surface of logos? Klein is radically clear about this. On the other side of a web of brands there are dramas of slums, poverty and misery[104]. Of course, there is no parallel between the life of monks and poor people the work of which is abused by transnational companies, however the play with authenticity on the market is real and raises many ethical questions. It concerns not only the question of identity, but also of real and dignified work – particularly of young people[105]. Following Klein it might be called a war between authenticity and international corporationism[106]. Individual micro-emancipatory practises, decentralisation of market-determined subjectivity are only two examples of tools

---

100 See Kappelman, «Not Just Sex That Sells», quoted above.

101 See, for instance http://www.imonaci.it/ or_http://www.dingdangdong.fr/_[access: 2.10.2017]

102 November/December 2014, retail-merchandiser.com, 43-45.

103 I. Jonveaux, *L'économie des monastčres : Recomposition d'une utopie dans la modernité Religieuse en comparaison européenne*, doctoral thesis defended in Ecole des Hautes Etudes en Sciences Sociales de Paris Università degli Studi di Trento (Italie) Département de "Sociologia e Ricerca Sociale" 2007, 305-309.

104 Klein, *No logo*, 19-20.

105 Klein, *No logo*, 278-279.

106 Klein, *No logo*, 332-333.

accessible in this battle. As Douglas Holt suggests, the consumers should form and cultivate conscious and authentically free choice to accelerate the fragmentation of global market. Is is a creative resistence of consumers[107]. However, it will never be a real and efficient resistance, rather a "market-sancioned cultural experimentation through which the market rejuvenates itself"[108].

This resistence of singular consumers against big corporations includes also a fight for authenticity. Brand, basing on authenticity is at the same time dangerous for it. Because of financial reasons it cannot respect all its forms, particularly the smallest and most fragile ones. As Thompson observes *corporate power and antibrand activism are counterveiling forces in a dynamic system of shifting and perpetually morphing relationships between power and resistance. This dialectical dynamism will appear to be paradoxical when framed by the trope of inside versus outside the marketplace.* This is a battle between power of market and our individual dreams of freedom and real authenticity[109] what is so much more important, as much modern and successful corporations produce brands as opposed to products[110]. Just this fact of producing and selling "brand" inserts the fight for authenticity in a specific context. What counts, are the images and impressions, an ideological and multi-sensual message. The "brand essence" is gradually invented and produced though a psychological/anthropological examination of potential meanings of brands to the culture and to people's lives[111]. Defining brand in opposition to the product means that *brand is conceived as an immaterial form of mediation*[112].

The search for the true meaning of brands - or the "brand essence," as it is often called - gradually took the agencies away from individual products and their attributes and toward a psychological/anthropological examination of what brands mean to the culture and to people's lives. This was seen to be of crucial importance, since corporations may manufacture products, but what consumers buy are brands. In this case, as Holt rightly notices, authenticity is becoming an endangered species[113]. He adds explicitly that *brands now cause trouble, not because they dictate tastes, but because they allow companies to dodge civic obligations. Postmodern branding is perceived as deceitful because the ideals woven into brands seem so dis-*

107 Holt, «Why Do Brands Cause Trouble?», 72.
108 Holt, «Why Do Brands Cause Trouble?», 89.
109 Thompson, «Marketplace Mythology and Discourses of Power», 174-175.
110 Klein, *No logo*, 25.
111 Klein, *No logo*, 29.
112 Manning, *The Semiotics of Brand*, 36.
113 Holt, «Why Do Brands Cause Trouble?», 86.

connected from, and often contrary to, the material actions of the companies that own them[114]. The analysts see that for consumers authenticity is a crucial value. Brands when their emotional-branding promises are viewed as inauthentic are avoided[115]. So, the conflict between corporations and public and individual space is inevitable. Its consequences are far reaching and may concern youthful identities, the concept of nationality but also the borderline of marketing[116].

3.2. Redefinition of service: sensibility for various needs, better efficiency, satisfaction of needs

Brand is a powerful tool in forming societies. Implicitly it would mean a new vision of service a monastery can render to people and society. Knowing how it works maybe not only helpful in dealing with various problems it brings but also may redefine some classical ideas about social and individual life. One of these ideas is visibility. It is important. Visibility establishes the first contact, invites – or not – to an interaction. It also plays an important role in distinction and recognition of our identity[117]. Visual identity is a new form of public representation and presence in social discourse[118].

Another idea is benefit. To be useful/ helpful means to offer a benefit to somebody. The benefits brand brings to consumers may be a model of successful relationships which satisfy our needs. Bambang Wijaya distinguishes four types of such benefits that are commonly offered by brand, namely:

- functional benefits (benefits that address the physical needs of the consumer),
- emotional benefits (benefits that address the affective needs of the consumer like feeling secured, self-confidence, love, etc),
- symbolic benefits (benefits that address the illusive needs of consumers in actualising, expressing and showing the meaning of themselves and their lives to the surrounding environment for the sake of self-existence, such as symbolic lifestyle, prestige, masculinity, power, etc)
- social benefits (benefits that address the spiritual needs of the consumer in self-reflection and appreciation of life through positive contribution to the

114 Holt, «Why Do Brands Cause Trouble?», 88.

115 Thompson-Rindfleisch-Arsel, «Emotional Branding», 63.

116 Klein, *No logo,* 27.

117 A.T. Shirley, «Denominational Logos: Religious Symbols or Branding Imagery?», *The International Journal of Religion and Spirituality in Society* 3 (2013) 47-59,48.

118 Shirley, «Denominational Logos», 49.

surrounding environment, such as: concern for education, life environment, health, local cultural values, social welfare, entrepreneurship, and so on)[119].

All this does not mean that to be good, to rend a service one need to be like ...a brand. However, some mechanisms applied by brands maybe useful perhaps (and at least) in increasing of our sensibility.

Brand can also stimulate a better management. Since authenticity is important in an efficient promotion of brand, a coherence between vision and the real situation of a product becomes crucial. Applied to a monastery if can be only helpful. To communicate its spiritual and existential message the monastery should be accessible, i.e. visible and audible in the society – at least partially. For instance, the monasteries which would like to be visited by pilgrims or tourists, it would seem necessary to develop touristic facilities[120]. It implies a coordination of some internal and external activities. Visibility should fit the internal content and, on the other hand, the internal content should correspond with visibility.

In particular, this better management can result in a better economic profit. Better presented and publicised products certainly are better sold. More visible and accessible monasteries may fulfill their spiritual and existential vision better.

3.3. Play with identity: between disappointment, abuse of image, competition and celebritism

Both visibility and service elaborated and seen in a new light, cause a new reflection on identity. The challenge of its coherence with visibility as well as its social aspect are both danger and chance.

Quite often brand softens identity. If the discrepancy between visibility and content is considerable, there is a danger of disappointment. If visibility is not sufficient – or wrong – it can abuse the image and reputation of monks. Finally, similar brands can compete (more or less consciously). As Klein notices, branding is, at its core, a deeply competitive undertaking in which brands are up against not only their immediate rivals (Mike vs. Reebok, Coke vs. Pepsi, McDonald's vs. Burger King, for example) but all other brands in the mediascape, including the events and people they are sponsoring[121]. It brings a danger

119 Wijaya, «Dimensions of Brand Image», 61.

120 A.-M. Drule, *The Importance of Infrastructure and Tourism Facilities in Case of Religious Sites. Evidence from Romania* in: *Marketing from Information to Decision,* Babeş-Bolyai University, Faculty of Economics and Business Administration, 2014, 91-106, 91.

121 Klein, *No logo,* 53.

of shifting towards superficiality and celebrity and of dissolving or even loosing identity. Instead of exploring and deepening it, a producer tries to please both sponsors and clients. A real rapport requires a clear identity. When it is scarified for the smoothness of relationship, there is something that does not work. Wijaya observes that for brand, the most important is brand image, that is, brand visibility. Other aspects of brand, such as brand identity (sic!), brand personality, brand associations, brand behaviour & attitude and brand competence & benefit) only serve to expose and re-inforce the brand image[122]. Here again, we come across the conflict between identity and visibility. In time of social media authenticity of "personal brand" is crafted by a special Social Media Influencer just in view of consumer outreach[123].

Today, in this endeavour of commercial communication, the phenomenon of celebrity is more and more important. A celebrity is the most visible person and thus, has the best possibilities of communicating anything. No wonder than for many people achieving some kind of celebrity status "has come to seem as reasonable a life goal"[124].

> The celebrity embodies exemplary forms of selfhood models how those forms of selfhood might be achieved and lived, and functions as a catalyst in and through which desire and power are seen to coalesce, [...] the long, conflicted, and constantly changing relationship between modes of subjectivity, self-presentation and economic value. The celebrity is a constructed subjectivity comprised of distinct sets of self-referential, attention-seeking, market-aware practices[125].

Celebrity-ism is a meaningful ethical switch - from a real hero into a person just promoted by media. Paradoxically, although the identity of celebrities is so much exposed, at the same time it is only "produced" what does not mean that its aspirations are "appeal", "trust", "aspiration", "Influence"[126]. Again, also here it is not identity that counts but efficient relationship. Through celebrity, identity just slipped into being "simply a metaphor for value", becoming "direct-

122 WIJAYA, «Dimensions of Brand Image», 62.

123 A. HEARN, S. SCHOENHOFF, «From Celebrity to Influencer. Tracing the Diffusion of Celebrity Value across the Data Stream», in *A Companion to Celebrity*, edd. P.D. Marshal-S.Redmot, Hoboken (NJ) 2016, 194-211, 194.

124 HEARN-SCHOENHOFF, «From Celebrity to Influencer», 194.

125 HEARN-SCHOENHOFF, «From Celebrity to Influencer», 195-196.

126 HEARN-SCHOENHOFF, «From Celebrity to Influencer», 197-199.

ly value-producing in and of itself"[127]. If so, identity is no more disinterested and important for itself. It is becoming a mean for production (and so, inconsequence, for gain). Visibility, identity and commerce entwine very tightly, as though penetrating one another up to mutual dependence. *In the modern "culture of image-based socialised production, attention-getting forms of self-presentation become crucial to survival". A Producer should be like a performing artist*[128], artist performs in view of economic success.

In this new context identity achieved a dynamic profile, however, at the cost of losing its dependence. It simply became involved in production and promotion of brand, being just – especially in celebrity-ism – conditioned by it. In this way authenticity and originality of human relation are gradually replaced by interactions with celebrities, giving impressions of being intimate and exclusive ones. What remains more and more open and worrying is the question of values and the final measure of this reputational capital and its benefits[129]. In consequence, such procedures leads to a drainage of identity by brand. As Holt notices, in post postmodern branding the paradigm citizen is considered an artist but as consumer (s)he is cultivating her/his self through branding[130]. According to this practice, *consumers will view brands as valuable resources for identity construction when brand meanings are perceived to be authentic—original and disinterested*[131].

These branding practices reflect and influence the cultural and ideological movement of the entire society[132], in a certain way undermining the traditional understanding of authenticity and reliability. The increasing importance of brand leads towards instrumentalisation of identity. At the same time the borderline between real and virtual live is disappearing. Instead of a real situation, a game of expectations and desires is launched. Brands promise better life and access to a world of better qualities, creating the "real" through simulacra such as "fake brands"[133]. Brand become a tool of corporations – against individuals[134]. The corporal, globalised identity displaces the real individual one. The idea of brand goes beyond products but is extended for non-profit organisations, cul-

127 HEARN-SCHOENHOFF, «From Celebrity to Influencer», 201.
128 HEARN-SCHOENHOFF, «From Celebrity to Influencer», 201.
129 HEARN-SCHOENHOFF, «From Celebrity to Influencer», 204-205.
130 HOLT, «Why Do Brands Cause Trouble?», 81.
131 HOLT, «Why Do Brands Cause Trouble?», 85.
132 MERZ-HE-VARGO, «The evolving brand logic», 14.
133 AGHA, «Tropes of Branding», 18.
134 HOLT, «Why Do Brands Cause Trouble?», 70.

tural festivals, tourist destinations or sports teams[135]. Brand organises our whole life. Everywhere a characteristic image or personality is created to attract consumers. Identity not only produces, but it itself becomes a product – or rather a projection of an ideal self-concept[136], where desires or complexes are managed via associations with the brand[137]. Global brands usually connote better quality, provide status and prestige[138].

All this battle for identity is somehow analogous to the essential challenge of monasticism, i.e. discovering one's own identity in relation to God and through various ascetic practices. If brand seems to offer opposite movement, its consequence should be interpreted as a strong appeal for return to monastic values which ensured authentic human growth to many generations of men and women.

3.4. Ambiguities in front of basic values: between expectations, illusion and humbug

Finally, brand reorganises the thinking on values. Blurring identity one arrives at a question about essentials. Some firm points of reference are necessary, especially in a modern, liquid society. Everything that circulates around brand to create it successfully has very little to do with values. It mainly refers to competitors as well as partners actions. The key criterion is satisfaction of the consumer which may have very different sources[139]. However, as Klein notices, brand producers are aware that marketing and advertising is also somehow spiritual. Brands can conjure feelings that go beyond standard consumption[140]. Klein continues: *The brand re-invented itself as a cultural sponge, soaking up and morphing to its surroundings*[141]. Branding is no more limited to specific products of a company. It touches the outside culture as well by sponsoring cultural or sport events widening the field of associations and connotations related to brand itself. According to Klein, *it is about thirstily soaking up cultural ideas and iconography that their brands could reflect by projecting*

135 Miwichian-Polyorat, *Temple Personality*, 3.

136 Swaminathan-Stilley-Ahluwalia, «When Brand Personality Matters», 987.

137 Swaminathan-Stilley-Ahluwalia, «When Brand Personality Matters», 993.

138 J.E. E. M. Steenkamp, R.Batra, D. L. Alden, «How Perceived Brand Globalness Creates Brand Value», *Journal of International Business Studies* 34 (2003) 53-65, 61.

139 K. L. Keller-D. R. Lehmann, «Brands and Branding: Research Findings and Future Priorities», *Marketing Science* 25 (2006) 740-759, 753.

140 Klein, *No logo*, 28.

141 Klein, *No logo*, 37.

these ideas and images back on the culture as "extensions" of their brands[142]. Is it a research of external, firm points of reference, values or simply another attempt of annexing new neutral spaces for branding? Branding may strip *the hosting culture of its inherent value and treating it as little more than a promotional tool*[143]. Klein is alarming saying that *the brand managers are now doing what they have done in music, sports and journalism outside the schools: trying to overwhelm their host, to grab the spotlight. They are fighting for their brands to become not the add-on but the subject of education, not an elective but the core curriculum*[144].

According to some experts, the only hope might be in esthetical dimension of brand and its application to education. Perhaps in this way our sensibility could be increased and well oriented (if not even ...tempered)[145]. This education, however, is rather a formation in esthetics of experts in marketing than a real esthetic education[146]. Although consumism facilitates the strategies of socialisation, it may reduce aesthetics to personal gratification mostly limited to pleasure[147]. The only chance can be seen in the perception of the human being, especially in the dimension of corporality but, again, the question remains of essential values one could make reference to[148]. These values seem necessary to keep the right balance between identity, visibility and commerce.

The values may be seen in the key of religion. But, given the global religious pluralism causing competitions between religions, religious values may also be subject to the market rules. Some scholars notice that spiritual consumers are likely to see spirituality or religion as a "product" which can more or less fit their needs[149]. It is not only a danger, but quite a popular practice. Moreover, as some experts notice *the consumers do not react to reality but rather to what they perceive as reality*. They perceive brand as a set of associations, as impression resulting from the context of competition with other brands in the same category. They chose a brand just to understand themselves, *to know their self-concept through an identity that is displayed and offered by the brand, as well as a medium to com-*

142 Klein, *No logo*, 47.
143 Klein, *No logo*, 56.
144 Klein, *No logo*, 105.
145 S.C. Lowry, «Canon corporal y educación estética de la existencia», in *Controverias del pensamiento. Homenaje al profesor Quintín Racionero*, edd. C. De Peretti *et al.*, 2016, 91-118, 113.
146 Lowry, «CAnon corporal y educación estética de la existencia», 22.
147 Lowry, «CAnon corporal y educación estética de la existencia», 24.
148 Lowry, «CAnon corporal y educación estética de la existencia», 25.
149 Shirley, «Denominational Logos», 48.

municate the aspects of themselves to others[150]. It means a fusion of brand with human identity. Brand has become a privileged instrument of definition of a person since it permits to express easily something people are not but what they aspire to be[151]. Following Holt, one can call it a cultural engineering in which brands become *concrete expressions* of valued social and moral ideals[152], cultural resources and useful ingredients *to produce the self as one chooses.* And to do it really, *branded cultural resources must be perceived as authentic,* that is *disinterested, [...] perceived as invented and disseminated by parties without an instrumental economic agenda, by people who are intrinsically motivated by their inherent value*[153]. Such authenticity may be regarded itself a value, becoming a chance of liberation from the weave of visibility, identity and profit – or just opening a transcendent perspective for this weave. It is possible unless the economic aspect finally will not prevail. So, brand may be a chance of reading our culture in a new way, bringing it again closer to our life. As Holt reports, *companies now work hard to weave their brands into cultural epicentres. Firms gain market power by effectively controlling the movement of culture that flows through these epicenters*[154].

This interaction of brand with identity, somehow transforming our understanding of values, is symptomatic for the condition of modern human being. People replace true self-fulfillment by some kind of entertainment, becoming ready to listen to all kinds of propaganda and to accept what fits them. In this situation any communication encompassing various facets of human relations always creates highly desired emotional appeal and any promise of integration appears as an incomparable remedy[155]. So, paradoxically, brand participates in the constant research of sense of human existence. It is difficult to judge whether it is a help or just a substitute. Gjoko Muratovsky is rather clear about this:

> When people find a brand that gives them the social and emotional support that they need, but cannot find elsewhere, they begin to form a 'tribe' around this brand, and follow it with a blind faith. The need to believe and to seek meaning in life is a common human characteristic that is both philosophical and religious in nature. Many people believe that owning branded objects will make their lives better, help

150 Wijaya, «Dimensions of Brand Image», 58.
151 Viñarás-Cabezuelo-Herranz, «Filosofía corporativa y valores de marca», 398.
152 Holt, «Why Do Brands Cause Trouble?», 80.
153 Holt, «Why Do Brands Cause Trouble?», 83.
154 Holt, «Why Do Brands Cause Trouble?», 84.
155 Muratovski, «*Icons of Popular Culture*», 33.

> them identify who they are, or give them a sense of belonging. That is why some scholars [...] argue that consumerism is the furthest reaching 'religion' of today[156].

At this point we arrive directly to an important, delicate and sometimes ambiguous rapport between brand and religion. As it was mentioned above, brand may be regarded as a substitute for religion. However, at the same time a constant transfer is going on: brand uses religious symbols and associations for its purposes and religion is more visible in the world also thanks to some brand mechanisms. Does it always serve for deepening authenticity and identity? It does not look like this. As Kappelman soberly notices regarding beer branding

> Religious references in beer branding often participate in the commodified authentic and cultivate an image of a nostalgic past through idyllic portrayals of monastic brewing. Alternately, beer branding via religion may employ irreverent, blasphemous, or offensive representations. Both the idealised and the indicting representations acknowledge a disparity between the real and the ideal in society[157].

So, brand lives from different narrations, mythologies opening in this way a new approach towards identity but the latter is practically losing its importance letting brand to construct an ideal consumer lifestyle. This construction, however, as Thompson notices, is channelled in a particular ideological direction[158]. The question about basic values remains open. Ideology will never be disinterested. It rather serves rather economy and profit. In such case brand will never fully satisfy human deep expectation, eventually remaining as a game of infinitively changing illusions and always able to avoid final humbug of its narration.

CONCLUSION: BENEFITS AND RISKS OF FURTHER PERSPECTIVES OF THE DIALOGUE

Resuming the whole discourse the ambiguity of brand in reference to monasticism should be always remembered. As every human invention, it may be used both for good and bad purposes. Everything depends on personal decision involved people. The fact that till now brand has been rather draining our identity

156 Muratovski, «Icons of Popular Culture», 34.

157 Kappelman, «Not Just Sex That Sells», 2.

158 Thompson, «Marketplace Mythology and Discourses of Power», 170.

and value than enriching it does not exclude possibilities of a future positive influence of brand on our life.

For the moment, a small balance of mutual interaction between monasticism and brand can be presented in the following table. The first left column shows different categories of affinity between brand and monasticism. The second column an intuitive evaluation of the influence monasticism has on brand. For the clarity, there are also two possible values – positive (+) and negative (–). The last column presents the opposite influence – of brand on monasticism.

	monasticism→brand	brand→monasticism
Sense of transcendence	+	–
Narration	+	+
Importance of rite	+	–
Reliability	+	–
Responsibility	+	+
Relationships	–	+
Community	+	+
Intimacy	–	+

Even if such evaluation must remain intuitive, it shows a certain balance in mutual relations. It means that both brand and monasticism gain rather than lose on their interaction As everywhere, the old monastic rule of discernment (*discretion*) and vigilance is the only way to keep the right proportion in this specific and inevitable rapport. Naturally this rule goes easier with monasticism than brand but, who knows? Perhaps soon the affinity which has been described above is in train to be extended also on discernment and vigilance. If so, it will not be just to see definitively brand as a new value which could compete with monasticism – as its substitution or an easier form. The attention, however should be kept.

Abstract

Brand is one of the key-concepts of modern marketing. The most recent researches and practices have revealed its affinity with religious discourse. Church, faith, rite, religious community are among the categories which mark this affinity. Monasticism began his encounter with branding not long ago but it had been "working" (of course, unconsciously) for many centuries to make this encounter interesting and meaningful. The most essential components of branding, such as reliability, solidity, quality, trust, sense of community are strongly present in monasticism. For example, the expression *Benedictine work* has always been a synonym of the highest quality. No wonder that monastic products have always been highly estimated what in the last decades has been abundantly exploited by various commercial producers, not necessarily connected with monastic entities. It provoked – or still should provoke – juridical counteractions. Special brands, like Trappist beer, Benedictine cheese or various herbs, medicines as well as Gregorian chant are values in themselves. They should be protected not only because they guarantee maintenance of many monastic communities but also because they are an authentic testimony of huge monastic tradition. On the other hand, the monasteries, trying to remain visible, to fulfill their mission in the society and to have new vocations, must accept to be regarded as a brand essentially very attractive for tourist or cultural activities. So, the market of "leisure industry" seems to be one of very few opportunities to offer an access to monastic spirituality for many secularised and religiously indifferent people. However, focusing only on this aspect of external activity of monasteries may provoke a risk of losing the right proportion in living their charisma. These dilemmas may be seen and analysed on the base of cases of particular brands, such as Westvleteren, Maredsous, Silos, Heiligenkreuz, *Benedictine blue*, *L'Artisanat Monastique* but they also need a broader, theological interpretation what, in the context of Pope Francis' ecological concern about economy, seems particularly important.

LIVING BY GODLY WISDOM: MONASTERIES AND MANAGEMENT IN THE AGE OF CORPORATIZATION

John H. SMITH

INTRODUCTION

For thirty years, first as a guest and then as an oblate, I have been privileged to absorb and enjoy Benedictine hospitality, prayer and community life as it is expressed at Holy Trinity Abbey, New Norcia. St Benedict and New Norcia have enriched my life immeasurably and I have gained support and stability in my work within my own church, the Uniting Church in Australia. I gratefully honour that community and the gifts they have given so freely to me. While I speak to you from outside the monastic tradition, I do so to share some insights that have germinated from working through a problem that has been a challenge to me and to my church and may affect the church generally[1].

Drawing on Benedictine life and the *Rule,* this paper explores what it means to operate a faith-based organization in a context in which managerialism has achieved ideological status. As Stephen Cummings has shown[2], Management theory and practice is a Modernist construction that is steeped in assumptions based on scientific method coupled with the experience of industrialization. Supremely confident in its own ability, its goal is to create efficient organizations that produce predictable and measurable results that make profit for their owners. Managerialism has crept into all areas of life resulting in the church being obliged to comply with an expanding number of regulatory controls. This paper discusses what it means for the church to meet its compliance obligations without its mission being undermined by the imposition of a foreign ideology that pays little or no attention to its ethos, and devalues or ignores its heritage. For

---

John H.Smith, Benedictine Oblate, New Norcia, Honorary Research Associate, University of Divinity.

1 Thanks to the Rev Dr. Michael Owen, teacher, colleague and friend of many years whose unpublished paper «Stewardship of Property – Stewardship of Truth» was an especially helpful resource for my thinking for this paper.

2 S. CUMMINGS, *ReCreating Strategy*, London-Thousand Oaks-New Delhi 2002, 84-85.

the Church risk management includes remembering whose it is, and what it is called to do and be in the world, so that while rendering what is due to Caesar, it remains true to the core of its vocation.

1. MANAGEMENT IN THE RULE OF ST. BENEDICT

Benedict employs management in the running of his communities. For example, RB 53.21 states that the guesthouse is to be entrusted to a «wise and God-fearing brother». It is notable that even when arranging to have enough beds and facilities on hand to cope with unpredictable arrivals, Benedict gives priority to the capacity to govern with the wisdom that grows from a life lived in the fear of God. This wisdom is not theoretical; it is theological knowledge lived faithfully and prayerfully in the service of God, the community of the monastery, and in this case, the strangers who called. In the guesthouse manager practical knowledge is to be coupled with the spiritual wisdom that is consistent with the faith of Benedict's central tenants of seeking God and preferring «nothing before Christ» (72.11). Benedict also says: «the house of God should be in the care of wise [community members] who will manage it wisely» (53.22). Terrence Kardong comments that the Latin word for manage that is used here, *administretur,* contrasts with God being the proprietor of the house[3]. This means the members of the community and the managers within it are not owners but stewards: stewards of the mysteries of God, and also stewards of all that is in their care.

Other individuals will be asked to shoulder responsibility within the community: the Cellarer (31.2), the monk responsible for the infirmary (36.7), and the Porter (66.1). Each role requires a relevant set of skills but in every case, and no less for the Abbot, the first requirement is the capacity to function according to the faith-based wisdom that springs from living in «the fear of the Lord»[4]. This is a founding disposition, a permanent, original element that lies at the heart of Benedictine community life, and, I argue in this paper, is integral to all Christian behaviour. This disposition has implications for all those who seek to live in the poverty of humility that grows from baptism into Christ, as it affects

3 T.A. Kardong, *Benedict's Rule: A Translation and Commentary*, Collegeville (MN) 1996, 430.

4 Kardong, *Benedict's Rule.* In relation to the Abbot (3.11) fear of God and observance of the *Rule* are the two principle restraints on authority proposed by Benedict. Of the two, fear of God is «...integral to all religious behaviour», 74.

the way they relate to all whom they meet, within the community, and beyond its walls[5].

The foundational disposition of fear of the Lord/reverence for God/ humility, applies not only to the monastery. The scriptural designation the House of God (the *domus Dei*)[6] recognizes solidarity with the chosen people, and stands for the community of believers, the members of the household that constitutes the church, the body of Christ. The designation can be applied with equal validity to the Monastery, to a Congregation or Parish, or the whole people of God – the worldwide Church of God. All of these entities, however they choose to manage their life, are communities of faith that give priority to aligning themselves with an understanding of faith that Benedict described as «God-fearing» (36.6) or living in the «fear of the Lord» Prologue 29. He later crystalized this understanding into meaning that his communities were to live preferring «nothing whatever to Christ» (72. 11). The fear of the Lord will be defined further in the next section, but the priority this has in the community of faith means that, by definition, the church is not a corporation that is working to maximize the wealth of its owners or shareholders. It is a fellowship of human beings who align themselves with faith, in this case, faith grounded in God's work in Christ for us. The church is not just another organization, God has gathered it together in Jesus Christ and formed it into a community of faith that seeks to bear witness to the riches of God's self-giving love for the world[7]. Christ's work for us, in all its aspects, inaugurated the Kingdom, God's reign amongst us, and it is this that shapes what the church is and how it lives out its life in the world.

In the community of Christ, can there be a happy marriage between modern forms of corporatized governance and the Spirit that drives the ecclesiastical polity of the House of God? What does it mean to seek God and live preferring «nothing before Christ» while also being accountable to the many domains of

---

5 A. De Vogue, *The Rule of St Benedict*: a doctrinal and spiritual commentary (Cistercian Studies Series 54) Kalamazoo (Michigan), 1983, 123, «Whether you envisage it from the standpoint of the text from Isaiah or from that of the Psalm, the fear of God appears as a permanent, given element in the monastic life. It is not only at its origin, it is at its heart».

6 1Timothy 3,15, 1Peter 4,17, Ephesians 2,19, *Interpreter's Dictionary of the Bible*, vol. E-J, 610 and vol. A-D, 658, Nashville (TN) 1962. Almost all descriptions of the church in the New Testament utilize images and concepts that have been applied to God's people, suggesting recognition of solidarity with Israel.

7 The inspiration for these thoughts is from M. Owen, *Stewardship of Property – Stewardship of Truth*, unpublished paper, 5, referring to *The Basis of Union* of The Uniting Church in Australia, 1992 edition, sections 4-8.

interest – legal, financial, ethical and moral, to name just a few – that intersect with our life and work? How can the church ensure it does not become captive to the foreign ideology that inhabits the doctrines of management thinking? What does it really mean to live in «the fear of the Lord»?

2. LIVING IN THE FEAR OF THE LORD

The language of the «fear of the Lord» (*timentes Dominum*) saturates the Hebrew Scriptures, where a positive connotation dominates. The fear of the Lord is the beginning of wisdom (Proverbs 9:10) and is synonymous with living in fidelity to God's Covenant with Israel. This positive understanding continues into the New Testament where Gentiles who affiliated with Jewish Synagogues are referred to as «God Fearers»(Acts 10:2)[8]. The «fear of the Lord» is also used to describe the awe and wonder resulting from Jesus' works of power (Mark 4:41)[9]. Within the Christian tradition the influence of apostolic texts such as 1 John 4:18, («There is no fear in love, but perfect love casts out fear; for fear has to do with punishment, and whoever fears has not reached perfection in love») has brought forth the meaning that love is the opposite of fear, and fear is even said to be abolished. This means that, thanks to God's love, which never ends (1Cor. 13:8), fear for ourselves may and should come to an end. But reverence and awe for God grows deeper as we draw closer to God (Ps 19:9).

Living in the fear of the Lord involves reverent submission to God, which means emptying ourselves to allow the sovereignty of God to have first claim in all matters. This means giving priority to the narrative of the Gospel and the imagination that brings to birth, rather than subordinating ourselves to whatever ideology becomes prominent in our time. This stance is manifest in the life of the prophets of Israel, whose priority was to allow the word of God to stand first, even if it meant having to speak truth to power. This stance is seen to be supremely at work in Jesus of Nazareth who, in reverent submission (Heb 5:7) and self-emptying, did not grasp at equality with God (Phil 2:5-11). Instead he entrusted himself (1Pet 2:23) to live in complete openness to the creative, life-giving power we know as God-with-us. Paradoxically this openness to God led Jesus to be more fully human and to demonstrate what true humanity is. Put another way, his relationship with God was the resource that enabled him to live an inclusive, healing and empowering life that embraced the poor and the out-

8 All biblical quotes are from the *New Revised Standard Version*.

9 Kardong, *Benedict's Rule*, 17.

cast in his community, brought liberation in place of oppression, allowed him to speak truth to power, and embodied all that is meant by Kingdom of God.

Benedict's strong reliance on scripture means the fear of the Lord is a central theme in the *Rule.* For him this is the basis for a reverential community in which practical concern for the other is practiced. The Cellarer is to be «God-fearing... like a father to the whole of the community» (31.2), the Infirmarian is to be «God-fearing, attentive and concerned» (36.7), and «all guests who present themselves are to be welcomed as Christ, for he himself will say: *I was a stranger, and you welcomed me»* (Matt 25:35) (53.1). For Benedict the full meaning of the fear of the Lord bears fruit in attentive hearts that overflow «with the inexpressible delights of love» (Prologue 49) as the community members show pure love to each other, loving fear to God, unfeigned and humble love for their Abbot, and live together preferring «nothing whatever to Christ» (72.8-11). The fear of the Lord proven as love is a necessary disposition of monastic life. As Adalbert de Vogüé says: «it is not only at its origin, it is at its heart»[10]. Similarly so for the whole church that seeks to maintain reverence, for God, reverence for all people, particularly the stranger and the vulnerable and, in the days of climate change, reverence for the whole of Creation. Furthermore, living in the fear of the Lord, understood as living faithfully on the basis of the Gospel, becomes the measure of all knowledge and action.

3. MANAGEMENT AND MODERN LIFE

Benedict was familiar with management because human beings have long acted in groups to achieve particular outcomes, the construction of the Pyramids being an obvious, ancient case in point. However, the conventional history of management practice locates its origins in the late nineteenth century, a period typified as Modern, which was deeply impacted by industrialization, and the rise of scientific method. At that time a group of people who were trying to make machines more efficient moved on to experiment and theorize about improving efficiency in *human* performance[11]. Prominent thinkers in the movement were Frederick Taylor, Henri Fayol and Max Weber. Taylor's work replaced a «rule of thumb» approach with scientific methods. Fayol conceived of management as a separate field that was applicable to all situations in which it would

10 De Vogue, *The Rule of St Benedict*, 123, I have extrapolated de Vogue's point to fit all Christian life.

11 In this section I am relying on the work of Cummings, *ReCreating,* 84-85, my emphasis.

deliver outcomes through practices that were regarded as universal functions: planning, organizing, directing, coordinating, and the principle of the division of labour. Weber consolidated the work of these two men in his principles of organization[12]. By 1947, management science was born, and was soon established as a discipline to be studied. In 1954 the American Management Association (A.M.A.) found that the 'functions of planning, organizing (the division of labour) and executing... corresponded to an understanding that management was about *improving efficiency*'[13] notably with the introduction of a powerful management body placed over the organization. This stance, evolved from rationalistic principles drawn from industry and scientific thinking that privileged productivity, gave weight to mechanical functions, and tended to treat people as unrelated entities rather than as real people.

Management science inherited Modernism's belief in progress, cared little for tradition or history and was blatantly optimistic about its own potential, believing that «efficient management has the ability to solve almost any problem»[14]. Stephen Cummings comments that the history of management highlights only what modernists believed was important: namely, their contribution to the world[15]. Modernism did not delve into the past to discover the true story but read back into history the view that all clever civilizations have attempted to use the same methods as rationalist modernist thinkers[16]. Cummings, who is open to pre-modern and post-modern ways of thinking, follows Foucault in advocating that we must interrogate historical conceptions[17] and «get in touch with an ocean of mutually incompatible alternatives» that are available to us[18]. This emphasis is important for socially oriented organizations such as those that are artistic or community based, which seek social outcomes that are harder to measure than those in industry. The Church belongs in this category. It is not a

12 Cummings, *ReCreating*, 85.

13 Cummings, *ReCreating*, my emphasis, 89.

14 S. Bellamy, «*Management*», in *An Informed Faith: the Uniting Church at the beginning of the 21st Century*, ed. W.E. Emilsen, Morning Star, Northcote 2016, article by 123. See also Owen, *Stewardship of Property*, 31-32. Owen, who draws on Z. Bauman, *Postmodern Ethics*, Oxford/Cambridge MA, Blackwell 1993/1996, 42 and E.H.. Carr, *What is History?* London 2008, 109-111 who says this view «depends on the modern belief in progress» and is a «secular adaptation of biblical faith in the final fulfilment of God's purposes».

15 Cummings, *ReCreating*, 89.

16 Cummings, *ReCreating*, 6.

17 Cummings, *ReCreating*, 6.

18 Cummings, *ReCreating*, 245.

time-bound community but has a long history, which includes the memory of managing people and organizations. Its traditions also allow it access to transcendent resources that motivate the loyalties of its people towards objectives that are personal and community oriented, that are extensive and diverse, and often prove resistant to rational, secular methods of measurement[19].

Since the 1970s, reforms have been introduced in a number of countries, including Australia, known as «New Public Management» (N.P.M.), which is a synonym for management based on the business model that imposes a powerful management body over organizations. New Public Management is driven by efficiency, keeps discipline under tight control and measures accountability based on results[20]. Sometimes referred to as «New Managerialism», New Public Management has been embraced by many not for profit organizations, and non-government organizations including the health system and universities. For example, in my context, formerly professional academics were in charge of universities and administrative staff did their bidding. But the introduction of N.P.M. reversed these roles. Universities are now regarded as part of an education industry that is subject to quantifiable measurements more related to economic rationalism than to creative, artistic or social output. Sheila Bellamy has argued that New Managerialism is «more than a cult» it is deeply embedded in our society[21]. It must be engaged with because good governance is an obligation not an option. But faced with pressure to be «more business-like» it is important to remember that management principles do not always transfer easily from one organization to another, and may be based on «inappropriate assumptions about reality» that restrict the ability to think of alternative approaches to problem solving[22]. For the church, openness to alternative approaches to problem solving include those learned through its long history of managing communities according to vision of and values of the Kingdom, grounded in the Gospel of

19 Bellamy, *Management*, 118. Typically, in the Australian church organizations Accountants have been found to accept the importance of transcendent agendas, but clergy will be resistant to making decisions based on economic rationalism because mission, not finance should determine objective, see Bellamy, *Management*, 121.

20 Bellamy, *Management*, 118, 121-2. This is different from a conciliar form of government in a faith-based organization that is intended to be open to the God, and the wisdom of the people gathered in council under God. Such governance is grounded in structures of mutual submission that do not privilege behaviour that is dominating or competitive.

21 Bellamy, *Management*, 123.

22 Bellamy, *Management*, 125, quoting from P. Drucker, «Management's New Paradigms», *Forbes* (05-10-1998) 1.

Jesus Christ. Cummings himself makes a further point that alerts us also to the dangers of accepting the tutelage of management science and speak. He says:

> Given the extent to which management now permeates the way we judge life, management's limits now potentially undermine our ability to think differently... in other spheres. We have begun to witness an outpouring of creative works in other applied fields such as medicine, architecture, physics and art through their revisiting different dimensions or styles *from their pasts*...However, the danger is that one of our most unidimensional and least creative applied subjects is now being increasingly employed to monitor and judge our most creative. This may mean that instead of the multidimensional society necessary to enable creative development to continue, the unidimensional logic of management and strategy could end up overriding other fields in such a way as to limit us to...the twentieth century's mantra of «development in the name of efficiency»[23].

As Benedict has shown, church structures do need to be managed. The challenge is that management is now so central to modern living that it has become an ideology with a life of its own, which, if employed unthinkingly, can impact the church's identity and purpose and undermine its understanding and practice of its faith. The Church that loses its grip on its theological heart, soul and mind risks compromising its identity and starts to act according to the rules of a corporation, rather than according to the spirit of the body of Christ.

4. FAITHFUL MANAGEMENT – LIVING BY GODLY WISDOM – REMEMBERING

What matters is that the Church maintains its accountability to God for its faithful living. This means that, as it confronts the challenges of corporatization it must continue to think theologically about its life so that its identity and integrity as a community of faith, that lives in the sovereignty of God as inspired by Gospel of Jesus Christ, remains intact. Through reflection on Scripture and participation in the liturgy the church constantly chooses to remember its origin and purpose in the world[24]. In doing so it remains a conscious body and remains in control of the vision that inspires its actions in the community, alert

23 CUMMINGS, *ReCreating*, 8, my emphasis.

24 In Scripture the *Shema*, in the harvest liturgy (Deuteronomy 26,4-9), is a classic "remembrance". In Benedictine spirituality prayer is understood as the *memoir Dei.*

to the many traps that the world throws up, including corporatization, which have the potential to undermine its heritage in faith, and disfigure its life.

Remembering whose it is, and what it is for, is the key. Remembering involves coming to the awareness that the self-serving love for innovation that inhabits Managerialism can overlook the long history of learning that is the heritage of the church, and cut off the opportunity to think of creative alternatives that might apply. For example, in the 1980s my church went through a process of re-branding an agency called «Good Samaritan Industries» that provided a sheltered workshop for disabled people. The marketing department decided that people did not know what «Good Samaritan» meant and, since the company name was regularly shortened to «G.S.I.» or «Good Sammies», they invented a logo of «Sammy the Seal» and dropped all reference to the parable from which the organization took its cue. If it was true that people did not know what the original name meant, an explanation given by staff who had been inducted into the true knowledge of why the organization existed and the parable that inspired their work would have not only been honest, it may have opened up new levels of meaningful conversations for those involved. In this way the organization may have served another purpose, it may have become a living hermeneutic for the Gospel.

The church is ruled by Christ the Good Shepherd whom we remember as one who cares for the sheep, while the hired hand does not[25]. The use of hired hands is the biblical equivalent of outsourcing, a common practice with many pitfalls. In the process of corporatization, consultants, whose historical origin is in the Modernist heritage outlined above, are usually called in to assist with making changes[26]. The consultant's language and ethos are based on assumptions that are often quite fixed, and differ from the body they are hired to assist. Also there is a danger that the principles that apply to one sector cannot always be easily transferred to another[27]. It is not just a problem of translation. Relying on the consultant's preferences rather than the resources of faith and the people's wisdom can distort the process and lead to incomplete or inappropriate outcomes. For example, in my church a large debt incurred when a new school project failed created an urgent need to address the financial liability. While in principle

25 John 10,1-6, 11-15.

26 CUMMINGS, *ReCreating*, 165. He cites Alastair Macintyre who said that consultants represent the merger of two characters thrown up by Modernism: the therapist who dispensed objective advice about behaviour, and the expert manager committed to increased efficiency.

27 CUMMINGS, *ReCreating*, 263-264.

the Uniting Church is organized as a flat structure of Councils, designed to allow for a wide and ordered sharing of responsibility in decisions affecting its life, panic or fear of reputational risk lead to a breach of normal processes. A series of management decisions were made under the provision of «special circumstances» that ran contrary to the spirit that is normally meant to rule in the church. The central office adopted a top-down approach, and hired non-church staff and consultants with property experience to help solve the problem of the debt. The hired hands were strongly focussed on monetary values rather than the deeper, self-giving values of the church, and normal protections were lost. The resulting outcomes were damaging and distressful for many congregations and individuals, the ramifications of which will be felt for many years to come. The employment of hired hands added to the problems the church was confronted with. It exacerbated the loss of trust that occurred between the congregations and councils of the church, especially regarding the operations of the central office, and it allowed continuing patterns of behaviour to become established that were outside the ethos of the church. Remembering means recalling whose we are and the need to manage our communities faithfully. This translates into being willing to critically evaluate a consultant's ability to genuinely care for the community they have been hired to help, through being able to enter into their ethos and understand it, and to work within it with deft sensitivity.

Remembering also means being aware that management thinking relies on an ideology of progress that is at vastly at odds with our understanding of life in the Reign of God. The belief that «efficient management has the ability to solve almost any problem»[28], depends on the modern belief in progress and is a secular adaptation of biblical faith in the final fulfilment of God's purposes[29]. Remembering means being reminded that the Kingdom is God's gift to us, not something we create. It is quite different from progress, and is not measurable in the way that management seeks to measure results. On the basis of 1 Corinthians 7, Michael Owen argues that:

> We are not called to transform the life of this world, but [to allow] ourselves to be transformed within its structures. Change for change's sake can be of little significance[30]. Christian presence, witness, and mission within a society and culture may lead to positive changes over time, but they are always side benefits,

28 Bellamy, *Management*, 123.

29 See footnote 13, I am relying on Owen, *Stewardship of Property*, 38, for these ideas.

30 1Corinthians 7,8-11,17-28.

consequential to active witness to Jesus Christ and God's promises in him; and they are always at risk of being overridden or distorted by forces at work in the particular society and culture[31].

Remembering means continuing to be aware that the church is not a corporation with a powerful management body placed over it. The church is «uniquely anti-authoritarian»[32]. It is communitarian, a fellowship of human beings who form a living body with Christ the Good Shepherd at its head. Corporate life in the body of Christ is measured by the quality of the relationships it maintains within the fellowship and offers to people in the world[33]. This includes an attitude of loving respect and mutual submission to one another, as the faithful grow towards the new order of life gifted to them in the promised Kingdom[34]. In the community of Christ who drank the cup of suffering to the full there is to be no lauding over others, and sacrificial service is the counter-intuitive measure of greatness (Matt 20,26-7). The difference in focus means that *how* the Church goes about things is just as important as what it seeks to achieve. We see this reflected in the quality of love Benedict expects of the Abbot and his managers. And it is seen in the respect for the wisdom of the people that is present in the Catholic doctrine of subsidiarity, which acknowledges the social nature of human life, and calls for those closest to the outcome of decisions to be involved in making them[35]. In my own church a cost cutting exercise decided upon by the central office without consultation, threatened the theological college with re-

31 OWEN, *Stewardship of Property*, 38.

32 BELLAMY, *Management*, 124

33 John 13,34-35,1 John 4,7-12, 1Corinthians 13:1-13

34 Both the *Rule* and the *Basis of Union* of The Uniting Church in Australia strongly affirm this point, and build it into the structure of community life as well as processes of decision-making.

35 Caritas Australia Website site, http://www.socialjustice.catholic.org.au/social-teaching [access 25/11/2016]: Subsidiarity: Just as it is gravely wrong to take from individuals what they can accomplish by their own initiative and industry and give it to the community, so also it is an injustice and at the same time a grave evil and disturbance of right order to assign to a greater and higher association what lesser and subordinate organizations can do. PIUS XI «Litterae Encyclicae *Quadragesimo Anno* (15 maii 1931)», *AAS* 23 (1931) 179.
The principle of subsidiarity protects people from abuses by higher-level social authority and calls on these same authorities to help individuals and intermediate groups to fulfil their duties. This principle is imperative because every person, family and intermediate group has something original to offer to the community. Compendium of the Social Doctrine of the Church par. 187.

dundancies. The college responded saying it did not support the plan and would find an alternative way of solving the problem. The principal and the staff collaborated in a confidential process that resulted in the choice to raise the money that would otherwise be saved by redundancy through their own salary sacrifice. The plan succeeded because a collaborative style was used instead of the method employed by the head office.

CONCLUSION – WHEN IS A CHURCH NOT A CHURCH?

The danger for the Church as it confronts the need to comply with a new regulatory environment and corporatize its structures is that the received trend in Management is to acknowledge only one set of historical influences, which are Modernist, in which the role of religious belief is routinely played down. Being prepared to think theologically and live in the «fear of the Lord» means remembering that for the Church – as for all religious communities – faith is fundamental to identity and gives meaning and purpose to the shared life and work. The practice of remembering faithfully leads to the church being itself, and by this means it may serve to open up managerialism to a wider range of influences as well as continue to remember its own calling and purpose in the world. When is a church not a church? When it fails to remember whose it is and what it serves in the world, and begins instead to think and act like a corporation rather than live as the body of Christ.

Abstract

Drawing on resources that Benedictine life and the *Rule* have to offer this paper explores what it means to operate a faith-based organization in a context in which management thinking and practice has achieved ideological status. Managerialism is a Modernist construction that is steeped in assumptions based on scientific method, coupled with the experience of industrialization. Supremely confident in its own ability, its goal is to create efficient organizations that produce predictable and measurable results to make profit for their owners. This paper discusses what it means for the church to comply with the governance obligations that are expected of it without becoming trapped by the imposition of a foreign ideology that pays little or no attention to its ethos, and devalues or ignores its heritage. Benedict was aware of the risks outside influences posed, and sought to enable his communities to live preferring «nothing whatever to Christ» (72.11). In this way he laid a foundation for thinking about how to prioritize seeking to live as the Body of Christ and avoid being dominated by the principles of corporate management, and the values of the free market economy.

GOOD PRACTICES

ESEMPI DI VALORIZZAZIONE DEL PATRIMONIO IPOGEO APPLICABILI ANCHE A STRUTTURE MONASTICHE

Carla GALEAZZI – Carlo GERMANI – Mario MAZZOLI

INTRODUZIONE

La cultura delle strutture monastiche presenta numerosi aspetti di grande interesse. Alcuni di questi sono stati resi evidenti grazie al lavoro, al pensiero, all'attenzione e alla concreta testimonianza di numerosissimi monaci che, in larga parte, sono riusciti a trasmetterli anche alle comunità laiche. Altri elementi degni di attenzione quali peculiarità delle opere architettoniche, storie di persone e di luoghi (e talvolta misteri) sono meno noti. Molto più spesso di quanto si possa pensare queste tracce si sono smarrite nel tempo e non è raro che gli stessi monaci possano averne perso completamente memoria. Si può trattare di documenti, reperti, racconti, tradizioni, mestieri oppure, come nel caso di questa testimonianza, di una vera e propria «dimensione»: la terza.

Lo scopo di questo contributo è di accendere una luce sulla dimensione sotterranea delle grandi opere di fede e di architettura perché possa essere considerata dalle Comunità Monastiche come una prospettiva da riscoprire, conoscere e, in alcuni casi, valorizzare. È in questo contesto che subentrano le competenze speleologiche e progettuali, strettamente correlate ed indispensabili alla concreta conoscenza di *cosa ci sia sotto*, affinché l'eredità lasciata dai predecessori possa essere riletta ed analizzata sia dal punto di vista culturale che destinata a nuovi progetti di sostentamento delle Comunità Monastiche.

La speleologia è un'attività di studio multidisciplinare che comprende l'insieme delle scienze necessarie alla comprensione di un fenomeno ipogeo. Speleologo è chi indaga il mondo sotterraneo dopo aver acquisito una specifica preparazione tecnica e scientifica, attraverso corsi dedicati e, soprattutto, lunga esperienza.

Carla Galeazzi, Carlo Germani: speleologists, researchers at Egeria Centro Ricerche Sotterranee.
Mario Mazzoli: speleologist, researcher at A.S.S.O. (Archeologia Subacquea Speleologia Organizzazione).

Per attività speleologica si intende l'esplorazione del mondo sotterraneo, la sua osservazione diretta, la ricerca di vie precluse, l'analisi dei parametri ambientali, la stesura del rilievo topografico e l'acquisizione della documentazione, anche bibliografica, di grotte e, come nel caso in oggetto, di cavità artificiali intese come opere sotterranee di interesse storico ed antropologico realizzate dall'uomo o da esso riadattate alle proprie necessità. Sono infatti considerate cavità artificiali sia le opere realizzate dall'uomo – scavate, costruite in sotterraneo o divenute ipogee per sovrapposizione stratigrafica – sia quelle naturali da esso riadattate almeno in parte alle proprie necessità quali, per esempio, le grotte naturali dell'arco alpino utilizzate come rifugio durante la prima guerra mondiale, gli eremitaggi in ripari naturali, i rifugi abituali dei pastori durante la transumanza.

1. STRUTTURE EREMITICHE E SOTTERRANEI DELLE STRUTTURE MONASTICHE

Gli eremiti e le piccole comunità monastiche operavano il distacco dal mondo anche in termini pratici, utilizzando frequentemente i primi ambienti di grotte naturali chiusi o suddivisi internamente con muretti a secco e forniti di ingegnosi sistemi di raccolta delle acque di percolazione, stalle per animali, luoghi per seppellire i defunti e piccoli orti di sussistenza che, in presenza di condizioni avverse quali forti pendii, venivano ospitati in riquadrature nel terreno.

Nelle zone in cui la struttura geologica è caratterizzata dalla presenza di rocce tenere e facilmente aggredibili, l'uomo ha scavato per millenni. Anche gli eremiti, quindi, approfittarono della facilità di scavo in alcuni luoghi per realizzare strutture insediative semplici, composte da celle per riposare e pregare, camere di alloggiamento per animali, captazione e trasporti di vene d'acqua, ecc.

Nelle comunità monastiche cenobitiche, invece, le strutture erano molto più complesse, spesso caratterizzate dalla presenza di ambienti sotterranei quali cantine, magazzini, cripte, vie di fuga, cisterne, ecc.

Dal punto di vista speleologico tutte le strutture monastiche, sia nelle forme eremitiche che cenobitiche, rappresentano tipologie di grande interesse. Mentre le chiese bizantine e i complessi monastici caratterizzati dalla presenza di dipinti, affreschi, iscrizioni sono stati presi in esame dal mondo archeologico, molte altre strutture, o parti di esse, abbandonate nel corso dei secoli, attendono di essere riscoperte e valorizzate.

Da qualche anno alcune equipe speleologiche specializzate nel settore delle cavità artificiali esplorano e documentano anche questi ambienti che frequente-

Fig. 1 Eremo di Fosso di Loppieda in Valnerina.

mente meritano approfondimenti e che, molto spesso, potrebbero proficuamente essere inseriti in percorsi di visita o in altri progetti di valorizzazione. Questa è la convinzione degli autori e delle due organizzazioni no profit di grande esperienza e credibilità alle quali afferiscono: Egeria Centro Ricerche Sotterranee ed A.S.S.O. Le due associazioni vantano un lungo e documentato curriculum in materia che può essere reso disponibile a supporto dell'intera Comunità Monastica.

Allo scopo di agevolare la comprensione delle diverse prospettive, tutte complementari, con le quali sia possibile affrontare la tematica, in questa sede vengono presentati cinque diversi casi di studio: il censimento di tutte le strutture sotterranee del Monastero Esarchico di Santa Maria di Grottaferrata (Roma), condotto nel 2004 in occasione del millenario dell'Abbazia e mirato alla ricerca dei resti dei Padri fondatori; l'indagine speleologica della Grotta Rumice (Palestrina, Roma); lo studio di antiche strutture idrauliche sotto la Chiesa di Santa Sabina (Roma); la riscoperta delle dimenticate Grotte di San Famiano (Faleria, Viterbo) e lo studio, rilievo e valorizzazione dei sotterranei del Palazzo Caetani a Cisterna di Latina (Latina).

1.1. I sotterranei del monastero esarchico di Santa Maria di Grottaferrata (Roma)

Il Monastero di Santa Maria di Grottaferrata, detto anche Abbazia Greca di San Nilo, fu fondato dai discepoli del Santo ed è l'ultimo dei numerosi monasteri bizantini che nel Medioevo si erano diffusi in tutta l'Italia meridionale e nella stessa Roma. L'abbazia, situata pochi chilometri a sud-est di Roma sulle prime propaggini dei Colli Albani, fu portata a termine da San Bartolomeo con l'aiuto dei monaci che si erano raccolti intorno al primo nucleo, lavorando venti anni alla costruzione della chiesa ed utilizzando materiale di riporto proveniente dalle rovine di una preesistente villa romana: colonne e lastre di marmo, trabeazioni scolpite, blocchi di peperino.

Nel corso dei secoli la chiesa ha subito vari interventi architettonici e di restauro. L'aspetto attuale è in gran parte dovuto alle fortificazioni erette nel XV secolo dal cardinale Giuliano della Rovere. Le modifiche più gravi furono apportate nel 1754 dal cardinale Guadagni, che sovrappose alle antiche strutture un pesante stile barocco. Nei primi decenni del secolo scorso alcune opere di ripristino, finanziate dal Ministero della Pubblica Istruzione restituirono parzialmente all'Abbazia tratti dell'aspetto originario.

Nel 2004 l'abbazia di San Nilo ha festeggiato il millenario dalla sua fondazione. Fra gli innumerevoli progetti voluti e coordinati dal Rev.mo Archimandrita Padre Emiliano Fabbricatore, si è inserita la completa esplorazione e rivisitazione degli ipogei ricadenti nel territorio dell'Abbazia.

Fig. 2 Abbazia di Santa Maria di Grottaferrata discesa sotto alla Cappella Farnesiana.

L'iniziativa fu proposta ed accolta dall'associazione A.S.S.O. che volle come partner nel suggestivo progetto il Centro Ricerche Sotterranee Egeria. Le due organizzazioni hanno condotto un lavoro organico di grande interesse pubblicato nel 2005 sulla rivista Opera Ipogea alla quale si rimanda per la trattazione completa delle evidenze sotterranee censite. In considerazione della complessità stratigrafica e storica del contesto, nell'affrontare lo studio fu indispensabile individuare un metodo che consentisse di presentare nel modo più organico possibile il risultato delle indagini. Si procedette classificando, documentando e rilevando accuratamente tutte le strutture ipogee presenti, ascrivendole alle rispettive epoche di realizzazione: compito di certo non semplice, stante la complessa storia dell'architettura abbaziale.

Le indagini, condotte con la massima accuratezza e rispetto per la sacralità del luogo, si sono indirizzate a documentare un aspetto della millenaria struttura finora sostanzialmente ignorato: quello ipogeo.

Fig. 3 Esplorazione ipogei dell'Abbazia di Santa Maria di Grottaferrata.

Il corso delle esplorazioni rese evidente anche a Padre Emiliano ed ai Monaci l'importanza dell'attività poiché, anche nel caso di San Nilo, le testimonianze del passato si conservano più chiare e leggibili al "di sotto", attraverso l'attento esame delle opere spesso non monumentali, ma indispensabili alla vita di tutti i giorni: quelle destinate all'approvvigionamento idrico, alla conservazione degli alimenti e del vino, allo smaltimento fognario e alle sepolture.

Lo studio, inoltre, costituì la base per successivi approfondimenti tematici condotti dal Centro Ricerche Sotterranee Egeria nei dintorni dell'Abbazia (Valli Molara e Marciana) e verso il sud d'Italia, percorrendo a ritroso il lungo cammino di San Nilo e documentando le tracce lasciate sul territorio dalle comunità grecaniche. Parallelamente, A.S.S.O. realizzò un documentario, a cura di Massimo D'Alessandro, dal titolo "Il mistero di San Nilo" che ha ottenuto grande apprezzamento a livello internazionale e che sarà proiettato nel corso del Simposio.

Purtroppo le indagini non hanno avuto esito positivo nell'individuazione delle spoglie di San Nilo e San Bartolomeo, ma il lavoro svolto ha gettato una nuova luce sull'Abbazia e sulla possibilità di intraprendere ulteriori ricerche, in collaborazione con la Comunità e gli Enti preposti alla tutela del patrimonio storico, religioso ed archeologico, e di valorizzare alcuni ipogei integrandoli in un avvincente e alternativo percorso di visita.

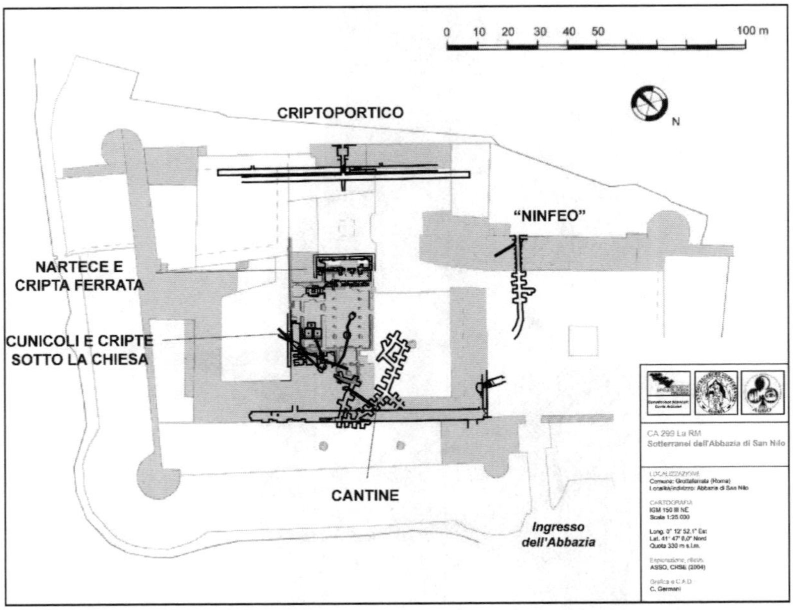

Fig. 4 Abbazia di Santa Maria di Grottaferrata
rilievo topografico delle strutture sotterranee.

1.2. La Grotta Rumice (Castel San Pietro Romano, Palestrina, Roma)

Il toponimo "rumice" richiama il termine romitorio. La grotta naturale si trova nell'area soprastante il quartiere degli Scacciati a Palestrina, sulla via di costa che anticamente saliva sino a Castel San Pietro consentendo il collegamento fra la città di *Praeneste* e la sua acropoli. L'ampia visuale sul paesaggio sottostante e l'evocazione propria della "salita al monte" suggerisce la frequentazione devozionale del luogo.

Fig. 5 Grotta Rumice: l'ingresso.

La grotta si apre a circa metà dell'antico sentiero. Qui la tradizione, tramandata sino ai nostri giorni, vuole che nel VI secolo d.C. tre eremite (Herundine, Romola e Redenta) si rifugiassero per astrarsi dal mondo civile raccogliendosi in preghiera. Note sulla vita delle tre eremite si ritrovano nella *Historia delle Sante Vergini Romane* e negli *Annali Ecclesiastici tratti da quelli del Cardinal Baronio.*

Dall'analisi dei testi nei *Secoli Agostiniani* le eremite potrebbero essere state quattro. Si trattò quindi di una piccola comunità eremitica femminile che cercò rifugio nella Grotta Rumice vivendo in isolamento, per motivi religiosi o per assistere Romola nel momento finale della malattia.

Fig. 6 Grotta Rumice: l'interno.

La grotta è facilmente accessibile dalla strada con un percorso di grande suggestione, mentre risultano scarse le indicazioni turistiche e completamente assenti quelle relative all'uso come eremitaggio. Le ricerche effettuate dal Centro Ricerche Sotterranee Egeria suggeriscono che con interventi economici assolutamente esigui e minimo impatto ambientale il luogo potrebbe divenire un sito di grande interesse nonostante l'ubicazione in un territorio come quello di Palestrina, già fortemente caratterizzato da importanti evidenze archeologiche.

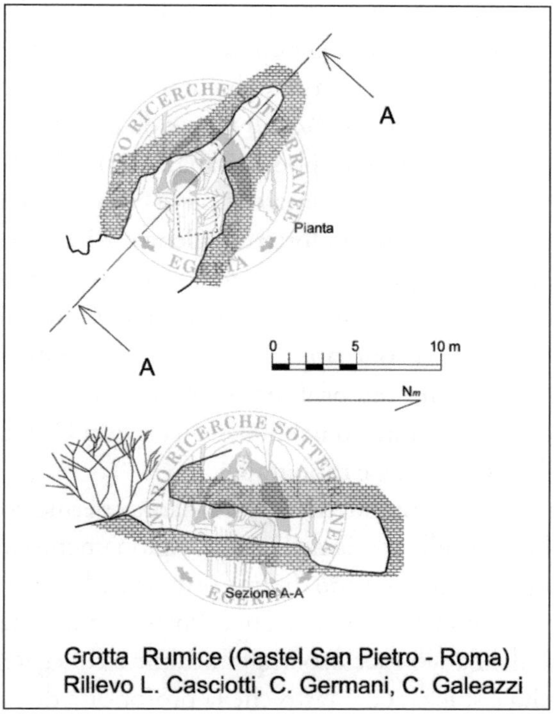

Fig. 7 Rilievo topografico della Grotta Rumice.

1.3. I cunicoli idraulici della Basilica di Santa Sabina (Roma)

Nel 1855 il padre domenicano Besson diresse lo scavo di una porzione di terreno tra la Basilica di S. Sabina e il fianco verso il Tevere. Le notevoli scoperte furono descritte e studiate da Ch. Descemet[1]. Fra queste il ritrovamento di cunicoli profondi ubicati a 15 metri sul livello del mare (s.l.m.) e a -30 metri dal piano di calpestio attuale, costituiti da una galleria principale che dava accesso a cunicoli trasversali, alcuni dei quali raggiungevano ambienti di età romana con pavimenti a mosaico.

La galleria fu esplorata per 380 metri e fu interpretata da Descemet come un braccio dell'Acquedotto Appio (312 a.C.). Tra il 1936 e il 1939 F. M. D. Darsy[2]

1 Ch. Descemet, «Mémoire sur les fouilles exécutées a Santa Sabina (1855-1857)», *Mémoires présentés par divers savants à l'Académie des inscriptions et belles-lettres de l'Institut de France* 6 (1864) 165-205.

2 F.M. Darsy, *Recherches archéologiques à Sainte Sabine* (Monumenti dell'Antichità Cristia-

riprese gli scavi di Descemet e risistemò il pozzo di accesso ai livelli più profondi ed eseguì opere di consolidamento per contenere i dissesti presenti nelle gallerie e nei cunicoli. Darsy ipotizzò che la rete di cunicoli del livello più alto fossero fogne realizzate nel 184 a.C. da *M. Porcius Cato* e da *L. Valerius Flaccus* nell'ambito di un vasto programma di sviluppo e risanamento dell'abitato urbano e attribuì, come il Descemet, all'Acquedotto Appio il cunicolo più profondo.

Nel 2005, grazie allo studio condotto dal Centro Ricerche Sotterranee Egeria in collaborazione con il geologo Leonardo Lombardi, sono stati nuovamente esplorati i cunicoli appartenenti sia alla rete posta a 36 metri s.l.m. sia a quella posta a 15 metri s.l.m. Essi sono apparsi in buono stato di conservazione, ad eccezione di alcuni ambienti più profondi occlusi da detriti e non più raggiungibili. Lo studio è stato pubblicato nel 2007 sulla rivista Opera Ipogea e ad esso si rimanda per i dettagli tecnici e topografici.

Vale però sottolineare che i dati acquisiti hanno permesso di trarre alcune importanti conclusioni sulla storia dell'approvvigionamento idrico in rapporto allo sviluppo abitativo dell'Aventino. In una prima fase l'acqua fu ottenuta dalla pioggia e conservata in cisterne sotterranee, costituite da una rete di cunicoli scavati all'interno del banco roccioso impermeabile e collegati alla superficie da pozzi. Questa scelta è spiegata dal fatto che la profondità dell'acquifero era notevole (-30 metri dal piano di calpestio delle abitazioni di età romana) cosa che rendeva l'attingimento dell'acqua assai difficoltoso. È probabile che in questa fase fossero anche sfruttate le sorgenti nella porzione bassa del colle sul versante occidentale e, forse, meridionale.

Il primo acquedotto che raggiunse il colle fu l'*Aqua Marcia*, inaugurata secondo le fonti nel 144 a.C. La costruzione dell'opera comportò, probabilmente, il graduale abbandono del sistema di conservazione d'acqua in cunicoli e l'obliterazione dei pozzi da parte delle nuove strutture in opera reticolata. All'acquedotto furono collegati i castelli terminali presenti sull'Aventino e rimase la principale fonte di approvvigionamento idrico dell'area in età imperiale.

In base alle osservazioni degli autori è da escludere, infine, che il lungo cunicolo presente a 15 metri s.l.m. fosse una derivazione dell'Acquedotto Appio, inaugurato nel 312 a.C.: più probabilmente la sua realizzazione aveva lo scopo di incrementare il volume d'acqua disponibile nel sistema cunicolare, drenando la più importante falda acquifera dell'area[3].

na II serie, 9) Roma-Città del Vaticano 1968.

3 Recenti ritrovamenti avvenuti durante lo scavo della linea C della Metropolitana di Roma hanno però riportato in discussione questa ipotesi.

L'indagine dei cunicoli idraulici della Chiesa di Santa Sabina, oltre a restituire un importante rilettura della storia dell'approvvigionamento idrico della zona, ha consentito di ampliare il percorso di visita sotterraneo, anche se con necessità di attrezzatura minima per la progressione come casco e relativa illuminazione che, anziché recare disturbo ai visitatori, contribuiscono a rendere la visita più emozionate.

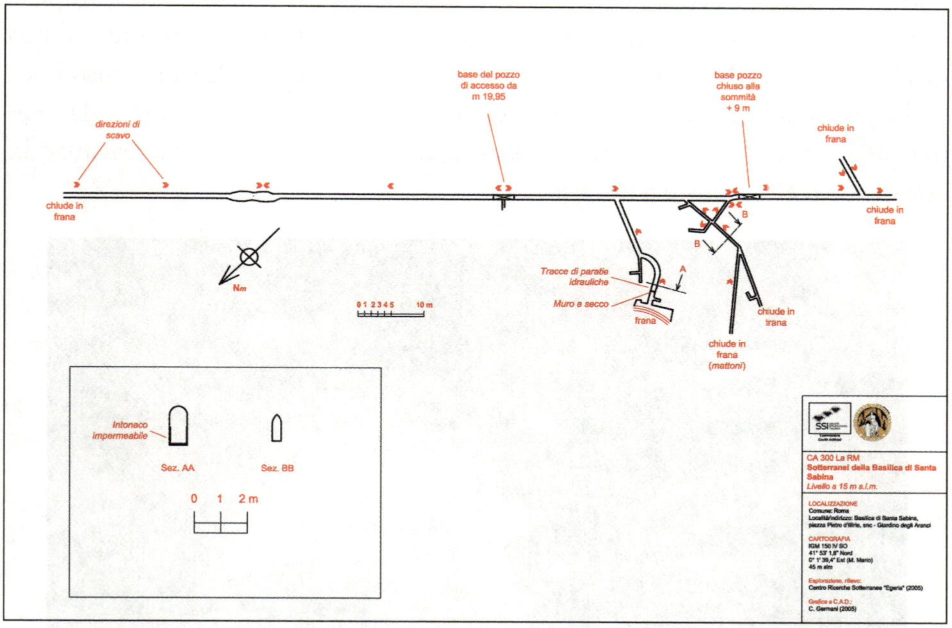

Fig. 8 Rilievo topografico dei cunicoli idraulici di Santa Sabina.

1.4. Le grotte di San Famiano (Faleria, Viterbo)

San Famiano era un frate cistercense nato a Colonia che condusse per molti anni vita eremitica in Spagna. Morì a Gallese (VT) nell'agosto del 1150. Dopo la morte fu canonizzato da Adriano IV e le sue spoglie furono deposte in una grotta sulla quale, nel 1155, fu eretta la chiesa che porta il suo nome. Nella grotta, che si trova oggi all'interno della chiesa, è custodito il prezioso sarcofago con il corpo del Santo, patrono del paese. A tre km dal centro storico di Gallese si trova, in un'altra chiesa dedicata, la cappella di San Famiano a Lungo. Il culto del Santo e la custodia delle due chiese sono affidati all'antica confraternita di San Famiano, ricostituitasi nel 1990.

Esiste però un terzo luogo di culto legato a San Famiano sino ad oggi sconosciuto in letteratura: le grotte di San Famiano, riscoperte dal Centro Ricerche Sotterranee Egeria, che devono la titolazione alla tradizione secondo la quale l'eremita trascorse qui i suoi ultimi giorni. Si trovano nel territorio di Faleria (VT), all'interno del bosco di Fogliano e sono costituite da una serie di ambienti di datazione incerta scavati lungo le pareti di una profonda forra sottostante il castello di Foiano. All'esterno la fascia tufacea evidenzia chiari segni di intervento antropico, soprattutto in corrispondenza dell'ingresso alle grotte. Di particolare interesse una nicchia con affreschi oggi quasi completamente obliterati dagli agenti atmosferici.

Le grotte si presentano con un piccolo ingresso dal quale, con una scala molto ripida, si accede alla camera soprastante, caratterizzata da sedili risparmiati in fase di scavo e una piccola finestra.

Fig. 9 Grotte di San Famiano la scala di accesso al piano superiore.

Tutta la struttura richiama la tipologia più frequente di cella eremitica. Oltre l'ingresso una clessidra scavata nel fianco tufaceo, molto alta, serviva probabilmente a tenere legato un cavallo. A fianco si trovano un piccolo sedile scavato nella roccia, protetto dal vento che in inverno arriva impetuoso dalla valle sottostante e altri due ambienti ipogei.

Il sentiero per arrivare alla grotta presenta un certa difficoltà di percorrenza nei mesi invernali perché scivoloso ed esposto al vento ma la bellezza del luogo e la particolarità della struttura ne suggeriscono la valorizzazione o, quanto meno, la ripulitura e l'integrazione in un percorso turistico.

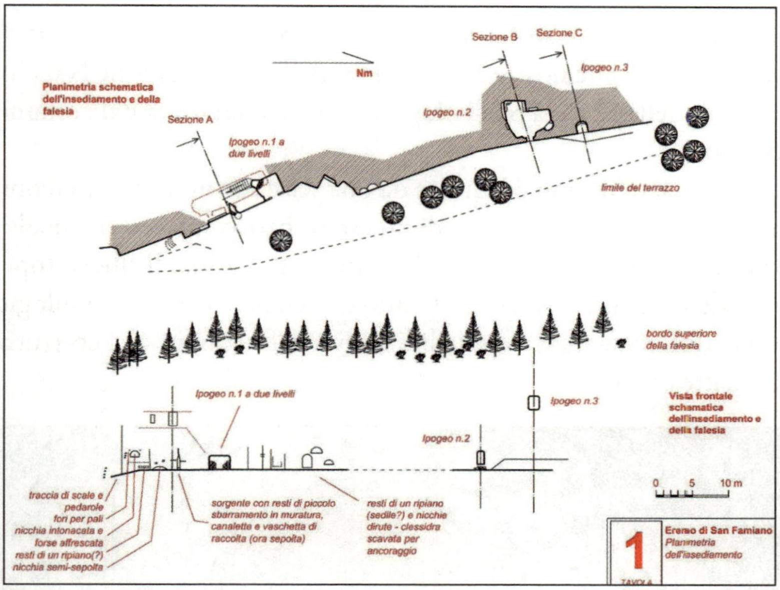

Fig. 10 Grotte di San Famiano planimetria dell'insediamento.

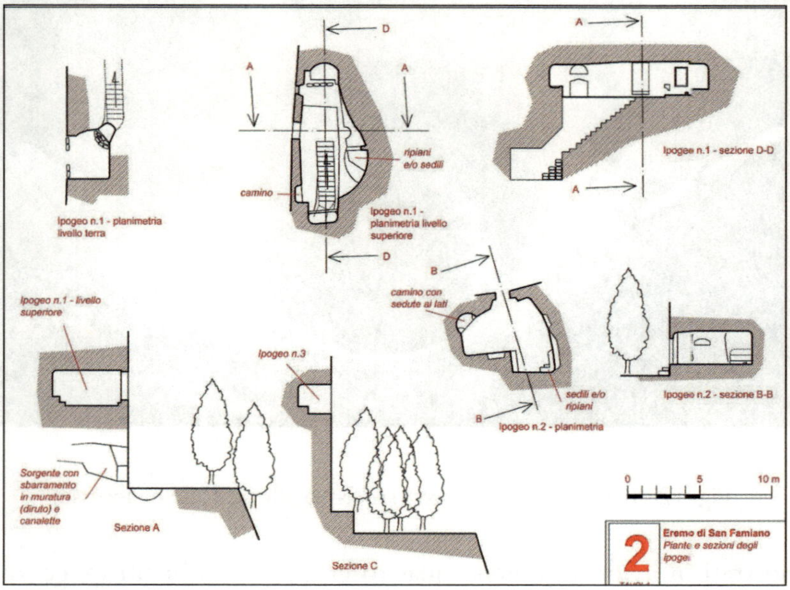

Fig. 11 Grotte di San Famiano pianta e sezioni degli ipogei.

1.5. Studio, rilievo e valorizzazione dei sotterranei di Palazzo Caetani (Cisterna di Latina, Latina)

Il progetto di studio dei sotterranei del Palazzo Caetani, denominati "Grotte Caetani" fu affidato alle nostre Associazioni dalla Commissione Nazionale Cavità Artificiali della Società Speleologica Italiana contattata dal comune di Cisterna di Latina.

Le Grotte Caetani sono costituite da una serie continua ed interconnessa di ambienti ipogei scavati all'interno di un esteso banco tufaceo, sul quale è sorto il primo nucleo storico del comune di Cisterna di Latina. Il rilievo topografico e lo studio dell'articolata struttura hanno evidenziato caratteri tipologico – architettonici differenziati, riconducibili a diverse funzioni e fasi costruttive cronologicamente distinte.

Fig. 12 Grotte Caetani il pozzo interno allo scalone di accesso.

Sono stati individuati almeno quattro gruppi di ambienti ipogei originari e autonomi, per alcuni dei quali permangono alcune incertezze interpretative. L'esteso ed eterogeneo ipogeo risulta attualmente interconnesso attraverso an-gusti cunicoli e irregolari brecce aperte dall'abbattimento di alcuni diaframmi murari di separazione tra ambienti originariamente contigui ma distinti.

La demolizione e la rimozione di tali diaframmi è avvenuta, molto probabilmente, quando la popolazione di Cisterna, spinta dall'emergenza dell'ultimo conflitto mondiale, realizzò i varchi per ottenere un unico grande ricovero antiaereo. Testimonianze orali e scritte riportano che in tali rifugi trovarono riparo, durante l'ultima guerra, oltre 4.000 cittadini di Cisterna.

Fig. 13 Le «cantine» delle Grotte Caetani.

La cavità ipogea più ampia ed estesa è costituita da una lunga ed alta galleria che inizia a partire dal termine di una scala elicoidale discendente, profonda circa 10 m rispetto al sovrastante Palazzo rinascimentale, commissionato dalla famiglia Caetani, proprietaria di una vasta parte del territorio circostante comprendente gli antichi insediamenti di Cisterna, Ninfa e Sermoneta, realizzato nel 1560 quale sfarzosa residenza di campagna. Nel 1570 l'architetto veneto Andrea Palladio descrive la realizzazione delle cantine: *si deono fare sottoterra, rinchiuse, lontano da ogni strepito e da ogni umore e fetore, e deono avere il lume da levante.* Anche quelle di Cisterna erano state così realizzate al riparo sia della calura estiva che del clima rigido invernale, quindi idonee alla conservazione delle derrate alimentari e dei vini e con l'uscita di servizio realizzata a Nord Est.

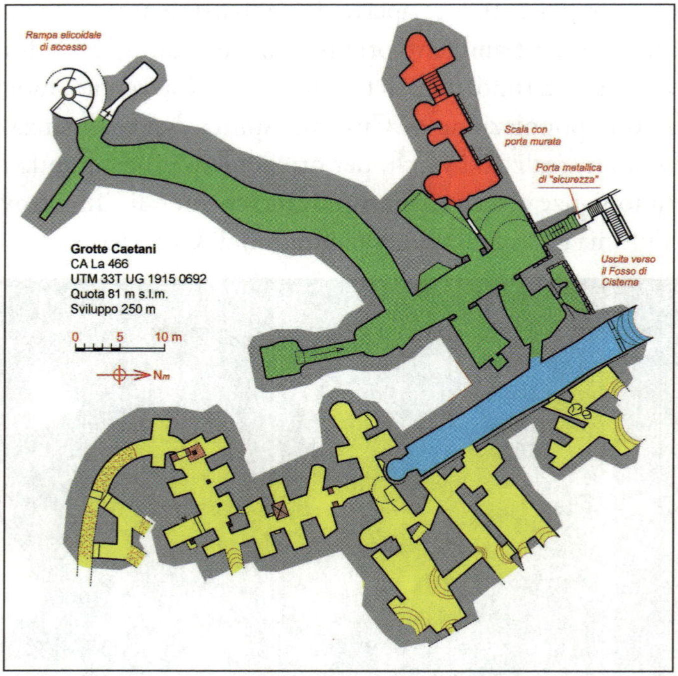

Fig. 14 Grotte Caetani: planimetria complessiva.

La scala elicoidale è stata probabilmente realizzata sul modello della nota scala del "Pozzo di San Patrizio" con pozzo di luce centrale, progettata dall'architetto Antonio da Sangallo il Giovane nel 1536-37 per la città di Orvieto.

Furono eseguite analisi preliminari dei gas (Radon e CO_2), analisi geologica, rilievo topografico e documentazione fotografica. Si analizzò inoltre la documentazione desunta dai testi storici integrandola con la ricerca di antiche mappe e documenti catastali. Il lavoro e le fonti resero possibile una ipotesi di restituzione grafica dell'antico borgo al XIX secolo stilata dall'Arch. Luigi Casciotti (Centro Ricerche Sotterranee Egeria). In particolare, dall'esame della Mappa 91 del Comune, appartenente all'antica Comarca (provincia) di Roma desunta dal Catasto Gregoriano dello Stato Pontificio (elaborata nel 1819), fu possibile elaborare una ricostruzione paesaggistica dell'abitato con la restituzione della presumibile volumetria cittadina relativa al XIX secolo, probabilmente non molto dissimile dal borgo del XVI secolo.

Le Grotte Caetani non presentano particolari valenze archeologiche ed architettoniche, ma rappresentano una importante testimonianza storica – sia pur recente perché risalente all'ultimo conflitto mondiale – per tutta la popolazione. Nel convincimento che ogni azione umana è il frutto della cultura del suo tempo, si progettò un percorso turistico per riscoprirle attraverso la rilettura e la comprensione delle originarie e distinte funzioni, confrontando tutte le possibili aggiunte e le variazioni d'uso intervenute nelle utilizzazioni successive. Il percorso ipogeo fu integrato con un ideale tragitto cittadino di superficie, rivolto alle testimonianze più significative della vita dell'antico centro storico di Cisterna ed esteso, inoltre, alla visita di quei resti che hanno delle dirette connessioni con le grotte. Il percorso turistico sotterraneo è stato progettato secondo un percorso ad anello per iniziare il tragitto indifferentemente dai diversi luoghi toccati dal tracciato ed è stato suddiviso in tre parti per evidenziare le originarie differenze funzionali consentendo di frazionare eventualmente la visita secondo tempistiche diverse.

Si tratta del «percorso ipogei e cantine», idealmente legato alla visita delle Cantine Caetani pertinenza diretta del soprastante omonimo Palazzo; il "percorso ipogeo e cisterna" che consente di visitare l'interno della grande cisterna rettangolare, per comprenderne il funzionamento e il "percorso di altri ipogei" che esplora gli altri ambienti ipogei verso il Fosso riscoprendone le destinazioni originarie e le modificazioni intervenute nel tempo, a partire dalle più antiche come cave di materiale, ipogei funerari, cantine e depositi vari.

Fig. 15 Ipotesi di percorso turistico integrato delle Grotte Caetani.
Progetto e restituzione grafica Arch. Luigi Casciotti.

2. CENNI DI TECNICHE SPELEOLOGICHE E SPELEO SUBACQUEE IN IPOGEI ARTIFICIALI

Le competenze necessarie ad affrontare in modo produttivo l'esplorazione, la documentazione e la progettazione di interventi tecnici e gestionali di valorizzazione di ambienti sotterranei trova grande vantaggio nell'avvalersi di team esperti, organizzati e specializzati. Andrebbero evitati approcci che privilegino *imprese for profit* senza competenze specifiche, che rischiano di trascinare le ricerche senza apprezzabili risultati, procrastinando di anni gli eventuali progetti di sviluppo. In relazione alle condizioni dell'ambiente fisico in cui sono state realizzate e si sono modificate le cavità artificiali, è necessario osservare criteri esplorativi le cui tecniche e attrezzature sono, in larga parte, le medesime della progressione in grotta ma alle quali si dovranno abbinare specifiche e maggiori cautele per evitare rischi legati alle persone e alle cose e quindi, ad esempio, evitare danneggiamenti alle strutture ipogee e segnalare la presenza di eventuali reperti archeologici.

Non esiste quindi un «metodo standard» per affrontare le indagini speleologiche in strutture antropiche sotterranee e ancor meno uno per prospettarne la valorizzazione. Ogni situazione avrà connotazioni proprie che dovranno coniugare le esigenze tipicamente scientifiche con la morfologia dei siti, la sicurezza degli interventi e il rispetto del carisma proprio di ogni organizzazione religiosa.

In alcuni casi si preferisce condurre esplorazioni preliminari tramite piccoli robot motorizzati oppure aeromobili a pilotaggio remoto, come nel caso del rilevamento delle volte della Domus Aurea di Nerone a Roma condotto dal team di A.S.S.O. L'esplorazione e lo studio di particolari strutture ipogee possono inoltre richiedere il supporto di subacquei specializzati, anche questi facenti parte delle competenze del team A.S.S.O.

Lo scopo delle immersioni, come nel caso dell'esplorazione e rilevamento dell'antico emissario sommerso del Lago Albano (RM), ad esempio, è stato finalizzato al reperimento di informazioni diversamente non ottenibili ed è per questo che, dopo una prima immersione conoscitiva, si rivelò fondamentale acquisire dati e immagini direttamente sott'acqua. Nella maggior parte dei casi, infatti, le strutture ipogee sommerse hanno perso la loro funzione primaria e la condizione di allagamento è dovuta ad abbandono con conseguente rischio di degrado strutturale e ambientale. Una immersione, quindi, oltre a difficoltà di carattere tecnico può presentare elevati rischi biologici. Questo è uno dei principali motivi per i quali, nonostante le scarse profondità, la progressione subacquea in cavità artificiali richiede grande attenzione, esperienza specifica di immersioni in ambienti chiusi e talvolta complesse attrezzature per la protezione dello speleo-subacqueo, il cui impiego non sempre è compatibile con le condizioni logistiche ed ambientali del luogo.

Fig. 16 Il team ASSO si prepara all'immersione nell'emissario del lago Albano.

CONCLUSIONI

Le strutture ipogee definite «cavità artificiali» sono strutture sotterranee di interesse storico realizzate dall'uomo o da esso riadattate alle proprie necessità e costituiscono interessanti prospettive di valorizzazione anche turistica e culturale. Come è facilmente riscontrabile, sempre più frequentemente città piccole e grandi creano percorsi sotterranei che rappresentano un valore aggiunto per l'offerta turistica (Napoli sotterranea, Rieti sotterranea, Cagliari sotterranea, ecc.). Al pari, il turismo cultuale legato all'ospitalità nelle strutture monastiche ha subito negli ultimi anni un deciso incremento, al punto che sono sorti portali dedicati e pubblicate guide di riferimento.

Il crescente interesse per il mondo sotterraneo e per le strutture a vocazione religiosa, potrebbero proficuamente coniugarsi, stimolando nuovi progetti di conoscenza e di adattamento alla fruizione turistica di sotterranei abbaziali, eremi, cripte, pozzi, camminamenti, ecc. Indagini specialistiche condotte da esperti del sotterraneo, che abbinino competenza tecnica interdisciplinare a capacità progettuale, possono integrare e favorire progetti di sviluppo sociale ed economico anche in realtà attualmente scollegate da percorsi e flussi turistici. Si tratta di una importante opportunità di *riscoperta della memoria* e di sviluppo socio-economico per le Comunità Monastiche e di accrescimento della conoscenza per il Team rappresentato dagli autori.

Per rafforzare la prospettiva e tornare all'aspetto turistico, va ricordato che la cultura internazionale del viaggio si basa sempre più su una offerta originale. Nel novembre 2015, a titolo di esempio, un noto tour operator (Viaggi e Avventure nel Mondo) ha indetto un concorso a premi per tesi di laurea riguardanti «L'uomo ed il suo ambiente, la sua storia, le realizzazioni dell'ingegno nel campo materiale e spirituale, le sue tradizioni, la religione, i rapporti interculturali con altre civiltà, l'ambiente naturale nei suoi molteplici aspetti».

Ciò conferma come chi muove i flussi turistici guardi con interesse alle strutture religiose intese prevalentemente come riscoperta di luoghi dimenticati. Da una indagine condotta da Trip Advisor, inoltre, i viaggiatori del 2016 hanno cercato soprattutto nuove esperienze, benessere, cultura. Il 63% dei viaggiatori italiani si dice interessato a provare qualcosa di nuovo e salgono i trend dei viaggi d'avventura: al 10% piacerebbe cimentarsi in esperienze più «forti», come l'alpinismo o il rafting. Se gli aspetti culturali e sociali di una destinazione, per quanto riguarda le ragioni che spingono a scegliere una determinata meta, costituiscono ancora il motivo principale per il 61% degli italiani, il rapporto rivela che anche i documentari sono una valida fonte d'ispirazione.

In sintesi: riscoperta di luoghi sotterranei dimenticati (anche piccoli, ma che raccontino una storia) + documentazione + valorizzazione = ampliamento dell'offerta culturale e turistica e della conseguente ricaduta economica.

Abstract

This contribution focuses on the size of the underground heritage of Monastic complexes, which may become a source of livelihood for the surrounding communities. To facilitate understanding the different aspects of this complex issue, we will present case studies related or applicable to monastic complexes, based on an interdisciplinary approach. Nowadays, small and large cities are opening to the public underground areas, which represent an added value to tourism attraction.

Accommodation in Monasteries for touristic purposes has recently increased, and has been greatly advertised in dedicated web sites and guides. This confirms the interest of tourists in what could be defined as the discovery of unusual or forgotten places.

In addition to the catacombs and crypts, the ancient aqueducts, mills, silos, cellars, wells, trenches and other underground structures may become of great interest for tourists. In order to properly start the exploitation and enhancement of this precious heritage, it is necessary to carefully analyze the underground heritage, integrating technical knowledge with an approach of project planning and design. Cost-effectiveness and time scheduling should also be carefully defined. Examining underground environments requires specific skills, professional experience and knowledge. The exclusive use of for-profit companies may entail the risk of focusing only on the building and plant-engineering aspects and neglecting the potential, artistic and historical value, and charisma of the Monastic complexes.

Crediti

Repertorio iconografico: ove non espressamente specificato le immagini sono degli Autori (archivi Egeria Centro Ricerche Sotterranee – ASSO).

Rilievi topografici: ove non diversamente indicato sono dell'archivio Egeria CRS; restituzione grafica: Carlo Germani, Egeria CRS.

Figura 15 progetto Arch. Luigi Casciotti, Egeria CRS.

WITH EYES FIXED ON HEAVEN ... AND THE BOTTOM LINE. THE SPIRITUAL AND ECONOMIC SUSTAINABILITY OF NEW NORCIA, A TOWN LIKE NO OTHER

John Herbert

The Benedictine mission at New Norcia, 130 kilometres north of Perth, Western Australia, was founded on 1 March 1847. It was one of three Catholic missions which set out to Christianise and civilise the indigenous populations of Western Australia, but the only one to have survived. José Serra and Rosendo Salvado were the two Benedictine monks who founded the Mission, though Serra left soon after to take up other clerical duties, leaving Salvado, later Bishop Salvado, to establish and develop the Mission over the next fifty years, until his death in Rome in December 1900 at the age of eighty-six.

In those early days of the Mission's establishment life was very hard. In his 1883 *Report to Propaganda Fide*, Salvado tells us that in the beginning he became as a nomad and a wanderer, like the *selvaggi* who shared with Salvado «the best parts of the snakes, lizards, worms, roots and other similar tasty mouthfuls they had with them»[1]. Even after the monastery was founded, life did not get any easier:

> For 22 months, eating meat was out of the question for us. It was impossible to recognise our monastic habits and everywhere they were falling to pieces; we patched our trousers with pieces of kangaroo skin abandoned by the *selvaggi* as useless. Suffering greatly and unable to walk without shoes any longer, since our feet were often torn to the point of bleeding, we made ourselves shoes with wood covered also with kangaroo skin... The future of the mission seemed to us full of life, but the present was a cause of pain[2].

John Herbert, abbot of the Benedictine Abbey of New Norcia (Australia).

1 R. Salvado, *Report of Rosendo Salvado to Propaganda fide in 1883*, ed. & trans. S Girola, Melbourne 2015, 22.

2 Salvado, *Report of Rosendo Salvado*, 26.

Even in later years, life at the Mission was not without its hardships, difficulties, hazards and dangers. Recurring droughts, a series of epidemics and plagues which beset the missionaries and Aborigines alike, and constant bushfires were daily reminders of the difficulties of life in the Mission. One occasion happened in December 1847—and remember, December is summertime in the southern hemisphere and it can get very hot. A disgruntled Aboriginal worker deliberately lit a fire, which Salvado described as:

> ... an inferno of flames devouring grass and areas alike and rapidly spreading towards our crop of corn...A high wind was blowing and within a short time a wide area of about a mile was burning furiously. Both we monks and the natives ran to meet this danger to our crop and to the mission...[but] we realised our helplessness...[and] unaided we could not prevent the complete destruction of the mission. [However,] we had recourse to God's infinite Mercy through the motherly intercession of the special Patroness of our Mission. We took the beautiful picture of Our Lady and placed it against the standing corn which seemed about to catch fire at any moment... Merciful Heaven! No sooner was the sacred image of Mary placed in front of the raging fire than the wind blew in the opposite direction, carrying the flames away to where everything was already burned black[3].

Quite apart from the physical hardships, money was also in very short supply. In his 1883 report Salvado tells us that all the money that had been given to him by the first Catholic bishop of Perth, John Brady, amounted to just £3, or in today's terms €335, and with this Salvado was expected to found and establish the Mission[4]. Clearly this was not enough and some dire measures were taken to try to raise more funds, including begging « at the door of the church in Perth », where he managed to raise another 20 francs (€110)[5]. But the funds were not enough and so he decided to perform a piano concert in the capital.

George Russo in his work *Lord Abbot of the Wilderness* devotes two whole pages to the concert and from this we learn that seventy people from the colo-

---

3 This version of the story appears in *A town like no other: the living tradition of New Norcia*, ed. D. Hutchison, Fremantle Arts Centre Press, Fremantle 2007 44. It is a rewording of the original, found in R. Salvado, *The Salvado memoirs*, ed. & trans. E J Stormon, Perth, 1977, 66-67.

4 Salvado, *Report of Rosendo Salvado*, 24.

5 Salvado, *Report of Rosendo Salvado*, 24; the *franc* was the currency Salvado quoted in his *Report*.

nial élite attended—few of whom if any, interestingly, were Catholics[6]. Salvado gave a solo performance for three hours, which he recorded in his memoirs:

> I wore my usual monastic habit, but it was in a very sorry shape indeed. My tunic reached only as far as my knees and from there on was a thing of rags and tatters: my black trousers were patched with pieces of cloth and thread of all different colours; my socks, after I had darned them, looked fairly respectable, but my shoes—a good pair which I had bought in Italy—had parted company with the soles somewhere in the Australian bush, so that my toes were kissing Mother Earth. Add to that a beard which needed more than a touch of the comb, and a deep tan on my face and hands, close enough, for all intents and purposes, to the colour of the natives. Altogether I cut a comical and pitiful figure[7].

Nevertheless, £70 (€7.600), was raised, which Salvado used to buy provisions, seeds and a few tools to take back to the monastery.

Despite his self-deprecation, it was an important and pivotal moment in the monastery's fortunes. Money, or rather the lack of it, was a source of constant anxiety for Salvado in the early years. Not only did he experience enormous difficulties in securing any, but when he did he found it was being siphoned off by Bishop Brady or by his erstwhile friend and *confrère*, José Serra. Throughout the 1883 report there are constant references to «debts» and «scandals» and suggestions of financial incompetence, which resulted in enormous sums of money going missing which Bishop Brady could not account for[8]. In 1851, Serra succeeded the hapless Brady but, as John Smith notes in his *Story of New Norcia*, Serra regarded New Norcia as «little more than a source of revenue and supplies to meet diocesan needs»[9]. On another occasion in 1853, Salvado returned

---

6 G. Russo, *Lord abbot of the wilderness: the life and times of Bishop Salvado,* Polding Press, Melbourne, 1980, 44-45.

7 Salvado, *The Salvado memoirs,* 43.

8 Salvado, *Report of Rosendo Salvado*, 32: «...I had seen [Brady] in his room walking hurriedly and almost out of his mind uttering half and disconnected words every now and then. I asked him if something was troubling him but he did not answer. He went on walking round the room...and maybe a quarter of an hour later he told me with broken words that somebody had robbed him because all the money he owned had disappeared. I asked him if it was a lot of money and he answered that he did not know. I replied that if he had a look at his account books it would be easy to find out and remove all doubts. But where were these books? They did not exist at all.»

9 *The story of New Norcia*, ed. J. Smith, Benedictine Community of New Norcia [=BCNN], 2015, 14.

from one of his many overseas trips during which he would raise funds and find recruits, with forty-three Benedictine postulants and £7,000 (€674.300) but again these funds were diverted to the diocese and in aid to the increasing Catholic settlement in Perth[10]. Fortunately Serra left for Europe soon after and the running of the diocese was left to Salvado.

Following his initial failed attempt to found his mission on somebody else's land in 1846, Bishop Salvado became a very astute landowner and it was perhaps this that generated such caution in future dealings. From an initial allocation of twenty acres (or just slightly over eight hectares), Salvado almost immediately increased this to fifty. By 1848, as Russo notes,

> Salvado had succeeded in acquiring the lease of 18,000 acres. This meant that with the 50 acres of the original grant...a flock of sheep and a few domestic animals, the mission was a pastoral enterprise of no mean economic status[11].

By the end of the 1880s Salvado owned or leased nearly a million acres of land—more than 4,000 square kilometres—making him the second largest landholder in Western Australia[12]. To put this area into perspective, his landholdings were almost twice the size of Luxembourg. His astute business sense is indeed a perfect example of keeping the eyes on the bottom line! George Russo again:

> Salvado calculated to the penny the costs of his leases. He discovered early that application forms for renewal of leases usually cost 2/6^{d} (25 cents) for each lease, so he decided to put as many leases as possible on the one form, and it was accepted. He wrote: "I have tried it and find that you can write 30 runs quite clearly on one form, and consequently there is no difficulty in applying for the renewal of 30 leases on a single form at the cost of only 2/6^{d}"[13].

By the time Torres became abbot, following Salvado's death in late 1900, the Mission had struggled through the hardships of the 19th century to become a hugely successful enterprise, not only as a pastoral empire famed for its horses—which were sold in India to the British army—and its agricultural products—

10 *The story of New Norcia*, 14-15.
11 RUSSO, *Lord abbot of the wilderness*, 64.
12 R. RIOS, *History of the Benedictine mission and Abbey Nullius of New Norcia*, BCNN, New Norcia Archives [=NNA], 00518, 108.
13 RUSSO, *Lord abbot of the wilderness*, 58.

which were famous at European exhibitions—but as a leading and enlightened mission to the Aborigines. In 1908 the Rev James Flood wrote a book entitled *New Norcia*, the subtitle to which was *The Remarkable Aborigines Institution of the Australian Commonwealth: A Monument of Benedictine Courage, Patience and Charity*—a wonderful example of understatement if ever there was one![14] For the Aborigines, who had held him in such high esteem, Salvado's death came as a terrible blow. And not only to the Aborigines: Salvado himself was a celebrity and mixed with the aristocracy of the day, with state governors and captains of industry. Amongst his personal friends were cardinals and abbots, Pope Pius IX and Queen Isabella II of Spain.

However, even before his death the next round of hardships was already taking shape. The colonial government (the Swan River Colony became the State of Western Australia in 1901) had, in the 1890s, reduced subsidies to missions, an act which did not begin to take its toll until after Salvado's death. Throughout his life, Salvado had attempted to educate the Aborigines by opening a school for their children: St Mary's for the boys in December 1847 and St Joseph's for the girls in August 1861. Then, Aborigines began to join the monks in their work, such as tilling the fields, building roads and bridges and land was soon allotted to the Aboriginal workers. In 1860 a larger school for the Aboriginal children was built. However, also in 1860, a measles epidemic decimated the Aboriginal population and Salvado had to look further afield for workers and therefore children. His agitating for changes in education resulted in the Industrial Schools Act of 1874, which gave Salvado (and other institutional directors) the same authority over Aboriginal children as their fathers. Aboriginal families at New Norcia consequently increased so that by 1892 the number of Aborigines at New Norcia reached 134. But, with the government subsidies cut, many Aboriginal families were forced to leave New Norcia and the grand pastoral empire which, in 1900 at the time of Salvado's death, encompassed some 400,000 hectares, fell to just over 41,000 in 1909[15].

Torres, like Salvado half a century before, was finding himself short of money. Torres changed the Mission's policies as a result—he had to look for Aborigines from even further afield and so established a mission in the far northwest of the state at Drysdale River following the government's encouragement. To

14 J. Flood, *New Norcia: the remarkable Aborigines' institution of the Australian Commonwealth situated in the State of Western Australia: a monument of Benedictine courage, patience and charity. The tribute of an Irish secular priest,* London 1908.

15 *A town like no other: the living tradition of New Norcia*, 63.

attract more income, he changed the focus from Christianising and civilising the Aborigines to providing education on an impressive scale. Communications were difficult in rural Western Australia in the early 20th century and local farmers needed schools for their children. In 1908 and again in 1913 he opened two very impressive colleges for non-Indigenous students: St Gertrude's and St Ildephonsus'. Sr Anne Carter, in her history of St Gertrude's College, states that «it is not possible to give a total cost for the construction»[16], but Fr Rios in his *History of New Norcia* (written in 1924) puts the cost of building the College at £30,000 (€3.15M) and St Ildephonsus', constructed between 1909 and 1913 even more, at £40,000 (€4.4M)[17]. Where did that money come from? Most likely Torres got the money from the sale of land—remember that by 1909 New Norcia's landholdings were down to a tenth of what they had been only nine years earlier. The financial intricacies of the Torres period are not easy to fathom and it leads one to suspect that Torres had acute cash flow problems and that much of those dealings were hidden, censored or not even recorded.

If one does a rough calculation of all the expenses listed for 1904, it comes to about £8,500, the highest sum being £980 paid to somebody in Southern Cross, nearly 400 kilometres away. 1905 has a slightly higher number of entries (564 vs 448) but the highest amount was a £500 deposit on a farm called Berkshire Valley. Averaged out, these are entries that feasibly total £10,000. 1906 has 603 entries, the highest being £254 for doors, and these average out at about £11,000. The entire expense over those three years suggests that it did not even come to the amount apparently paid for the college[18].

The Rev Flood in his 1908 work on New Norcia confirms this when he says that the annual expenditure of the Mission for 1901–1906 amounted to over £9,000[19]. Interestingly however, Fr Rios notes that Torres, upon his appointment,

> ...set himself the task of perusing, cataloguing and archiving all the documents, books of accounts, correspondence etc etc, which covered a period extending over fifty years. Thus he became acquainted with, and had a firm grasp on, any matter of importance, old and new, concerning New Norcia[20].

16 A. Carter, *A rich harvest: St Gertrude's College*, South Perth 2006, 18.
17 Rios, *History of the Benedictine mission*, 132.
18 Monastery Accounts Book 1901-1912, BCNN, NNA, 02969-33.
19 Flood, *New Norcia*, 286.
20 Rios, *History of the Benedictine mission*, 131.

The evidence would suggest though that while he kept meticulously neat expense accounts, they did not show the true nature of the monastery's finances—in this instance we can't say for certain what the bottom line was!

Despite his problems the enormous scale of buildings during Torres' reign, as he transitioned away from the original concept of a mission for the Aborigines, is breathtaking. Fr Rios lists, among considerable minor improvements and smaller additions, the extraordinary catalogue of construction that Torres (who was an architect in his own right) achieved:

1901–1903	A third storey added to the monastery and 550 metres of covering between the balconies and verandas;
1903	The erection of the three-storey central part of the monastery;
1904–1906	The building of St Gertrude's College, which was originally intended for native girls but changed to accommodate white Australian fee-paying girls;
1907–1908	The erection of a new campanile and façade to the monastery church;
1909	The building of St Joseph's Orphanage for native girls;
1909–1913	The building of St Ildephonsus' College;
1913	The construction of handball courts for St Ildephonsus';
1914	The erection of walls surrounding the different buildings[21].

He also repeats the pun that the Romans had made of Pope Urban VIII, on account of Urban's great love of building: that he was a man of «great edification»[22].

Other problems within the Community were surfacing too: when Torres took over in 1901 he saw to it that the whole monastic community was housed in the monastery itself; that the habit was standardised and he insisted on the Community living by stricter Benedictine principles. This met with considerable resistance from some of the Community and, according to the Smith was even roundly criticised, not only by settlers in the new state of Western Australia, but even by the state's leadership[23]. Furthermore in his new building programme the walls previously mentioned meant that Salvado's open family atmosphere was now under Torres very much a segregated community.

21 Rios, *History of the Benedictine mission*, 132.
22 Rios, *History of the Benedictine mission*, 132.
23 *The story of New Norcia*, 23.

To add to Torres' woes, the state government in 1905 introduced The Aborigines Act which took effect from April 1906. It was «an act to make provision for the better protection and care of the Aboriginal inhabitants of Western Australia», and it governed the lives of all Aboriginal people in Western Australia for nearly sixty years[24]. The Act created the position of a Chief Protector of Aborigines, who became the legal guardian of every Aboriginal child up to the age of sixteen, and permitted authorities to «send and detain» Aboriginal children in institutions and in «service» (in other words, work). The Aborigines Act 1905 was finally repealed by the Native Welfare Act of 1963.

As the director of a designated institution and as of 12 June 1906 an appointed Protector of Aborigines, Torres was obliged to accept Aboriginal children placed in his so-called «orphanages» by government agencies. An analysis of Aboriginal boys at St Mary's Orphanage shows a sudden jump in numbers from nine in 1904 to thirty-three in 1905. Things weren't going too well for the government either, as the following letter from Henry Prinsep, Chief Protector of the Aborigines, written to Torres on 21 August 1906 shows:

> I am directed by the Honourable the Colonial Treasurer to inform you that in re-considering the amounts to be granted to missions and other charitable institutions, the strictest economy will have to be exercised owing to the present financial condition of the State and that it will be necessary for him to know how such sums are expended and that there is justification for each grant. I shall therefore be obliged if you [would] kindly forward to me a statement, not only showing how the grant to your institution for the recently expired year has been expended, but also *showing your general financial conditions*[25].

Torres replied on 10 September with a very detailed account of what had been spent on the Aboriginal children, but he was less forthcoming about the monastery's expenses:

> It is true that the Mission is self-supporting at present, but I must say that the economics of the mission for the first five years are employed in the building of a

24 Aborigines Act 1905 (1906–1964), *Find & Connect*, (2017), <https://www.findandconnect.gov.au/guide/wa/WE00406>. [accesso 01-06-2016]

25 H. Prinsep, personal correspondence to F Torres, 21 August 1906, NNA, 05118; emphases are those of the author.

great college of some thousands of pounds, in which there will be places for over a hundred native girls.

Then he goes on to say:

> Considering the great expenses the mission has expended in favour of the natives, I hope the government will see the necessity of increasing the yearly grant[26].

Perhaps understandably there is no record of a reply from Mr Prinsep.

In the face of all his difficulties, Torres' other great achievement was the establishment in 1908 of the mission mentioned earlier at Pago on the Drysdale River, which later moved to Kalumburu in 1937 owing to the failure of the local water supply. In the preface to his 1977 history of Kalumburu, then Premier of Western Australia Sir Charles Court said:

> [This history] is the story of many lives spent in unselfish dedication to the Christian commitment to carry the comfort of the faith to the four corners of the earth. Despite its isolation, the mission represents the most sustained attempt by Western Australians to incorporate Aboriginal people into the community at large[27].

Hilton Deacon, who wrote the foreword to the history, went further when he noted that:

> ...the difficulties [Bishop Torres and his party] were to face required the stuff of which heroes and heroines are made. The countryside was inhospitable, the wandering groups of Aborigines...had suffered immeasurably from death and disease and were suspicious of new intruders, and the lines of communication with the south...were long and unreliable[28].

Access to the Mission was only by ship, a distance of well over 2000 kilometres from Perth, yet the Mission survived until 1982 when it became self-gov-

---

26 F. Torres, personal correspondence to H Prinsep, 10 September 1906, NNA, 05132, 96-99; emphasis is that of the author.

27 E. Perez, *Kalumburu: the Benedictine mission and the Aborigines, 1908–1975,* Wyndham 1977, III.

28 Perez, *Kalumburu*, I.

erning and was returned to the local Indigenous population. It suffered badly during World War II when it was bombed by Japanese aircraft and one monk and several of the local population were killed[29].

Smith sums up Torres thus:

> Torres brought a new vision to the mission and the town, which laid the foundations for New Norcia to become a rich source of religious, educational and cultural life for Western Australia and beyond... But, Torres did not see his impressive efforts reach fruition; he died in 1914, worn out and weakened in health by the hardships of establishing the Kimberley mission and developing New Norcia itself[30].

By 1914 the infrastructure as we know it today was more or less in place. Torres' successor Anselm Catalan was a first-rate administrator, if rather lacking in charisma. He had his difficulties of course, but by and large they were not on the scale that Salvado had endured, nor even compared with Torres' problems. Catalan's problems were the same problems that everybody else faced and were not especially peculiar to New Norcia: World War I brought about a drop in available manpower, as did World War II, and the Great Depression of 1929 ushered in its own special difficulties. However, these were offset by a marked upturn in enrolments at the Colleges, following a general post-WWII boom. Abbot Catalan extended the buildings a little further—he built the hostel for College children's visiting parents in 1927 (which became the Hotel in 1955) and a second classroom block for St Ildephonsus' College in 1931.

Perhaps his most astute investment though was the purchase of many of the works of art that today form the nucleus of New Norcia's very valuable art collection. However, it was not until a robbery at the Art Gallery in 1986 that the full potential of the collection was realised, and a concerted effort was made not only to install adequate security measures but also to restore and conserve the paintings which had been stolen—all apart from one were recovered—and then to build on the collection. Careful selection of art works based on the advice of experts has resulted in one of Australia's most important collection of religious

29 For an account of Kalumburu's wartime tribulations, see *Kalumburu war diary, eds.* E. Perez-R. Pratt-J Millington Perth 1981.

30 *The story of New Norcia*, 27.

art, which now regularly receive works by Australia's very best artists. Catalan retired in 1951 and eventually passed away in 1959.

He was succeeded by the first abbot to be elected from the Community, Gregory Gomez. Sadly Abbot Gomez' years were marred by unfortunate planning, which not only caused strife within the Community but also led to losses of various types being experienced by the monastery[31]. Outside the monastery society was changing, becoming more affluent, and a young Australia was finding its own feet. More Australian monks joined the Community leading to tensions within and to a change in the language of the monastery, from Spanish to English. Roads outside Perth were being built and this directly affected the two large Colleges—St Gertrude's and St Ildephonsus'—since local children could now be educated in Perth at a number of similar institutions with arguably better facilities only two to three hours' drive away. The Marist Brothers who ran St Ildephonsus' from 1913 to 1963 left to establish their own schools in Perth and the College was taken over by the monks. Then in 1977 the Sisters of St Joseph who had been associated with St Gertrude's also departed. A merging of the two Colleges eventually occurred but by then the New Norcia colleges had had their day, and they were shut down in 1992. Changes in government policy too had seen the closure of the Orphanages in 1972.

Under Fr Bernard Rooney, an Australian who became abbot in 1972, a marked shift in focus occurred—away from the second great phase of New Norcia's life: education—to one that embraced a modern and affluent age, which included the new phenomenon of mass tourism, but which interestingly coincided with, and echoed, the very roots of the Benedictine monastic principle of hospitality. In addition to establishing the Art Gallery and Museum in the now deserted St Joseph's Orphanage, Abbot Bernard extended the Guesthouse, thereby making a visit to New Norcia a much more attractive proposition.

The closure of the schools however saw the once thriving and bustling town of New Norcia reduced to little more than a ghost town. Under the leadership of Placid Spearritt (initially as prior administrator and eventually abbot) the Community was forced to «reinvent» itself. With hospitality clearly identified as its new primary focus, the former schools became available for school camps, an Education Centre was established, the Archives and libraries were made more available, and camping grounds were provided. Most recently the Community has looked to the future by entering into an arrangement with the

31 *The story of New Norcia*, 32.

European Space Agency who have a deep space telescope ten kilometres to the south; the ESA has a dedicated room at New Norcia especially for educational purposes.

My own election as the seventh abbot in 2009 coincided with events bringing new difficulties. A significant portion of the Community's off-shore investment portfolio for example was totally wiped out by the global financial crisis, resulting in a substantial loss of revenue. The state government redress scheme (*Redress WA*), offering compensation payouts to victims of neglect and abuse while in the care of government run or funded institutions (in which New Norcia fitted the latter category), has resulted in thousands of complainants turning to Church authorities for additional redress. To date I have, on behalf of the Community, met some three-hundred individuals (mostly Aboriginal) through the *Towards Healing* process, a pastoral response providing an opportunity for complainants to have their story listened to in a compassionate way, to be believed, to receive an apology, and to receive some form of financial assistance as tangible evidence that their story matters. This is important work which, although taxing, I consider a privilege to undertake. But it has nonetheless had its effect on the bottom line, to the tune of several million dollars. And it's not over—the Royal Commission into institutional responses to child sexual abuse currently underway in Australia will undoubtedly require further response.

A national review of the not-for-profit sector in Australia provided the impetus for the Community to reassess its status as an incorporated association resulting in a major process of corporate re-structure. Although the old entity recognised and covered the legal operations of the Community, the complexity and ever-increasing regulation and legal oversight of the Community's growing operations often led to operational difficulties when dealing with the rising number of lay staff who were now being employed by the Community. In my opinion (and experience) industrial relations and compliancy issues have become two of the foremost difficulties in running any organisation these days. The process determined that the transfer of all operational and day-to-day activity to a registered private company was the safest and most efficient method to comply with the growing legal and legislative requirements. The complex and difficult task of creating the necessary «Deed of Gift» documents and the other related issues regarding land title, charitable status, tax exemption, etc eventually led to the establishment of the company, appropriately named Monochorum, which commenced operating on the 1 March 2014, the 200th anniversary of the birth of Rosendo Salvado.

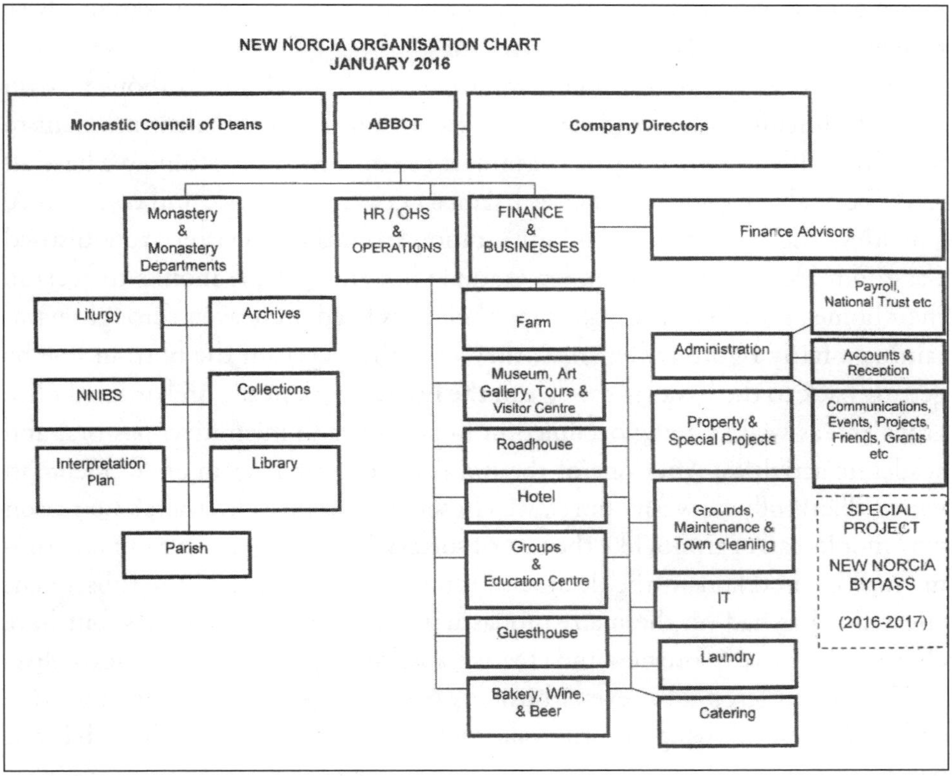

A brief look at the current organisational chart illustrates the complexities involved in running an autonomous private monastic town reliant mostly on its own resources and responsible for its own infrastructure—water, sewage, rubbish collection etc. The top sections include executive, councils and advisors. Unlike public companies we don't employ senior management—the abbot is the managing director and CEO, the accountant is the company secretary and procurator, our consultants and advisors are predominantly volunteers. We are not exempt however from the responsibilities of governance or from corporate legislation. Although at times challenging, it means we are both transparent and accountable, desirable attributes in an era in which the church is often criticised for its self-regulatory, self-investigative nature.

The organisation is divided into two main sections: 1) monastic departments, which include: the Archives, Museum Collections and the Library; and 2) the revenue earning businesses, which include: the Farm, Group Accommodation, Education Centre and the Museum and Art Gallery. Both these main sections are supported by administration and services. Each department has its own manager or supervisor and is overseen by a committee, which meets monthly to review operational, HR and financial issues.

Still in its early days the company structure, although not without its own suite of difficulties, is providing a safe, secure and legally efficient mechanism for both staff and the monastic community to operate successfully. We have already been able to achieve a better balance between monastic and commercial activities. The removal of all administration from the monastery to a disused classroom block in the village for example has allowed the monks to reclaim their home and while clearly keeping their eyes fixed on heaven through maintaining a fairly rigorous *horarium*, they keep their eyes on the bottom line by getting back to the basics—they clean the house, work in the orchard and olive grove etc, as well as being occupied in important administrative, pastoral and academic activities. After one of the monks wrote off a car in an accident (in which thankfully he wasn't hurt), we chose not to replace it. There's no reason why monks can't carpool like the rest of society attempting to save our environment. We could lament the decline in monastic vocations and the subsequent effect this has had on the many monastic revenue-earning activities, but have chosen rather to explore new and creative ways to keep these «industries» alive.

We have entered into several business partnerships, which means the wine and beer are still flowing, we still wake each morning to the smell of fresh bread baking in our wood-fired oven, and the once dormant printery is up and running again, offering print workshops. Monastic culture is continually celebrated through our well-attended annual Library Lecture, Archives' Studies Day, and Writers' Festival. Monastic spirituality is also kept alive and well via the offerings from our Institute for Benedictine Studies and retreat programme in the Monastery Guesthouse, enhanced by the involvement of the Benedictine Sisters of the Good Samaritan.

So while all seems well, and indeed the restructure has produced a somewhat healthier bottom line, an analysis of the past ten years and a projection into the next ten, don't paint a very pretty picture. Like all prudent companies, we too must work on our strategic planning, and it will need to be radical panning if we are to be a sustainable entity. This isn't the place to go into detail, only to mention Dr Elena Lasida's recent article entitled «When fragility becomes promise of renewal»[32]. That a positive approach to fragility might be the key to future

32 E. Lasida, «When fragility becomes promise of renewal», *AIM Monastic Bulletin* 109 (2015) 49-55.

planning inspires me and encourages me to enter this radical path with a real sense of hope.

The on-going responsibilities in our stewardship of Australia's only monastic town at times leaves me feeling somewhat overwhelmed: the relentless maintenance, restoration and conservation issues, and the associated funding required to respond to these, sometimes leaves me wondering why we do it. We do it of course because we are seeking God and we want to share our desire with all who pass our way. In this sense heaven and the bottom line are one and the same, because in all of it—from a missionary monk in 1847 walking 130 kilometres to Perth to play the piano to raise £70 to keep the Mission going, to the current abbot in 2017 wondering where on earth he's going to find the $250,000 to repair the sewage well in danger of collapse—we are attempting to give glory to God.

In conclusion, Rev Flood's remarks made in 1908 are just as true now as they were then:

> It must be borne in mind that everything the Mission has made and spent has been squeezed out of the land by hard toil, and by the practice of the most rigid economy[33].

Abstract

With the building of two boarding colleges in the early 1900s, the monastic town of New Norcia (Est. 1847) experienced its first major transition from an Aboriginal mission to an era of education, spanning most of the 20th century. After the closure of the last of these colleges in 1991, the community was again faced with the enormous challenge of reinventing itself. In this current era of extended hospitality, New Norcia continues to be a financially self-sustaining organisation which conducts a wide range of commercial endeavours, including a substantial farm, museum & art gallery, and hotel, and non-commercial activities such as archives, library and an Institute for Benedictine Studies. As an historic site, this monastic community is the steward of a physical, cultural and spiritual heritage of state, national and international importance.

To remain a Benedictine monastery, to be economically viable, to preserve and conserve the unique heritage, and to share this heritage and the spiritual life of the monks with their guests and visitors have always been aspirations;

33 Flood, *New Norcia*, 288.

these aspirations have become the present day key objectives, but sustained by traditional monastic values.

This paper will trace the slow but steady evolution of a community which includes heroic pioneering endeavours, long years of conflict, difficulty and hardship. It will explore the complex web of relationships and the vast possibilities and significant challenges involved in attempting to create an environment in which the monastic goal of seeking God and the corporate realities of running a monastic town can co-exist – the complex and delicate task of holding oratory and boardroom in balance.

MODÈLES D'ÉCONOMIE MONASTIQUE EN EUROPE ET EN AFRIQUE : ENTRE ÉCONOMIE ALTERNATIVE ET ÉCONOMIE DE DÉVELOPPEMENT

Isabelle JONVEAUX

Depuis les Pères du Désert, le travail et l'économie ont toujours représenté une question critique dans l'histoire du monachisme. Selon Jean Séguy, le monastère peut être défini comme une utopie du Royaume de Dieu déjà là et encore à venir. « On appelle utopie tout système idéologique total visant implicitement ou explicitement par l'appel à l'imaginaire (utopie écrite) ou par passage à la pratique (utopie pratiquée) à transformer radicalement les systèmes sociaux globaux existants »[1]. Comment est-il alors possible d'intégrer le travail et l'économie qui ont pour rôle de subvenir aux besoins de la communauté dans l'utopie religieuse sans altérer la qualité de vie monastique ? La Règle de saint Benoît offre une forme d'intégration où le travail devient une part même de la définition du moine (RB 36,8). Toutefois, l'économie demeure une question délicate dans la vie monastique, notamment dans la nécessité de trouver la forme de travail et d'économie la mieux adaptée aux valeurs monastiques. Parallèlement, alors que la société fait face à une crise du capitalisme et cherche d'autres formes d'économie, les monastères peuvent témoigner envers le monde de modèles alternatifs. L'économie constitue ainsi une forme non religieuse de communication avec le monde séculier.

Cet article s'appuie essentiellement sur des enquêtes de terrain menées dans 26 monastères de cinq pays d'Europe depuis 2004 et de 10 monastères en dehors de l'Europe. A partir de 2013, des enquêtes ont été conduites au Togo, Kenya, Argentine et Sénégal. En outre, j'ai pu avoir accès à des rapports de contrôle des comptes de huit monastères africains[2].

Isabelle Jonveaux, sociologist, researcher at the University of Graz (Austria)

1 J. SEGUY « Une sociologie des sociétés imaginées : Monachisme et utopie », *Annales. Économies, Sociétés, Civilisations* 2 (1971) 331.

2 Je souhaite remercier vivement le Frère Ardouin pour m'avoir donné accès à ces données.

Une comparaison internationale permet de distinguer ce qui serait inhérent à l'économie monastique – si cela existe – de ce qui dépendrait d'un contexte socio-économique spécifique. Une première partie présentera les différents modèles d'économie monastique et explorera quelques cas spécifiques. Dans une seconde partie, j'analyserais les modèles d'économie des monastères africains en lien avec le modèle du fondateur et le contexte local. Enfin, nous verrons dans une troisième partie en quoi l'économie monastique peut être force de changement et de développement.

1. L'ÉCONOMIE MONASTIQUE : TYPOLOGIE DES MODÈLES

Il est évident que les monastères, comme groupes de personnes qui se consacrent à la recherche de Dieu, ne sont pas premièrement des groupes d'action économique orientés vers la performance et la recherche du gain. Toutefois, les monastères peuvent se définir selon Max Weber comme des « communautés de régulation de l'économie (*wirtschaftsregulierende Gemeinschaften*) »[3], c'est-à-dire des communautés « qui ont un côté économique, mais qui ne sont pas des communautés économiques, c'est-à-dire dont les organes n'exercent ni par leur activité propre ni par leurs prescriptions, ordres et interdictions, une action constante sur le développement économique, mais dont les statuts règlent néanmoins le comportement des personnes qui leur appartiennent »[4]. Parce que les religieux vivent ensemble et partagent tous les aspects de l'existence dans le même lieu, les communautés monastiques sont confrontées au nécessaire aspect économique de l'existence même si elles aimeraient se libérer des conditions terrestres.

Le modèle économique qui ressort de la Règle de saint Benoît est un modèle autarcique de production interne qui permet de protéger l'espace monastique. Les moines doivent pouvoir produire dans le monastère ou proche de celui-ci tout ce dont ils ont besoin. Mais cette forme véritablement autarcique est le plus souvent restée dans l'histoire un idéal jamais réellement atteint plutôt qu'une réalité. Les monastères développèrent ainsi différentes formes d'économie qui purent dans certains cas être extrêmement performantes et devenir, ainsi que le dit Weber, « des lieux d'économie rationnelle »[5].

3 M. WEBER, *Économie et Société*, tome 2, Paris 1995, 53.

4 WEBER, *Économie et Société*.

5 M. WEBER, *Sociologie des religions*, Paris 1996, 422.

1.1. Modèles de sources des revenus

Si nous comparons les formes d'économie monastique des communautés de la famille bénédictine dans le monde actuel, nous pouvons définir cinq modèles principaux de sources des revenus :

- *Travail direct des moines avec une économie interne de production.* La France illustre cette catégorie où plus de la moitié des revenus de la majorité des monastères proviennent du travail direct des moines et moniales. Les communautés monastiques développent des (plus ou moins) petites sociétés de production dans lesquelles travaillent les religieux avec aussi parfois des employés laïques[6].
- *Économie d'activités extérieures ou économie externalisée.* Cette forme d'économie se trouve notamment dans les monastères belges où ce ne sont pratiquement que des laïcs qui travaillent dans les entreprises monastiques. La communauté peut aussi vendre le processus de fabrication à une entreprise laïque et recevoir ainsi les dividendes liés à la marque. À Maredsous par exemple, 46% des revenus provenaient en 2006 des dividendes pour la bière et le fromage.
- *Économie de patrimoine.* L'Autriche correspond parfaitement à ce modèle où la majeure partie des revenus (jusqu'à 95% parfois) provient de l'exploitation des propriétés foncières et immobilières. Les moines sont alors le plus souvent engagés dans des activités intellectuelles et de pastorale.
- *Économie du don.* Dans ce modèle, les moines et moniales travaillent dans des activités qui ne sont cependant pas rentables pour la communauté, qui vit alors essentiellement des dons. Cela peut être le cas de nouvelles fondations, par exemple en Afrique.
- *Économie de la vieillesse.* Ce modèle est souvent le fruit de la situation présente de petites communautés féminines vieillissantes. Pour deux monastères de femmes étudiés en France en 2007, la pension des anciennes représentait respectivement 44% et 36% des revenus.

1.2. Origine des différences des économies monastiques

Pour leur majorité, ces différences dans les modèles d'économie monastique prennent leur origine non pas en premier lieu dans les décisions des communau-

6 Pour une description de ces types d'économie, voir I. Jonveaux, *Le Monastère au travail. Le Royaume de Dieu au défi de l'économie*, Paris 2011.

tés, mais de l'histoire politique et religieuse du pays dans lequel elle se trouve. Les exemples de la France et de l'Autriche permettent illustrer ce propos. Dans le contexte des Lumières en Autriche, l'Empereur Joseph II, suivant les théories de l'économiste français Quesnay, édita une loi pour éliminer toutes les communautés religieuses qui n'auraient pas d'activités jugées « utiles » pour la société. En conséquence, les monastères durent ouvrir des écoles et développer le travail dans les paroisses, tandis que l'État leur imposa aussi de nouvelles paroisses. Il est courant encore actuellement que les monastères aient la charge de 20 à 30 paroisses. Les données statistiques sur la vie monastique en Europe montrent encore parfaitement l'héritage de ces différences historiques, notamment à travers les activités des moines et moniales. Par exemple, seulement 61% des monastères bénédictins autrichiens ont un magasin tandis que cela concerne 79% des monastères bénédictins français [7]. La majeure partie des activités des moines autrichiens se trouvent à l'extérieur du monastère. Ainsi 63% des moines du monastère de Kremsmünster – abbaye bénédictine en Haute-Autriche – travaillent en dehors du monastère, et 54% sont ou étaient actifs dans les paroisses. Les revenus des communautés autrichiennes proviennent essentiellement de leur patrimoine foncier et immobilier. À Kremsmünster, les revenus de l'exploitation forestière représentent 80% des revenus du monastère. Les activités directes des moines sont quant à elles rémunérées par le diocèse lorsque les moines sont curés de paroisses et par l'État lorsqu'ils enseignent à l'école. Cette situation est cependant remise en question par la nouvelle génération de moines qui ne souhaite pas habiter en paroisse ou même être prêtre, mais les diocèses se refusent à reprendre les paroisses du fait du manque de prêtres.

À l'opposé, l'histoire monastique française est marquée par deux suppressions qui ont conduit à la perte de leur patrimoine immobilier et foncier, mais aussi par le scandale de la révélation du « milliard des congrégations » [8] au début du XXe siècle. Dans ce contexte, l'économie de patrimoine n'est plus possible et les moines ont dû développer une économie interne de production intégrée à un mode de vie très contemplatif. La vie monastique fut en effet refondée à la fin du XIXe siècle et au début du XXe par des prêtres qui avaient en tête un idéal romantique de la vie monastique du Moyen Âge [9].

7 I. Jonveaux, «Mönchtum in Zahlen. Benediktinerklöster in Österreich im Spiegel der Statistik», *Erbe und Auftrag: Benediktinische Monatsschrift* 2 (2014) 204.

8 C. Sorel, La République contre les congrégations, Histoire d'une passion française 1899-1904, Paris 2003.

9 Voir D. Hervieu-Leger, *Le Temps des moines*, Paris 2017.

Ces deux exemples montrent parfaitement à quel point les modèles d'économie monastique actuels sont influencés par l'histoire politique et religieuse de la société plus que la conception interne des ordres religieux.

1.3. Économie de production : une typologie des réponses à la tension entre économie et vie monastique

Économie et vie monastique sont deux réalités soumises à des contradictions constantes. Considérer le monastère comme une utopie signifie qu'il est une institution entièrement religieuse qui n'admet théoriquement dans son cadre que les activités qui servent les buts religieux de l'institution. Nous pouvons construire ainsi une typologie des types de confrontation entre économie et vie monastique.

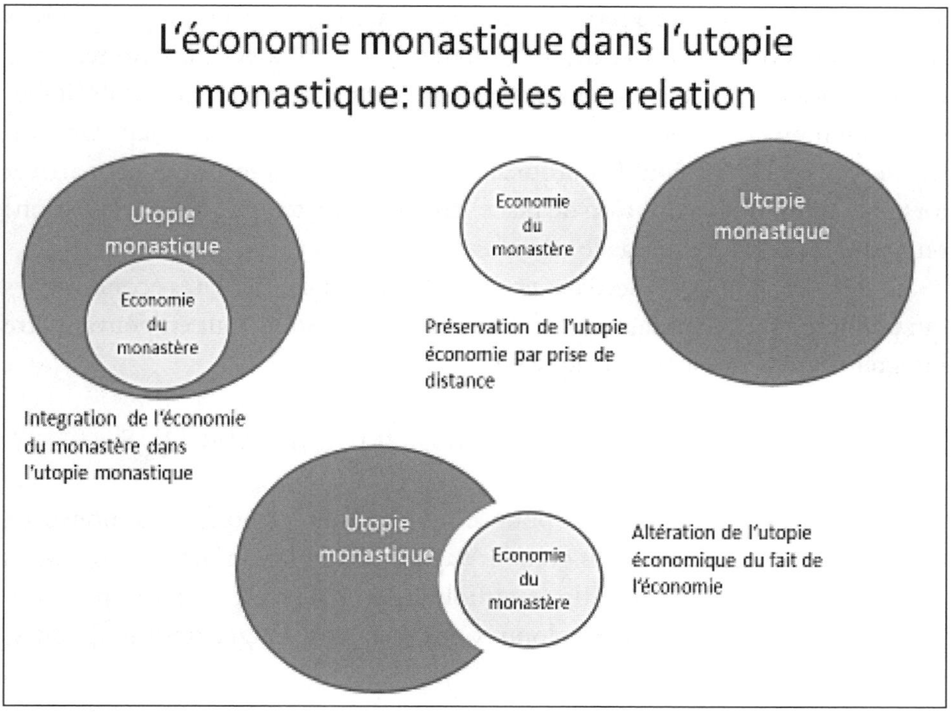

Nous obtenons ici trois modes possibles de relation entre l'utopie monastique et l'économie. La première est l'intégration de l'économie dans l'utopie qui requiert une redéfinition de l'économie de telle manière à pouvoir l'intégrer dans la vie monastique sans altérer cette dernière. Cela signifie pour les moines de donner une signification religieuse à leur travail et à l'économie de telle manière à ce qu'ils ne s'opposent plus. C'est évident dans le cas des productions religieuses comme les hosties ou les icônes, le plus souvent présentes dans les communautés féminines, mais ces activités sont de moins en moins rentables faute de demande. Les travaux d'art ou d'artisanat permettent aussi de donner une nouvelle définition au travail qui se trouverait par-là libéré de sa dimension économique et recevrait une dimension religieuse comme continuation du travail divin de création. Enfin, l'écologie prend de plus en plus de place dans l'économie monastique pour donner aux activités un sens de respect de la création. Le second mode de relation entre la vie monastique et l'économie consiste à garder cette dernière à distance pour préserver l'utopie monastique. Une manière de le faire est de nier l'économie en créant des espaces alternatifs pour le don ou le troc, même si les moines sont conscients que ces formes d'échange ne le suffiraient par pour vivre. Un processus d'externalisation de l'économie est aussi possible. Il consiste à retirer les moines des activités économiques pour les remplacer par des laïcs ou à extraire les ateliers économiques de la clôture. Cette externalisation peut être appliquée au cellérier, par exemple à Camaldoli (Italie) où la communauté a choisi de laisser la charge de l'économat à un laïc. Un troisième type est l'altération de l'utopie à cause de l'économie, ce qui peut arriver lorsque l'économie prend trop de place (en termes de temps ou préoccupation) ou prend la préséance sur la vie religieuse.

Le défi des moines et moniales et donc de trouver des activités économiques qui permettent à la communauté de subvenir à ses besoins tout en pouvant être intégrées dans l'utopie monastique sans l'altérer.

2. MODÈLES D'ÉCONOMIE MONASTIQUE EN AFRIQUE

L'Afrique et l'Asie représentent pour le monachisme catholique de nouveaux continents monastiques où les grandes vagues de fondation datent des années 1960. La situation du monachisme catholique en Asie n'est toutefois pas comparable à celle de l'Afrique étant donné que l'Asie a une longue tradition monastique hors-christianisme.

2.1. Rupture ou continuité par rapport au modèle des fondateurs ?

La plupart des monastères africains actuels sont des fondations exogènes de communautés européennes – avec l'exception notable de l'Éthiopie qui a sa propre tradition depuis le Ve siècle selon la fameuse légende dite des « Neufs Saints ». Les fondateurs viennent pour la plupart du temps des anciens pays colonisateurs. Nous appelons communautés exogènes les communautés fondées par des moines venus d'autres milieux culturels, le plus souvent d'autres continents. À l'opposé, émergent depuis une trentaine d'années en Afrique des communautés endogènes qui sont soit le fait d'une communauté locale existante (fondation d'une fondation) par exemple Séguéya, fondation de Keur Moussa (Sénégal) en Guinée Conackri, soit par des moines individuels indigènes comme Boniface Tiguila au Togo. Quel modèle économique observe-t-on alors dans ces monastères ? Dans quelle mesure les fondateurs exportent-ils leur modèle économique dans les fondations exogènes ? Une question qu'il faudra encore étudier est celle de savoir si l'on observe des différences dans la structure économique entre fondations exogènes et fondations endogènes.

Un croisement des observations entre monastères européens et africains montre tout d'abord des similarités entre le modèle des fondateurs et celui du monastère fondé. Ainsi, on observe que la majorité des monastères fondés par des communautés françaises en Afrique, développent un modèle d'économie interne de production. Par exemple, l'abbaye de Dzobegan, qui a été fondée par la communauté française d'En Calcat en 1961 (Congrégation de Subiaco) a différentes activités de production (café, thé, huiles essentielles...). La même structure s'observe au monastère de Keur Moussa au Sénégal, qui a été fondé en 1962 par la communauté de Solesmes. Les moines développent, comme en France, des activités internes de production, comme l'atelier de kora, l'agro-alimentaire, les fruits secs, le parfum, etc. Les moniales de Koubri au Burkina Faso sont essentiellement actives dans une production de yaourts à l'intérieur du monastère comme l'a étudié Katrin Langewiesche[10].

Inversement, les communautés bénédictines que j'ai pu visiter au Kenya ont été toutes fondées par des communautés allemandes. L'hospitalité et les offres spirituelles (retraites, parcours « African Bible on the ground ») sont les activités principales du monastère Our Lady of Mount Kenya dans le centre du pays. Les sœurs de Karen à Nairobi sont essentiellement actives dans un petit dispensaire qu'elles ont ouvert dans l'enceinte du monastère. En outre, les communautés fondées par des Français en Afrique de l'Ouest ont presque toutes un magasin (Keur Moussa, Keur Guilaye, moines et moniales de Koubri au Burki-

10 K. Langewiesche, « Economic management under a Vow of Poverty: Monastic Mangement in Burkina Faso », in *Monasticism in Modern Times*, edd. I. Jonveaux-S. Palmisano, London 2016, 63-78.

na, ...) où ils vendent leurs propres productions ainsi que des produits des monastères voisins. Ce n'est pas le cas au Kenya. Toutefois, il faut souligner que les monastères bénédictins kényans appartiennent presque tous à la Congrégation de Sainte-Odile pour les hommes et de Tutzing pour les femmes qui ont clairement un but missionnaire et s'engagent dans des activités sociales directes envers la population locale.

De prime abord, le modèle économique des fondations exogènes en Afrique reflète le modèle de la communauté fondatrice. Mais comme nous l'avons expliqué plus haut, ces modèles sont eux-mêmes le fruit d'une situation contingente et d'une longue histoire. L'exportation en Afrique du modèle des fondateurs ne correspond donc pas à une définition absolue de la vie ou de l'économie monastique, mais à la situation spécifique de leur société. Des ruptures conscientes avec la tradition des fondateurs peuvent aussi s'observer. C'est le cas du monastère d'Agbang au Togo, fondé par Boniface Tiguila[11]. Celui-ci débuta sa vie monastique au monastère de Dzobegan qui reflète le modèle contemplatif des fondateurs français. Considérant ce modèle inapproprié dans le contexte local, il quitta sa communauté et fonda en 1985 un nouveau monastère qui est ensuite entré dans la Congrégation de Sainte-Odile. Son but était de développer une vie monastique « fondée par un Africain pour les Africains ». Son modèle économique repose essentiellement sur un encastrement local pour pouvoir répondre à des besoins des habitants de la brousse autour du monastère.

2.2. Déterminants spécifiques de l'économie monastique en Afrique

En comparaison de l'Europe, l'économie des monastères africains est influencée par différents facteurs internes ou externes à la communauté. Le premier est celui de la structure des communautés selon la taille et la distribution des âges. Si nous nous référons aux statistiques démographiques de la Congrégation de l'Annonciation (2012), nous trouvons une moyenne d'âge de 42 ans pour les communautés en Afrique et de 40 ans en Asie. En regard, de nombreuses communautés européennes présentent une moyenne d'âge supérieure à 65 ou

11 J'ai rencontré Boniface Tiguila la première fois en 2012 lors du chapitre général d'une congrégation bénédictine. J'ai ensuite effectué une enquête au Togo en 2013 alors qu'il n'était plus prieur d'Agbang et l'ai à nouveau rencontré au Kenya en 2014.

70 ans[12]. Une moyenne d'âge plus jeune a des effets positifs sur la dynamique de la communauté et plus spécialement pour les activités économiques. Toutefois, une communauté jeune doit aussi investir dans la formation des jeunes moines, ce qui n'apporte pas de résultats immédiats pour la communauté. Par exemple, pour le monastère de Séguéya fondé en Guinée Conackri en 2006, les charges de formation ont été multipliées par huit en trois ans.

L'absence d'histoire monastique dans la plupart des pays africains a aussi des conséquences sur l'économie. Les monastères africains sont *a priori* libres du poids de l'histoire qui a pu dans d'autres contextes, comme en Autriche, déterminé en grande partie la structure des activités monastiques. En conséquence, les communautés monastiques peuvent théoriquement choisir par elles-mêmes les activités les mieux adaptées à leur projet monastique et à leurs besoins financiers.

Mais la nouveauté du monachisme en Afrique occasionne en outre une moindre compréhension de la vie monastique et de son « inutilité » théorique dans le sens où les monastères n'ont pas pour but direct d'être socialement actifs ou de développer une activité économique contrairement aux congrégations apostoliques qui se sont souvent implantées plus tôt dans ces pays. Un moine français affirme : « Tant qu'on n'a pas compris que le monachisme "ne sert à rien" on passe à côté de sa véritable signification, car il ne se situe pas du côté de l'efficacité. »[13] Du point de vue économique, cela signifie aussi que les produits monastiques ne bénéficient pas d'une valeur ajoutée parce qu'ils sont produits par des moines ou moniales comme cela peut être le cas en Europe[14]. Toutefois, le cellérier de Keur Moussa affirme que leurs produits sont reconnus pour leur qualité :

> Les gens trouvent que les produits monastiques sont de bonne qualité, ils sont sûrs de la qualité du produit. Donc ils apprécient beaucoup les produits monastiques de Keur Moussa. On est très connus. Parfois à Dakar, quand je marche, les gens m'arrêtent et me disent : "Vos fromages de chèvre, comment faire pour les avoir ?" Il n'y a pas longtemps une dame m'a contacté pour signer une convention avec nous par rapport aux fromages de chèvre. La personne a dit : "Vos fromages sont de bonne qualité". (4.07.2016)

12 Jonveaux, « Mönchtum in Zahlen », 202-209.

13 Un moine bénédictin « Le Mystère monastique », Paris 1977, 32.

14 Jonveaux, *Le Monastère au travail*, Paris 2011.

Une autre caractéristique de l'économie des communautés monastiques africaines actuelles est un accent plus grand donné à l'autosuffisance. De nombreux monastères d'Afrique de l'Ouest comme Agbang, Keur Moussa ou Koubri, possèdent à l'intérieur de leur enceinte des ateliers de mécanique ou de menuiserie nécessaires à sa maintenance comme Benoît le recommande. L'autoconsommation est aussi plus importante que dans les monastères européens d'après les rapports des visites économiques. La sœur économe au monastère de Karen à Nairobi explique :

> We also have our garden, so we also try to be self-sustainable. We plant our own vegetables, we try as much as possible not to buy the things we are able to produce ourselves. We also have some cows over there, so we find that we try to reduce the cost of things, of buying things from outside. (21.02.2014)

Ou à Keur Moussa : « L'idée de ces produits c'est d'abord d'être autosuffisant, mais aussi de vendre parce que ça fait vivre la communauté. » (4.07.2016).

Le plus grand recours à l'autosuffisance s'explique en partie par le contexte socio-économique local où l'autoconsommation est une stratégie pour contourner la pauvreté. C'est pour cette raison que les sœurs de Karen enseignent aux gens dans les villages des techniques pour devenir plus autosuffisant.

2.3. Caractéristiques de l'économie monastique en Afrique

L'étude des comptes de communautés monastiques africaines fait ressortir plusieurs particularités dans la structure de l'économie comparée aux communautés françaises[15]. Parmi ces spécificités, on peut noter que les communautés monastiques africaines ne reçoivent pas de dons ni de legs contrairement aux communautés françaises, qu'elles ont souvent beaucoup d'activités disparates, dont la plupart s'éteignent à peine commencées et enfin que de nombreuses activités sont déficitaires. Parmi les questions d'actualité, celle de la couverture sociale, autant pour les membres autochtones des communautés que pour les employés, se pose. Un problème rencontré est souvent celui des débouchés, car la population locale ne constitue en général pas la demande pour les produits monastiques. Ainsi les plus grands clients du magasin de Keur Moussa sont les expatriés européens de Dakar et les touristes. De même, les koras se vendent plus

15 Je m'appuie pour cette partie sur les rapports des comptes de communautés auxquels j'ai pu avoir accès.

à l'étranger qu'au Sénégal ou même qu'en Afrique. Comme le souligne le rapporteur économique concernant le monastère de Kokoubou au Bénin, le pouvoir d'achat se situe dans les capitales et les grandes villes, ce qui rend difficile le développement des activités d'artisanat.

Les monastères de fondation récente ont une structure économique qui repose pour plus de la moitié des revenus sur des dons de différentes provenances comme c'est le cas à Séguéya ou Agbang. Les gros investissements, en bâtiments notamment, sont le plus souvent permis par l'aide la congrégation ou de l'AIM. La question des bâtiments est une question brûlante, notamment parce que les communautés sont encore assez récentes et doivent souvent – dans le sens contraire où le vivent les communautés ouest-européennes actuelles – se poser la question de l'agrandissement, de la construction de locaux pour une nouvelle activité économique ou d'une hôtellerie dédiée à un public particulier (groupes, familles, etc).

La répartition des dépenses des communautés dans les rapports de comptes comparés entre l'Afrique et l'Europe de l'Ouest illustre parfaitement bien, comme mentionné dans les rapports, la loi d'Engel qui montra en 1857 que la part dédiée à l'alimentation baisse avec l'augmentation du budget. Ainsi la part de l'alimentation est-elle un poste important dans les communautés africaines et représente même le premier poste de dépenses pour le monastère masculin de Koubri au Burkina (30%) alors qu'il est de l'ordre de 8 à 15% en France. Le poste d'énergie est particulièrement important en Afrique du fait du coût de l'électricité. De même, le transport occasionne de grosses dépenses à cause du mauvais état des routes qui engagent des frais élevés de véhicule (33% à Séguéya). Du côté des employés, les communautés africaines présentent la particularité d'embaucher des journaliers qui sont absents des monastères européens. On y trouve aussi certains emplois spécifiques comme gardien ou chauffeur.

Comme nous l'avons vu dans les modèles exposés plus haut, l'économie des monastères ne repose pas nécessairement sur le travail direct des moines et moniales ou des activités de production. Il est bon néanmoins de rendre cette approche de l'économie plus concrète en présentant les activités de quelques monastères africains[16] :

16 Ce tableau ne rapporte pas l'ensemble des activités sources de revenus, mais seulement les principales. Les communautés africaines peuvent en effet avoir de très nombreuses petites sources de revenus éparses.

Pays	*Communauté*	*Sexe*	*Ordre*	*Fondation*	*Activités*	*Nb. employés*
Bénin	Toffo	F	Bénédictines	1966	Alimentaire - tissage – vêtements liturgiques - artisanat -magasin	30
Bénin	Peporyakou	F	Bénédictines	2008	Hosties - farine enrichie – ferme - magasin - hôtellerie – teckeraie - potager	4 + journaliers
Bénin	Kokoubou	H	Trappistes	1972	Fromage frais – sirop – miel – phytothérapie – boutique – soja – poulailler	
Burkina	Koubri	H	Bénédictins	1962	Verger – confiserie – provenderie – ferme – hôtellerie - boutique	7+ journaliers
Burkina	Koubri	F	Bénédictines	1963	Yaouterie – spiruline – magasin – jardin	
Congo-Brazzaville	La Bouenza	H	Bénédictins	1958	Laboratoire médicaments - hôtelleries 1 et 2 - poulailler - cultures	2+ journaliers
Sénégal	Keur Moussa	H	Bénédictins	1963	Kora – agroalimentaire – hôtellerie – magasin – fromagerie – verger – parfumerie	7+ journaliers
Sénégal	Keur Guilaye	F	Bénédictines	1967	Pain d'autel – magasin – confiserie – verger - poulailler	3+
Guinée	Séguéya	H	Bénédictins	2003	Bananeraie – ananas – élevage – alimentation pour bétail	9+20 journaliers

3. L'ÉCONOMIE MONASTIQUE COMME MOTEUR DE CHANGEMENT

Quel que soit le modèle économique développé par les communautés, on observe tout au long de l'histoire monastique que les monastères ont toujours été forces de changement social. Philibert Schmitz, historien de l'Ordre Bénédictin, parle d'« œuvre civilisatrice »[17] des moines en Europe. Dans quelle mesure le monachisme actuel peut-il jouer un rôle d'innovation et de développement ?

3.1. Pourquoi les monastères sont-ils des lieux d'innovation ?

Si les monastères ont toujours été au cours de l'histoire des lieux d'innovation et de développement alors que cela ne constituait en aucune manière leur but premier, cela signifie que la structure monastique présente des caractéristiques propres qui peuvent conduire à cette dynamique. Selon Olivier de Sardan, l'innovation peut se définir comme une « greffe de techniques, de savoirs ou de modes d'organisation inédits (en général sous forme d'adaptions locales à partir d'emprunts ou d'importations) sur des techniques, savoirs et modes d'organisation en place »[18]. Il souligne aussi que l'innovation doit être considérée comme un processus social.

Tout d'abord, une communauté monastique n'est pas un groupe économique qui a pour but de faire du profit. L'économie demeure théoriquement au service de la subsistance de la communauté. Cela a pour conséquence la possibilité de prise de risque parce que le but immédiat de la communauté n'est pas le résultat d'excédent d'exploitation en fin d'année. La communauté monastique est en outre durable ; ce groupe a une durée de vie plus élevée qu'une entreprise et peut ainsi prendre des risques ou investir en capital humain. La communauté monastique se projette dans un temps long qui est à mettre en lien avec l'idée de stabilité (*stabilitas loci*). De plus, ce groupe est la plupart du temps en paix sociale ; il se définit lui-même comme un groupe de personnes qui cherche Dieu. La dimension durable de la communauté rend aussi possible la transmission d'expériences et de connaissances. On se souvient par exemple des travaux de copie des moines qui ont permis de conserver et de transmettre pendant tout le Moyen Âge leurs

17 P. Schmitz, *Histoire de l'ordre de saint Benoît, tome II. Œuvre civilisatrice jusqu'au XII*ème *siècle*, Maredsous 1943.

18 J.-P. Olivier De Sardan, « Anthropologie et développement. Essai en socio-anthropologie du changement social », Marseille-Paris 1995, http://classiques.uqac.ca/contemporains/olivier_de_sardan_jean_pierre/anthropologie_et_developpement/anthropo_et_developpement.pdf [accés: 11-11-18].

connaissances en médecine, agriculture, botanique, etc. Enfin, la longue histoire du monachisme permet d'améliorer différentes dimensions et de prendre exemple sur l'expérience vécue par d'autres communautés ou d'autres époques. « The remarkable stability of monasticism is in large part a stability of memory, a continuity of understanding spanning thirty generations »[19]. Même si la communauté est récente, chaque monastère s'intègre dans la longue tradition du monachisme, ce qui constitue un moyen sa légitimation[20].

3.2. Économie et développement en Afrique

Dans les pays en voie de développement où le monachisme est souvent une implantation récente, les communautés jouent un rôle important pour le développement économique et social. Jean-Pierre Olivier de Sardan définit le développement comme un « ensemble des processus sociaux induits par des opérations volontaristes de transformation d'un milieu social, entreprises par le biais d'institutions ou d'acteurs extérieurs à ce milieu, mais cherchant à mobiliser ce milieu »[21]. Dans le cas du monachisme, le développement prend cependant différentes dimensions. Comme déjà mentionné, innovation et développement ne sont pas en soi des buts de la vie monastique, mais peuvent devenir des externalités positives. Cela signifie que le développement est une conséquence d'activités motivées par un but monastique, c'est-à-dire qui servent le but religieux de la vie monastique. Par exemple, les moines au Moyen Âge développèrent la force hydraulique pour gagner du temps pour la prière[22].

Le développement occasionné par les monastères en Afrique contemporaine est le plus souvent une externalité positive qui découle des activités ou innovations du monastère. Ainsi que le dit l'abbé de Keur Moussa : « On ne cherche pas le développement, il vient avec ». Les communautés d'inspiration bénédictine ont dans leur tradition de développer dans et autour du monastère les conditions qui leur permettront de subvenir aux besoins de la communauté. Cela signifie dans le cadre d'une nouvelle fondation que les moines et moniales travailleront à rendre leurs terres arables, à s'assurer de la présence d'eau et amener ou produire de l'électricité. L'abbaye de Keur Moussa au Sénégal a adopté pour devise cette phrase

---

19 R.H. Winthrop, «Leadership and Tradition in the Regulation of Catholic Monasticism», *Anthropological Quarterly* 58 (1985) 30.

20 B. Delpal, « Le Silence des moines, Les Trappistes au XIXème siècle », Paris 1998, 15.

21 Olivier De Sardan. « Anthropologie et développement ».

22 M. Derwich, « La Vie quotidienne des moines et chanoines réguliers au Moyen-Age et Temps Modernes », Wroclaw 1995.

biblique « Et le désert fleurira » (Esaïe 35, 1) et elle a en effet rendu possible l'agriculture de ses terres auparavant arides et introduit de nouvelles espères dans l'environnement. L'embauche de salariés locaux contribue aussi au développement local en donnant du travail aux gens des environs. Pour un moine kényan du monastère Our Lady of Mount Kenya, il s'agit de la dimension principale de leur activité de développement. Enfin, la formation des moines et moniales est aussi une part directe du développement. De manière indirecte, le monastère participe au développement de sa région lorsqu'il attire des populations qui vont venir s'installer dans les alentours pour bénéficier d'un travail, d'un dispensaire ou d'une école.

Une autre dimension du développement monastique vient en effet de la réponse des moines et moniales à des demandes locales. Etant donné que les premières communautés religieuses présentes en Afrique étaient des congrégations missionnaires qui avaient pour but de développer des écoles, dispensaires et hôpitaux, ce même type de demande est adressé aux moines lorsqu'ils s'installent dans un nouvel environnement. C'est pour cette raison que les moines de Keur Moussa qui venaient de Solesmes et apportaient avec eux un modèle strictement contemplatif et cloîtré de vie monastique, ont dû ouvrir une école et un petit dispensaire. Ils ont toutefois aussitôt que possible confié l'école à des laïcs et le dispensaire à une congrégation apostolique de sœurs. Comme le dit un moine en entretien : « Les femmes venaient pour accoucher et les moines devaient le faire, alors que ce n'est pas la mission d'un moine de le faire ! ». Les communautés monastiques soutiennent aussi parfois des programmes sociaux, par exemple le monastère Our Lady of Mount Kenya participe à un projet d'agriculture dans des sacs pour aider les familles pauvres à devenir autosuffisantes.

3.3. L'économie monastique comme économie alternative

L'économie monastique peut aussi constituer une force de changement à l'intérieur-même de l'économie en apportant des façons alternatives de la vivre. En contexte européen par exemple, les monastères tentent d'offrir une alternative à l'approche capitaliste et développent dans certains cas des réelles réflexions et proposent des cours sur ce sujet[23]. La sœur française Nicole Reille parle ainsi de l'économie des congrégations comme d'une « économie prophétique » grâce au témoignage qu'elle peut rendre au monde par les placements éthiques.

La dimension alternative de l'économie des monastiques africains s'observe aussi en lien avec le contexte spécifique, car l'altérité ne se construit que par

23 Jonveaux, *Le Monastère au travail*, Paris 2011.

rapport aux normes de la société. Une première dimension concerne la manière dont le travail est vécu et justifié dans la vie monastique. Etant donné que le travail pourrait à première vue entrer en contradiction avec l'idéal monastique, les moines et moniales utilisent différentes formes de justification dans les entretiens. Par exemple, une jeune sœur à Karen :

> I do it with love, not just doing it, I do it with a lot of love. Until they feel themselves that this cloth is washed with love. Even when you sweep you sweep a place with love and somebody will look at it and say "Yes, this was done with love." It doesn't matter what you have gone to school for but what matters is what you give to the community. (04.2014)

Un exemple intéressant vient de Séguéya en Guinée Conackri et de la situation particulière de cet État communiste où les moines contribuent à donner une nouvelle valeur au travail :

> Les moines travaillent de leurs mains, ils essaient de tout faire pour avoir une activité. Je prends l'exemple de nos frères qui sont en Guinée Conakry. La Guinée a comme particularité qu'ils n'ont pas vraiment la culture du travail, à cause du système politique. Les gens ont perdu la culture du travail. Et le fait de voir nos frères travailler et labourer la terre a donné aux gens l'envie de faire la même chose. Je pense que c'est un message qui passe. (04.07.2016)

Une seconde dimension est le management humain et social développé par les communautés envers leurs salariés. La dimension sociale du recrutement est un critère qui prévaut parfois sur la performance économique. À Keur Moussa, le cellérier explique :

> C'est d'abord la dimension sociale. Dès le départ, on a eu cette exigence sociale de vouloir aider ceux qui n'ont pas de travail autour de nous, qui viennent demander du travail. On voudrait faire plus, mais on est limité dans nos moyens. On aide beaucoup de gens autour de nous. (4.07.2016)

En outre, certaines communautés africaines paient des cotisations sociales pour leurs salariés, ce qui n'est pas toujours répandu dans la société.

Enfin, le développement durable et l'écologie sont des sujets qui s'implantent aussi de plus en plus dans les communautés africaines. Ainsi la communauté de Keur Moussa s'engage actuellement dans l'agriculture biologique. Ou au Kenya, les moines développent l'énergie solaire et le recyclage de l'eau pour contourner cette difficulté en attendant d'être raccordés au réseau central. Le monastère d'Agbang, qui vit aussi de l'énergie solaire, constitue une source d'électricité pour les Peuls de la brousse qui viennent recharger leur téléphone au monastère.

CONCLUSION

Qu'est-ce que l'économie monastique ? À ce point, nous pouvons dire qu'il n'existe pas une économie monastique en soi, mais différentes formes d'économie des monastères qui dépendent de l'histoire politique et religieuse de chaque pays et du présent contexte économique et social. Toutefois, certaines tendances communes s'observent dans le sens que les communautés souhaitent imprimer à leur activité économique. La forme de l'économie joue un rôle important pour la plausibilité de la vie monastique dans une société parce qu'elle constitue souvent l'un des premiers vecteurs de communication avec le monde. Elle influence en outre la forme de vie monastique et inversement.

L'économie des monastères africains est une économie qui cherche encore souvent la stabilité et reflète les spécificités du contexte socio-économique ainsi que les influences du modèle du fondateur. Mais c'est aussi le plus souvent par leurs activités économiques que les monastères peuvent jouer un rôle dans le développement de leur environnement. Sans qu'il soit un but de la vie monastique en soi, on observe, selon les termes de Max Weber, une « affinité élective » entre économique monastique et développement économique, social et culturel de l'environnement dans lequel le monastère est intégré. La vie monastique peut donc avoir une influence sur son environnement local et même, lorsque la matrice monastique est suffisamment dense, influencer la société elle-même comme on a pu le voir dans l'histoire européenne.

Abstract

The paper discusses differences from the sociological point of view models of monastic economy. Application of these models depend on geographical and cultural context in which monasteries live. The difference between Europe, Africa and Asia are meaningful. To maintain monasteries alive, not only a prudent flexibility and openness are important but also sensibility for local conditions. Such approach requires changes but, succesfully implemented, may be an inspiration also for the lay society.

MONASTIC MANAGEMENT IN BURKINA FASO

Katrin LANGEWIESCHE

I would like to draw attention to the fact that research into monasticism not only sheds light on little known aspects of Christianity in Africa, it can also make an important contribution to the understanding of the processes of social change and debates on globalization in African societies.

The contemplative orders develop alternative economic forms, interact with their local environment, and build transnational networks or integrate into them. They emerge as local and transnational actors, change in the course of these processes, and contribute to the social change in the societies in which they participate. Like the current proponents of the solidarity economy, monasteries oppose the doctrine of constant economic growth and support instead the self-limitation of needs, forms and rhythms of work determined by the actors themselves, and non-monetary exchanges.

The idea of a "solidarity economy" is linked – like the label "alternative economy" with the concept of the "moral economy" as coined by E.P. Thompson[1] (Edelman, 2012). Thompson related it to the values and norms that influenced the economic activities of the English working class of the eighteenth century independently of the maximization of profit and principle of individual utility. After Thompson it was used by numerous authors to summarize all of the factors of economic trade that could not be described as individual rational value addition[2]. The analysis of organized alternatives to the capitalist economy (like the Occupy and Attac movements) shows that the redefinition of values is the precondition for the spread of alternatives to capitalism. And this is precisely what monastic communities have been doing for centuries when they base their production and consumption activities on religious and social values rather than market-economy ones.

Katrin Langewiesche, antropologist and researcher at the Department of Anthropology and African Studies at Johannes Gutenberg University Mainz.

1 Cf. M. EDELMAN, "E.P. Thompson and Moral Economies", in *A Companion to Moral Anthropology*, ed. D. Fassin, Wiley-Blackwell 2012, 49-66.

2 Cf. C. HANN, «Moral Economy», in *The Human Economy*, edd. K. Hart-J.-L. Laville-A.D. Cattani, Cambridge 2010, 187-198.

However, the alternative economy propagated by the religious actors should not be taken for granted in any way here and it is the object of this study. Hence, the main question is: Could monasteries provide a model for a solidarity economy in West Africa?

Thus, the focus here is on how the contemplative nuns can influence not only the Catholic Church but also their immediate environment, from which they try to separate themselves through their seclusion[3].

A comparative analysis approach in Africa is particularly appropriate to answer these questions. Chabrel Gravrand from Aiguebelle Abbey wrote in the early nineties "*Black Africa has become a vast monastic, spiritual and material building site*" [4].

My study is part of a research project, which will conduct a detailed analysis of the monastery landscape of Burkina Faso, Ghana and Senegal[5]. The initial research carried out as part of the project in Burkina Faso supports the assumption that an uniform picture does not emerge when questions are made about the social change initiated – consciously or unconsciously – by the monasteries[6]. The attempt to combine market-economy integration with the monastic ethos and overcome the contradiction between neoliberal economics and religious live is prompting changes that affect the religious activities and have at the same time social impacts that are worth recording and analysing.

In this paper, I focus on two female monasteries in Burkina Faso, which belong to the large family of the Benedictine order: the Cistercian Monastery of Bafor (Bernardine Cistercians of Esquermes) near Dano around 300 km south

---

3 The analysis of the link between habitus and economic action is based on Weber's concept of wordly/otherworldly asceticism and on the debate surrounding the moral economy initiated by Thompson. Cf. L. KAELBER, *Schools of Asceticism. Ideology and Organization in Medieval Religious Communities*, Pennsylvanie 1998; D. FASSIN, «Les économies morales revisitées», *Annales* 6 (2009) 1237-1266.

4 C. GAVRAND, *Fils de Saint Bernard en Afrique. Une fondation au Cameroun 1950-1990*, Beauchesne-Paris 1990, 9.
30 new monasteries were established there between 1997 and 2007 by the Benedictine family alone.

5 DFG project "Kontemplation und Gesellschaftsengagement. Westafrikanische Klöster, transnationale Netzwerke und alternative Ökonomien ("Contemplation and Societal Involvement") (2016-2019). The first stage of this research was made possible by a travel grant from the Fritz Thyssen Foundation.

6 K. LANGEWIESCHE, «Hors du cloître et dans le monde. Des Sœurs catholiques comme actrices transnationales», *Social Sciences and Missions* 25/3 (2012) 195-224.

of the capital city Ouagadougou, and Koubri Abbey (Benedictines of Our Lady of Koubri) which is around 30 km south of Ouagadougou.

First, I will provide a very brief account of Burkina Faso's monastery landscape before I will describe and compare the economic activities of the Bafor and Koubri monasteries. Then, I will outline the importance of integration in monastery networks for the economic development of both monasteries, and in the conclusion, I will try to answer my initial question: could these monasteries provide a model for a solidarity economy in Burkina Faso?

1. THE MONASTERY LANDSCAPE OF BURKINA FASO

In 2017, Burkina Faso has seven monasteries and 61 religious institutes, which together accommodate some 4,100 nuns and monks. The four indigenous institutes of consecrated life founded in former Upper Volta and now run by Burkinabe Catholic sisters have the most members. Approximately 100 nuns live in Burkina Faso's five contemplative women's monasteries. Most of them are African women of different nationality. Following the foundation of the monastery in Koubri (1963), the Redemptorist sisters settled in Diabo and were followed by the Augustinians de la Miséricorde de Jésus in Banfora, the Carmelites in Dédougou[7] and the Cistercians near Diébougou (in 2005).

7 The Carmelites left Burkina Faso in 2015.

Based on the assumption that the age of the monastery and the size of the area available for economic activities are factors in the success and stability of their economic activities, I selected for this preliminary study Burkina's oldest monastery (Koubri), which has around 100 hectares of land, and its youngest one (Bafor), which encompasses 20 hectares.

The Cistercians in Bafor, near Diébougou, belong to a special branch of the Benedictine order, the order of the Bernardine Cistercians of Esquermes. Their mother house is in the north of France, however the sisters who established the Burkina branch originated from a monastery in Goma in the Democratic Republic of the Congo. The establishment of new monasteries in Africa by existing African monasteries, is typical of the new Benedictines foundations. Monasteries of the same order exist also in England, Vietnam and Japan.

In 2015, six Congolese nuns and one from Benin were living in Bafor monastery,[8] which was established as recently as 2005. The analysis of the economy of Bafor monastery, which is still under development, provides an insight into the development and ups and downs of monastery foundation.

8 The number of nuns decreased between 2011 and 2015 as several of the Congolese sisters could not tolerate the climate in Bafor. One Burkinabe postulate wanted to complete her studies before entering the order and a young sister who had taken her first vows eventually decided to take a different path in life.

The other monastery, which I will describe in more detail, are Koubri Abbey. The oldest monastery in Burkina Faso, which has existed since 1963. It is a twin monastery; there is a male monastery located near the female one. In 2015, there were 26 sisters and five novices living at the nuns' abbey while the nearby monks' abbey was home to 23 monks and four novices. Koubri was established by the Abbey of Notre Dame de Protection in Valognes in France (Normandy, France).

Both monasteries, Bafor and Koubri, were established at the request of a bishop. Both belong to the large Benedictine family, they are as different as people themselves and are fully autonomous in status[9]. They have different constitutions, which,

9 At international level the Benedictines are subdivided into 20 congregations, one of which is the Cistercian order, which, in turn, has several subsidiary orders. The large Benedictine

however, are both based on the *Regula Benedicti* (Rule of Saint Benedict). Individual poverty and the community-based management of resources enable the members of both institutions to benefit from medical and old age aid. In the context of Burkina Faso this is worth mentioning, because this is an unattainable luxury for the majority of women in Burkina Faso, one of the poorest countries in West Africa. The spirituality, charisma and formalization of everyday life at Koubri and Bafor monasteries are similar in many respects.

However, two key differences between them consist in the fact that, first, the Bernardine Cistercians of Esquermes are not tied to a local monastery: in their case, the *stabilitas loci* relates to the order itself and not a particular monastery. Second, they have integrated the mission of education into their charisma. In some of the locations where they have established a presence, they have schools from which they obtain most of their income and many of their new members. However, they have not opened a school in Burkina Faso as the Bishop requested that they establish a place of prayer and hospitality.

Through this decision, the option of establishing a school was excluded despite the fact that both the constitution and charisma of the Bernardine Cistercians of Esquermes would have allowed it. As a result, the economic activities of Bafor monastery were severely limited and the Cistercian sisters have been forced to try out a very wide range of activities since its establishment with a view to identifying the economic sectors best suited them. They are guided in this endeavour by the experience of the nuns and monks in Koubri and in the other West African abbeys[10].

I will first give some details about the economic activities of the Koubri female abbey and than about the Bafor monastery.

---

family is a federative association, within which the individual abbeys enjoy considerable autonomy. This association was established by Pope Leo XIII in 1893. A summary of the diversity of this religious family can be found on the website of the Alliance Inter-Monastère: http://www.aimintl.org/index.php?option=com_content&view=article&id=63&Itemid=88&lang=de, [access: 12-08-2012]. Different Benedictine congregations are represented in West Africa: the congregation of Solesmes, the congregation of Subiaco, the federation of Cœur Immaculé de Marie, the congregation of Sainte Bathilde and other diocesan-law communities.

10 An association was founded in 1980 which links the five oldest Benedictine monasteries in West Africa and also involves other congregations in its exchange of experience: *La solidarité entre les bénédictines d'Afrique de l'Ouest*. http://www.aimintl.org/index.php/fr/2015-05-29-13-29-48/bulletin-74/la-solidarite-entre-les-benedictines-d-afrique-de-l-ouest, [access: 03-05-2014].

1.1. Monastic economy in Koubri

During the first ten years of the abbey's existence, the Koubri nuns tried out various activities to secure their material existence: i.e. breeding laying hens, selling fruit and vegetables, running a guesthouse, operating a photocopying service for the diocese, and making liturgical vestments. It was only with the development of their yoghurt production, which they launched in the early days of the abbey's existence that they succeeded in attaining financial independence. The artisan yoghurt operation established in 1964 has now evolved into one of Burkina's biggest yoghurt factories. Nowadays, the yoghurt is based on imported dried powdered milk. This alleviated the problem posed by the hygienic storage of the milk and means that interruptions in production can be avoided. Moreover, the powdered milk is imported by the state and subsidised by Europe, and is cheaper than local fresh milk as a result. The decision to use powdered milk instead of fresh milk was made by the nuns as a profit-oriented measure. They are criticized by various parties for this practice as the labelling of their yoghurt as "*Yaourt du Burkina*" ("Burkina yoghurt") does not clearly indicate the origin of the milk whereby preference is given to imported powdered milk over locally produced milk[11].

Today, Koubri's monastery economy is characterized by its diversification. Despite being cloistered, the nuns have developed a large variety of economic activities with various partners and considerable contact with the local population through the abbey employees and their families, their own families and, of course, through their integration into the local Christian community. The nuns are involved in agriculture (domestic subsistence farming with the barter or sale of surplus produce), in the services sector (guesthouse) and in several manufacturing activities – like production and marketing of yoghurt, mango jam, spirulina, and kora music CDs recorded by the nuns. But, the monastery's main source of income is the yoghurt factory[12]. All of the community's running costs

11 Article by Father Frans Balemans, published in Le Pays, No 3219, Tuesday 28 September 2004. Consulted on 20 May 2013 on: http://www.lefaso.net/spip.php?article7965&rubrique21. The nuns are also criticized by Oxfam for this practice: http://www.oxfamsol.be/fr/IMG/pdf/dossier_lait_2FR.pdf [access: 13-11-18].

12 The nuns indicated that the yoghurt production is their most important source of income. In the eyes of the sisters it is a profitable operation as it enables the community to cover its operating costs. However, in the opinion of the abbey's external accountant, the yoghurt factory is not economically viable and he has advised the nuns that they should diversify their economic activities. Koubri has been investing in an innovative project for

are covered by the nuns' income. Investments in new machines or buildings, the maintenance of existing buildings and the further training of the nuns have to be funded by the mother house, the Alliance for International Monasticism (AIM) or other organizations.

1.2. Monastic economy in Bafor Monastery

Like Koubri, the Bafor community embarked on a wide variety of attempts to find profitable activities during the first ten years of its existence. They planted mango, cashew, teak and citrus crops, purchased and bred cattle, produced milk and yoghurt, opened a small printing press, and developed a large guesthouse. These economic activities were not selected solely on the basis of financial criteria but also on the basis of the community's composition. When the printing press was set up, it was intended to provide jobs for the monastery's 14 postulants at the time. However, as none of these postulants ultimately entered the order, the printing press could not operate as efficiently as planned. The nuns identify a lack of education as the reason for this high rate of termination. It is very difficult to make the monastic lifestyle understandable and clear to the young girls if they have no school education. The nuns reported on one postulant who wanted to enter the convent with her young baby.

As was the case in Koubri, in the early years, the nuns in Bafor encountered a considerable lack of understanding in their immediate surroundings. Over the past ten years, their tree plantations have been burnt down regularly, sometimes intentionally and often as a result of the careless management of bush fires which are common in the area. The cows the monastery acquired for milk production with the help of an NGO were poisoned. The milk and yoghurt production was a good source of income for the nuns so they decided to continue to produce yoghurt without cows using powdered milk. Because the yoghurt produced in Koubri is not supplied in this region of Burkina, the two monasteries do not compete with each other with their yoghurt[13]. It would seem that yoghurt production is also emerging as the most profitable source of income for the nuns in Bafor. Just as the brewing of beer became a regional speciality and profitable form of business for

two years: the cultivation of spirulina, a microalga which is used as food additive.

13 Due to a lack of employees, the nuns have only been able to supply yoghurt as far as Diébougou, Dano and Gawa. Moreover, they have a guaranteed outlet for their products in the small seminary located nearby.

Bavarian monasteries[14], the yoghurt industry appears to be a profitable business for Burkinabe monasteries. According to Bafor's administrator, 40 percent of the monastery's running costs are covered by its business activities. Everything else is covered by the main house.

When the economic activities of the two monasteries are compared, it becomes clear that they are both highly diversified in their working activities, i.e. they are engaged in the primary, secondary and tertiary sectors. Manufacturing generates the highest income after the guesthouse. In both regions, the nuns face the greatest difficulties in establishing their agricultural and forestry activities. After over ten years, the nuns in Bafor have noticed a slow decrease in the bush fires and that their neighbours are becoming a little more cooperative. The reason they give for this is the increasing education and awareness-raising about bush fires among the local population. The founding sister in Koubri also reported that the nuns there had experienced many years of difficulties with their agricultural activities.

An important element of the monastic economy is the number of members who are fit for work and the relationship between the nuns and their lay employees. In Bafor, which has only six nuns[15], three permanent lay employees[16] and six to ten casual workers, the ratio of internal to external staff is unusually high and, accordingly, cost intensive. In contrast, Koubri has over 30 nuns and novices who are fit for work, seven permanent members of staff and around ten casual workers[17]. Moreover, unlike Bafor, Koubri also has an additional source of income from the pension of one of the French nuns. Unlike in European monasteries, the level of income obtained from pensions and property in African monasteries is low. The female monasteries also have the disadvantage that they do not carry out any pastoral activities like the monks, who are also priests and are paid for this work by the dioceses. On the contrary, the sisters are frequently expected that to provide financial assistance or support to the diocese.

14 H. Jaschke, *Wirtschaftsmanagement in benediktinischen Männerklöstern Deutschlands*, Berlin 2010.

15 Two nuns work in the yoghurt factory, one in the hotel, one in the kitchen, one takes care of the office and printing works and the other acts as manager for the community.

16 One of these employees is a student who helps the nuns with the farming during his holidays. The latter pay his study expenses in return.

17 The permanent employees work in the yoghurt factor and as drivers, while the casual staff are assigned to the agricultural work and gardens. Agriculture is an intensive activity, which is only profitable if a large number of internal (i.e. unpaid) workers are available.

For example, if a priest from the diocese comes to Bafor, he is given accommodation in the guesthouse free of charge.

I have had the impression during the interviews with the procurators of the two monasteries and the sisters of the yoghurt factory in Koubri that the nuns' idea of business volume is highly variable and confused. Turnover and profitability are not their main concern. I asked one of the responsible of the yogurt production in Koubri if their production increased in the past year. She answered

> I am really not able to answer this question [whether yoghurt production increased in the past year]. I calculate how much milk and containers we need each day. I would have to calculate from the papers whether it increased over the past year. And who has the time to do that? (Laugh) Do you really need to know the figure?[18]

This is where the utopian component of the monastic economy comes to the fore[19].

In the opinion of the nuns, productivity and individual utility are not values from which they take guidance. In response to the question as to what work she does at the monastery, a nun from Koubri declares: *"I don't know whether I work (laugh). I don't do much. I answer the telephone. We are not here to work, we pray and glorify God. I can't do more than that (laugh)."*[20] These are the words of a nun who works in the garden and in the reception of the monastery. But she seems not to consider this occupations as work, more than a part of prayer, meanwhile answering on the telephone seems to be work for her.

The nuns' utopia culminates in their observation that society derives no utility from their presence. They exclude themselves from the mentality of profitability and define their own criteria so that they can make themselves available

---

18 Sister Emilia, 1 August 2012, Interview on monastic work.

19 Regarding the concept of "utopia" in a monastic framework and of "practised utopia", see J. Séguy, «Instituts religieux et économie charismatique», *Social Compass* 39 (1992) 35-51. Like this author and our examples confirm – as a criticism of the dominant economy or an attempt to transform class and gender relationships – the coenobitic utopia ends up being sucked into the support of the ruling classes and maintenance of the established order. Cf. Séguy, «Instituts religieux et économie charismatique» 348; K. Langewiesche, «Transnational monasteries. The economic performance of cloistered women», *Social Compass* 62/2 (2015) 132-146; C. Lenoble, *L'exercice de la pauvreté. Economie et religion chez les franciscains d'Avignon (XIIIᵉ-XVᵉ siècle)* (Collection Histoire), Rennes 2013.

20 Sister Maria, 9 August 2010 Biographical Interview.

to serve God and the community. For example, in 2014 the nuns in Bafor decided not to cultivate any land of their own as they held their general chapter that year and it had coincided with the sowing period. All of their actions run contrary to a spirituality of productivity and are based instead on the principle of moderation[21].

There is a constant tension between individual poverty and the need for financial viability as a community, however. Because the aim is to liberate the individuals from economic constraints, the monastic community must assume responsibility for the professional management of its economic affairs through the procurator and, sometimes also, with the help of lay experts. Due to the shift in their economic activities, the nuns or some of them, at least, become more and more involved in worldly management. In small communities which are still being developed, as is the case in Bafor, strict seclusion from the society must sometimes give way to daily contact with the society to ensure the basic survival of the monastery.

I will finish the comparison of Bafor and Koubri economic activities by giving you some details about the regional differences in which the monasteries are involved and of the changes in the neighbourhood since the establishment of the monasteries. I think that these are a main elements to understand transformation of the economic activities of a monastery and whether their succeed or not in the search of autonomy over time.

Like the missionaries, nuns and monks have disseminated new methods and technologies, for example in the areas of architecture, medicine, engineering and cattle breeding, and introduced new trade links[22]. In Africa, detailed social scientific studies on the economic and social changes to the surrounding population instigated by the establishment of monasteries have yet to be carried out, however. I would like to mention just a few examples here which apply to Koubri and require more in-depth research.

In the course of the establishment of Koubri Abbey in 1963, the subsequent electrification and dam construction, and the improvement of the roads, three new villages were established in close proximity to the abbey and the bush was

---

21 Joan Chittister, a Benedictine in Pennsylvania, describes the idea that the consecrated life is associated with special tasks (like caring for the sick, education, charity etc.) and legitimized through them. Cf. J. Chittister, *The Fire in These Ashes. A Spirituality of Contemporary Religious Life*, Leominster 1995.

22 For example: P. Harries, *Butterflies and Barbarians. Swiss Missionaries and Systems of Knowledge in South-East Africa*. Oxford 2007; J.-M. Bouron, «Le paradigme médical en milieu catholique», *Histoire et Missions Chrétiennes* 21 (2012).

increasingly curtailed. In the late 1960s, lions could still be found in the bush around Koubri, however, they gradually disappeared. All of the land around Koubri is now farmed and highly sought after by urbanites from the nearby capital. While the land in the immediate vicinity of the abbeys is completely farmed, the remaining two hundreds (232) hectares of the abbey have been developed into a biodiversity reserve.

Since the foundation of the abbey, 120 dams have been funded by the monks and nuns. Numerous farmers established their farms around the dams to benefit from this irrigation service. Due to climate conditions, agricultural production in Burkina Faso, which is dominated by cereal and cotton cultivation, is subject to enormous fluctuations. Hence, dams, which also enable consistent irrigation during the dry period, are very important. The irrigated area of Burkina Faso has increased overall and is promoted by the state in the context of the national programme for the rural sector (MAFAP, 2013). The Koubri plain, which benefits from its rich soil, is now referred to as the vegetable, fruit and rice supplier to the capital. The economic success of the products, the demand for labour and the market possibilities in Ouagadougou make this area an attractive arena for state initiatives, agro-speculators and humanitarian projects. Thanks to the establishment of the abbey, the development of the area around Koubri also includes the improvement of educational opportunities through the construction of schools and health service provision through the establishment and equipping of health centres (*dispensaires*). The integration of the orders into global Catholic networks and their relationships with development aid organizations had a significant influence on their economic activities and their integration into the local society as it was only with this support that the monasteries could develop social activities for the local population.

The area around Bafor is rainier than Koubri. Various vegetables are cultivated on the harvested rice fields during the dry season. The farmers generally harvest the crops once or twice during the dry season depending on the amount of water remaining in reservoirs. Most of the people living in the area are of the same ethnic origin (Dagara) while the population of the Koubri plane is of heterogeneous ethnic composition (most of them are at least Mossi). Up to now the monastery has not triggered the emergence of new villages, however the nuns believe that this will quickly change when the electricity can be made available to the local population. The distance from the capital city (300 km) is so great that the market for the monastery's products is limited. The distance from the capital also results in the fact that the more comfortable guesthouse in Bafor only accounts for barely ten percent of the monastery's income while the simple Koubri guesthouse attracts more visitors and accounts for around 30 percent of the Abbey's income.

2. MONASTIC NETWORKS

I come now to the second point of my argument, the importance of the integration into global networks for the monastic economy. In the context of the anthropological research on contemporary trends of globalization, many authors focus on the role of the Pentecostal churches, which are analysed as a global religion per se[23]. However, Catholic nuns are more and more engaged in civil and religious trans-national networks and involved in development cooperation.

From a sociological and historical perspective, integration into monastic networks appears to be particularly important for the economic development of monasteries[24]. Personal acquaintanceships within the Benedictine family and Catholic community in the broadest sense enable both monasteries to work with well-trained agronomists, architects and energy experts without having to pay the standard fees. Some nuns also benefit from their training in associated monasteries. For example, one sister from Bafor was trained in yoghurt-making at the monastery in Parakou (Benin). A monk from Keur Moussa monastery (Senegal) gave kora lessons to the nuns in Koubri and Bafor. The financial support of associations like the Alliance for International Monasticism (AIM) or Cistercians Solidarity (*Solidarité cistercienne* founded by the Belgian abbey of Chimay) and *Entraide dans la Congrégation de Subiaco* are indispensable[25]. Wi-

23 Cf. *Transnational Religion and Fading States*, edd. S. Hoeber Rudolph-J. Piscatori, Colorado 1997; *Globalization and Identity. Dialectics of Flow and Closure*, edd. B. Meyer-P. Geschiere, Oxford 1999; *Between Babel and Pentecost: Transnational Pentecostalism in Africa and Latin America*, A. Corten-R. Marshall-Fratani, Bloomington 2001; *Entreprises religieuses transnationales en Afrique de l'Ouest*, edd. L. Fourchard, Laurent-A. Mary-René Otayek, Paris 2005.

24 Historical studies provide a convincing presentation of the transnational network-like spread of the orders over different periods. The medieval monasteries (in particular the Cistercian reform movement) were linked far beyond political territories and linguistic borders through their properties. Cf. J. Schmiedl, «Orden als transnationale Netzwerke der katholischen Kirche», *European History Online* (2011) [online] available from http://www.ieg-ego.eu/schmiedlj-2011-de Schmiedl refers to the Cistercians as the first multinational concern [access: 13-11-2018].

25 Solidarité cistercienne is the not-for-profit umbrella organization of the Abbeys of Rochefort, Orval and Chimay (Beligian). Since 1961, all member congregations of the Benedictine federation can obtain support for their projects from the AIM.

thout the financial support of these organizations and their mother houses, the new African abbeys would not be able to survive.

Finally, the nuns in Koubri can rely on the cooperation with the nearby monk's abbey. Both abbeys operate independently of each other but are involved in the joint planning for 200 hectares of land. It could be assumed that twin monasteries become self-sufficient faster and are more viable than single monasteries. This hypothesis will be tested on the basis of other twin monasteries in Senegal and Benin.

Apart from these special Benedictine or Cistercian networks, the abbeys have links with various Catholic and secular organizations. Several secular NGOs provide support for the yoghurt factory in Koubri and the relatively new spirulina production operation in the form of consultancy, personnel and material resources[26]. These NGOs unite many individual initiatives in the context of town partnerships, school projects and youth exchanges and save the abbey from having to negotiate with multiple partners. The Burkinabe Catholic charity Organisation (OCADES) also supervises the spirulina cultivation in Koubri. The monks and nuns cooperate with different thematic networks, e.g. the *Centre International pour le Développement Agro-Pastoral* training centre[27]. In Bafor, the cattle breeding project was carried out with the help of financial support from English sisters and the afforestation project received support from the Jean-Paul II Foundation.

Koubri also received support from an international programme for the conservation of biodiversity[28]. Bafor does not yet benefit from an international project, however in view of the increasing interest of international organizations in partnerships with Catholic monasteries, particularly in the area of environmental protection and organic agriculture, this could well change in the near future[29].

The general trend that can be observed from this analysis of monastic networks is the increasing recognition of religious communities by international organizations and secular NGOs. While the nuns from Koubri have experience support from Benedictine and Catholic networks since the establishment of

26 These NGOs include: G.H.I.M.A.O. www.ghimao.org , Essenciel cooperative http://huilerit.essenciel.free.fr/ferme-solidaire-en-afrique.html, Terre solidaire connaissance, partage et développement ccfd-terresolidaire.org consulted on August 2015

27 www.cidaptogo.org consulted on August 2015.

28 Global Environment Facility (GEF), United Nations Development Programme (UNDP) and United Nations Office for Project Services (UNOPS).

29 Langewiesche, «Transnational monasteries».

their abbey, the support from secular NGOs and international bodies is a relatively new development since the 1990s. Catholic monasteries, have the reputation of not associating local development with aggressive evangelization as practised by some Protestant and Muslim groups[30]. They also present to the secular NGOs as ideal partners for development. Whether these development projects meet the expectations and succeed in evolving into a model for sustainable development stay ambiguous.

The case studies of Koubri and Bafor highlight another general trend: African monasteries are living communities which, unlike their European counterparts, continue to attract young people[31]. Nevertheless, like the local churches, they can only survive with the help of money from the North. This situation could be summarised in somewhat exaggerated terms as the vocations coming from the South and the money from the North.

CONCLUSIONS

Following this brief comparison of the economic aspects of the monasteries in Koubri and Bafor, I would like to conclude by answering the question raised at the outset: Can these monasteries be viewed as testing grounds for alternative forms of production and trade? In other words, could they provide a model for a solidarity economy in Burkina Faso?

In accordance with their founding charisma, the nuns reject inhuman structures and development through their lifestyle. However, monasteries are also subject to market conditions if they aim to sell their products at a profit. Therefore, the nuns in Koubri made a conscious decision to opt for the importation of subsidized powdered milk from Europe rather than use fresh local milk in the production of their yoghurt. This shows how profit-oriented calculations can overlap with local development efforts. The nuns in Bafor have also resorted to the use of powdered milk – albeit involuntarily – so that they can stay in the yoghurt business despite having no cows.

---

30 On the topic of religious elites in the development arena, see the introduction by M. Kaag-M. Saint-Lary, «The New Visibility of Religion in the Development Arena», *APAD Bulletin* 33 (2011) 23-38.

31 I have published my reflections on the attractions of contemplative and active congregations for young women in Africa elsewhere: Langewiesche, «Hors du cloître et dans le monde», Id., «Émancipation et obéissance: Religieuses catholiques au Burkina Faso durant un siècle» *Autrepart* 61 (2012) 117-136.

The changes in the immediate environment of the monasteries and the differences between the regions clearly demonstrate that many unintended side effects arise which are not always in tune with an economy based on solidarity and long-term development (e.g. the land speculation arising as a result of the improvement of living conditions and cultivation options in the areas around Koubri Abbey). Further comparison of African Monasticism would permit analysis of the differences between monastic economies as a result of the social context variable. It is reasonable to expect that a country's social and religious history will be a discriminating variable in explaining different kind of economic choices.

Koubri Abbey has been economically independent for over 35 years[32] and Bafor is aiming to achieve this state. Both monasteries can only put their ideas about work and prayer into practice because they belong to networks that guarantee their financial security. In this sense, they are integrated into the globalized society. Thanks to their transnational structure and their status as 'global players' they can continue to pursue economically non-viable activities from religious conviction[33]. As deteritorrialized religious communities[34], the orders are not locations that can provide the rest of society with models for an ideal solidarity economy. However, thanks to their transnational networks, they can tests alternatives and develop a moral economy without having to fear collective poverty and, in this way, provide inspiration for the general public. The moral economy of the monasteries is based on norms that are religiously legitimized and governs the monasteries' activities to a far greater extent than economic imperatives. It is based on the exchange of goods and services and principles of justice, respect and human dignity, which adapt to the pressure of the liberal economy to a greater or lesser extent at different times. Based on the training they receive through their vow of poverty and strengthened by the spirituality of moderation, the nuns are able to act as models for a life of limitation and re-

32 According to the sisters' own assessment, the abbey has been financially independent since the late 1970s. https://sites.google.com/site/benedictinefrance/suscipe-me-domine, [access: 3-06-2013].

33 Religious orders feature as 'global players' in the areas of refugee aid, peace work, ecology and international relations, in particular. On this point, see *Religionen – Global Player in der internationalen Politik?*, edd. I.-J. Werkner-O. Hildalgo, Wiesbaden 2014, LANGEWIESCHE, «Hors du cloître et dans le monde».

34 Cf. J. CASANOVA, «Rethinking Secularization: A global comparative perspective», in *Religion, globalization, and Culture*, edd. P. Beyer-L.G. Beaman, Leiden 2007, 101-120.

nunciation and to spread a doctrine of discipline based on ecological and social principles.

The aura of sanctity that envelopes the monasteries attracts donations; the culture of asceticism of daily life generates a profit; the mutual support of the nuns and monks reduces subsistence costs and facilitates the mobilization and accessing of talent and employees; and finally the individual renunciation of property facilitates the accumulation of collective goods[35]. Especially in an African context, these social and economic characteristics of religious accumulation stressed already by Jean Seguy, one of the founding father of monastic research are worth emphasizing. My analysis suggests that we have to shift attention from the idea of monastic social economy as a model for the civil society to monastic social economy as a resource privileging cultural creativity and change. It seems productive to examine to what extend the monastic social economy is generative of new meanings which are perceived as being relevant today.

Abstract

The argument presented in this paper is based on field surveys of two female monasteries in Burkina Faso. The first, the abbey of the *Benedictines of Our Lady of Koubri,* was established in Burkina in 1963 by five French nuns. It now has a community of 27 African sisters who have developed a successful yoghurt industry and guesthouse. The second, the Monastery of Our Lady of Bafor, is run by sisters from the order of the *Bernardine Cistercians of Esquermes* and was founded by Congolese Bernardine Cistercian sisters from the Monastery of Our Lady of the Lake of Goma in 2005. Its establishment is a work in process.

The two case studies identify the differences arising from the social and economic contexts in which the monasteries are located. The comparison of these examples, their integration into the West-African monastic landscape and the latter's links with international monastic networks highlight the importance of transnational links for the success of the nuns' economic ventures.

This paper highlights the economic characteristic of religious accumulation with a view to focusing attention on the radicalism of the monasteries which propose alternative lives far removed from fundamentalist temptation.

35 Séguy, «Instituts religieux et économie charismatique», 39.

CONTROLLING THE ENTREPRENEURIAL ACTIVITIES IN MONASTERIES

Karin NIEDERWIMMER – Birgit FELDBAUER-DURSTMÜLLER

INTRODUCTION

Today[1], the modern monastic world is faced with complex economic conditions[2], which require an intensive discussion with business topics. This is a significant challenge for the primarily spiritually oriented type of organisation. A management control system system can effectively support today's demands[3].

In this lecture, the above statement is illustrated by using in particular the example of the male communities of the Benedictines. St. Benedict (d. 547) created with his Rule (*Regula Benedicti* = RB) the still valid basis of monastic life for his communities. Benedict required his monks to earn their own living[4] in order to maintain an inner independence apart from relatives and benefactors by having a secure economic independence[5]. Similarly, the daily work should help the monks to balance inner seclusion and outward actions.

Katrin Niederwimmer, Assistant at the Institute for Management Control and Consulting at the Johannes Kepler University Linz (Austria); Birgit Feldbauer-Durstmüller Professor and Director of Instituts für Controlling und Consulting at the Johannes Kepler University Linz.

1 This article is also presented on ISTR's 12th International Conference in Stockholm, June 28-July 1, 2016. Moreover, sub-areas are published in the "Praxishandbuch Controlling" (SpringerGabler) in 2016.

2 Cf. S. SANDBERGER-B. FELDBAUER-DURSTMÜLLER, «Beraten, Beschließen und Überwachen – Aufgaben von Kapitel und Wirtschaftsrat in der Sicherstellung materieller und finanzieller Ressourcen eines Benediktinerklosters», in *Ressourcenmobilisierung durch Nonprofit-Organisationen. Theoretische Grundlagen, empirische Ergebnisse und Anwendungsbeispiele. Dokumentation des 11. Internationalen NPO-Kolloquiums,* edd. A. Andessner-D. Greiling-M. Gmür-L. Theuvsen, Linz 2015, 391.

3 Cf. B. FELDBAUER-DURSTMÜLLER, S. SANDBERGER-K. NIEDERWIMMER-M. NEULINGER, «Controlling im Kloster. Ein Fallbeispiel eines österreichischen Benediktinerklosters», in *Jahrbuch für Controlling und Rechnungswesen,* ed. G. Seicht, Wien 2013, 578.

4 Cf. M. CASEY, *Einführung in die Benediktusregel. Ein geistliches Ausbildungsprogramm,* Sankt Ottilien 2010, 243.

5 Cf. A. GRÜN, «Bete und arbeite - Kurzformel benediktinischen Lebensstils», in *Heraus-*

To earn one's keep today is subject to other conditions as in St. Benedict's times. Declining yields in the often highly diversified economic sectors, the lack of young monks, the superannuation of the members of the monastery and the large, maintenance-intensive buildings put a strain on the finances of the monasteries. The subsequent resulting demands on the management committees of monasteries to comprehensively deal with financial issues and strategic change processes can lead to resistance by internal and external stakeholders. Restructuring can become difficult in grown and for centuries deadlocked organizational structures. In addition, different ways of thinking, certain expectations and resource problems may have a blocking effect[6].

If the introduction or expansion of a management control system is considered in order to support the monastery management, an examination of the traditions and values of the organisation is recommended to avoid resistance. It is important to take into account the particular human, structural and economic conditions, which have evolved over the centuries.

The aim of this article is to anticipate those conditions that are highly relevant for a well-performing management control system in monasteries. Then, in a further step, recommendations for the design of such a system are derived. Thus, the following research questions emerge:

Which special conditions have to be considered by implementing a management control system in a monastery?

Which suggestions can be deduced to avoid resistance against reorientations?

1. METHODOLOGY

The use of a management control system in monasteries has so far received little attention in the existing accounting literature[7]. Corresponding publications deal mainly with the importance of accounting (in general) for religious institutions[8]

forderung der Mönche. Benediktinische Spiritualität heute, ed. G. Braulik, Wien 1979, 160.

6 Cf. M.P. del Val-C.M. Fuentes, «Resistance to change: a literature review and empirical study», *Management Decision* 41 (2003) 148.

7 Cf. P. Tracey, «Religion and Organization: A Critical Review of Current Trends and Future Directions», *Academy of Management Annals* 6 (2012) 87-134; L. Parker, «Financial Management Strategy in a Community Welfare Organization: A Boardroom Perspective», *Accountability & Management* 19 (2003) 341-374.

8 Cf. P. Booth, «Accounting in Churches. A Research Framework and Agenda», *Accounting, Auditing & Accountability Journal* 6 (1988) 37-69; R. Laughlin, «Accounting in its Social Context: An Analysis of the Accounting Systems of the Church

or with the influence of religion on the development and use of management techniques and corporate governance[9]. The implementation of a management control system in a monastery is not in the focus of the current journal literature.

In order to provide a better understanding of the complex coherences that may result from an implementation of a management control system in a monastery, the literature analysis is complemented by results from a concrete case study. Case studies support the research of social phenomena by providing a holistic and meaningful depiction of real events[10].

Subject of the investigation was an Austrian Benedictine abbey where, amongst other things, an operations management system was implemented. The team established, consisted of university employees, the abbot and the accountant of the monastery. Temporarily, other secular employees and monks were involved. Between October 2011 and December 2015, workshops were held with secular employees and members of the monastery. In May 2016, semi-structured exploratory interviews were conducted, transcribed and analysed. The focus of this type of survey is on subjective and relevant opinions as well as attitudes on the subject matter[11]. Excerpts are recorded in chapter 8.5. The aim of the interviews and the documentation of the workshops was to determine potential conflicts and resistance problems and to find a starting point for solving them.

---

of England», *Accounting, Auditing & Accountability Journal* 1 (1988) 19-42; R. Laughlin, «A model of financial accountability and the Church of England», *Financial Accountability and Management* 6 (1990) 93-114; M. Lightbody, «Storing and shielding: financial management behavior in a church organization», *Accounting, Auditing & Accountability Journal* 13 (2000) 156-174; P. Quattrone, «Accounting for God: accounting and accountability practices in the Society of Jesus (Italy, XVI–XVII centuries)», *Accounting, Organizations and Society* 29 (2004) 647-683; A. Berry, «Accountability and control in a cat's cradle», *Accounting, Auditing & Accountability Journal* 18 (2005) 255-297.

9 Cf. K. Rost-E. Inauen-M. Osterloh-B. Frey, «The corporate governance of Benedictine abbeys. What can stock corporations learn from monasteries», *Journal of Management History* 16 (2010) 90-115; K. Rost-G. Graetzer, «Multinational organizations as rule-following bureaucracies - the example of catholic orders», *Journal of International Management* 20 (2014) 290-311; B. Feldbauer-Durstmüller-S. Sandberger-M. Neulinger, «Sustainability for Centuries. Monastic Governance of Austrian Benedicitine Abbeys», *European Journal of Management* 12 (2012) 83-92.

10 Cf. R.K. Yin, *Case Study Research: Design and Methods,* Sage, Los Angeles [4]2009, 4.

11 Cf. A. Aghamanoukjan-R. Buber-M. Meyer, «Qualitative interviews», in *Qualitative Marktforschung,* edd. R. Buber-H.H. Holzmüller, Wiesbaden 2009, 422.

2. THEORIES TO EXPLAIN THE PECULIARITIES OF MONASTERIES

In considering the management structures in monasteries the following theories may help to explain the peculiarities of these forms of organisation.

The principal-agent theory assumes interactions between a principal and an agent[12]. It is believed that there exist conflicts of interest between the two. Agent and principal strive for individual utility maximization and thus, may perhaps pursue opportunistic goals. Furthermore, the principal-agent theory is based on the assumption that the agent has information advantages against the principal with respect to the decisions to be made by the agent. Those decisions may have a positive or negative effect for the principal. Thus, in turn, the latter handles the situation with attempts to influence the behaviour of the agent and to distribute potential risks between himself and the agent[13].

Management control systems contribute to solving the above principal-agent problems in two ways: a) to support the establishment of a planning, monitoring and reporting system in order to compensate information differences and b) to assist the implementation of incentive systems that makes the agent to acquire an attitude that is target-compliant and in line with the principal's interests[14].

Principal-agent-relationships can also be found in the management structures of monasteries. This concerns, for example, the relationship of the abbot to his officials (office holders such as the cellarer, novice master, etc.) who are appointed directly by the abbot. They are liable to account towards the abbot and have to report to the chapter in defined cases. Other principal-agent relationships are those between the abbot and secular employees or internal decision-making bodies such as the chapter or the council of elders[15]. Depending on the situation the abbot can also take on the role of the agent. This is the case, if he acts on behalf of his monastic community or towards umbrella organisations of his religious order or towards governing bodies of the church.

12 Cf. K.M. Eisenhardt, «Agency Theory: An Assessment and Review», *Academy of Management Review* 14 (1989) 57-74.

13 Cf. S. Schaefer-C. Lange, «Informationsorientierte Controllingkonzeptionen – Ein Überblick und Ansatzpunkte der Weiterentwicklung», in *Controlling – Theorien und Konzeptionen,* edd. E. Scherm-G. Pietsch, München 2004, 116.

14 Cf. Schaefer-Lange, «Informationsorientierte Controllingkonzeptionen – Ein Überblick und Ansatzpunkte der Weiterentwicklung», 117.

15 Cf. Österreichische Benediktinerkongregation, *Die Satzungen der österreichischen Benediktinerkongregation,* Melk 2006, 167-237.

Classical solutions of the principal-agent theory are implemented in the Rule of Benedict and in the statutes in the form of decision-making and monitoring mechanisms, responsibilities, reporting requirements, sanctions etc. Due to limited personnel and time resources of the principal's approval and reporting processes can often not take their controlling effect. Here, especially in monasteries, mechanisms determined by loyalty and mutual trust are effective. Amongst them are informal structures which are based on traditions and conventions[16]. The strong binding to the monastery and its objectives accompanied by intrinsic motivation is characteristic. Thus, this would rather indicate conditions that belong to the stewardship theory[17].

In contrast to the agent the steward considers partnership and cooperative behaviour more useful than the pursuit of personal gain. The personal claim to self-control and self-responsibility comes to the fore. Here we need information and clarity on strategic objectives. It's not about controlling the employee, but to ensure the action and the decision-making ability and the necessary intrinsic motivation of stewards[18].

Another theory to explain the particularities in Benedictine monasteries is the stakeholder approach. Thus, organisations can only be successful in the long-run, if they meet the needs of central interest groups (stakeholders). Carroll and Buchholz define stakeholders as "any individual or group who can affect or is affected by the actions, decisions, policies, practices or goals of the organisation"[19]. These may be highly heterogeneous due to the regional roots and the diverse activities of a monastery. Payer-Langthaler and Feldbauer-Durstmüller[20] take the case of an abbey in order to distinguish between monastery-internal stakeholders (monks, employees) and monastery-external stakeholders (beneficiaries and the wider environment).

16 Cf. Feldbauer-Durstmüller, Sandberger-Niederwimmer-Neulinger, Controlling im Kloster. Ein Fallbeispiel eines österreichischen Benediktinerklosters», 583.

17 Cf. J.H. Davis-D.F. Schoorman-L. Donaldson, «Toward a Stewardship Theory of Management», *Academy of Management Review* 14 (1997) 20-47.

18 Cf. P. Velte, «Stewardship-Theorie», *Zeitschrift für Planung & Unternehmenssteuerung* 20 (2010) 285-286; M. Hernandez, «Promoting Stewardship Behavior in Organizations: A Leadership Model», *Journal of Business Ethics* 80 (2007) 122.

19 Cf. A.B. Caroll-A.K. Buchholtz, *Business & Society: Ethics and Stakeholder Management,* South Western, Mason (OH) [7]2008, 84.

20 Cf. S. Payer-Langthaler-B. Feldbauer-Durstmüller, «Performance Management im Kloster: Das Beispiel der Benediktiner in Österreich», in *Performance Management in Nonprofit-Organisationen: Theoretische Grundlagen, empirische Ergebnisse und Anwendungsbeispiele,* edd. M. Gmür-R. Schauer-L. Theuvsen, Wien 2013, 105.

3. MANAGEMENT CONTROL SYSTEMS

Within the Anglo-American literature a distinction is made between "management accounting", "management accounting systems" and "management control systems". The latter two are comparable to the conceptions of the German term "Controlling" in the common German-speaking world. There are considerable differences between the existing definitions[21].

Anthony, to whom the term "management control" is ascribed, prioritised the application of the accounting information to the techniques of information retrieval. He developed the three process levels "strategic planning", "management control" and "operational control", whereby "management control" establishes the connection between the "strategic" and "operational" level[22].

Chenhall[23] describes "management accounting" (MA) as a "collection of practices: such as budgeting or product costing", whereas he defines "management accounting systems" (MAS) as a "systematic use of management accounting to achieve some goal". "Management control systems" (MCS) are then regarded as an extension of MAS including the components "personnel" and "clan controls". Broader conceptions can also involve strategic development, strategic control and learning processes. These are factors that are usually not associated with management control system[24].

Malmi and Brown[25] suggest that management accounting systems, whose application is not monitored, are not to be counted to the group of management control systems. If mechanisms to monitor the goal congruence of the employees are missing, then they are rather to be considered as support systems for decision-making or information systems than management control systems. Ac-

---

21 Cf. H.G. Baum-A.G. Coenenberg-T. Günther, *Strategisches Controlling,* Stuttgart ^{5}2013, 5.

22 Cf. T. Günther, «Conceptualisations of "controlling" in German speaking countries: analysis and comparison with Anglo-American management control frameworks», *Journal of Management Control* 23 (2013) 270.

23 Cf. R.H. Chenhall, «Management control systems design within its organizational context: findings from contingency based research and directions for the future», *Accounting, Organizations and Society* 28/2-3 (2003) 129.

24 Cf. K.A. Merchant-D.T. Otley, «A review of the literature on control and accountability», in *Handbooks of management accounting research,* edd. C.S. Chapman-A.G. Hopwood-M.D. Shields, Amsterdam ^{2}2007, 785.

25 Cf. T. Malmi-D. Brown, «Management control systems as a package - Opportunities, challenges and research directions», *Management Accounting Research* 19 (2008) 290.

cording to Malmi and Brown[26] (Malmi and Brown 2008, pp. 291 et seqq) management control systems include cybernetic controlling tools such as classical budgeting, monetary and non-monetary measurement systems as well as their combination. But they also comprise corporate culture, corporate planning, incentive and compensation systems and administrative control approaches. (The latter includes corporate governance beside the design of the organisational structure).

This broader concept of management control systems is the basis for this respective article. It matches the complex framework of a monastery better than narrowly defined system approaches, such as that of Anthony which is designed towards a primarily finance and accounting-base[27]. Thus, the essential factors in the control of a monastery are the *cultural* control such as the religious community, religious values, dress codes, etc. and the *administrative* control comprising the Regula Benedicti (as corporate governance control) and the statutes of the monastery. The combination of financial and non-financial measurement systems according to the cybernetic system of Malmi and Brown is very suitable for the monastic organisation that is strongly influenced by normative objectives (see chapter 8.1).

4. RESISTANCE IN PROCESSES OF CHANGE

The durability of Benedictine monasteries shows that these organisations have managed to exist successfully for many centuries, not least due to their strong management structures and principles[28]. Nevertheless, monasteries are currently in a radical change. Recruitment problems, increasing economic complexity and growing competition make it necessary for monasteries to review existing structures and, where appropriate, to initiate processes of change.

Changes of structures and habits that have grown for decades can provoke refusals and blocking behaviour by the internal stakeholders. Not infrequently, the resistance of employees becomes the cause of failure in processes of change[29].

---

26 Cf. Malmi-Brown, «Management control systems as a package - Opportunities, challenges and research directions», 291.

27 Cf. Günther, «Conceptualisations of "controlling" in German speaking countries: analysis and comparison with Anglo-American management control frameworks», 285.

28 Cf. E. Inauen-B.S. Frey, «Benediktinerabteien aus ökonomischer Sicht. Über die außerordentliche Stabilität einer besonderen Institution», *Erbe und Auftrag* 86 (2008) 13.

29 Cf. A. Michel-R. Todnem-B. Burnes, «The limitations of dispositional resistance in relation to organizational change», *Management Decision* 51 (2013) 761-780.

Rumelt[30] even assumes that any changes in strategy, structures and administrative processes are difficult, expensive, risky and time-consuming, because lethargy and low mobility within the company have a blocking effect.

Resistance to change can be considered a phenomenon slowing down, delaying and obstructing the processes of change and increasing costs[31]. Another definition describes resistance as any behaviour that attempts to maintain the status quo and equates it with the conception of lethargy. Both lethargy and resistance can have a positive impact, since changes may not necessarily be of an advantage for organisations. A study by del Val and Fuentes[32] shows that most resistance occurs when strategic changes come about in connection with deeply rooted values. The authors recommend, if necessary, checking and adjusting the compatibility of the new objectives with the existing culture of the organisation before starting the process of change. These considerations can be applied to processes of change in monastic organisations. If the life and value system receives too little consideration when introducing a management control system, resistance of the members of a monastic community can be the result.

5. CONDITIONS FOR A MANAGEMENT CONTROL SYSTEM IN A BENEDICTINE MONASTERY

5.1. The Value System of Benedictines

The value system of the Benedictines is largely determined by the Regula Benedicti. Hereby, the therein contained call to "truly seek God" and that "in all things God may be glorified"[33] is considered the primary organisational objective for all members of the Benedictine order worldwide[34].

30 Cf. R. Rumelt, «Inertia and Transformation», in *Resources in an Evolutionary Perspective. Towards a Synthesis of Evolutionary and Resource-Based Approaches to Strategy,* ed. C. Montgomery, Kluwer Academic Publishers, Norwell 1995, 101-132.

31 Cf. del Val-Fuentes, «Resistance to change: a literature review and empirical study», 148.

32 Cf. del Val-Fuentes, «Resistance to change: a literature review and empirical study», 148-153.

33 Cf. Monastery of Christ in the Desert, «Introduction to Study the Holy Rule of Saint Benedict and Abbot Philip Lawrence's accompanying commentary», (n.d.), https://christdesert.org/prayer/rule-of-st-benedict/, [accessed: 24-05-2016].

34 Cf. U. Soegtrop, *Nachhaltiger Wandel im Kloster: Organisationale Veränderungsprozesse in der Benediktinerinnenabtei Burg Dinklage*, Baden-Baden 2003, 35; Feldbauer-Durstmüller, Sandberger-Neulinger, «Sustainability for Centuries. Mona-

In the very centre of monastic life there is God as the source and goal of all ministry. In the Benedictine monasteries all live by the principle of "ora" (pray) – "labora" (work) "et lege" (and read) respectively "communion" (communion)[35]. This also means that sound economic thinking and acting have to have its place in order to contribute to the long-lasting existence of a monastery[36]. Nevertheless, busyness should not be the main purpose of life, rather, Benedictine existence proves to be the absence of a purpose in order to create "a space of emptiness", and "thereby makes the glory of God visible"[37]. Moreover, St. Benedict warns his monks not to lapse into the motive of greed. He orders his monks to establish prices "which should, therefore, always be a little lower than people outside the monastery are able to set"[38].

The fundamental values and objectives as described in the RB are not economic in nature, but rather stimulate concrete virtues, practices and behaviours[39]. Economically oriented, however, are those principles that pursue considerations of sustainability. The key objective of the monastic economy is to secure the viability of the monastery for future generations. "All utensils and goods of the monastery" are regarded "as sacred vessels of the altar"[40]. The implementation of this rule can be seen in the considerations of sustainability such as in a) activities in the primary sector like eco-friendly energy production and its usage and in b) the global awareness of this issue[41].

---

stic Governance of Austrian Benedicitine Abbeys», 90.

35 Cf. SOEGTROP, *Nachhaltiger Wandel im Kloster: Organisationale Veränderungsprozesse in der Benediktinerinnenabtei Burg Dinklage,* 14.

36 Cf. D.A. TREDGET, «"The Rule of Benedict" and its relevance to the world of work», *Journal of Managerial Psychology* 17 (2002) 222.

37 Cf. SOEGTROP, *Nachhaltiger Wandel im Kloster: Organisationale Veränderungsprozesse in der Benediktinerinnenabtei Burg Dinklage,* 38.

38 Cf. MONASTERY OF CHRIST IN THE DESERT, «Introduction to Study the Holy Rule of Saint Benedict and Abbot Philip Lawrence's accompanying commentary», [accessed: 24-05-2016].

39 Cf. MONASTERY OF CHRIST IN THE DESERT, «Introduction to Study the Holy Rule of Saint Benedict and Abbot Philip Lawrence's accompanying commentary», [accessed: 24-05-2016].

40 Cf. MONASTERY OF CHRIST IN THE DESERT, «Introduction to Study the Holy Rule of Saint Benedict and Abbot Philip Lawrence's accompanying commentary», [accessed: 24-05-2016].

41 Cf. B. FELDBAUER-DURSTMÜLLER-M. NEULINGER, «Stabilität über Jahrhunderte - Corporate Governance österreichischer Benediktinerklöster», in *Corporate Sustainability,* ed. H.K. Prammer, Wiesbaden 2010, 231.

5.2. Motives for the Entrance into a Monastery and Qualifications of its Members

An investigation of a Benedictine monastery in Germany has shown that in addition to spiritual motives the desire to live in a community and the positive experience of monastic ceremonies are relevant for the decision to enter a monastery. Another motive of entry is the desire "to slow down life" away from the rest of the world and to be able to develop by the constant exchange of work and prayer, community and solitude[42]. The qualification of (young) men entering a monastery or their training after their entry also shows a rather spiritual orientation. Moreover, positions that require specific knowledge like those of the cellarer are filled by members of the monastery, which correspond primarily to requirements of the Regula Benedicti. Professional qualifications, however, are given less importance[43].

5.3. Human Resources and Social Responsibility

With a few exceptions, the number of monks in monasteries declines or is stagnant. Superannuation raises an additional support effort, which is to be provided internally or externally[44]. Positions with specific demands on the personality and professional knowledge such as the executive of an enterprise can only partially be filled with secular employees[45]. Increasingly, external staff must be employed to deal with internal tasks such as household services and care for the elderly.

The impact of recruitment problems becomes evident when filling those offices that are reserved for monks only. Especially for those positions that are less spiritually oriented like that of the cellarer, a member of the order who is both professionally suitable and sufficiently motivated to take on this role may not be found. This "personnel shortage actually forces [...] a superior to find a

42 Cf. H. Jaschke, *Wirtschaftsmanagement in benediktinischen Männerklöstern Deutschlands*, Berlin 2010, 127-130.

43 Cf. M.R.W. Hiebl-B. Feldbauer-Durstmüller, «What can the corporate world learn from the cellarer? Examining the role of a Benedictine abbey's CFO», *Society and Business Review* 9 (2014) 65.

44 Cf. Jaschke, *Wirtschaftsmanagement in benediktinischen Männerklöstern Deutschlands*, 176-180.

45 Cf. Feldbauer-Durstmüller, Sandberger-Niederwimmer-Neulinger, «Controlling im Kloster. Ein Fallbeispiel eines österreichischen Benediktinerklosters», 584.

person; not one who is suited for the job, but one who is free and could assume obligations"[46].

An increase in the proportion of secular people, particularly on the management levels of the monastic enterprises, results in an increase of principal-agent-relationships. As there is the claim for timely, correct and understandable information about the economic activities and services of the agent, the burden of control for the monastery leadership is raised.

At the employee level hiring and release decisions burden the high social responsibility of the monasteries. Moreover, the tendency to employ underachieving (disabled or for other reasons disadvantaged) personnel or to postpone necessary staff reduction is rather typical[47].

5.4. Industrial Sectors and Assets Structures

Significant agricultural and silvicultural estates characterise the assets structure of Benedictine monasteries. These estates passed into the ownership of the monasteries due to donations and endowments in the past. Processing and converting facilities complement the existing entrepreneurial structures. Additional income is obtained in the areas of craft and tourism as well as in the trade and services sector[48].

The strong network of the different entrepreneurial facilities of a monastery can lead to a lack of transparency in assessing the profitability of the individual profit centres. Mistakes are detected too late and incorrect strategic decisions are made. It is therefore particularly important to ensure readability and clarity when presenting a report. In some monasteries, the growth of their entrepreneurial facilities could be promoted successfully in terms of securing their livelihood. Especially, the controllability and transparency of the increasingly elaborate structures and data volumes can be ensured by means of a management control system[49].

---

46 Cf. Jaschke, *Wirtschaftsmanagement in benediktinischen Männerklöstern Deutschlands*, 66.

47 Cf. Feldbauer-Durstmüller, Sandberger-Niederwimmer-Neulinger, «Controlling im Kloster. Ein Fallbeispiel eines österreichischen Benediktinerklosters», 589.

48 Cf. Payer-Langthaler, Feldbauer-Durstmüller, «Performance Management im Kloster: Das Beispiel der Benediktiner in Österreich», 100.

49 Cf. W. Gehra-G.M. Hanke-H.L. Schmidt-G. Schuster, «Controlling im Kloster: Ein Praxisbericht aus der Benediktinerabtei Plankstetten», *Zeitschrift für Controlling & Management* 51 (2007) 119.

But monasteries are also historically grown organizations, often modified, partially supplemented and therefore at risk of becoming non-transparent. This applies in particular to the allocation of tasks and responsibilities within the areas of the monastery as well as the roles of its members. In these cases, it would be obvious to initiate a revision of structures and responsibilities to improve transparency when introducing a management control system.

5.5. Reporting Obligations

5.5.1. Internal Reporting Obligations

There is an individual accountability to the abbot for individual members of the order. The abbot himself has to inform the chapter at least annually on the financial and staffing situation of the monastery. This is usually done with the completion of the annual statement of accounts. Every six years the structural condition of the monastery is the subject of an additional report, which has to be issued by the abbot or an appointee[50].

5.5.2. External Reporting Obligations

Exceeding the internal reporting obligation, there is the obligation of an annual report of the independent monasteries to the Economic Council of the Congregation. An account has to be given on the financial status, as well as on the sales, human resources and performance indicators by the end of March. The reporting process is completed when presenting the annual statement of accounts by December and receiving an opinion of the Economic Council[51].

Every six years the Economic Council of the Congregation will review the economic situation of the monasteries during a visitation. Its aim is to uncover abuses in time and to end them by giving recommendations; all for the purpose of securing the livelihoods of the communities[52].

50 Cf. Österreichische Benediktinerkongregation, *Die Satzungen der österreichischen Benediktinerkongregation,* 180.

51 Cf. Österreichische Benediktinerkongregation, *Die Satzungen der österreichischen Benediktinerkongregation,* 318.

52 Cf. Österreichische Benediktinerkongregation, *Die Satzungen der österreichischen Benediktinerkongregation,* 325-337.

6. DESIGNING A MANAGEMENT CONTROL SYSTEM IN A MONASTERY

6.1. Objectives of management control systems

Regarding the challenges a monastery is confronted with today, the satisfaction of the need for information is highly relevant. Structures that have grown over decades have to be examined and adapted to altered requirements[53].

Limiting the objectives of management control systems to performance and liquidity targets is not valid for monastic organisations. The supplementation with non-monetary measures according to the MCS-concept by Malmi and Brown[54] is recommended. In a case study by Payer-Langthaler and Feldbauer-Durstmüller normative objectives were derived from the RB and a first stakeholder analysis:

- Searching for God
- Securing the inventory for future generations under the premise of sustainability
- Contentedness of the central entitlement groups, “Nobody should be sad in the house of God”[55].
- Accordingly, similar to Non-Profit organisations the sheer maximisation of profits is not discernible. Rather the focus lies on the *regula benedicti* that targets qualitative characteristics and central stakeholder interests[56].

6.2. Instruments of management control systems

Within the context of the strategic process the management control system supports the management by designing and using or applying strategic planning

53 Cf. Feldbauer-Durstmüller, Sandberger-Niederwimmer-Neulinger, «Controlling im Kloster. Ein Fallbeispiel eines österreichischen Benediktinerklosters», 584-585.

54 Cf. Malmi-Brown, «Management control systems as a package - Opportunities, challenges and research directions», 292-293.

55 Cf. Payer-Langthaler, Feldbauer-Durstmüller, «Performance Management im Kloster: Das Beispiel der Benediktiner in Österreich», 105.

56 Cf. Payer-Langthaler, Feldbauer-Durstmüller, «Performance Management im Kloster: Das Beispiel der Benediktiner in Österreich», 103; Feldbauer-Durstmüller, Neulinger, «Stabilität über Jahrhunderte - Corporate Governance österreichischer Benediktinerklöster», 239.

and control systems that are supervised in a coordinating manner[57]. At the beginning of the strategic process of forming objectives is the vision. “The vision is the consciousness of a pipe dream about changing the environment”[58], according to the vision foundations for entrepreneurial activities can be derived in form of “basic principles” or “mission statements”. With these the purpose of the enterprise’s existence should be founded and its legitimacy described.

The next step is generating strategic objectives based on normative regulations. Before these are integrated into the strategic planning, possible opportunities and risks in the surrounding of the enterprise and within have to be anticipated by strategic foresight[59]. The recognition of external opportunities and risks and their coordination with the strengths and weaknesses of the enterprise supports the traditional long-term, strategic objective of the “sustainable securement of the enterprise’s existence”. Also, Benedictine communities strive for this primary objective, which can be differentiated according to the so-called Triple Bottom Line into social, ecological and economic sustainability. This way the lived principle in Benedictine communities of “*ora-labora-et lege*” demands a long-lasting safeguard of existence and therefore economic sustainability.

The social component of sustainability aims can be found in some verses of the RB, for example in RB 2 – “He [the abbot] must so accommodate and adapt himself to each one’s character and intelligence that he will not only keep the flock entrusted to his care from dwindling, but will rejoice in the increase of a good flock”[60]. This does not only mean the growth of the monastic community but rather the long-term sustainability regarding the structures of age and competences that should suffice to deal with succession questions and therefore the continuity of the monastery. Crucial application areas of ecological sustainability considerations are in the fields of renewable energy as well as the primary production, like agriculture and forestry[61].

57 Cf. B. Feldbauer-Durstmüller, *Handels-Controlling: Eine Controlling-Konzeption für den Einzelhandel,* Trauner Verlag, Linz 2001, 134.

58 Cf. H.H. Hinterhuber, *Strategische Unternehmensführung: II Strategisches Handeln,* Berlin [7]2004, 44.

59 Cf. Baum-Coenenberg-Günther, *Strategisches Controlling*, 16.

60 Cf. Monastery of Christ in the Desert, «Introduction to Study the Holy Rule of Saint Benedict and Abbot Philip Lawrence’s accompanying commentary», [accessed: 24-05-2016].

61 Cf. Payer-Langthaler, Feldbauer-Durstmüller, «Performance Management im Kloster: Das Beispiel der Benediktiner in Österreich», 106.

The leadership of monasteries is confronted with particular challenges in formulating a strategy. It is posed by the complicated measurability of non-monetary objectives of social and ecological dimensions as well as a conflict of goals between the dimensions (especially social and ecological sustainability versus economic sustainability)[62]. A joint elaboration of success potentials within a SWOT-analysis can help to develop a uniform perspective on the monastery's starting position and its future orientation. The SWOT-analysis is an instrument that detects "the dominance of opportunities and risks that were determined in the analysis of the environment and the strengths and weaknesses that were recognised by analysing the enterprise"[63].

The discussion process, which was prompted by the execution of the SWOT-analysis, supports the achievement of a shared evaluation of development possibilities of the organisation. The insights of participants from different fields (convent members, employees) help to discover strategic knowledge gaps and developing a mutual future perspective[64].

Tasks of the strategic planning process are the construction and receipt of success potentials afterwards the derivation of operational measures follows. Here, Malmi and Brown speak about "action planning" as an important connecting link for the realisation of strategies[65]. The strategic planning mostly bases on qualitative information and its concreteness is too little to formulate immediate actions[66].

6.3. Organisation of management control systems

The organisational design of management control systems can differ depending on the size and organisation of an enterprise and its existing resources. According to an investigation by Jaschke[67] more than half of the male Benedictine monasteries in Germany can be classified as small or middle-sized. Therefore, the institutional elaborations in this article are suited to the needs of small and medium organisations.

---

62 Cf. Baum-Coenenberg-Günther, *Strategisches Controlling*, 10.

63 Cf. Baum-Coenenberg-Günther, *Strategisches Controlling*, 99.

64 Cf. Baum-Coenenberg-Günther, *Strategisches Controlling*, 402-403.

65 Cf. Baum-Coenenberg-Günther, *Strategisches Controlling*, 6.

66 Cf. K.M. Welge-A. Al-Laham, *Planung: Prozesse – Strategien – Maßnahmen*, Gabler Verlag, Wiesbaden 1992, 411.

67 Cf. Jaschke, *Wirtschaftsmanagement in benediktinischen Männerklöstern Deutschlands*, 17-18.

A fundamental decision is whether the management control is designated to internal or external responsible entities. If the maintenance of management control is internal, the tasks can be either assigned to existing departments (not-institutionalised management control) or executed by newly established units (institutionalised management control).

Regarding institutionalised Management and Accounting the position on a hierarchical level (first, second or lower levels) has to be clarified. In general, a high allocation of the management accounting unit in the hierarchy of an enterprise is recommended, as the management accounting can be orientated cross-divisionally and it faces tasks that deal with the organisation as a whole[68]. In a monastery this would correspond to the level of the abbot. Alternatively and with regard to the relief of the abbot, the allocation of management accounting to the scope of duties of the cellarer (second leading level) is possible. The latter can execute the role himself, if he has the corresponding education, experience and resources at his disposal, or entrust a member of the staff with the assignments of management accounting.

6.4. Resistances to the design of management control systems in a monastery

Monastic communities are characterised by their historic connection to the past[69]. The orientation on the future of management accounting might be understood as disparagement of the tried and trusted and may provoke a disapproving attitude. Furthermore, at the first sight, the common utilisation of success and liquidity measures in operational management accounting seem contrary to the non-profit orientation of Benedictine communities, where the RB puts a fulfilled human life and the search for God into the centre of attention[70]. A subsequent interpretation of the management control system to be an instrument that neglects the normative objectives of the Benedictines may cause resistance of convent members and employees. Additionally, first results of management accounting analyses may have straining effects, if they show a pressing necessity of adaptation to the altered environmental conditions. Centuries-old

68 Cf. B. Friedl, «Controlling», in *Grundwissen der Ökonomik, Betriebswirtschaftslehre*, edd. F.X. Bea-E. Dichtl-M. Schweitzer, Stuttgart 2003, 113.

69 Cf. Feldbauer-Durstmüller, Sandberger-Niederwimmer-Neulinger, «Controlling im Kloster. Ein Fallbeispiel eines österreichischen Benediktinerklosters», 585.

70 Cf. Feldbauer-Durstmüller, Neulinger, «Stabilität über Jahrhunderte - Corporate Governance österreichischer Benediktinerklöster», 239.

rules, structures and traditions, which are regarded as inviolable, frequently pose decisive barriers for necessary transformation processes.

The challenge in designing management control systems is reaching an increased orientation towards the future and simultaneously maintaining the values and aims of the monastic community[71]. In a further step, the careful design of the strategy finding process is highly relevant. Areas of tension may occur in the coordination of social, ecological and economic sustainability goals whose practicability largely depend on the financial room for manoeuvre.

6.5. Experiences of the implementation workshop in an Austrian Benedictine monastery

6.5.1. Initial Situation

The monastery, which was examined between 2011 and 2016, is led by a small community of monks and its existence can be traced back to the 11th century. Its founder already equipped the monastery with an extensive property that still affects the economic activities of today in agriculture, fishing and rental and leasing. At the beginning of the investigation 19 Benedictine monks were living in the monastery. Additionally, 35 workers were employed in the administration and other enterprises. In the period of observation, the number of monks was reduced by a fourth due to death and resignations and, as a result of cutting measures, the ancillary staff declined by a third.

A variety of further areas like a kitchen, a building department or an administration unit, support the maintenance and the daily life of the monastery. Moreover, next to its ecclesiastical and cultural tasks, the monastery also keeps a "Gymnasium" (=middle school) and a business school.

The economic situation of the monastery has worsened over the last decades due to declines in revenues in substantial business areas. Despite various efforts, no further profitable business divisions could be erected. Bottlenecks in liquidity have been compensated by sales of real estate, however, the income position still shows a declining trend.

Before the start of the project there was no continuous and extensive planning and reporting system. Ambiguous accounts made the use for controlling purposes hardly possible. The accounting was supervised by an administration employee and mainly focused on the fulfilment of legal record-keeping obligations, their comple-

71 Cf. Feldbauer-Durstmüller, Sandberger-Niederwimmer-Neulinger, «Controlling im Kloster. Ein Fallbeispiel eines österreichischen Benediktinerklosters», 585.

tion was executed by an external tax adviser office. The internal reports primarily supported cost centre perspectives whereas the urgently necessary general overview was neglected. Foresight and planning calculations were missing completely.

6.5.2. External Conditions and influencing factors

During the management accounting project, specific external conditions could be identified, which partly had a supporting effect but some also provoked resistances and tensions.

The flat hierarchy and the direct access to the abbot as the central decision maker for all employees had a positive effect. It eased the execution and coordination of policies that were necessary for the design of management control systems and accelerated the steps in the process.

Missing financial and personnel resources made the realisation of organisational policies difficult, which were necessary for the introduction of management control systems. Additional expenses of work and time had to be kept as low as possible and investments in IT facilities were forgone with the exception of some marginal adaptions.

While urgent needs in saving and restructuring were detected during the first analyses, tensions and resistant reactions were arising from the influence of external conditions of the monastery. These included the personal attitudes of monks and ancillary employees about economic questions as well as the social role the monastery has or has had.

The predominantly theological and less economic education of the convent members made the understanding of economic connections difficult. Differences between the life goals and corporate objectives (faith versus economy) led to an insufficient willingness to occupy oneself with financial problems. Whilst it was possible to compensate missing knowledge with simple and comprehensible presentations of information fast and well, the creation of awareness about the necessity of the restructuring policies took more time and sensitivity on the part of the abbot and the project team. Also, many ancillary employees assessed the connections wrongly. Not least, this results from the missing transparency of the economic situation over years and the occurring lack of knowledge about relevant influential factors.

Also, the social starting position of the monastery had straining effects. This became evident with a considerable large share of members of the staff that were employed due to social reasons and only restrictively efficient. Furthermore, a special amount of prudence and sensitivity was essential by planning personnel reduction policies and eventually led to delayed realisations.

6.5.3. The implementation of the management control system: process and resistance problems

For the start of the project a broad range of persons from the monastic community and the ancillary employees were included. Next to extensive information about and coordination of the project aims, a process to find ideas about the new design of single sections was initiated. The awareness of the monks about the necessity of the project saw person 1 as *"differently distinctive, from a positive to a suspicious and expecting mood."* Person 2 observed negative reactions especially of older brothers:

> Particularly older brothers, who bore responsibility and were in leading positions in former times and are no more today, reacted with an offended and cross behaviour, because they have the feeling, that their work from the past is no longer appreciated.

The introduction process differentiated itself into an operational part, in which the focus lay on the installation of a structured and useful information and planning system as well as the realisation of initial – expenses-sided - policies for the improvement of the income situation. The utility of the installed operational management accounting instruments was seen differently by the monks, depending on their understanding of the economic situation. Person 2 explained: *"For those, who understand what is at stake, for those it is an important basis for decisions, for those, who do not know, it is a closed book, ...then, they are not really interested in it ...".*

With the newly portrayed income statement, a monthly comparison of estimates and results with the possibility to drilldown to the document level was provided. For the first time, an overview of the monastery in a current and permanently retrievable manner, which could be decomposed easily and quickly for economic sections as well as cost centres, offered meaningful information to the abbot and supported him in making decisions.

The present accountant of the monastery took over the role of the management accountant, his field of activity was analysed and shifted accordingly to create room for future tasks of management accounting. A management accountant of the university team accompanied him during and after the phase of implementation. Partly, there were sceptical reactions from the convent about the professional expertise for monasteries. In principle, the external support was welcomed positively, because the monastery members who were responsible for economic issues were also in favour of this approach. Person 1 explained: *"The examination of economic questions is perceived as an existing reality, where a high degree of trusting delegation to incumbents (abbot, economist, economic councillors) occurs".*

The need for a second – strategic – part crystallized, when problems were recognisable during the implementation, which required a fundamentally new strategic orientation. This proved far more difficult than the installation of operational instruments. The external conditions, which were described above, especially aims in life and missing economic awareness led to distinct resistances, particularly because accustomed processes and roles were questioned. Moreover, the real extent of the strategically critical initial situation was not understood or acknowledged. Person 2 stated: *"Some people, mainly the younger ones, have not realised what would happen, if we continue like that"* and criticised, that some only regard the strategically critical situation as temporary *"because they have not really had a good look at the whole story."*

In order to avert a direct liquidity crisis, it was necessary to realise initial saving policies in the immediate daily routines of the monks at relatively short notice. Person 1 describes the reactions of the monks as: *"generally positive, even though single policies were experienced as agonising".*

Although person 2 detected age specific differences:

> The older brother grew up with an image of a priest, that no longer corresponds to today's time and they do not want to deal with thrift due to their understanding of their role in society without wanting to insinuate that they would have lived a high life, that would not be true.

Saving measures at ancillary employees partly led to moral conflicts of monks. Person 2 about it: *"For some, the Christian conscience stood in the way, also concerning people, where one had to objectively say that they would have to be dismissed in the short or long-term regardless of the economic situation due to lacking motivation and effort."*

Single members of the convent even considered leaving the monastery in view of the perceived future perspectives. Reduction measures in personnel partly led to a shift of single working processes from employees to monks. Although, according to person 1, this was seen as: *"Mainly positive, the question arose how much is possible next to the traditional working fields of the monks".*

According to person 2, timely and accomplishment-related overtaxing occurred because *"nobody was relieved of other tasks in return for taking over additional tasks."*

Also, inequalities in the new distribution of tasks occurred:

> Then there were those, who wanted to take part and had realised it, they had very many tasks. Other people, who rather blocked, did not have any tasks and so it resulted in a big imbalance within the convent, so that people, who did not want to participate, did not have to and the whole burden was left to a relatively small number of brothers".

The hierarchical thinking among the monks led to further conflicts, because the positioning in the hierarchy was not improved by the expansion of tasks rather the acceptance of simple household chores was regarded as inferior. Person 2: *"... because they were very many practical aiding tasks, like doing the laundry, cooking etc., one was rather downgraded in the hierarchy by some brothers, one is not suitable for more, so to say."*

Furthermore, taking over household chores did not correspond to the views of the lives of some monks. *"Some simply came into the monastery with the attitude of simply wanting to be priest and not having to deal with practical things, that is the task of other people and suddenly they are confronted with them".*

The ancillary employees faced the project with a high degree of worry for the monastery and their own place of work, although according to the statement of person 1 *"the worries about the monastery"* were *"often pithy and not honest".* There also were frank and vehement counter-reactions. According to person 1 *"behind one's back single persons openly criticised the policies devoid of loyalty and reported incompetence and intellectual/mental deficits ... about the principal and tried to influence convent members and employees."*

The reactions of the employees differed according to education and operating range. Administration employees with a basic economic education were more positively minded than simple workers, who according to person 2 *"... often did not understand the connections. They also did not understand what the reasons might be, that there is need for saving. There mainly was a completely understandable worry about their own work place in the centre of attention."*

In the course of the project two groups formed, which person 3 describes as the pro and contra factions. *"The "contra-faction" put their personal interests and ideas above the ones of the monastery. The "pro-faction" remained faithful to the leadership of the monastery and went along the way of management accounting. Some employees created "realms" that had to be preserved at any price."*

External Stakeholders were concerned by the restructuring policies in some economic sections, according to person 1 emotions *"were partly exploited by employees" and "the pastoral care of single convent members was occupied by the topic and partially straining".*

In this context, person 2 regarded the unrealistic image, that the public had about the financial situation of the monastery, as one reason for the existing conflicts. "... *that the monastery appears to the outside as rich and it naturally is not in reality*" and ".... *because the newspaper reports provoke the impression that we make the personnel pay.* The public is not really aware of...that we have to work more."

Overall, according to person 1 the duration of affiliation and the sense of belonging played a special role in the resistance process: "*non habitus facit monachus –it is not the habit that makes the monk*".

Person 1 felt the resistance to be fiercest by external stakeholders, "*leading resistant employees and one – in separation living – brother*".

6.5.4. Recommended courses of action to avoid resistance

The identified external conditions and results of the case study allow the following recommended courses of action to be drawn:

- Organisational knowledge of external management accounting advisors:
- The gain of appropriate previous knowledge about the structure, hierarchy and rules of a monastery as well as its informal norms and traditions is fundamental for the acceptance and trustful collaboration with the convent members.
- Basis business knowledge of decision makers:
- Ensuring or conveying basic business knowledge poses a pre-requisite for understanding status reports and prognoses. In small groups, the people affected should be met at their level of education without making them lose face.
- Clarification about the actual initial economic situation:
- Contemporary, simple and clear depictions, adapted to the respective target group (monks, mundane employees, external stakeholders) can support the conveying of a realistic picture of the initial situation and the expecting developments.
- Here it is recommendable to coordinate and agree on uniform ways and contents of information that should be carried outside in advance.
- The punctual communication of essential policies (like reduction of personnel, closure of institutions, etc.) and their comprehensible reasons help to prevent rumours.
- Causes of crises and former leading executives (monks):

- In contrast to mundane enterprises retired abbots, economic councillors etc. remain further in the community of the monastery. If causes of crises are traced back to their tenure, gentle and appreciating dealings can avoid resistance and blocking behaviour.
- Cultural Components of new task distributions in the convent (after reduction in personnel):
- New task distributions can also be seen as a chance to deal consciously with the personal aims in life, the content of the Regula Benedicti and the over time developed understanding of the role of monks. Important is the accompaniment and moderation by the abbot (perhaps supported by an external organisation advisor) and a commitment of all involved monks.
- Accomplishing component of new task distributions in the convent:
- In order to prevent overtaxing and a resulting resistance, the examination of possible tenable service reductions of the monastery (to the inside as well as to the outside) is worth considering. Possible, synergy effects with other monasteries can be found and exploited.

SUMMARY

External economic conditions, that have become more complex, as well as disadvantageous developments of personnel resources in monasteries have led to a gain in relevance of intensive examinations of business topics in this primarily spiritual orientated form of organisation. A management control system can support the management in planning and controlling from a cultural, personal, cybernetic and administrative perspective.

When installing a management control system in a monastery, the specific external conditions, which distinguish this form of organisation, have to be regarded in order to fulfil the demands for effectiveness and efficiency and to prevent the resistance of the stakeholders. Therefore, a limitation of management accounting objectives to performance and liquidity aims, similar to non-profit organisations, is inappropriate. Rather the orientation to holistic organisation aims like, for example, searching for God, contentedness of the stakeholder and the pursuit of sustainability goals, is in the centre of attention.

The analysis of external opportunities and risks, as well as their comparison with the strengths and weaknesses of the monastery in a SWOT-analysis can be applied as an effective instrument to detect strategic gaps and development possibilities. The budgeting and reporting system, as instrument of operational management accounting, is suitable to support the planning and controlling process within smaller structures.

The organisational incorporation of a management control system into the monastery depends on the prevailing resources and on the educational level of the considered task managers. The allocation to existing departments like the accounting section or to the range of tasks of the cellarer is a possible alternative. Special attention should be paid to resistances. A system, which is mainly used in profit-orientated organisations, can trigger worries about the securement of the existing value culture in a monastic surrounding. In order to avoid blockades and delays during the implementation phase, an intensive examination and the inclusion of the characteristics of Benedictine communities are recommended.

Abstract

At first sight, entrepreneurial thinking and acting does not seem to have anything in common with monastery life. On closer examination, however, another picture arises. In particular, the Benedictine congregation is characterised by its claim for economic self-reliance to ensure political independency. However, the burden of complex economic conditions, youth problems and obsolescence constitute big challenges to monastic management. Therefore, the implementation of a management accounting system seems to be self-evident. The ensuing change processes can provoke resistance and have to be carefully prepared.

The present paper describes the most relevant frame conditions to ensure a well-performing management accounting system in an abbey. The subsequent implications for the design of this system are deduced given the resistance problem. Derived from this, the following research questions are answered:

- *Which special frame conditions have to be considered by implementing a management accounting system in an abbey?*
- *Which suggestions can be deduced to avoid resistance against reorientations?*

This paper is based on the results of qualitative interviews, document analysis and workshops in an Austrian Benedictine monastery.

The analysis of the explicit research questions is based on various theoretical approaches, particularly principal–agent theory and stewardship theory. To derive the specific frameworks for functioning control within the monastery, stakeholder theory is applied.

Considering the specifics of Benedictine monasteries, the containment of management accounting targets on earning and liquidity targets similar to non-profit organisations is not recommended. Rather, the focus is on holistic organisational goals such as God-seeking, stakeholder satisfaction and the pursuit of sustainable development goals. Particular attention should be paid to resistance problems. A system such as management accounting which is mainly used in for-profit organisations, may cause concern for the protection of the existing culture of values in a monastic environment. The prevailing collective thought – in the sense of stewardship theory – within monasteries should be strengthened for strategic and structural changes with sensitivity to the particularities of a monastic community and used for a successful reorganisation

FINAL LECTURE

QUAND'È CHE LAVORO E CARITÀ COMINCIARONO A FAR PARTE DELLA VITA DEI MONACI EGIZIANI?

Ewa Wipszycka

Dimentichiamo per un momento ciò che sappiamo sul ruolo del lavoro nel monachesimo europeo. Non intendo mettere in dubbio l'idea che i monaci egiziani tardo-antichi abbiano contribuito al plurisecolare processo storico grazie al quale la civiltà europea di oggi, nelle sue manifestazioni migliori, attribuisce al lavoro un valore fondamentale. Ma se vogliamo fare ricerche sulla storia delle comunità monastiche, non è lecito presupporre che i più antichi monaci sapessero già che il lavoro è necessario in una vita che aspiri alla perfezione.

Dobbiamo vedere che cosa esattamente dicano i testi scritti nei primi tempi del movimento monastico, fino ai primi decenni del V secolo, seguendo l'ordine cronologico della composizione delle opere, e non quello delle vite dei personaggi di cui le opere nate dopo parlano[1]. Procedere in questo modo è indispensabile, se vogliamo evitare il pericolo di attribuire troppo peso a testi tardi che parlano dei monaci celebri delle prime generazioni: gli autori di tali testi, infatti, descrivevano il lontano passato secondo modelli che erano in vigore al loro tempo.

Però prima di cominciare a esaminare e commentare le fonti, ricordiamoci dei passi del Nuovo Testamento che erano per i monaci i più importanti per la questione del modo di trattare il lavoro. Su quei passi essi si fondavano nel loro pensiero e nel loro comportamento.

> Perciò vi dico: per la vostra vita non affannatevi di quello che mangerete o berrete, e neanche per il vostro corpo, di quello che indosserete; la vita forse non vale più del cibo e il corpo più del vestito? Guardate gli uccelli del cielo: non seminano, né mietono, né ammassano nei granai; eppure il Padre vostro celeste li nutre. Non

---

Ewa Wipszycka, storica, studiosa del monachesimo antico in Egitto, professoressa emerita dell'Università di Varsavia.

1 La documentazione dettagliata per tutte le considerazioni che seguono si trova nel mio libro *Moines et communautés monastiques en Égypte (IVe-VIIIe siècles)*, Varsovie 2009, e in vari miei articoli accessibili *on-line*: http:/www.academia/ edu e.wipszycka [accesso: 11-11-18].

contate voi forse più di loro? E chi di voi, per quanto si dia da fare, può aggiungere un'ora sola alla sua vita? E perché vi affannate per il vestito? Osservate come crescono i gigli del campo: non lavorano e non filano. Eppure io vi dico che neanche Salomone, con tutta la sua gloria, vestiva come uno di loro. Ora se Dio veste così l'erba del campo, che oggi c'è e domani verrà gettata nel forno, non farà assai più per voi, gente di poca fede? Non affannatevi dunque dicendo: Che cosa mangeremo? Che cosa berremo? Che cosa indosseremo? Di tutte queste cose si preoccupano i pagani; il Padre vostro celeste infatti sa che ne avete bisogno. Cercate prima il regno di Dio e la sua giustizia, e tutte queste cose vi saranno date in aggiunta. Non affannatevi dunque per il domani, perché il domani avrà già le sue inquietudini[2].

Guarite gli infermi, risuscitate i morti, sanate i lebbrosi, cacciate i demòni. Gratuitamente avete ricevuto, gratuitamente date. Non procuratevi oro, né argento, né moneta di rame nelle vostre cinture, né bisaccia da viaggio, né due tuniche, né sandali, né bastone, perché l'operaio ha diritto al suo nutrimento[3].

Gesù rispose: In verità, in verità vi dico, voi mi cercate non perché avete visto dei segni, ma perché avete mangiato di quei pani e vi siete saziati. Procuratevi non il cibo che perisce, ma quello che dura per la vita eterna, e che il Figlio dell'uomo vi darà[4].

Voi ricordate infatti, fratelli, la nostra fatica e il nostro travaglio: lavorando notte e giorno per non essere di peso ad alcuno vi abbiamo annunziato il vangelo di Dio[5].

Sapete infatti come dovete imitarci: poiché noi non abbiamo vissuto oziosamente fra voi, né abbiamo mangiato gratuitamente il pane di alcuno, ma abbiamo lavorato con fatica e sforzo notte e giorno per non essere di peso ad alcuno di voi. Non che non ne avessimo diritto, ma per darvi noi stessi come esempio da imitare. E infatti quando eravamo presso di voi, vi demmo questa regola: chi non vuol lavorare neppure mangi[6].

In un altro passo di Paolo, tuttavia, i monaci trovavano un'altra indicazione molto importante:

---

2 Mt 6,25-34.
3 Mt 10,8-10.
4 Gv 6,26-27.
5 1Ts 2,7.
6 2Ts 3,7-10.

> Vi esortiamo, fratelli: correggete gli indisciplinati, confortate i pusillanimi, sostenete i deboli, siate pazienti con tutti. Guardatevi dal rendere male per male ad alcuno; ma cercate sempre il bene tra voi e con tutti. State sempre lieti, pregate incessantemente, in ogni cosa rendete grazie; questa è infatti la volontà di Dio in Cristo Gesù verso di voi[7].

Teniamo presente che i monaci tardo-antichi interpretavano e usavano i singoli passi della Sacra Scrittura alla lettera, senza prendere in considerazione il contesto né le convenzioni letterarie. L'insieme di passi biblici che ho citato poteva essere compreso in vari modi. A seconda delle interpretazioni, se ne potevano trarre due indicazioni opposte: da un lato, la conferma che il lavoro fosse un elemento importante dell'ascesi (chi non vuol lavorare neppure mangi); dall'altro, la conferma che esso fosse nocivo all'ascesi, allontanasse cioè il monaco dal vero scopo della sua vita (la preghiera), testimoniasse mancanza di fede nella provvidenza divina (il Padre vostro celeste sa di cosa avete bisogno). Trovando nelle Sacre Scritture due indicazioni che sembravano inconciliabili tra di loro, i monaci sceglievano una delle due, tacendo dell'esistenza dell'altra, oppure tentavano, con scarso successo, di conciliare l'una con l'altra.

In questa prospettiva sono interessanti i ragionamenti di Agostino nell'operetta *De opere monachorum*, scritta verso il 410 su richiesta del vescovo di Cartagine. Il primate dell'Africa, Aurelio, si era detto inquieto a causa della presenza di monaci che erano convinti di non dover lavorare. Agostino rispose appunto con il *De opere monachorum*. Qui egli critica quei monaci servendosi di artifici retorici, ricordando le parole evangeliche sugli «uccelli dell'aria» e i «gigli del campo», insistendo sull'esperienza personale di Paolo (e tacendo delle sue parole «pregate incessantemente», che erano sempre invocate da coloro che erano contrari al lavoro monastico ...). I sostenitori della tesi opposta, egli li presenta come uomini pigri che entrano in un monastero sperando di trovarvi una vita comoda. Scrive (22):

> Ma, tornando a questa gente che si consacra al servizio di Dio e ne fa la professione, la più parte di essi o provengono di tra gli schiavi o son dei liberti che per motivo religioso hanno ottenuto la libertà o son lì per ottenerla; ovvero, son dei contadini vissuti nei campi o artigiani che hanno esercitato l'uno o l'altro mestiere o attività in uso fra i plebei. [...] Né sempre consta con sicurezza se siano venuti con l'intenzione di servire Dio o non piuttosto perché, fuggendo a tasche vuote una vita in-

7 1Ts 5,14-18.

tollerabile e per il lavoro e per la povertà, si son ripromessi di venir mantenuti, vitto e vestito, dalla comunità. Tanto più che vengono anche a riscuotere onori da parte di coloro da cui non solevano ricevere se non disprezzo e umiliazioni. Orbene, costoro, non potendosi sottrarre al lavoro con la scusa della salute malferma (debbono ammetterlo per forza a causa del genere di vita condotto fino allora!), pretendono di farla franca celandosi all'ombra d'una dottrina erronea: per cui, interpretato falsamente il Vangelo, s'adoperano per stravolgere le norme fissate dall'Apostolo. Uccelli dell'aria per davvero, che si levano in alto sulle ali della superbia, e insieme gramigna della terra per il loro fin troppo umano sentire.

Affermando che la maggior parte dei monaci contrari al lavoro monastico sono uomini di origine sociale bassa (schiavi, liberti, contadini, artigiani), Agostino intende discreditare la loro opinione. Noi non abbiamo alcuna ragione per pensare che non ci fossero tra di loro molti uomini di origine sociale più elevata.

Nel concludere le sue considerazioni, Agostino si sente in dovere di scrivere (30): «... non potrebbe infatti Paolo, servo di Gesù Cristo, inculcare una dottrina in contrasto con quella del suo Signore»[8].

Fatta questa introduzione, passo ora all'essenziale del mio discorso. Cominciamo dall'inizio, cioè da Antonio. Dalla *Vita Antonii* di Atanasio sappiamo che quando il santo decise di chiudersi in un antico sepolcro all'orlo del deserto per lottare con Satana, chiese a uno dei suoi conoscenti (*gnorimoi*) di portargli ogni tanto del pane[9]. Quest'uomo un giorno lo trova disteso per terra, battuto dai demonii, e, credendolo morto, lo trasporta in una chiesa (8, 1-4). Antonio riprende i sensi e chiede di essere riportato nel sepolcro. Qualche tempo dopo, si trasferì in una fortezza abbandonata dall'esercito, situata nella zona coltivata a poca distanza dal deserto[10] – uno spazio circondato da un muro e che si poteva chiudere; l'acqua c'era; pane per sei mesi, Antonio l'aveva portato con sé; più tardi, due volte all'anno, qualcuno gli buttava da fuori del muro altre scorte di pane (12, 3-4). Questo stato di cose dura per quasi vent'anni. Finalmente gli ammiratori dell'ascesi di Antonio sfondano la porta della fortezza e persuadono il santo a

8 *De opere monachorum*, ed. J. Zycha, *Corpus scriptorum ecclesiasticorum latinorum*, vol.: 41, Wien 1900; Aurelius Augustinus, *I monaci e il lavoro*, ed. introduzione e note A. Sanchez, Roma 1984.

9 Edizione: Athanase d'Alexandrie, *Vie d'Antoine*, ed. G.J.M. Bartelink (Sources Chrétiennes 400) Paris 1997, 248-265. Si noti: all'orlo, non all'interno del deserto. Dove esattamente, non lo sappiamo.

10 Sappiamo esattamente dove essa si trovasse: là dove oggi c'è il villaggio di Burumbul; vd. il mio libro *Moines et communautés monastiques* (citato sopra, nota 1), 248-265.

uscirne e a prendersi cura di coloro che desiderano imitarlo: nasce così la prima *laura*. Poi, per sottrarsi ai visitatori che lo disturbano, Antonio si rifugia in una piccola oasi deserta vicina al Mar Rosso[11]; qui il pane gli viene portato ogni tanto da carovane di Saraceni e da monaci che vengono a fargli visita; egli si nutre anche di datteri di palme che crescono accanto a una sorgente. Desiderando risparmiare la fatica ai suoi visitatori, egli chiede loro di fornirgli degli strumenti e un po' di sementi; da allora in poi coltiverà un pezzetto di terra accanto alla sorgente. «Facendo questo ogni anno, aveva da ciò il pane, rallegrandosi di non dare disturbo a nessuno e di mantenersi in tutto non gravoso» (50, 6). In questa frase avvertiamo reminiscenze delle epistole di Paolo: *2 Cor.* 11,9; *1 Tess.* 2.9; *2 Tess.* 3,8.

È vero che, secondo il racconto di Atanasio, Antonio, nella prima fase della sua vita ascetica, quando viveva nelle vicinanze del suo villaggio natale, avrebbe lavorato «con le sue mani» per potersi mantenere e anche per poter aiutare i bisognosi (3, 6). Tuttavia le decisioni che Antonio prese più tardi per quanto riguardava la scelta del luogo e del modo dell'ascesi, provano che quell'accenno al lavoro del santo nella prima fase va trattato come un elemento convenzionale del modello di monaco costruito da Atanasio. Scrivendo la *Vita di Antonio* all'inizio degli anni Sessanta del IV secolo, l'autore sapeva bene che i monaci del suo tempo, o almeno la maggioranza di loro, lavoravano; perciò trovò opportuno scrivere che Antonio lavorava nei primi anni della sua vita ascetica. Commentando questo passo, l'editore della *Vita di Antonio* G.J.M. Bartelink (come del resto altri commentatori) ha creduto di poter osservare che il lavoro fu fin dall'inizio un elemento della vita ascetica; ma non ha tenuto conto del séguito della biografia.

Epifanio di Salamina, nella sua opera *Panarion*, descrive i costumi dei monaci egiziani – che, secondo lui, sarebbero un modello per tutti i monaci – contrapponendoli agli eretici messaliani, i quali, interpretando letteralmente l'insegnamento di Paolo in *1 Tess.* 5,17, ritengono che la preghiera continua escluda il lavoro[12].

> Come l'ape, che sulle zampe ha la cera, frutto del suo lavoro, e sulla bocca una goccia di miele, con la propria voce inneggiante inneggia il Signore dell'universo per quanto glielo consentono i suoi sensi, come attesta anche Salomone che dice: *Avendo onorato la sapienza è stata esaltata* (Prov. 6, 8c LXX), così anche i servi

11 Più di trecento anni più tardi, in questo luogo sorse il Monastero di sant'Antonio, che esiste ancora oggi.

12 Epiphanius, «*Panarion*» 80, 4, in *Ancoratus und Panarion*, vol 3, ed. K. Holl (GCS 37), 1933, 489; traduzione: Epifanio di Salamina, *Panarion, eresie 74-80. Compendio della fede* (Collana di testi patristici), Roma 2015, 225.

di Cristo, che si fondano veramente sulla solida roccia della verità e costruiscono saldamente la loro casa, realizzano le loro minuziose opere con le loro mani in base alle capacità di ciascuno. Ripetono con la loro bocca praticamente tutta la divina Scrittura, fanno lunghe veglie con facilità e diligenza, un po' pregando e un po' salmodiando, prendono continuamente parte alle riunioni che sono fissate secondo l'usanza e secondo le regole. In ogni tempo scandiscono il giorno ora per ora, innalzando preghiere a Dio legittimamente e con molta umiltà e faticosi gemiti. Pur fra le opere spirituali, lavorano con le proprie mani, come ho detto, per non diventare indigenti e non cadere nelle ipocrisie umane, perché altrimenti non sarebbero più in grado di rinfacciare la verità all'empio, né di essere immuni dalla sordidezza di chi si è arricchito ingiustamente e ha defraudato i poveri, né di fare a meno dei loro sussidi alimentari: non potrebbero da giuste fatiche trarre il nutrimento quotidiano, ma sarebbero costretti per il bisogno dovuto alla loro inerzia a condividere la tavola dei ricchi.

Prima di diventare vescovo di Salamina nel 367, Epifanio era stato per molti anni monaco in Egitto; possiamo dunque ritenere le sue informazioni degne di fede, pensare che esse siano fondate sulla sua esperienza personale. In questo brano di *Panarion* troviamo anche la prima attestazione della pratica della *melete* (lat. *meditatio*), che consisteva nel recitare canticchiando passi biblici o brevi preghiere, ripetendoli spesso a brevi intervalli. Se il monaco camminava o faceva un lavoro che non richiedesse molta attenzione, la *melete* poteva benissimo accompagnare tale attività[13]. Il guaio è che da altre fonti risulta che il lavoro dei monaci non consisteva sempre nel confezionare corde, cesti, reti; molti di loro copiavano libri, tessevano, confezionavano oggetti di cuoio, e queste attività richiedevano una piena concentrazione dell'attenzione. Il *Panarion* ci permette di capire come sia nato un *topos* letterario secondo cui i monaci avrebbero potuto lavorare senza venir meno al dovere di pregare continuamente. Questo *topos* sarà ripetuto innumerevoli volte. L'autore della *Historia monachorum in Aegypto*[14], scritta tra il 395 e il 404, sa che i pii monaci a volte lavorano (1, 32). Egli scrive anche che tutti i monaci partecipano alla mietitura, ottenendo come pagamento una certa quantità di grano (18, 1). Questa informazione, egli la dà nel contesto di un elogio dei

13 A. Guillaumont, *Le problème de la prière continuelle dans le monachisme ancien*, in *Études sur la spiritualité de l'Orient Chrétien* (Spiritualité Orientale 66), Abbaye de Bellefontaine 1996, 131-141.

14 *Historia monachorum in Aegypto*, ed. A.-J. Festugière (*Subsidia Hagiographica* 34), Bruxelles 1961.

monaci: scrive infatti che i monaci usano una parte del loro guadagno per dare elemosine ai poveri dei dintorni e anche a quelli di Alessandria. Ciò non diminuisce il valore di questa informazione: essa è del tutto degna di fede. Proprio in questo modo si comportavano i poveri delle città di tutto il mondo mediterraneo – non solo nell'antichità. Tuttavia la *Historia monachorum in Aegypto* più spesso parla di asceti che Dio nutre miracolosamente (o a cui Dio toglie questo aiuto se essi perdono l'umiltà). Viaggiando attraverso i luoghi monastici dell'Egitto, l'autore conversò con parecchi monaci: probabilmente questi non collocavano il lavoro abbastanza in alto nella scala dei valori da poter convincere l'autore che il lavoro fosse uno dei doveri principali della vita monastica. Egli era un monaco del Monte Oliveto di Gerusalemme: è lecito supporre che anche l'ambiente da cui proveniva non considerasse il lavoro indispensabile per i monaci. Traducendo questa operetta in latino, Rufino di Aquileia vi introdusse vari cambiamenti, a volte importanti, ma nessuno di questi cambiamenti riguarda la posizione del lavoro.

Press'a poco contemporaneamente alla *Historia monachorum in Aegypto* fu scritta la prima versione della famosa opera di Palladio sui monaci egiziani. Palladio la compose durante il suo soggiorno in Egitto, nel centro monastico dei Kellia, dunque tra il 388 e il 399. Questa prima versione si è conservata solo in parte e solo in traduzione copta, ma ciò che resta contiene esplicite dichiarazioni positive riguardanti l'importanza del lavoro nella vita dei monaci[15]. Nella versione dell'opera scritta negli anni 419-420 e dedicata a Lausos, ciambellano della corte imperiale (da cui il titolo *Historia Lausiaca*[16]), Palladio afferma più volte, parlando di quei monaci che sono gli eroi positivi della sua narrazione, che essi vivevano del lavoro delle loro mani. Racconta che il famoso monaco Macario di Alessandria biasimò un certo monaco che non lavorava, ma pregava ininterrottamente arrivando fino a settecento preghiere, mantenendosi per mezzo dei doni che riceveva; Macario gli avrebbe detto: «Io dopo sessant' anni di vita recito ogni giorno cento preghiere stabilite, compio il lavoro necessario a procurarmi il nutrimento e soddisfo all'obligo di concedere colloqui ai confratelli, e la mia ragione non mi condanna come se avessi mancato di diligenza» (21,3). A un altro monaco, Pambo, Palladio attribuisce delle parole significative (10, 6): «non mi ricordo di aver mangiato un pezzo di pane dato in dono, fuori dell'opera delle mie mani». Il maestro di Palladio, Evagrio Pontico, copiava libri (38, 10), sebbene non fosse costretto dal bisogno a

15 *Quatre ermites égyptiens d'après les fragments de l'Histoire Lausiaque,* edd. G. Bunge-A. De Vogüé (*Spiritualité Orientale* 60), Abbaye de Bellfontaine 1994.

16 Palladio, *Storia Lausiaca*, ed. G.J.M. Bartelink (Fondazione Lorenzo Valla), Milano 1974.

fare questo (come apprendiamo dalla versione copta (p. 97; 162, 18) l'economo che si occupava delle cose materiali riguardanti Evagrio e i suoi discepoli, aveva a sua disposizione più di duecento *solidi*: questo denaro, proveniente da doni, serviva per accogliere i numerosi ospiti).

Nel trattato intitolato *Antirretikos* (una specie di antologia di passi biblici, destinata a servire ai monaci in situazioni pericolose per l'anima), Evagrio (che soggiornò nel centro monastico dei Kellia negli anni 383-399) scrive:

> 61. «Contro i pensieri che inducono la nostra anima a non voler fare provviste per mezzo del lavoro manuale, e a non decidersi a ricevere qualcosa dai famigliari, perché questi sono poveri e abitano lontano, e invece le consigliano di prendere ciò di cui ha bisogno da altri» ... ; segue una citazione di Paolo, *Epistola ai Filippesi* (4, 5-6): «Il Signore è vicino! Non angustiatevi per nulla, ma in ogni circostanza fate presenti a Dio le vostre richieste con preghiere, suppliche e ringraziamenti».
> 64. «Contro il pensiero che ci impedisce di lavorare con le nostre mani e ci costringe a mangiare pane e a saziarci» ... ; anche qui segue una citazione di Paolo, *Seconda Epistola ai Tessalonicesi*: «chi non vuol lavorare neppure mangi» (3, 10).

Si osservi che nel primo di questi due passi i doni che un monaco riceve dai suoi parenti sono collocati, nella scala dei valori, allo stesso livello di ciò che il monaco stesso produce col lavoro delle sue mani. Per Evagrio è evidente che il monaco ha diritto a una parte degli averi famigliari, perciò trova naturale che egli faccia uso di questi in caso di necessità, mentre l'uso di doni fatti da persone estranee costituisce un problema. La dichiarazione di Evagrio ci permette di constatare un fatto importante: i monaci del suo tempo sono per lo più uomini che prima di abbandonare il «mondo», avevano posseduto dei beni e che per lo più li possiedono ancora e li usano nella vita monastica. Contrariamente a ciò che gli storici moderni hanno pensato per molto tempo, il movimento monastico attirava uomini di diverse condizioni sociali ed economiche. Ricordiamo che i genitori di Antonio erano dei proprietari di terra benestanti, come è attestato da Atanasio. Per molti monaci il lavoro era una scelta, non una necessità economica.

In certi casi però esso era una necessità economica. Tale fu il caso di Pacomio e delle comunità cenobitiche che si formarono sotto la sua direzione, a cominciare dalla più antica, quella di Tabennese (nata verso il 323). Pacomio fondò questa comunità in un villaggio abbandonato, situato all'interno della valle del Nilo, densamente popolata. Non sembra che lui stesso o i suoi primi monaci possedessero averi propri consistenti: per la loro comunità, dunque, il lavoro era una necessità economica. La congregazione pacomiana nacque senza alcun aiuto da parte della Chiesa gerarchica. A partire da un certo momento, quando il monastero di Tabennese era ormai famoso, cominciarono ad affluire dei doni (come sappiamo dalle biografie di Pacomio); ma durante la prima fase i monaci dovettero lavorare per procurarsi cibo e vestiti. Notabene: le biografie di Pacomio raccontano che questo santo lavorava fin dall'inizio della sua vita ascetica, al tempo in cui era guidato da un vecchio anacoreta, Palamon: insieme essi producevano sacchi con pelo di capra. Questo dettaglio non è banale: di solito infatti, nei racconti riguardanti i monaci egiziani, questi fanno canestri o corde. Può darsi che la memoria collettiva dei pacomiani abbia conservato un ricordo di racconti fatti dal maestro stesso. In passi dove si tratta di tempi posteriori, le stesse biografie raccontano che i monaci pacomiani producevano stuoie. Questa è un'attività che richiedeva un impianto tecnico e la collaborazione di più persone. Essa non è menzionata in altri testi monastici. È probabile che l'informazione sulla produzione di stuoie nei monasteri pacomiani corrisponda alla realtà dell'economia di questi.

Introducendo Pacomio nelle mie considerazioni, non ho detto niente della datazione delle fonti che narrano la sua vita. Lo studio della genesi delle biografie di Pacomio è, per lo storico del monachesimo egiziano, uno dei compiti più difficili. Nessuno dei testi che possediamo appartiene al IV secolo, né al V (il manoscritto più antico, purtroppo incompleto, appartiene al VI secolo, o forse al VII) [17]. Questo fatto però non mi preoccupa, perché, se si considerano il carattere e le dimensioni del primo dei cenobii pacomiani, è inevitabile pensare che il dovere di lavorare esistesse fin dall'inizio di questa comunità. Tuttavia non dimentichiamo che non tutti i monaci erano in grado di lavorare intensamente: quelli malati o molto vecchi dovevano farsi mantenere dalla comunità. Più tardi, i priori dei cenobii non accoglievano tra i monaci uomini in queste condizioni; ma tutto ciò che sappiamo di Pacomio ci autorizza a pensare che egli si comportasse diversamente, nonostante gli inconvenienti economici.

Verso la fine del IV secolo la situazione economica della congregazione pacomiana cambiò, perché il crescente prestigio di questa suscitava un afflusso di doni. Sembrerebbe naturale pensare che nella nuova situazione i pacomiani non avessero bisogno di lavorare. Tuttavia, contrariamente a ciò che potremmo aspettarci, questi doni non diminuivano la quantità di lavoro che i monaci erano tenuti a svolgere. Da un lato, la necessità di assicurare i mezzi di sussistenza a un numero crescente di monaci, e dall'altro lato, la comparsa di un nuovo fattore economico, cioè l'accumularsi di beni provenienti da donazioni, spinsero la

17 Cf. *Pacomio servo di Dio e degli uomini*, ed. L. D'Ayala Valva, Magnano 2016.

congregazione pacomiana a impegnarsi sempre di più in attività economiche: era necessario lavorare di più sui campi, nell'artigianato, nel trasporto su barche, per evitare che i beni donati si sprecassero e che i monaci, sempre più numerosi, patissero la fame. Si aumentava perciò la quantità di tempo da dedicare al lavoro, diminuendo il tempo da dedicare alla preghiera.

Nel grande insieme degli apoftegmi il problema del lavoro del monaco è ancora presente, sebbene coloro che, verso la fine del V secolo, in Palestina, redassero la prima collezione di essi (l'*Alphabetikon*) facendo una selezione all'interno di un materiale più antico, risalente al IV secolo, facessero indubbiamente parte di coloro che disapprovavano quei monaci che non volevano lavorare. Questi ultimi non scomparvero affatto dagli ambienti monastici. Ciò è testimoniato dalla lettera 84 di Cirillo al vescovo del Fayyum, Kalosirios – lettera riguardante i monaci di Kalamun[18].

Il fatto che la tendenza che considerava il lavoro un dovere aveva prevalso tra i monaci egiziani, ebbe grande importanza per i monaci palestinesi, che erano fortemente influenzati dal monachesimo egiziano. Ciò risulta chiaramente da fonti del VI secolo: dalla corrispondenza tra Barsanufio e Giovanni, due monaci che vivevano presso Gaza, e dai racconti precisi e attendibili di Cirillo di Skythopolis sui monaci del Deserto di Giuda.

Basilio di Cesarea è un convinto sostenitore della soluzione egiziana (era stato in Egitto verso il 357). Nelle sue *Regole esposte per esteso* (*Horoi kata platos*)[19], scritte verso il 377, egli parla della necessità di lavorare richiamandosi alle epistole di Paolo. È significativo che egli metta insieme il discorso sul lavoro e quello sulle ore delle preghiere: questo rivela un'intenzione polemica contro i fautori della preghiera continua (37). Inoltre egli scrive:

> Indicare con precisione alcuni lavori non è facile perché si richiede l'uno o l'altro a seconda delle caratteristiche di ciascun luogo e delle attività proprie di ogni regione. Tuttavia si può delineare un criterio generale: bisogna preferire quei lavori che permettono di custodire la pace e la tranquillità della nostra vita, che non richiedono traffici eccessivi per l'acquisto del materiale necessario, né troppa competizione per la vendita dei prodotti ottenuti e che non comportano rela-

18 Cyril of Alexandria, *Selected Letters*, ed. and trans. by L.R. Wickham, Oxford 1983, 214-221.

19 Edizione: Basilius Magnus, *Regulae fusius tractatae*, 37-38, ed. J.-P. Migne, Paris (*PG* 31), 1009-1017; traduzione: Basilio di Cesarea, *La cura del povero e l'onere della ricchezza. Testi delle Regole e delle Omelie,* ed. L.F. Pizzolato, Milano 2015, 176-184.

zioni sconvenienti o dannose con uomini o con donne. Ma in ogni cosa bisogna pensare che il nostro intento è quello di ricercare ciò che è semplice e di uso comune, evitando di servire le insensate e funeste passioni umane lavorando per ciò cui esse ambiscono. Per la tessitura dobbiamo accettare solo quanto viene usato normalmente e non quello che viene escogitato da gente senza scrupoli per accattivarsi i giovani e gettarli nelle loro reti. Lo stesso vale per il mestiere del calzolaio: serviremo con il nostro lavoro solo chi richiede cose necessarie per i suoi bisogni. I mestieri di muratore, di falegname, di fabbro e di contadino sono per se stessi necessari per vivere e presentano notevoli vantaggi; non dobbiamo quindi rifiutarli per motivi particolari, a meno che non siano per noi fonte di disordini o disgreghino la vita comune dei fratelli; allora è indispensabile evitarli. (38)

Vale la pena notare che Basilio ritiene che il lavoro agricolo sia per i monaci un'attività normale. In realtà non era così: la terra appartenente a un monastero non era lavorata dai monaci stessi se non raramente; di solito veniva data in affitto a contadini, oppure veniva lavorata da schiavi o da persone molto povere (mi affretto però ad aggiungere che da questo punto di vista le due grandi congregazioni egiziane, quella di Pacomio e quella di Shenoute, fanno eccezione). In uno degli apoftegmi (*Poimen* 22) è detto che il lavoro sui campi non è un'occupazione per un monaco. Questa dichiarazione non è accompagnata da alcuna argomentazione, il che presuppone che tutti sapessero perché il lavoro sui campi fosse da evitare. Perché lo era? Forse perché era troppo pesante? O perché obbligava ad assentarsi dalla propria cella per vari giorni? O perché costringeva i monaci a entrare in contatto con gli abitanti dei villaggi – cosa per loro non gradita? Purtroppo le fonti tacciono.

Contrariamente ai monaci egiziani e palestinesi, la maggior parte dei monaci siriaci, che agivano in un ambiente formato da una tradizione presente in Siria fin dal III secolo (o anche prima), cercavano di seguire l'indicazione paolina che esortava a pregare senza interruzione, pensavano che fosse loro obbligo dedicarsi interamente alla preghiera[20]. Quella tradizione era il frutto dell'attività di gruppi ascetici fortemente legati alla Chiesa gerarchica e noti sotto il nome di Figli e Figlie dell'Alleanza – gruppi che erano mantenuti dalle comunità cristiane. Altrettanto importante era la corrente siriaca degli asceti-insegnanti, attestata dalle cosiddette Lettere Pseudo-Clementine (III secolo) e dal *Liber Graduum*, opera più tarda (IV secolo), ma fondata su una concezione siriaca più antica,

20 Ph. Escolan, *Monachisme et Église. Le monachisme syrien du IVe au VIIe siècle: un monachisme charismatique*, Paris 1999, capitolo V: *Le financement du monachisme: travail ou aumône?*, 183-225.

che divideva l'insieme dei cristiani in due gruppi – quello dei «giusti» (cioè dei cristiani ordinari, rispettosi dei comandamenti) e quello dei «perfetti» (cioè degli asceti). Uno dei tre «gradini» più difficili che il «perfetto» deve salire nel suo cammino verso il cielo, consiste in questo: «egli non deve lavorare per ottenere cibo per sé stesso e vestito per il corpo, se vuole liberarsi da tutto ciò che possiede (20,1)» [21]. A partire dall'inizio del V secolo la posizione del lavoro negli ambienti monastici subì dei cambiamenti in conseguenza dello sviluppo delle comunità cenobitiche, specialmente di quelle più grandi, che contavano alcune decine, a volte (ma raramente) alcune centinaia di monaci. Vivendo in piccolissimi gruppi (due o tre persone), abitando in eremi raggruppati in quegli insiemi debolmente strutturati che chiamiamo *laurai*, gli anacoreti eseguivano regolarmente per sé stessi varie attività di tipo domestico: cucinavano i cibi, andavano a prendere acqua, spazzavano il pavimento o il cortile ... eccetera; queste attività, essi non le consideravano un lavoro, perché, pur essendo faticose, esse non generavano ciò che era indispensabile per vivere: cibo e vestiti. Invece nei grandi monasteri cenobitici questo genere di attività costituisce uno spazio di lavoro interno, organizzato dalla comunità. Quando macinano il grano o preparano il pane o vanno a prendere acqua per tutta la comunità, i monaci concepiscono queste attività come un lavoro e hanno buone ragioni per essere convinti di compiere il dovere di lavorare secondo l'insegnamento di san Paolo.

Dal punto di vista economico, tutte queste attività interne non producevano guadagni per il monastero. Per poter esistere, il monastero aveva bisogno di beni provenienti dall'esterno.

Nella prospettiva storica un fattore si mostrò determinante per le sorti del lavoro monastico: l'afflusso costante di doni – sia dei modesti doni che i comuni fedeli portavano agli eremi e ai monasteri all'occasione di visite o della partecipazione alla messa domenicale, sia di grandi doni sotto forma di pezzi di terra o sotto forma di somme di denaro. È per mezzo dei doni che i monasteri, o almeno la maggior parte di essi, ottenevano un fondamento economico stabile, e ciò creava per i loro monaci la possibilità di vivere senza lavorare, nonostante che il valore psicologico del lavoro, come mezzo per disciplinare la mente e i sensi e combattere il pericolo della noia, fosse evidente. La consapevolezza dell'esistenza di questa funzione del lavoro è chiaramente attestata negli *Instituta* di Giovanni Cassiano[22], scritti negli anni 420–424: nel libro X di quest'opera egli

---

21 *The Book of Steps: The Syriac* Liber graduum, edd. R. Kitchen-M. F.G. Parmentier (Cistercian Publications), Kalamazoo 2004.

22 J. Cassien, *Institutions cénobitiques*, ed. J.-Cl. Guy (*Sources Chrétiennes* 109), Paris 2001.

tratta dell'*acedia*, pericoloso *spiritus* (o *cogitatio*: cioè, nel linguaggio di Evagrio, *logismos*) che le forze del male suscitano nel monaco per distoglierlo dall'ascesi, e sostiene che per combatterlo è necessario il lavoro manuale (*opus manuum*)[23]. Cassiano era stato in Egitto negli ultimi anni del IV secolo. Sebbene le sue opere debbano essere trattate come un programma destinato ai monaci delle Gallie – un programma in cui la descrizione del monachesimo egiziano doveva servire soprattutto come modello ideale – non c'è dubbio che ciò che egli scrive sul lavoro sia fondato su ciò che egli aveva visto in Egitto.

Gli scrittori cristiani che esortavano i fedeli a offrire doni ai monaci citavano alcuni passi dei libri deuterocanonici del Vecchio Testamento in cui è detto che l'elemosina purifica dai peccati. Eccoli[24]:

> Buona cosa è la preghiera con il digiuno e l'elemosina con la giustizia. Meglio il poco con giustizia che la ricchezza con ingiustizia. Meglio è praticare l'elemosina che mettere da parte oro. L'elemosina salva dalla morte e purifica da ogni peccato[25].

---

23 Cassiano illustra le sue considerazioni a proposito delle dichiarazioni di san Paolo sul dovere di lavorare, per mezzo di una storiella divertente perché paradossale – una storiella del tipo di quelle che leggiamo nelle collezioni di apoftegmi:
«L'abate Paolo, che, tra i padri, fu uno dei più sperimentati, viveva in un deserto molto vasto denominato Porfirio [*il Mons Porphyrites nel Deserto Orientale* – EW], e poteva ricavare un nutrimento sufficiente e sicuro per il suo sostentamento dai frutti delle palme e da un piccolo orticello. Non avrebbe avuto alcun bisogno di dedicarsi a qualche lavoro allo scopo di potersi mantenere, anche perché la sua dimora in quel deserto era lontana dalle città e dalle terre abitabili per almeno sette giornate di cammino e anche più, e, del resto, il prezzo che a lui sarebbe stato richiesto per il trasporto era più grande del compenso del suo lavoro, fosse pure a prezzo di sudore! E allora egli raccoglieva le foglie delle palme e si obbligava così ogni giorno a una certa quantità di lavoro, come se soltanto a quel prezzo egli dovesse sostentarsi. Giunto alla fine dell'intero anno, quando la sua grotta ne era ormai tutta ripiena, appiccatovi il fuoco, dava alle fiamme tutto quello che durante ogni anno aveva ammucchiato faticando con grande sollecitudine. E intanto egli comprovava che un monaco, senza il lavoro delle sue mani, non poteva restare a lungo al suo posto e neppure giungere, un giorno, al culmine della perfezione. Perciò, sebbene non lo inducesse a lavorare il bisogno del nutrimento, tuttavia egli lo faceva per la sola purificazione del cuore, per la salvaguardia dei suoi pensieri, per la permanenza duratura nella sua cella e per la sconfitta vittoriosa della stessa accidia». (X, 24) Traduzione di L. Dattrino: GIOVANNI CASSIANO, *Le istituzioni cenobitiche*, Abbazia di Praglia 2007.

24 D.J. DOWNS, *Alms, Charity, Reward, and Atonement in Early Christianity*, Waco 2016 (cf. la *Conclusion*, 273-286); cf. anche i saggi, estremamente interessanti e brillanti, di P. BROWN, *The Ranson of the Soul. Afterlife and Wealth in Early Christianity,* Cambridge 2015, e *Treasure in Heaven. The Holy Poor in Early Christianity*, London 2016.

25 Tb 12, 8-9.

Per mezzo delle elemosine e della fede si spazzano via i peccati[26].

L'acqua spegne un fuoco acceso, l'elemosina espia i peccati. Chi ricambia il bene si ricorda del futuro, al momento della sua caduta troverà un sostegno[27].

Riscatta i tuoi peccati per mezzo dell'elemosina e le tue ingiustizie per mezzo della compassione per i poveri, forse Dio sarà paziente verso le tue colpe[28].

Su questa base si formò l'idea che l'elemosina fosse una specie di prestito fatto a Dio e che Dio avrebbe restituito al creditore al momento della morte di questo: chi fa la carità al povero fa un prestito al Signore che gli ripagherà la buona azione[29].

È chiaro che i passi ora citati dei libri deuterocanonici testimoniano la nascita di una concezione nuova – nuova rispetto alle parti della Bibbia più antiche – della vita oltretomba e anche delle forme che può e deve assumere la penitenza per i peccati commessi, per ottenere la salvezza eterna. La concezione presente in questi libri, il cristianesimo l'accolse già nel I secolo. Essa compare nel Nuovo Testamento, specialmente in un passo del Vangelo di Luca, 11, 38-44:

Dopo che ebbe [Gesù Cristo] finito di parlare, un fariseo lo invitò a pranzo. Egli entrò e si mise a tavola. Il fariseo si meravigliò che non avesse fatto le abluzioni prima del pranzo. Allora il Signore gli disse: «Voi farisei purificate l'esterno della coppa e del piatto, ma il vostro interno è pieno di rapina e di iniquità. Stolti! Colui che ha fatto l'esterno non ha forse fatto anche l'interno? Piuttosto date in elemosina quel che c'è dentro, ed ecco, tutto per voi sarà mondo. Ma guai a voi, farisei, che pagate la decima della menta, della ruta e di ogni erbaggio, e poi trasgredite la giustizia e l'amore di Dio. Queste cose bisognava curare senza trascurare le altre. Guai a voi, farisei, che avete cari i primi posti nelle sinagoghe e i saluti sulle piazze. Guai a voi perché siete come quei sepolcri che non si vedono e la gente vi passa sopra senza saperlo».

Molte altre testimonianze si potrebbero citare da opere del II e del III secolo. Citerò invece un testo scritto in Egitto più tardi, all'inizio del V secolo, e che illustra questo atteggiamento in un modo particolarmente netto. Si tratta di un

26 Prv 15, 27a.
27 Sir 3,30-31.
28 Dn (Th 4, 27); traduzione mia dal testo della Septuaginta, ed. A. Rahls, Stuttgart [8]1965.
29 Prv 19, 17.

testo normativo attribuito erroneamente ad Atanasio (canone 85) [30]. L'autore afferma che se un uomo ricco, a cui sia morto un figlio, offre, per la salvezza dell'anima di questo, molto denaro o doni generosi alla Chiesa perché questa li distribuisca ai poveri, il Signore certamente accetterà questa offerta e salverà l'anima di suo figlio a causa della sua misericordia verso i poveri. A conferma dell'ortodossia di tale affermazione, egli cita un passo dei *Proverbi*, 13, 8: «Riscatto della vita d'un uomo è la sua ricchezza».

Perché i passi biblici da me menzionati potessero venir usati per sostenere che bisognava offrire doni ai monaci, occorreva trattare tali doni come una forma di elemosina e i monaci come poveri – poveri in quanto avevano rinunciato al «mondo».

Poiché, a partire dal IV secolo, esistevano degli uomini – i monaci – che venivano considerati eletti da Dio, dotati di grazie particolari, e per mezzo dei quali si riteneva possibile entrare quasi materialmente in contatto con la sfera del *sacrum*, i cristiani trovavano naturale fare dei doni a questi santi uomini per ottenere il loro aiuto in questo mondo e nell'altro. Dalla coscienza dei singoli donatori dipendeva capire in quale misura tale intercessione presupponesse un miglioramento del loro comportamento. Molti credevano che le richieste e le offerte fatte ai monaci avessero automaticamente efficacia. Citerò una sola delle innumerevoli testimonianze: un'omilia su un passo del Vangelo di Matteo, pronunciata da Giovanni Crisostomo ad Antiochia nel 390/391. Qui Giovanni Crisostomo, che in altre omilie esorta i fedeli a offrire doni agli asceti, critica coloro che credono che i doni e le preghiere dei santi siano sufficienti e dice: «le preghiere dei santi hanno grande efficacia, ma soltanto se ci saremo convertiti e saremo diventati migliori» (V, 4)[31].

Siamo ormai sulla strada che porterà alla fondazione, da parte di imperatori e di membri dell'alta aristocrazia costantinopolitana, di monasteri come istituzioni aventi lo scopo di salvare le anime dei fondatori e dei loro parenti. In tali monasteri i monaci, divisi in cori, innalzavano costantemente preghiere secondo l'intenzione dei fondatori. Nell'Occidente carolingio gli imperatori fondavano splendidi monasteri per monaci che avevano il compito di pregare per il successo delle campagne militari imperiali; in questo caso le preghiere dei monaci avevano uno *status* analogo a quello delle prestazioni a cui i sudditi laici erano tenuti nei confronti del sovrano: come questi pagavano le tasse e andavano in

30 *The Canons of Athanasius of Alexandria*, edd. W.E. Crum-W. Riedel, London 1904.

31 *In Matthaeum homiliae, PG*, 55-62.

guerra, così i monaci pregavano. In questa nuova situazione non c'era più posto per l'antica, appassionata controversia sul ruolo del lavoro nella vita monastica.

Mentre il rispetto per il lavoro fu una novità legata al monachesimo, nel campo delle attività di beneficenza i monaci non furono degli innovatori. L'idea che soccorrere il prossimo bisognoso di aiuto fosse un dovere, faceva parte della dottrina cristiana fin dagli inizi. La Chiesa gerarchica era la principale organizzatrice degli aiuti ai bisognosi; tutti i fedeli erano convinti che questo fosse uno dei compiti principali del vescovo. Quando nacquero grandi monasteri che avevano dei proventi stabili e dunque anche la possibilità di svolgere attività caritativa su ampia scala, presso di essi nacquero anche degli ospedali, degli orfanotrofii, delle locande per viaggiatori non ricchi. Constato però che queste forme di attività sembrano essere assenti nei monasteri pacomiani del IV secolo. (Nel dossier pacomiano è menzionato un locale separato per i malati, ma si tratta di monaci malati, e non di malati esterni.) Inoltre si dava naturalmente l'elemosina ai poveri davanti alle porte dei monasteri (accenni a questo si trovano nelle regole). Anche su questa forma di carità gli autori pacomiani tacciono: verosimilmente essa era una cosa evidente e non generava dei casi che meritassero di essere menzionati in opere letterarie. Mi chiedo: forse la congregazione pacomiana non aveva mezzi sufficienti per costruire, per esempio, degli ospedali? o forse non era psicologicamente pronta a creare delle forme istituzionali di aiuto? Pacomio non voleva avere persone estranee dentro i monasteri; d'altra parte, poiché i suoi monasteri avevano la forma di villaggi monastici, può darsi che proprio questa forma non favorisse la delimitazione di spazi destinati all'esercizio di attività caritative. I centri monastici dei Kellia e di Sketis, che ebbero un ruolo decisivo nella formazione della tradizione monastica, erano situati nel deserto all'orlo del Delta: troppo lontano per avere ogni giorno delle folle di bisognosi in cerca di aiuto. Nel modello di asceta creato da Atanasio l'attività caritativa non è messa in risalto.

*

Tutto ciò che ho detto fin qui può sembrare un contributo erudito privo di importanza per gli storici del monachesimo. Si può infatti pensare che il tratto di cammino percorso dalle comunità monastiche nei loro inizi non sia molto interessante, che ciò che importa sia soltanto l'effetto di questa evoluzione – effetto raggiunto in un tempo relativamente breve. Tuttavia, a parte il fatto che il seguire questo processo leggendo e commentando le fonti fa parte del dovere di ogni storico, sono convinta che una ricerca dettagliata in questo campo possa contribuire a capire la mentalità monastica. Tutti i monaci avevano buoni motivi nel compiere la loro scelta tra suggerimenti biblici contrastanti: sia quelli che decidevano di lavorare, sia quelli che decidevano di dedicarsi esclusivamente alla preghiera. Dobbiamo ascoltare le loro ragioni attraverso i testi che essi ci hanno lasciato, partendo dal presupposto che tutti agissero in buona fede. Dobbiamo rispettare entrambe le parti, qualunque sia la nostra simpatia. È bene non imitare Agostino nella sua polemica retorica.

Abstract

At the very beginning of monasticism, it was not evident that working is necessary for those who aspire for a perfect life. The passages from the Gospels according to Matthew and John as well as from two letters of S.Paul to the Thessalonians show a tension between work and the life of prayer. Augustine, Athanasius, Epiphanius of Salamina, Palladius, Evagrius, Basilius and other monastic authors develop and describe the praxis of monastic work, where an ascetical dimension is intervowen with the economic one. Everything was related to the geographical context and was evolving with the development of various forms of monastic life within the passage of time.

INDEX OF NAMES

INDEX OF PLACES

STUDIA ANSELMIANA

Diego León Fioravanti
Signum audibile gratiae invisibilis
Interacción dinámico-estético sacramental entre la P(p)alabra y el lenguaje musical
Studia Anselmiana 175, 2018, 552 pag.,
ISBN 978-3-8306-7916-5

Gregor Maximilian Weiermüller
Von der Anpassung zur Selbstreflexion
Eine kritische Untersuchung der Frage nach der Zuschreiben jüdischer Identität
Studia Anselmiana 176, 2018, 360 pag.,
ISBN 978-3-8306-7918-9

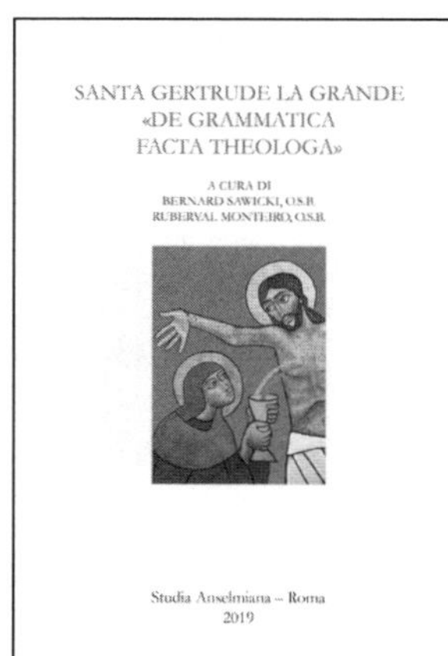

Gianluca De Candia, Philippe Nouzille (edd.)
Sancta morum elegantia
Stile e motivi di un pensare teologico.
Miscellanea offerta a Elmar Salmann
Studia Anselmiana 177, 2018, 672 pag.,
ISBN 978-3-8306-7920-2

Bernard Sawicki, Ruberval Monteiro (edd.)
Santa Gertrude la Grande
«de grammatica facta theologa»
Atti del Convegno, Roma, Aprile 2018
Studia Anselmiana 178, 2019, 320 pag.,
ISBN 978-3-8306-7943-1